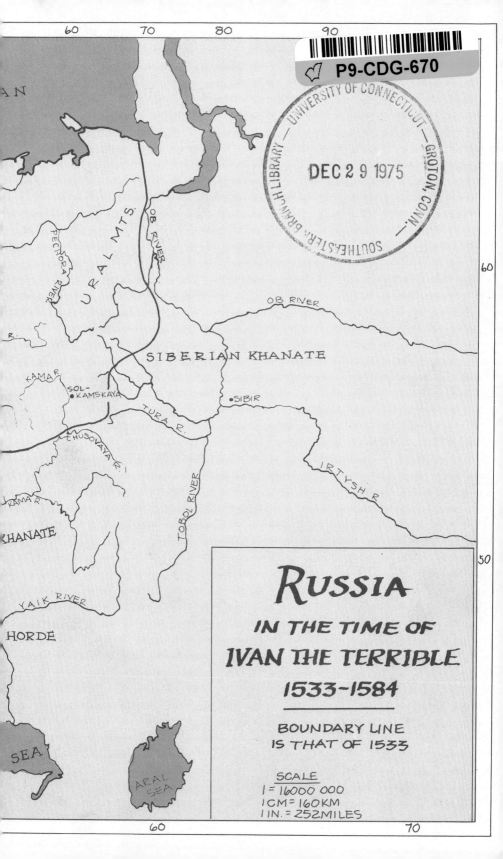

60 70 80 90

60

50

PECHORA RIVER

URAL MTS.

OB RIVER

OB RIVER

SIBERIAN KHANATE

KAMA R.

SOL-KAMSKAYA

SIBIR

TURA R.

CHUSOVAYA R.

IRTYSH R.

TOBOL RIVER

KAMA R.

KHANATE

YAIK RIVER

HORDE

SEA

ARAL SEA

RUSSIA

IN THE TIME OF

IVAN THE TERRIBLE

1533–1584

BOUNDARY LINE
IS THAT OF 1533

SCALE
1 = 16 000 000
1 CM = 160 KM
1 IN. = 252 MILES

60 70

Ivan the Terrible

IVAN
THE TERRIBLE

*Robert Payne
and Nikita Romanoff*

THOMAS Y. CROWELL COMPANY
New York   Established 1834

All pictures except where otherwise credited were obtained in the Soviet Union.

Designed by Ingrid Beckman
Manufactured in the United States of America

ISBN 0-690-00582-2

Library of Congress Cataloging in Publication Data

Payne, Pierre Stephen Robert, 1911–
    Ivan the Terrible.

    Bibliography: p.
    1. Ivan IV, the Terrible, Czar of Russia, 1530–1584. 2. Russia—History—Ivan IV, 1533–1584.
    I. Romanoff, Nikita, joint author.
DK106.P39   947'.04'0924 [B]   74-13374
ISBN 0-690-00582-2
                1 2 3 4 5 6 7 8 9 10

For Janet and Patricia

Contents

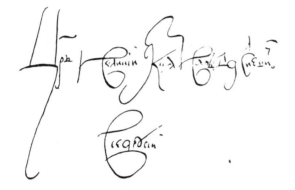

Ivan's signature. Some historians believe he never signed documents, but ordered his chief secretary to sign for him. It reads: "Tsar and Grand Prince Ivan Vasilievich of all Russia."

The Grand Prince Vasily III

OF ALL THE PEOPLE in Russia the Grand Prince Vasily III regarded himself as the most miserable. He could trace his descent back to Rurik, the legendary founder of the Russian state, and through his mother, Sophia Palaeologina, to a long line of Byzantine emperors, but he had neither sons nor daughters to continue the line. One day, walking in the countryside around Moscow, he saw a bird's nest and gazed at the chicks with a feeling of shame. "Whom do I resemble?" he asked. "Not the birds of the air, for they are fertile. Not the beasts of the earth, for they produce young ones. . . ." A few days later, talking to his boyars, he again bewailed his fate. "Who will rule after me in the Russian land, in all my cities, within my frontiers?" he exclaimed. "Shall I give them up to my brothers? But they do not know how to order affairs in their principalities!" The boyars replied: "Lord, Grand Prince, the barren fig tree must be cut down and cast out of the orchard!"

The Grand Prince Vasily III was a mild-mannered prince, well-liked by the people. Unlike his more famous father, Ivan III, known to history as Ivan the Great, who conquered large territories and fought the Tatars, Vasily III possessed none of the gifts of a conqueror. He had fought desultory wars against Lithuania, drawn Pskov, Smolensk, and Ryazan into his kingdom, and shown himself to be a cautious and sensible man who rarely permitted himself the luxury of showing his full strength. A portrait of him on the walls of the Cathedral of Michael the Archangel, which he built at the beginning of his reign, depicts him as a tall, heavy-set man, sad-eyed and vulnerable, with pursed lips and a huge beard which flows heavily across his chest. He wears an air of settled melancholy and looks more somber than any of the other somber figures who crowd the cathedral walls.

His wife, the Grand Princess Salomonia, the daughter of a rich boyar, was regarded at the time of her marriage as the most beautiful woman in Russia. She was devout, gentle, and loving, and no one had found any fault in her. Now at the age of forty-seven, having reigned for nearly a quarter of a century, the Grand Prince found a fault in her that was beyond curing. She was barren and must be cast out of the orchard. She protested that she had committed no crime, it was God's will that she was barren, the Church categorically forbade divorce on the grounds of barrenness alone. She had powerful allies. They included the Metropolitan Varlaam, the great theologian known as Maxim the Greek, and Prince Simeon Kurbsky. The Metropolitan was banished to a monastery in the far north, Maxim the Greek was put on trial on the charge of heresy and banished to Tver, and Prince Simeon Kurbsky was banished from court. The Grand Princess Salomonia was divorced and sent to a nunnery in Suzdal. It was said that she raged against the injustice of her divorce to the very end and cursed the husband who had cast her out. It was said, too, that an even more terrible curse was laid on him. Mark, Patriarch of Jerusalem, heard about the coming divorce and thundered: "If you should do this evil thing, you shall have an evil son. Your nation shall become prey to terrors and tears. Rivers of blood will flow, the heads of the mighty will fall, your cities will be devoured by flames." And all this came about.

Vasily III entered upon his new marriage joyfully and light-heartedly. His bride was Princess Elena Glinskaya, by origin Lithuanian, now living as a refugee in the Russian court. She was the ward of her uncle, Prince Mikhail Glinsky, whose adventurous career had led him to fight in the armies of the Emperor Maximilian and Albert of Saxony. His ward was about twenty, strong-willed, exuberant, beautiful. To please her the Grand Prince shaved off his beard, even though the Orthodox Church regarded it as a sin for a man to shave off his beard. But though he doted on her, he was not especially enamored of her family. Prince Mikhail

Vasily III with his coat of arms in the foreground. (From Herberstein's *Rerum Moscoviticarum Comentarii*)

Glinsky was at that time spending his days in a Russian prison; he had been arrested for treason, he was in chains, and his lands were confiscated. He was not finally released until February 1527.

The boyars viewed the coming wedding with mixed feelings. They resented Elena as a foreigner and suspected that she might have more love for Lithuania than for Russia. Almost inevitably she would outlive her husband, and unless she quickly produced a son and unless the Grand Prince survived long enough to superintend the education of his son, there was no certainty that the succession could be maintained. They observed that she had a will of her own and might prove intractable. Her ancestors were Lithuanian princes who had fought against Russia, but she also claimed descent from Mamay, the Tatar prince who had laid waste Muscovy until he was defeated by the Grand Prince Dmitry Donskoy at the battle of Kulikovo.

Yet there were many who saw advantages in the marriage. She was young, eager, well-educated. She was not so devout as Salomonia, and she had a fund of gaiety which kept Vasily amused and happy. The court would be rejuvenated by her presence. She brought excitement and pleasure to a court that had become monotonous and stuffy.

The marriage took place on January 21, 1526. The day appears to have been carefully chosen, for it was the Feast of the Assumption of the Virgin. The marriage ceremony began the moment she walked into one of the painted halls of the Golden Palace in the Kremlin, with two noblemen bearing candles leading the way and accompanied by her matrons of honor. She wore a sumptuous robe inlaid with jewels and sat on a chair upholstered with forty black sable skins. Prince Yury of Dmitrov, one of Vasily's two brothers, called out, "Lord, come to the place where God summons you," and then Vasily, dressed in equally sumptuous garments, entered, prayed before the icons, and then took his place beside Elena on another chair upholstered with forty black sable skins. The nuptial candles were lit, prayers were read, the matrons of honor combed the hair of the bride and groom, and over Elena's head there was placed the headdress appropriate to a married woman and a kerchief of the finest silk. Hops were sprinkled on the couple to assure fertility. Bread and cheese were offered to the wedding guests. It was a long ceremony and they needed refreshment.

The second part of the ceremony took place in the Cathedral of the Annunciation, the smallest and most beautiful of the cathedrals in the Kremlin. Vasily walked to the cathedral; Elena drove in a horse-drawn sleigh. A carpet of red damask bordered with sables was spread out for them in the cathedral. The Metropolitan Daniel offered them a glass of Italian wine, and when they had both drunk from it Vasily tossed the glass on the floor and ground it to pieces under his heels. There were many hymns, many blessings, many prayers. The boyars and the court nobility passed in procession, offering their congratulations, while the choir sang a hymn invoking God's blessing on them and the hope that they would enjoy a long life.

There followed the wedding feast, where a roast cock was served to the wedded couple, and later they were escorted to the bedroom and the nuptial candles were stuck into tubs of wheat. On the bed were laid twenty-seven sheaves of rye. In each corner of the room sable furs and wheat loaves were laid, and arrows were shot into the corners. The arrows signified that the enemies of the marriage would be laid low, while the wheat loaves signified the hope of fertility.

Unfortunately, as the months passed, Elena appeared to be no more fruitful than her predecessor. Vasily, who had gone to so much trouble to procure a new wife, remained childless. An absolute monarch, possessing more personal power than any European king, he was unable to produce what peasants produced with the greatest ease.

Baron Sigmund von Herberstein, the ambassador of the Emperor Maximilian to the Kremlin, was a remarkably observant man who came to know the workings of Vasily's mind and the dazzling complexities of the Russian court. He knew a good deal about Elena and her brothers Yury and Mikhail, and he had a certain fondness for Vasily. What struck him most of all was that Vasily was more absolutely supreme over his subjects than any other monarch in the world. "The will of the Lord is the will of God," said the Muscovites, and in their eyes Vasily was "God's steward and gentleman of the bedchamber." Yet the autocracy was not absolute; Vasily and his Boyar Council decided upon all important issues; the Metropolitan had the right to intercede for anyone who had fallen into disfavor; the concept of the Third Rome, with Muscovy taking the place of fallen Byzantium, was still being debated.

When Herberstein turned his attention to the machinery of government, he realized that it was often very erratic indeed. Decisions were made by the sovereign in consultation with the Boyar Council, a carefully selected group of noblemen, but the carrying out of these decisions depended upon an army of clerks. He estimated that half the people he met in the government offices inside the Kremlin were clerks. Whenever he went to see a boyar about some matter connected with his diplomatic mission he would find two or three clerks present; if he asked a question, the clerks would whisper the answer into the boyar's ear. Since they were usually more competent than the boyars, they could do very nearly whatever they pleased; and if a boyar annoyed them, they would threaten to haul him off to the Grand Prince. Herberstein relates that he once saw an important noble, the head of a department, dragged away by force to the Grand Prince by an army of enraged clerks.

These clerks were a law unto themselves. They were the bureaucracy, the permanent civil service. They took bribes, made promises that they promptly forgot, and worked continually to their own advantage. We understand Vasily better when we realize that he was all-powerful but at the same time he was dependent upon them, often submitted to them, and found them indispensable. The boyars called the clerks "nettle seeds," as we might call them "hillbillies," for they usually came from priestly or poor families. Sometimes the real power was in the hands of half a dozen trusted clerks.

These clerks ran the country when Vasily and his young bride absented themselves from Moscow and visited the holy shrines in the hope that the saints would intercede and grant them a son. Vasily enjoyed hunting and traveling, and on these expeditions he was usually accompanied by his brothers, Prince Yury of Dmitrov and Prince Andrey of Staritsa. Dmitrov and Staritsa were the appanage principalities bestowed on them by their father.

The Muscovites saw very little of their Grand Prince except on ceremonial occasions. The new Grand Princess was presented to them, and they rejoiced and went about their business. The city had a seething life of its own; the vital center of this life was a vast field stretching from the Moskva River to the Neglinnaya River outside the Kremlin wall. In those days it was called simply "the Square"; today it is called "the Red Square." The field served many purposes. It was the main marketplace with painted booths set up in orderly rows, where men could buy anything from silks and damasks to iron stirrups and leather saddles, from wooden vats to wooden sleighs. When the booths were cleared away, the Square became a parade ground or a fairground with clowns and jugglers and performing bears. Here executions were held, and here a man might pray for mercy in one of eight or nine wooden churches, or get a letter written by a scribe, or watch a religious procession with great painted banners waving in the wind, or listen to the herald proclaiming a decree signed by the Grand Prince himself with his royal seal.

The Grand Prince Vasily III, from a contemporary French engraving.

On any ordinary day the most remarkable thing about the Square was the noise. Merchants were shouting their wares, horses were galloping, farm carts were rumbling. There was the incessant sound of creaking wheels and cracking whips. Dogs barked, women screamed, children wailed, barkers shouted at the top of their lungs.

But if the noise was deafening, the individual human speech was wonderfully rich and vibrant, for in those days the common speech was closer to the rhythms of Church Slavonic and even more resonant and emphatic than the speech of today. Amid all the uproar there would suddenly appear a naked *yurodivy*, a fool of God, with tangled beard and glaring eyes, calling upon men to repent their sins and walk in the paths of righteousness.

Life in the Square was hot-blooded and human, with little righteousness in it. There was a good deal of thieving, and most men carried daggers in their sleeves or in their boots. Drunkards wandered about merrily. Mead and vodka were the favorite drinks; the mead, which was served boiling hot, kept the cold away on long bitter winter nights. Anthony Jenkinson, who was in Moscow in 1558, heard of men and women selling off their children in the taverns and then selling off all their earthly goods to buy a drink until finally there was nothing left but to pawn themselves. Then the taverner would throw them out and beat them over the legs with a cudgel until a sympathetic passerby took pity on them and ransomed them. "All the burden lieth on the poor people," he wrote.

The poor suffered atrociously; a growing middle class lived comfortably; the rich were unbelievably rich. There were nobles who owned scores of towns and villages and lived in breathtaking luxury. A class of rich wholesale merchants was rising to prominence; they owned the shops in the area called Kitay Gorod, which lies immediately behind the Square. They controlled the grain marts and fur markets, financed fishing fleets in the far north, traded with Persia, the Baltic, France, and Italy. Banking was in its infancy, but complicated barter deals were practiced. Foreign merchants had their agents in Moscow, and a Frenchman selling cloth would receive its worth in furs, leather, and jewelry. Foreigners spoke of the honesty and probity of the merchants of Pskov and of the shrewdness and hard dealing of the merchants of Moscow, always eager for a profit. Bargaining with foreigners, they would ask for five, ten, or twenty times what their merchandise was worth, and sometimes made fantastic profits. The Tatars too were known as good traders. They brought their sturdy ponies for sale in the field reserved for them on the south bank of the Moskva River and rode off to the south and east with furs, cloth, silks, jewelry, mirrors, finished leather goods, and whatever knickknacks took their fancy. They were nimble men with slant eyes and flat noses, bowlegged and smaller than the Russians. Giles Fletcher said, "Their speech is very sudden and loud, speaking as it were out of a deep hollow throat. When they sing, you would think a cow lowed or some great bandog howled." They were absolutely fearless, as befitted a people who had once conquered the whole of Russia except the northern principality of Novgorod and made the Russians pay tribute to them. But the great days of the Golden Horde had passed away and the Tatar empire had dissolved into quarreling khanates.

In October, when the rivers were frozen over, the booths that were formerly on the Square were set up again on the ice of the Moskva River, which became a fairground, a merchandise mart, a main thoroughfare. Sleighs, wooden vats, pots and pans, cattle, horses, poultry, bread, and every kind of food were sold on the ice. The Muscovites regarded the ice as their friend, for it preserved meat and made travel easier. Winter was a time for feasting and great religious processions.

But what the Muscovites loved most of all was their Square, with the high Kremlin wall towering over it. Then, as now, history passed through it. The parades, the processions, the flags, the banners, the gaily striped awnings of the shops, the bright clothes of the people—for everyone who could afford it dressed to the hilt—the bustle and movement intoxicated them. Here, too, on a summer evening the youths practiced fisticuffs. Herberstein once watched them at it after hearing a low whistle which summoned the youths together. They fought well, attempted to hammer each other into insensibility, and sometimes had to be carried off the field. "They fight in this way," he wrote, "to prove that they can give blows and tolerate punishment."

On the Square, late in the evening of August 25, 1530, the Muscovites learned that the Grand Princess Elena had at last, after four years of marriage, given birth to the long-awaited heir to the throne. The birth took place in the Terem Palace in the Kremlin at six o'clock in the evening. The chroniclers report that in various parts of Russia the birth was accompanied by sudden terrifying storms which shook the foundations of the earth. Auguries, real or imaginary, attend the birth of great princes, and these sudden storms on a day of clear summer skies seemed an appropriate augury for a child who was to be known as Ivan Grozny, for *grozny* means "dreadful" or "terrible," and derives ultimately from *grom*, meaning "thunder."

All Vasily's past miseries were forgotten in the celebration of the birth of his firstborn. Church bells rang. Solemn thanksgiving services were held. Presents were heaped upon the mother and on the tombs of the saints who had interceded with God so that the holy work of the dynasty of Rurik should be continued. The christening took place at the Troitsa-Sergeyevsky Monastery fifty miles northeast of Moscow on September 4, 1530. The fortresslike monastery was sacred to the Holy Trinity (*Troitsa*) and to St. Sergius of Radonezh who was buried there in an ornate tomb. On this tomb the newborn child would receive his name, and they believed he would be protected throughout his life by the Holy Trinity and by the divine influence of the saint.

In the great cathedral behind the high walls of the monastery Vasily solemnly presented Ivan to Abbot Ioasaf. Almost the entire court was present. For the occasion everyone wore sumptuous garments. Vasily wore his crown, the candles flickered on the walls painted with scenes from the life of St. Sergius, prayers were offered, and the choir sang. The Abbot advanced solemnly through the royal gate of the iconostasis to the altar and implored blessings on the child. Then he emerged from the sanctuary and gave the child back to Vasily, who placed his son on the saint's tomb, praying tearfully: "O Sergius, by your prayers to the Holy Trinity, you gave me my son. Protect him from all evil, seen and unseen, until he has grown in strength. All my faith is placed in you."

By being placed on the tomb, the child was officially dedicated to St. Sergius. He was christened by a saintly monk known as Cassian the Barefoot, and given the name of Ivan, the Russian equivalent of John, after John the Baptist. He was also blessed before an icon of the Virgin. At his christening, therefore, the Holy Trinity, the Virgin, St. Sergius, and John the Baptist were all invoked, and to the end of his life Ivan believed he was under their special protection. In time he would accumulate many more saints, praying to them fervently and trusting in their powers of intercession, but he never wavered in his allegiance to the saints who attended his christening.

After giving costly gifts to the monastery, Vasily returned to Moscow with his son who, in the words of the chronicler, "had been sent by God for the comfort of his soul, the alleviation of his hopes, and the strengthening of the Tsardom." Elena was not present at the ceremony, and the chroniclers relate that he journeyed home in a great hurry "because a loving mother cannot suffer to be separated for long from her child."

A year later, on the anniversary of his birth, Ivan made his first public appearance. A small wooden church, dedicated to John the Baptist, was erected at Vasily's orders just outside the Kremlin walls. Large crowds assembled to watch the church being built and to pay tribute to Vasily, Elena, and their infant son, who was solemnly presented to the people. The church was built in a single day.

A year passed, and once again Ivan attended the consecration of a church. This time it was the Church of the Ascension, built in gratitude for the birth of the long-awaited heir on the family estate at Kolomenskoye ten miles west of Moscow. The church was built on a rise above the Moskva River in the grounds of the wooden palace of Kolomenskoye, among orchards and rolling fields. With its outer galleries and slender tent-shaped steeple, faced with white stone and wonderfully proportioned, this church was to be the supreme architectural achievement of Vasily's reign; and though quite small, for the interior was scarcely larger than a living room, it gave an impression of great size and the steeple could be seen twenty miles away. On one wall of the church stood the Grand Prince's throne emblazoned with the double-headed eagle, and here he sat with his son sitting on a smaller throne beside him to receive the congratulations of the nobles and the church dignitaries.

For three days there were prayers, chants, festivities, and feasts. The Metropolitan Daniel presided over the religious ceremonies. Vasily's brothers, Yury and Andrey, were present. All eyes were on the small, red-haired, bright-eyed boy, in whose honor the church was erected and who therefore played an important role in the ceremonies.

These ceremonies came to an end on September 5, 1532, and soon Vasily was hurrying once more to the Troitsa-Sergeyevsky Monastery for the annual memorial service for St. Sergius. Ivan remained in the Kremlin with his mother, who was expecting her second child. Yury was born on October 30. We learn from the chronicler that "there was great rejoicing in Moscow." The parents may not have rejoiced, for Yury was born deaf and dumb, and so he remained to the end of his life.

We have a few brief glimpses of Ivan in his early childhood. On February 2, 1533, the two-and-a-half-year-old Ivan attended the wedding of his uncle, Prince Andrey of Staritsa, in the Kremlin, where he gracefully presented gifts to the wedding couple. We learn, too, that both Ivan and his mother suffered from ill-health. Elena was afflicted with headaches, earache, and various bodily pains, and Ivan suffered from boils. Vasily learned of these illnesses while he was on his travels, and wrote to his wife:

> From Grand Prince Vasily Ivanovich of Russia to his wife Elena.
> Thou hast written to me on Friday that Ivan became ill. Now thou writest that he is suffering from a hard boil on the nape of his neck. Thou didst not mention this in thy previous letter. Now thou writest that on Sunday morning at one o'clock the boil on his neck became larger and redder, and that it was painful, and there was no pus.
> Why didst thou not tell me this before? Why didst thou not write about it before? Previously thou saidest only that Ivan was ill. Thou shouldst write to me, telling me how God watches over him and exactly what it is that appeared on his neck. How did it come about? When did it begin? How is it now? Speak to the princesses and the ladies of the court, and ask them what our son Ivan is suffering from, and whether it is customary among small children. If it is customary, then find out whether it comes from birth or from some other cause. Speak to the ladies of the court and ask them about all these things, and write to me so that I shall know what is happening. Tell me what they think will happen. Does it happen often? What do they think? How does God watch over thee and our son Ivan? Write to me about everything.

There was no doubt that Vasily was deeply shocked by the news from his wife, and feared that there might be even more severe ailments in store for his son. Elena had mentioned her own aches and pains, but he was more concerned with those of his son. She wrote to her husband describing how Ivan's boil had opened, and he seemed to be recovering. Vasily was still not satisfied, and he wrote another urgent letter:

> From Grand Prince Vasily Ivanovich to his wife Elena.
> Do not keep me without news of thy health. How does God watch

over thee, and how art thou? Write to me, too, about our son Ivan. How does God keep him? As for me, thanks to God and the prayers of His most perfect Mother and of all the saints, I am alive and in good health.

Thou hast written to me that the boil on our son Ivan's neck has opened and the pus came out, but now only lymph comes out. Thou shouldst write to me about whether there is anything else coming out, and what condition the boil has reached, whether it is larger or smaller. Write to me also how God is keeping thee. Does half thy head and ear and side ache? Write to me about everything.

These letters appear to have been written in the summer of 1533. Boils were very serious matters in those days, for complications often set in and people were known to have died of blood poisoning after a boil had been lanced. Vasily had reason to be concerned.

On September 21, 1533, he set out from Moscow once more for the Troitsa-Sergeyevsky Monastery. His whole family accompanied him. This time there would be only a brief visit, for he intended to hurry on to his estate near Volokolamsk, some ninety miles northwest of Moscow, for some hunting. As usual, the monks welcomed him at the monastery with candle-lit icons, and there were services and prayers beside the tomb of St. Sergius. Later Vasily invited all the monks to a feast, and then with a large retinue he went on his way. He had prayed to St. Sergius to watch over his health, but his prayers were unavailing, for on the first stage of the journey to Volokolamsk he developed a sore on the inside of his left thigh, presumably caused by chafing against the saddle.

The journey to Volokolamsk and to his hunting lodge at the small village of Klop took four or five days, and by the time he reached the hunting lodge he was in considerable pain. He was able to attend a banquet in his honor given by his favorite chamberlain, Ivan Shigona, and on the following day he was observed making his way painfully to the bathhouse. But there were clear skies, the weather was perfect for hunting, and he could not resist the temptation. After resting for a day or two, and summoning Prince Andrey of Staritsa to join him, he went hunting on his estate. The horns sounded, the hounds were let loose, Vasily and his retinue set out for the chase on their small nimble ponies. They had ridden little more than a mile when Vasily complained he was in such great pain that it was impossible for him to go on. The hunt came to an abrupt end, and they all returned to the hunting lodge. For a few minutes Vasily sat down at a table with his brother, and then took to his bed. He knew now that he was a very sick man.

Doctors were summoned, but they could do little to relieve the pain. The sore had developed into a huge abcess, which was beginning to fester. A poultice of fresh honey, wheaten flour, and baked onions was applied. It had little effect. The boil grew larger and more painful, ripening slowly; the pus came out; the swelling increased. Vasily was carried to Volokolamsk on a litter, and there once more the huge abcess was examined and poulticed, and he complained of pains in his chest. The doctors gave him a purgative of seeds, but the only effect was to make him weaker, so that he had difficulty in talking.

Because he was so ill, and because his death might bring about an upheaval in the nation, he became increasingly concerned about the succession. He was afraid his brother Prince Yury would attempt to seize the throne. Prince Andrey remained with him, but when Prince Yury arrived at Volokolamsk he was ordered to return to his principality because Vasily did not want him to know how sick he was. At all costs he was determined that the throne should pass to his son Ivan.

Two confidential secretaries, Yakov Mansurov and Grigory Putiatin, were sent on a secret mission to Moscow. The mission was so secret that neither Elena nor the Metropolitan Daniel nor any of the boyars were informed. Their task was to secure the last will and testament of the Grand Prince and those of his father and grandfather and bring them in great haste to Volokolamsk. It was especially important that they should find Vasily's will, because it had been drawn up before his marriage to Elena. This will was to be destroyed, the other documents were to be studied. The secretaries succeeded in removing the will without attracting attention, and on their return to Volokolamsk they attended the secret council appointed to help Vasily draw up a new will.

Meanwhile his condition was growing worse. The swelling had gone down, but huge amounts of pus continued to pour out of the wound, and it was clear that his whole system was infected. For a few days he seemed to be holding his own, but toward the end of October it became obvious that they would have to employ desperate measures to save him. Already the heavens were provid-

The young Ivan (left) accompanies Vasily III and Elena to the Troitsa-Sergeyevsky Monastery and receives the blessing of the abbot. (From the *Nikon Chronicle with Miniatures*)

ing the appropriate auguries of his death, for on the night of Friday, October 24, on the eve of the Feast Day of St. Demetrius, falling stars were seen all over Russia. According to the chroniclers the stars fell "like hail or rain."

To a monk called Missail Sukin, summoned from Moscow to hear his confession, Vasily announced that even if he was saved from death by the intercession of the saints, he would cease being the ruler of Russia. He would become a monk and live out his days in a monastery.

The days passed and he still clung to life, though growing progressively weaker. Perhaps a miracle might save him. The life-giving tombs of saints were generally acknowledged to possess miraculous powers, and there happened to be such a tomb nearby. Some twelve miles north of Volokolamsk stood a fortresslike monastery founded by Joseph Sanin, later canonized under the name of St. Joseph of Volokolamsk. At a famous church council held in 1503 Joseph Sanin defended monastic wealth against a certain Nilus Maikov, who firmly believed in monastic frugality. Joseph insisted that there could be no charity without wealth and Nilus insisted just as emphatically that unless a man stripped himself of all his possessions he could not come to Christ. The Russian Church in its wisdom canonized both Joseph and Nilus, who became known as St. Joseph of Volokolamsk and St. Nilus of Sorsk.

Joseph of Volokolamsk died in 1515, and his tomb lay in the sumptuous Church of the Assumption within the monastery. Vasily could scarcely stand and had to be supported by two of his nobles. He prayed before the tomb with Prince Andrey of Staritsa, Elena, and his two young sons at his side. Elena was in tears, and Vasily became so weak during the ceremony that he had to be carried out and laid down in the outer gallery. He spent the night in the monastery, and the next morning set off for Moscow.

He was driven in a sleigh, with many cushions and pillows, for every jolt was excruciatingly painful. Two of his nobles rode with him, and from time to time they turned him to avoid bedsores. They traveled in slow stages, and they were in some doubt whether he would reach Moscow alive. If possible, they hoped to enter Moscow unobserved, for it was essential that Vasily's real condition should remain unknown until all the arrangements for the succession had been completed. Also, there were ambassadors and foreigners in Moscow, who would listen to rumors, tell tales, and inform their governments. Winter was coming down, the snow was falling, and ice covered the rivers.

Vasily reached the outskirts of Moscow on November 21. He possessed a large estate on the Sparrow Hills overlooking the city, and remained there for two days. The Metropolitan Daniel and the great boyars of his court came to visit him. They found him emaciated, for he had been able to eat very little during the journey. To Metropolitan Daniel he said: "There are some who do not want me to become a monk, but let no one dissuade you—make me a monk, for it is God's wish and so I have vowed." The Metropolitan hesitated, for the great boyars were not yet ready to see their monarch transformed into a monk, and their counsels prevailed.

The ice on the Moskva River was not thick enough to allow the passage of a sleigh, and therefore it was decided to throw a bridge across the river. The wooden bridge was constructed quickly—too

Vasily III during his last illness. He is returning to Moscow on a sleigh and pausing to receive medicines. (From the *Nikon Chronicle with Miniatures*)

quickly. When on the morning of November 23 the sleigh carrying the dying Vasily drove over the bridge, part of the bridge collapsed, the horses fell into the water, and the sleigh itself was saved only because the drivers had the presence of mind to cut the traces of the four horses. All this happened very quickly, Vasily was not hurt, the sleigh was pulled off the bridge, new horses were procured, and they drove back to the Sparrow Hills.

Later in the day Vasily and his retinue crossed the Moskva River on the ferryboat at Dorogomilovo without incident. There was little time to lose. As soon as he reached his quarters in the Kremlin Palace, he summoned a meeting of the Privy Council to discuss the succession. The meeting was attended by Princes Vasily and Ivan Shuisky, and the boyars Mikhail Zakharin, Mikhail Vorontsov, and Mikhail Tuchkov-Morozov. Peter Golovin, the chief treasurer, and Ivan Shigona, the chamberlain, were also present, and in addition there were two secretaries to take down the Grand Prince's words. Finally, there was Prince Mikhail Glinsky, Elena's brother, a huge, burly man, who was invited to the meeting because it was necessary that someone should represent the Grand Princess.

Lying in bed, Vasily dictated the terms of the will prepared in Volokolamsk, and already written, but never previously divulged. It was a very simple will. He gave Russia to his three-year-old son Ivan, who would rule until the age of fifteen under the regency of his mother with the advice of the Council of Boyars. Vasily was too ill to discuss the succession in any greater detail, and for the next two days he rested.

On the third day, November 26, he was well enough to receive Holy Communion and to address a much larger meeting of church dignitaries and boyars. The Metropolitan Daniel, Prince Yury, Prince Andrey, and all the high officials of the court attended. Vasily was concerned to emphasize the strong bonds which attached the boyars to the sovereign, and he wanted above all that these bonds should endure during the reign of his son. They must swear an oath of loyalty to his son, they must assist Elena, and they must not allow divisions among themselves. It was as though he foresaw a long peaceful reign, his son Ivan working in perfect harmony with the boyars. There would be no friction, no quarrels. Ivan would draw strength from the boyars, and the boyars in turn would draw strength from their sovereign. He said:

> As you well know, our sovereignty over Moscow, Vladimir and Novgorod descends from Vladimir, Grand Prince of Kiev. We are your hereditary sovereigns, and you have been our boyars from time immemorial. With me, you governed the land, and I held you in honor and especially favored your children, and my fame reached all countries. You have all taken the oath to serve me and my children. So now, on your lives, I commend to you my Princess and her son, Grand Prince Ivan. Brethren, preserve the Russian land, his sovereign state, and preserve Christianity entirely from all its enemies. . . .
>
> I know now that I am near to death, and therefore I have written in my will how it must be with Princess Elena, my sons, and my brothers in the years to come. If you wish to see good come to pass, then put your names to the will and kiss the Cross as a sign that you will keep your oaths. And if I have written anything unworthy, it can be changed.

All the boyars agreed to sign the will, some with their signatures, others by affixing their seals. It was not expected that the Grand Prince would survive for more than a few days.

Surprisingly, he was still alive six days later. He was very weak, but in no pain. Gangrene had set in, and the smell of the wound was almost unendurable. The doctors, and Prince Mikhail Glinsky, hovered over the bed. A doctor, Nikolay Bulev, pronounced that there was no more hope, no medicines would cure him, and only divine aid would save him. Vasily overheard him and said to the nobles of the bedchamber: "Brethren, Nikolay has just said my sickness is incurable. The time has come for me to save my soul from perdition!" The nobles wept. Soon Vasily lost consciousness. From the depths of unconsciousness he was heard chanting, "Alleluya! Alleluya!" And when he became conscious again, he said, "Let God's will be done! Let God's name be blessed now and forever!"

Such at least were the words which the monkish chroniclers record, and since Vasily was very devout and desperately ill, it is likely that he said words like these. In the early hours of the following morning Abbot Ioasaf, of the Troitsa-Sergeyevsky Monastery, came to the bedchamber. Vasily was wide awake, and asked for a blessing. "Pray, father, for the well-being of the country, and for my son Ivan, and for my sins," he said. "God and St. Sergius, the great miracle-worker, through your prayers, gave me my son. He was baptized before the miracle-worker's tomb, and I presented him to the saint, I placed him on the tomb, I gave him into your arms. Pray God, the pure Virgin and the great miracle-worker for my son Ivan, and for my poor wife, and do not leave the city."

This time the words have a more authentic ring, for the chronicle reflects the passion of a dying man. Later that day, when he felt he was failing rapidly and wanted to say goodbye to his wife and son, he summoned them and then changed his mind. Only his wife must be allowed to see him, for as he explained, "My son is young and I am in great sickness. He might shudder at the sight of me." Then he changed his mind again, and Ivan was brought into the bedchamber in the arms of Prince Mikhail Glinsky. The Grand Prince removed the Cross of St. Peter the Metropolitan from his own neck, pressed it to his son's lips, and then placed it round the boy's neck. To Agrafena Cheliadnina, the boy's governess, he said, "Guard my son closely and never leave him for a single moment." And then hearing the sound of sobbing—for the Princess was on her way to the bedchamber—he dismissed Ivan and the governess, and prepared to receive his wife, who was being supported by Prince Andrey of Staritsa.

The Princess was weeping uncontrollably, and he did his best to console her. He said he was in no pain, which was true, and that he felt better, which was untrue. He was dying, and he was now saying farewell to his family. She asked him about the inheritance, and he replied that Ivan would inherit Russia, she would receive an appanage, according to the custom, and Yury would receive the principality of Uglich. She would be the ruler of Russia until Ivan came of age. He was going to speak to her about the art of governing, but she was weeping so violently that he had to let her go away.

The time had now come for him to receive the last rites of the Church and to exchange the vestments of a Grand Prince for a monk's gown. The relics of St. Catherine of Alexandria were brought to him and he kissed them reverently, and when Prince Yury of Dmitrov came close to the bed, he said, "Brother, do you remember how our father was overcome with weakness on the day and night of his death? In the same way, brother, I am approaching the hour of my death." Then he reminded the priests that he wanted to be made a monk, and at once an argument broke out. Prince Andrey of Staritsa objected strenuously, reminding everyone at the bedside that the heroic Grand Prince Vladimir of Kiev "did not die a monk but instead received the peace of the righteous, and so did many other Grand Princes." It was an unseemly quarrel beside the bedside of a dying man. The boyar Mikhail Zakharin argued that the ordination should proceed, and Prince Andrey aided by the boyar Mikhail Vorontsov argued that it was quite unnecessary. The Metropolitan flared up in anger, looked straight into the eyes of Prince Andrey, and said: "I will grant you no blessing either in this life or the next!" The quarrel subsided. The Grand Prince was dressed in a monk's robes. The Metropolitan Daniel presided over the ordination, but the ceremony was conducted hurriedly, for he was sinking fast. The man lying on the bed was no longer the Grand Prince Vasily III, lord of Pskov, Novgorod, and a hundred other cities. He was the monk Vassian.

He died at midnight on December 3, 1533. Ivan Shigona said that at the moment of his death the Grand Prince's soul leaped from his body taking the form of a thin silvery vapor.

The dead man became a Grand Prince again when he was buried in the Cathedral of Michael the Archangel in a stone coffin beside his father. The bells tolled, the choirs sang, the funeral service was conducted with all the panoply due to a reigning monarch. Elena, too weak to make the journey on foot, was carried the short distance from the Kremlin Palace to the cathedral on a sleigh. Ivan was not present, perhaps because the mournful ceremony would be harmful to an impressionable child. It was a long and exhausting ceremony with many invocations and anthems, and in the crowded cathedral ablaze with lamps and candles there were few who did not feel that a good man had perished and the future was dark and uncertain.

The chroniclers relate that the people of Moscow wept like children watching the burial of their father.

For more than seventy years under Ivan III and Vasily III Russia had been in strong and capable hands. No one could remember a time when there had not been an experienced man on the throne. Now Russia was rudderless and adrift.

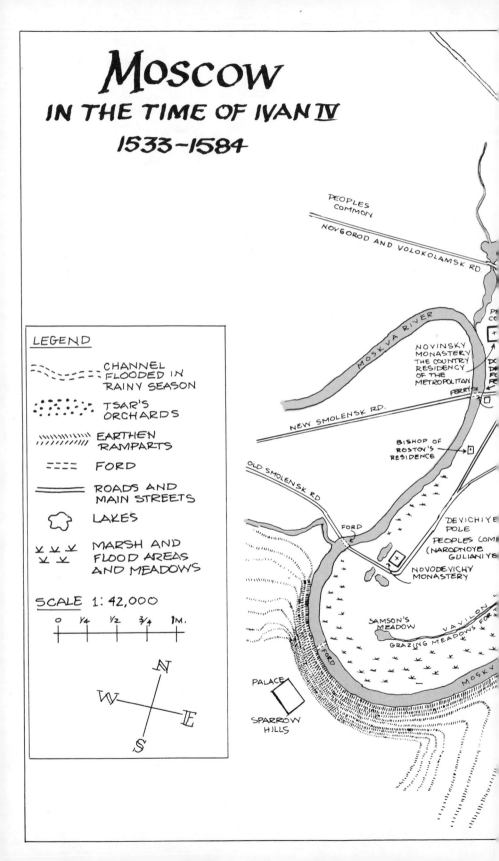

Moscow
IN THE TIME OF IVAN IV
1533–1584

LEGEND

- - - - - CHANNEL FLOODED IN RAINY SEASON
:::::: TSAR'S ORCHARDS
\\\\\\ EARTHEN RAMPARTS
- - - - FORD
———— ROADS AND MAIN STREETS
◯ LAKES
v v v MARSH AND FLOOD AREAS AND MEADOWS

SCALE 1: 42,000

0   ¼   ½   ¾   1 M.

N
W   E
S

PEOPLES COMMON

NOVGOROD AND VOLOKOLAMSK RD.

MOSKVA RIVER

NOVINSKY MONASTERY THE COUNTRY RESIDENCY OF THE METROPOLITAN

PEOPLES COMMON

FERRY

NEW SMOLENSK RD.

BISHOP OF ROSTOV'S RESIDENCE

OLD SMOLENSK RD.

FORD

DEVICHIYE POLE

PEOPLES COMMON (NARODNOYE GULIANIYE

NOVODEVICHY MONASTERY

SAMSON'S MEADOW

VAVILON

GRAZING MEADOWS FOR

MOSKV

FORD

PALACE

SPARROW HILLS

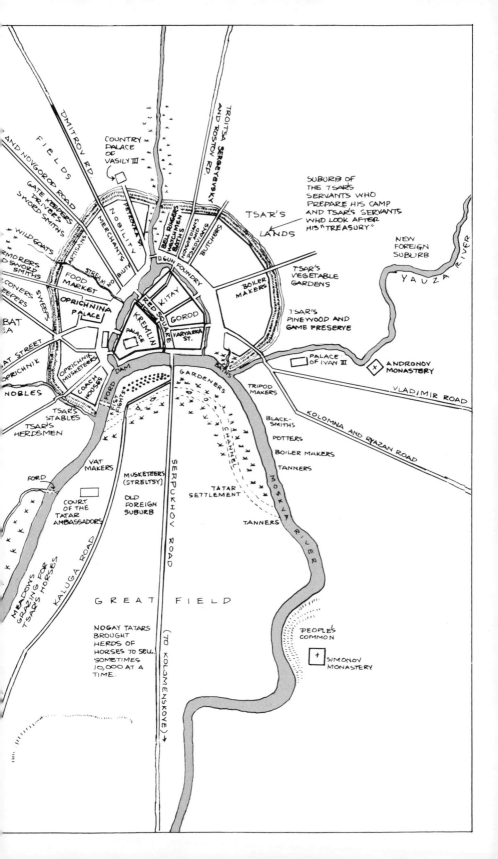

A Child on the Throne

IN THEORY all power was vested in the three-year-old Grand Prince Ivan Vasilievich.

A few days after the burial of his father he was present at a ceremony held in the Uspensky Cathedral, where he was proclaimed the true Sovereign of all Russia. The small, red-headed boy sat on his throne wearing a crown and royal vestments while the Metropolitan Daniel intoned the proclamation: "May God bless you, Sovereign, Grand Prince Ivan Vasilievich of Vladimir, Moscow, Novgorod, Pskov, Tver, Smolensk, Yugorsk, Perm, the land of the Bolgars, and many other lands, Tsar and Sovereign of all Russia! And may you remain in good health upon the grand-princely throne of your father!" The orb and scepter, the emblems of kingship, were placed in his hands, and the assembled princes, boyars, clergy, courtiers, and all those who had been invited to the ceremony swore allegiance to him and sang the anthem "Long May He Reign." At the end of the ceremony they passed in procession before him, laying rich presents at his feet.

The country he ruled over was vastly smaller than the Russia we know today. The total population was about eight million. It stretched from the Arctic Ocean to the southern steppes where the Tatars roamed. To the east it was bordered by the powerful Khanate of Kazan and to the west by Livonia, Lithuania, and Poland. Most of what is now known as the Ukraine, including Kiev, belonged to Lithuania.

For the young Ivan, living out his ceremonial life within the Kremlin palaces, rarely penetrating beyond the high Kremlin walls except to go on pilgrimage to the shrines of the saints, there could be little consciousness of the vast powers he had inherited from his father. He was treated with great deference, shown to visiting ambassadors, propped on his throne on ceremonial occasions, and made to listen to many speeches in which he was addressed as sovereign, lord, autocrat, Tsar and Grand Prince, while at the same time it was deeply impressed on him that he possessed no powers at all. As a child he appears to have spent his life in the company of adults, his only playmate being his deaf-mute brother Yury. Priests attended to his education. He was a quick student with an agile mind, given to brooding. He was being brought up in an atmosphere which was far from being conducive to a proper education. Scarcely anywhere else in the world was there such an ostentatious display of luxury as in the small area within the Kremlin, somewhat smaller than a city block, occupied by the palaces of the Grand Prince.

The young Ivan receiving the boyars. Elena is at top left. (From the *Nikon Chronicle with Miniatures*)

Here palaces crowded on palaces; gold domes proliferated; everything was new and splendid; an army of palace servants kept everything spotless. The palace area contained three separate but adjoining palaces, three cathedrals, five churches, a chapel, a treasury, government offices and council chambers, storerooms, bathhouses, prisons, and an establishment supervised by the Tsaritsa for weaving silk embroidery and gold cloth. Most of these buildings were quite new, having been designed by Italian architects during the reign of Ivan's grandfather. Thus the Uspensky Cathedral (the Cathedral of the Assumption of the Virgin), the center of the religious life of the rulers of Russia, was designed by Rudolfo Fioravante of Bologna between 1475 and 1479. The Cathedral of Michael the Archangel, where the Grand Princes were buried, was designed by Marco and Aloisio Novi some twenty years later. Marco Ruffo and Pietro Antonio Solario designed the Granovitaya Palata, the principal palace, so named because the stones were faceted like pomegranates. The impressive bell tower, which dominated most of the buildings around it, known as the bell tower of Ivan the Great, was designed by Marco Bono.

Except for the Granovitaya Palata, which resembled a small and luxurious Italian *palazzo*, few of these buildings betrayed their Italian origins. The architects steeped themselves in traditional Russian architecture, traveling widely and studying the great cathedrals of Vladimir and Novgorod, and working closely with Russian architects. What they added was a certain grace and lightness; they rejoiced in subtle proportions; and they took care to conceal the influence of the Italian Renaissance while making it all the more manifest.

Among these palaces and cathedrals Ivan spent most of his boyhood, dimly aware that this small corner of the Kremlin generated the royal power which stretched beyond the Kremlin walls to the remotest regions of Russia.

This concentration of power within a small space was deliberate; it expressed the needs of the ruling dynasty, and followed the Byzantine model. Here all the important ceremonies of royalty were performed; here, usually, the Grand Princes were born, here they were married and were crowned, here they died and were buried. It was not really necessary for a Grand Prince to travel outside this well-guarded area, except to lead his armies. The palaces and cathedrals were designed as expressions of his authority, his majesty, his preeminence above all other mortals. In this setting everything was designed to exalt the person of the sovereign.

Yet life in the Kremlin was not altogether pleasant or rewarding. A strict protocol was observed; complexities abounded; there were subtle gradations of rank; and power moved from the throne room in mysterious ways. Titles might mean much or little, depending on the owner. Traditionally the boyar families, who belonged to the untitled aristocracy, wielded great power. There were about fifteen boyar families; they possessed enormous prestige as the hereditary lords of Moscow under the Grand Prince. The history of Moscow was very largely the history of these fifteen families—the Cheliadnins, Morozovs, Zakharins, Saburovs, Saltykovs, Vorontsovs, Sheremetevs, Pleshcheyevs, Kolychovs, and a few more. To be a prince was not necessarily to be wealthy or powerful, but to be a Morozov or a Zakharin was to have wealth and power beyond the wildest dreams of ordinary men. All this Ivan had to learn in his boyhood.

Titles had not yet proliferated, and there were in fact only two titles: *veliky knyaz,* or Grand Prince, the title of the sovereign, and *knyaz,* a title held by about a hundred princely families. In these families the sons of princes were princes and all their daughters were princesses; hence the multitude of princes and princesses, some wealthy and powerful, others living in modest circumstances. Here again there were infinite gradations. To be a Prince Belsky or a Prince Mstislavsky, who were closely related to the sovereign on the maternal line, meant a great deal. The Princes Shuisky, who descended from the Grand Princes of Nizhni-Novgorod, were also held in high respect. Descendants of Grand Princes who had once ruled over vast principalities counted far more than princes who had ruled over lesser principalities. The greatest princes were the princes of the blood royal, the brothers and uncles of the reigning Grand Prince.

The throne rooms and reception rooms in the Kremlin palaces were approached by narrow outside stairways which led from the ground floor to the first floor. In all the Kremlin there were no wide flights of steps. These stairways were well guarded; only two or three people could climb up them abreast; and they could be watched from above and below. Access to the Grand Prince depended upon an exact protocol. If a visitor was very important, if for example he was one of the princes of the blood royal, descended from Rurik, the ancient founder of the dynasty, then even the Grand Prince himself might welcome him at the foot of the stairs and at the very least there would be high-ranking nobles to escort him up the stairs. If he was less important, if for example he was a boyar, he might be met by another boyar or by a prince attached to the court. Depending on his importance, the visitor would be greeted at the foot of the stairs or half way up or at the top by noblemen or by palace servants or simply by a solitary tipstaff. An ambassador would know from the moment he approached the stairs whether he was likely to be received with favor or disfavor in the throne room. His value in the social organism had already been precisely calculated and the degree of deference to be paid to him was expressed in smiles, bows, greetings, the number of steps he climbed unescorted, the number and rank of the people who welcomed him. It was a complex maneuver which satisfied an age that delighted in hierarchies.

Just as the steps leading to the palace were deliberately made narrow, so too, within the palace, the openings that led from one room to another were narrow. They were very low, and a man had to bow his head in passing from one room to the next. These small openings testified to the fear that reigned over the palaces. The young Ivan, who learned protocol before he learned his letters, soon learned that royalty was dangerous. The greatest danger always came from his close relatives: uncles, cousins, princes of the blood royal were likely to be contenders for the throne. The guards who stood at the doorways were not there for ceremonial purposes: they were fully armed.

As a child Ivan saw very little of the great world beyond the Kremlin wall. His secluded and cloistered life was spent largely in the Terem Palace, where the Grand Princess Elena lived in great state among her ladies-in-waiting. This long palace, five stories high, was luxuriously decorated; there were ornate carvings around the windows and the walls were painted with enormous flowers; on the second floor were the looms where immense quantities of gold cloth and embroidered silk were produced for the use of the grandprincely family, who wore sumptuous clothes on all ceremonial occasions. This cloth was also bought by the princes, boyars,

Seventeenth-century painting of the Kremlin Palace. At bottom left the Cathedral of Michael the Archangel, with the Cathedral of the Annunciation above it. The Zolotaya Palata, or Golden Palace, is in the center, with the Hall of Facets center right, and the Uspensky Cathedral on the right. The Terem Palace is the high building behind the Hall of Facets.

and priests, and there were shops in Moscow which sold the cloth from the royal looms. One of Ivan's earliest memories was the incessant clicking of the looms.

Behind the palaces were two small gardens, the summer and winter gardens, where he was permitted to walk and take exercise under the watchful eyes of armed guards. He was also permitted to visit the houses of his relatives, who lived nearby. His world was minutely organized within the stifling protocol of a Byzantine court. Within the Kremlin plots and counterplots flourished, the wildest rumors sped along the shadowy corridors, and treason filled the air like incense.

The most powerful man in Russia was a man once regarded by Vasily III as an arch traitor. This was Prince Mikhail Glinsky, the uncle of Elena, astute and tough-minded, possessing a formidable instinct for survival. He exerted vast power at court; nor was he in any mood for half-measures. Once he was chief minister in the

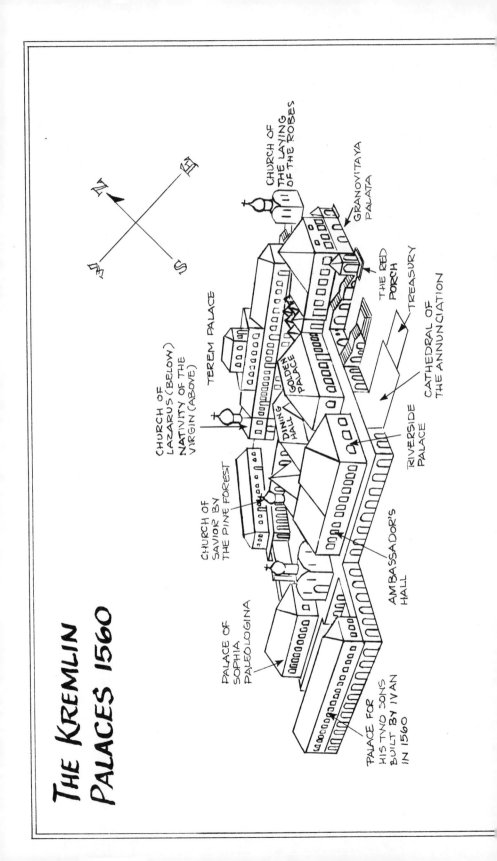

THE KREMLIN PALACES 1560

N

PALACE OF SOPHIA PALEOLOGINA

CHURCH OF SAVIOR BY THE PINE FOREST

CHURCH OF LAZARUS (BELOW) NATIVITY OF THE VIRGIN (ABOVE)

TEREM PALACE

CHURCH OF THE LAYING OF THE ROBES

GRANOVITAYA PALATA

THE RED PORCH

TREASURY

DINING HALL

GOLDEN PALACE

CATHEDRAL OF THE ANNUNCIATION

RIVERSIDE PALACE

AMBASSADOR'S HALL

PALACE FOR HIS TWO SONS BUILT BY IVAN IN 1560

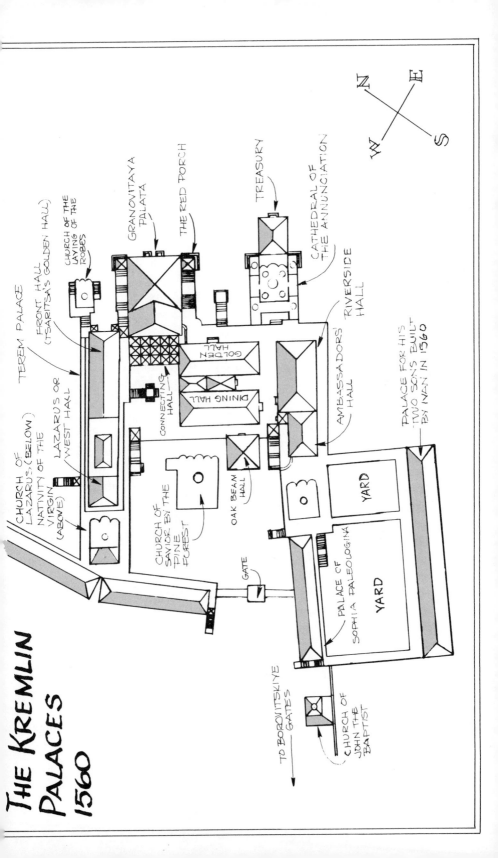

THE KREMLIN PALACES 1560

N E S W (compass rose)

CHURCH OF LAZARUS (BELOW) NATIVITY OF THE VIRGIN (ABOVE)

TEREM PALACE

FRONT HALL (TSARITSA'S GOLDEN HALL)

CHURCH OF THE LAYING OF THE ROBES

GRANOVITAYA PALATA

THE RED PORCH

TREASURY

CATHEDRAL OF THE ANNUNCIATION

LAZARUS OR WEST HALL

GOLDEN HALL

DINING HALL

CONNECTING HALL

AMBASSADORS' HALL

RIVERSIDE HALL

CHURCH OF THE SAVIOR BY THE PINE FOREST

OAK BEAM HALL

GATE

PALACE FOR HIS TWO SONS BUILT BY IVAN IN 1560

YARD

PALACE OF SOPHIA PALEOLOGINA

YARD

TO BOROVITSKIYE GATES

CHURCH OF JOHN THE BAPTIST

court of Sigismund Augustus, King of Poland and Grand Prince of Lithuania, but fell out with him, turned traitor, swore allegiance to the Grand Prince of Moscow, and then turned traitor again because Vasily refused to grant him the great city of Smolensk, and he was returning to Lithuania when he was arrested. Insanely proud, contemptuous of death, despising everything except power, he was brought before Vasily III to answer for his latest treachery. He replied that he had himself captured Smolensk and therefore deserved to have possession of the city. As for the accusation of treachery, he answered, "I have never been disloyal, and if you had been true to your promise to me you would have had in me the most loyal of servants. I have always despised death, and eagerly welcome it, if only because I shall no longer see your tyrannical face!"

Many men had suffered many deaths for lesser acts of treason and for lesser boasts, but Vasily was in a forgiving mood. Prince Mikhail Glinsky was thrown into prison, and released in 1527, after his niece married Vasily. Thereafter he grew in Vasily's favor. His fiery temper and outrageous pride were excused because he had spoken honestly and bluntly, and never dissembled.

Prince Mikhail Glinsky was now the de facto ruler of Russia, the man who made all the final decisions. When he learned that there was an obscure plot to place Prince Yury of Dmitrov on the throne—or perhaps it was no more than the rumor of a plot invented by Prince Andrey Shuisky, for everything about this plot smells of the agent provocateur—he had no hesitation in arresting Prince Yury. Only eight days had passed since the death of Vasily. Prince Yury, loaded with chains, was removed to a prison within the Kremlin Palace by order of the Regent Elena and the Council of Boyars. Two and a half years later, Prince Yury died in his cell and was buried in the Cathedral of Michael the Archangel "in the place reserved for disgraced princes." The chroniclers also remembered that before burial his body was laid out and rubbed with oils in an attempt to remove the marks left by the chains.

A prince's life was one of perpetual danger, for he was at the mercy of jealousies, rumors, and suspicions. It was not necessary that he should commit an act of treason to find himself in prison or without a head. If someone in authority found some advantage in throwing him into prison or beheading him, this was reason enough. The Regent Elena was strong-willed like her uncle, and inevitably there were quarrels. When she took as her lover the young and handsome Prince Ivan Obolensky, Prince Mikhail Glinsky protested vigorously. It was unseemly; it was disgraceful; it was against state policy. It was also a threat to his own position as the wielder of power behind the scenes. He argued so persistently that Elena used the only weapon left to her. He was summoned before the Boyar Council and accused of wanting to rule despotically. Arrested on August 5, 1534, he was sentenced to life imprisonment, having enjoyed supreme power for a little more than seven months. Like Prince Yury of Dmitrov, he was loaded with chains. He died, according to the chroniclers, in "the stone building behind the Kremlin Palace" on September 15, 1536, having outlived Prince Yury by little more than six weeks. Elena ordered that he should be buried quietly, without honors, in the Church of St. Nikita on the farther side of the Neglinnaya River. Once again the chroniclers remembered that an attempt was made to remove the marks left by his chains. A few months later Elena suffered a change of heart, and the body of the man who had once held all the reins of power in his hands was dug up and reburied in the Troitsa-Sergeyevsky Monastery with all the pomp appropriate to the burial of a great prince.

The young and personable Prince Obolensky was now the power behind the throne. His sister Agrafena was Ivan's nurse. The Regent Elena had appointed him Master of the Horse and a member of the Boyar Council. He was therefore in a position to dominate the small circle around the Regent, and since Ivan liked and trusted him, and Elena loved him to distraction, there appeared to be no reason why Prince Obolensky should not continue in power. The Boyar Council, consisting of about fifteen members, was torn by factions, with the Belsky and Shuisky families playing the leading roles. As the only member of the Boyar Council continually in touch with the throne, Prince Obolensky was able to maneuver the councillors according to his wishes. His power, as he knew, depended on the survival of Elena. If she died, he could expect to feel the full weight of all the enmities he had aroused, and to this extent he was at the mercy of the councillors.

Prince Dmitry Belsky, who presided over the Boyar Council, was one of those calm, sober, cautious men, who are so accustomed to being in positions of authority that they show very little interest in the intrigues swirling around them, knowing that they can scotch these intrigues with a stroke of a pen. As he presents himself to history, he is superbly detached while remaining consummately loyal to the throne. He was descended from one of the daughters of Ivan III and from the Grand Princes of Lithuania and Ryazan. Royal blood flowed in his veins, and he was well aware of it. His younger brothers Ivan and Simeon lacked his innate self-discipline and engaged in desperate stratagems, but no one ever suggested that the older brother aided them. He seemed to live apart from them in a world of his own.

The Shuisky princes were violent and predatory, none more so than Prince Andrey Shuisky, whose curious intrigues led to the arrest and imprisonment of Prince Yury of Dmitrov. For his pains he was thrown into prison; few regretted his absence, and his cousins Vasily and Ivan Shuisky, both members of the Boyar Council, both enormously powerful, did nothing to help him. Prince Andrey Shuisky was the black sheep of the family. His reputation tarnished beyond redemption during a later period when he ruled over Pskov and oppressed the inhabitants as though they were no more than the instruments of his avarice. The Shuiskys descended from the Grand Princes of Nizhni-Novgorod and Suzdal, which were conquered by the Grand Prince of Moscow at the beginning of the fifteenth century. The task they gave themselves was to seize power at the first opportunity, and they were prepared to wait patiently.

The intrigues lapped at the gates of the Kremlin Palace, but rarely penetrated them, for Prince Obolensky took care that the inner citadel should remain intact and inviolable. Ivan, in the care of his nurse and priestly tutors, performed his royal duties with distinction. He was present at all ceremonial occasions: a grave, wide-eyed boy well aware that he must be treated with the utmost deference. When the ambassadors came from the Tatar Khans he would address them in their own language, and he would listen politely and perhaps uncomprehendingly when treaties were read out and formally signed in his name by his mother. He was six years old when he received an ambassador from the Khan of the Crimea, and thereafter he was nearly always present when ambassadors arrived at his court.

Nervous, passionate, easily excited, and incapable of concealing his emotions, Ivan as a child showed many of the characteristics he would reveal later. He was fascinated by Church rituals, pilgrimages, sacred relics, the panoply of kingship. At an early age he learned long passages of the Scriptures by heart. From his tutors he acquired an absorbing interest in sacred and profane history: his heroes were David, Solomon, Augustus, Constantine, and Theodosius. The kings and emperors of Jerusalem, Rome, and Byzantium interested him as much as the Grand Princes of Moscow, his ancestors. The emperors of Byzantium were also his ancestors, and he could thus convince himself that he was descended from a long line of royal personages reaching back to King David. He was fascinated by the Russian chronicles, the sermons and homilies of the Church Fathers, Roman and Byzantine histories. He walked with kings and saints, and knew very little about the lives of ordinary people.

All through his childhood the macabre dance of the princes around the throne continued. Prince Andrey of Staritsa, who was Ivan's uncle, possessed many of the qualities of Vasily III. He was proud, stubborn, generous to his friends, conscious of his rights as a member of the ruling family. His brother had bequeathed to him in his will the rich principality of Volotsk; the Regent Elena refused to grant him this bequest, but gave him the customary gifts offered to the brothers of deceased Grand Princes. Prince Andrey was given some horses with richly adorned saddles and many furs and goblets, and he was told that the principality of Volotsk would remain in the possession of the Regent. When he complained that the terms of the will were not being fulfilled, he received more horses, more furs, and more goblets. He retired to Staritsa profoundly dissatisfied but in no mood to intrigue against the Regent. His brother, Prince Yury of Dmitrov, was languishing in prison on a trumped-up charge of treason. It was clear that some people in the court hoped that Prince Andrey would suffer the same fate.

Soon rumors reached Moscow that he had been heard to complain bitterly over the loss of his promised principality. Prince Ivan Shuisky, as a member of the Boyar Council, was sent to Staritsa to negotiate with him and to invite him to Moscow for a conference with the Regent. He refused to make the journey without a safe-conduct signed by Elena, and when at last he set out for the capital he seems to have gone with a heavy heart, knowing that no good would come from the conference even though the Metropolitan Daniel had offered to act as the mediator. Elena was forthright. "We have heard that you have spoken angry words against us," she said. "You should be loyal and not listen to troublemakers. Tell us who these troublemakers are, and there will be no further quarrel between us."

It was the classic gambit of the prosecutor. Prince Andrey denied everything; he was not the kind of man to surround himself with troublemakers; he was loyal to the throne, though gravely provoked. Elena made him sign a document promising he would reveal the names of any future troublemakers and that he would never take into his service anyone who served the Grand Prince. Ivan was present, and watched the solemn oath-taking. Prince Andrey was treated with the greatest honor and attended all the ceremonial functions in the Kremlin Palace, but he was under no illusions. His freedom and his life were in danger. He returned to Staritsa to brood on his powerlessness, the loss of Volotsk, the imprisonment of his older brother, and the prospect that he too might find himself in a stone cell near the Kremlin wall.

When he learned, in August 1536, that his brother had died in prison, he appears to have taken the news calmly. He had expected it; and he suffered in silence. Months passed before the Regent heard, or pretended to hear, that he had decided to flee the country. She therefore sent word that he must immediately appear in Moscow, together with the nobles of his principality, their horses, weapons, and servants, because the Tatars of Kazan were about to wage war against Russia. The Tatars were in fact on the rampage, and large areas around Nizhni-Novgorod were being devastated, but she had never previously called upon him to serve in the army and he was afraid of a trap. He replied that he was unable to come to Moscow because he was ill. The Regent sent a doctor to Staritsa, and when the doctor reported that the illness was not serious—"He says he is suffering from a sore on his thigh and he is forced to lie in bed"—Elena, accustomed to being obeyed, suspected a plot, sent more nobles to Staritsa to report on the strange behavior of Prince Andrey, and learned without too much surprise that the reason why he refused to come to Moscow was that he was mortally afraid of what would happen to him. Nevertheless she was determined that he should appear before her court. Twice she summoned him; twice he rejected her summons. On the third summons he composed a letter written ostensibly to the Grand Prince Ivan, in whose name he had been summoned to appear in Moscow. He wrote:

> My Lord, you have commanded me most categorically to appear before you. It grieves me sorely that you place no credence in my sickness and demand my immediate presence. My lord, in former days it was not considered proper that we should be dragged on a stretcher in order to appear before you, our lords. From sickness, calamity and sorrow I have lost my mind and reason.
>
> Therefore, my Lord, you should shew me mercy and favor, thus warming the body and heart of your servant. Thus your servant, receiving your favor, will be released from fear and sorrow, as God guides your heart.

While the letter was still on its way to Moscow, the Regent decided to act vigorously. She sent a delegation of clergy to Staritsa to urge Prince Andrey to come to her court, and at the same time she sent a column of troops to Volotsk to intercept him in the event that he should attempt to flee to Lithuania. The matter was so important that she ordered her lover, Prince Ivan Obolensky, to take command of the troops. At all costs he must arrest Prince Andrey. There were spies on both sides. About the same time that Elena heard that Prince Andrey had finally decided to leave the country, the Prince heard that Obolensky's troops were racing toward Staritsa. He had wanted to be left in peace; he had never intended to be disloyal; and now disloyalty was forced on him.

On May 2, 1537, Prince Andrey, accompanied by his family, his armed nobles, and all his court, rode out of Staritsa. He rode due north to Torzhok, and it was expected that he would then turn west and make for the Lithuanian frontier. Instead, he rode on to Novgorod at a leisurely pace, confident that Obolensky would not catch up with him. He had forgotten that spies were everywhere and that all his movements were known. He issued proclamations to the people of Novgorod province to come out in open revolt against the Regent and the Grand Prince, and some thirty nobles from Novgorod joined his forces. Prince Nikita Obolensky, a young cousin of Elena's lover, was ordered to race with a column of troops to Novgorod to place the city in a state of defense. Prince Andrey was outmaneuvered, for the young Obolensky reached Novgorod in good time, the city fathers swore allegiance to the Regent Elena and her son Ivan IV, and the entire population was set to work building fortifications. Novgorod was impregnable. Reluctantly Prince Andrey was forced to the conclusion that he could be safe only if he crossed the Lithuanian frontier. His nobles were deserting him, and his hopes of raising a revolt were fast vanishing. He was forty miles from Novgorod, on his way to Lithuania, when the troops of Prince Ivan Obolensky caught up with him. There was nothing left for him but to fight. Just as the two small armies were about to do battle, Prince Obolensky sent an envoy promising him in the name of the Regent and the Tsar that if he returned to Moscow no harm would befall him. He would be allowed to return to Staritsa and all his past sins would be forgiven him.

In this way the trap cunningly prepared in Moscow was sprung.

Trusting in the words of Prince Obolensky, Prince Andrey rode to Moscow, where he was treated with ceremony and permitted to take up residence with his wife Efrosinia and his two-year-old son Vladimir in his own house inside the Kremlin walls. He thought himself a free man, but in fact he was closely guarded. For two days Elena and her lover debated what they would do with their prisoner; then they sentenced him to a lingering death in the same cell once occupied by his brother. Loaded with chains, Prince Andrey of Staritsa died in his cell six months later.

Elena's victory was not yet complete, for it was necessary to punish all those who had assisted and followed the Prince during his short-lived rebellion. The members of his court, his boyars and nobles, were arrested, flogged, and thrown into prison, while a special punishment was reserved for the thirty Novgorod nobles who had joined him on his northward march. Their bodies hung on gibbets along the Moscow-Novgorod road, so that all travelers to Novgorod would know what fate to expect if they rebelled against Moscow.

The Regency was secure; it had no more enemies. Elena would reign until Ivan came of age, for Russia was at peace and the Boyar Council supported her. She was in her late twenties, young, proud, and vigorous, with a full life in front of her. Then quite suddenly, without any warning, the Regency came to an end. Early in the morning of April 3, 1538, she died. She may have suffered a heart attack; someone may have administered poison. On the same day she was buried without pomp in the Church of the Resurrection in the Kremlin. Her sudden death and unobtrusive burial hinted at murder, but Ivan himself seems to have believed that she died a natural death. Her death terrified him, but still more terrible was the behavior of Vasily Shuisky, who seized power and became the new Regent. Within a week Ivan Obolensky was thrown into prison while his sister Agrafena, Ivan's nurse, was ordered into a nunnery. Vasily Shuisky had no sympathy for Ivan. The boy would serve as a figurehead, and his very welfare depended upon his total submission to the Regent. At Vasily Shuisky's orders all the jewels and gold vessels belonging to Elena were unceremoniously bundled up and carried off to the well-guarded State Treasury.

Many years later Ivan remembered vividly what happened after his mother's death. He wrote:

> Thus by God's will it came to pass that our mother, the pious Tsaritsa Elena, went from the earthly kingdom to the heavenly, and we and our brother Yury were orphaned, being without parents and having no one to look after us, but trusting in God. We threw ourselves upon the mercy of the Most Pure Mother of God and the prayers of all the saints and the blessings received from our parents. . . . When I entered my eighth year, then our subjects achieved their design to have a kingdom without a ruler. They did not regard me as their Sovereign, worthy of their loving attention, but instead they set about pursuing wealth and glory, and quarreled violently with one another. And what did they not do? How many boyars and well-wishers of my father, how many generals were killed by them! And they took my mother's treasures and carried them to the Great Treasury, furiously kicking them and poking them with sharp instruments, and some of the treasures they divided among themselves.

The world, which was beginning to open wide, now enclosed Ivan in its iron claws. He was living on sufferance, in fear and trembling. His mother worshipped him, his nurse doted on him, Obolensky talked to him, and now they were all swept away. Guards were set over him to watch and report on all his actions and everything he said: his only weapons were cunning, secrecy, and the knowledge bred into him that he was indeed the rightful Lord and Grand Prince of Russia. This knowledge would sustain him through all the trials ahead.

Vasily Shuisky was not inexperienced in the art of governing. He was in his sixties, a hard-bitten soldier and administrator, a man of few words. They called him "the silent one," and silence was one of his most formidable weapons. Totally without scruples, totally merciless, he had once, when governor of Smolensk, arrested the traitors who preferred to be ruled by the Grand Prince of Lithuania and hanged them on the city walls garlanded with the gifts they had received from the Grand Prince. One of his first tasks when he came to power was to open the prisons and release all those sentenced by Elena for treachery. Two months after her death he married Anastasia, Ivan's first cousin, the daughter of his aunt Evdokia. The princess had not the least desire to be married to him, but he was the Regent with power of life and death over everyone and she submitted to his will. By marrying into Ivan's family Vasily Shuisky was legitimizing his usurpation of power. The princess was doubly royal, for she was the granddaughter of the Grand Prince Ivan III and of Ibrahim, a former Khan of Kazan. Immediately after the marriage Vasily Shuisky moved with his young bride into the Kremlin palace of Prince Andrey of Staritsa.

The chronicles record that Ivan "gave away his sister[1] Anastasia in marriage," and he must therefore have been present at the wedding, wearing his crown and robes of state. He did not attend the wedding as a free agent, but as a puppet manipulated by the Regent and mechanically reciting the words put into his mouth. He feared and detested the Regent, all the more so when he learned that Vasily and Anastasia Shuisky were living in the palace of his dead uncle, close to his own palace. Above all, it was necessary not to show any fear. While still a child he was acting out many roles and learning to dissimulate, knowing that a false move would bring about his death or imprisonment.

Three people remained close to him. They were the Metropolitan Daniel; Fyodor Mishurin, who had once been his father's secre-

---

[1] By Russian court usage quite distant female relatives of the Tsar were regarded as "sisters." Evdokia, the sister of the Grand Prince Vasily III, married Kudaikul, Prince of Kazan, the younger brother of the reigning Khan Alegam. Kudaikul was converted to Christianity and given the name of Peter. The marriage of Peter and Evdokia took place on January 25, 1506.

tary; Prince Ivan Belsky, the ambitious younger brother of Prince Dmitry Belsky, who presided over the Boyar Council. Prince Ivan Belsky was playing for the highest stakes: he wanted to ensure the survival of Ivan with himself as the closest friend of the throne. The blood of the Grand Princes of Moscow flowed in his veins and he saw himself as the future Regent. His elder brother, who had a greater claim to high position, was totally disinterested. As president of the Boyar Council he was immersed in the day-by-day operations of government and showed no interest in exchanging real power for the panoply of power.

The cards were being dealt out afresh; new groups of intriguers were being formed; inevitably Prince Ivan Belsky would attempt to bring down Prince Vasily Shuisky, and inevitably there would be palace revolts with the losers exiled, tortured, or loaded with chains in a small prison cell. Those who were prepared to revolt knew the risks they were taking. Prince Ivan Belsky, unknown to the Regent, was attempting to pack the Boyar Council with his own friends and relatives. This was the first step. The next step would be to reduce Vasily Shuisky to the rank of a Boyar Councillor. The third step would be to deprive the Shuisky family of its wealth and influence.

If Ivan knew of these intrigues, he was silent about them. Every year he made a ceremonial visit to the Troitsa-Sergeyevsky Monastery to pray at the saint's tomb and to call down blessings on his reign from heaven. Accordingly, on the birthday of St. Sergius, he appeared at the monastery with the usual large retinue, which included his deaf-mute brother Yury, the Regent, and the Regent's brother, Prince Ivan Shuisky. Ivan offered presents to the monks and conducted himself in a manner that showed he was accustomed to following the most complicated rituals. In Moscow Prince Ivan Belsky was preparing a revolt against the Regent. The revolt failed, perhaps because Prince Belsky lost his nerve or more likely because it was badly organized. When the Regent returned to Moscow he ordered the arrest of all the conspirators.

Prince Belsky was placed under house arrest, his close friends were banished to their country estates, and the main punishment fell on the hapless secretary, Fyodor Mishurin, who was stripped naked before being executed. Since Prince Belsky was related by ties of blood to Ivan, he received no further punishment. The quarrels of the princes had a strangely unreal character and ended when, very conveniently, the Regent died shortly after the execution of Fyodor Mishurin. His successor was his younger brother Prince Ivan Shuisky.

The macabre dance of the princes, which would not end until Ivan was crowned Tsar, continued relentlessly. It was a ring dance with Ivan at the center, the Belskys and Shuiskys circling around him in the candlelit darkness. Sometimes mysterious figures would emerge out of the darkness to join them and then vanish. Ivan would try to slip past the dancers, but always in vain. To the end of his life he would remember the suffocating presence of those dimly seen dancers, armed with swords and axes, as they revolved around him; and he vowed that when he was in power he would make them dance to his tune.

Once again he had lost his friends: Fyodor Mishurin was dead, Ivan Belsky arrested, the Metropolitan Daniel under suspicion. On February 2, 1539, Prince Ivan Shuisky demanded of the Boyar Council that they should pass judgment on the Metropolitan Daniel, whose chief crime was that he had taken part in the Belsky conspiracy. The new Regent did not, however, mention the conspiracy. Instead, he drew up a catalogue of the Metropolitan's vices. "The Metropolitan acted with merciless cruelty to all," he declared. "He has thrown people in prison, put them in chains, and starved them to death. He has acquired an immense fortune." The Boyar Council decided that it was simpler to argue the merits of banishing the Metropolitan than to let him continue in office. Ioasaf, the chief abbot of the Troitsa-Sergeyevsky Monastery, who had officiated at Ivan's baptism, became the new Metropolitan.

No decision had been reached about the fate of Prince Ivan Belsky, who was still under house arrest. Guards stood outside the house with orders to prevent him from leaving, but on July 25, 1540, he quietly slipped out, entered the Kremlin Palace and was immediately received by Ivan, who was overjoyed to find the man he regarded as a friend and a confidant. Ivan Shuisky, who had been taken by surprise, raged but could do nothing against the combined forces of Prince Belsky and the Metropolitan. Indeed, he found some comfort in doing nothing, for he rejected all invitations to discuss the situation with Ivan and the Boyar Council. He accused the Metropolitan Ioasaf of engineering the coup and implicated some members of the Boyar Council, but refused to participate in the government.

Ivan Belsky became Regent. His first task was to decide what should be done to Ivan Shuisky, and he came to the sensible conclusion that he should suffer no punishment, since his fall from power was punishment enough. Even-handed and sober-minded, tolerant and intelligent, Ivan Belsky, who was descended from the Grand Princes of Lithuania, ruled Russia well. For two years his moderating influence was felt, and then the wheel turned full circle and once more Ivan Shuisky came to power in one of those sudden upheavals which threatened to make a mockery of the throne.

Ivan was now nearly ten years old. From his childhood he had known nothing but coups and countercoups, intrigues, treachery, the great princes continually attempting to seize power by surprise attacks on the Kremlin, by murder or by stealth. Sensitive, widely read, with a knowledge of political affairs far in advance of his years, Ivan was well aware of the dangers of his high position. Many of the tragedies of his reign have their source in his childhood fears and childhood terrors.

Meanwhile there was a brief period when fears and terrors fell away and for the first time during a war against the Tatars he was allowed to play a kingly role.

Facing the Tatars

ALL THROUGH THE YEARS of the Regency of Elena and of her successors Russia remained in little danger from her foes. A two-year war with the Grand Principality of Lithuania at the beginning of the Regency could be regarded as little more than a succession of border skirmishes. Lithuanian embassies were received, a peace treaty was signed, more skirmishes took place, and sometimes one of the Russian nobles, dissatisfied or fearing for his life, crossed the frontier, swore allegiance to the Grand Prince of Lithuania, and was rewarded with large estates in the hope that he would not betray his adopted country. Lithuania and Russia were sworn enemies doomed to fight until one was beaten to her knees or both were reduced to a state of exhaustion.

But if Lithuania no longer threatened her existence, Russia possessed another and more dangerous enemy in the southeast—the remnant of the Golden Horde. The Tatars, of mixed Turkic and Mongolian ancestry, yellow-skinned and slant-eyed, still occupied vast regions of the southern steppes, their khans ruling over Kazan, Astrakhan, and the Crimea, all of them with powerful armies at their disposal. The Grand Princes of Muscovy made treaties with them, invited Tatar ambassadors and traders to Moscow, arranged marriages between the princely families of Russia and the families of the khans who entered the Tsar's service, and always addressed the khans with the respect due to royalty. Tatar blood flowed in the veins of many Russian princely families, and many claimed that both Rurik and Jenghiz Khan were among their ancestors. Russian culture was deeply colored by the culture of the Tatars, and the Russian language borrowed [1] lavishly from the rich, earthy language of these tribesmen who rode bareback on shaggy ponies and thought nothing of riding across the whole length of Asia. Their songs and heroic poetry deeply influenced Russian poetry, and their way of life subtly influenced the Russian character.

All this was inevitable, for the Tatar armies had swept across Russia, burning, pillaging, and raping as they pleased, demanding and receiving tribute from the Russian princes who were compelled to appear in person before the Khan of the Golden Horde in his tent-city of Sarai on the Lower Volga. The first wave of invaders came in 1223 at the orders of Jenghiz Khan. It was led by Sabutai and Jebei the Arrow, who was one of the world's greatest conquerors, for he led the invasion against China, and then against Persia, and then against Georgia, and then against Russia. The invaders fought the Russian army led by Prince Mstislav of Galich on the Kalka River between the Don and the Caspian, and when the battle was over, nearly all the Russians lay dead and all southern Russia lay open to the invaders. Sabutai and Jebei the Arrow then turned to attack the Bolgars on the Upper Volga. For the moment Russia was forgotten, while they attacked and destroyed the army of the Bolgars.

Fourteen years later Batu, the grandson of Jenghiz Khan, ordered Sabutai to conquer Russia. Sabutai was prepared to accept the submission of the Russian princes without fighting. Ambassadors were sent ahead with the Mongol prince's demands: Surrender a tenth of all property and a tenth of the population, or else you lose everything. The Russians killed the ambassadors, and Batu ordered the second invasion. Ryazan fell after a six-day siege, and then it was the turn of Vladimir. The Russian army fell back on the river Sit, two hundred miles northwest of Vladimir, and was completely destroyed. Sabutai's army rode north until it was within sixty miles of Novgorod, and was within a few days of establishing an empire reaching from the Pacific to the Baltic when the order

---

[1] Many familiar Russian words, especially those dealing with trade, food, clothing, horses, and precious stones, were borrowed from Tatar. Among them were *tma* (ten thousand), *dengi* (money), *kazna* (treasury), *tamozhnia* (custom house), *balagan* (booth), *bashmak* (shoe), *tabun* (drove of horses).

was given to turn back. The spring thaws would soon be coming, and soon the North Russian plains would become an impenetrable morass of mud and melting snows. The city that called itself Lord Novgorod the Great remained unharmed, but all the Russian principalities had ceased to exist or existed only by favor of the invaders.

Thus most of Russia became a colony of the Golden Horde with the princes acting as agents and tax gatherers of the conquerors, a role which they performed sometimes with fervor and sometimes with distaste but nearly always with alacrity. Tribute was sent regularly to the reigning Khan, and the princes appeared at Sarai to receive their titles and to pronounce oaths of loyalty. Occasionally a prince rebelled against the Tatar yoke, murdered the envoys from Sarai, called out his army, and proclaimed a holy war against the infidels. Then from Sarai there would come the abrupt order commanding one of the other princes to suppress the rebellion or lose his principality. In this way Russians fought against Russians to maintain the *pax tatarica.*

Gradually the principality of Moscow, which received many favors from the Khan for putting down many rebellions, grew to become the preponderant power in Russia. Moscow in the time of Jebei the Arrow was no more than a small frontier post on the edge of the marshes. It grew to become a large city, pushing out its boundaries and forming alliances on a scale that threatened the power of the Golden Horde. Mamay, the commander of the Tatar army in the reign of Khan Murid, decided that the time had come to put an end to Russian insolence. He advanced on Russia and met the army of Grand Prince Dmitry of Moscow at Kulikovo Field on September 8, 1380. Mamay fled after losing half his cavalry, Dmitry lost half his infantry. Here, on the banks of the Upper Don, the Russians showed that they were determined to wrest power from the Tatars. Never again were they to live in abject fear of the Golden Horde.

The invasions continued, large areas of southern Russia were continually being raided, but the invaders were no longer capable of enforcing their demands for tribute. By the time of Ivan IV the once-powerful Golden Horde had disintegrated into the separate khanates of Astrakhan, Kazan, and the Crimea, and some marauding tribes under their chieftains. Astrakhan and Kazan were fortified cities; Bakhchisaray in the southern Crimea was a city of palaces; and all were ruled by khans who claimed descent from Jenghiz Khan. Still another khanate was deliberately created by the Grand Prince of Muscovy within his own territory. It lay on the Oka River south of Moscow and was called Kasimov after Khan Kasim, its first ruler. Kasimov served as the headquarters of the Tatars who took service under the Grand Prince. This khanate, completely under the jurisdiction of the Grand Prince, also served to remind the Khans of Astrakhan, Kazan, and the Crimea that Muscovy could call upon thousands of Tatars to defend its territory. Within this small territory people who were once subjects of the Great Khan had become the subjects of the Grand Prince.

The Khanate of Kasimov provided the Grand Princes of Muscovy with a powerful psychological weapon against the Tatar khans on the Volga and in the Crimea. The very fact that it had been possible to create such a state showed that the Tatars were divided; and the resourceful Russians took care to sharpen this thorn in their side. Kasimov's khans were given precedence above all Russians except the Grand Prince and his family. They were received in the Kremlin with the honors due to kings, even though they ruled over a comparatively small territory consisting of the town of Gorodets, which means "little town," and the surrounding area. For the Russians Kasimov was a gateway to the East, a trade mart, an intelligence center, a recruiting office. Here disaffected Tatar princelings found aid and comfort offered on a lavish scale and prepared themselves for endless intrigues against the khans.

These khans were also engaged in far-reaching intrigues. When Ivan Belsky came to power, he had the mortification of knowing that his younger brother Simeon, who had fled to Lithuania in 1534, was now acting as chief adviser to the Khan of the Crimea and planning an invasion of Russia. This was treachery on a grand scale. Simeon Belsky never hesitated in his efforts to destroy Russia. All his life he had been a destructive influence, an ambitious intriguer, corrupt and volatile, hating and despising his older brothers perhaps because they occupied high positions at court which were denied to him.

This time there was a very real possibility that the invasion would be successful. Khan Saip Guirey was in close alliance with the Sultan of Turkey, Sulayman the Magnificent, and could count on heavy Turkish guns and trained Turkish gunners. He was also in alliance with the Grand Prince of Lithuania. The plan of attack involved a massive concentration of forces from three directions, from Lithuania in the west, from Kazan in the east, and from the Crimea in the south. Three large armies reaching Moscow simultaneously would hammer it into submission, and all of Russia would be divided between the Tatars and the Lithuanians.

Khan Saip Guirey was a proud and forceful man with a clear understanding of what he wanted to do. In a letter addressed to the Grand Prince Ivan, not yet eleven years old, he announced that he was coming to destroy the state of Muscovy and enslave its peoples. He wrote in the authentic tones of the early Khans of the Golden Horde: "I shall come upon you, I shall stand before Moscow in your estate on the Sparrow Hills, I shall let loose my army in all directions, I shall enslave your land." It was not an empty boast. He had a vast army, massive armaments, trusted allies. In addition he had Simeon Belsky, who could speak authoritatively about the strength and disposition of the Russian forces.

In July 1541 a scout in one of the forward frontier posts reported that the khan was advancing with his troops along the upper course of the Donets River. He said he had followed them for a whole day and estimated there were a hundred thousand troops. Later another scout reached Moscow with the news that the enemy had crossed the Don River, and there were so many of them that they were beyond counting. Later still it was learned that the new stone fortress at Zaraisk, the strongest fortress on Russia's southern frontier, had been attacked, but the garrison fought off the invaders and even captured some Tatar soldiers. They were carried off to Moscow where they boasted that their khan would soon cross the Oka River and ravage all the territories surrounding the capital. They also confirmed that Simeon Belsky was traveling with the khan.

Moscow was placed in a state of alert. Dmitry Belsky assumed overall command of the army, while Ivan Belsky directed the defense of the capital. Ivan Shuisky with his own army joined forces with the army of Shigaley, the Khan of Kasimov, at Vladimir, where they hoped to head off an invading army led by Safa Guirey, the Khan of Kazan. Dmitry Belsky made his headquarters at Kolomna directly in the path of the Crimean Tatars.

Although Ivan was a mere boy, quite incapable of making military decisions, he played an important role in the defense of Moscow. He was the totem, the figurehead, all the more appealing because he was young, vigorous, deeply religious, and perhaps in direct communion with God and the saints. His kingdom was threatened; never before in his reign had there been a full-scale invasion by the Tatars. Accompanied by his brother Yury, arrayed in the royal robes, he prayed earnestly with tears in his eyes for divine intercession. The brothers fell on their knees before the icon of the Virgin of Vladimir in the Uspensky Cathedral. "Oh, most holy Sovereign Mother of God, be merciful unto us Christians," he prayed. "Be merciful to us, your children, and save us and all Christendom from the infidel Khan Saip Guirey, who is advancing against me and against all the Russian land with great confidence. Protect me and all the Russian land, and be merciful lest the infidels say: Where is their God in whom they put their trust?"

Then, rising from their knees, the brothers made their way to the tomb of St. Peter the Metropolitan, who was believed to have taken the city of Moscow under his special care. Ivan urged the saint, who resembled "a bright candle guarding over our family and over all Orthodox Christians," to pray earnestly to God on behalf of Muscovy threatened with extinction. There were more icons to be visited, and then at last Ivan returned to the Kremlin Palace, where the Boyar Council was waiting for him.

The question to be decided was whether Ivan should remain in Moscow or whether he should be removed to a safer place. The decision, Ivan said, remained in their hands and he appealed to them to offer their arguments and come to a conclusion. Historical precedents were discussed. It was remembered that in 1408 Khan Edigey came up to the walls of Moscow, and the Grand Prince Vasily I, leaving his brothers to defend the city, rode off to Kostroma and during the journey was very nearly captured by the Tatars. Such were the dangers of leaving Moscow, and these dangers would be compounded when the Grand Prince set out from Moscow. "Our Grand Prince is young and his brother is even younger," one of the boyars said. "Their endurance is short and they are not experienced horsemen. How fast can one ride with little children?"

The Metropolitan Ioasaf wanted Ivan and Yury to remain in the Kremlin, urging that there was really nowhere else for them to go. In the past, when the Tatars invaded Muscovy, the Grand Princes had sometimes taken refuge in the fortified towns in the east, but today these towns stood in the path of the army coming from Kazan. Retreat to Novgorod or Pskov in the north would bring them too close to the Lithuanian frontier. The Metropolitan spoke about the holy churches and holy relics within the Kremlin, and how they would serve to protect the Grand Prince and all of Muscovy. Woe to those who abandoned them!

The Metropolitan carried the boyars with him: it was decided that Ivan should remain within the Kremlin. Orders for the defense of Moscow were issued in Ivan's name. Gunners and musketeers were stationed along the walls and at the towers. Kitay Gorod, the densely populated section of Moscow east of the Kremlin, was heavily fortified, and the people were ordered to bring all their movable property behind the defense works. The chroniclers report that morale was high, and the people went about promising one another they would be steadfast unto death for the holy churches, for the Grand Prince, and for their own homes.

When news reached Moscow that the Tatars were building pontoon bridges over the Oka River, a proclamation was drawn up in the name of the Grand Prince and immediately dispatched to Dmitry Belsky. The proclamation called upon the army to resist the aggressors to the uttermost and on no account must they be permitted to cross the river. "But if it should happen that the Khan succeeds in crossing the river, then you must hold fast for the sake of the holy churches and the Orthodox Christians and fight the Tatars with God's help. I shall reward you and your children, and those of you whom God shall take will have their names entered in The Book of Life, and I shall give rewards to their wives and children."

The proclamation had the desired effect of demonstrating that Ivan was deeply concerned with the welfare of his army. Dmitry Belsky read the proclamation first to his generals and then to the assembled troops, who replied that they were all ready to lay down their lives for Orthodox Christianity. "We are well armed," they declared, "and we are prepared now to drink the cup of death with the Tatars." The proclamation reached the army just in time. Dmitry Belsky, observing the enthusiasm of the soldiers, gave the order for the advance on the Oka River.

The Army of the Crimea reached the Oka River at three o'clock in the afternoon of July 30, 1541. The Tatar engineers had already laid down pontoons near the small town of Rostislavl, and a massive crossing was about to take place when the Russian army appeared on the opposite bank. Khan Saip Guirey set up his headquarters on a hill overlooking the river. Only the first detachment of Dmitry Belsky's army had reached the river bank, but they were so numerous that for a while the Khan thought he was confronted with the entire Russian army. It was a hot summer day, and the arms and armor of the Russians glittered in the sun. The Khan pressed his advantage: his troops raced across the pontoons, the Turkish guns opened up, the Tatar archers drew their bows and the arrows fell on the Russians thick as rain. This relentless, massive attack sent a shudder through the Russian lines, which faltered and were close to breaking. But more and more Russian troops came up and the lines held.

Soon the heavy Russian guns were answering the fire of the Turkish guns, and the Tatars were being forced off the north bank of the river. From his headquarters Khan Saip Guirey saw the Russians coming up, column after column, all in good order. He turned angrily to Simeon Belsky and said, "I was told the Grand Prince's army was off to Kazan and there would be no one here to challenge me. Never have I seen so many well-equipped men on excellent horses in one place, and my old Tatars—men who have taken part in many campaigns—say the same." Simeon Belsky had encouraged the Khan with the promise of an easy conquest, but there was to be no easy conquest.

The Khan held a council of war with his princes and learned that what he feared above all was taking place—endless columns of Russians were converging on the river. When night fell, the fighting slackened off. During the night the Russians mounted more guns on the river bank, more troops came up, and the Khan became more and more convinced that his forces would never succeed in establishing themselves on the north bank. Before morning he had decided to break off the engagement. The Russian chroniclers relate with some satisfaction that he lost his nerve to such an extent that he was unable to mount his horse and had to be carried away in a cart. The whole Tatar army fled south.

Dmitry Belsky was confronted with a serious problem: whether to pursue the retreating Tatars. He feared an ambush; he feared, too, the consequences of breaking a traditional practice, for the Russian armies rarely pursued a retreating enemy. He solved the problem by resorting to half-measures. A small force made up of men chosen from all the regiments was ordered to follow the Tatars in the hope of picking off the stragglers, capturing prisoners, and hurrying the Tatar retreat across the southern steppes. From the prisoners it was learned that the Khan was in a state of abject despair and had told his princes that in spite of all his efforts he had achieved only dishonor. At the very least he had hoped to wound Russia grievously, and now, even though in full retreat, he was determined to exact vengeance by taking the town of Pronsk, a well-fortified outpost in Ryazan province. If he could capture its treasure, enslave its people, and put it to the flames, he would be partially rewarded for an ignominious defeat.

The Khan's army arrived before Pronsk on August 3, and immediately attacked the town with a barrage of gunfire from Turkish guns and missiles hurled by catapults. The town was defended by a small garrison without heavy weapons. Tatars who attempted to scale the walls were thrown back by men armed only with pikes and stones. The walls held; the people of Pronsk were confident they would be rescued; the commander of the garrison troops knew that a Russian column was on its way. A delegation of Tatar dignitaries rode up to the city walls to parlay with the commander, offering him rich rewards if he surrendered the town, "because the Khan will not depart until he has taken it." The commander replied, "This town was built by the will of God and therefore it cannot be taken without God's will. The Khan should be patient! Soon the Grand Prince's officers will be following in the footsteps of the Tatars."

The threat was well-founded, but the Khan was determined to take the town. Wooden towers and scaling ladders were brought up; orders were issued for a general assault on all sides; the garrison commander urged the townspeople to mount guard on the walls with whatever weapons lay at hand: knives, rocks, boiling water. About this time seven men, forerunners of the relief column, slipped into the town with the news that the column was only a few miles away. When one of the townspeople was captured by the Tatars and brought into the presence of the Khan, the prisoner declared boldly that the Tatars would soon have to meet the full force of the Russian army. The Khan panicked, ordered the siege lifted, and sped south in the direction of the Don River. When the relief column arrived at Pronsk, all the Tatars had already fled.

In Moscow the church bells rang in celebration of the victory. Ivan's triumph was complete. "Sovereign, we conquered by your angelic prayers and your good fortune," they told him, and he believed them.

Figurehead, talisman, object of adoration, symbol of Russian dynastic traditions, offerer of angelic prayers, he was all of these and much more, but he was also a child who could be manipulated by desperate men. No one in Moscow was more popular, more beloved, more angelic, but he was at the mercy of the boyar factions. He was very close to Ivan Belsky, a man of steady intelligence, and it seemed that at long last the Regency was being managed skillfully, without brutality. The Regent had deliberately allowed Ivan Shuisky to go free after he was toppled from power: no savage reprisals, no secret arrests. On the contrary, Ivan Shuisky was given command of the army at Vladimir, a position of trust, for the Muscovites expected an attack by the army of the Khan of Kazan. But there was no attack. Ivan Shuisky, restless and ambitious, determined once more to become Regent and saw his opportunity. He possessed an army, a power base, in Vladimir, and spies working for him inside the Kremlin. He had long family connections with the people of Novgorod, and the nobles and gentry from Novgorod joined his faction. With the help of Prince Ivan Kubensky, Prince Dmitry Paletsky, and the state treasurer Ivan Tretiakov, he engineered a plot so breathtakingly simple that it was almost bound to succeed. The plot called for the simultaneous arrests of the Grand Prince Ivan, the Metropolitan Ioasaf, and Ivan Belsky in the depths of the night. On the following day Ivan Shuisky, accompanied by three hundred armed men from Vladimir, would enter the Kremlin in triumph.

Everything happened exactly as the conspirators wanted it to happen. Ivan Belsky knew nothing whatsoever about the plot and had taken no precautions for his own safety. On the night of January 2, 1542, armed men burst into his palace, arrested him, and carried him off to the well-guarded Treasury building near the Kremlin Palace.

About the same time, at five o'clock in the morning, when it was still very dark, Ivan was roughly awakened by a group of boyars who burst into the Kremlin Palace. They ordered the terrified boy to get up and to say his prayers in front of the icons in his bedroom. While he was at his prayers the Metropolitan Ioasaf arrived at the Kremlin Palace. He had been awakened by stones thrown at his window, and suspecting a plot he had fled along the covered arcade leading from his own palace to the Kremlin Palace, hoping to warn Ivan and lead him to safety. In fact he fell into the trap. The boyars who arrested Ivan were about to arrest the Metropolitan, but he slipped away and reached the lodging house belonging to the abbot and priests of the Troitsa-Sergeyevsky Monastery near the Troitsky Gate of the Kremlin, while a group of nobles from Novgorod followed hot on his heels. There was a good deal of wild shouting. Prince Dmitry Paletsky, one of the leaders of the conspiracy, arrived just in time to prevent the killing of the Metropolitan. The conspirators had achieved their aims: Ivan Belsky and the Metropolitan were under arrest, Ivan was at their mercy, and the Kremlin gates could now be opened to Ivan Shuisky and his three hundred armed men from Vladimir.

The first task of the new Regent, who reached the Kremlin later in the day, was to decide the fate of Ivan Belsky and of the Metropolitan. This was a pleasant and satisfying task: he consigned both of them to Beloozero (White Lake) in the far north where Ivan Belsky spent the few remaining months of his life in prison, while the Metropolitan Ioasaf was consigned to a cell in the Kirillov Monastery. Some of Ivan Belsky's close companions and advisers were exiled to their country estates. Makary, Archbishop of Novgorod and Pskov, became the new Metropolitan.

The coup d'etat had become the normal means of acquiring power, and the Muscovites were growing accustomed to a quick succession of rulers. Foreign affairs suffered little change. When ambassadors arrived in the Kremlin, they were received by Ivan with the traditional ceremonies. So it happened that when Lithuanian ambassadors arrived in March, Ivan welcomed them, attended by the new Regent and by Dmitry Belsky, who as permanent president of the Boyar Council had the place of honor on Ivan's right side. A seven-year truce with Lithuania was signed in the great hall of the Kremlin Palace on March 25, 1542. The treaty was placed on a salver, a cross was placed over the treaty, and Ivan solemnly kissed the cross. The chroniclers remembered that the eleven-year-old boy presented the ambassadors with goblets filled with a cherry cordial and spoke to them with grave dignity. In public he behaved with decorum; in private he seethed with rage.

He had reason to rage, for he was suffering from intolerable frustrations. No sooner had he settled down with a new Regent than the Regent himself vanished from the scene. Life had become a series of brutal submissions all the more galling because the Grand Prince was surrounded with the panoply of power and was continually addressed as though he, and he alone, was in full possession of power. Ivan Belsky had treated him with deference, but Ivan Shuisky treated him with contempt. He was made painfully aware that he was not the master of his own household. Many years later he could still remember the slights he had received at the hands of the Regent and the other Shuiskys who filled his court. He wrote:

> The Shuiskys treated us—myself and my brother—as though we were foreigners or the most wretched menials. What sufferings I endured through lack of clothing and from hunger! For in all things my will was not my own (I had no will); everything was done contrary to my will, in a manner unbefitting my tender years. I recall one incident. I and my brother were playing together when we were quite young, and there was Prince Ivan Vasilievich Shuisky sitting on a bench, his elbows on my father's bed, his leg up in a chair, and he did not even incline his head toward us either in a parental manner or as a master, nor did he show any humility toward us. Who can endure such arrogance?

Such wounds festered and in time they would poison his whole organism. The study of revenge became his main preoccupation, his main solace. He was waiting impatiently for the moment when he would be able to break through his bonds and overthrow the tyranny of the princes who ordered his life and regarded him as a puppet. In theory he would come of age at fifteen. Then he would rule in his own right and no one would give him orders again.

Ivan Shuisky did not long enjoy his power. He died in May 1542 of natural causes and was succeeded by his cousin Andrey. In the same month Ivan Belsky died in prison in Beloozero. According to one report he was starved to death, according to another he was murdered. What is certain is that Andrey Shuisky wanted him out of the way and deliberately destroyed him. At his death Belsky was about forty years old, a quiet, scholarly, and deeply religious man who appears to have accepted his fate with equanimity.

Andrey Shuisky was a man trained in conspiracy and a notorious mischief-maker. Many years earlier he had been responsible for the arrest of Prince Yury of Dmitrov, who was Ivan's uncle, charging him with treason. In 1539 he became governor of Pskov, where he displayed such a talent for exacting bribes that it became necessary to remove him. An able extortionist, he was now at the height of his powers and determined to use Ivan for his own ends. As the senior member of the Shuisky clan, the most cunning and the most experienced, he set about consolidating his power. At all costs Ivan must be prevented from forming close friendships with people outside the Shuisky faction.

Among Ivan's close friends was Fyodor Vorontsov, a middle-aged man belonging to a well-known boyar family. He had served Ivan's father and was known to possess an intense loyalty to the throne and a deep affection for the person of the Grand Prince. His presence in the Kremlin Palace infuriated the Shuiskys, who decided to rid themselves of him.

On September 9, 1542, there was a meeting of the Boyar Council in the dining hall of the Kremlin Palace. The Shuiskys were present in force. Ivan sat on his throne, and the Metropolitan Makary sat on another throne at a lower level. Suddenly there was a commotion, for the Shuiskys had caught sight of Fyodor Vorontsov. There was some wild shouting, and then the Shuiskys and their followers jumped up and hurled themselves on Vorontsov, who defended himself as best he could, but was no match for his enemies. They manhandled him, tore at his clothes, beat him across the face, and carried him off into an anteroom. Ivan was appalled. He asked Metropolitan Makary and the two boyars Ivan and Vasily Morozov to run after them. It was clear that the Shuiskys intended to murder Vorontsov either within the palace or just outside.

The Metropolitan had been appointed by the Shuiskys and they may have expected he would be obedient to him. But he was a man of peace who had been outraged by the uproar in the dining hall, and he acted vigorously. He demanded and received on the cross the promise that Vorontsov would not be killed. He then asked that Vorontsov should be freed, but this was refused. Vorontsov was carried off to a private prison on the farther side of the Neglinnaya River.

Although the Shuiskys had promised not to kill Vorontsov but to exile him to some far distant place, Ivan feared the worst. The Metropolitan and the Morozovs were again sent to parley with the Shuiskys. Hot words were exchanged, a crowd gathered around the Metropolitan, and a certain Foma Golovin deliberately stepped on the hem of the Metropolitan's robe so that it was ripped to shreds. The Morozovs were attacked from behind. Nevertheless they were able to report to Ivan that they were certain Vorontsov would suffer no bodily harm if he agreed to go into exile in Kostroma. Ivan bided his time. He had developed a towering hatred for Andrey Shuisky and in due course he would exact a terrible vengeance.

Within the Kremlin Palace and during the long pilgrimages to the outlying monasteries, the ceremonial life continued. The Shuiskys ruled in Ivan's name, and from time to time Ivan received ambassadors, recited statements written by people he detested, and mechanically fulfilled the rituals demanded of a Grand Prince. When he looked back on his short life, he realized that he had been continually slighted and used by others for their own advantage. The rigid mask he presented to the world on ceremonial occasions concealed a ferocious despair and a consummate understanding of the uses of violence. He brooded, read the Scriptures, especially the passages dealing with the conspiracies in the courts of the Kings of Israel, and sometimes acted like a normal boy, playing games with his deaf-mute brother Yury. But violence was in the air, and the time was soon coming when he would use it for his advantage.

In September 1543, shortly after his thirteenth birthday, Ivan set out for the annual pilgrimage to the Troitsa-Sergeyevsky Monastery. That year the pilgrimages were unusually protracted and he did not return to Moscow until the end of November. The weather was exasperating; there were heavy rains, the Moskva River overflowed its banks, and because it was so cold ice floes formed, causing considerable damage. In winter, under gray skies, the

Kremlin is a forbidding place. Ivan, returning reluctantly to the Kremlin Palace, was in the worst of tempers.

What he dreaded most of all was the audiences he was compelled to grant to the Shuiskys, especially the Regent, Andrey Shuisky who had been a thorn in his side during all the years he could remember. He decided to act. Andrey Shuisky attended an audience on December 29, 1543. He came alone, unarmed, without his private guards. Suddenly Ivan ordered his arrest. In the normal course of events a man arrested in the Kremlin Palace would be given over to the palace guards, chained, and carried off to one of the small cells near the Kremlin wall. Instead, Ivan arranged that his prisoner should be given over to the tender mercies of the keeper of the hounds. The dog boys clubbed the Regent to death and then flung his body outside the Kuriatny Gate.

According to the Moscow chronicle written a decade later, Ivan merely ordered the arrest of Andrey Shuisky. "The Grand Prince was unable to bear the lack of decorum and the willful acts of the boyars who exceeded their authority," wrote the chronicler. "With their fellows they committed many unauthorized killings and subjected the land to many wrongs during the minority of the Sovereign. So the Grand Prince gave orders to arrest their leader Prince Andrey Shuisky." Many years later Ivan himself edited the chronicle, adding the words: "The boyars committed many shameful acts in the presence of the Grand Prince and offended his dignity." The Moscow chronicler wrote: "From this time the boyars began to fear the Grand Prince." To this statement Ivan added words which must have given him a grave satisfaction. He wrote: "and became obedient to him."

At the age of thirteen Ivan committed his first murder. He would learn that murder was an effective weapon, wonderfully satisfying in its speed and finality. He learned, too, that there are degrees of murder and that the effects of murder are sometimes incalculable. Machiavelli had observed that when a man seizes power, it is incumbent on him to be cruel, for otherwise the people will not grant him their untrammelled respect. Ivan had learned his lesson. Henceforth he would be murderous whenever he pleased.

escapades that he was merely demonstrating his manly qualities.

In September 1545, when Ivan had just turned fifteen and was about to embark on his annual pilgrimage to the Troitsa-Sergeyevsky Monastery, he was incensed because a certain Afanasy Buturlin, a young courtier from a well-known noble family, had not behaved with the absolute deference he demanded from his courtiers. Buturlin had said "some rude words," and therefore must be punished. The punishment must fit the crime. Ivan decided that the offending courtier should have his tongue cut out in full view of the people of Moscow. A stage was erected outside the prison, and Buturlin suffered his punishment. Later, Ivan appears to have regretted this action, invited Buturlin to his court, and even appointed him to the Boyar Council.

Satisfied that he had inflicted an appropriate punishment on an offending courtier, Ivan accompanied his brother to the Troitsa-Sergeyevsky Monastery, where he was especially solicitous of the welfare of the monks, giving them sumptuous gifts of money and grain. Then he went off to his hunting lodge at Alexandrova Sloboda, where he spent several weeks before returning to Moscow. The fruit of his meditations in the hunting lodge was a stream of harsh orders, which were directed chiefly at the Vorontsovs, who were now in disfavor. Fyodor Vorontsov's crime was that he was continually preventing Ivan from granting privileges and favors unless he had first examined and approved them. Ivan would explode with anger when his warnings were disobeyed. Dmitry Belsky, who worked long and patiently as president of the Boyar Council, was also in disfavor. Some members of the Shuisky faction like Prince Dmitry Paletsky, who had saved the life of the Metropolitan Ioasaf, were also summarily dismissed and in grave danger. Some weeks later, on the intercession of the Metropolitan Makary, they were pardoned. Ivan was demonstrating to his own satisfaction that he was quite capable of dismissing his favorites.

Trouble was brewing with the Tatars, but exactly what form the trouble would take was unclear. Intrigues among the khans and the pretenders in the Khanate of Kazan were continually being fanned by the Russians. In January 1546, while in Vladimir during a tour of inspection of the provinces, Ivan learned that there had been an uprising in Kazan. Khan Safa Guirey, and his friends and advisers from the Crimea, had fled the city and the pro-Russian faction wanted Shigaley to become Khan of Kazan under Russian protection. The unexpected news delighted Ivan, who was well aware of the difficulty of working with the Tatars and therefore acted cautiously. Not until June did an official embassy accompany Khan Shigaley to Kazan, where he was enthroned and where in the presence of Dmitry Belsky he swore an oath of loyalty to the Grand Prince. The Khanate of Kazan was once again a vassal state.

The Khan of the Crimea threw himself into a frenzy of activity. At all costs it was necessary to destroy Muscovite influence in Kazan, which had formerly been ruled by his nephew Safa Guirey. There had been a palace revolution brought about by Russian intrigues and Russian money. He, too, could create a palace revolution and in addition he could wage another war against Muscovy. Spies from the Crimea reported that Khan Saip Guirey intended to lead an army against Moscow by way of Kolomna on the Oka River. Accordingly the Russians transformed Kolomna, a town of about 4,000 inhabitants, into an armed camp. In May 1546 Ivan established his temporary capital in this southern town at the junction of the Moskva and Oka rivers. He was in good spirits. A vast army was gathered around him, there were processions and parades, and good hunting in the nearby forests. The radiant young Grand Prince was enjoying a prolonged summer holiday.

According to the Piskarevsky Chronicle he especially liked to amuse himself with people of his own age. He plowed the fields, sowed buckwheat, dressed himself up in strange costumes, walked on stilts, and enjoyed a game called "playing at boyars," which apparently had nothing to do with boyars but was a kind of rowdy charade with young men carousing on the eve of an imaginary wedding. Boating, hunting, holding military reviews, acting in charades, and playing games filled his days. The Khan of the Crimea had called off the invasion, or at least there was no sign of his army. Kazan, having become a Russian vassal state, immediately threw off the Russian yoke. Khan Shigaley reigned for a few days and then fled for his life to the safety of Russian territory.

In Moscow power was now being wielded by the Glinskys—the Princes Yury and Mikhail Glinsky who were Ivan's uncles, and his grandmother, Princess Anna Glinskaya. The Muscovites detested them, for they were cruel and grasping. Ivan adored them, because they permitted him to do whatever he pleased and removed from his shoulders the burden of making decisions.

The long summer made longer by the interminable waiting for the Khan's army was half over when Ivan demonstrated once more that he was capable of ferocious brutality. He was hunting near Kolomna when about fifty musketeers from Novgorod approached him with a petition. He was in no mood to receive petitions, ordered his nobles to send them away, and was exasperated when the Novgorodians instead of departing peacefully began to pelt the nobles with clumps of mud and to knock off their hats. Ivan, who was at a safe distance, called upon the nobles riding in the rear of his party to join forces with the rest. The Novgorodians were armed with long staves and muskets; the nobles were armed with swords and bows and arrows. There was a skirmish, five or six people were killed on each side, and Ivan was terrified. He gave orders to abandon the hunt and to return to his wood-and-stone palace in Kolomna. The musketeers were still standing in his way, and he was therefore compelled to take a roundabout route.

The Novgorodians had disobeyed his orders and affronted his dignity. It was necessary to give them exemplary punishment. It was also necessary to discover who was behind the conspiracy, for he was firmly convinced that they were conspirators. His private secretary, Vasily Gniliev-Zakharov, was given full powers to investigate the actions of the Novgorodians. It seems never to have occurred to Ivan that they might have had legitimate cause for complaint.

Vasily Gniliev-Zakharov was one of those men who thrive on investigations. He assured Ivan that the conspiracy had been organized by the boyars Ivan Kubensky and Fyodor and Vasily Vorontsov, all of whom held commands in the army at Kolomna. Kubensky was second in command of all the armed forces and Fyodor and Vasily Vorontsov held commands in the field. Implicated in the conspiracy were Vasily Vorontsov's brother Ivan and a certain Ivan Cheliadnin, the Master of the Horse, who belonged to a famous boyar family. Ivan Vorontsov was put to the torture and sentenced to exile. Ivan Cheliadnin, who knew the Grand Prince well, realized that his life depended upon agreeing to all the charges levelled against him. His clothes were stripped off him and he was forced to plead naked. Ivan sentenced him to exile in Beloozero, and all his vast possessions—for he was one of the richest men in Russia—were forfeited to the Grand Prince.

The main brunt of punishment fell on Ivan Kubensky and Fyodor and Vasily Vorontsov. They were powerful and important dignitaries, and Fyodor Vorontsov had once been Ivan's closest friend and confidant. It was known that Fyodor Vorontsov profoundly distrusted the Glinskys, and it is possible that the Glinskys assisted Vasily Gniliev-Zakharov in manufacturing evidence against him. On July 21, 1546, with their hands tied behind their backs, all three were brought before Ivan, who sat on a portable throne outside his tent. In a rage Ivan ordered their immediate execution. A contemporary miniature in the *Tsarstvennaya Kniga* (The Book of the Kingdom) shows how they were forced to lie on the ground while their heads were chopped off by an executioner with a long-handled ax. About this scene, as drawn by a monkish illustrator, there hovers an air of quiet inevitability

The execution of Prince Ivan Kubensky and the Vorontsov brothers. (From the *Nikon Chronicle with Miniatures*)

with the victims casually accepting their fate; and their heads rest lightly on the earth.

The Glinskys were now completely in power, with Mikhail Glinsky occupying the office of Master of the Horse, a title which concealed immense powers and privileges. Prince Kurbsky wrote that Mikhail Glinsky was "the root of all evil," but this was to underestimate Ivan's own involvement in the affairs of the nation. The *Tsarstvennaya Kniga* says: "The Glinskys were close to the Grand Prince and in his favor, and they permitted their followers to rob and oppress the people, doing nothing to stop them." Some contemporary historians believe the note was added in Ivan's own hand.

Three weeks after the executions in Kolomna Ivan returned to Moscow, and in September, in great state, he made his annual ceremonial visit to the Troitsa-Sergeyevsky Monastery to pray at the tomb of St. Sergius. A few days later he set out on a ceremonial tour of the great monasteries and churches, as though to prepare himself spiritually for his forthcoming coronation. He went on to Mozhaisk, Volokolamsk, Rzhev, Tver, and Novgorod, which he reached early in the morning of Sunday, November 14, 1546, to be met by Archbishop Feodosy and a huge concourse of people, the clergy carrying crosses and icons. He stayed in the palatial house of a prominent citizen, Kazarin Dubrovsky, who was later, for the crime of bringing up the artillery too late during a battle in Livonia, hacked to pieces at Ivan's orders. But for the moment everything in Novgorod was arranged to please the young Grand Prince, and as he continued his journey to Pskov and then to the great Pechersky fortress-monastery, which stood on the Livonian border and was heavily guarded by a detachment of musketeers, he seemed to be enjoying a triumphal progress. His brother Yury and his first cousin Vladimir of Staritsa accompanied him in these journeys and shared in the adoration showered on him.

These ceremonial visits were always costly, and inevitably the ordinary people had to pay for them. The Pskov Chronicle hints at some disquieting aspects of Ivan's character. "While Prince Yury caused not the slightest harm to his patrimony," wrote the chronicler, "the Grand Prince raced about all the time on post horses, causing much expense and hardship."

From Pskov Ivan returned to Novgorod, and then made the long and exhausting journey to Tikhvin, far in the north, where in the Cathedral of the Dormition he worshipped a wonder-working icon of the Virgin. This long pilgrimage had many purposes, and not the least of them was to acquire spiritual merit through the contemplation of as many icons as possible. He reached Moscow on December 12, 1546. During the following month preparations were made for the coronation, which was expected to be the most splendid and the most sumptuous in Russian history.

In Russia, where Church and State were closely intertwined, subtle changes were continually taking place in order to redefine their relationship. The nature of spiritual and earthly power were changing. New concepts, new legends, new arguments were constantly being brought forth to buttress the claims of Church and State. Some legends were invented out of the whole cloth, while others arose by a process of spontaneous generation to fulfill the human need for certainties or to fill up gaps in history. A certain Spiridon Savva, appointed Metropolitan of Kiev by the Patriarch of Constantinople in 1471, was removed from office by the Grand Prince Kazimir of Lithuania and expelled from the country. He came to Russia and went to live in the Ferapontov Monastery in Beloozero and devoted his time to writing imaginative history. In 1510, when he was already an old man, he sent a long epistle to the Grand Prince Vasily III in which he recorded the august descent of the Grand Princes of Moscow. Ultimately the Grand Prince's authority derived from Noah, Sesostris, "the first King of Egypt," Augustus Caesar, and the Byzantine Emperors. Spiridon Savva wrote that at his coronation Augustus Caesar had worn the kingly robe of Sesostris and "the crown of King Porus of India, which Alexander of Macedon brought from India." Augustus Caesar commanded the whole earth and sent his brother Prus to rule over the regions bordering on the Baltic. In the course of time Rurik, the direct descendant of Prus, became the first ruler of Russia and the ancestor of all the Grand Princes of Moscow. But this was only one of the streams of authority that reached out to the Grand Princes. In 1114 Prince Vladimir Monomakh of Kiev was crowned by an envoy of the Byzantine Emperor with all the insignia of the imperial dignity; it was as though the Byzantine Emperor himself had been present. The evidence of the coronation lay in the jewelled "crown of Monomakh." Thus from imperial Rome and imperial Byzantium the Grand Princes of Moscow derived their imperial authority.

Even before Spiridon Savva wrote his epistle to Vasily III the theory that Moscow was "the Third Rome" was widely current. The monk Filofey of Pskov had spoken about "the Third Rome" about 1500, and it is likely that other monks had used these words before him. Indeed, with the capture of Constantinople by the Turks in 1453, there were many Russians who felt that the leadership and defense of Orthodox Christianity had fallen by default on Moscow and its Grand Prince.

Gradually these ideas had begun to penetrate the minds of the Russian people, who saw in Ivan IV more than a Grand Prince. In their eyes he possessed almost the dimensions of a divinely appointed world emperor.

The Russian Church was well satisfied with this new concept and the Metropolitan Makary went to great lengths to create a coronation ceremony which would reflect the new importance of the new ruler of Muscovy. Previous coronations were studied. Unhappily there was some doubt about the validity of the documentary material. It was known that Vasily III had never been crowned. There existed however a lengthy account of the coronation of Grand Prince Dmitry, the eldest grandson of Ivan III. The Grand Prince had been deposed, but his coronation ceremony was closely followed by the Metropolitan Makary when Ivan was crowned.

Such ceremonies were always immensely long and intricate. There were prayers, acclamations, blessings, recitals from Holy Scripture. The coronation platform, covered with purple cloth, was erected in the middle of the Cathedral with steps leading down to the Royal Gate. The Icon of the Virgin of Vladimir, said to have been painted by St. Luke, was prominently displayed. On a table near the Royal Gate rested the regalia, which consisted of a jewelled cross, a scepter, a jewelled stole known as *barmy,* and the crown of Monomakh. The thrones of Ivan and the Metropolitan on the coronation platform were covered with cloth of gold. Ivan, the nobility, and all the boyars wore gold vestments which flashed and gleamed in the light of a myriad candles. It was as though the Cathedral had suddenly become transformed into a golden radiance.

On that day, January 16, 1547, the Grand Prince of all Russia received for the first time the title of Tsar. This title had been used tentatively and discreetly in the past. Henceforth the ruler of Russia would be known as Tsar and Grand Prince, and the title was in no way tentative. This was what he called himself and how he expected to be addressed.

At the coronation ceremony Ivan delivered a speech in which he claimed the title of Tsar and Grand Prince. He said:

> Father, Most Holy Metropolitan by the will of God, our ancestors, the Grand Princes, have from the earliest times to the present day handed down the Grand Principality to their eldest sons. Thus my father, Grand Prince Vasily Ivanovich of all Russia during his lifetime endowed me with the Grand Principality of Vladimir and of Moscow and of Novgorod and of all Russia, and commanded that I should ascend the grand princely throne and be anointed and crowned with the Tsar's crown, according to our ancient customs. And my father, the Grand Prince, wrote about this in his testament.
>
> Therefore, our father, thou shouldst bless my ascension to the throne and pronounce me Grand Prince and Tsar crowned by God. Thou shouldst crown me now with the Tsar's crown according to the ancient ceremonies of the Tsars and according to God's will and the blessing of my father, Grand Prince Vasily Ivanovich.

Here the formula is still not completely crystallized, but we are able to see it emerging through veils of mythology and tradition. What in the past had been called the grand princely crown has become the Tsar's crown, and what is now the Tsar's throne is described as the grand princely throne. Ivan's father is not the Tsar but the Grand Prince, and Tsardom belongs to Ivan alone.

These were not small matters for they involved immense changes of attitude and new definitions of the powers possessed by Ivan. In the eyes of Makary, who wrote Ivan's speech, a new dispensation of time had come into existence. Ivan was given absolute authority over everything that belonged to Caesar, but the Metropolitan warned him that he must seek to inherit the Kingdom of Heaven "by the performance of virtuous deeds" and he commanded the new Tsar to be obedient to the Church.

The very word "Tsar" invoked a new absolutism, but Makary went to some pains to insist that the rights of an absolute monarchy were outweighed by its duties. He must dispense justice without fear or favor, preserve the people from their enemies, and walk humbly in the sight of God. He was urged to succor the poor and respect all priests, and to ensure that no high offices were bought with bribes. He must be compassionate and accessible to all, so that at the time of the Second Coming he will be able to say: "Here I am, O Lord, and here are the people of Thy great Russian Tsardom, whom Thou hast entrusted to me." "Then," said Makary, "thou shalt hear the sweet voice of the Tsar of Heaven saying: 'Good and faithful servant, O Russian Tsar Ivan, thou hast been faithful to me over a few things, I will make thee ruler over many things: enter then into the joy of thy Lord.'"

Makary's sermons and invocations were all designed to exalt the Caesar who wore a heavy jewelled cross on his chest, the jewelled *barmy* over his shoulders, and a jewelled crown. In addition he wore a gold chain which was said to have been a gift from the Emperor of Byzantium. Finally he was anointed with holy oil on his ears, chest, shoulders, palms, and the back of his hands, and when he left the Cathedral to show himself to the people his brother Yury three times showered him with gold and silver coins.

It was a long and exhausting ceremony; many hymns were sung; many bishops, archimandrites, and abbots took part; many precise movements were made; and Ivan acquitted himself well. But the Ivan who entered the Cathedral that morning and the Ivan who left it later in the day were like two different people. The new autocrat of all Russia henceforth believed firmly that he had been crowned by God, and that the destiny of every Russian lay within the anointed palms of his hands.

Headstrong, nervous, wildly erratic and excitable, Ivan had all the makings of a bad Tsar. Only one thing could save him—a good wife. To Makary he had expressed a desire to marry immediately after his return from Novgorod and Tikhvin, saying that he intended to marry a Russian woman and not a foreign princess. Makary was overjoyed, and it appears that he already had a bride in view. She was Anastasia Zakharina, the daughter of a boyar, Roman Zakharin, who had died a few years earlier, and the niece of Mikhail Zakharin who had been one of the prominent members of the court of Grand Prince Vasily III. In those days surnames changed with alarming rapidity, and the Zakharins were known at various times as the Koshkins, the Yurievs, and the Romanovs.

The Coronation of Ivan. (From the *Nikon Chronicle with Miniatures*)

According to tradition the family descended from a Prince Kobyla who had entered Russia from the region now known as East Prussia during the thirteenth century, but the name first appears in historical records in 1347 when Andrey Kobyla was a trusted boyar attached to the court of Grand Prince Simeon of Moscow. Anastasia was beautiful, sweet-tempered, and deeply religious. She was also distantly related to Ivan through the marriage of a granddaughter of Fyodor Koshkin to the Grand Prince Vasily II. There were no possible impediments to the marriage, which was celebrated with great pomp on February 3, 1547, less than three weeks after the coronation.

At the wedding ceremony in the Cathedral Ivan and Anastasia stood side by side on a carpet of red damask bordered with sables. Makary gave them a glass beaker filled with wine, and after they had sipped the wine, Ivan tossed the beaker on the ground and ground it under his heels. After the ceremony they breakfasted together, and Ivan spent the rest of the morning on horseback visiting the neighboring monasteries. The festivities continued in the bedroom, where the bride and groom were surrounded with the symbols of ancient fertility cults and symbols representing long life, wealth, and contentment. They followed the same rituals practiced at the wedding of Vasily and Elena. At night Anastasia's younger brother, Nikita Zakharin, slept beside the bed, while Mikhail Glinsky, the Master of the Horse and the second most powerful man in Russia, rode on a stallion with a raised sword in his hand below the bedroom windows. Over the bed hung an icon of the Nativity, an icon of the Virgin, and a crucifix. The arrows shot into the corners of the room signified that all enemies would be kept at bay.

On the following morning Ivan and Anastasia went to their respective bathhouses. Nikita Zakharin accompanied Ivan, and they poured hot and cold water over each other. Then the bride and groom returned to the bedroom and were served bowls of *kasha*.

The festivities lasted for several days, the church bells pealed, and the Muscovites rejoiced. A miniature in the *Tsarstvennaya Kniga* shows Ivan and Anastasia wearing their crowns while being blessed by the Metropolitan and in another scene we see them sitting at table among their courtiers who lift their goblets and wish them long life. Two weeks after the wedding Ivan and Anastasia set out on foot in pilgrimage to the Troitsa-Sergeyevsky Monastery where, accompanied by the members of the court, they spent the first week of Lent attending services and every day praying at the tomb of St. Sergius. Expensive gifts were showered on the monks, who showered them with blessings. It was generally believed that Ivan under the guidance of Makary and with Anastasia beside him would settle down to a life of quiet and purposeful activity.

Yet there was very little to justify this belief. He refused to permit marriage to restrain his natural impulses and rarely listened to Makary. The coronation ceremony had intoxicated him with his own glory. He was Grand Prince, Tsar, Autocrat, successor to Sesostris and Augustus Caesar, and nothing could be denied to him. The Glinskys ruled insolently and corruptly, apparently unaware that they were detested both for their actions and their Lithuanian origins, appointing corrupt governors at their pleasure and deliberately indulging Ivan's whims so that he would have less time to deal with government affairs. At the coronation ceremony Makary urged Ivan to cherish the people, but he was indifferent to them and hated them when they got in his way.

The people of Pskov, suffering under a corrupt governor, Prince Turantay-Pronsky, who had been appointed by Mikhail Glinsky, sent a deputation of seventy citizens to Moscow to plead for the

After the coronation gold and silver coins were showered on Ivan by his brother Yury. (From the *Nikon Chronicle with Miniatures*)

removal of the governor. They caught up with the Tsar at the village of Ostrovka near Moscow. It was March, with the snow on the ground, and the deputation of elders solemnly presented the Tsar with the petition, expecting that at the very least he would listen to their arguments and treat them respectfully. Instead he cursed and abused them, poured hot wine over their heads, set their beards on fire, and then commanded them to strip and lie naked in the snow. He was contemplating more indignities when suddenly messengers galloped into the village with news that the great bell that summoned people to church in Moscow had fallen. Ivan ordered his horse to be saddled and galloped off to see something more exciting than seventy elders lying in the snow.

Moscow was dry tinder, always in danger of going up in flames. Every year there were conflagrations; whole streets went up in flames and the fires burned themselves out. Long ago a system of fire watchers had come into existence but had not proved to be especially efficient. In the spring of 1547 there were two large fires. Many houses and shops were destroyed and a powder tower inside the Kremlin blew up, the bricks scattering like projectiles in all directions. Both of these fires had suspicious origins, arsonists were suspected, and many people were arrested and put to the torture until they confessed, and they were then beheaded or impaled or thrown into a bonfire. But no one knew in fact whether arsonists were responsible. It was the year of Ivan's coronation and marriage, a year of evil omens. Moscow was full of strange rumors that ghouls called *serdechniki* were wandering abroad and removing people's hearts. There was an air of expectancy: something dreadful was about to happen but no one knew for certain from what direction it would come.

On June 21, 1547, at ten o'clock in the morning, a fire began in the Church of the Exaltation of the Cross on crowded Arbat Street and within an hour the entire area beyond the Neglinnaya River had gone up in flames. A strong wind was blowing, the fire took the form of sheets of flame moving at will across the city, and when the wind changed direction, the flames stormed across the Kremlin walls. The Tsar's palace caught fire. His stables, his armory, his treasury went up in flames. Within the treasury he kept his regalia, vast stores of gold plate, and the jeweled cross containing a fragment of the True Cross. The golden-domed Cathedral of the Annunciation, which stood next to the treasury, caught fire, and all its treasures, including the great icon of the *Deisis* by Andrey Rublev, perished. The roof of the Uspensky Cathedral caught fire, but although the interior was filled with smoke, its treasures survived and the icon of the Virgin of Vladimir was untouched. Makary was in the cathedral when the roof burst into flames. He escaped and succeeded in making his way to the Tainitskaya Tower on the Kremlin wall, where others had taken refuge. At midnight, when flames were still lapping the city, he was lowered down by a rope to the river bank below, but the rope broke and he had a bad fall. Half dead, he was carried to the Novinsky Monastery.

Long-famous buildings inside the Kremlin vanished. The Chudov Monastery was destroyed, and eighteen monks and eight servants perished. The Voznesensky Monastery, where the wives of the Grand Princes were buried, also burst into flames; the charred bodies of ten monks were found in the ashes. The wooden galleries along the top of the Kremlin wall vanished; the powder kegs blew up; and nothing was left of the stone building that housed Ivan's extensive wardrobe. The gilded roof of the Golden Palace melted in the heat of the flames.

In Kitay Gorod only two churches, ten shops, and a few private dwellings, including some of the palatial houses on the Varvarka,

Ѝженнлⷭⷨ съⷭ равⷭⷬсїнцрⷭь йоелⷭⷨїссїн гдⷭрь .
Ѳеѡрала мцⷶⷶ , г҃ . очеⷪⷭⷭⷭвеⷶⷬдныⷭⷨⷣ не
лн... йоенⷬⷶⷶⷶⷶⷶⷶⷶчалⷭⷭьⷪⷪⷪⷪⷪⷪⷪⷪниⷭⷭⷣⷣхⷬⷬⷬⷬⷬⷬ со собⷭⷭрⷣⷣⷣⷣⷣⷣⷣⷣнонцрⷭⷭⷭⷭⷣⷣⷣⷣⷣⷣⷣⷣкон
преⷭⷭⷭⷭⷭⷭⷭⷭⷭⷭⷭⷭⷭⷭⷭⷣⷣⷣⷣⷣⷣⷣⷣⷣⷣⷣⷣⷣⷣⷣⷣⷣⷣⷣⷣⷣⷣⷣⷣⷣⷣⷣⷣⷣⷣⷣⷣⷣⷣⷣⷣⷣⷣтⷭⷭⷭⷭⷭⷭⷭⷭⷣⷣⷣ...ⷭⷭⷭⷣⷣⷣⷣⷣⷣⷣⷣⷣⷣⷣⷣⷣⷣⷣⷣⷣⷣⷣⷣⷣⷣⷣⷣⷣⷣⷣ

The wedding of Ivan and Anastasia in the foreground and the wedding feast at top right. (From the *Nikon Chronicle with Miniatures*) survived. The fire spread beyond the walls east and north of Kitay Gorod; the houses and the vegetable gardens and all the vegetables were reduced to cinders. The roaring of the flames drowned the cries of the helpless. Moscow was transformed into a great crackling bonfire under a black cloud of smoke which was torn into ribbons by the strong winds. Flames fed on flames; stone buildings crumbled or exploded; wooden houses became puffs of smoke; people with smoke-blackened faces wandered desolately through fields of ashes. In the eyes of the Muscovites the city was being punished for its sins, and it was especially remembered that God had not spared the churches or the relics of saints. The Nikon Chronicle says:

> The fire came to an end at the third hour of the night. God punished us for our sins because they had multiplied and He did not save the relics of the saints and a vast number of our churches. In a single hour seventeen hundred men and women, not counting small children, perished in the houses and gardens. For God, in his just judgment, brings us to repentance through fire and famine and plague and war.

For Ivan, too, as he watched the flames from his palace on Sparrow Hills, the fire of Moscow seemed to be a visitation of God. He was visibly shaken when, on the second day after the fire, he attended a meeting of the Boyar Council at the Novinsky Monastery. The meeting was convened at the monastery so that Makary could attend, and it was here that Ivan first learned from the lips of his own confessor, the archpriest Fyodor Barmin, that the people of Moscow thought they knew how the fire had come about. The mysterious *serdechniki* had been removing people's hearts, soaking them in water and then sprinkling the city with this water which had acquired the magical power of setting fire to everything it touched. This, they said, was how the fire of Moscow had been brought about. The archpriest's words were supported by the boyars Fyodor Shuisky and Ivan Cheliadnin, who had been pardoned and had now returned to court. This was a matter worth investigating and Ivan gave orders for the establishment of a commission to examine the problem of the *serdechniki*.

The people of Moscow were naturally credulous, a prey to rumors, but they were also hardheaded and resolutely conspiratorial. They may have deliberately spread the rumor in order to incriminate the Glinskys and their followers who oppressed the people and metaphorically tore out their hearts. On Sunday, June 26, five days after the great fire, the commission of boyars met outside the Uspensky Cathedral in the presence of a large gathering of Muscovites who were in an angry mood. Many people had lost all their possessions; they had lost their families; they hated the Glinskys and feared the Tsar. They could not blame the Tsar directly but they could blame Princess Anna Glinskaya, the Tsar's grandmother, and all her descendants. They told the boyars: "Princess Anna Glinskaya and her children and her servants have practiced magic, and she herself has taken out the hearts of people, soaked them in water, and she has gone driving through Moscow, sprinkling the water, and thus Moscow was burned down."

At this time Prince Mikhail Glinsky and his aged mother, the Princess Anna Glinskaya, were living on their estates at Rzhev, and out of reach. But Prince Yury Glinsky, Mikhail's brother, had recently arrived in Moscow and was actually present on the square outside the cathedral. He, too, was being accused of practicing magic against the people. He was recognized, and fled for safety into the cathedral, hoping to receive sanctuary. But the crowd surged after him, killed him, dragged his body through the main gates of the cathedral and carried it triumphantly to the place of execution on the Red Square, where it was exposed for everyone to see. In this way they wanted to show that Prince Yury Glinsky had been justly executed for his crimes.

Having disposed of Prince Yury, the crowd turned against the members of his household, his servants and retainers, hounding them to death and pillaging whatever property of the Glinskys had survived the fire. The chief enemy was still Princess Anna Glinskaya, and the crowd was now demanding her death, shouting that she was the magician who had set fire to Moscow by transforming herself into a magpie and dropping the magical water that caused the fire. This was perhaps easier to believe than that she had driven through the city in a carriage, tossing water out of the window.

Soon the rumor spread that Princess Anna and Prince Mikhail were hiding in Ivan's palace on Sparrow Hills and simultaneously there came the rumor that the Glinskys were in secret communication with the Tatars who had pitched their tents on the southern frontier and were preparing to invade Russia, or so it was believed. At all costs the witch and her brood must be executed. With the double purpose of destroying the Glinskys and defending Moscow from the invaders, the crowd rushed to Sparrow Hills, having armed themselves with whatever weapons they could lay their hands on. Ivan saw the mob approaching Sparrow Hills and was terrified. He had good reason to be terrified. The mob demanded that Princess Anna Glinskaya and Prince Mikhail Glinsky should be handed over to them, and it was obvious that they proposed to deal with Ivan's grandmother and uncle exactly as they had dealt with Prince Yury Glinsky. Ivan succeeded in convincing the mob that he was not hiding the Glinskys and they finally left him in peace. Infuriated that he should have been placed in such great danger, he ordered an investigation, and the arrest and execution of the ringleaders. Most of them had fled. Prince Mikhail Glinsky and his mother had also fled. They abandoned the family estate at Rzhev and took refuge in a monastery.

In later years Ivan complained in a famous letter to Prince Kurbsky that the boyars deliberately spread rumors that the Glinskys started the fire. They also spread rumors that Ivan knew all about it. In the letter Ivan defended himself at considerable length and with great heat. "Who would be so mad or ferocious," he asked, "as to destroy his own property out of rage against his own subjects?" He had lost his palaces, his treasury, much of his inherited wealth. Dogs and traitors were at work, for how otherwise could one explain the murder of his uncle in the Chapel of St. Demetrius of Salonica in the Uspensky Cathedral? Ivan proclaimed his total innocence; he had nothing whatsoever to do with the fire, and it was beyond belief that his grandmother could have sprinkled magic fire-breathing waters on the city from a great height. He raged against the boyars "who assembled without our knowledge like a pack of dogs" on the square outside the cathedral and then murdered Prince Yury Glinsky, and he found it hard to understand why the Glinskys were so fiercely hated. He was determined to find an explanation for these terrible events.

Sylvester, a priest who had recently arrived from Novgorod and was attached to the Cathedral of the Annunciation near the Kremlin Palace, provided the explanation. He was a man who

The killing of Prince Yury Glinsky, June 26, 1547. Ivan appears at top right. At center Prince Glinsky is being dragged out of the Cathedral and at bottom he is dead.

possessed innate authority; Ivan was taking spiritual guidance from him. According to Sylvester the fire was a punishment sent by God; the murder of his uncle was also a punishment; henceforth he must walk in the paths of righteousness in the fear of the Lord. Sylvester's hold on Ivan was all the greater because he was not afraid to speak of prophecies, apparitions, and miracles; he was a practical man of the world, but he was also a mystic; and he convinced Ivan that he knew the answers to many mysteries. Prince Andrey Kurbsky later suggested that Sylvester was compelled to practice deception. He wrote: "In this way perhaps did that blessed man deceive Ivan for a good purpose, healing and purifying his soul from leprous sores and restoring his depraved mind, thus leading him along the path of truth." Sylvester was like a surgeon who cuts away gangrened limbs to save the patient from death.

Henceforth for a few years we shall see Ivan standing in fear and trepidation before God, the stern figure of Sylvester beside him. He is trying to do good and setting aside his childish ways, trying to act responsibly and behaving with cautious dignity toward the boyars. The good Tsar Ivan, almost beyond hoping for, had finally emerged.

Nevertheless, as we shall see, Sylvester's strong medicine was too strong. Without being aware of it, the clever priest planted in Ivan the seeds of a rebellion which was perhaps even more dangerous than the original rebellion. In due course Ivan would turn away from Sylvester and abandon the strict code of morality enforced upon him by a man much older and wiser than himself. He would throw morality to the winds and destroy everything in his path.

The Youthful Warrior

THE REIGN OF IVAN IV, which had begun so inauspiciously, now seemed to be full of promise. The Glinskys were no longer in power, the government was once more in the hands of experienced boyars and court nobles, and there was no reason why Russia should not become a powerful and contented state. Ivan, intelligent, God-fearing, and remorseful, presented himself as a man who had only one purpose in life—to be a good ruler.

Contemporary miniatures show him round-faced, with thick curly hair, beardless, carrying himself well under the weight of his heavy vestments. He wears a heavy crown with curling leaf-shaped plaques of gold set with jewels. Since the miniaturists drew and painted in order to illustrate chronicles written by monkish scribes, we often see Ivan in the presence of monks and priests, and indeed he appears to have spent a good deal of time among them. They were teaching him to be good and at the same time they were advancing the interests of the Church.

Sylvester was the acknowledged chief adviser, a man of remarkable persuasiveness, energy, charm, and something that could be called fanaticism if it was not so severely controlled. His qualities were those particularly associated with Novgorod, where clarity and compassion and a certain generosity of spirit were regarded as eminently desirable. He was not a simple priest; he was an administrator, a scholar, a man with an intricate and systematic mind, which he proved when some years later he wrote the

Domostroy (The House-Order), a manual of Christian conduct which set out to show the precise duties of everyone in every Christian household. To the surprised Muscovites Sylvester seemed to have emerged like a clap of thunder or like Elijah the Tishbite who solemnly proclaimed the wrath of God upon the evil King Ahab. But in fact Sylvester, who was close to Makary and had assisted him in compiling lives of the saints, had known Ivan for some time and already possessed considerable influence over him.

Another figure soon emerged among the Tsar's principal advisers. This was Alexey Adashev, who had formerly served at court as a *batozhnik,* or wielder of the baton, a post of some trust, for he not only cleared the way for the Tsar but was also one of the many who guarded over the Tsar's security. At the time of the fire of Moscow he was a gentleman of the bedchamber. He now presided over the Chosen Council, a small and rather informal group of advisers who effectively ruled Russia in the name of the Tsar during the following years. Adashev was known for his fairness and straight-dealing, and Kurbsky records that during the Livonian war enemy towns under siege would surrender to Adashev "on account of his goodness." A quarter of a century after his death Adashev's memory was still alive. A Polish archbishop was heard asking what manner of man Boris Godunov was, only to be told "he was like Adashev in his goodness."

Not that Adashev was entirely virtuous. He was a man of affairs with a penetrating intelligence and he could act very firmly when he chose. But he was scrupulous and incorruptible, acting always in the best interests of Russia. One of the chroniclers says that Adashev and Sylvester "governed the Russian land together," but Sylvester, who rarely attended the meetings of the Chosen Council, preferred to rule behind the scenes. Later Ivan or one of his secretaries wrote in the margin of the *Tsarstvennaya Kniga,* "Sylvester was all powerful, and all obeyed him, and none dared oppose him in anything."

The Chosen Council, chosen by Adashev and Sylvester, included among its early members Prince Andrey Kurbsky, Prince Ivan Mstislavsky, Ivan Sheremetev the Elder, Ivan Cheliadnin, Ivan Viskovaty, and Mikhail Morozov, who was married to the daughter of Prince Dmitry Belsky. With a few exceptions they were comparatively young men in their early thirties. The Boyar Council still met regularly and there appears to have been a good deal of overlapping of powers, with the same people sometimes appearing on the Chosen Council and the Boyar Council.

They were living in difficult times, for there was a succession of bad harvests and Russia was at war with the Tatars, who were continually sending armed raiders into Russian territory. It was thought that an attack on Kazan would put an end to these raids or at the very least inflict a suitable punishment on them. Accordingly Prince Dmitry Belsky set out at the head of an army against Kazan early in December to be followed a few days later by an army commanded by Ivan, who left Moscow on December 11 and arrived at Vladimir nine days later. He was forced to stop at Vladimir for more than two weeks because the heavy artillery had become bogged down in torrential rains. He reached Nizhni-Novgorod on January 26 with his artillery. Usually at this time of the year the Volga River was thickly covered with ice and the heavy cannon could be dragged over the ice without any difficulty. But the weather turned unseasonably warm, the ice began to melt, and many cannon were lost. Ivan took this as a bad omen and returned to Moscow.

It was not the intention of the Russians to capture Kazan and no serious effort was made to do so. It was enough if they could challenge the Tatar's army under the city walls and maul it. This was done. Khan Safa Guirey met the Russian vanguard on the Plain of Arsk to the east of the city and was defeated. Prince Dmitry Belsky immediately sent couriers to Moscow to announce the victory. This was the first significant battle to be won during Ivan's reign and the Russians took heart, seeing themselves as a people with a mission to destroy the vast empire of the Tatars.

Meanwhile they rested on their laurels, for they had nothing to lose by waiting. The Tatar Khanates were at odds with one another. In the following year the Khan of the Crimea sent an expedition against the Khan of Astrakhan, whose army and defense works were pathetically weak. He conquered the city, tore down the walls, and led a large number of prisoners to the Crimea. Thereafter he considered himself the overlord of a vast area stretching between Kazan and the northern slopes of the Caucasus.

The Khan of the Crimea wrote to Ivan, "You were young, but now you are grown up. Let me know what you want: my affection, or bloodshed? If you want my affection, do not send us trifles. Instead, like the King of Poland, who sends us 15,000 gold pieces annually, you should send us substantial gifts. If you desire war, I am prepared to march on Moscow and your land will lie under the hooves of my horses."

These were serious threats and they were taken seriously. At the Chosen Council it was decided to act firmly. When it was learned that the Crimean Khan was employing captured Russian merchants as domestic servants and ill-using the Russian envoy at his court, they ordered the summary arrest of the Crimean ambassador in Moscow. And when Safa Guirey, Khan of Kazan, died during a drunken quarrel in the spring of 1549, leaving a two-year-old son Utemish Guirey, and the nobles of Kazan sent a delegation to the Khan of the Crimea to ask for military assistance, the Russians succeeded in intercepting the delegation and bringing it in chains to Moscow. Accident and circumstance were gradually bringing Russia into full-scale confrontation with the Tatars.

Another and even more important confrontation was taking place: Ivan was confronting the people and attempting to wrestle with their problems. He was holding long conferences on the necessity of reforms and discussing plans for the complete reorganization of the state. Adashev had appointed himself Examiner of Petitions, which included both personal petitions concerning grievances and various petitions concerning the welfare of the state, and he had come to the conclusion that a great deal was wrong and there was much that needed to be remedied.

During this period we hear very little about Ivan's personal life or the private affairs of the court. We learn that his deaf-mute brother Yury married the daughter of Prince Dmitry Paletsky on November 3, 1547. The bridegroom's grandmother, Princess Anna Glinskaya, and his uncle, Prince Mikhail Glinsky, who were living obscurely on their estate in Rzhev, did not appear at the wedding. Believing that Ivan would be very busy superintending the wedding, it occurred to them that this was the time to flee to Lithuania. Ivan possessed a quick and dependable intelligence service, and the news of the escape of the Glinskys reached Moscow two days later. The intelligence service learned that Prince Turantay-Pronsky was also making his way to the Lithuanian frontier. The Tsar's frontier troops, led by Prince Peter Shuisky, began closing in on the fugitives in the thick forests near the border, and the Glinskys and Prince Turantay-Pronsky did a quick turnabout and raced to Moscow to place themselves under the protection of the Tsar. If asked, they would say that they had been on a pilgrimage to a monastery that happened to be near the Lithuanian border. They thought they would be able to shake off the agents of Prince Shuisky, but almost as soon as they reached Moscow they were arrested. Nothing more is heard about Princess Anna Glinskaya, who was presumably pardoned because she was Ivan's grandmother, but Prince Glinsky and Prince Turantay-Pronsky were put on trial and would have been condemned to death but for the intervention of Makary. Their lands and property were confiscated, and nobles related to them were compelled to guarantee against heavy fines that they would make no more attempts to escape from Moscow.

The adventures of Prince Glinsky demonstrated the power of Ivan's intelligence service which could reach out to the farthest limits of the kingdom, acting with extraordinary speed and efficiency. But the Glinskys were a spent force and it scarcely mattered what happened to them. Far more important tasks awaited Ivan and the Chosen Council.

The reformers were at work, seeking new methods, new formulas, new conceptions of the nature of the state. Inevitably many of the reformers came from the priesthood, for they were the best educated. They were often well-traveled, they felt a sense of responsibility to their flocks, and while Sylvester was in a position of authority they had easy access to the Kremlin. Among those who took advantage of the new dispensation were two priests from Pskov, Ermolay Erazm, who was attached to the Church of the Savior by the Pine Forest inside the Kremlin wall, and another who was known simply as Artemy of Pskov. Artemy's proposals were sweeping. He wanted the great monastic estates broken up and given to the poor, for he was opposed to ownership of land by the monastic foundations. He said the root of all evil was money and great wealth was the devil's work. The problems of Russia could only be solved if the Tsar displayed the utmost humility toward the people and obeyed God's commandments. Artemy was close to Sylvester, and we learn that "he was invited to the Tsar's table."

Ermolay Erazm approached the problem of government with somewhat more discretion in a pamphlet called "Concerning the government and the economy as seen by the benevolently disposed rulers." Erazm believed that he had discovered the key to perfect government. He wrote that the Tsar should give primacy to the peasantry, not to the nobility, and submit himself to the higher power of the Church, which represented the will of God and was not bound to earthly interests. Since the peasantry produced food and clothing, and were ultimately responsible for the wealth of the country, they should be taxed lightly. He believed that the petty nobility should live in the towns, thus making it easier for them to mobilize for war, and that the peasants should be permitted to pay their taxes in grain, not in coin or in cattle. Peasants working for landlords should be exempt from all state obligations, by which he seems to have meant that the landlords should pay the peasants' taxes. With regard to the great monastic foundations Erazm felt that since the monasteries served the purposes of God they should be permitted to keep their lands, but he later changed his view, saying that the ownership of land by monasteries was reprehensible because it prevented the monks from living lives of perfect asceticism. "The monks," he wrote, "should be as humble as angels."

Erazm's blueprint for reform was aimed at improving the material well-being of the peasants and at undermining the powers of the hereditary nobility. He wanted to stop the sale of alcoholic beverages and demanded that all wineshops should be closed. "In this way," he wrote, "we shall put an end to drunkenness in the land and there will be no murder." The fact that people murdered one another obviously weighed heavily on him, for he suggested that the manufacture of knives with sharp points should be forbidden by law.

The fact that these sweeping reforms were discussed at the Tsar's table and in the Chosen Council speaks well for the liberality of the new rulers of Russia. However impractical they were, the reforms were eagerly debated by the people who had the most to lose if they were put into effect. None of those who made suggestions for reforms were punished. By the beginning of 1549 it was becoming clear that some elementary reforms would soon be put into the law books.

Ivan prepared himself for some momentous announcements on the subject of reform by going into a retreat, giving himself up to fasting and prayer. This lasted for several days. The idea was that he should cleanse himself of all sin before inaugurating a new era of reform. The reforms would be introduced first at a great convocation of Church dignitaries and the nobility in the Kremlin Palace and this would be followed a few days later with a convocation of the people on the Red Square. Because so many interests were at stake, the reforms were relatively minor but at least a beginning had been made.

The convocation at the Kremlin Palace opened on February 27, 1549. Ivan acknowledged that during the period of his minority many serious errors had been made by the ruling boyars and princes. Henceforward these errors would cease, for he would no longer tolerate them. He would permit the provincial nobility and the people to lodge complaints against their oppressors and offered to act as judge and final court of appeal. At the same time he appears to have accepted the proposition that the slate must be wiped clean and that there would be no punishments for any crimes committed in the past, for he said, "I have no rancor against any of you for what has happened in the past and I will not punish you, but you must not do these things in future." One of the immediate results of this convocation was to place the provincial nobility outside the jurisdiction of the governors of the provinces except in matters relating to robbery and manslaughter.

The convocation of the people on the Red Square took place on March 3 with great ceremony. A procession of priests carrying banners and crosses emerged from the Kremlin, followed by the great princes and boyars of the court. The Red Square was crowded with people who had assembled from all the regions around Moscow. A religious service was performed, and then at last the young Tsar stepped onto the *Lobnoye Mesto*, a stone platform on the highest part of the Red Square and the traditional place for public pronouncements.

The Tsar turned to Makary at the beginning of his speech, begging for his prayers, and then delivered himself of an apology for the crimes committed during the rule of the Glinskys and all the other princes who had usurped the powers of the lawful ruler of Russia. He said:

> I was very young when God took away my father and mother. The powerful boyars and nobles, who wished to rule over the country,

failed to look after me. In my name they acquired high rank and honors and enriched themselves unjustly and oppressed the people, and there was no one to stop them. In my poor childhood I appeared like someone deaf and dumb. I did not listen to the groans of the poor, and being young and isolated from affairs, I did not reprimand the evil ones.

At this point Ivan turned toward the boyars and princes who were standing close by and cursed them, saying, "You were corrupt and rapacious, fabricators of false justice, and what answer will you give now? How many tears and how much blood has been shed because of you! I am guiltless of these crimes, but God's judgment awaits you!"

It appears that these words were not part of the prepared speech. They were designed to placate the people. Only a few days before, while addressing the boyars and princes, he had wiped the slate clean. Now, quite suddenly, he saw that there were advantages in pleasing the crowd and showing that he was on their side against the most powerful men in the land. He went on:

> God's people were given to us by God. I beg you to have faith in God and to love me. It is not possible to remedy all the injustices and depredations you have suffered during my childhood as the result of wrongdoings by boyars and government officials. So I beg you to forget your quarrels with one another and the wrongs you have suffered, unless they were great wrongs. Concerning all these matters I shall be your judge and protector in the future. I shall stamp out these wrongdoings and I shall return to you all that has been taken from you.

Afterward it was remembered that the Tsar turned in all directions and bowed to the people.

What was curious about this speech was its theatricality. The drama of the setting, with the Kremlin wall as a backdrop, evidently excited him. Never before had he addressed a mass meeting of ordinary people; nor had he ever played so many roles in so short a space of time. He saw himself as Tsar and Grand Prince, as the aggrieved child, as the dedicated enemy of the boyars, as the protector of the people from the rapacity of the boyars and princely families, and as the man who would return to the people everything that had been wrongly taken from them.

According to the chronicler, Ivan wept and the people wept with him, so moved were they by the fervor of his words. The millennium was at hand, for had he not promised to return all their stolen possessions and punish the guilty? They did not know that he had promised to wipe the slate clean and punish no one.

In his first public appearance Ivan showed himself a consummate actor. He was not lacking in sincerity, for he genuinely believed in all the roles he was playing; and some of these roles were in conflict. He could not simultaneously protect the people against the boyars and the boyars against the people. He could not expropriate the land of the boyars and give it to the people. The Church owned nearly one-third of the land held in private possession in Russia, but he could not expropriate the Church lands without exacerbating his relations with the Church. Inevitably the great reforms would dwindle into little reforms.

Artemy of Pskov and Ermolay Erazm had presented the case for the peasants. Another reformer, Ivan Peresvetov, presented the case for the petty nobility, landowners who received their land on condition that they put a stated number of farm workers into uniform, trained them, and led them into battle. On September 8, 1549, the feast day of the Nativity of the Virgin, Peresvetov placed in the Tsar's hand his first petition on behalf of the petty nobility. The petition took the form of an allegory about a certain Sultan Mehmet who acquired a powerful state by executing all the princes who committed treason, uttered falsehood, took bribes, or were indolent. Sultan Mehmet placed his faith on the petty nobility, who were paid in coin of the realm raised in taxes. In their military service they received advancement by merit, not by seniority. Peresvetov believed that men of great wealth were incompetent military commanders because they were incurably indolent. He regarded indolence as a crime.

Peresvetov believed implicitly in Russia's mission to conquer the Tatars and to regain the lost lands in the West. Hence the need for military reforms and the importance he attached to the petty nobility, who were the mainstay of the army. He believed that Russia would sooner or later find herself in conflict with the Ottoman Empire and liberate the Greeks and the Slavonic people in the Balkans. He was one of the first to envisage an imperial destiny for Russia.

Peresvetov's reforms were not much more helpful than the reforms of Artemy and Ermolay Erazm, but they had the merit of offering practical solutions to practical problems. Neither Ivan nor the ruling boyars were quite ready to reform the basic concepts of the state. The princely families remained enormously powerful, the petty nobility received their land and titles at the pleasure of the Tsar, and the peasants were at the mercy of the landowners. Only the Church was open to immediate reforms, and these could be brought about all the more readily because the Church was divided between the followers of Joseph of Volokolamsk, who believed that the great monasteries should be permitted to own large estates and entire villages, and those who believed that the Church had no business acquiring wealth. Between the Josephites and the rest battle lines had already been drawn.

At the beginning of January 1551 Ivan convoked an assembly of churchmen at the Kremlin Palace. The Boyar Council was invited to attend and so were many court dignitaries. This was known as the *Stoglav*, meaning "a hundred chapters," because the laws and recommendations reached by the assembly were included in a hundred articles.

Ivan addressed the assembly in his customary manner, robustly depicting himself as a sinner, demanding rather than seeking forgiveness, and blaming the boyars for the evils that had fallen on Russia. He said:

> No one can describe or relate with the tongue of man all the evil things I have done through the sins of my youth. At first God humbled me by taking away my father, who was your shepherd and protector. The boyars and nobles, pretending to wish me well, were seeking power for themselves and because their minds were filled with darkness they dared to arrest my father's brothers and murder them. On the death of my mother the boyars ruled the Tsardom like despots. Because of my sins, because I was an orphan and young, many people perished in civil strife, and I grew up neglected, without instruction, and accustomed to the evil ways of the boyars, and since that time to the present day how greatly have I sinned before God! How many punishments has God sent down on us!
>
> More than once we attempted to revenge ourselves upon our enemies, but without success. It was beyond my understanding that God was inflicting great punishments on me, and therefore I did not

repent my sins and continued to oppress the poor Christians with all manner of afflictions. God punished me for my sins with floods and plague, and even then I did not repent. Then God sent great fires and terror entered my soul, and my bones trembled and my soul was humbled; I was filled with great spiritual emotion and I knew I had sinned. I asked and received forgiveness from the priests and I forgave the princes and boyars.

Ivan's *mea culpa* would have been more impressive if it had come from the heart; it is too contrived to be altogether convincing. "Do not spare me for my shortcomings, but boldly reprove my weaknesses so that my soul may live," he went on. It appeared later that the only shortcomings to be discussed at length were to be found in the Church, and among the nobility, and in the private habits of ordinary citizens. The Church had a horror of the clowns who ran about in front of wedding processions, and they were banned. The Church also disapproved of the musicians who attended wedding feasts and sang bawdy songs; the priests were ordered to leave at the moment when the musicians began to play. The Church was appalled by the existence of soothsayers and fortunetellers, who were henceforth forbidden to ply their trade. Icon painters who led immoral lives were forbidden to paint. The Church gained easy victories for morality but suffered many financial defeats.

In an age demanding reforms the Church was vulnerable. Although Church lands remained inviolable in theory, decrees were issued that severely limited further acquisitions of property. The existing tax privileges were abolished; lands donated to the Church during Ivan's minority were sequestered by the government; and all lands received by the Church in payment of debts incurred by the petty nobility and by the peasants became government property. The Church could hold land, but was forbidden to increase its holdings. This was not new, for in the time of Ivan's father and grandfather there were laws forbidding the sale of land to the monasteries in many provinces. Now these laws were reaffirmed. The Chosen Council was determined to limit the financial power of the monasteries.

One of the most important rulings of the assembly of churchmen was designed to introduce universal education in Russian cities. Priests and deacons "well versed in reading and writing" were to establish schools in their own homes and the parents were ordered to pay whatever they could afford. These schools had existed for many years but had no legal basis. Now they were demanded by law. There were as yet no universities and education remained in the hands of the priests.

Another ruling concerned the copying of manuscripts by priestly scribes. So many defective or hastily written manuscripts had come into existence that the assembly gave orders that copies should be carefully compared with the original. Only good translations were permitted, and no copies could be sold until they had been checked for accuracy. Icons too must be accurate, following accepted traditions. Badly painted icons must be destroyed and self-taught icon painters must be taken in hand and taught to paint properly. The Church was taking a much larger role in education, and Ivan himself seems to have been largely responsible for these changes.

The chroniclers have very little to say about the early years of Ivan's marriage. Anastasia remains a shadowy figure, beautiful, sweet-tempered, generous, deeply religious, the epitome of all the feminine virtues. Very occasionally they offer a brief glimpse of her. Thus we learn that on the night of August 10, 1549, she gave birth to her first child, a daughter, who was christened Anna. Two days later she was sitting up in bed, receiving a delegation led by the Metropolitan and including all the important churchmen, the boyars and their ladies. To all of them she gave sweetmeats with her own hands.

On the following day Ivan led another large group into the bedchamber. Once more the Metropolitan blessed Anastasia and her newborn daughter, and then Ivan asked the guests to sit down while Yuliana, the wife of his brother Yury, served the guests from a table heaped with sweetmeats. That night Ivan invited all his guests to attend a feast, and after dinner they trooped back to the bedchamber to congratulate Anastasia again, to drink wine, and to eat sweetmeats. Then the Metropolitan and clergy took their leave, and the guests returned to the dining hall and continued feasting. There were more feasts and festivities to celebrate the baptism of the princess, which took place a few days later, and largesse was distributed to the poor. Ivan's joy was brimming over. He did not know that his firstborn would live less than a year.

Meanwhile Ivan and the Chosen Council were preoccupied with

the coming war against Kazan. The days of skirmishes were over. More and more it was becoming an article of faith that the power of the Tatars must be destroyed. On November 24, 1549, Ivan set out from Moscow with 60,000 men on his second campaign against Kazan. At Vladimir, which he reached on December 3, he learned that there were dissensions within the army, especially among some of the officers who felt that they had received appointments not commensurate with their rank or ability. Makary made a long speech urging them to put aside their differences and to remember that they were all taking part in a war against the enemy of the Orthodox faith. If they believed they had received commands below their dignity, they should so inform the Tsar who would arrange matters and give them satisfaction. "You should not be separated from one another by pride but bound to one another by love as befits Christian men," Makary warned them. "In this way you will receive laurels from Heaven and honors from the Tsar." Then he gave his blessing to the entire army.

The quarrels over appointments were patched up and the army moved on to Nizhni-Novgorod, where Ivan arrived on January 18, 1550. A severe Russian winter had set in, and many of the soldiers froze to death. It took nearly three weeks for the army to reach Kazan along the icy roads, and when at last the heavy guns were posted outside the city and the white tents went up, the military commanders congratulated themselves that they had brought a vast army and overwhelming firepower against the enemy. Ivan, the first Grand Prince of Russia to set eyes on Kazan, took part in the military councils, showed himself to the soldiers, exhorted them to fight until victory was achieved, and hugely enjoyed himself.

It appeared that everything was working for the Russians. Kazan was close to civil war, the Khan was a child, the Regent was unpopular, and many Tatars inside the city were working for Ivan, who possessed a formidable Tatar army of his own, for Khan Shigaley, a claimant to the throne of Kazan, was commanding Tatar troops against the Tatar city. The Russian army was under the overall command of Prince Dmitry Belsky and Prince Vladimir Vorotynsky.

The plans were well laid; everything was ready for an assault on the city; and then the weather changed and all their carefully contrived plans came to nothing. First came tremendous winds, then the weather became unseasonably warm, and then the torrential rains fell. The ice melted, the rivers and streams overflowed their banks, the heavy guns were bogged down in the mud, the powder used in firing the muskets became damp. Soon everyone realized that the siege would have to be lifted. During eleven days of torrential rains the army waited patiently for the weather to change, but it did not change. Food was running out. The artillery captains were wondering how they would be able to dig out their guns. Finally on February 25 it was decided to raise the siege.

Returning to Moscow along the still-frozen surface of the Volga River, Ivan granted himself a pleasure reserved for kings and emperors. About twenty miles from Kazan he observed near the mouth of the Sviaga River a rounded hill with a lake beyond it. With a suite of about thirty boyars and nobles of his court Ivan rode to the top of the hill and announced: "On this hill we shall construct a Christian city. From here we shall attack Kazan and God will deliver the city into our hands." In this way the fortress town of Sviazhsk came into existence.

The raising of the siege gave encouragement to the Tatars, who were troublesome throughout the summer and the following winter. Ivan spent a month in the late summer on the southern front, awaiting a Tatar attack that never came. In the winter the Nogay Tatars raided the southeastern borders of Russia. An expedition was sent out against them, and this time the weather favored the Russians, for many of the Tatars froze to death and most of the survivors were rounded up. Ivan was so pleased with the success of this expedition that he gave large rewards to the commanders and banqueted them in the Kremlin.

The Khan of Kazan was Utemish Guirey, grandson of the Nogay chieftain Yusuf Mirza, whom Sulayman the Magnificent once described as "the prince of princes." Khan Utemish was about five years old, and the real power lay in the hands of the Crimean nobleman Ulan Korshchak, who detested the Russians and was prepared to fight to the death to preserve Kazan in Tatar hands. In the spring of 1551 the third expedition against Kazan set out from Moscow under the command of Khan Shigaley, and on May 18 an advance detachment of Russian cavalry under Prince Peter Serebriany fell on the suburbs of Kazan and succeeded in doing considerable damage during a dense fog. The Tatars were taken by surprise, many prisoners were taken, many Russian prisoners in Tatar hands were released, and the Russians were able to celebrate a small victory.

Six days later, on May 24, Khan Shigaley and the main body of the army arrived at the rounded hill overlooking the Sviaga River, to be greeted by Prince Serebriany and his soldiers carrying trophies of victory. The lumber for building the fortress town of Sviazhsk had now arrived, the trees on top of the hill were cut down, the walls of the town were marked out, priests walked in procession, carrying banners and icons and sprinkling holy water. Within four weeks the town was solidly built and ready for occupancy. There was even a wooden church dedicated to the Nativity of the Mother of God. The Cheremiss tribesmen living nearby were suitably impressed by the speed with which the Russians were able to build a fortress so close to Kazan.

Here on the right bank of the Volga many tribesmen of many different origins were living under the suzerainty of the Khan of Kazan. There were Cheremiss, Chuvash, and Mordvins, all speaking Finno-Ugric dialects. The tribal chieftains were aware of the power of the Russian army and swore allegiance to Ivan. Delegations arrived at the Russian camp and were rewarded with charters confirming the chieftains in their positions and exempting the tribesmen from taxes for three years. Administratively they were attached to the new, gleaming town of Sviazhsk. Throughout the summer the tribesmen, traveling in groups of five or six hundred, traveled to Moscow to pay their respects to Ivan and were royally feasted. The chieftains received gifts of armor, horses, money, bolts of cloth, and velvet coats embroidered with gold and with fur trimmings. Ivan was scattering largesse to an extent that amazed the chroniclers who reported they had never seen anything like it. In fact he was acting sensibly, since he intended to use the tribesmen to help him to conquer Kazan. Within a month of Khan Shigaley's arrival at Sviazhsk, an army of Cheremiss tribesmen was recruited to fight against the city. Outgunned and outnumbered by the Tatars, they were forced to withdraw, leaving a hundred dead and some fifty captured. They had proved their loyalty and thereafter they were used as scouts.

The news that the tribesmen were going over to Ivan brought

consternation to the Tatars in Kazan. Ulan Korshchak promised eventual victory, but no one knew how it would come about, for the Tatars had less than 20,000 soldiers, the surrounding countryside was in Russian hands, and the Russians were united under Ivan while the Tatars were divided among themselves. The Russian plan to conquer Kazan by threats, by intimidation, and by negotiation with dissident Tatar nobles was succeeding. Soon even Ulan Korshchak realized he was in danger and with three hundred Crimean followers he fled the city, having first looted the treasury. As the Tatars were crossing the Kama River, the Russian cavalry suddenly fell on them, destroyed their rafts, and captured about fifty of them. Ulan Korshchak was caught, sent to Moscow, and executed.

Tatar embassies arrived in Moscow and offered to accept Ivan's vassal, Khan Shigaley, as ruler of Kazan. Ivan demanded the surrender of Suyun Beka and her young son Khan Utemish. The ambassadors agreed, but demanded that the right bank of the Volga should be returned to Kazan. On this subject Ivan was adamant; he would return nothing he had conquered. Alexey Adashev was sent to Khan Shigaley to explain the situation. The Khan answered quite intelligently, "If you do this, how shall I be able to rule? Can I demand the affection of my subjects when I have ceded to Russia a large part of their land?" More ambassadors came from Kazan to discuss and argue, but there was nothing to discuss and no arguments were permitted. Ivan had said the right bank belonged to Russia, and so it was.

On August 11 Suyun Beka arrived with her son, having prostrated herself at her husband's tomb before setting out on the journey. Weeping, she left her weeping people; and although she received all the honors due to her rank, she found no comfort in captivity. She became a hostage for the good behavior of Kazan.

Khan Shigaley entered Kazan and took up his residence in the palace formerly occupied by Suyun Beka and her young son. Three hundred of his own Tatar guards from Kasimov and two hundred Russian musketeers accompanied him. According to the Russian chronicler there was an enthronement ceremony superintended by Prince Yury Bulgakov, a member of an old and powerful boyar family, who represented Ivan and officially proclaimed Khan Shigaley as the rightful Khan of Kazan, but it is more likely that

Prince Bulgakov remained in the background for fear of offending Tatar sensibilities. Ivan had taken possession of Kazan but he had not yet convinced the people that he was their rightful sovereign and it was necessary to act cautiously.

A new law went out from the palace: Any Tatar found using Russians as slaves would be executed. Suddenly, from all the crannies of Kazan, Russians captured in Tatar raids emerged to claim their freedom. There were a surprisingly large number of them, and many of them had been woefully ill-used. They were taken to Sviazhsk, where they were clothed and fed and sent back to their towns and villages. We hear of sixty thousand Russian slaves being set free, and although the figure appears to be inordinately large it is not impossible. Later it was learned that the Tatars still had many Russian slaves hidden away in cellars and holes in the ground.

Ivan appeared to have succeeded far better than he expected. He had conquered Kazan without losing a single Russian life; he had annexed the right bank of the Volga and freed countless Russians who had been enslaved by the Tatars, and he had appointed a vassal Khan who appeared to be amenable to his commands. Khan Shigaley was determined that there should be no opposition to his rule, and he therefore invited some of the Tatar nobles to a feast of reconciliation and then massacred them. Seventy were killed, others escaped in the uproar, some made their way to Moscow, and others joined the Nogay horde. The classic method of solving disputes is not always the best, and Kazan was no happier under Khan Shigaley, the creature of Ivan, than under the appointees of the powerful Khan of the Crimea.

Khan Shigaley's relations with Moscow grew worse, for he kept insisting that without the right bank it was impossible to rule the city. The Tatar nobles who escaped the massacre accused him of being a bloodthirsty monster and said he should be deposed, and if a successor could not be found, then it was up to Ivan to appoint a viceroy. But the viceroy could not take power until the last remnants of opposition within the city had been quashed. Khan Shigaley was ordered to present himself with his nobles at Sviazhsk after first rendering the city defenseless.

The plot was carried out with exemplary cunning. On March 6, 1552, having spiked some of Kazan's guns and removed many barrels of gunpowder and many muskets secretly to Sviazhsk, Khan Shigaley left Kazan ostensibly to go fishing in a nearby lake. It is unlikely that anyone really believed that he was going fishing, because he was accompanied by a massive retinue which consisted of nobles from his own court of Kasimov, some eighty-four nobles from Kazan, and five hundred Russian musketeers, whose presence gave authority and force to whatever he might say.

Once outside the walls of Kazan Khan Shigaley had the nobles from Kazan surrounded and then addressed them at some length, promising them a just retribution for their sins. "You wanted to kill me and you petitioned the Tsar to have me dethroned because I was treating you so badly, and then you asked that a Viceroy should be appointed instead of me!" he declared. "Well, the Tsar has ordered me to step down from the throne of Kazan, and I am going to him now. We shall settle our score there!" Khan Shigaley was in an ugly mood, and he appears to have hoped that the entire nobility of Kazan would be wiped out at the orders of Ivan. This did not happen, for when they reached Sviazhsk they were told that if they swore allegiance to Ivan, they would be permitted to return and continue to enjoy their high positions. Ivan had evidently concluded that to rule Kazan it would be necessary to use the Tatar nobility.

The way was now clear for the Viceroy, Prince Simeon Mikulinsky, to make his official entry into Kazan, accompanied by his servants and bodyguards and some of the Tatar nobles who swore allegiance to the Tsar at Sviazhsk. In addition he took with him Ivan Sheremetev and Alexey Adashev, who were among the most powerful men in Russia. The Tatar nobles promised Prince Mikulinsky that he would be received with great ceremony and cordiality. He set out in high spirits and was pleased when he encountered a delegation of Tatars from Kazan who greeted him with much flattery and provided him with suitable entertainment. He decided to send on his luggage and servants in advance. Why hurry to enter Kazan when he could enjoy a rest in the meadows in delightful company? In this way the Russians fell into the trap. Some Tatar nobles rode ahead with the luggage and spread the rumor that the Muscovites intended to kill off all the inhabitants of Kazan, and when at last the prince arrived outside the gates, he found them closed against him and there were armed Tatars on the walls.

For a day and a half the Russians were compelled to waste their energies in vain negotiations outside the gates. Kazan was defiant: it would not let the Viceroy in and it would not let the Russian servants out. The people were aroused and determined to defend themselves. Yediger Makhmet, the son of a former Khan of Astrakhan, was now proclaimed Khan of Kazan, after promising the people that not a single Muscovite would ever enter the city gates. Prince Mikulinsky returned to Sviazhsk, and wrote a long dispatch to Ivan describing the latest act of Tatar treachery.

All the carefully contrived negotiations and the intricate plotting of many months had come to nought. Tatar armies were now successfully attacking the Cheremiss on the right bank of the Volga; the Chuvash and the Mordvins were flocking to the Tatar banners. Kazan appeared to be more powerful than ever, threatening Sviazhsk, where there was an epidemic of scurvy and where morale was low. It appeared that the Russian soldiers in this fortress outpost had become incapable of fighting.

Ivan looked for remedies and found none. Yediger Makhmet could not be bribed into vassaldom; he refused to negotiate; he was determined to attack. He had brought with him five hundred armed Nogay Tatars and they succeeded in stiffening the determination of the people of Kazan to remain independent.

The news from Sviazhsk was especially disquieting. Large numbers of women and girls freed from Tatar captivity were enjoying their freedom in the warm spring weather. Horrified priests reported to Moscow that the town was a den of iniquity. They reported that the soldiers were shaving off their beards to please the women, that grown men were going to bed with boys, and that Sviazhsk was both Sodom and Gomorrah.

This dreadful news reached Ivan in May, and he immediately sought the help of Makary, who believed in the power of the saints to remedy all the evils affecting the Russian people. He therefore ordered that all the available relics be gathered together in the Uspensky Cathedral and held a service in which he called upon God to protect the purity and vigor of the soldiers of Sviazhsk. Makary was unable to go to Sviazhsk himself, but sent a priest from the Church of the Annunciation instead. With the priest went bottles of holy water blessed within sight of the relics, certain instructions about the ceremonial purification of the town, and a long sermon. Makary hoped that when they heard the sermon, the soldiers of Sviazhsk would change their ways.

> Blessings from the most holy Makary, Metropolitan of all Russia, to the new town of Sviazhsk, to the princes, boyars, voyevodas, and nobles, and to the army, and to all the Christian people!
>
> By the will and mercy of God, by the prayers of the Virgin and the saints, and by the unwavering faith, the prayers and vigorous efforts of our God-loving Tsar Ivan, and by our own blessed meekness, and by the prayers of the entire priesthood and of all Orthodox Christians, God deigned that this town together with its churches should be built. And so it was built and it was filled with people and with good cheer. And then God gave to our God-loving Tsar and to all our God-loving army a joyful and bloodless victory, for Kazan yielded, the people on the right bank submitted to the Tsar, and millions of captive Christians, men, women, youths, girls, and children were freed from the infidels and went joyously and freely to their homes. And all this was due to the mercy of God, the will of the Tsar and your own valor. . . .

All this was merely the opening flourish of a sermon of immense prolixity. The people of Sviazhsk were not let off lightly. Their gluttony, their drinking, their unseemly laughter, their chatter, their shamelessness, their adulteries, their addiction to sodomy and other acts of lewdness, all these were passed in review and solemnly excoriated. Makary was especially incensed because the men had shaved off their beards, "according to the customs of the heretical Latins, although it is foreign to Christian tradition and is sinful." Shaving off their beards showed that they had forgotten the fear of God and the commandments of the Tsar. Worse still, they had forgotten that God had created man in His image, for God was bearded. Therefore He had sent them a plague of scurvy and permitted many of them to drown in the Volga after drunken orgies. "Let them remember the hour of their deaths and the Last Judgment and the Coming of Christ," he thundered. And then more mildly: "Let them go to church and listen attentively and with pure thoughts, and let them give to the priests and to the poor such gifts as they can afford from their well-deserved earnings, and they will receive rewards in heaven."

On May 21, 1552, the Archpriest Timofey left Moscow with the sermon and the holy water for Sviazhsk. It was becoming clear that neither sermons nor holy water would solve the problem of Kazan. The negotiations continued, but were fruitless. There was only one solution—conquest.

The March on Kazan

FORTIFIED BY THE PRAYERS of the Church and with the certain knowledge that he had been called upon by God to punish the treacherous Tatars, Ivan resolved to conquer Kazan with a deep awareness of his responsibility as the divinely appointed ruler of Russia. He saw himself as another Joshua or another Gideon leading his people to the promised land, smiting the enemy with terrible blows. No longer would he direct the course of battles from a distance; he himself, in all the panoply of kingship, would lead the Russian army in the field. He was then twenty-one years old.

First it was necessary to ensure that divine influences would work in his favor and he therefore set out on the inevitable pilgrimage to the Troitsa-Sergeyevsky Monastery, which he regarded as a fountain of spiritual power, a place charged with the energy of the Holy Trinity. He had given many gifts of gold, jewels, and precious stones to the monks, and the Icon of the Holy Trinity, the chief object of worship in the monastery, was thickly studded with gold and pearls from his own treasury. It was to this icon therefore that he offered his prayers, falling on his knees and crying out in a loud voice:

> O merciful Creator, hear the prayers and entreaties of thy sinful servant, and do not remember my trespasses, those which I committed when I was a youth and those which I committed when I became of age. I have recourse to Thee, my Creator and Lord. Behold my

sighs and my tears, the sighs and tears of thy slave, and forgive me my sins and accept my repentance as Thou hast done for David and Hezekiah and Manasseh and the thief and the people of Nineveh.[1] Have mercy upon me in Thy great compassion, O Lord, and grant me victory over our enemies, so that the godless shall not say: "Where is God?" and so that all shall know Thou art the true God and under Thy mercy we shall defeat our enemies.

The Tsar then knelt beside the relics of St. Sergius, weeping profusely, calling upon the saint to protect him and his Christ-loving army. Had not the saint aided and protected Dmitry Donskoy, Grand Prince of Moscow, who was the Tsar's ancestor? His parents had brought him to be christened at the saint's tomb, and had they not beseeched him to protect the infant prince? Therefore it was incumbent upon the saint to protect the Tsar, who had given so much treasure to the monastery. In this way, cajoling and bargaining, the Tsar impressed upon St. Sergius the need for his holy protection, demanding it as a right, not as a gift. A little while later he received the blessings of the abbot, the clergy, and the monks, and after presenting gifts to the brethren, he returned to Moscow.

At the thought of committing his army to battle against the infidels, Ivan felt an overwhelming need for divine protection. A few days after his visit to the Troitsa-Sergeyevsky Monastery, he entered the Uspensky Cathedral in the Kremlin and prostrated himself before the Icon of the Savior, a twelfth-century work of great beauty and elegance. He beseeched the Savior to show him mercy and to grant victory to his army. Had not Abraham triumphed over the King of Sodom, Joshua over the seven kings of Jericho, Gideon over the Midianites, and Hezekiah over Sennacherib? He reminded the Savior of the circumstances of all these triumphs at great length and with fervor, and tearfully begged for divine assistance. If this assistance were given, "then all our enemies will know we are Thy true servants and our enemies will be defeated because we have faith in Thee."

Another wonder-working icon in the Uspensky Cathedral was the Icon of the Virgin of Vladimir, also painted by a twelfth-century Byzantine master. This icon, showing the Child's face nestling

---

[1] The reference to Manasseh, the wicked king of Judah, is to be found in II *Chronicles*, 33, and the repentance of Nineveh is described in *Jonah*: 3, 5–10.

tenderly against the face of the Mother, was, if possible, even more elegant and beautiful than the Icon of the Savior, and by common consent was regarded as the wonder-working icon above all wonder-working icons. To this icon Ivan also prayed tearfully, calling upon the Virgin to intercede for him and to grant him victory, "so that our enemies will know we are victorious not because we are strong and brave, but because God has helped us through the prayers and the intercession of the Virgin and the saints." Then he prayed at the tomb of St. Peter the Metropolitan, whose prayers had assisted Dmitry Donskoy to overcome the Golden Horde, and afterward asked for the blessing of Makary. The Metropolitan blessed him and promised to pray for him at all times "when we are gathered together and when we are alone in our cells."

It remained to tell Anastasia about the coming war against the Tatars. No doubt she had known for many days that he had decided to conquer Kazan but he appears to have felt the need to inform her officially, in the presence of his brother, his cousin, and his nobles. So he walked in procession from the cathedral to his private apartments in the Kremlin Palace. The highly emotional speech delivered by Ivan to Anastasia was recorded by a priest called Adrian Angelov:

> Wife, it is my wish and desire to make war against the infidels, placing my trust in Almighty God, who loves mankind. I desire to wage war on behalf of the Orthodox faith and the holy churches, not only unto the shedding of my blood, but even unto death, for it is sweet to die for the Orthodox faith, and to endure death for the sake of Jesus Christ is to enter eternal life.
>
> Thus did the martyrs undergo their sufferings, and so did the apostles, and the former Tsars who lived in fear of God, and their kinsmen, and for this they received on earth not only Tsardom from God, but also glory. For their valor they were feared by their enemies, and they also received a glorious and long life on earth.
>
> Why, then, do I speak so much about what is mortal and perishes? It is because God gave them a place in Heaven because they were God-fearing and because they suffered for the sake of Orthodoxy, and when they passed from the world they lived in perpetual happiness and joy in the Lord together with the angels and the righteous, as it is said in the Scriptures: Eye hath not seen, nor ear

heard, neither have entered into the heart of man, the things which God hath prepared for them that love him and keep his holy commandments.

Therefore, Wife, I bid thee not to grieve while I am away. I bid thee to fast, to perform works of grace, to go often to God's holy church and to say many prayers for me and for thyself. Give alms plentifully to the needy. I bid thee to grant pardon to the many poor wretches living under the Tsar's displeasure, and I grant thee the power to release prisoners at thy pleasure. Thus we shall receive great rewards from God: I for my valor, and thou for thy good works.

Adrian Angelov records that Anastasia was so disturbed by her husband's speech that she would have fallen if he had not supported her, and for some time she remained speechless, weeping bitterly. At last, addressing herself to "My Lord, the God-fearing Tsar," she begged him to return victorious and unharmed to the greater glory of God and of the Orthodox faith. "How will I endure the absence of my lord?" she asked, like every good Russian wife seeing her husband go off to the wars.

Thus the rituals of departure were observed in the proper medieval style with long speeches, sermons and prayers, with Ivan exultantly proclaiming his coming victory over the Tatars while simultaneously abasing himself before God and the saints. He saw himself as a warrior by divine grace, the brother of Abraham, Joshua, Gideon, and Hezekiah, and all the legendary warriors of the past. He walked in legends, and if he had come upon Abraham under the tree of Mamre he would not have been in the least surprised.

At the head of a formidable army, drums rolling and banners waving, Ivan set out for Kazan early in the morning of Thursday, June 16, 1552, leaving Anastasia, Makary, and his brother Yury to govern his country. The army marched through the village of Kolomenskoye on the Moskva River, and here Ivan rested for a while, ate some food, and pondered what course to pursue. The boyars had cautioned him against a march on Kazan, thus leaving Moscow open to attack by the Crimean Tatars. He decided there was no danger, but a few hours later, when he was on the march again, a messenger from Putivl, a town on the Russian border far to the south, brought news that the Crimean Tatars had crossed the border. Ivan held a council of war and decided that the greater evil

Ivan IV leaving Moscow and arriving in Kazan with his army and
standard-bearer. (From an early, seventeenth-century edition with miniatures
of the *Kazansky letopisets*)

was presented by the Crimean Tatars with their declared aim of "destroying the Orthodox faith," not by the Kazan Tatars who were merely guilty of treachery and of killing many Christians. He ordered the army to march to the heavily defended fortress city of Kolomna and arranged to strengthen the defenses along the north bank of the Oka River which commanded the river crossings. Instead of marching to Kazan, the army waited for the Crimean army to attack. In this way the Russians lost their momentum and were placed on the defensive.

For a few days nothing more was heard about the advance of the main forces of the Crimean Tatars. No scouts returned with reports of enemy movements, no hard-riding messengers brought news from the south. Ivan was in a quandary, for this silence was ominous. Then there came a report that a force of about seven thousand Tatars had appeared before the gates of Tula only to vanish again. A scouting party had been sent to explore the state of Tula's defenses. A few hours later, while he was at dinner on the evening of June 23, Ivan learned that Devlet Guirey, Khan of the Crimean Tatars, had reached Tula with his vast army composed of Tatars and Janissaries, and with heavy Turkish cannons. Without finishing the meal Ivan hurried to the cathedral of Kolomna to pray for divine help and then gave orders for his whole army to march on Tula, a distance of about 75 miles as the crow flies. His own royal guard, composed of nobles, formed the rear of the army.

The siege of Tula was soon over, for the defenders were emboldened by the news that the Tsar's army was on its way and they fought brilliantly, even the women sallying out to attack the Tatars. The Khan lifted the siege and ordered a retreat as soon as he learned that the Russian army was approaching. Many of his heavy guns were captured outside the walls of Tula, together with stores of gunpowder. The Khan with the remnants of his army fled to the south, abandoning camels and baggage carts and huge stores of provisions.

Ivan was overjoyed by the victory and returned to Kolomna to offer thanks to the Icon of the Virgin in the cathedral. This icon was believed to have accompanied Dmitry Donskoy at the time of his great victory on the Don River. In Ivan's eyes the Virgin had blessed his army. In fact, he had not covered himself with glory; he had simply waited on events and owed the victory chiefly to the courage of the ordinary people of Tula, where there was only a small garrison. The people armed themselves against the enemy. Tula was heavily bombarded by the guns of the Janissaries, and flaming arrows set fires raging through the town.

From Tatar prisoners the Muscovites learned a strange story. The Khan of the Crimea was far from being a redoubtable warrior. Some miles south of Tula he held a council of war and decided it was too dangerous to proceed farther. He had thought, or half-believed, that the Tsar was in the neighborhood of Kazan, leaving Moscow open to attack. He panicked when he learned the Tsar had reached Kolomna and immediately ordered a general retreat. At the last moment one of his advisers suggested that it was intolerable to march so deep into Russian territory with so little profit. A sudden attack on Tula would bring great stores of booty, and there was still time to raid the villages. The Khan agreed with his adviser, ordered the attack on Tula, and sent groups of Tatars fanning out into the villages to capture young Russians to be sold in the Crimea as slaves. He was not so much a military commander as the captain of an army of looters.

With this defeat of the Khan of the Crimea the way was now open for the march on Kazan.

The plan of campaign was carefully worked out. From Kolomna the army would march to Sviazhsk in two columns, the northern column taking the road through Vladimir and Murom, the southern column taking the road through Ryazan and Meshchera. The two columns would meet at a crossing of the Sura River before advancing on Sviazhsk. The northern column was commanded by Ivan and the southern column by Prince Ivan Mstislavsky and Prince Mikhail Vorotynsky. Khan Shigaley, too fat and too indolent to ride on horseback, was given permission to make the journey by riverboat. The southern column, which was intended to shield the Tsar from attacks by marauding bands of Nogay Tatars, amounted to about 15,000 men, while the main army including the troops in Sviazhsk amounted to perhaps 125,000 men.

While preparations were being made for the march, there was some murmuring in the army. It came principally from the petty nobility of Novgorod, who complained that they had been fighting the Tatars without respite for many months, and had neither the money nor the strength to endure a long campaign. The problem was a real one, for they had to equip and maintain their own troops, and Ivan listened to their complaints with an outward show of sympathy. He ordered a list to be made up of all those who wanted to go on the march and another list of those who wanted to stay behind, promising substantial rewards to those who marched and hinting at substantial punishments for the rest. He learned that many of the petty nobles from Novgorod possessed no land and simply could not afford to campaign any longer. Finally he convinced them that he would take care of all their needs when he reached Kazan, and they promised to follow him.

On July 3, 1552, after once more praying before the Icon of the Virgin in the Cathedral at Kolomna, Ivan gave the order to march. In five days the main army reached Vladimir. Here, following his custom, he prayed before the relics of the saints, invoked on his army the blessings of God and the Virgin, and learned, as though in answer to his prayers, that the plague of scurvy which threatened to kill off the entire garrison at Sviazhsk had come to an end. It appeared that the whole town had been sprinkled with holy water, the priests led the people and the army in procession through the town and round the walls, and prayers were offered up in the churches. The people of Sviazhsk had surrendered to sensuality and license. Now in their despair, seeing death all round them, they gave themselves up to good works in thankfulness to God, who had spared them and pardoned their sins. Ivan was very pleased. Once more God had favored him. He regarded these acts of divine mercy without the slightest incredulity. It was as though God was speaking through him, and he was the intercessor between God and the Russian people.

He spent a week in Vladimir, and on July 13 reached Murom, where he received a long and strenuous letter from Makary, at once blessing and rebuking him. "Be pure in heart, be humble in glory, do not despair in adversity," wrote the Metropolitan. "Remember that a virtuous Tsar is the salvation of his country." The Metropolitan went on to stress the paramount importance of virtue, courage, wisdom, truth, purity, justice, and mercy. All this, of course, was predictable, but the Metropolitan had more serious matters to discuss. He reminded Ivan that the garrison at Sviazhsk had behaved abominably, giving themselves up to pride, drunkenness, and the lusts of the flesh. Did not the Apostle say that sinners would have no place in the Kingdom of Heaven? Had not many men of virtue succumbed to sinfulness? Who possessed more virtue than King David? "But David fell by the wayside and suffered grievously, and for all the remaining years of his life he soaked his bed with tears." This was only one example; there were many others. Noah had made himself a laughingstock by his drunkenness, and Solomon in old age became proud and fell into sin and perished. He begged Ivan to remember his ancestors, who had lived chastely and soberly in holy wedlock, and were therefore rewarded by God with victory over the heathen. "We therefore beseech you, pious Tsar Ivan, and your brother Vladimir Andreyevich and all your great lords, princes and boyars and voyevodas, and all your Christ-loving army, that you remain pure, humble, wise, chaste and repentant, while keeping all the other virtues as well."

Ivan replied in a letter that was uncharacteristically brief and to the point:

> To our father, His Holiness Makary, Metropolitan of all Russia, greetings from the Tsar and Grand Prince Ivan Vasilievich.
>
> You wrote to us instructing us to abjure sin and to be pious. We promise, lord, to do as you request.
>
> Now we go forth with Vladimir of Staritsa, the boyars, and all the Christ-loving army, calling upon God, the Holy Virgin and all the saints to help us.

On March 20 Ivan marched out of Murom with his troops and two weeks later reached the Sura River, which marked the boundary of Russia and Tatary. Here he received a delegation of Cheremiss chieftains who had revolted but were now willing to renew their allegiance to the Tsar. Ivan forgave them, presented them with food from his table, and flattered them with kind words. On the same day by prearrangement the southern column also crossed the river. Prince Andrey Kurbsky, who rode with this column, remembered the journey to the Sura River with horror, for their food soon ran out and while riding across the uninhabited steppe they lived on fish and whatever wild animals they were able to catch. They had encountered no enemies and fought no battles. What dismayed the prince most of all was the endless loneliness of the steppe and the lack of bread. When they came up to the main army, their chief thought was for dry bread, which they begged, borrowed or bought at inflated prices, happy to get their teeth in any crust.

The worst part of the march was now over, for in little more than a week they would be reaching Sviazhsk. Bread was still uppermost in Prince Kurbsky's mind as they rode north to the great Russian stronghold on the Volga:

> From the Sura River we rode with the army for eight days across the steppe and through woods and sometimes through forests. We saw few villages, for these people conceal their houses behind natural fortifications invisible even when you are quite close to them. But we were getting food now, and as we traveled through these places we were able to buy bread and meat, though we paid dearly for them. Yet, because we had been faint with hunger, we were grateful. As for malmsey wine and other liquors and sweetmeats—we could forget about them! We found Cheremiss bread tasting better than our costly biscuits.
>
> Above all, we were joyful and grateful because we were fighting for our Orthodox Christian fatherland against the enemies of the Cross of Christ and because we were marching with our Tsar. We felt no distress at all, vying with one another in good deeds, and the Lord God Himself helped us.

In this mood the great cavalcade came in sight of Sviazhsk to be greeted by the townspeople overjoyed at the safe arrival of the Tsar. The entire garrison came out to welcome them in a grand parade which included companies of Cheremiss soldiers who had only recently submitted to the Tsar. There were feasts and processions and prayers, solemn meetings and conclaves, more parades, more inspections. The Tsar inspected the town, visiting the churches, the arsenal, the fortifications, and the private houses, and he found it all good and especially admired the view from the walls. In fact, Sviazhsk was beautifully situated on the shores of the green Sviaga River which flows into the Volga less than a mile away. On one side there were the plains, hills, woods, dark forests, and on the other there were the wild cliffs of the Volga and the white islands in midstream. Here and there you could see the Chuvash villages half lost among the hills.

Prince Kurbsky felt that it was "like coming home after a long and arduous journey." All of Russia seemed to be pouring into Sviazhsk, for the merchants of Moscow, Yaroslavl, and Nizhni-

Ivan crossing the Volga to attack Kazan. (From the *Nikon Chronicle with Miniatures*)

Novgorod had sent ships downstream laden with every conceivable article of merchandise. The sandy shores of the river were transformed into a marketplace, and every day more ships came to unload their treasures.

In Sviazhsk it was hoped that the Tsar would occupy one of the larger houses, but instead he set up his tent in a meadow outside the walls. In this sumptuous tent he held another council of war attended by Vladimir of Staritsa, the boyars, and voyevodas. Khan Shigaley also attended the conference. He was instructed to write a letter to Khan Yediger Makhmet demanding his submission. If he came to the Tsar, he would have nothing to fear and would receive many rewards from the Tsar's hands. At the same time the Tsar sent another letter addressed to the chief mullah and all the Tatars living in Kazan, promising that if they submitted all their past acts of rebellion would be forgiven. These letters were sent on August 15, two days after the army reached Sviazhsk.

Ivan had no real hope that Khan Yediger Makhmet would surrender the city. The letters therefore were merely formal statements of his claim to Kazan.

Without waiting for a reply, he ordered the army to begin crossing the Volga the next day. Two days later, on August 18, he crossed the river with his bodyguard, and it was not until the following day that the whole army reached the left bank of the Volga. The days of clear sunshine had come to an end, torrential rains filled the sky, the river rose and the low-lying plains became lakes and marshes. In the darkness and the rain the army drove toward Kazan, the wheels of the carts and gun carriages clogged with mud. The heavy guns, which had come down by boat, were landed at a point only four miles from Kazan. The chief obstacle was the small and swift-flowing Kazanka River, but it presented little difficulty. Six bridges were thrown over it, and by August 20 the whole army had crossed over.

The weather cleared a little, but the skies were still gray and there would be more torrential rains in the days to come. From his camp at the mouth of the Kazanka River the Tsar saw the fortress city of Kazan four miles to the east standing dark against the sunrise, with its citadel perched on a high rock, while the rest of the city sloped toward the surrounding meadows. The Tatars had closed the gates and were waiting for the attack. The Tsar, too, was waiting. He would conquer the fortress in his own leisurely time.

Conquest

IF YOU STOOD in Ivan's camp on the shores of the Volga River, you would have seen a city on a hill with towers and pinnacles and walls made of huge balks of timber from the surrounding forests, and this city would have something of the appearance of a medieval castle in a fairy tale. On the western heights overlooking the Kazanka River there were minarets, mosques, palaces of white stone, flags flying, battlements thrusting up against the sky. These formidably defended heights offered little comfort to conquerors. They could be stormed only by scaling the sheer cliffs on the west or climbing the steep pathways on the east. The defenders, who regarded their city as impregnable, saw no reason to be especially alarmed when they saw Ivan's army. They could see every boat coming up the Volga and every Russian soldier in the plains, while their own soldiers remained invisible behind fortress walls.

If all of Kazan had stood on a high cliff, then the problem of conquering it would have been nearly insurmountable. But in fact the city followed the pattern of many ancient and medieval cities: there was the acropolis, the fortress on the heights, while below it, sprawling across the plain, lay the lower town with its huddled streets and long avenues leading to heavily fortified gates. Here and there the lower town was cut by ravines, and sometimes the huddled streets opened out into gardens and lakes. In the lower town lived the merchants, the artificers, the workmen, the poor, and the soldiers who manned the wooden towers.

To defend the city Khan Yediger Makhmet had an army of about 30,000 well-trained soldiers and about 2,700 Nogay tribesmen. They were armed with bows and arrows, spears, swords, lances, maces, and muskets. They also had heavy guns and ample supplies of gunpowder, and there was enough food in the city to take them through a long siege. Both the Tatars and the Russians wore chain mail and pointed iron helmets, so that it was sometimes difficult to tell them apart.

Ivan was under no illusions about the dangers confronting him. Khan Yediger Makhmet was a determined, daring, and ruthless adversary, who could be expected to use every ruse to prevent the city from falling into Russian hands. There was no possibility of a sudden surprise attack. It was not simply a question of conquering a well-defended city, but there was also the problem of how to deal with the Tatar armies outside the city, the many soldiers based in the town of Arsk which lay on the other side of a dense forest stretching almost to the walls of Kazan. The Russians would have to defend themselves against sudden sorties from the forest and against marauders from all directions. All together there were about 35,000 Tatar and Cheremiss troops loyal to the Khan outside the city, most of them hidden in the forest of Arsk. Of necessity Ivan would have to take special measures to protect his rear, his lines of communication with the supply ships moored on the Volga, and his own person, for the Tatars well knew that if the Tsar was killed or captured the siege would be lifted.

The plan of campaign was carefully worked out by the Tsar's war council, which consisted of about a dozen generals, many of them princes and many of them related to his own family. For the most part they were young men in their twenties and thirties, who already had experience in fighting the Tatars. Each army was led by two generals, one senior and one junior. Thus the main army was led by Prince Ivan Mstislavsky with Prince Mikhail Vorotynsky acting as his second-in-command. His brother, Prince Vladimir Vorotynsky, commanded the Tsar's elite corps, with Ivan Sheremetev the Elder acting as his second-in-command. The Sheremetevs were not princes, but members of an ancient boyar family which regarded itself as at least the equal of any princely family. In addition to the main army and the elite corps, there were seven other armies. They were called the vanguard, the rear guard, the

right wing, the left wing, the scouts, and the armies of Vladimir o
Staritsa and Khan Shigaley. Each army was given its own separate
task, and all the armies were under the command of Prince Ivar
Mstislavsky, who was then only twenty-five years old. He had the
curious distinction of being descended from Rurik, from Jenghiz
Khan, and from the ancient line of the Grand Princes of Lithuania
His grandfather, Prince Kudaikul of Kazan, had married the sister
of Vasily III, and his mother was their daughter. He was therefore a
quarter Tatar. He was an outstanding commander and Ivan had
complete trust in him.

These generals were arrayed like peacocks, for they rode about in
shining armor, wore plumes in their helmets, and trailed richly
embroidered capes from their shoulders. The elite corps, numbering
about twenty thousand men, and consisting mostly of nobles and
their retainers, was also magnificently arrayed. The watchmen,
looking down from the acropolis of Kazan, could see at a glance
the progress of the nobles in their finery.

Ivan was accompanied by his retinue and a full court. His
Keeper of the Signet, Master of the Horse, his state secretaries,
equerries, heralds, armorers, pages, and royal clerks were con-

A war banner carried by Ivan IV's standard-bearer, now in the Armory Museum
in the Kremlin.

stantly with him. In addition there was a large number of priests attached to his court including his father confessor, the priest Andrey Protopopov. There were also innumerable messengers all wearing the Tsar's livery and a host of servants.

By August 20 this entire army with its heavy cannon and war machines was standing on the shores of the Volga, waiting for the order to storm Kazan. But the order did not come. Prince Ivan Mstislavsky and the council of generals decided to move cautiously, wanting to learn more about conditions inside the city before attacking. On that day two persons entered Ivan's camp, each of them bringing information of the utmost importance. One was a Russian, a former prisoner of the Tatars, who was allowed to go free on condition that he give a letter written by Khan Yediger Makhmet to Khan Shigaley. This letter denounced Khan Shigaley as a scoundrel and traitor, and went on to denounce the Tsar and the Orthodox Church with extraordinary savagery. "We are preparing a banquet for you!" the letter concluded, and there was not the least doubt what kind of banquet was meant.

The letter from Khan Yediger Makhmet gave some indication of the temper of the defenders. Kamay Mirza was the second person to escape from Kazan. He was a Tatar nobleman who slipped out of the city with seven companions, the survivors of about two hundred men who had hoped to join the Tsar's forces but had been arrested and executed. He brought news about the city's defenses. He reported that the Tatars were well-armed and well-equipped, numbered about thirty thousand, and there was another Tatar army under Prince Yepancha hiding in the forest of Arsk. This was alarming news. During the two following days the council of generals decided upon the final disposition of the troops outside the walls of Kazan. The order to march was given during the early hours of the morning on August 23.

The plan of campaign was based on the assumption that Kazan could be conquered only after a lengthy siege. The main army would be stationed outside the east and south walls, the vanguard outside the north wall, the rear guard and left wing outside the west wall, and the scouts in the marshy ground south of the Kazanka River facing the acropolis in the east. The brunt of the fighting would fall on the main army, which would also have to fight the Tatar troops coming from the forest of Arsk. Since the walls of Kazan were over twenty-four feet thick, they could be breached only by blowing them up with gunpowder. All round the city the soldiers were ordered to build earthworks, which took the form of enormous wicker baskets about eight feet high and seven feet in diameter, known as gabions. They were solidly packed with earth to protect the guns and to provide defense works against the Tatars issuing out of the gates in sudden attacks against the Russian troops.

On that early morning, as the army moved toward Kazan, Ivan was in a deeply reflective mood, feeling the need for divine guidance and protection. When the army had traveled about three-quarters of the way across the plain known as the Khan's Meadow, he called a halt and unfurled his great standard which bore an image of Christ "not made by human hands." There was the sound of trumpets, the drummers beat their drums, and the Tsar and all his generals dismounted to pray for victory and to celebrate the glorious deaths of those who would fall in the coming battles. "I am ready to give my life for the triumph of Christianity," Ivan said, and Vladimir of Staritsa encouraged him, saying: "Go forth, O Tsar! We are all united before God and before you!" According to the chronicles, Ivan gazed at the great standard with the image of Christ throughout the ceremony. Addressing himself to Vladimir of Staritsa, the boyars and voyevodas, and all the men in his army, Ivan declared that the time had come for a decisive battle, and he went on:

> Therefore strive together to suffer for piety, for the holy churches, for the Orthodox Christian faith, summoning God's merciful aid with the purest trust in Him, and strive on behalf of our brothers, those Orthodox Christians who have been made captive for many years without reason and who have suffered terribly at the hands of the infidels of Kazan. Let us remember the words of Christ, "Greater love hath no man than this, that a man lay down his life for his friends." Let us therefore pray to Him with a full heart for the deliverance of the poor Christians, and may He protect us from falling into the hands of our enemies who would rejoice over our destruction.
>
> I therefore bid you serve us as much as God will help you. Do not spare yourselves for the truth. If we die, it is not death, but life! If we do not make the attempt now, what may we expect from the infidels in future? I myself have marched with you for this purpose. Better

that I die here than live to see Christ blasphemed and the Christians, entrusted to me by God, suffering at the hands of the heathen Tatars of Kazan. No one can doubt that God will hear your continuous prayers and grant us His aid. I shall bestow great rewards on you, and I shall favor you with my love, and provide you with everything you need, and in every way I shall reward you to the extent that God in His mercy offers His aid. And I shall take care of the wives and children of those of you who die!

In this way, making vast promises, the Tsar ensured the loyalty of his troops, who shouted enthusiastically, wept, prayed, and gave every indication of being swayed by religious emotion. For about an hour they gazed at the standard of Christ fluttering above their heads, and at last, speaking in a voice that carried across the plain, the Tsar said, "Lord, in Thy name we march!" Then he ordered them all to make the sign of the Cross, and they rode toward Kazan.

When the soldiers looked up at the walls of the city, they saw no sign of life. No guards manned the towers, the gates were closed, the city seemed silent and deserted. Many Russians rejoiced, imagining that the Tatars had been overcome by fear and had fled to the forest. Others, who knew the enemy better, advised caution. The Bulak River, little more than a muddy stream, followed the west wall of Kazan, and beyond the river and a small ridge lay the Plain of Arsk. Suddenly, as an advance patrol of about seven thousand scouts marched over the ridge, the great Nogay Gate flew open and streams of Tatars poured out of the city to attack them. The Russians were taken by surprise. About five thousand Tatar cavalry armed with lances hurled themselves on the scouts, and another thousand Tatar bowmen came running out of the gates. The scouts were forced back over the ridge and they would have been cut down to the last man if the vanguard under Prince Ivan Turantay-Pronsky had not rescued them. Finally the Tatars were driven back to the gates. They fought well; they had achieved surprise, and only ten prisoners had fallen into Russian hands, but they had lost the skirmish. The Tsar was well pleased with his small victory, but he knew that at any moment the gates would open again and the Tatars would come streaming out.

His own camp was established in the Khan's Meadow about a mile to the west of the city. Before erecting his own tent, he gave orders that three church tents should be erected. These tents were dedicated to the Archangel Michael, St. Catherine the Martyr, and St. Sergius the Miracle-Worker. Beside the tent of St. Sergius he dismounted and offered prayers for his army. Throughout all the weeks of the siege the Tsar would continue to pray in these tents which were richly furnished with icons and relics. When he spoke of "continuous prayers" to be uttered by his soldiers, he meant precisely what he said, and prayers were continually on his lips. Only by "continuous prayer" could final victory be assured.

But God listened only intermittently to the Tsar's prayers, for on the night of August 24 there rose a storm so terrible that it could be understood as a sign of divine displeasure. Many Russian ships were sunk, and vast supplies of food and ammunition were lost, so that it became necessary to send to Sviazhsk and as far as Moscow for replenishments. All the Tsar's tents including the church tents were hurled down by the storm, and the Khan's Meadow became a shallow lake. The storm lasted throughout the night and subsided early in the morning. On August 25 the Tsar was seen riding round the walls of the city and inspecting his troops. The heavy gabions were rolled into place during the day and the following night, and by morning Kazan was surrounded by a ring of earthworks. Then the heavy guns were brought up and placed behind the gabions. While all this was happening, the Tatars made a number of sorties against the Russian lines and sometimes they were able to reach the gabions, but no farther. Sometimes, too, the Tatars opened fire from the walls with muskets and cannon. They did little harm, for by this time the Russians were protected by their earthworks.

With Kazan enclosed within a wall of earth, it soon became clear that Prince Yepancha would attempt to break out of the forest of Arsk. Although the Russians knew about this force, they had not expected it to emerge for some time and had merely stationed a few detachments of cavalry along the edge of the forest. The first sortie from the forest took place on August 28, a Sunday. The Tatars came surging out of the forest, taking the Russians by surprise, killing the commander of the cavalry detachment, and routing them, so that they would all have been killed if reinforcements from the vanguard and the main army had not arrived in time. This first battle on the Plain of Arsk taught the Russians a lesson they would not forget: there was no safety as long as Prince Yepancha

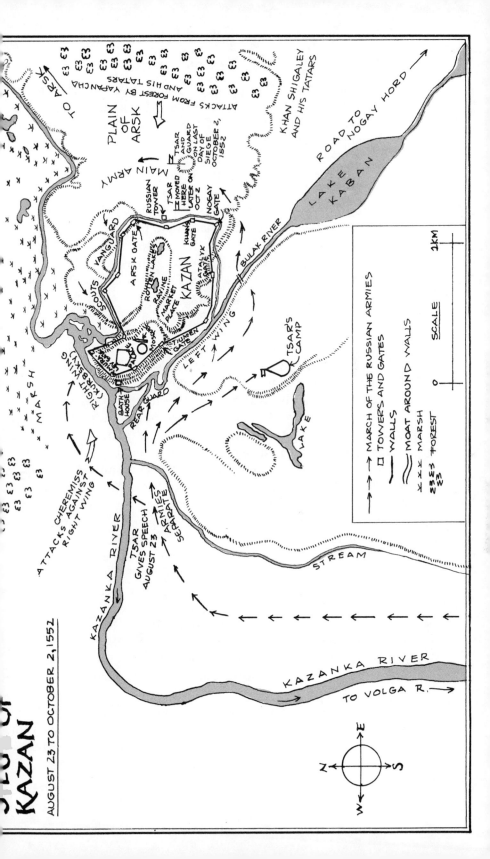

SIEGE OF KAZAN

AUGUST 23 TO OCTOBER 2, 1552

remained in the forest. The fighting was so severe that Ivan ordered a detachment from his own army to help them, and mounted his horse, saying he would fight with them. He was, however, dissuaded and he appears to have spent the rest of the day praying to St. Sergius the Miracle-Worker. His prayers were answered, for the Tatars were thrown back. On the Plain of Arsk there were more Russian than Tatar bodies.

On the following day the Tatars again appeared on the edge of the forest, but this time the Russians were prepared for them. The Tsar gave strict orders that his troops were not to engage the enemy. All that day the Russians and the Tatars stood watching each other warily. The Muscovites could only guess how many more Tatars were hiding in the dark forest.

There had been many strange signs and portents, but the strangest of all came during the last days of the month when the city was already invested. According to Prince Andrey Kurbsky, the Tatars began to practice magic spells which were surprisingly effective. Just after sunrise some old men and women appeared on the acropolis plainly visible to the army below. They uttered incomprehensible words and made obscene gestures, turning their backs and lifting up their garments. A moment later the wind rose, clouds formed, and rain fell, even though there was not a single cloud in the sky before they appeared. "Then all the dry places became swamps," reported Prince Kurbsky, "and the rain fell directly above our army, not elsewhere, and there was nothing in the sky to suggest this was about to happen." Clearly the Tatars were using magic powers not possessed by the Russians.

But the Russians had magic powers not possessed by the Tatars. Ivan remembered that he possessed a piece of the True Cross. He sent for it, ordering his messengers to travel as quickly as possible to Moscow. Within eight or nine days they were back again in Kazan, having traveled by fast carriage from Moscow to Nizhni-Novgorod and thereafter by one of the small swift Viatka sailing vessels. The True Cross was carried in procession through the army, and Prince Kurbsky relates that thereafter all traces of the pagan magic disappeared.

Nevertheless there were no easy victories, and neither Ivan's incessant prayers nor the presence of a holy relic saved the Russians from savage maulings at the hands of the Tatars, who had

y this time taken the measure of their adversaries. Attacks from
ιe forest were concerted with sudden sorties from the city gates.
ιccasionally, too, the Cheremiss tribesmen attacked the Russians
om the northwest, pouring out of another forest. They were
ι-equipped and no match for their enemies, but they tried men's
atience. The Tatars on the acropolis signaled to their friends on
ιe edge of the forest of Arsk by means of battle flags flying from
ιe huge tower dominating the city. The Muscovites also had a
ιrefully worked out signaling system, using heavy drums.
hroughout the day, and sometimes at night, there could be heard
ιe booming of the great drum of Prince Ivan Mstislavsky, giving
recise orders to every army gathered around Kazan. The drum
as so large and so heavy that it had to be supported on the backs
ⁿ four horses.

Already Ivan was coming to the conclusion that the siege might
st through the winter. He had lost all hope of a speedy victory, for
s soldiers were half-starved, living on dry bread, water, and
hatever they could purchase at sharply inflated prices. "They
ιuld not even eat their fill of dry bread because there was so much
ιrassment from the enemy," wrote Prince Kurbsky, who went on
· describe his own misery at night when he had to remain awake in
der to guard the guns against a sudden enemy attack. Within ten
ιys of arriving outside Kazan the army was showing signs of
ιhaustion.

Ivan himself had no doubt that Kazan would be conquered. His
ιpes rested on God, his army and his sappers, skilled and
ιtermined men who enjoyed tunneling under the earth and
ιwing up fortifications. Through Kamay Mirza the war council
ιrned that the main source of Kazan's water supply was a hidden
ring which rose on the banks of the Kazanka River and fed into
ιe city through a secret underground passage. Since the spring lay
ιtside the walls, the Russians could blow up the passage if they
ιuld find it, and the people of Kazan would die of thirst. There
ιre no springs inside the city, only some brackish pools and lakes.
A stone bathhouse on the northwest of Kazan had already been
ιptured. It was logical to assume that the secret passage passed
ιar the bathhouse. A certain Razmysl, an engineer of Lithuanian
ιigin, took charge of the operation, and Alexey Adashev, the
ιar's favorite, was given overall command, thus emphasizing the

importance of a ruse that might bring the siege to a quick end. Th
sappers started digging on August 26, and in ten days reached
point underneath the secret passage. The sappers heard the voic
and the footsteps of the Tatars overhead. Eleven barrels o
gunpowder were rolled into the tunnel. At dawn on Sunda
September 4 the gunpowder was ignited in the presence of Iva
who had the satisfaction of seeing the explosion, which tore dow
part of the wall. Huge logs, stones, and rubble were hurled into th
air; the wall caught fire; many Tatars were killed. The people o
Kazan were dumbfounded by the destruction of their water suppl
and many began to talk of surrender. They dug into the rock fo
another source of water, but found only a small spring so brackis
that it was scarcely drinkable, and some people became ill an
swollen from drinking it, and some died. Nevertheless the Tata
went on fighting.

The sappers continued to dig tunnels under the walls of Kaza
Two fortified towers, one on the southwest corner and the other o
the eastern wall, were both mined. The work proceeded slowly an
was not completed until the end of September. At the same time th
Russians bombarded the Arsk Gate with their heavy guns, finall
destroying it, but since the Tatars were able to put up a ne
wooden gate very quickly, little was gained. Meanwhile morta
kept lobbing stone balls over the walls day and night to keep th
Tatars from resting.

Prince Yepancha, from his hiding place in the Arsk fores
continually made sorties against the Russians, and this incessa
harassment grew costly. Finally the Russians lured him into th
open plains, defeated him, and sent the remnants of his arm
running back into the forest, where they took refuge in a fortre
built of huge balks of timber, situated on a hill surrounded t
swamps. From this base at the proper time they intended to mak
further sorties against the Russians.

At a council of war the decision was made to destroy th
formidable stronghold, whatever the cost. Prince Alexander Go
baty-Shuisky was entrusted with the command of the puniti
expedition; he was ordered to destroy the fortress and capture
many prisoners as possible. If the fortress was destroyed within
short time, his next task was to advance on the town of Arsk, whi
lay on the shores of the Kazanka River some twenty miles beyor

the forest stronghold. Prince Kurbsky described Prince Gorbaty-Shuisky as "a very wise man, well versed in military affairs." In addition to his own troops the prince was given command of the Tatars of Khan Shigaley and some Cheremiss tribesmen who served as guides through the forest pathways.

Prince Gorbaty-Shuisky rode into the forest with his cavalry as though it was the most natural thing in the world to capture and destroy a fortress hidden deep in the interior. The Tatars had warning of his coming and were ready for him. When the Russians reached the swamps at the foot of the hill, the cavalry dismounted and split into two groups, one group mounting a frontal assault on the fortress with bowmen and musketeers, while the other, led by the prince, made a surprise attack on the right of the fortress after hacking their way through dense forests. The battle was all over in two hours, the Tatars fleeing with the Russians in pursuit. About a hundred Tatars were captured, and a vast amount of booty.

Two days later the Russians reached Arsk to find the town deserted. Here in the plains beyond the forest were the estates of the Tatar nobles, rich fields, cattle, and grain, stores of honey, and many villages, which the Russians raided at their pleasure. On these estates they found Russians working as slaves. They were now liberated, and they joined the Muscovites in marauding expeditions that led them to the banks of the Kama River. Ivan gave strict orders that Prince Gorbaty-Shuisky should return in the shortest possible time, but the prince was in no hurry. He had found a land of milk and honey, and his soldiers were enjoying themselves.

As the days passed, Ivan became more and more disturbed by the prince's long absence. As always, he was full of foreboding. His spirits revived a little when the monk Adrian Angelov reached his camp, bearing gifts from the Troitsa-Sergeyevsky Monastery. Ivan was deeply moved by the gifts, which included many icons. Angelov describes Ivan falling on his knees before the icon of the Holy Trinity, saying, "Glory to Thee, my Creator, who comest to me, sinner that I am, in these far away lands. I gaze upon this icon of Thee, and it is as though in very truth I see my God, and I pray for mercy and help for myself and my army!" Then he ate the holy bread and drank the holy water and raised his arms to heaven, saying, "Holy Trinity and the most holy Mother of God, help us!"

Ivan spent half the day praying and the other half in conference or inspecting his troops. Angelov was struck by the Tsar's extraordinary religious fervor and also a little puzzled by it. He therefore questioned Ivan, taking the greatest care not to offend him. Why, he asked, was the Tsar so relentlessly determined to conquer Kazan? The Tsar answered that he had been sickened by the depredations of the Kazan Tatars. They had made too many Russians captives, they had spilled too much Russian blood, and they had brought desolation to too many Orthodox churches. Then, abruptly, the Tsar began to speak of himself and his own responsibilities. He said:

> I have been appointed Tsar by God through the mediation of the Virgin and all the saints, and I am the shepherd over the Orthodox land and its people, and this has come about in order that I might govern God's people, being unwaveringly faithful to the Orthodox Christian faith, and that I might protect them from all the evils they may encounter and take care of all their needs, because I am their Tsar by God's favor and they must have fear of me and be obedient in all things. For I have received this power not from man but from God.

These breathtaking claims show that the Tsar, who had just passed his twenty-second birthday, regarded himself as possessing powers given to him by God for the furtherance of the divine cause. Since he was God's representative on earth, he demanded blind obedience from his people, and it was proper that they should fear him. "They must have fear of me and be obedient in all things." Throughout his life he would continue to make the same claim, justifying his most terrible acts by the self-evident fact that not only God but the Mother of God and the entire assembly of saints had commanded him to exercise his powers. A strange divinity had fallen upon him, and he accepted it with open hands.

Meanwhile Ivan continued to rage over the long absence of the army of Prince Gorbaty-Shuisky. His rage, however, turned to joy when the army finally returned to Kazan, bringing not only the liberated Russians and a multitude of prisoners but also herds of cattle and wagonloads of furs and treasure. The Russians, on short rations, found themselves in plenty. Cows could be bought for five copecks, and a large ox cost little more. The Tsar hurried to his tent church as soon as he heard of their safe arrival and ordered thanksgiving services to be held for the successful outcome of the campaign. He embraced Prince Gorbaty-Shuisky, permitted the officers to kiss his hand, gave them costly gifts, entertained them with banquets, and praised them. The Russians liberated from the Tatar yoke presented themselves at his camp, where he gave them new clothes, fed them for three days, and then sent them under escort back to their homes in Russia. At intervals he vanished into one of his tent churches, wept, prayed, and gave thanks for the victory that swept the Tatars out of the forest of Arsk and the plains beyond.

The siege was going well, though outwardly there was little to show for the constant hammering on the walls of Kazan. Ivan was waiting for the moment when Razmysl would report to him that he was ready to blow up the two towers. Through these breaches his army would pour into the city.

Ivan's faith in eventual victory was confirmed by the presence of St. Sergius inside Kazan. People who had somehow succeeded in escaping over the walls reported that they had seen an old man in tattered robes sweeping the roads. He was evidently a monk and wore a thick but not very long beard. Asked why he was busy sweeping the roads, the old monk answered, "I am doing this, because soon I shall have many guests here." When people tried to touch the monk, they discovered that he was as insubstantial as the air.

Such a visitation by his favorite saint was only to be expected, but Ivan gave orders that it should be kept secret. This was a matter that related to the divine economy, and should not be revealed until the grace of God was fulfilled.

Nor was Ivan content to rely on icons, prayers, and the presence of St. Sergius. A powerful siege engine was being built secretly some distance south of Kazan. It took the form of an enormous wooden tower forty-two feet high, considerably higher than the walls of the city. The formidable armaments, arranged on the top stages of the tower, consisted of ten heavy guns and fifty light cannon, the heavy guns being ten feet long and the cannon seven feet. They were manned by the best gunners in the army.

The tower, which took two weeks to build, was rolled up to the Khan's Gate during the night. At dawn there was a thunderous roar as the guns fired directly into the city, causing fearful damage and killing vast numbers of women and children. The Tatar soldiers behind the Khan's Gate quickly dug trenches or put up earthworks, but the presence of the huge tower bristling with guns was a constant reminder of the massive power of the invaders.

As they saw themselves more and more tightly encircled, the Tatars made more sorties, fighting desperately at the gates, hoping to bring about such heavy losses that the Russians would raise the siege. In Ivan's eyes the huge losses were immaterial, for a Russian soldier went straight to heaven the moment he fell on the field of battle. Had not God told him he would conquer Kazan? The Metropolitan Makary sent him an icon of the Assumption ornamented with pearls and precious stones, and another icon of the Annunciation, similarly ornamented, was sent to Vladimir of Staritsa. There was such an accumulation of relics and icons in the tent churches that they threatened to burst open under the weight of treasures.

Everything now depended on the sappers, who had been digging for a whole month. Ivan, who liked things done quickly, appears to have been incensed by the long delay and to have threatened to punish the sappers for malingering. A famous ballad composed some years later describes Ivan standing among the sappers and threatening them with instant death because the fuse leading to the barrels of gunpowder was burning so slowly. In the ballad the sappers answered:

> A candle burns up quickly in the wind:
> Under the earth it burns more quietly.

The quiet work under the earth was completed on Saturday October 1, the Feast Day of the Intercession of the Virgin Mary. On that day Razmysl reported that all the tunnels had been completed, the gunpowder barrels were in place, and it remained only to light the fuse. The war council decided that the city should be stormed at dawn the next day.

On that Saturday the final preparations were made. There was an especially heavy bombardment, as though to prepare the Tatars for what was to come. Wherever possible, the moat around the city was filled with earth and tree trunks, so that the Russians could break through wherever the walls showed signs of weakness. The Tsar ordered all his soldiers to make their confessions and receive the sacraments, thus placing them in a state of grace beyond the reach of fear. When he addressed his troops, he dwelt on the theme of suffering, saying that the more they suffered, the more certain would be the victory. It was a subject he had pondered at great length and he had arrived at some definite conclusions, among them that suffering was good in the sight of God and of the Tsar. He said to the troops:

> Those who suffer truly will receive glory on earth and laurels in heaven. Your names will be inscribed in the books of Heaven, and here on earth in the most famous city of Moscow, in the great cathedral,[1] your names will be celebrated during divine services for everlasting, and they will be remembered throughout the whole of Russia. Should you die, I shall take care of your wives and children and pay your creditors. The estates handed down to you by your ancestors or granted to you by me will remain in the possession of your wives and children.
>
> As for myself, dear brothers and friends, I too am prepared to suffer unto death for the sake of the holy churches, the Orthodox faith, the Christian blood, my own patrimony.

The Tsar's speech was uttered with great fervor, and when his soldiers shouted that they were ready for any suffering he imposed on them, he wept with joy.

On the morning of October 2 Ivan awoke early, buckled on his armor, went to the tent church of St. Sergius, and prayed before the icons, tears streaming down his face. He asked the Virgin to intercede for him and begged for a special favor: that his own sins should not be counted against him in God's sight. When the priest who performed the morning service came to the words, "There shall be one fold, and one shepherd," there was a sound like thunder, the earth shook, and Ivan rushed to the door. In the dawn light he saw a huge black cloud rising into the sky and there were balks of timber and Tatars flying through the air. A few minutes later there was another thunderclap as the second tower was blown sky-high.

With the two towers blown up, the general assault began on all

---

[1] By "the great cathedral" Ivan clearly meant the Uspensky Cathedral in the Kremlin, where the Tsars were crowned, important decrees were proclaimed, and the most solemn ceremonies were held. The Metropolitans of Moscow were buried there.

sides of the city, but especially along the east and south walls, where the Russians hurled themselves through the breaches. The noise of the attack was deafening, but Ivan seemed not to hear it. He was still praying when one of his officers entered the tent and said, "Lord, the time has come for thee to leave the tent, for there is fierce fighting in the city and the soldiers are expecting thee." Ivan replied, "Let us wait until the end of the service. If we do so, we shall receive greater mercy from Jesus Christ and all the more will our prayers serve as weapons against our enemies." Another entered the tent, summoning him urgently to the battlefield. Weeping, he addressed an icon: "Do not forsake me, O God, do not abandon me, help me!" Then he went to the icon of St. Sergius, kissed it, and said, "Help me with thy prayers," and drank the holy water and ate the holy bread.

In the eyes of Ivan the icons were machines generating spiritual power, and the longer he remained in the tent the greater the spiritual power massed against the enemy.

At last he was prevailed upon to leave the tent, and with Vladimir of Staritsa and Khan Shigaley he rode from his camp to a position on high ground somewhere near the Khan's Gate on the south of the city. As he rode, he could see Russian standards already flying from the city walls.

While the Russians were fighting ferociously in the city, pushing the Tatars back until they were being forced toward the ravine at the foot of the acropolis, something happened so unexpectedly that the commanders of the army could scarcely believe their eyes. Scores of Russians were slipping away from the city not because they were being vanquished by the enemy but because they wanted to safeguard their loot and bring it back to their camps. They were streaming out of the Khan's Gate. The Tsar's military advisers ordered the elite corps of mounted cavalry, all of them noblemen, to be thrown into the battle, to fight the enemy, and also to put an end to the looting. Usually the elite corps was held in reserve, acting as the Tsar's bodyguard. The Tsar was terrified. Men pleaded with him to move closer to the Khan's Gate, where his standard had been planted. He did so reluctantly, and Prince Kurbsky relates that "his councillors took his horse by the bridle and placed the Tsar close to the standard whether he liked it or not, ınd among these councillors were some men of the generation of ɔur fathers."

Prince Kurbsky was not present at the Khan's Gate and he was merely relating what he had heard from others. With his brother Roman, he was fighting strenuously along the north wall of the city, attempting to capture the acropolis. The Tatars fled beyond the Kazanka River, and while Prince Kurbsky was charging them with

van watches as his army storms Kazan. (From the *Nikon Chronicle with Miniatures*)

three hundred of his cavalry, he fell from his horse and would hav
been trampled to death if he had not been wearing heavy armor. "
had so many grievous wounds that I lost consciousness," he wrote
"When I came to about an hour later, I saw two servants of min
and two soldiers of the Tsar standing over me, weeping an
sobbing as though I were dead. And I saw myself lying naked
wounded in many places but still alive, for I had been wearing
very strong armor inherited from my forefathers." He recovered
but did no more fighting that day.

By this time the fighting was nearly over. Khan Yedige
Makhmet retreated to his walled palace on the acropolis an
continued to fight off the invaders. At last they broke into th
palace, where they slaughtered men, women, and children indis
criminately, until the whole acropolis was running with blood. Ku
Sherif, the chief mullah of Kazan, led a desperate charge agains
the Russians, but the mullah and all his men were slaughtered
Everywhere the dead lay in heaps. They lay in the narrow alleyway
of the city, in the palaces, in the mosques, and they were piled high
against the walls. The Russian chroniclers speak of the whole Plai
of Arsk being carpeted with bodies, suggesting that the Tatar
made massive sorties before they were cut down.

Escaping from his palace, Khan Yediger Makhmet took refuge ii
one of the fortified towers still remaining in Tatar hands. Her
Prince Dmitry Paletsky parleyed with him, urging that he surrende
because his cause was lost and it was time to put an end to th
fighting. From the tower the Khan saw a city in flames and th
Russians in full possession of the acropolis. He offered to surrender
but the remnant of his army, observing the fate of their country
men, decided on flight. While the Khan, his wife, and his cour
went into captivity, the remaining Tatar soldiers succeeded ii
scrambling over the walls in the hope of making for the forest
beyond the Kazanka River. Most of them were killed by the
Russian cavalry.

Elsewhere in Kazan all resistance came to an end, and there wa
only the wailing of the women and the crackling of the fires. The
fighting, which began at dawn, was over by early afternoon.

The Tsar's faith in divine help was rewarded. He assured his
soldiers that victory had come "by the grace of God and the

Ivan IV trampling Khan Yediger Makhmet of Kazan. (From the *Kazansky letopisets*)

prayers of the Most Pure Mother of God and of the saints of Moscow and of all Russia." His own ancestors, the saintly Tsars and Grand Princes, had fought by their side. He paid tribute to his fighting men, his nobles, boyars, and voyevodas, Khan Shigaley and Vladimir of Staritsa, but above all they owed the victory "to the inexpressible mercy of God." Embracing Vladimir of Staritsa, he cried out, "God has made me for my humility Lord of Great Russia and of the eastern kingdom of Kazan." In this way he simultaneously invoked the humble Ivan and the other Ivan who was dazzled by his own success.

The ceremonies of victory were performed in the manner of the medieval romances. The Tsar remained on horseback, while all his generals and even Vladimir of Staritsa bowed low before him, the sole victor, the lord of many lands, Ivan Vasilievich, Tsar and Autocrat. Khan Yediger Makhmet, his wife, and his courtiers were brought to the Tsar in chains, and prostrated themselves before him. To the interpreter the Tsar said, "Tell them that according to our merciful custom we reprieve them from the sentence of death and order them to be released from their bonds." Then Khan Yediger Makhmet rose and walked up to the Tsar's horse and kissed the Tsar's stirrup.

It was a moment of exquisite triumph, never to be repeated. There would be many wars, many cities would be sacked, and many countries would be invaded, but never again would the Tsar achieve so complete a victory with the knowledge that God was walking by his side.

The Tsar's Sickness

ALTHOUGH HE HAD TAKEN NO PART in the fighting and was never in great danger, Ivan genuinely believed that Kazan had been conquered by him and that by his presence on the battlefield he had induced God to favor Russian arms. Divine energy had flowed through him, and from him it had flowed out among his soldiers. There would have been no victory without his prayers—those continual prayers which he uttered while moving from one tent church to the next. The sacred relics, the great banner portraying a stern Christ which fluttered above his head, and the many priests in his camp—all these had played a part in his victory.

He was therefore in a very solemn mood as he gazed at Kazan and decided how he would celebrate his triumph. His first act was to order that a church should be immediately built on the place where he had stood during the last stages of the attack. Since the church was made of wood and there was a good deal of lumber available, his master carpenters had no difficulty in building it in a single day. His second act was to send messengers to all his armies with orders that they should convey his gratitude and approbation, promising that he would himself congratulate them at the proper time. His third act was to make a ceremonial visit to the city. Some time elapsed before he could make the visit because the dead lay everywhere, and it was necessary to clear a passage for him.

The Tatars had captured many Russians in their raids, employing them as slaves. Now, as he rode through the city, they knelt beside the road, shouting in gratitude for their deliverance from bondage. Once, seeing some Tatar dead lying where they had fallen, women and children among them, Ivan said with tears in his eyes, "They are not Christians, but still they are people like us!" He rode up the winding road to the Khan's palace on the acropolis, gazed across the plains, and then returned to his camp. Then he went to pray in the tent church of St. Sergius.

Later in the day he summoned his troops and addressed them, praising them for their courage, their steadfastness, their faith in God. He ordered the spoils to be divided among them. The most valuable of the spoils were the Tatar women and children, and these were accordingly distributed among the troops. "With my own eyes I saw vast numbers of prisoners being led away like herds of cattle," wrote Angelov. Ivan's share of the spoils consisted of Khan Yediger, his regalia, and heavy guns.

On October 4, when Kazan had been cleared of corpses, Ivan made his second triumphal entry accompanied by his court and a retinue of priests. His purpose was to select a site for the cathedral to be erected on the acropolis and to attend divine service for the first time on a spot where future generations of Christians would worship. Since the victory owed so much to the intercession of the Virgin, he decided that it should be called the Cathedral of the Annunciation. When the service was over, Ivan, still accompanied by his court and by a retinue of priests, made a processional journey around the walls, which the priests blessed with holy water. In this way Kazan became a Christian city.

Meanwhile there were other solemn ceremonies to attend, and many rituals. From all around Kazan there came tribesmen to swear allegiance to Ivan and to prostrate themselves at his feet. They brought presents, and received presents from the hands of the Tsar. Then there were the great banquets offered to his generals and boyars, and more banquets for the soldiers. It was necessary, too, to make decisions about the government of the city and about whether all the surrounding tribes should be subdued, and how many soldiers would be needed to occupy the khanate. Prince Gorbaty-Shuisky was made governor and Prince Vasily Serebriany vice-governor. In the belief that the conquest of Kazan had struck terror into the hearts of the Tatars, it was decided that only a small token force needed to be left behind. These troops amounted to about fifteen hundred cavalry, three thousand musketeers, and some detachments of Cossacks. Prince Kurbsky and others thought this policy completely mistaken and urged Ivan to remain with his army in Kazan until all the Tatars within the Kazan khanate had been conquered. Ivan refused. Had not God, the Virgin, and the saints fought by his side? Who would dare to raise his hand against the victorious Tsar?

There were, of course, many other reasons why the Tsar rejected this advice. He was eager to return to Moscow, he wanted to enjoy the fruits of victory in his own capital: the acclamations, the processions, the new majesty that accrued to him as the conqueror of Kazan. The nobles and boyars, who raised their own private armies and supported them, were anxious to disband them and return to their estates. Anastasia would soon be giving birth. She had already presented him with two daughters, and he was now hoping for a son, who would inherit the throne. He knew, too, that he was more powerful in Moscow, the mystical center of his empire, than when he was in the field. His task, as he saw it, was to return to Moscow as quickly as possible, to disband the greater part of the army, and to see that Kazan was well-governed. Kazan was one of the jewels of his crown, but there were many others.

There is no evidence that he gave much weight to Prince Kurbsky's advice, which was remarkably sound and based on a wide knowledge of the Tatars. In fact, during the following years there were continual uprisings in the region of Kazan, and army after army had to be sent out to suppress them. Ivan had not struck terror into the hearts of the Tatars; he had merely wounded them.

The Cathedral of the Annunciation at Kazan was built in an astonishingly short space of time, for Ivan attended a thanksgiving service in it before leaving the city. Prayers were offered to Christ, the Virgin, and the saints to protect the city and its people, and then, while the people knelt in the streets, he made his ceremonial departure at the head of his army, which accompanied him to Sviazhsk, where he spent a night before making the long journey by boat to Nizhni-Novgorod. The cavalry rode along the banks of the Volga and the infantry traveled by boat. He was as well guarded on the boat as it was possible to be. Nevertheless in later years he convinced himself that during the journey from Sviazhsk to Nizhni-Novgorod he had been in terrible danger.

Ivan was not a man of great physical courage and he remembered in excruciating detail all the occasions when he felt himself to be in mortal danger. He especially remembered the times when he was abandoned by those whose duty was to protect him, when he would have perished if God had not saved him. Writing to Prince Kurbsky twelve years later in one of those strange and brilliantly written letters full of the fury of denunciation, he spoke of the ignominy and misery he suffered during the journey:

> After God in His unfathomable mercy gave us victory over the Muslims and we were returning safe and sound with all the Orthodox Christian army—what shall I say about those "well-wishers," whom thou callest martyrs? Let me say this: they placed me like a prisoner on the ship, and conveyed me with a very small escort through a godless and most unbelieving land. Had not the all powerful hand of the Almighty protected my humility, then I would certainly have lost my life. Such are the "well-wishers," whom thou defendest, and thus do they lay down their lives for us by striving to deliver our soul into the hands of our enemies!

If Ivan in his hours of triumph could give way to irrational fears, then it could be expected that he would be even more irrational and fearful when triumph eluded him.

The journey to Moscow was one long triumphal progress. Everywhere he was acclaimed and worshipped. The peasants came down to the banks of the Volga to acclaim him, and the priests recited the litanies of thanksgiving only to have their words drowned by the shouts of the kneeling peasants, who called him their deliverer, the mighty one, the Tsar who had lifted the fear of the Tatars from their souls. Sometimes his ship anchored near the shore, and he presented himself to them, and there were more praises, more litanies. The news of the victory had long since reached Moscow, and from time to time he was met by messengers bearing letters from Anastasia, his brother Yury, or the Metropolitan Makary, all urging him to return quickly and offering congratulations for his victory.

The ceremonial mustering out of the army took place at Nizhni-Novgorod, where he formally thanked the soldiers for their services and gave them permission to return to their homes. Then he continued his journey to Moscow by way of Vladimir, the former capital of Russia.

On the road to Vladimir he was met by Vasily Trakhaniotov, Anastasia's messenger, a boyar of Greek origin. He brought news that Anastasia had given birth to a son. Ivan was so overjoyed that he jumped off his horse, embraced Trakhaniotov, prayed, thanked heaven, wept, and ran about like a madman. To celebrate such an occasion he needed to give Anastasia's messenger a present, but what present? Impulsively he threw off his mantle and pressed it on the messenger, and for good measure added his horse. Anastasia's brother Nikita Zakharin was sent posthaste to Moscow to present the Tsar's congratulations.

The birth of a son so quickly after the conquest of Kazan made Ivan delirious with joy. He already had two daughters, Anna and Maria—Anna died at the age of eleven months—but daughters counted for nothing compared with the birth of a son. God had once more shown him favor, for now the dynasty was secure.[1]

In Vladimir and Suzdal he paused only long enough to pray in the churches and to receive congratulations. He hurried on to Moscow, but first it was necessary to pray at the tomb of St. Sergius in the Troitsa-Sergeyevsky Monastery and to break bread with the monks. He spent the night on his estate at Taininskoye, where his brother Yury met him, and together they set out early the next morning for what would evidently be a tumultuous reception in Moscow.

Long before they reached Moscow, the people came out to welcome him. The crowds were so thick that he had difficulty making his way among them and was in danger of being cut off from his guards and retinue. He rode through the throng, bowing right and left, while the people kissed his hands and feet, and shouted, "Long live our God-fearing Tsar, conqueror of the barbarians, savior of the Christians!" At Sretinsky Monastery he was met by a procession headed by the Metropolitan Makary, the clergy carrying crosses, banners, and icons. Here he dismounted and kissed the Icon of Our Lady of Vladimir and many other icons. The old boyars, Prince Mihailo Bulgakov and Ivan Morozov, who

---

[1] Anastasia and Ivan had six children in all: Anna, born August 10, 1549, died July 20, 1550; then Maria, born March 17, 1551, the exact date of her death being unknown; then Dmitry, born October 1552, died June 1553; then Ivan, born March 28, 1554, died November 19, 1582; then Evdokia, born May 11, 1556, died June 1558; then Fyodor, born May 11, 1557, died January 1598. Only the last of his six children survived him.

had served his father and grandfather and who had ruled over
Moscow in his absence, were also waiting for him. He embraced
these and many other nobles, and then it was time for the
Metropolitan to deliver a special blessing. Ivan, in return, explained
the circumstances that led to the conquest of Kazan, his armies
having gone forth in defense of Christ and the Church. He said

> Before I set forth on the campaign against Kazan, I took counsel
> with the Metropolitan Makary and the clergy about how the Khan of
> Kazan and his people were devastating the Russian land, the towns
> and villages, the churches and monasteries, and how countless
> Christians including priests and monks, boyars and princes, youths
> and children, men and women, had perished or had been taken
> prisoner and dispersed over the face of the earth. All this happened
> because of our sins and especially because of my sins.
>
> Thus it was that on your advice we set out to make war against
> them. I urged you to pray to God, the Virgin and all the saints for our
> well-being and for the forgiveness of our many sins and for our
> deliverance from the barbarians. Thanks to God, the Virgin and the
> saints, and also thanks to your prayers and the watchful care and
> courage of Vladimir of Staritsa and of all our boyars and generals and
> our Christian army, which was ready to suffer great hardships for the
> true and holy Christian faith and for the holy churches and for our
> Orthodox Christian brethren, we reached Kazan safely and in good
> health. And God in His great mercy overlooked our sins and granted
> us victory. He gave into our hands the royal and populous city of
> Kazan, and he threw down the Muslim falsehood and established the
> Cross. And by the judgment of God, the Muslims who lived in that
> city perished without a trace and only Khan Yediger Makhmet
> remained alive in our hands.
>
> Together with Prince Vladimir of Staritsa, I and all my army give
> thanks to thee, holy father, and to all the holy priesthood, for it was
> owing to your prayers that this miracle came to pass.

Ivan spoke as a conqueror who genuinely believed in the power
of prayer, and he was not being in the least ironical or deceitful
when he ascribed the victory to their prayers. Nor did he need any
assistance in composing these speeches which read like sermons, for
his mind had long since acquired an ecclesiastical coloring.

One phrase in the speech stands out: "All this happened because
of our sins and especially because of my sins." It is a phrase to
remember, and we shall hear it again and again in the chronicle

Seventeenth-century portrait of Ivan the Terrible. (Courtesy British Museum)

that follows. Sometimes he speaks the words very softly, in hushed expectation of punishment, but no punishment comes. Sometimes he speaks them boldly and defiantly, brazenly, with a sound like rolling thunder. To the end of his days he would speak publicly about his sins.

Now, in the Sretinsky Monastery just outside of Moscow, in the presence of the richly robed priests and the Metropolitan, he appeared as a figure of martial dignity and magnificence. He was wearing full armor: plumed helmet, brightly polished cuirass, greaves, gantlets, all the accoutrements of a warrior. Makary addressed him in a welcoming speech of inordinate length, with many quotations from many texts. He called upon God to witness the splendor of Ivan who had saved the Orthodox people and the Orthodox churches from the depredations of the Tatars. "The grace of God has been with you, as it was with all the ancient rulers who were favored by God," he said, and went on to speak of Ivan's ancestors, beginning with Constantine the Great and going on to Alexander Nevsky and Dmitry Donskoy. Then the Metropolitan and all the priests knelt before Ivan.

The time had now come for Ivan to change his role. He exchanged his shining armor for the robes of a Tsar. The jeweled fur-lined crown of Monomakh was placed on his head and the royal breastplate called the *barmy,* inset with jewels, hung from his shoulders. In addition he wore on his breast a jeweled cross that contained a small fragment of the True Cross. He entered Moscow in a blaze of jewels.

The solemn processions continued. In the Uspensky Cathedral he prayed before the icons and at the tombs of St. Peter and St. Iona, who were Metropolitans of Russia. In the Cathedral of Michael the Archangel he prayed at the tombs of his ancestors. One by one he visited all the churches in the Kremlin, for this was expected of him and he rejoiced in these liturgical processions. Only when he had performed all his religious duties did he permit himself the pleasure of seeing his wife and newborn son.

Anastasia lay in bed in the Kremlin Palace. He praised her for giving birth to his son and she praised him for conquering Kazan. This is all that the chroniclers tell us. We can therefore deduce that he closed the doors and permitted no one to observe him when he saw his wife for the first time in many weeks.

For a week he remained in seclusion, and then on November 8, 1552, he celebrated the victory with a banquet in the Granovitaya Palata attended by the Metropolitan Makary, all his generals, and all the great officers of state. The banquet lasted three days. He rewarded all who had helped to bring about the victory, and accordingly the first gifts went to the Metropolitan, the bishops, and the clergy, whose prayers had powerfully influenced the course of battle. An honor roll was drawn up, listing the names and titles of those who had fought most bravely, the great deeds they had accomplished and the wounds they had suffered. The names were read out and the soldiers were led up to the Tsar's high table to be rewarded with gifts. These gifts took many forms. A soldier might receive a horse, another a suit of armor, another a velvet robe embroidered with gold and trimmed with sable. Many received jeweled Italian drinking cups and gold goblets, while others received estates and governorships. All together, in those three days, the Tsar gave away money, furs, robes, goblets, horses and armor worth 48,000 rubles. "No man had ever seen such splendor, so much celebration and merriment and generosity in the Kremlin Palace," wrote the chronicler.

All Russia rejoiced, and all through the winter the battle of Kazan was the main topic of conversation. Ballads were written about it, legends accumulated round it, the story of the battle assumed the dimensions of an epic describing the forces of light overcoming the forces of darkness. More than Alexander Nevsky or Dmitry Donskoy, Ivan was exalted in the Russian imagination. A mere youth, almost single-handed, he had overcome the Asiatic hordes and cast off the Tatar yoke, which had pressed heavily on the Russians for two and a half centuries. If he had accomplished nothing else in his life, the Russians would have been profoundly grateful.

This was a moment of grave importance in Russian history. Soon the Russians would extend their power beyond Kazan and take possession of the Khanate of Astrakhan at the mouth of the Volga, and beyond the Volga lay Siberia. They would reach down to the Crimea and westward toward the Baltic, never content until they had pushed back their boundaries to the farthest possible limit. Russia would become an imperial power, ruling over many nations and countless tribes. Ivan was the true founder of this empire, which would always bear the imprint of his character, his violence his rages, his towering ambitions, his pride and strange humility

Now more than ever he was determined to rule as an autocrat independent of the nobles and boyars. One day, shortly after the conquest of Kazan, he addressed them, saying, "God protected me from you! I could not torment you while Kazan stood on its own. I needed you for all manner of things, but now I am free to inflict upon you my torment and my wrath!"

Many of his councillors observed this new authoritarian manner with misgivings. Men like Adashev and Sylvester were deeply disturbed, and not only because their positions were threatened. Sylvester was still Ivan's spiritual adviser. Ivan still relied heavily on Adashev's counsel, but he was becoming increasingly reserved and remote. The poison of absolute power was working on him.

In December he journeyed again to the Troitsa-Sergeyevsky Monastery for the baptism of his son, who was given the name Dmitry. The christening took place at the tomb of St. Sergius, thus insuring a long, godly, and prosperous life for the boy, or so Ivan believed. He was accompanied by Anastasia, his brother Yury, and his cousin Vladimir of Staritsa.

There were more baptisms during the following months. The six-year-old Utemish Guirey, who had inherited the Khanate of Kazan only to be replaced by Khan Shigaley, was baptized by the Metropolitan Makary in the Chudov Monastery and given the name Alexander. After the ceremony the boy solemnly dined with the Metropolitan and was then taken to Ivan, who proclaimed that the boy should henceforth live within the Kremlin Palace. His policy was to keep a cautious eye on all claimants to the throne of Kazan, since he was himself the Tsar of Kazan.

During the same month Yediger Makhmet, the last Khan of Kazan, informed the Metropolitan that he would like to be baptized and to enter the Christian faith. To make sure that the Khan's request was sincere, the Metropolitan arranged that he should be closely interrogated by priests for a number of days, but they found no evidence that he was embracing the faith because it was politically expedient. The Metropolitan reported the priests' findings to Ivan, who received Yediger Makhmet and embraced him. On February 26, 1553, the convert to the faith, wearing only a white linen shroud, walked out of the Tainitskaya Gate in the deep snow, and in the presence of Ivan, Yury, Vladimir of Staritsa, and the Metropolitan Makary he was led across the frozen Moskva River to a place where the ice had been chopped away. He was asked whether he had changed his faith through compulsion and replied, "I desire sincerely and with love to worship Jesus. As for the false Mohammed and his evil book I curse them!" He then entered the icy water and was baptized under the name of Simeon. A large house within the Kremlin walls was set aside for him, and a retinue of servants was provided for him.

Thereafter Khan Simeon occupies only a minor place in the history of the Russian court. As a Khan, he was permitted to have his own courtiers and a boyar called Ivan Zabolotsky acted as his chief adviser and reported directly to the Tsar. He was treated like royalty, but had no power.

In this way the rebellious Tatar Khans were appeased, becoming as gentle as lapdogs. They were reduced to insignificance while retaining all the outward panoply of power. They were merely decorations at the Tsar's court.

A few days later, perhaps because he caught a cold during the Khan's baptism, Ivan took to his bed. The monkish chronicler wrote in March 1553: "Because of our ingratitude and our many sins the Orthodox Tsar was visited with a fiery sickness."

This fiery sickness, probably a virulent form of pneumonia which brought him within an inch of death, was one of the most shattering events in Ivan's life. It profoundly affected his attitude toward the many members of his court who refused for various reasons to swear allegiance to the Tsarevich Dmitry and it reduced him to helplessness at a time when he had hoped to exert the full powers of an autocrat. Terrible suspicions were awakened in his exhausted brain, as he fought with his illness. He had always been a suspicious man, who was inclined to see people in the worst possible light, and during his illness he grew even more suspicious, more resentful, and more cunning. His illness was a nightmare from which he emerged like a man clothed in the colors of a nightmare.

The chronicle known as the *Tsarstvennaya Kniga* contains the statement that Ivan suffered from a fiery sickness, and there are somewhat lengthy additions, which some scholars believe were written by Ivan in his own hand or at his dictation by his personal secretary Ivan Viskovaty, and these additions can be dated fairly accurately, being not earlier than the summer of 1566 and not later than the summer of 1570. From this document, from the letters of Ivan and Prince Kurbsky, from the deposition of Prince Simeon Rostovsky after his arrest, and from other sources it is possible to put together an account of what happened during the Tsar's sickness.

Here are the words written into the *Tsarstvennaya Kniga* by the Tsar or his secretary:

> After the baptism of Khan Simeon of Kazan on Wednesday March 1, 1553, the Tsar fell ill. The illness was very serious, and it was difficult for him to recognize people. He was so ill that many believed he would die. The Tsar's secretary Ivan Mikhailovich Viskovaty took it upon himself to remind the Tsar about his will, which the sovereign always kept handy. The Tsar gave orders that the will should be completed, signed and dated.
>
> When all this was done, Viskovaty reminded the Tsar about the oath of allegiance to the Tsarevich Dmitry which should be sworn by Prince Vladimir of Staritsa and the boyars. The same evening the following boyars gave their allegiance to the Tsarevich: Prince Ivan Fyodorovich Mstislavsky, Prince Vladimir Ivanovich Vorotynsky, Ivan Vasilievich Sheremetev, Mikhail Yakovlevich Morozov, Prince Dmitry Fyodorovich Paletsky, the secretary Ivan Viskovaty, and also the boyars Danilo Romanovich Zakharin, Vasily Mikhailovich Zakharin, and also the nobles who took part in the Council, Alexey Fyodorovich Adashev and Ignaty Veshniakov. . . .

These were all members of the Chosen Council. Mstislavsky and Vorotynsky were among Ivan's commanders at Kazan, Paletsky was the father-in-law of Ivan's brother Yury, and Danilo Zakharin was Anastasia's elder brother. Later in the evening it transpired that two other members of the Chosen Council, Prince Dmitry Kurliatev and the treasurer Nikita Funikov, were both ill, or pretended to be ill, and therefore were unable to swear the oath of allegiance.

Many boyars and nobles were reluctant to take the oath. There were rumors that Prince Vladimir of Staritsa was being pushed forward by his mother, Princess Efrosinia, as a candidate for the throne and they were supporting him either because they genuinely admired him and wanted him to be Tsar after Ivan's death or because—this was a more powerful argument—the death of Ivan

nd the elevation of the infant Dmitry to the throne would
ievitably bring about the regency of Anastasia with all her
elatives in positions of power. Prince Vladimir's role is obscure.
ccording to the chronicle, he frequently visited Ivan during his
Iness, but the boyars grew suspicious of him and finally kept him
way from the bedroom "in order to safeguard the throne."
ylvester thought he behaved quite normally and defended him. In
is deposition written in 1554 Prince Simeon Rostovsky wrote:

> At the time of the Tsar's illness in March 1553, we were all
> discussing what we would do if the Tsar died. A messenger arrived at
> my house from Princess Efrosinia and Prince Vladimir of Staritsa,[2]
> asking me to go and serve Vladimir of Staritsa and win over people to
> his side. I discussed the matter with many boyars and we thought that
> if we served the Tsarevich Dmitry, we would be ruled by the
> Zakharins, and rather than be ruled by the Zakharins, we would serve
> Prince Vladimir of Staritsa, and there were many boyars and princes
> who felt this way.

The names of the boyars who preferred to serve Vladimir of
taritsa are known. They were not self-seekers, but people who
ere distressed at the thought of having to live under another
egency so soon after the regency which took power during Ivan's
iinority. Some straddled the fence, offering to swear allegiance to
ie Tsarevich but not to the regency. Thus Fyodor Adashev, the
ither of Ivan's close friend and adviser Alexey Adashev, said:
God knows, and so dost thou, O Tsar, that we kiss the Cross for
iy sake and for the sake of thy son the Tsarevich Dmitry, but we
iall not serve the Zakharins, Danilo and his brothers. Thy son, O
ord, is still in swaddling clothes, and therefore we shall be ruled
y the Zakharins, Danilo and his brothers, and we have suffered
ıough from the boyars during thy minority."
To the Tsar, suffering from a raging fever, so weak that he could
ot stand and could scarcely speak, such speeches smacked of
eachery. All he had lived for, all he had fought for, was now in
opardy. He believed he was dying among traitors. In his agony he

[2] In Eisenstein's film *Ivan the Terrible* Vladimir of Staritsa appears as a simpleminded
uth without any talents, the victim of his mother's ambitions. He was an intelligent,
rthright man, not in the least simpleminded, and for a long time he had been Ivan's
separable companion.

held fast to one thought: Dmitry must rule. Finally, summoning all his strength, Ivan addressed the refractory boyars. He said:

> If you will not kiss the Cross in allegiance to my son Dmitry, means you have already found another sovereign. But you kissed the Cross more than once to swear allegiance to me, thus promising that you would seek no other sovereign than me.
>
> I hold the Cross to you, and I command you to serve my son Dmitry, not the Zakharins. I cannot speak much more. You have forgotten your oaths, because you do not want to serve me and my children. You no longer remember what you once swore to uphold. Those who refuse to serve a Tsar in swaddling clothes would not wish to serve him when he grows up. If you reject me, then let it be on your souls!

The Tsar was desperate for certainties, but there could be no common ground between "Dmitry must rule" and "the Zakharins will rule." It occurred to him that Anastasia and Dmitry were in mortal danger, and so he turned to those who had sworn allegiance to him the previous evening, and said:

> Yesterday you swore allegiance to me and my son Dmitry, but there are boyars who do not wish to see my son on the throne. If God wills that I should pass away, then remember your oath to me and to my son. Do not let the boyars use any means to destroy my son, but flee with him to a foreign land, which God will show you!

Finally in his distress the Tsar turned to the Zakharins, his brother-in-law Danilo and Vasily, who was Danilo's first cousin, and pleaded with them to save the lives of Anastasia and his son:

> And you, Zakharins, why are you so fearful? Do you imagine the boyars will spare you? No, you will be their first victims! You should sacrifice your lives for my son and for his mother, and you should not let my wife suffer indignities at the hands of the boyars!

These last words had the effect of silencing the quarreling boyars, for the Tsar's rage was terrible to watch, and he had never before spoken so nakedly. One by one they left his bedside and made their way into the anteroom, where they kissed the Cross in allegiance to the Tsarevich Dmitry. Some days later, when the Tsar had recovered from his sickness, Vladimir of Staritsa and his mother also swore allegiance to the Tsarevich.

For Ivan those days of sickness were fraught with terror, and he remembered them vividly in years to come. He had seen treachery when he thought he was dying; he had imagined his wife and son dead; was the autocrat of all Russia so weak that he could not even safeguard his own son? The quarrel was over in a few days, for his sickness lasted little more than a week, but it left wounds that never healed. Henceforth he would distrust everyone, even those who were closest to him.

His relationship with Vladimir of Staritsa was severely strained, and though they sometimes appeared together at court functions the old easy companionship was now a thing of the past. In the autumn of 1577, nearly twenty-five years after his illness and eight years after he had ordered the execution of Vladimir, Ivan still remembered his old hurts. Writing to Prince Kurbsky, who had by this time become his sworn enemy although at the time of the illness he was one of those who professed their loyalty to the Tsarevich, he said:

> Tell me why did you want to place Prince Vladimir on the throne and remove me and my children? Did I ascend the throne by robbery or by bloody feats of arms? I was born to rule by the grace of God, and I do not even remember my father bequeathing the Kingdom to me and blessing me. I grew up on the throne. Then why should Prince Vladimir be sovereign? He was born from the fourth appanage prince.[3] What qualifications did he have for ruling? Where did he stand in the order of succession? His only claim was your treacherous support of him and his own stupidity. What was my guilt before him?

The Tsar's guilt, real or imagined, and the guilt of others preoccupied him. The treachery and stupidity of others was also a subject of immense concern to him. In his own eyes he had never offended Prince Vladimir of Staritsa. Why, then, had the prince attempted to snatch the throne from him?

It was partly because he was so deeply aware of his own guilt that Ivan went constantly on pilgrimage to the holy places and fervently kissed the icons and relics. During his sickness he swore that if he

---

[3] Vladimir's father, Andrey of Staritsa, was the fifth son of the Grand Prince Ivan III. The eldest son Vasily became Grand Prince and the father of Ivan the Terrible. Andrey of Staritsa was thus the fourth appanage prince, and his son Vladimir could claim only a very remote place in the order of succession.

recovered he would go on pilgrimage to the Kirillov Monastery at Beloozero, far in the north. (St. Kirill had been one of the disciples of St. Sergius.) To this monastery Ivan's mother had traveled before he was born, to pray for the birth of a son. By making the same pilgrimage he was returning to the source of his own life, praying to be born again with new strength, his sins washed away through the intervention of the wonder-working saint. This pilgrimage would mark a new beginning of his life.

Nearly all his advisers attempted to dissuade him from making this long pilgrimage. They argued that it was unwise to undertake an arduous pilgrimage so soon after his illness, and the Tsarevich was too young to accompany him. Fighting had broken out near Kazan, with the Tatars gaining the upper hand. Kazan was in danger; the forest of Arsk was once more a refuge for a Tatar army who had built a new fortress deep in the interior. Sviazhsk, too, was under attack. These uprisings demanded his presence in Moscow. There were many other reasons why he should remain in Moscow, but Ivan rejected all of them. He had made up his mind. No one could dissuade him from undertaking a journey so close to his heart.

He took with him the people he liked and trusted most. Anastasia, his brother Yury, Danilo and Vasily Zakharin, Prince Ivan Mstislavsky, Prince Andrey Kurbsky, and Alexey Adashev were his companions on the journey. He also took with him his confessor, the Archpriest Andrey Protopopov, who had accompanied him to Kazan. Significantly, Vladimir of Staritsa did not accompany him.

The first stop was the Troitsa-Sergeyevsky Monastery, where Ivan visited the cell of Maxim the Greek, an old scholar who had been brought to Russia by the Grand Prince Vasily III to translate church books. Maxim was an ascetic, stern and uncompromising, and he had set his face against the monastic ownership of land. He had also corrected many errors in the Russian translations of Greek texts, to the confusion and consternation of Russian theologians, who found reasons for putting him on trial as a heretic. He was exiled and received the treatment reserved for heretics, being chained to the wall in a small cell and fed only when his jailers remembered him. Finally the Metropolitan Makary interceded for

Maxim the Greek. (From a contemporary manuscript)

him, and Ivan gave orders that he should be permitted to stay at the Troitsa-Sergeyevsky Monastery.

Maxim was a very old man by this time, and was believed to possess extraordinary spiritual powers. Ivan visited him to obtain his blessing, and instead received a rebuke. What particularly disturbed Maxim was that Ivan had promised faithfully to look after the widows and orphans of the soldiers killed at Kazan, and had done nothing at all. He was also disturbed because Ivan insisted on making a pilgrimage to the far north with his wife and seven-month-old child.

Prince Andrey Kurbsky, who had a high regard for Maxim and knew him well, has left an absorbing account of the meeting between the saintly Maxim and the formidable young Tsar. Here Maxim explains to Ivan that he is undertaking the pilgrimage for the wrong reasons:

> You made a vow that you would pray to St. Kirill to intercede for you with God, but such vows are not in accordance with wisdom. For the following reason: When you were waging war against the proud and strong Muslim kingdom, many who fought strenuously for the Orthodox faith were slaughtered by the infidels, their wives were widowed, their children orphaned, their mothers left without sons, and they could only grieve and lament. You would be far better

advised to reward these people and put their affairs in order, comfor
them in their sorrows and troubles, and summon them to your capita
instead of fulfilling vows that are contrary to reason.

Know that God is everywhere, He accomplishes all things, He see
all places with His sleepless eye, as the Prophet sayeth: He tha
keepeth Israel shall neither slumber nor sleep.[4] And another Prophe
sayeth: The eyes of the Lord are seven times brighter than the sun.
Likewise not only does St. Kirill see in the spirit, but also all th
spirits of our just forefathers, whose names are inscribed in th
heavens and who now serve before the throne of the Lord, for the
possess the clear-sighted eyes of the spirit, which see more from o
high than the rich in Hell; and they pray to God for all men wh
dwell on earth, especially those who repent from their sins an
willingly turn away from their transgressions to God.

Maxim was displeased because Ivan showed no intention o
departing from the way of the transgressor. Why did he want to g
to St. Kirill, when he could pray directly to God here at th
Troitsa-Sergeyevsky Monastery, or in the Kremlin, or anywhere h
pleased? An ostentatious pilgrimage would not bring him nearer t
God, and abandoning widows and orphans would only remove hin
from God's sight.

Suddenly the old priest became a figure out of the Old Testamen
uttering prophecies. Ivan had been saying, "I must go to St. Kirill,
must go to St. Kirill," like a man obsessed. Maxim turned on hin
and said:

> If you do not harken to me when I advise you according to God, i
> you forget the blood of the martyrs slaughtered by the infidels whe
> fighting on behalf of Orthodoxy, if you overlook the tears of th
> widows and orphans, if you set forth stubbornly on your pilgrimage
> then know that your son will die and will not return from thenc
> alive. But if you harken to me, then both you and your son will enjo
> health.

It was an age when many priests and saints uttered prophecies
and Ivan appears to have paid little heed to these dramatic words
According to Prince Kurbsky, Maxim was so convinced of th
truth of his prophecy that he repeated it to four people intimat

[4] *Psalm*, CXXI, 4.
[5] *Ecclesiasticus*, XXIII, 19.

with the Tsar, begging them to remind the Tsar that the Tsarevich was in grave danger. The four people were the Archpriest Andrey Protopopov, Prince Ivan Mstislavsky, Alexey Adashev, and Prince Kurbsky himself. "But the Tsar paid no attention to these words, and went on his way."

So the pilgrimage continued through the thickly wooded and marshy region north of Moscow, sometimes on horseback, sometimes by riverboat, sometimes on foot. Whenever possible, they spent the night in a monastery, and there was much kissing of relics and icons and usually there were special services to celebrate the Tsar's arrival. One of the monasteries they visited was the Pesnoshsky Monastery near the city of Dmitrov. The monastery lay in a low swampy hollow near the river and Prince Kurbsky felt grave misgivings as they approached the place because it was the residence of Vassian Toporkov, formerly bishop of Kolomna, who had been deposed for acts of cunning and cruelty ten years earlier. At all costs Toporkov was determined to get into Ivan's good graces.

According to Prince Kurbsky, everything happened exactly as though "the devil had aimed directly at the heart of the Tsar." Ivan entered the monk's cell and asked the question uppermost in his mind: "How may I rule in order to make my great and noble subjects obedient to me?" Toporkov answered: "If you wish to be an autocrat, do not let a single councillor wiser than yourself stand near you. Be firm, and you will hold all men in the hollow of your hands." Ivan kissed the monk's hand and said: "If my father were alive, even he would not have given me such sound advice."

The prophecies of Maxim were forgotten in the happy contemplation of Toporkov's celebration of absolute autocracy.

By way of Uglich, the upper reaches of the Volga and the Sheksna River, they came at last to the Kirillov Monastery. The monastery, which was built around the relics of St. Kirill, was immensely rich. It was a fortress, a trading post, almost a principality, possessing vast landed estates, warehouses, shops, and ships. Trade in fish and salt kept Beloozero alive, and much of this trade passed through the hands of the monks.

They arrived by ship outside the monastery walls and set up tents between the monastery and the river Sheksna. It was June, and pilgrims were coming from all over Russia to pray at the Saint's shrine. There was a special service to honor the Tsar's coming, and afterward Ivan distributed gifts to the monks. He visited the nearby Ferapontov Monastery, which was famous for the great swirling frescoes painted by Dionysius earlier in the century, and went on to visit other monasteries and hermitages. He stayed only a few days at Beloozero, and then gave the order to return to Moscow.

While they were boarding the ship which would take them down the Sheksna River on the first stage of the return journey, there took place an event so extraordinary and so unexpected that it seems to belong to legend rather than to history. A nurse carrying the Tsarevich Dmitry stumbled near the landing stage, and Dmitry fell out of her arms into the river. The child was quickly pulled out of the water, but was already dead.

The prophecy of Maxim the Greek was fulfilled at the very moment when they were leaving Beloozero. Lightning had struck out of a cloudless sky.

Slowly, sunk in hopeless grief over the death of the heir to the throne, Ivan returned to Moscow.

In a chastened mood, he continued to conduct affairs of state with the help of the Chosen Council. He was now disposed toward forgiveness, and the Chosen Council was disposed to practice moderation and compromise. There were no reprisals against those who failed to kiss the Cross and swear allegiance to the Tsarevich. The proud Ivan had given way to the humble and God-fearing Ivan, who realized obscurely that God had His own mysterious reasons for taking away his infant son.

In November 1553 Khan Simeon of Kazan, the former Yediger Makhmet, married Maria Kutuzova, who belonged to an ancient and noble Moscow family. At the wedding many nobles who had been reluctant to swear allegiance to the Tsarevich were present. Already, in June 1553, Fyodor Adashev, the father of Alexey Adashev, had been promoted to the rank of boyar in spite of his behavior at the time of Ivan's illness. It was an unprecedented appointment, for the rank of boyar was the prerogative of the great nobility, while the Adashevs belonged to a good but modest noble family.

Sylvester remained a powerful influence at court, and there was a complete reconciliation with Prince Vladimir of Staritsa. The processes of reconciliation could scarcely have gone further.

Another child was on the way, and Ivan's grief was tempered by the knowledge that there might soon be another Tsarevich. On March 28, 1554, Anastasia gave birth to a son, who was given the name of Ivan. The baby was carefully measured and his exact measurements were marked on a board. Later, on this board, there was painted an icon depicting the boy's saint. This was St. John Climacus, whose church stood within the bell tower of Ivan the Great in the Kremlin.

The birth of an heir to the throne was an occasion for rejoicing all over Russia. Messengers were sent in all directions to announce the glad tidings and well-wishers flocked to the palace to congratulate Anastasia, saying, "We are happy with you." Monks and hermits came to bless the newborn child and were feasted at the royal table. The prisons were opened. Soon Ivan and Anastasia were journeying on foot to the holy shrines to render thanks to God and the saints for the favor they had received, bringing sumptuous gifts to the monasteries and dispensing alms to the poor.

Very little is known about the upbringing of the Tsarevich Ivan. One day, when he was about two years old, he was sitting on the lap of his nurse Frosinia when something very strange happened— the jar of holy water on the shelf behind her began to froth and bubble, making curious sounds. The nurse jumped up with the Tsarevich in her arms, lifted the lid of the jar, and watched the holy water pouring out. Obviously this was a miracle, perhaps directed toward the Tsarevich, and she poured the water over the boy, saying: "May this mercy shown by God bring long life and happiness to your noble parents and to you, my lord, and to all the kingdom." News of the miracle reached Anastasia, who came hurrying to see the jar. Once more the holy water bubbled out, and she poured it over her face and body. Soon everyone in the palace heard about the miracle and came hurrying to wash themselves in the holy water.

A few weeks after the birth of his son Ivan received welcome news. He was staying with his family on the Kolomenskoye estate when a courier arrived with a letter from Prince Yury Shemiakin-Pronsky announcing the fall of Astrakhan at the mouth of the Volga. He learned that the Russian army had entered the city unopposed; the people had fled; the Khan of Astrakhan was in full flight. The Russians now commanded the full length of the Volga

River and could sail across the Caspian at will. The Metropolitan was staying at Kolomenskoye and a solemn thanksgiving service was immediately held in the small and beautiful Church of the Ascension built by Ivan's father to celebrate the birth of his son. Some weeks later Prince Shemiakin-Pronsky reached Moscow; he brought with him the captured wives of the Khan and was richly rewarded. At that moment it seemed that all of Tatary would inevitably fall to Russian arms.

In May of this year Ivan wrote his will, which was witnessed by Makary. The will proclaims that in the event of the Tsar's death Prince Vladimir of Staritsa will become regent, and in the event of the death of the Tsarevich in childhood Prince Vladimir will become the lawful successor to the throne. Formerly Ivan was concerned to prevent the prince from ever ascending the throne. Now he saw that there might be no alternative. A curious clause in the will demanded that Prince Vladimir, if he should become regent, should not spare his own mother if she were to attempt some mischief against Anastasia and her son. Another clause demanded that the prince should keep no more than a hundred soldiers in his Moscow palace. He was to rule "without being vengeful and without partiality," and at all times he must consult with the Metropolitan, the Boyar Council, and Anastasia.

In this way Ivan attempted to insure that after his death his wishes would prevail. While the will testified to a certain magnanimity, it also acknowledged a fact that had become especially apparent after the death of the Tsarevich Dmitry—the fact that he had very few options.

The goddess of Irony, who presides over Russian history, also presided over the will. As we shall see, Anastasia soon died, and Ivan murdered both his son and Prince Vladimir of Staritsa. The will therefore fell into abeyance and became one more of those documents which gather dust on the shelves of history and are remembered only because they illuminate the hopes and fears of a monarch confronted with the problem of the succession. From time to time we shall see him wrestling with the same problem, but with little success. It was as though he knew in his heart of hearts that the dynasty would die with him.

The Coming of the English

ON MAY 9, 1553, Sebastian Cabot, a Venetian by birth and an Englishman by adoption, finished writing a long and detailed set of instructions for the captains and crew of the three ships he was sending from London to Cathay. He was in his seventies, very old, very venerable, and very powerful, for he had been appointed governor for life of an extraordinary institution called the "Mystery and Company of the Merchant Adventurers for the Discovery of Regions, Dominions, Islands, and Places Unknown." The three ships were the *Edward Bonaventure*, 160 tons, the *Bona Speranza*, 120 tons, and the *Bona Confidentia*, 90 tons. He believed that in the space of a few weeks they would reach Cathay by way of the northeast passage.

Cabot's instructions were contained in thirty-three paragraphs which distilled the learning acquired during many voyages of discovery. The crew were instructed to dress properly at all times, to be obedient to their captains, to avoid blasphemy, drunkenness, and the telling of filthy stories, and to make careful notes of everything they saw. They should not be afraid of foreigners wearing lion skins or bear skins, for such people are usually less dangerous than they seem to be, but they should be especially on guard against naked swimmers armed with bows and arrows, who might attempt to clamber on board and seize "the bodies of men, which they covet for meat." Cabot paid particular attention to the first confrontations with foreigners and suggested that when they rowed ashore in their pinnaces, the sailors should sing and play musical instruments to show that they came joyfully, but afterward they should attempt to entice some of these foreigners onto their ships and make them drunk on wine or spirits, thus learning their secrets. It was sensible advice, and there was some evidence that it was faithfully followed.

Two days after drawing up his set of instructions Cabot watched the three ships sailing down the Thames. They sailed past Greenwich Palace, where the fifteen-year-old King Edward VI lay dying, and they fired a salute in his honor. A few days earlier the King had signed a letter addressed to the Emperor of Cathay and all other kings and potentates in the northeast parts of the world, which, it was hoped, Sir Hugh Willoughby, the captain-general of the fleet, would place in their hands. The fleet vanished into the North Sea and nothing more was heard of it for a year. In the summer of 1554 the *Edward Bonaventure* returned to England with the news that the *Bona Speranza* and the *Bona Confidentia* had been caught in the ice off the coast of Lapland and all their crews had perished. Richard Chancellor, captain of the *Edward Bonaventure*, had reached Moscow and been entertained by the Tsar of Russia.

Chancellor's account of his journey to Russia is one of the most satisfying documents of the time. He sees vividly and directly, and we have the feeling of being present by his side. He liked the Russians, marveled at their hardness and straight living, and was impressed by the brilliant luxury of the Tsar's court. The Russian soldiers were unbelievably tough, living on oatmeal and water, capable of defying the cold for months on end. "Yea and though they lie in the field two months, at such time as it shall freeze more than a yard thick, the common soldier hath neither tent nor anything else over his head. The most defense they have against the weather is a felt, which they set against the wind and weather, and when snow cometh he doth cast it off, and maketh him a fire, and layeth him down thereby." But if the soldier was wonderfully capable of resisting cold, Chancellor had not much good to say of him as a fighter. "They run hurling on heaps," he wrote, "and for the most part they never give battle to their enemies; but that which they do, they do it all by stealth."

He was appalled by their poverty and half-admired the poor for being able to eat rotten fish and then proclaiming that it was sweeter than fresh meat. They told him that life in prison was better than life outside, and would have been paradise "except for the great beating." In prison men get meat and drink without labor; there is always merriment in prison, and well-disposed people give them charity. "But being at liberty they get nothing."

From the mouth of the Dvina River on the White Sea Chancellor made his way to Moscow and was cordially received by Ivan. He was almost blinded by the glitter of sumptuous gold garments when he entered the throne room in the Kremlin. Ivan sat on his high, gilded throne, wearing "a long garment of beaten gold, with an imperial crown upon his head, and a staff of crystal and gold in his right hand, and his other hand half leaning on his chair." Chancellor presented the letter signed by Edward VI, and Ivan then graciously asked about the health of the King of England, and Chancellor replied that he believed the King was in good health; in fact he was dead, and "bloody Mary" was on the throne of England. A little while later Chancellor was invited to dine with the Tsar. By this time Ivan had changed into a gown of silver and sat on a high chair apart from his nobles, who were dressed in cloth of gold. Chancellor was struck by the profusion of massive gold plates, cups, and salvers; liveried servants with napkins over their shoulders waited upon two hundred guests at tables spread with white tablecloths. Great handfuls of bread were given out by the Tsar to his favorites, and the master of ceremonies announced that these gifts came from the hands of Ivan Vasilievich, Tsar of Russia and Grand Prince of Muscovy. The Tsar's cups flashed with jewels. Chancellor observed that Ivan had a good appetite for drink and sometimes drained his cup at a single throw.

The great meals enjoyed at Ivan's court were to become familiar later, and we have many accounts of them. But Chancellor preserves details which many forgot. He observed that when Ivan took bread or a knife in his hands, he always crossed himself on his forehead, and that the servants changed their uniforms three times during the course of a meal. Dinner was a lengthy affair, beginning in the afternoon and going on into the evening, when the candles were brought in, and the Tsar, in bidding his guests farewell, recited all their names apparently to assure them that they were in good standing. It was a remarkable feat of memory and Chancellor was suitably impressed.

But what chiefly impressed him was the Tsar's majesty, his ease and dignity. "There was a majesty in his countenance proportionable with the excellency of his estate," Chancellor wrote. He was impressed, too, by the astonishing luxury of the Tsar's appointments, for even his tents were made of cloth of gold and hung with jewels; and he observed that the Tsar liked to wear different crowns at different times of the day, and he might wear two crowns during the course of a single dinner.

Chancellor was a man of many gifts, and had no difficulty making himself pleasant to the Tsar, who rewarded him with a letter to King Edward VI that was remarkable for its generosity of feeling. The Tsar granted all Chancellor's requests. Henceforth the English might have "their free Mart with all free liberties through my whole dominions with all kind of wares to come and go at their pleasure." The letter, dated February 1554, was written in Russian and accompanied by a Dutch translation. Attached to it was the great seal of the Tsar, which showed a man on horseback treading a dragon underfoot.

In the following year Chancellor returned to Moscow, this time bearing a letter from Queen Mary written in Greek, Polish, and Italian, for in all England there was apparently no one who knew Russian sufficiently well to write in it. Once again there was a set of instructions: the travelers were earnestly requested to make inquiries about the sea and land routes to Cathay, and to abstain from drinking and fighting while in Russia. George Killingworth was appointed the first English agent in Muscovy, and the Tsar was much taken with this former draper who sported a beard "which was not only thick, broad and yellow coloured, but in length five foot and two inches of assize." Killingworth reported that the great secretary of state, Ivan Mikhailovich Viskovaty, whom he calls Ivan Mecallawich Weskawate, was regarded as "their very friend"; and indeed the Englishmen received nothing but friendship at court.

One of the fruits of the second journey to Moscow was a detailed inventory, signed by the Tsar, of the rights and duties of English traders in Russia. It could scarcely have been more favorable. The English were permitted to trade without paying duty throughout Russia; disputes between English and Russian merchants would be decided by the Tsar himself; no Englishmen could be arrested for

A contemporary German engraving of Ivan the Terrible.

debt provided they possessed surety; and disputes among the English were to be judged by the agent and, if necessary, the Russian authorities would imprison the guilty one or provide the instruments of punishment. If an English ship sailing to or from Russia was in any way damaged, robbed, or attacked by pirates, the Tsar himself promised to indemnify the shipowners. The exact words were: "We shall doe all that is in us to cause restitution, reparation, and satisfaction to bee duely made to the said English marchants by our letters and otherwise, as shall stand with our honour, and be consequent to equitie and justice." No doubt there were legal loopholes in the ten separate clauses of the agreement, but it gives the impression of having been drawn up by men of good faith, who were determined to bring about an equitable understanding between the two countries.

Ivan wanted more trade, especially in materials of war, and proposed to send an ambassador to England when Chancellor made the return journey. His choice for ambassador fell on Osip Nepea, a high official in Vologda, who was apparently celebrated for his oratory, for he was described as "ambassador and orator." The letters written by the Tsar to the English court were addressed to monarchs whose titles were as lengthy as his own. Mary, the daughter of Henry VIII and Catherine of Aragon, had married Philip II of Spain, who thus became King of England. Ivan's letter was accordingly addressed to "the most famous and excellent princes, Philip and Mary by the grace of God, King and Queen of England, Spain, France and Ireland, Defenders of the Faith, Archdukes of Austria, Dukes of Burgundy, Milan and Brabant, Counts of Hapsburg, Flanders and Tyrol." So many possessions in the hands of the King and Queen of England powerfully disposed Ivan toward them, and he was very hopeful that the embassy would be successful.

On July 20, 1556, Chancellor sailed from the White Sea in the *Edward Bonaventure* with a cargo of wax, train oil, tallow, furs, felt and yarn to a value of £20,000. In addition the ship carried an enormous collection of sables, including four live sables, as a gift to the King and Queen of England, who were also presented with a large white gerfalcon with a gilded lure. Nepea, who was a merchant as well as an ambassador, brought with him a cargo valued at £6,000, which represented a considerable fortune. Three other ships, the *Philip and Mary*, the *Bona Confidentia*, and the *Bona Speranza*, accompanied the *Edward Bonaventure*.

Of all these ships only one, the *Philip and Mary*, reached London after being blown off course and taking nine months to make the journey. The *Bona Speranza* vanished and was never heard of again. The *Bona Confidentia* struck on the rocks of Norway and sank with its whole crew. The *Edward Bonaventure*, after a stormy passage of four months, came to grief during a storm in the Scottish Bay of Pitsligo, where it was dashed to pieces on the rocks. Chancellor went to the aid of the Russian ambassador, and was drowned. His son was drowned; most of his crew was lost; and of the sixteen Russians who accompanied the ambassador seven were lost. Nothing was left of the ship, and what cargo spilled ashore was plundered by the villagers living nearby. The shipwreck occurred on November 10, 1556; news of it reached London on December 6; and it was not until December 23 that two envoys, sent at the express command of Queen Mary, reached Edinburgh to placate poor Nepea, who had been ill-treated by the villagers and had watched what remained of his cargo being "conveyed away, concealed and utterly embezzled." Sometime later the Queen ordered a commission of inquiry to discover exactly what happened to the cargo. One hundred and eighty witnesses were examined; they all told their stories, but none professed to know what had happened to the treasure of gold, silver, jewels, costly furs, and rich apparel which had once been on the *Edward Bonaventure*. All that was ever discovered were a few small parcels of wax.

The Russian ambassador finally arrived in London on February 27, 1557, escorted by a bevy of noblemen. He was lodged in a merchant's house, was given gold cloth, silks, and velvet, and a fine horse with rich trappings, and received with honor wherever he went. When he rode out to meet the Lord Mayor of London, three hundred horsemen accompanied him, and it was more like a triumphal procession than the visit of an ambassador. People in the streets ran after him, to feast their eyes on the first Russian ambassador who ever set foot on English soil. Since the merchant's house was somewhere in the north of London, it was decided to give him lodgings closer to the center of London. Lodgings were found for him in Fenchurch Street, with a rich cupboard of plate and the best furniture and hangings available, and as he entered his new lodgings a messenger arrived from Queen Mary with more gifts of cloth of gold, damask, and crimson and purple velvet. Finally on March 25 he was received by King Philip and Queen Mary at Westminster. The letters from Ivan were translated into English and Spanish; their Majesties embraced him, and all kinds of entertainments were prepared for him before he returned to his lodgings by ship along the Thames.

Nepea made a good impression on the English. He was very grave, very courteous, and carried himself with stately demeanor, as befitted the representative of a great imperial power. As a special honor, he was invited by King Philip and Queen Mary to attend the annual celebrations of the knights of the Order of the Garter, which always took place on St. George's day, April 23. Six days later there was a banquet in his honor at Draper's Hall. But there were agreements to be concluded and much business to be done, and on May 3, 1557, he left London for Russia on board the *Primrose*, Anthony Jenkinson being the captain-general of a small fleet of four well-equipped ships which all reached the White Sea safely.

Jenkinson was no ordinary seaman; he had the modern temper: cool, restrained, with a gift for clear-cut observation, wildly adventurous. He was scarcely out of his teens when he traveled across Europe, visiting France, Spain, Portugal, Flanders, the Netherlands, Germany, and Italy. He knew all the islands and seaports of the Mediterranean, and had been to Damascus and Jerusalem. His secret ambition was to reach China, and for him Russia was only a way station, a temporary halting place, on a longer journey. He reached the bay of St. Nicholas in the White Sea with his fleet on June 12, and while Nepea immediately set off for Moscow to report to the Tsar, Jenkinson deliberately delayed his journey at Kholmogori and Vologda, then the major centers of the salt trade and the chief entrepôts of the north. He wanted to study the Russian way of building boats, how they traded, how they went about their affairs; and mostly he traveled by boat, spending the night on the river bank. When he reached Moscow in December, he knew more about northern Russia than any Englishman and most Russians.

He had his first audience with Ivan on Christmas Day. The Tsar sat on his throne, wearing a richly jeweled crown. He was robed in cloth of gold, and in one hand he held a gold scepter. His brother

Yury and the twelve-year-old Utemish Guirey, Khan of Kazan, sat beside him. Jenkinson evidently made a good impression on the Tsar, who invited him to dinner and set him down at a small table immediately facing him. Like many others who were invited to dine in the Kremlin, Jenkinson was awed by the splendid barbarity of the scene: the gold and silver plate on his own table, the jewel-studded goblets, the cupboards filled with sumptuous plates on display. Jenkinson calculated that a single gold cup set with precious stones was worth four hundred pounds sterling. A gold receptacle, decorated with fortress towers and dragons' heads, dominated the rest, for it was six feet long. Never had he seen such a display of conspicuous wealth, and his head reeled.

At the end of the banquet the Tsar called him by name and gave him a goblet filled with wine, and everyone rose to salute him.

A few days after Christmas came the ceremony of blessing the water. Jenkinson wore Russian dress and accompanied the procession to the river, which was frozen over. The Tsar stood bareheaded among his nobles while a hole was cut in the ice, and then the Metropolitan blessed the water and sprinkled it on everyone around him.

> That done, [wrote Jenkinson] the people with great thronging filled pots of the said water to carry home to their houses, and divers children were thrown in, and sick people, and plucked out quickly again, and divers Tatars christened, all which the emperor beheld. Also there were brought the emperor's best horses to drink at the said hallowed water. All this being ended, he returned to his palace again and went to dinner by candlelight and sat in a wooden house very fairly gilded. There dined in the palace above three hundred strangers, and I sat alone as I did before directly before the emperor, and had my meat, bread, and drink sent me from the emperor.

Jenkinson was a proud man, and felt that he was receiving his due. He was fascinated by Russia and by the Tsar, but still more fascinated by the prospect of exploring the vast regions of the Orient, with China hovering like a mirage at the end of the journey. Accordingly, with the hope of reaching China, he acquired safe-conducts from the Tsar which permitted him to travel down the Volga to Astrakhan and beyond. He never reached China, but he succeeded in sailing across the Caspian and arrived in Bokhara shortly before it was sacked by the Prince of Samarkand; then, sadly, he returned to Moscow, bearing presents for the Tsar—a white cow's tail and a Tatar drum—and a Tatar girl called Aura Sultana, who was later presented to Queen Elizabeth.

As he journeyed along the Volga, Jenkinson observed that the Nogay Tatars were suffering terribly from famine, plague, and war. Many of the survivors fled to Astrakhan, hoping to find food and shelter, but the Russians drove them away or sold them into slavery, and the banks of the Volga near the city were strewn with dead and decaying bodies. They were "like to beasts unburied, very pitiful to behold," and Jenkinson found himself wondering why the Russians had not made greater use of them. They were an admirable people, proud, independent, and resourceful, but helpless against famine and the plague.

The Russian attitude toward the Tatars was ambiguous: they were admired and detested, feared and loved. Many of the Tatar princely families married into the Russian nobility, and there was scarcely a family in Russia which had not received some admixture, however slight, of Tatar blood. But the Tatars were predators, by instinct and training hostile to settled government, and capable of extraordinary savagery. The Khan of the Crimea, with the support of the Sultan of Turkey, continually raided Russian territory. The Russians, in turn, raided the territories of the Khan. In the spring of 1558 a particularly successful raid was carried out by Prince Dmitry Vishnevetsky in the regions immediately north of the Crimea. This was a deep thrust into Tatar territory, and the Khan was determined upon revenge. Later in the year, hearing that Ivan was marching with his troops against Livonia, the Khan raised an army of a hundred thousand men and ordered a three-pronged attack on Ryazan, Tula, and Kashira. In fact, Ivan was still in Moscow, the Russian army had not set out for Livonia, and the Tatars withdrew when they reached the Mecha River, a tributary of the Upper Don. The Russians drew the inevitable inferences. The time had come to attempt the conquest of the Crimea.

By February 1559 all the preparations had been completed and the plan of attack had been worked out. Daniel Adashev, the younger brother of Alexey Adashev, was given command of an army of 8,000 men and ordered to sail down the Dnieper and attack the Crimea by sea from the west. Simultaneously Prince

Dmitry Vishnevetsky was ordered to sail down the Donets and the Don to Azov. There they would build ships, cross the Sea of Azov, and attack the Crimea from the east. The double attack was well conceived, but only Daniel Adashev's army succeeded in engaging the enemy. At the mouth of the Dnieper they captured two Turkish ships and forced the captains to sail toward Perekop. Suddenly the Russians spread out and attacked all the Tatar camps and settlements near the coast. The maneuver was brilliantly conducted. The Tatars were taken by surprise, many were killed, many more were captured, and huge herds of camels were destroyed. The pillage continued for more than two weeks. Daniel Adashev was specially pleased because he was able to bring about the release of many Russian and Lithuanian prisoners of the Tatars.

The Russians had no navy, but the two Turkish ships served them well. Filled with plunder and prisoners of war, the ships were forced to sail back to the Turkish fort of Orchakov at the mouth of the Dnieper. To the commanders of the fort, Adashev explained with perfect politeness that he had no quarrel with the Sultan of Turkey and surrendered the two ships together with some Turkish captives, and then transferred his army to the same small boats which brought them down the Dnieper. The Turks, though allied to the Tatars, were equally polite, showered gifts and provisions on the Russians, and murmured understandingly when Adashev explained that the expedition had been undertaken as an experiment and there would be more such expeditions in the future. And when Adashev's small fleet sailed up the Dnieper, the Turks bade them a courteous farewell.

The Lower Dnieper has hundreds of islands and is surrounded by marshlands. Traditionally it was the home of pirates and outlaws. Here twenty men could stand up against an army of a thousand and vanish into the morning mists. The Tatars marched along the banks of the river in search of the elusive Russian fleet and sometimes found it. But the Tatar arrows were no match for the Russian muskets, and there were few serious engagements, even though the Khan of the Crimea swore that at all costs he must avenge the insult to his honor. After six weeks the Russians reached Monastyr Island, which they fortified, having learned that the Khan had sworn to destroy them on the island. But the expected attack never came, the Khan retreated to the Crimea, and from

Moscow Ivan sent a delegation to the island to congratulate Adashev on his victory and to distribute gold medals to his soldiers. The supremacy of Russian arms had once more been vindicated. According to the chronicles, Ivan was inclined to give himself much credit for the success of the expedition. "As a result of the Tsar's prayers, his wisdom and courage, a great miracle occurred," wrote the chroniclers. Prince Vishnevetsky's expedition was less miraculous. He failed to reach the Crimea, but succeeded in destroying a column of Crimean Tatars who were attempting to slip into Kazan. Soon there came the welcome news that the Crimea was suffering from famine and that the Cossacks left behind by Adashev were continually raiding the enemy's camps. Ivan began to believe that the Crimea would soon be added to his crown.

But there were enemies nearer home who demanded his attention. These were the Livonians, who occupied the southern shores of the Gulf of Finland, ruled by the Knights of the Livonian Order. The knights were German, who commonly spoke German in their great cities of Riga, Reval, Dorpat, and Narva, while permitting their peasants to speak in their own Latvian and Estonian dialects. Rich and powerful, dominating the Baltic, the knights were determined to prevent Russia from expanding westward to the sea. In 1242 the knights were defeated by Alexander Nevsky, Grand Prince of Novgorod, in a famous battle on the ice of Lake Peipus, but their essential aims remained unchanged. Livonia was a hammer poised over Russia.

There was no love lost between the Germans and the Russians. The feudal knights were masters of the arts of blockade. They permitted no guns, no gunners, no armor, no armorers, no metal-smiths, no skilled artisans to enter Russia under pain of death. Determined to isolate Russia from the military inventions of the West, they succeeded only in alienating the Russians, who regarded the Germans as interlopers and all of Livonia as their own ancestral property. For more than fifty years Livonia and Russia had lived together in an uneasy peace. Tempers on both sides were wearing thin, and by the late fall of 1557, on the excuse that the city of Dorpat had failed for fifty years to pay tribute to the Grand Princes of Muscovy, Ivan mounted an army of 40,000 men on the Livonian frontier under command of Khan Shigaley of Kasimov. The failure of Dorpat to pay tribute was merely one of many things that exasperated Ivan, who wanted to break the blockade and to acquire a seaport on the Baltic.

The Livonians acted quickly. They preferred to fight at a time and place of their own choosing, and therefore sent ambassadors to Moscow to negotiate a truce. In particular, they offered to pay a yearly tribute of 1,000 gold ducats and a lump sum of 45,000 talers. Ivan asked them whether they had brought the money with them, and learned that they had not. He therefore invited them to a state dinner at which they ate off empty plates. Then, still hungry, they were permitted to return to Livonia. In the following month Ivan unleashed his army. It was to be a punitive expedition designed to ravage and destroy as much of Livonia as possible, with no frontal assaults on the fortresslike cities. Those who suffered most were the peasants, not the knights and the landowners. Next time the Livonians would come to the conference table with money in their pockets.

The war against Livonia was protracted, inconclusive, curiously unreal. Senseless and inexplicable acts were continually taking place. For example, the German gunners in Narva suddenly opened fire on the nearby Russian city of Ivangorod during a period of truce and while Livonian ambassadors were in Moscow negotiating a peace treaty. The bombardment continued for two weeks, thus demonstrating that the guns were not being fired accidentally. Ivan was enraged, dismissed the ambassadors after demanding an increased indemnity, and ordered that Narva should be bombarded in turn. This was done, a new embassy arrived from the people of Narva, and the Tsar graciously accepted their allegiance, promising them the same freedoms they possessed under the Livonian Order—freedom to trade as they pleased, freedom to retain their ancient customs. Suddenly and unpredictably, at almost no cost, Ivan had obtained what he wanted above all—a window on the west. For twenty years Narva remained a Russian city and Russian merchandise flowed uninterruptedly into the Baltic.

The Order of the Livonian Knights was dying of a familiar disease: they had lost confidence in themselves. Each feudal city cherished its independence at the expense of the other cities. Having acquired Narva, Ivan resolved to capture Dorpat, the largest and richest city in central Livonia. The city had to be taken by assault or by demonstrating overwhelming force. In July 1558,

Prince Peter Shuisky surrounded the city, which had been abandoned by the knights and was defended by 2,000 mercenaries. Hermann Vieland, Bishop of Dorpat, took command. He was no match for Prince Shuisky, who under cover of darkness and fog built towers against the walls and dug tunnels under them. At the appropriate time he ordered the beating of drums to attract the attention of the populace and then announced that they had two days to decide whether to surrender or be annihilated. He threatened that not a single man, woman, or child would be left alive if they refused to surrender.

The prince-bishop was a man who knew the Russians well and was aware that the Russians had no real intention of destroying the city. He drew up a long list of conditions. The religious beliefs of the people must be respected, the nobility must be allowed to retain their lands, no Russian soldiers must be billeted on the good citizens of Dorpat, all crimes must continue to be judged by the city courts, and no citizen of Dorpat could be deported to Russia or indeed to any other place. All together fourteen conditions were presented to Prince Shuisky, and they were all accepted. On that same day, July 18, 1558, the city gates were opened and the Russian army marched in. The prince kept his word, the people of Dorpat were treated courteously, the nobility retained their land and took the oath of allegiance to the Tsar while Bishop Vieland and some of the people left the city. At a banquet given for the dignitaries of Dorpat Prince Shuisky announced, "My house and my ears will be open to all. I have come to punish the wicked and to protect the good."

Such sentiments from the lips of Russian military commanders were highly unusual, but there was a simple explanation. Ivan had reached the conclusion that all of Livonia could be conquered without the loss of a single soldier; all that was necessary was to employ blandishments and threats. By promising the Livonian cities their freedom once they had sworn allegiance to the Tsar he was ensuring their submission. In this way some twenty fortified towns in Livonia surrendered without resistance.

Not all the Livonian towns surrendered. Reval, although promised greater privileges than before, refused to submit and the Russians therefore devastated the countryside around it. Punishment for smaller towns which resisted was swift and sure: they were burned to the ground and the people were massacred. Prince Shuisky's campaign ended in the fall. The Tsar offered an exuberant welcome to his victorious generals at the Troitsa-Sergeyevsky Monastery, where prayers were offered in celebration of so many victories, and then he escorted them to his small palace at Alexandrova Sloboda, where they were presented with furs, jeweled goblets, and suits of armor. In addition he offered them great estates and permitted them to choose horses from the royal stables. To the provincial nobility, who made up most of the army, he gave estates in Livonia.

Although Russian garrisons were left behind in the Livonian towns, the bulk of the army was disbanded. The Knights of the Livonian Order took this opportunity to mount an offensive against the fortress at Ringen, which they captured. The Russian prisoners, numbering between two and three hundred, were thrown into the fortress dungeons. A few days later, fearing that Russian reinforcements might soon arrive, the knights abandoned the fortress, leaving the prisoners to die of starvation in the dungeons.

In January 1559 the Russians returned in force to resume a war of devastation. Gottgard Kettler, Grand Master of the Livonian Knights, turned in desperation to Gustavus Vasa, the Swedish King, for help and was rejected. The city of Reval sought the help of King Frederick II of Denmark, who obligingly wrote to the Tsar, urging him to send no more troops into Livonia. Ivan thundered that he had every right to send as many troops as he liked into Livonia, because it was his own property. "Since the days of our ancestors all the Livonians have been our subjects," he declared. Nevertheless he was prepared to declare a truce to please the King of Denmark. Let Gottgard Kettler come to Moscow and swear allegiance to the Tsar: peace would be immediately established. Kettler turned for help to Sigismund II Augustus, King of Poland and Grand Prince of Lithuania. At all costs he was attempting to avoid coming under Russian dominance. Sigismund II Augustus offered him a treaty of alliance on condition that the southeastern region of Livonia was ceded to him; the German states sent soldiers; it appeared that a Grand Alliance of Germany, Poland, Lithuania, and Livonia was about to come into being, with inevitable disastrous results to the Russians. But the campaigns fought during the winter were inconclusive, and in January 1560

Sigismund II Augustus sent ambassadors to Moscow with instruc
tions to seek out a settlement on the basis that the Grand Master o
the Livonian Knights had become a vassal of the King of Poland
and Grand Prince of Lithuania. Ivan was not amused by this
argument. He wrote to Sigismund II Augustus:

> God knows, and so do all the rulers and all the people, to whom
> Livonia rightfully belongs. From the time of our ancestors until this
> day Livonia has always belonged to us. With our knowledge and
> agreement Livonia chose German Grand Masters and German
> priests, but always paid tribute to us. Your demands are laughable
> and improper.
>
> It has come to my knowledge that the Grand Master has been to
> Lithuania and illegally offered you some fortresses. If you desire
> peace, remove your people from them, do not take up the cause of
> traitors, for their fate must depend upon my mercy. I have sincerely
> desired an alliance with you against the infidels, and do not now
> refuse to conclude an alliance. I await your ambassadors and expect
> them to offer reasonable proposals.

The Tsar's claim to Livonia was not so well-founded that he
could dismiss all counterclaims simply as examples of effrontery
Sigismund II Augustus wrote back: "You call Livonia yours. But
how was it that the war between Moscow and Livonia at the time of
your grandfather was brought to an end by a truce? What ruler
concludes a treaty with his subjects?" It was a hard thrust, and
there was no reply. The German Emperor sent an envoy to Ivan
with a polite and friendly letter, pointing out that Livonia was an
imperial province and therefore the Russians should not wage war
against it. Ivan replied with an ill-tempered admonition to the
German Emperor to send ambassadors rather than messengers if he
wanted to discuss important affairs.

The Russian campaigns in Livonia continued in their desultory
fashion. Ivan was aware that little was being accomplished and sent
his close friend and confidant, Prince Andrey Kurbsky, to Dorpat
to take charge. The best troops had been sent to the south to guard
against Tatar invasions, and the Russian troops in Livonia were no
match for the enemy. Ivan urgently wanted to put more mettle into
them. Prince Kurbsky described how one day in the early spring of
1560 he was summoned to an audience with the Tsar: "He led me
into his bedchamber and then said to me with much kindness,

amiability and many promises: 'Because so many of my generals have run away, I am forced myself to march against the Livonians or to send you, my beloved friend, so that, God aiding you, my troops may become brave again. Therefore go and serve me faithfully.' Whereupon I left in haste."

The raids, the battles, and the skirmishes continued until there was scarcely a square yard of Livonia which was not devastated. Prince Kurbsky attacked the German knights at Weissenstein, soundly defeated them, took 170 high-ranking prisoners, and retired to Dorpat. Ivan ordered a massive attack on the fortress of Fellin with 30,000 cavalry, 10,000 musketeers, and 90 guns. Alexey Adashev, Prince Peter Shuisky, and many other Russian generals took part in the siege, which was made memorable by the bravery of a German, Philipp von Bell, who attacked the Russians near Fellin with his small army consisting of five hundred knights and five hundred foot soldiers. Philipp von Bell was one of those rare soldiers who command the admiration of their enemies. The chroniclers described him as "the last defender and last hope of the Livonian nation." Captured by Alexey Adashev, he was brought before the Russian generals and replied to their questions so eloquently and bravely that they made him their dinner companion, finally sending him to Moscow with a letter to the Tsar urging that he should be well-treated, for, wrote Prince Kurbsky, "all of Livonia regarded him as a father."

Philipp von Bell was as brave and eloquent in Moscow as he had been at Fellin. Brought before the Tsar, he described the terror let loose on the people of Livonia by the Russian armies. "You are attempting to conquer our fatherland in bloody, unjust ways," he declared. "You are not behaving like a Christian Tsar." Ivan was so enraged that he ordered the immediate execution of the German knight. Too late Ivan had second thoughts, ordered the execution stopped, and learned that the knight was already dead.

Fellin surrendered to the Russian forces, but on its own terms. The German soldiers were allowed to leave on safe-conducts, only the knights being made captive. The most distinguished of these knights was Wilhelm Fürstenberg, a former Grand Master of the Livonian Knights, and he was treated with the decorum due to a princely ruler. The other knights were less well-treated. The story was told that a Tatar prince fighting for the Russians spat at the knights as they were being led out. "Serves you right, you Germans!" he shouted. "You gave the Tsar a whip, which he beat us with! Now it's your turn!" The former Grand Master was invited to sup at Ivan's table and given an estate in the province of Kostroma, but the knights were paraded through the Moscow streets and fared badly.

With the surrender of Fellin the Livonian war came to a temporary end. Large areas of Livonia were in Russian hands, but most of Estonia and all of Courland remained in the hands of the knights. Livonia had become a patchwork, a no-man's-land. Soon it would be given over to civil war, for the peasants began to fight the knights who for so long had burdened them with heavy taxes and made them foot soldiers in their interminable wars. With some pleasure Ivan watched the disintegration of a country which was once rich and powerful.

In the summer of 1560 he enjoyed few other pleasures. His wife, the Grand Princess Anastasia, was dying. She had been ill of a wasting sickness for more than six months; the doctors had failed to diagnose her sickness; and though her condition improved somewhat during the spring, the summer brought a relapse. Hearing that a certain Katrina Schilling, a widow living in Dorpat, was renowned for her ability to cure diseases, he sent for her, examined her closely, and promised her half the income of the bishopric of Dorpat for life if she could save the Grand Princess.

Anastasia was a woman of great faith.

"You can certainly help me," she said, when Katrina Schilling was brought to her bedside. "Help me!"

But instead of getting better, Anastasia became worse. Ivan sent her to his palace in Kolomenskoye, hoping she would benefit from the quieter life outside of Moscow, where the usual summer fires were breaking out. To amuse himself and to forget his sorrow, he led the fire-fighters. A large area around the Arbat went up in flames on July 17, and two days later there was another fire. Ivan and Prince Vladimir of Staritsa fought the flames with a company of musketeers. In the intervals of fire-fighting Ivan made plans for the construction of a new palace for his two sons, the seven-year-old Ivan and the four-year-old Fyodor, near the Kremlin wall. For some unexplained reason he wanted the new palace built with

xtraordinary speed. The order for the construction of the palace
vas dated August 6, 1560.

On the following day Anastasia died at Kolomenskoye. Her
leath threw Ivan into paroxysms of grief. At the funeral he wept
bitterly and noisily, and those who accompanied him had to hold
aim up, for otherwise he would have fallen to the ground. The
burial took place within the Voznesensky Monastery near the
Florovsky Gate, the main entrance to the Kremlin. Thousands of

The fire of Moscow in 1560 and Ivan IV escorting the sick Anastasia to
Kolomenskoye. (From the sixteenth-century edition of the *Nikon Chronicle with
Miniatures*)

Muscovites attended the ceremony and followed the coffin to the grave. They wept unrestrainedly, for she was greatly loved. She was one of those who shed a benign influence around them, beautiful and devout, quiet and merciful. They knew they would not see her like again.

Many years later Jerome Horsey, who probably came to know Ivan better than any other Englishman, made some inquiries about Anastasia. He wrote: "This empress became wise and of such holiness, virtue and government, as she was honored, beloved, and feared of all her subjects. He, being young and riotous, she ruled him with admirable affability and wisdom." Horsey believed she deserved full credit for whatever successes Ivan achieved during the early years of his reign.

The Glory and the Splendor

OF ALL THE WORKS OF ART created in Ivan's reign the most splendid
is the many-domed and brilliantly colored Cathedral of the
Intercession of the Virgin in the Red Square. We know it better as
the Cathedral of St. Basil, but this was not its original name; nor
was Basil a saint of any eminence; nor, except by accident, did he
have anything to do with the cathedral. Basil was a *yurodivy*, a holy
fool, who was buried in the cathedral yard. The Muscovites loved
him and it pleased them to call that wildly improbable cathedral by
the name of a fool.

Nevertheless this cathedral with its domes and towers melting
into one another belongs to the Virgin, and for good reason. Ivan
firmly believed she had interceded for him to bring about the
victory at Kazan, and the cathedral was built because he owed a
special debt to her. The cathedral was to be her dwelling place,
shimmering with her radiance and reflecting her divine glory and
triumphant majesty. The architects were instructed to build something so new and unprecedented that it would astonish everyone
who set eyes on it. To this day it continues to astonish us, and even
the presence of Lenin's granite tomb nearby cannot detract from its
soaring splendor.

At first there was only a small wooden church near the *Lobnoye
Mesto*, on the high ground just before the Red Square dips toward
the Moskva River. This wooden church, built in 1553, was taken
down less than two years later and work was begun on the

The Cathedral of the Intercession of the Virgin (St. Basil's), Moscow.

cathedral under the direction of two architects from Pskov, Postnik and Barma. By the Tsar's orders it was to enclose eight altars; the architects, who are described as "ingenious and competent men," were of another opinion. We learn from a seventeenth-century document that "they, by God's Providence, built nine altars, which was not according to their instructions."

Postnik and Barma are shadowy figures, and there is even some doubt about their names. Recently Soviet scholars found documents that suggested they were one person called Postnik Yakovlev, nicknamed Barma. Whether they were one or two matters as little as the legend that they were killed when the cathedral was completed so that their secrets would die with them. The legend is certainly untrue. What is certain is that the cathedral was both an affirmation of victory and of faith in the powers of the Virgin.

The ground plan was based on the eight-pointed star of the Virgin, an emblem which appears on her robe and headdress in innumerable Byzantine and Russian icons. From this rigid ground

lan the architects improvised a cluster of domed chapels of
different heights and colors around the central spire crowned with a
small golden dome. In this way they were able to suggest an
effortless and springing grace, the thrust of flowers, vegetables, and
young trees. The secret lay in building the domes at different
heights and in defying the normal laws of symmetry. Originally the
platform supporting the cathedral was broken by archways leading
to a vast subterranean gallery filled with what remained of the
eleven wooden chapels once scattered around the Red Square; and
these archways were conceived as essential elements of the design,
adding to the illusion of ease and weightlessness, so that the visitor
ascending the slope from the Moskva River was made suddenly
aware of a spontaneous flowering. And yet everything about the
building, which seems to be so spontaneous, so haphazard, was in
fact carefully calculated to produce this precise effect. Out of white
stone, red brick, many-colored tiles and golden domes the builders
created an image of youthful daring and unself-conscious power.

When, after nearly five years of work, the cathedral was finally
consecrated on October 1, 1559, in the presence of Ivan and
Anastasia, the central spire had not yet been completed and it must
have had a somewhat ungainly appearance. Since this central spire
is the kingpin around which the eight colored domes revolve, it
would appear that there were formidable problems of design, with
many false starts and many delays, until the soaring pinnacle
acquired its final shape. But all these delays were worthwhile. The
spire, as we see it today, holds the entire complex structure together
and gives it a unity it would not otherwise possess. The whole
building has the quality of inevitability, which is the sign of
mastery.

In later years many additions and alterations were attempted. In
1588 a new domed chapel was erected over the tomb of St. Basil.[1]

---

[1] St. Basil was canonized by the Orthodox Church in 1588. He was born in 1469, the son of
peasants belonging to the village of Yelokhino near Moscow. While apprenticed to a
shoemaker, he discovered that he possessed the gift of second sight. A customer entered the
shop and asked for a pair of boots that would last for several years. Basil took the order and
smiled. When he was asked later why he smiled, he said the customer would not need a long
lasting pair of shoes because he would die tomorrow. And so it happened.

Soon he left the shoemaker's shop and became a *yurodivy*, wandering naked about the city,
wearing heavy chains, and sleeping under the stars. One day, in the marketplace, he scattered

Turrets were placed over gateways and vaulted galleries were bui
late in the seventeenth century, and in the nineteenth century th
archways on the platform were blocked up. But none of thes
changes could affect the simple majesty of a cathedral built out c
so many complex elements. The Cathedral of the Intercession c
the Virgin remains the supreme architectural achievement of Ivan'
reign.

Only one other surviving church from this time displays thi
originality. This is the Church of St. John the Baptist at Dyakov
near the royal estate of Kolomenskoye on the outskirts of Moscov
The church stands on the edge of a ravine in proud isolation fror
all the other churches on the estate, most of them built by Ivan'
father. It was built, at Ivan's orders, to commemorate his adoptio
of the title of Tsar and as a votive offering for the birth of an heir t
the throne. What is chiefly remarkable about the church is hov
faithfully it reflects the exaltation of the Tsar, his sense of surgin
power and self-conscious triumph, and this is largely brought abou
by the powerful thrust of short pillars supporting the massive dom
These pillars, actually half-cylinders, leap to the eye. Even if th
dome weighed a thousand tons these pillars would support it, an
indeed they give the impression of being powerful enough t
support the whole sky. This prodigious invention was neve
repeated. Both the Cathedral of the Intercession of the Virgin an
the Church of St. John the Baptist derive from the early years o
Ivan's reign, when he was still in his twenties. There is a sense i
which both buildings may be regarded as abstract portraits of Iva
in the eagerness of his youth and the consciousness of a grea
destiny, when the people were buoyed up with vast hopes and a
exultant Tsar sat on the throne.

---

a tray of cakes on the ground. It had been revealed to him that the cakemaker had adde
chalk to the dough. On another occasion he was walking in the square wrapped in a fur coა
given to him by a rich benefactor. A thief approached him, pointing to another pretending t
be dead, and asked Basil for his coat, saying that it would pay for the funeral expenses. Bas
saw through the ruse and said to the man pretending to be dead: "You will surely die fc
your wickedness, for it is written that the wicked shall perish." And so it happened.

Ivan honored Basil, and with Anastasia visited him when he was lying on his deathbe
When Basil died in 1552, Ivan accompanied the bier to the small cemetery of the Troits
Church on the Red Square. Over this cemetery the Cathedral of the Intercession of th
Virgin was built, but Ivan ordered that Basil's bones should remain untouched. The toml
with the chains lying on it, became an object of veneration and many miracles were said t
have been performed there. In this way Basil became one of the many saints of Moscov

Church of the Ascension, Kolomenskoye.

The Crown of Kazan.

This sense of exultation reappears in the crown of Kazan, which was especially made for Ivan to celebrate his victory. This crown, in its delicacy and grace, must be counted among the most superb achievements of the goldsmith's art. Formed of leaf-shaped plaques of gold, fretted and jewel-studded, flaring up like fire, the crown represents a departure from existing Russian crowns and may have been modeled on the original crown of Kazan worn by the Tatar Khans. Many Russian crowns have perished, but the crown of Kazan survives to this day and can be seen in the collection of treasures in the Armory Museum in the Kremlin.

Another splendid creation was the gilded wooden throne, which at Ivan's orders was set up in the Uspensky Cathedral in 1551. In twelve panels carved in walnut, four on the back and four on each side, are carved the legendary incidents in the life of the Grand Prince Vladimir Monomakh, "the greatest of the princes of Greater Russia." According to the legend, which was elaborated toward the end of the fifteenth century, the prince, who died in 1125, received his regalia from the Emperor of Byzantium and was crowned by the Bishop of Ephesus as sovereign ruler of Russia. The twelve panels depict the reception of the ambassadors from Byzantium, his coronation, and his wars against Thrace. The carving is at once hieratic and full of movement, with a kind of monumental calm, as befitted a ruler whose historical significance was outweighed by his towering legend. This throne can still be seen in the cathedral, but most of the gilding has worn off and time has smoothed away the delicacy of the carving.

The throne was a magnificent object in its own right. For Ivan, who identified himself with Vladimir Monomakh, the throne was something more. It was the visible sign that he derived his powers from Byzantium, and he found comfort in contemplating that princely figure who was so heroic, so handsome, so deeply religious and so conscious of his imperial destiny.

If Ivan turned slightly while sitting on the throne, he would see hanging on the wall of the cathedral an enormous icon thirteen feet long and about four and a half feet wide. In the cathedral inventory the icon was called "The Blessed Army of the King of Heaven." The knights were Russian princes and saints carrying spears and banners and moving in three columns toward the Heavenly Jerusalem, where the Virgin and Child stand at the gates to welcome them. The columns are led by the Archangel Michael, riding a winged scarlet horse, and immediately behind the archangel comes Ivan on a gray mare, wearing armor, jewel-studded boots, and a gold cuirass, and holding high a scarlet banner. Both Ivan and the archangel are looking over their shoulders at the huge and monumental figure of Vladimir Monomakh, who dominates the entire panel. He rides a black charger, wears sumptuous jeweled vestments and a gold crown, the perfect portrait of a Byzantine emperor even to the elongated jeweled cuff which he alone was allowed to wear. His features are clearly discernible, and it is not surprising that he should resemble an idealized portrait of Ivan himself with his long nose, penetrating eyes, and red hair. He wears a youthful red beard and carries himself with heroic grace, a cross in one hand, a white *sudarium* in the other, and he sits gracefully on a scarlet saddlecloth.

It is an amazing painting, filled with color and movement, crowded with angels who strew crowns of glory on the martyred saints and warrior princes who risked their lives in defense of the Orthodox Church and their Orthodox subjects. Above all, it is

Two of the gilt panels on Ivan's throne made in 1551, ostensibly describing the life and victories of Vladimir Monomakh. At top Vladimir Monomakh is receiving his boyars; at bottom he is starting out on a campaign.

notable because it depicts the apotheosis of the youthful Ivan raised
to sainthood and almost within reach of Jerusalem. In the figure of
Vladimir Monomakh we see Ivan as he saw himself in his
imagination: first among all the Grand Princes, greatest of conquerors, and especially dear to the Virgin and Child, who open their
arms in expectation of his coming.

Under Makary the Moscow school of painting undertook a
grandiose program of monumental designs demonstrating the
power and glory of Ivan's reign. Was not Russia especially favored
by God? Was not Moscow the third Rome? The imperial succession had been established, for while the Byzantine empire had gone
down to defeat before the Turks, it had been revived in the new
Muscovite empire under its sovereign autocrat, the Grand Prince
and Tsar Ivan Vasilievich.

All this was expressed in the icons, frescoes, and wood carvings
of the time. Most of them have perished. There survives an
astonishingly detailed account written in the seventeenth century of
the frescoes that once adorned Ivan's Golden Palace, the Zolotaya
Palata, where the Chosen Council met and foreign ambassadors
were received. The frescoes were designed to exalt Ivan and at the
same time to impress upon him a proper humility toward Christ
and the Church. It appears that Sylvester was in charge of the
arrangement of the frescoes and the choice of subjects. On the
ceiling was the inevitable Christ in Majesty seated on a rainbow,
with orb and scepter, reigning over the universe. Below Christ were
the four Virtues and the four Vices. There were panels representing
the four seasons, the sun, the moon, the sea, and the earth. Parables
and biblical episodes were also depicted. There was the rich
Lazarus in Hell and the poor Lazarus at his prayers, the parable of
the wedding feast, the parable of the lost sheep, Hezekiah rising
from his sickbed, Gideon waging war against the Midianites. Ivan
had a particular fondness for Gideon, and some of the incidents
depicted may well have been chosen by him. In the lower courses of
the fresco were the portraits of Ivan's father and grandfather, the
saintly Prince Alexander Nevsky and the Grand Prince Mikhail of
Tver, who refused to kneel down to Tatar idols and met a martyr's
death. Essentially the fresco took the form of a cosmic allegory,
with the great princes of the past supporting the weight of the
universe, while Christ, the Tsar of Tsars and Grand Prince of

The Church of St. John the Baptist, Dyakovo.

Detail from the icon called "The Blessed Army of the King of Heaven" painted to celebrate the victory of Kazan. The central figure on the black horse represents Vladimir Monomakh and is an idealized portrait of Ivan.

Grand Princes, crowned the edifice. Unfortunately the Golden Palace was torn down and rebuilt by the Empress Elizabeth many years later, and this brilliantly colored and rather confused fresco vanished with it. During the reign of Ivan the Moscow school of painters enjoyed painting immensely crowded scenes. Compositional rhythm was sacrificed, while harmony and simplicity were forgotten in an effort to include as many figures as possible.

Not all the Russians approved of these frescoes. Ivan Viskovaty, the Secretary of Foreign Affairs, objected to the painting of Lust, depicted as a harlot with loosely hanging sleeves dancing shamelessly in close proximity to Christ. No one appears to have been surprised when the Metropolitan Makary took issue with Viskovaty, who was placed on trial before the Church Council. A three-year penance was imposed on the unfortunate layman who dared to speak out against a picture of Lust in the Tsar's palace.

In the later years of Ivan's reign, when the entire country was plagued with disasters, famine, war, a kingdom divided against itself, and the oprichniki embarking on large-scale murder, artists emerged with the power and the energy to depict the cruelty of the age. They did not paint the horrors they saw in front of them; instead they painted icons which subtly reflected those horrors. The colors became somber and menacing. Scenes of triumph and glory disappeared. The gold backgrounds, common during the first half of the century, were replaced by stark green and brown backgrounds; the faces of the saints became more deeply lined and acquired an earthen color; the figures were strangely isolated, standing out stark and gaunt, full of unappeasable sorrow.

One of the most remarkable icons of this time shows a gaunt John the Baptist, winged like an archangel. He is thin and haggard, his deep-set eyes haunted by death—his own death. In his left hand he carries a bowl which contains his own bleeding head. So there are two heads, one living, the other dead. Nevertheless he raises his right hand in blessing over a world which has known too much of death. Beneath the bowl there is a small withered tree gashed by an ax, with an inscription reading: "Now also the ax is laid unto the root of the trees; therefore every tree which bringeth not forth good fruit is hewn down, and cast into the fire."

The bleak and muted color scheme offers no consolation: the background is green and brown, the flesh is earth-colored, there are scarlet lights on the ax and the saint's powerful wings. They are the same colors that will be seen later in Grünewald's *Crucifixion* at Colmar. Like Grünewald, the unknown icon painter has painted a moment of visionary terror—a saint, a tree, an ax, a bowl, all seen in the lightning flash. The saint blesses, the ax threatens, the world is entering into darkness.

From his own writings it appears that Ivan had very little visual imagination; his audial imagination was strong. It appears in the rush and roar of his sentences, his control over their turbulent music. We know that he wrote music, composed hymns, enjoyed singing and was a competent choir master. And when he writes prose, it sings vehemently.

It appears that Ivan himself may have been partly responsible for an important innovation introduced at a Church Council in 1551 Part-song, long practiced in Novgorod and Pskov, was made

John the Baptist carrying his head, from an icon once in the Monastery of the Holy Trinity at Alexandrov, now in the Rublev Museum, Moscow, circa 1570.

compulsory in the Moscow churches. Ivan enjoyed part-song and wrote at least two hymns in this mode, one addressed to the Icon of the Virgin of Vladimir, the other to St. Peter the Metropolitan. In Russian hymnology they have an assured place, and not only because Ivan wrote them. They were written with a sense of grandeur and of urgency, with deep religious feeling. Ivan wrote both the words and the music, which was transcribed with the cumbersome *kryuki* ("hooks") which Russian composers derived from ancient Byzantine sources.

Throughout his life Ivan showed a special veneration for the Icon of the Virgin of Vladimir, said to have been painted by St. Luke but in fact by a great Byzantine master of the twelfth century. This icon showed the Christ Child pressing his face with grave gentleness against the face of his Mother, and that somber painting conveys both a sense of human tenderness and divine dignity, so that it stands out among the conventional paintings of the Virgin with its sense of authority as though here, finally, there had been discovered the true lineaments of divinity in the sorrowing Mother and the compassionate Child. For the Russians the icon represented divine tenderness. It was almost the country's pallium, to which they always returned in times of danger. It was widely believed that when Timurlane turned back before the gates of Moscow, he did so because at that very moment the icon was being carried in procession and pointed in his direction. The eleven-year-old Ivan at the time of the Crimean invasion of 1541 had thrown himself down on his knees and prayed before the icon which hung in the Uspensky Cathedral in the Kremlin.

Thus there were good reasons why Ivan should compose a hymn to the icon to be sung on June 23, the feast day associated with the coming of the icon to Moscow. He wrote:

O WONDROUS MIRACLE
Composed by the Tsar

O Thou who art most compassionate toward sinners,
O most pure Mother of God, ready comforter, our salvation and
intercession,
Rejoice, O most great city of Moscow, to receive the miracle-working
icon of Vladimir.

O ye faithful, let us sing forth with the bishops and the princes.
Rejoice, O joyous one, the Lord is with Thee, grant us thy great
mercy.

Wondrous is thy mercy, O Sovereign Lady:
For when the Christians implore thee on their knees to deliver them
from awful ruin,
Then invisibly dost Thou pray to thy Son and by this holy image
saved the people.
O ye Christians, rejoice and sing forth.
Rejoice, O joyous one, the Lord is with Thee, grant us thy great
mercy.

The bishops and priests, the Tsars and princes,
The monks and clergy and all the people, women and children,
glorify thy intercession,
The lords and the Russian warriors kneel before thy holy icon.
They glorify Thee and sing forth unto Thee.
Rejoice, O joyous one, the Lord is with Thee, grant us thy great
mercy.

Trumpet forth the song on the day of our blessed feast.
The darkness shall perish and the light will come, shining brighter
than the sun:
For she is the Queen and Sovereign of all of us, Mother of God,
Mother of the Creator of all
human creatures, and of Christ
our Lord.
As she hears the prayers of her unworthy servants, she is full of
compassion and invisibly raises
her arms toward her Son and our
God,
And prays to him on behalf of all the Russians to deliver them from
evil and from the wrath of God.

O most compassionate and sovereign Lady!
O most merciful Empress and mighty intercessor!
O Mother of God, who by thy prayers to thy Son and our God
And by the coming of thy holy and most glorious icon, which is
beyond all praise,
Hast delivered the city and all its people from adversity and death.

Tsars and princes gather together, bishops and priests rejoice:
Let the assembled multitudes of the faithful of all ages sing out her
praises.

Rejoice, O dwelling-place of God and living city of Christ our Lord
and God.

Rejoice, O fountain of charity and mercy and providential assistance.

Rejoice, O refuge of those who come unto Thee for intercession,
deliverance and salvation.

Ivan's six strophes were trumpet blasts rather than polite
invocations. They demanded with great insistence, and there was
nothing humble in his prayers. He was speaking as one sovereign to
another, and because he was certain the Virgin heard his prayers he
spoke triumphantly.

The date of the composition of the hymn is unknown, but we
learn from the fifth verse that it was composed to celebrate the
deliverance of the city from the enemy. Quite probably it was
composed in 1551 or 1552, at a time when he was deeply influenced
by the Novgorod style of composition and by the victory over
Kazan, a city which he regarded as a perpetual threat to Moscow.
Yet there can be no certainty about the date of composition, for he
was pious in his own way throughout his life and there was no
period when he was not immersed in music.

St. Peter, Metropolitan of all the Russias, who lived in the time of
the Grand Prince Ivan Kalita, had been buried within the Kremlin
for over two centuries when Ivan composed a hymn in his honor.
He lay now in the ornate tomb built for him in the Uspensky
Cathedral, not far from the Icon of the Virgin of Vladimir. He had
become the patron saint of Moscow and was worshipped as the
"Sufferer for the Russian land," because he had lived in a time of
calamity when it seemed that Moscow could not survive against her
enemies, and yet he had prophesied that Moscow would become
one of the greatest and most powerful cities in the world if the
Muscovites would build a church to the Virgin. This was done, and
thereafter he always received men's prayers. He was preeminently
the saint of suffering surmounted and hope regained. His powers
were of course far less than those of the Virgin, but they were
believed to be sufficiently substantial to warrant the earnest
attention of the faithful. Ivan's hymn to St. Peter the Metropolitan,
like the hymn to the Icon of the Virgin of Vladimir, is composed of
six strophes. The first three strophes follow:

John the Baptist, from an icon once in the Church of Dmitrov, now in the
Rublev Museum, Moscow, circa 1560.

HYMN IN PRAISE OF ST. PETER,
METROPOLITAN OF RUSSIA
Composed by the Tsar Ivan, Despot of Russia

Let us now adorn the Bishop with crowns of praise.
He who lies in the Russian earth can be reached in spirit by all those
with pure hearts.
He defends the faithful and intercedes for them, and comforts all who
are sorrowful.
O Peter, stream of piety, whose waters bring joy to the Russian land,
Our ardent defender and guardian!

Opening verse with musical notation of the Hymn to the Virgin. The second line reads: "Composition by the Tsar."

With prophetical hymns we crown the Bishop,
Unshakable pillar of the Church, warrior against evil, upholder of
faith,
Blessed from the cradle, conqueror of Moslems, bringing shame to all
evildoers,
O Peter, stream of many miracles, whose waters bring joy to the
Russian land,
Our ardent defender and guardian.

With prophetical songs we praise the Bishop,
Who prophesies far into the future and brings it close to us,
Prophecies were the visions of this most pure priestly miracle-worker.

O Peter, stream of healing remedies, whose waters bring joy to the
Russian land,
Our ardent defender and guardian. . . .

That an emperor should also be a hymn writer was not regarded
as unusual in those times. Two Byzantine emperors, Leo IV the
Philosopher and his son Constantine VII Porphyrogenitus, were
famous for their hymns, which still survive.

But while Ivan was an eminent composer he has an even greater
claim to fame as a prose writer. His letters, which sometimes take
the form of long essays, are written in a style of violent invective—
he writes out of seething anger—and with a churchman's conscious
use of biblical rhythms. It is writing on the grand scale with all the
organ stops pulled out. Prince Andrey Kurbsky, whose letters drew
Ivan's fire, writes nearly as well but lacks the Tsar's sustained vigor.
In an age which produced little great prose the correspondence
between Ivan and Prince Kurbsky is outstanding.

Literature was largely dominated by the Church. The lives of
saints, theological arguments, homiletics, passionate statements
against heresy and abstruse discussions on the nature of God, all
these were produced by monks, copied and recopied, and dissemi-
nated throughout Russia. Many monasteries compiled their own
chronicles, but the chroniclers sometimes differ sharply among
themselves. A monk writing in Novgorod about the events of Ivan's
reign would necessarily see them quite differently from a monk
writing in Moscow. Nevertheless the chroniclers are in general
agreement on nearly all the main issues and they provide an
invaluable historical commentary on these times. From time to
time new chronicles, long buried in monastic archives, are found,
and one by one the gaps in our knowledge are being filled up.

The most representative work of the age was a manual of
instruction, the *Domostroy*, written by Sylvester to implant a proper
sense of morality into the Russian people. He explains how life
should be lived, and since he was hardheaded and practical he went
into all aspects of household economy, discussing not only the need
to be virtuous but going into such subjects as cooking, sewing,
embroidering, preserving food, cultivating vegetables and orchards,
the clothes to be worn in church and when visiting, and how to
entertain guests, with the result that we are provided with a detailed
picture of life as it was lived in the sixteenth century among the

middle classes. Sylvester was a stern man, with little joy in him. He prohibited amusements of all kinds. Dancing, singing, and unedifying games like chess were prohibited. Laughter was the invention of the devil. The entire family owed obedience to the master of the household. The wife was not so much the husband's helpmate as the chief of his servants, blindly executing his orders. She must rise before the servants, wake them, and spend every remaining moment of the day busily occupied, and even if guests came she must go on working.

Sylvester, with his pathological distrust of woman, treats her as a slave or beast of burden, and he enjoys describing the punishment to be meted out to her for her graver sins. A whipping on the bare back is recommended, but only birch twigs may be used. Iron staffs (like the staff Ivan habitually carried with him) are not recommended, nor is it permissible to punch a wife under the heart or to slap her face. Children, too, must be whipped when they do wrong. "Whip your child hard," he writes. "It will not kill him, but on the contrary does him good, since by beating him you save his soul from perdition." Servants fare little better than sons and daughters. "Beat your servant, even when he is in the right. Thus strife is brought to an end, and nothing is lost and there is no hatred." One would have thought that he was encouraging hatred, but he proclaims that gentleness and patience are the greatest virtues. He offers man a cheerless life in preparation for a more cheerful Heaven.

Puritanical, stubborn, self-worshipping, and without much kindness in him, Sylvester, without being aware of it, offers us a complete portrait of himself. He is well aware of his high priestly office and encourages good Christians to be equally aware of it. Priests should be revered, for do they not take care of our immortal souls and answer for us on the Day of Judgment? One should bow low to them, invite them into our homes, heap gifts upon them, and never even think of abusing or reproaching them. They are God's representatives on earth, but they are also God's watchdogs. Woe betide anyone who commits evil and forgets to say his prayers!

There were prayers in Russia for all occasions and all purposes. Sylvester urged lengthy morning prayers, more prayers in the evening, and this was not the end, for after having gone to sleep the good Christian must awake at midnight and pray tearfully to God concerning the sins committed during the day. He wrote in the *Domostroy*:

> When rising in the morning, you must pray for the forgiveness of sins, for the Tsar, for the Tsaritsa, for their children, for the Tsar's brothers, for his boyars, for his Christ-loving Army, for aid against the enemy, for the release of captives, for the clergy, for those who are sick and in prison, for all Christians, for those of one's own household, and for one's relatives and for one's spiritual fathers.
>
> You must always pray at Evensong in your houses. Every evening the husband, his wife, and their children and servants must attend Evensong with the singing of hymns and prayers and bowing to the ground. And before going to bed you must bow three times to the ground, and at midnight you must wake and rise and pray tearfully to God as much as you possibly can concerning your sins.

Sylvester's moral maxims and his detailed advice for leading the Christian life may not be very appealing to modern generations but they answered to the hard puritanical core in the ecclesiastical mind. Like Sylvester, the Russians of his age were exceedingly devout, believed firmly in the efficacy of prayer, adored ritual and flocked to the churches to take part in the awe-inspiring services. The Orthodox Church was a living force that penetrated into all regions of human life. And while Sylvester was the first to produce a manual of Christian instruction which described how men should behave at every moment of the day, much of what he said had long since been said by others. He practiced what he preached, and those who knew him well regarded him as an exemplary head of his household, who loved his dependents and provided well for their future, practical and honest, a man who engaged in trade and usually made a profit, and men liked to have dealings with him. But there was also a sharp, astringent side to his character, and too often he was overbearing. "Imitate me!" he wrote to his son. "See how I am respected by all, loved by all, because I have been able to please everyone!" He did not please everyone, for Ivan, who spent many years under his tutelage, rebelled violently against him and thought he had wasted his life in obedience to his stern taskmaster. Sylvester must bear some blame for Ivan's erratic conduct. He had pressed down too hard; insisted too often; demanded too much.

Ivan's rebellion took the form of a total repudiation of all the restraints imposed upon him.

Sylvester's book was widely read and hundreds of manuscript copies were distributed, but it was not printed until the following century. Printing came late to Russia, the first printed books appearing more than a hundred years after Johann Gutenberg printed the Vulgate Bible. After the conquest of Kazan Ivan began to think of the needs of the people living in the conquered territories, and ordered churches to be built and religious books to be provided for them. Someone pointed out that the available manuscript copies of Psalters and the New Testament were riddled with copyists' errors and only a very small number of accurate copies could be found. "When the Tsar heard this," wrote Ivan Fyodorov, the first Russian printer, "he began thinking that it would be good to have printed books like those which exist in Greece, Venice and Italy." With the blessing of the Metropolitan Makary Ivan set about finding a man who would learn how to print, and his choice fell on Ivan Fyodorov, the deacon of the Church of St. Nicholas Gostunsky, which stood in the Kremlin. The first Russian printing office was set up in the church.

Of the early trials of the printing office we know very little. It appears that Fyodorov learned his trade with the help of an Italian printer, for Italian technical terms were used from the beginning. The first book, *Triod Postnaya* (Lenten Psalms), was undated but was almost certainly printed about 1554. This was followed by *Triod Tsvetnaya* (Easter Psalms) and by a New Testament. The printing was unskillful, the red ink for the initials was smudgy, and some of the pages of *Triod Postnaya* were mixed up. The first dated book was the *Apostol*, containing The Acts of the Apostles and all of St. Paul's Epistles. Fyodorov began printing the book in April 1563 and completed it in March 1564. The work was painfully slow. Later in the year he produced a *Book of Hours* which was completed in two months, and in the following year he brought out another New Testament. But the first flowering of printing on Russian soil was very brief, and soon Fyodorov departed for Lithuania, taking his printing press with him. He complained that he left Moscow because certain ecclesiastical authorities were accusing him of heresy and making life difficult for him. "Because of this unreasonable envy and hatred," he wrote later, "we were expelled from our land, from our fatherland, from our people, to other lands unknown to us."

Ivan showed only a desultory interest in the printing of books. In 1568, at the height of the Oprichnina Terror in Moscow, two printers, Andronik Nevezha and Nikifor Tarasiev, both students of Ivan Fyodorov, were permitted to print a Psalter, and nine years later at Alexandrova Sloboda a second Psalter was printed by Andronik Nevezha. In Ivan's reign no more books were printed.

Because he possessed a vast private library of manuscripts, Ivan was among the most highly educated men in Russia. He wrote with passionate intensity in defense of his autocracy, his absolute dominion over the lives of his subjects; and if, even in his own time, he failed to be convincing, it was not for lack of any command of language. So Justinian might have spoken if anyone had dared to question his absolute supremacy over his subjects, and like Justinian he celebrated only those arts that served his own glory. It would never have occurred to him that any other glory was worth contemplating, for the glory of God was manifest in the Tsardom.

Thus he became a composer of hymns and a benefactor of architects and painters, but only when they celebrated his own greatness. The Cathedral in the Red Square and the Church of John the Baptist at Dyakovo showed to what heights Russian architecture might have risen if he had not succumbed to the overwhelming sense of anxiety that shadowed all his later years. The arts of his time reflected his early triumphs, but they also reflected his anxieties, his despairs, and the horrors of the closing years of his reign.

The Rages of the Tsar

AFTER THE DEATH OF ANASTASIA a change came over Ivan. Her restraining influence, intelligence, and deep religious faith had served him well and often saved him from disaster. Now she was gone, and there was only an emptiness in his heart. Within ten days of her death he commanded that all mourning should end abruptly and threw himself into a life of dissipation, drunkenness, and revelry.

She died at the wrong time and in the wrong way. He convinced himself that she had been poisoned, that spells had been cast on her, that in some mysterious way the boyars were determined to punish him by doing away with her. Grief, which had struck him so hard, loosened the bonds. Henceforth violence became a way of life; murder was his companion; to see the dead around him was his solace. In his rage he attempted to destroy everything he could lay his hands on—the state, the boyars, his friends. In him power assumed its ultimate form: the power to kill. After the death of Anastasia the story of Ivan is one of unrelieved tragedy. The Tsar as mass murderer entered the stage.

His character seemed to change overnight. The man who had been deeply religious and conscientious in his duties, carefully weighing the advice of his Chosen Council, acting for the most part mildly and judicially, rarely giving way to the cruelty that lay just below the surface, suddenly showed himself to be a harsh and tyrannical voluptuary. He lived riotously, drank heavily, surrounded himself with peculators, murderers, thieves, drunkards, and perverts, criminals who had no difficulty recognizing the latent criminality in him. Violent men urged him to hitherto unimaginable feats of violence. He enjoyed carousing all night, the tables laden with food, with the *skomorokhi* entertaining him. They were clowns who sometimes wore masks, singers of lewd songs, professional mimes, actors of vaudeville farces, storytellers, buffoons, and jesters, and while they represented an aspect of the degenerate taste of Ivan's court, they also derived from the ancient pre-Christian Russian culture; and though the Church inveighed against them, the masses adored them.

There were many weaknesses in Ivan. Like many men who appear to be outwardly bold and fearless, he was in fact very timid, easily terrified, likely to strike out at imagined enemies, at the mercy of uncontrollable fears. What he regarded as his greatest strength—his relentless and passionate determination to rid the world of evil—was in fact his greatest weakness, for he saw evil everywhere, and so there grew in him a monstrous appetite for murder. If necessary, he would destroy all Russia to save its soul. He succeeded in reducing Russia to a state of timidity, from which it never completely recovered. For nearly a quarter of a century, all the remaining years of his life, he gave himself up to a reign of violence and terror.

Prince Andrey Kurbsky, who observed him closely, believed that Ivan made a conscious choice between good and evil. "The Tsar came to detest the narrow pathway laden with sorrows which leads to salvation through repentance," he wrote. "Instead he ran joyfully along the broad highway that leads to Hell. Many times I heard from his own lips—when he was depraved he would say these things in the hearing of all: I must make my choice between this world and the other world! He meant: the broad highway of Satan or the sorrowful pathway of Christ."

Perhaps it was not quite so simple as that. Perhaps the choice was made for him and was dictated by his ancestors, his character, his upbringing. Within Ivan "this world" and "the other world" were never completely separated. He remained fervently religious and God-fearing even when he was committing atrocious crimes.

Already during the last months of Anastasia's life we can watch the process of corruption at work. In October 1559, at Mozhaisk, he learned that the Livonians had broken the truce and were advancing on Dorpat under the command of Gottgard Kettler, the Grand Master of the Livonian Order. The truce had been arranged by Alexey Adashev, his chief adviser on foreign affairs. He therefore raged against Adashev and against all those who had supported the policy of peaceful coexistence with Livonia. He felt that he had been outwitted and outmaneuvered, and suspected treachery. He wanted to hurry back to Moscow but the weather was terrible and for several days he was trapped in Mozhaisk like a prisoner. The news of the attack on Dorpat especially depressed him. As soon as the weather cleared, he drove off to Moscow with Anastasia, his family, and the entire court. The snow was on the ground, there was mud and slush everywhere, and progress was slow. To make matters worse Anastasia fell ill during the journey. He was not a man who could resolve two crises simultaneously, and the double blow was almost more than he could take. The Archpriest Sylvester was traveling with him and he appears to have been incensed by the priest's insistence that all human misfortunes —the war in Livonia, the illness of the Tsaritsa—were God's punishment for sins. Nor did he feel that Adashev and Sylvester were sufficiently solicitous of Anastasia; they could at least have provided her with medicines, but did nothing.

In this sullen mood, aware that great issues were at stake and that he was powerless to order them, he rode through the angry winter, allowing his own anger to boil up in him. His worries and frustrations precipitated an explosion. There were violent words addressed to Adashev or Sylvester, or both. We do not know exactly what happened, but when Ivan remembered the long exhausting journey he also remembered the "little, unbecoming word" uttered in a moment of rage. Since his little words were likely to be long tirades and since he later regretted having spoken them, it is possible that he deeply offended his former friends. Soon after reaching Moscow, Sylvester asked permission to retire from the scene and went to live at the Kirillov Monastery in Beloozero in the far north. For a few more weeks Adashev remained in charge of foreign affairs, but it was clear that he had lost the Tsar's confidence. Anastasia was seriously ill, and in his loneliness and misery Ivan "embarked on all sorts of things in an ungodly manner." These were the words of Prince Kurbsky and leave little doubt that Ivan, while Anastasia was still alive, was beginning to sow his wild oats.

In May 1560, Ivan got rid of Adashev by sending him to Livonia to take charge of one of the armies commanded by Prince Ivan Mstislavsky. This was a punishment, for Adashev had protested vehemently against continuing the Livonian war, preferring to direct the main forces of the Russian army against the Crimean Tatars. Adashev had never previously commanded an army in the field; he had none of the makings of a general but was admirably fitted to preside over the Chosen Council. His friends hoped he would be permitted to return to court, but the death of Anastasia on August 7, 1560, drove Ivan into a madness of grief. In his confused, unbalanced mind he convinced himself that Sylvester and Adashev were the authors of her death. Later he would say they practiced magic spells on her and half the nobility of Russia were in league with them.

There were always sycophants and provocateurs at court, and by the end of the year they were saying both Adashev and Sylvester should be placed on trial for casting spells on Anastasia. When Sylvester and Adashev heard about it, they asked to be allowed to confront their accusers face to face. Ivan refused, assembled a court which consisted of himself, the Metropolitan Makary, and the leading boyars and bishops, and eagerly listened to the two monks, Missail Sukin and Vassian Toporkov, who produced the necessary "evidence." Makary protested that it was unseemly to hold a trial in which the accused were not allowed to be present, but was drowned out by the voices of those who feared the presence of spellbinders. "They are well-known evil-doers and great sorcerers!" they cried. "They will bewitch the Tsar and destroy us, if they come here!" Adashev and Sylvester were pronounced guilty. Sylvester was ordered to leave the Kirillov Monastery and enter the Solovetsky Monastery, which lies on an island in the White Sea. Adashev was removed from his command and kept under house arrest. Two months later he caught a fever and died. Ivan ordered that his body should be buried in the family tomb in Uglich—a last salute to the man who had served him so well.

In this way, in a period of a few weeks, Ivan lost Anastasia, Adashev, and Sylvester, the three people who in their different ways had dominated his life and restrained him from his worst impulses.

In his mind Anastasia was the murdered innocent struck down by evil sorcerers, while Adashev and Sylvester were figures of incarnate evil. Concerning Adashev an early seventeenth century chronicler wrote that when he was in power "there was a great peace and well-being in the land, and also justice." Prince Kurbsky relates that he was a man of deep piety who "kept scores of sick people in his house, feeding and washing them and many times cleansing their sores with his own hands, and he did all this in secret." Meanwhile Ivan continued to rage against them, hating them most of all because their strength of character mocked his own weakness.

Henceforward he was determined to live his own life without interference. He would no longer deny himself the pleasures that Sylvester regarded as sinful. He would marry whomever he pleased, surround himself with agreeable flatterers and drinking companions, and conduct himself as though Russia were his private possession. Although as a youth he maintained that it would be disastrous for a Tsar to marry a foreign princess, he chose as his second wife the beautiful and high-spirited Princess Kocheney Temriukovna, the daughter of a Circassian chieftain, Prince Temriuk, who ruled over territories on the slopes of the Caucasus Mountains. The fame of her beauty had already reached Moscow, where two of her brothers were serving at court. Ivan had evidently seen pictures of her, and was properly impressed. She reached Moscow on June 15, 1561, with an immense retinue. Her sister, Princess Altynchach, who was married to the Tatar Prince Bekbulat, accompanied her. The young son of the princess, Prince Sayin, was a member of the retinue. In the course of time this Tatar prince would for a brief period become the Grand Prince of Russia, taking Ivan's place. Circassians and Tatars flocked to the court.

Ivan was well-pleased with Princess Kocheney when she was presented to him. He ordered that she should be instructed in the dogmas of the Orthodox faith. A month later she was solemnly baptized, taking the name of Maria. In August, just a year after the death of Anastasia, Ivan and Maria were married in the Church of the Annunciation in the Kremlin. Sir Jerome Horsey records that "the manner and solemnity of this marriage was so strange and heathenly as credit will hardly be given to the truth thereof." No doubt he was referring to the wild Circassian entertainments that followed the marriage ceremony.

Many persons at court expressed dismay and displeasure at the marriage of Ivan and Princess Kocheney. They found her willful, strange, with a streak of cruelty in her, preferring Circassians and Tatars to Russians. They suspected rightly that she would be unable to restrain her husband from his excesses and was herself violent to excess. She loved intrigue, attended bearbaiting, and enjoyed watching the public executions on the Red Square from a vantage point high on the Kremlin wall. Boyars who snubbed her did so at their peril. She was well aware of the power that went with her title: Tsaritsa Maria.

Deep down she appears to have feared and despised the Russians, and to have suffered from a corrosive loneliness and melancholy. A popular folk song of the period puts into her mouth the words:

> God grant that I should not be here
> In the Tsar's Moscow built of stone,
> Nor my children nor my grandchildren,
> Not only grandchildren but all my descendants!

But it was not her loneliness so much as her violence that people feared. As the historian Soloviev wrote, "One could see clearly what Ivan would gain by marrying a savage," but it was more difficult to understand what Russia would gain.

About the same time that he married Princess Kocheney Ivan received another visitor from abroad. This was no less a person than Ioasaf, Metropolitan of Kizikos, who came bearing a gift without price, a document signed by the Patriarch of Constantinople confirming Ivan in his title as Tsar. The Metropolitan was rewarded with costly presents, and Feodorit, the monk who made a special journey to Constantinople to secure this privilege, was offered three hundred silver rubles, a valuable sable coat, and any ecclesiastical distinction he chose. Feodorit smiled, said he had renounced all earthly possessions and honors, and wanted only to be allowed to live out his days in the silence of his cell. Ivan pressed him hard, reminding him that it was disrespectful to refuse the gifts of the Tsar. So Feodorit agreed to accept twenty-five silver rubles and the sable coat, which he sold, giving the money to the poor

At the end of the year Ivan's temper, which always grew more violent in winter, became increasingly explosive. What especially enraged him was the discovery that young Prince Ivan Belsky, the nephew of the former Regent bearing the same name, was in secret correspondence with King Sigismund II Augustus and preparing to flee to Lithuania, having already received a safe-conduct signed by the King. Prince Belsky was arrested; two noblemen implicated in the plot were publicly whipped; a musketeer officer, who prepared the escape map, had his tongue torn out. Prince Belsky was in grave danger. Makary pleaded for him, and when the spring came he was released after renewing his oath of allegiance to the Tsar and obtaining bonds from 124 noblemen who pledged to pay vast sums into the Tsar's treasury if he fled to Lithuania.

Meanwhile Ivan was engaged in a war of nerves with King Sigismund II Augustus. Lithuanian ambassadors came to Moscow, but the negotiations were at a standstill. The Russians had intercepted a letter from the King to the Khan of the Crimea, urging that they should attack Russia simultaneously and offering rich rewards. Ivan was displeased. He possessed an ungovernable hatred for the King and was determined to wreak vengeance. Accordingly he prepared for a massive invasion of Lithuania, set up his headquarters in Mozhaisk, and was about to order the attack when he learned that the Khan of the Crimea was invading Russia from the south. The Khan's forces were surprisingly small, amounting to no more than fifteen thousand men. Prince Mikhail Vorotynsky was ordered to attack them but failed to engage them after they ran off. Ivan then ordered his arrest. His possessions and vast ancestral estates were confiscated, and he was exiled to Beloozero. Since there was no formal trial, and since he ranked above all Russian princes except those connected by blood to the Tsar, his downfall came as a blow to the nobility. Some Russian historians suspect that his real crime was that he did not show sufficient respect for the Tsaritsa.

In October 1562 another nobleman, Prince Dmitry Kurliatev, who was one of Adashev's closest collaborators, was also arrested on a charge of treason. Ivan had an experimental attitude toward punishment and ordered him tonsured and sent him to a monastery on an island in Lake Ladoga together with his son. His wife and

wo daughters were ordered into a nunnery. Later the entire family
was strangled. Ivan's resentment against Prince Kurliatev was
expressed in a letter written to Prince Kurbsky in 1577. "And
Kurliatev—why was he better than me? For his daughters all sorts
of adornments were bought—well and good! But for my daughters
—rejection and funerals!" Ivan lost two of his daughters by
Anastasia in infancy and he was always blaming others for their
deaths.

By November 1562 Ivan had received information that led him
to believe that a winter campaign against Lithuania might be
successful. On the last day of the month he prayed for victory
before the Icon of the Virgin of Vladimir in the Uspensky
Cathedral, and soon he was marching off once more to Mozhaisk at
the head of his army. The staging point for the invasion of
Lithuania was Veliki Luki, which he reached early in January 1563.
The aim was to capture Polotsk, once an important town in Kievan
Russia. The journey through dense forests was slow and difficult;
some columns were lost; others blundered about in the darkness;
supply trains were in the wrong places. Ivan did his best to bring
order to the confusion. At the border fortress of Nevel, on January
19, 1563, where he rested for a day, Ivan for the first time killed
someone with his own hands. Tired and irritated by the difficulties
of the long march in the dead of winter, he fell into an argument
with Prince Ivan Shakhovskoy and struck him with a mace. The
wound was fatal.

Polotsk, defended by 500 Polish soldiers and some foreign
mercenaries, fell to the Russians without much difficulty. The easy
victory pleased Ivan, who made a triumphal entry into the town
and visited all the Orthodox churches to pray before the icons,
saying, according to the chroniclers, "Thou hast shown unto me,
thy unworthy servant, thy mercy and thou hast given me this city
without bloodshed. And what shall I give thee in return, O Lord?"
It was not, of course, a question he intended to pursue at any
length. The gold and silver vessels and all the valuables of Polotsk
were shipped to Moscow. The Polish soldiers who had defended the
city so ignominiously were given presents and allowed to leave
under safe-conduct.

Ivan was in an affable and triumphant mood as he returned to
Moscow by slow stages. Polotsk had satisfied, at least temporarily,

his lust for conquest. The announcement that the Tsaritsa Maria had given birth to a son also pleased him. But at Veliki Luki he quarreled violently with Prince Andrey Kurbsky, who was lucky enough to escape with a reprimand and exile in Livonia—Ivan accused him of taking morbid offense over "a small single angry word." Ivan had a vile tongue, and his small single ugly words were likely to be screaming insults.

When Ivan was a day's march from Veliki Luki, on March 5 1563, a messenger arrived from Mikhail Morozov, the governor of Smolensk. The messenger reported that the Russian commanders of Starodub were about to surrender the city to the Lithuanians. The news was almost certainly untrue, but Ivan became wildly excited. One of the commanders of Starodub was Ivan Shishkin, a close relative of Alexey Adashev. Obviously Shishkin was a traitor; just as obviously the entire Adashev family was tainted with treachery and sorcery. Ivan Shishkin, together with his wife and children, were executed. The matter did not end there. One by one Ivan rounded up all other relatives of Alexey Adashev and executed them. Daniel Adashev, Alexey's brother, the hero of the 1559 invasion of the Crimea, was among those killed, and his young son was killed with him. Altogether sixteen members of the Adashev family were put to death in a display of malicious fury unexampled in Russia until this time.

Another family to feel the weight of the Tsar's displeasure was the Sheremetevs. Nikita and Ivan Sheremetev were both members of the Boyar Council, rich, powerful, and well-liked. Both held high military rank, and Nikita bore the scars of many wounds. They belonged to the faction that insisted that the Tsar should make war with the Tatars, not with the Lithuanians and Livonians, and it was clearly for this reason that the Tsar decided to punish them. Ivan Sheremetev's punishment was graphically described by Prince Kurbsky in his *History of the Grand Prince of Moscow*:

> His torture chamber was a terribly cramped cell with a rough earth floor; heavy chains were fastened round his neck and his arms and legs, while a thick iron hoop girdled his loins with ten weights of iron hanging from it. The Tsar came to talk to him while he lay prostrate on the rough floor, wearing his heavy chains, half-alive and scarcely breathing. Among other questions the Tsar interrogated him in the following way.

"Where are your many treasures?" he asked. "Tell me, for I know you are very rich. Nevertheless I have failed to find in your treasure house what I expected to find."

"They lie hidden where no one can find them."

"You must tell me. Otherwise I shall add torture to torture."

"Do as you wish. I am near the end of my journey."

"I insist that you tell me about your treasure."

"I have already told you that even if I told you where they were, you would not be able to make use of them. The hands of the poor and the needy have removed them to the heavenly treasure house, to my Christ."

According to Prince Kurbsky the Tsar was sufficiently impressed by the brave words of Ivan Sheremetev to order the heavy chains removed. He was eventually released from prison and became a monk. His brother was strangled.

The Sheremetevs had long been a thorn in Ivan's side: like Adashev and Sylvester they represented the Russian humanistic tradition, reasonableness, sobriety, a deep awareness of the Tatar menace. Gleefully Ivan reported to the Khan of the Crimea: "Adashev, Sylvester, and Sheremetev, all those who have been creating troubles between the Tsar and the Khan, have fallen into disgrace." He was sacrificing Russians to be in the good graces of the Crimean Khan.

It was a year of many deaths, many executions. Three deaths moved Ivan deeply. The Tsarevich Vasily, his son by the Tsaritsa Maria, died on May 4, 1563, aged just over two months. On November 24 the Tsar's brother Yury died at the age of thirty-one. Yury was quiet, uncomplaining, and simpleminded, but there was a deep bond of affection between the brothers. Ivan took care that his brother should appear at all the ceremonies in the Kremlin, magnificently robed, receiving the honors due to the younger brother of the Tsar. The death of a brother can be a shattering thing, and it is possible that Ivan was as shattered by the death of Yury as by the death of Anastasia.

Finally on the last day of the year the Metropolitan Makary died, a weak but kindly man, scholarly and possessed of genuine piety. For twenty-one years he had ruled the Russian Church with gentle austerity. If he bowed too often to Ivan's will, he nevertheless took pains to plead for mercy. Under his rule important reforms were carried out, and they were embodied in the *Stoglav*, or Hundred Chapters. He edited and wrote a part of the *Minei Chetii*, a compilation of the lives of the Russian saints, a voluminous work with readings for every day of the year. With his death a chapter of the history of the Russian Church came to an end. In his lengthy testament, which was read out during the funeral service held in the Cathedral of the Annunciation, he forgave everyone and asked forgiveness from everyone, and he spoke of how, weighed down by sorrows, he had hoped to be permitted to lay down the burdens of his office and retire to the peace of a monastery, but the Tsar and the Church hierarchy always prevailed on him to remain.

If Ivan had possessed the leisure to take stock of this unhappy year, he would have found much that was pleasurable. There had been no battles after Polotsk. There were some skirmishes on the borders, many embassies flocked to Moscow, his relations with the Khan of the Crimea improved considerably, and the Lithuanians were unusually quiet. He had been on many pilgrimages and worshipped at many shrines. God had blessed him with a mild winter. Early in December there was a warm spell and the ice melted on the rivers.

There was another matter which gave him unrelieved pleasure. A certain Savliuk Ivanov, one of the secretaries of Prince Vladimir of Staritsa, had been thrown into prison. From his prison cell he smuggled out a letter accusing Prince Vladimir of abominable crimes. Ivan treated the letter with the importance it deserved, sent his agents to Staritsa, cross-examined witnesses, drew up an impressive bill of particulars, and finally confronted the Prince in the presence of the Metropolitan Makary and high ecclesiastical officials with his crimes. Since he regarded Vladimir of Staritsa as a potential claimant to his throne, this was an eminently satisfactory procedure. Vladimir confessed, or at least he realized the futility of defending himself. Ivan then forgave him on condition that his entire court was transferred to Moscow and a new set of courtiers was chosen for him. Princess Efrosinia, Vladimir's mother, was ordered to take the veil and sent to a nunnery at Beloozero.

Albert Shlichting, who learned Russian and served as an interpreter to Ivan's Belgian doctor, Arnold Lenzey, believed that the easy victory at Polotsk had an unsettling effect on Ivan. He thought Polotsk was the turning point. "After the capture of

Polotsk," Shlichting wrote, "the tyrant became arrogant with success and began to plan how to destroy his councillors, especially those who were distinguished by an ancient and illustrious lineage." Shlichting thought Ivan "lost his reason by virtue of his pride," the pride of a great military commander who conquers towns and cities by his mere presence. But it was more likely that the turning point came earlier with the death of Anastasia. The murder of Prince Ivan Shakhovskoy and the victory at Polotsk only reinforced his delighted awareness of his power over people's lives. Henceforth he killed his real and imagined enemies whenever he pleased, safe in the knowledge that no one would ever punish him. He became the pure tyrant, divested of all human sympathy, rejoicing in his ferocity, capable of acts of such obscene violence that they took the breath away and left people stunned and helpless; and it would be to underestimate his intelligence to suggest that he did not know the effect of his crimes. He knew very well what he was doing. He was ruling by terror, and terror is always effective.

Nevertheless there was some truth in Shlichting's contention. A military victory, even such an easy victory as Ivan gained at Polotsk, can corrode the mind of the conqueror with the knowledge that he is the supreme arbiter over the lives of all the people he has conquered. In fact, Ivan permitted all the Polish defenders to leave and offered them safe-conducts, thus publicly presenting himself as a man of mercy. But this act of mercy was designed to impress the Poles with his benign intentions toward them; he had no need to show acts of mercy to the Russians.

In his drunken rages Ivan was becoming increasingly murderous. Blood flowed at his drinking parties, which often lasted through the night. One day a certain courtier called Molchan Mitkov was commanded to drink from a huge bowl of mead. He had already drunk more than enough, and now in a loud voice he heard himself saying: "Accursed one, you force us to drink mead mixed with the blood of our brothers, the Orthodox Christians!" Ivan was so enraged that he transfixed the man with the iron point of his staff and then ordered him to be dragged out of sight and put to death.

On another occasion Ivan was carousing with his drinking companions. The *skomorokhi,* the masked clowns, were also present. The Tsar, who was drinking heavily, put on a mask and began dancing with the *skomorokhi,* and all joined him except

Prince Mikhail Repnin who was outraged at the sight of Ivan cavorting like a madman. He was so distressed that he began to weep and said through his tears, "Christian Tsar, it is unbecoming of you to do such things!" The Tsar, who liked Prince Repnin and wanted to be friends with him, urged him to do what all the others were doing. "Be of good cheer and play with us!" he commanded, and placed a mask over Prince Repnin's face. The Prince took the mask, flung it to the floor, and trampled on it, saying, "May I never perform such indecorous and insane acts." The Tsar was enraged and ordered him out of the room.

It was winter, a few days after the death of the Metropolitan Makary, and bad news had just come from the Lithuanian front, where fighting had broken out again. An army under Prince Peter Shuisky had been savagely mauled by the army of Christopher Radziwill. In his anger the Tsar began to cast about for a victim, and he settled on Prince Repnin. The Metropolitan was dead, no new Metropolitan had been appointed, the Tsar did not have to answer for any crimes before the ecclesiastical authorities. He gave orders that Prince Repnin should be killed while attending an all-night vigil in church. "He was killed," wrote Prince Kurbsky, "during the reading of the Gospel, while he was standing near the altar like an innocent lamb of God."

On the same day the Tsar ordered the death of Prince Yury Kashin, who was struck down as he entered the church. What crime he had committed is unknown.

When Prince Andrey Kurbsky wrote the first of his five long letters to the Tsar protesting against the endless murders and persecutions ordered and instigated by him, he had these two murders particularly in mind. "Why," he asked, "have you spilt their holy blood in God's churches and stained the thresholds with the blood of martyrs?"

Prince Kurbsky's letters and Ivan's two lengthy replies are among the most amazing documents of the age. They both wrote with vehemence, with raging tempers, in a style that reproduces the sound of clanging metal. Kurbsky accuses Ivan of committing abominable crimes against God and man, and Ivan answers that he is absolute Tsar ruling by divine right with the God-given power to root out evil wherever he sees it. Kurbsky keeps asking what devilish impulse has led to so much murder and concludes that

Ivan must himself be Antichrist. Ivan answers that he is the only true believer, the one man who stands between Russia and Satan, more God-fearing than any of his subjects. To Kurbsky, who was once his friend, Ivan opens out his heart to display all the griefs and sorrows written on it, his miserable childhood, the treachery of his advisers, the threats on his life, the murder of his uncle Prince Yury Glinsky, the dreadful rumors spread about his grandmother, Princess Anna Glinskaya; and as he recounts these episodes in passionate detail, he commends himself for his steadfastness, his sobriety, his fearful faith in God's justice. He is innocent, this above all, and to deny his innocence is to show oneself a traitor. He protests too much, screams too loudly, and denounces his enemies so violently that it becomes obvious that he is a man of uncontrollable brutality and ferocity. Again and again Prince Kurbsky asks, "Why did you kill?" and there is no answer.

Kurbsky did not of course write his letters from Russian soil. He would have been tortured to death very slowly if Ivan could have laid hands on him. Fearing that he was about to be arrested, he fled on the night of April 30, 1564, from Dorpat in Russian Livonia to Volmar which was under the control of Lithuania. The decision to flee was taken quite suddenly, although he had been contemplating it for some time and already possessed a safe-conduct from King Sigismund II Augustus. He asked his wife which she preferred: to see him dead at her feet or to lose him for ever. She answered that his life was more important to her than her own happiness, and then he bade her farewell, blessed his nine-year-old son, and slipped out of the house, abandoning all his possessions, his books, his manuscripts, and even his suit of armor. A servant was waiting for him outside the city wall with two horses. At the last moment twelve noblemen from his court—he had been governor of Dorpat and lived in great state—joined him in his flight. They rode through the night as fast as their horses could carry them, and at Volmar they were received with open arms.

On that same day Ivan had taken part in a curious ceremony. The virtuous Yuliana, the widow of his brother Yury, had decided to accept the fate reserved for nearly all widowed princesses: she became a nun. Fulfilling the vow she made at the death of her husband she made the journey from the Kremlin to the Novodevichy Nunnery on foot, followed by the Tsar, the Tsaritsa Maria,

Prince Vladimir of Staritsa, and a host of people who adored her, and did not want to see her vanish into the silence of a nunnery. The long procession wound its way silently through the streets of Moscow. Ivan demanded that in the nunnery she should be given every luxury. She wanted to live alone in a bare cell; he filled it with furniture and insisted that she should be provided with ladies-in-waiting, and granted her vast estates for her upkeep. Princess Yuliana, now known as the nun Alexandra, humbly submitted to the will of the Tsar.

Prince Andrey Kurbsky had not the least inclination to play the role of the humble spectator. Aroused to fury by the thought that Ivan had ordered his arrest and by the anarchy that prevailed in Russia, he wrote his first accusing letter in a seething rage, addressing it to "the Tsar, exalted above all by God, who appeared once to be most illustrious, especially in observance of the Orthodox Faith, but now as a consequence of our sins has been found to be the direct opposite." Having written the letter, Kurbsky sent it to the Tsar by his loyal servant Vasily Shibanov. We learn from a seventeenth-century chronicler that the Tsar glanced at it, realized that it was a deliberate attack on him, bade Vasily Shibanov come closer, and then pierced the servant's foot with the sharp point of his staff. Leaning heavily on the staff, he ordered the letter read aloud. The story may be true, for in another letter to Kurbsky the Tsar goes out of his way to praise the courage of Vasily Shibanov.

Kurbsky was well-equipped to engage the Tsar in argument. He was intelligent, well-read, courageous. He had distinguished himself at the battle of Kazan and at many other battles. His lineage was impeccable, for he descended from the Princes of Yaroslavl and was related through his grandmother to the family of Anastasia. Tall, swarthy, with gray eyes, diffident only in the presence of scholars and priests—among his closest friends was the great theologian known as Maxim the Greek—he belonged to the rare group of Russian princes who were also humanists. He translated the works of John Chrysostom, Basil the Great, Gregory of Nazianzen, Nil Cabasilas, Nicephorus Callistus, and many other Greek theologians into Church Slavonic, and he was so intrigued by the *Paradoxi* of Cicero that he set himself to learn Latin in order to translate them. He was a Renaissance man who turned easily

rom the study of weapons and fortifications to the study of
philosophy and theology.

The exchange of letters between Kurbsky and the Tsar has
become part of Russian history. For the first time we witness a
head-on collision between autocracy and freedom. The autocrat
presents himself as little less than divine while the man who loves
freedom or at least wants more freedom than autocracy can
provide asks why this particular autocrat should be in league with
the devil, accomplishing devilish things. Ivan answers sometimes
blandly, sometimes cunningly, and always menacingly—his crowns
were given to him by God, he is free to reward and punish his
servants as he pleases, no limit has been set to his earthly powers.
What Kurbsky calls insane killing is merely just retribution; no one
has been killed who did not deserve it a thousandfold. King David
killed, but was found pleasing to God. Constantine the Great killed
his own son, but what emperor was greater? "It is always proper for
Tsars to be perspicacious—now very gentle, now fierce—mercy and
gentle dealing for the good, ferocity and torture for the evil." He
depicts himself as one who stands in perpetual judgment. In a
breathtaking passage he pronounces judgment on Prince Kurbsky:
"If thou considerest thyself just and faithful to the Tsar, so why
didst thou not accept sufferings and the crown of death from us,
who are thy wicked master?"

Kurbsky accuses Ivan of having "a leprous conscience," of a
fierce addiction to sin, of surrounding himself with lewd and
debased flatterers, and of committing heinous murders. Ivan tends
to brush the murders aside. "As for 'blood in churches'—we have
spilt none," he writes, dismissing two murders with a wave of his
hand. Kurbsky accuses him of overweening pride, the sin by which
the angels fell, and Ivan replies calmly from the heights of his
superb arrogance:

> I boast not in my pride, and indeed I have no need for pride, for I
> perform my royal task and place no man higher than myself. It is
> rather you who puff yourselves up with pride, for being servants you
> usurp the royal and ecclesiastical dignity: teaching, forbidding,
> commanding.

It was a neat disclaimer, but not completely convincing. Ivan
claimed that the boyars were always attempting to take power by

transforming the government into a debating society with the debaters teaching him how to do his job. He thanks God that the days are over when he permitted others to do his own thinking for him. Accepting his premise that he has received his power from God, the argument he presents is unanswerable except on the one point that Kurbsky continually presses home: how can it be that God, through Ivan, should commit so many crimes and associate Himself with so many despicable villains?

Both Kurbsky and Ivan quote the Scriptures to bolster their arguments; they have a priestly cast of mind, a priestly dogmatism. Ivan had read widely in the Fathers of the Eastern Church, and quotes at length from the letter to the monk Demophilus written by Dionysius the Areopagite. In the letter Dionysius tells the story of Carpus of Crete, who learned that a pagan had entered a church and converted a Christian to paganism. The matter deeply disturbed Carpus. At night in his prayers he begged God utterly to destroy these two sinners, and at that moment the house where he was praying split in two and he saw a vast abyss opening below him with the two sinners clinging to the edge, trembling with terror. Serpents crept out of the abyss, twining round their feet and attempting to pull them down into the darkness below. Men came out of nowhere and rained blows on the heads of the sinners, hoping they would fall into the abyss. Carpus watches all this supremely content because the sinners are being punished. But Christ steps down from the heavens, stretches his hand toward the sinners and bids the angels lift them up, and then turns to Carpus saying: "Now lift your hand and strike Me, for I am ready again to suffer for the salvation of men. Which do you prefer, to be cast down into the abyss or to live with God and the kindly angels?"

The story of Carpus is worthy to rank with Dostoyevsky's "The Grand Inquisitor." It is something seen in a vision, in a lightning flash. Ivan quotes the story accurately and then tells it all over again in his own words, unable to resist the temptation to improvise on the theme. In this second version the men are tied with rope and forcibly dragged into the abyss, Christ is seated on the shoulders of the Cherubim, and as he turns to Carpus, he says: "If it is sweet to thee, Carpus, strike Me, for heretofore I offered my shoulders so that I might suffer wounds and bring all men to repentance." Then Ivan comments: "If the Lord of the Angels did not hearken to such a just and holy man, who justly prayed for the destruction of sinners, how much less will he hearken unto you, you stinking dog and evil unjust traitor, who desires only evil!"

In this way Kurbsky is rebuked, but Ivan has demonstrated that he is impervious to earthly mercy and has no understanding of the mercy of Christ. For his part Kurbsky is more generous, for he pleads and prays that Ivan will see the error of his ways. "Why do you not join the side of God and the angels who love mankind?" he asks in his last letter; and following John Chrysostom, he suggests that Ivan would do well to give himself up to tearful penitence, the divine antidote.

The Tsar remained impenitent; the murders continued; even more terrible murders were being contemplated.

Prince Kurbsky lived out the remainder of his life in Livonia. He had hoped the Tsar would spare his family, but his mother, wife, and son were thrown into prison. King Sigismund II Augustus loaded him with properties and estates and he received a new title: he became Prince of Kowel. Sometimes he fought with the Lithuanian army against the Russians but the days when he could cover himself with military glory were over; he fought well but without great distinction. He continued to write and translate, completing his *History of the Grand Prince of Moscow*, which is a prime source for the reign of Ivan, studied languages, corresponded with friends, and when he learned that his wife had died, he married again. His new wife was a certain Princess Golshansky, rich, well-connected, and influential. For five years they lived happily together, and then, fearing that death was approaching, she wrote a will bequeathing all her property to her husband. She recovered; her children by a former marriage learned about the will; there were family quarrels; Kurbsky took to his bed. While he was ill, the princess had an affair with a steward. Kurbsky found three witnesses who would attest to her infidelity and obtained a divorce. In 1579 he married again, this time to a much younger woman, who gave him a son and a daughter. He died in May 1583 after a short illness. He was about fifty-five years old.

In 1564, when Kurbsky fled to Lithuania, the Tsar was thirty-four years old and in the fullness of his power. He was still an impressive figure with his bright eyes, his rippling beard, his broad shoulders and barrel chest, but already his hair was thinning out, deep wrinkles were forming on his forehead, and the once handsome features had grown coarse. Drinking and self-indulgence were destroying him. Yet he still commanded the gestures of kingship, knew how to play his role, and inspired respect and fear. Crowned and sitting on his throne, robed in cloth of gold, he was a formidable presence.

One day in the summer of 1564 he invited Prince Dmitry Ovchina-Obolensky to a banquet, commanded him to drink a huge bowl of mead to the last drop, thus demonstrating how dearly he held the health and well-being of his lord, and watched closely while the prince struggled to perform the task entrusted to him. And when the prince, having successfully drunk half of the bowl, showed that he was incapable of drinking any more, the Tsar in his most caressing voice suggested that there was an effective medicine for people who were not too well disposed toward him. "Go to the wine cellar and drink anything you choose and as much as you want," he said. The prince then made his way to the cellar, where the Tsar's dog-keepers were waiting for him with a rope. They strangled him. His crime was that he had offended Fyodor Basmanov, the Tsar's favorite, with the words: "We serve the Tsar with useful labor; you serve him with sodomy."

A new Metropolitan had been appointed in the spring of 1564 several months after the death of Makary. This was Andrey Protopopov, who had been Ivan's confessor and took the name of Afanasy. The new Metropolitan and the boyars were deeply disturbed by these senseless acts of cruelty. Courageously the Metropolitan reminded the Tsar that it was unbecoming of a Christian ruler to destroy people as though they were cattle. For the shedding of innocent blood God punishes even unto the third generation. Shamed by the Metropolitan's words, and offering no justification for his crimes, the Tsar gave hope that he would correct his ways. For six months he committed no more murders.

This was the private Ivan; the public man continued to be on display. We have a glimpse of him in the memoirs of Rafaello Barberini, an Italian merchant of Antwerp, who visited Moscow in November 1564 to represent the interests of the Italian merchants of Flanders. He came with excellent credentials, being armed with letters of introduction from both King Philip II of Spain and Queen Elizabeth of England. Ivan gave him the seat of honor just below the throne. "The Tsar," Barberini wrote, "wore a gold crown studded with jewels, a rich black sable cape hung from his shoulders, and beneath it he wore a long robe of cloth of gold decked with pearls, falling all the way to his feet and fastened with gold buttons as large as small eggs. His tan leather boots had long points and were studded with tiny silver nails. In one hand he held a gilded silver staff like a bishop's crook."

Barberini witnessed the ceremonial procession which took place when the Tsar swept out of the room to change his clothes, always followed by young ax bearers who perhaps represented a link with the splendors of imperial Rome. He observed that the axes were made of gold and silver, and the ax bearers were all younger members of noble families, tall and robust, dressed in silver cloth with silver buttons and ermine linings, and they wore white velvet hats sprinkled with pearls and silver. They were suitably impressive.

He was less impressed by the continual toasting of the Tsar's health, for there were so many toasts and at each toast it was necessary to stand up and bow to the Tsar and this seriously interfered with his supper. In November there were only five hours of daylight and it was already dark when they sat down to eat by the light of tallow candles stuck in brass candlesticks. Some tables were high, some low, and this somehow added to the general air of confusion. Servants were rushing about, the Tsar was continually making the sign of the Cross, ambassadors were being led up to receive goblets of wine from his hands, and suddenly, quite unexpectedly, it was all over, for the Tsar had given the signal bringing the feast to an end. "Then the ambassadors, and I with them, were rudely chased out of the room," Barberini wrote. "We were rushed out as hurriedly as the Scribes and the Pharisees from the temple. Passing through unlit rooms, mingling with drunken and rowdy crowds, we came to the palace stairs. Some sixty feet away the grooms with their horses were waiting to take their masters home, but between the stairs and the horses lay a sea of mud that came up to our knees. It was a dark night, there were no lights, and we had a long way to go."

The Separate Kingdom

FOR ALL THESE YEARS Ivan had been straining at the leash,
determined to exert his will, but finding himself at every turn
confronted by powerful forces which attempted to reduce him to
the status of a constitutional monarch. He saw himself as an
autocrat ruling by imperial decree, his wishes instantly obeyed, his
demands immediately accepted, his slightest whispers becoming
laws. A profound study of the Old Testament had demonstrated the
existence of divinely appointed rulers who took counsel from no
one but God. Why then should he listen to the advice of the
boyars? He detested advice, just as he detested the traditional
usages of the court which decreed a balance of power between the
Tsar and his boyars. What he wanted above all was the freedom to
rule as he saw fit, without the interference of anyone, as a pure
autocrat. He had wanted this almost from the beginning of his
reign, and as he grew older he wanted it more insistently and more
imperiously.

There was nothing in the least strange in this desire. He lived at a
time when the divine right of kings was still an acceptable dogma,
and Queen Elizabeth believed no less emphatically in her divine
right to rule. She chose her ministers well, used them to advantage,
trusted them, rewarded them generously, rarely executed them, and
sailed serenely from one crisis to another. Ivan distrusted his
ministers, and there was no serenity in him. In his ideal world there
were no ministers at all, only servants obeying his commands. A

he wrote in a letter to Prince Kurbsky, the Tsar receives his power from God, and therefore the boyars must offer him implicit obedience. The Tsar needs no instruction from anyone and he has the right to bestow his favors on anyone he pleases and to punish at his pleasure.

The boyars, and Prince Kurbsky, thought differently. They remembered the years when Ivan ruled righteously, in purity and penitence, submitting to the restraints of kingship. "He humbled himself and ruled well," Prince Kurbsky wrote of those years. The Tsar remembered only that he had been ill-treated. Writing to Prince Kurbsky in July 1564 he complained that the boyars not only took the government out of his hands, but they regulated his daily life in the minutest detail. From this intolerable situation he was determined to free himself.

Gradually there emerged the plan to create a separate kingdom, over which he would rule with absolute authority. He was a timid man, and therefore he embarked upon the plan cautiously, by stages, reluctant to advance too far before he had assured himself that each stage had been accomplished safely. He was a master of stratagems and deceptions, and he went about the creation of the new kingdom with extraordinary cunning. Not all the steps he took are known, and it is possible that for some weeks he did not know precisely what form the new kingdom would take. He liked to shroud his acts in mystery, and he enjoyed spreading rumors about his plans to test the reactions of the boyars, and as likely as not he would do something completely different. At all costs it was necessary to conceal his real intentions.

In the winter of 1564 Moscow was full of rumors that the Tsar was about to abdicate in favor of his ten-year-old son, thus releasing him for a life of contemplation and solitude in a monastery. "My soul is satiated with power," he is supposed to have said, "but I only desire to have power over myself, to remove myself from the cares and temptations of this world and to flee from situations which breed sinfulness." Albert Shlichting, who records these words, goes on to describe the Tsar's formal abdication. But nothing so simple as a formal abdication took place. Instead, the Tsar summoned the clergy and the nobles, lectured them on their behavior, accused them of disloyalty and treason, and even of wanting to hand over the Russian state to a foreign power, and there in the Great Hall of the Kremlin took off his crown and royal robes. He did not abdicate; he accused. The theatrical gesture was intended to inspire fear, and the crown and royal robes remained in his possession.

He addressed the clergy and the nobles about the middle of November 1564. During the following days his actions became even more ominous. He went around Moscow plundering the icons and holy banners in the churches, kissing them before they were piled high on his sledges. All that was most holy in Moscow he reserved for himself. Then, on Sunday, December 3, 1564, about two weeks after his last meeting with the clergy and the nobles, he summoned them again to meet him in the Uspensky Cathedral, where the Metropolitan Afanasy was presiding over the morning service. After the service the Tsar gave his blessing to the Metropolitan, the archbishops, bishops, priests, monks, princes, boyars, voyevodas, nobles, and merchants, who were all gathered outside the cathedral. They all kissed his hand and he made the sign of the Cross over them, and then, accompanied by the Tsaritsa Maria and his two sons, he departed.

It was a strange leave-taking, for he made it abundantly clear that he was going into a kind of exile, but never for a moment did he declare his intentions. When he went on pilgrimages he always traveled in state with a large retinue, but never before had he left Moscow burdened by so many holy images or by so much gold plate from his treasury. There was an uneasy feeling that some strange silent drama was being performed in the dead of winter. Those farewells on a savagely cold day boded ill for Moscow, for if he was going into exile it could be expected that he would exact some terrible retribution from the city. He was not the kind of person who would simply leave Moscow and vanish from sight. He was one of those who made their presence felt even when they were far away.

He reached Kolomenskoye the same day, announcing that he intended to take part in the celebrations for the Feast of St. Nicholas on December 6. With him went a small army of mounted men in full armor, and it was observed that the wives and children of his favorites accompanied him. With the exception of a few government officials, who were brought along for a special purpose, the Tsar's companions belonged to his private and intimate court. They were sinister men going on a sinister errand.

The celebrations for the Feast of St. Nicholas passed without incident, but then the weather suddenly changed. The sun came out, the ice melted on the rivers, the snow turned into slush, travel became impossible. Ivan and his large retinue were forced to remain in Kolomenskoye on the outskirts of Moscow for two weeks. The improvement in the weather did not improve the Tsar's temper.

When travel became easier, the Tsar set out for the Troitsa-Sergeyevsky Monastery where on December 21 he celebrated the memorial day of St. Peter the Metropolitan, who died in 1328. St. Peter was the first Metropolitan of Moscow, a man of great sanctity. Formerly the Metropolitan ruled the church from Vladimir. St. Peter was responsible for making Moscow the religious capital of the country. Ivan possessed great reverence for the saint, and the ceremonies took place in an atmosphere of pious exaltation. Meanwhile Ivan was working out the last details of his extraordinary plan to carve out a separate kingdom for himself, to be called the *Oprichnina*, from the word *oprich*, meaning "separate." It was the word used to describe the portion of a man's estate set apart for his widow, and Ivan may have chosen the word because it suggests both separation and bereavement. His new capital would be the former hunting lodge of Alexandrova Sloboda. His new ministers and servants would be known as *oprichniki*, "the separated ones," mercilessly ferocious and instantly obedient to his orders. They wore black gowns, rode black horses, carried brooms to signify that they intended to sweep away all treachery, and tied dogs' heads to their saddles or under the horses' necks to indicate their determination to savage their enemies.

On the road to Alexandrova Sloboda the Tsar punished some of the boyars and courtiers who had been ordered to accompany him. Lev Saltykov, Ivan Chobotov, and others were summarily dismissed, stripped of their robes of office, and ordered to return to Moscow. They were naked, or nearly naked, and it is not known how they survived the journey in the depth of winter. Lev Saltykov was the Master of the Armory, one of the five most important officials of the court; he superintended all court affairs and had little to do with the armory. His abrupt dismissal was a warning to the establishment. Boyars in high administrative positions were expendable.

About the same time Ivan sent two letters to Moscow by the hands of Konstantin Polivanov. In these letters Ivan announced his intention of residing permanently in Alexandrova Sloboda and of resigning rather than abdicating from the throne. One letter was addressed to the Metropolitan Afanasy, the other to the people of Moscow. The complete text of these letters has not survived, but we know from contemporary sources that the letter to the Metropolitan was intended to be read by the church hierarchy, the boyars, and members of the Tsar's court, and contained the inevitable vitriolic attack against them. He accused the church hierarchy of continually interceding for the lives of malefactors who deserved to be punished, "wherefore the Tsar and Grand Prince, not wishing to endure these many acts of treachery, has abandoned the Tsardom with a heavy heart, and now travels wheresoever God may lead him." He reminded the boyars that during his minority they committed many acts of treason and embezzled the state treasury. He accused them, too, of failing in their duty to defend Orthodox Christianity against its foreign enemies—Tatars, Lithuanians, and Germans. These same accusations were made in Ivan's letter to Prince Kurbsky written during the previous summer and in a speech to the people of Moscow delivered on the Red Square fifteen years earlier. He had not changed, and he would never change, but now at last he possessed a strange weapon forged in secret: the threat to create a separate kingdom. He would retain all his powers, he would not abdicate, he would abandon Moscow and go wherever God directed him to go, and he would resign from the government of Moscow, leaving it in the hands of the scoundrels who now held office, but only as long as he saw fit, for he would return and gather up his powers whenever he felt it was necessary. He wrote: "If God and the weather permit, I shall go to Alexandrova Sloboda and I commit the Tsardom into the hands of traitors. Nevertheless the time may come when I shall once more demand the Tsardom and take it back."

The intention of the letter was clear: to sow confusion into the ranks of the clergy and the boyars. He was Tsar and not Tsar; he had abdicated and not abdicated; he was content that Russia should be ruled by traitors, and at a time of his own choosing he would wrest it from them. By creating so much confusion he was giving himself the maximum freedom to maneuver.

In his letter to the people, Ivan wrote that he had no quarrel with them at all and they were not in disgrace. His quarrel was with their masters, the church hierarchy and the boyars. He was obviously attempting to drive a wedge between the people and their rulers, pretending that he stood on the sidelines. He was also hinting that it was to the advantage of the people to rise in rebellion against the ruling boyar families. Although the letter to the people did not provoke a rebellion, it caused, as he had hoped, great distress among them. According to the chronicles they came in droves to the Metropolitan Afanasy, saying: "Woe on us who have sinned before God and angered the Tsar by our many wrongdoings against him. To whom shall we turn now, and who will save us

A seventeenth-century engraving on the base of a silver candlestick, showing a mounted oprichnik with broom and dog's head.

from the attacks of foreigners? How can the sheep live without a shepherd? How can we endure without a Tsar?"

These letters were received in Moscow on January 3, 1565, when for over a month there had been no news from Ivan. There was such consternation that the Metropolitan Afanasy and the boyars decided to act at once, drawing up a petition to the Tsar begging him not to resign and arranging for a delegation of dignitaries to present the petition. It was learned that Ivan had at last reached Alexandrova Sloboda, which he had transformed into an armed camp. Since his real intentions were unknown, the petition was carefully designed to uncover them by asking him to make a public announcement mentioning the names of the people he regarded as traitors. The petition read:

> With grave reluctance and sorrow in our hearts we have learned from our Great Lord, who merits every praise, that he is displeased with us and especially that he is abandoning the Tsardom and us. We are but poor and inconsolable sheep without a shepherd, and the wolves, our enemies, surround us. We therefore request and beg him to see fit to change his mind.
>
> In the past nations have been conquered and left without rulers, but that a mighty Sovereign should abandon his loyal subjects and his Tsardom needlessly—such things are unheard of, and not to be read in books!
>
> If the Tsar knows of the existence of traitors, then he should proclaim their names and they must answer for their crimes, for our Lord has the right to punish them and to pass exemplary sentences upon them.
>
> Should the Tsar agree to hear our petition, we shall gladly submit ourselves to his will.

Such was the petition drawn up with great care by the Metropolitan with perhaps some assistance from the leading boyars and immediately dispatched to Ivan with the delegation, which was led by Pimen, Archbishop of Novgorod, and the Abbot Levky of the Chudov Monastery, a man known to be among Ivan's favorites. The Metropolitan remained in Moscow, but many of the important boyars including Prince Ivan Belsky and Prince Ivan Mstislavsky accompanied the delegation. Hundreds of nobles, officials, merchants, and ordinary people of Moscow went with them. Everything was being done so quickly that many did not have time to go home to eat and change their clothes. They made their way to Alexandrova Sloboda in the snow, in the freezing cold, holding up banners and singing hymns as though they were going on pilgrimage.

All the approaches to Alexandrova Sloboda were guarded, and at the village of Slotino the whole procession came to a halt, while the guards sent messengers to discover whether he was prepared to receive the petitioners. The message came back that he was prepared to receive only the leading members. Accordingly only seven or eight dignitaries were permitted to make the rest of the journey.[1] They spent the night at Slotino, and rode the remaining twenty miles to Alexandrova Sloboda the next day. All the time they were under close guard.

The reception given to the petitioners was cold, formal, courteous. They were treated as though they were ambassadors from a foreign state. Ivan listened to Archbishop Pimen's long speech on the manifest duty of the Tsar to uphold Orthodox Christianity, and how could he do this if he exiled himself from his people? If he abdicated, the true faith would inevitably be tainted with heresy, for he alone had the power to instill fear into the hearts of heretics. Gravely the Archbishop repeated the argument contained in the petition: if there were crimes and shortcomings committed by the people, then the Tsar should be empowered to set things right either by acts of mercy or by employing the most terrible punishments. Having read the letter and listened to the Archbishop's plea, the Tsar dismissed the petitioners, saying he would make his decision on the following day.

At the reception on January 5, 1565, Ivan was in a rancorous mood. He spoke about the interminable rebellions against the Tsar's majesty, which were recorded in the chronicles, and therefore there was no reason why he should recite them. From the time of Vladimir Monomakh to the present Russia had been full of traitors who wanted to dethrone the reigning Sovereign and put someone else in his place. Officers of his court were continually

---

[1] One of the most brilliant passages of Eisenstein's film on Ivan the Terrible shows the vast procession of petitioners winding through the snow and singing hymns, while Ivan gazes down at them from a high tower at Alexandrova Sloboda like an eagle in his eyrie. In fact, the main body of petitioners was stopped twenty miles away and only a handful of people were allowed to enter his presence.

negotiating secretly with foreign powers: the King of Poland, the Sultan of Turkey, and the Tatar Khans all had secret agents in his court. The traitors wanted to kill him in the same way that the Tsaritsa Anastasia had been killed. All this was well-known to them. Then why did they expect him to return to Moscow except under the most stringent conditions? Only if they accepted these conditions would he condescend to put aside his wrath against the Muscovites.

There were two conditions: the right to strike down anyone he considered a traitor, and the right to form a separate kingdom with its own army, its own boyars, nobles, secretaries, and officials. For the first time the petitioners heard the dreaded word Oprichnina. Out of Russia there would be carved a new kingdom reserved for his own use, where his followers, the oprichniki, would be granted estates commensurate with their rank, and these estates would necessarily have to be taken over from their present owners. Whole towns and provinces would be included within the Oprichnina for the upkeep of his own court and the courts of his sons. The rest of Russia, known as the *Zemshchina*, meaning "the dominion," would be ruled by the boyars in obedience to his wishes. Over the Oprichnina he would rule directly and absolutely, without any restraint whatsoever.

The dignitaries, when they heard these conditions, were relieved, for they feared that the conditions might have been more onerous. They thanked the Tsar, accepted his conditions, and promised to conduct their affairs according to his commands.

"Thus," commented a Livonian knight who took service under the Tsar, "they prepared the whip and the birch with their own hands, and all those brightly painted devil-masks before which all the spiritual and secular orders bowed down."

The dignitaries returned to Moscow expecting that Ivan would soon follow, taking up his residence in that part of the city now reserved for the Oprichnina, which included a large area to the northwest of the Kremlin, but excluded his own palaces. The only part of the Kremlin which he claimed for himself was an area "where the Tsaritsa's palace stood formerly, behind the Church of the Nativity and St. Lazarus, including all the cellars, kitchens and ice-houses as far as the Kuriatny Gate." Exactly why he chose this area is unknown, but he clearly desired to have a foothold within the Kremlin walls.

When Ivan returned to Moscow a month, or perhaps six weeks later—the exact date is unknown—he was a changed man, and scarcely recognizable, for he had lost a good deal of hair and beard. The uncharitable Livonian knight wrote that his hair and beard "had been devoured and destroyed by his rage and by his tyrannical soul," but it is at least possible that they had fallen out as a result of illness. To the assembled nobles and dignitaries of the Church, he explained why he had abdicated and then changed his mind, feeling it necessary to curb his anger and to act with mercy.

In his speech, which was recorded by his secretaries and inserted in the chronicle, he explained his views on the new Russian state henceforth to be divided between the Oprichnina and the Zemshchina. For the first time he announced his intention to bequeath the Oprichnina to his younger son, while the Zemshchina would be inherited by the Tsarevich, and he urged the boyars to prevent any disputes arising between his sons, for, as he said, "your task is to root out injustices and crimes, while at the same time upholding order, peace and unity."

Unity, however, was precisely what he refused to grant. The cumbersome machinery of a divided state was not calculated to produce either order or peace, and he seems to have realized that there were inherent difficulties in the division of power. On all matters concerning the Zemshchina the boyars were permitted to make the final decisions, but he reserved for himself the right to intervene in military matters and great affairs of state. He did not define the powers of the boyars, though his own powers were adequately defined, for he remained the Tsar and the owner of a vast private principality. For his expenses in running his principality he demanded that the Zemshchina should contribute 100,000 rubles, a vast sum in those days, equivalent to perhaps 10 million dollars. The assembled dignitaries publicly assented to the new tablets of the law, while privately agreeing among themselves that the division of powers was dangerous, cumbersome, and perhaps unworkable. No one dared to protest. They held the Tsar in such awe that they would have agreed to almost anything so long as he resumed the throne.

Their fears were soon justified, for on the day following the Tsar's speech from the throne Prince Alexander Gorbaty-Shuisky was arrested together with his seventeen-year-old son on a trumped-up charge of treason, and they were executed a few days later. According to Prince Kurbsky, the son was about to lay his head on the block when the father suddenly asked permission to be the first to be executed. This permission was granted, and when his head was struck off, the boy lifted it up and kissed it, saying: "I thank Thee, Jesus Christ our Lord, who has deemed us worthy to be executed in our innocence, being like unto Thee, the innocent lamb, who was also slain!"

A shiver of horror ran through Moscow, for no one could guess what secret reasons compelled Ivan to execute them. Prince Gorbaty-Shuisky was one of the heroes of the battle of Kazan; his daughter Irina was married to Prince Ivan Mstislavsky, another hero of the battle. Still another daughter was married to Nikita Zakharin, the younger brother of Anastasia. A few days after the execution Ivan sent 200 rubles to the Troitsa-Sergeyevsky Monastery to pay for prayers for the soul of Prince Gorbaty-Shuisky. In this way he reduced the burden of responsibility, for some of the burden now rested on the well-rewarded monks of the monastery he favored above all others.

Ivan's rage against the men he regarded as traitors was not exhausted by the murder of Prince Gorbaty-Shuisky. Those who were very close to him, those who had received special marks of his favor, and those who thought they were very safe were in mortal danger. Prince Peter Gorensky was an accomplished courtier, young, rich, and well-connected. He was one of the leading members of the Tsar's intimate circle, and in a testament written in 1561 Ivan nominated him to be one of the regents in the event of the Tsar's death. In March 1564 he was still in high favor, but in the fall of the same year he was out of favor and serving on the Lithuanian frontier. Ivan appears to have believed that Prince Gorensky was plotting against him. Orders were given for his arrest, but he fled with fifty of his retainers into Lithuania, only to be pursued and overtaken by Ivan's security forces, who executed him on the spot. He was impaled, and his retainers were all hanged. About a week later Ivan sent fifty rubles to the Troitsa-Sergeyevsky Monastery to pay for prayers for the soul of the prince.

Those who had incurred Ivan's displeasure in the past also suffered, victims of his long memory. Prince Simeon Rostovsky had always been troublesome. He had criticized Ivan's marriage to Anastasia, and during the following years he complained frequently about the appointments he received, saying they were unworthy of his high birth. In 1553, when the Tsar was thought to be dying, he favored the succession of Vladimir of Staritsa. In the same year it became known that he had spoken slightingly about the Tsar to the Lithuanian ambassador to Moscow and had even gone so far as to reveal some secrets of the Boyar Council. It was said too that he had advised the Lithuanian ambassador against making peace with Moscow. A year later he attempted to flee to Lithuania, was caught, found guilty of high treason, deprived of boyar rank, and sent into exile. Later he was pardoned, but though he received important positions he never regained the rank of boyar. In the spring of 1565 he was made governor of Nizhni-Novgorod. The Tsar intensely distrusted him, and sent thirty oprichniki to Nizhni-Novgorod, with orders to bring back his head.

The oprichniki set out from Moscow with enthusiasm. It was the time before the thaws, the roads thickly covered with ice, but they accomplished the journey in a few days. Arriving in Nizhni-Novgorod, they learned that the prince was praying in church accompanied by some of his servants and retainers. They rushed to the church, shouted, "Prince, you are the Tsar's prisoner!" and arrested him. The servants and retainers were led off to jail. The prince, realizing that he was powerless, threw down the staff of office, which he had received from the Tsar's hands and which he carried with him wherever he went. The oprichniki then tore off his clothes, leaving him naked, for it was inappropriate that a doomed man should be seen wearing the costly vestments of his high rank. He was then wrapped in a soiled gown, bound hand and foot, and placed on a sledge. For some reason it was decided that the execution should not take place in Nizhni-Novgorod, but on the ice-covered Vetluga River three or four miles away. Two or three oprichniki were sitting on the prince to prevent him from escaping, while others rode beside the sledge. Suddenly the small procession came to a halt and some men were ordered to chop the ice on the river. As though awakening from sleep, Prince Rostovsky asked

Alexandrova Sloboda

THE FORMER HUNTING LODGE at Alexandrova Sloboda now became the capital of the separate kingdom. Surrounded by a moat and a wooden palisade which was later faced with stone, it stood amid gloomy forests some seventy-five miles north of Moscow. Like all the royal hunting lodges it consisted of many buildings: there was the Tsar's palace, his chapel, offices for his ministers, guest houses, residences for his large retinue, barracks for his bodyguards, guard houses, and in addition there were prisons, warehouses, store houses, and dormitories for the servants, butchers, bakers, cooks, stewards, grooms, falconers, bear-keepers, storytellers, tailors, priests, clerks and their families, all those whose presence was necessary for the upkeep of a royal residence. During the years of the Oprichnina the hunting lodge at Alexandrova Sloboda grew in size and splendor; there were more and more buildings; new churches were built; wealth poured in; and soon it came to resemble a thriving town. *Sloboda* means "a large village." But the visitor from Moscow would recognize at once that the village had been transformed into a royal town where the builders were continually at work. The basic industry of the town was the generation of royal power.

In its remoteness and isolation Alexandrova Sloboda fitted Ivan's mood. Here he could live in seclusion, safe from the tumult of Moscow. No one could possibly reach the place without being observed, for there were forts and guard posts scattered along the approaches, and two high towers or belfries served as observation posts enabling the watchmen to survey the countryside. A river flowed past the palisade, and there were lakes and pools nearby.

Ivan's palace, built of stone and brick, stood on high ground, and so did the *terem*, where the Tsaritsa Maria lived with the womenfolk of the court. But the region was marshy and insalubrious and there were times when much of the area enclosed within the palisade was under water. Wooden causeways extended from the ornamental gate, so that visitors on foot would not get their feet wet. For Ivan, life went on very much as it went on in Moscow with some special refinements due to the special nature of the separate kingdom. The councillors met, ambassadors were received, and high officials were entertained at meals where the Tsar presided at a high table. In the middle of the dining room there was the inevitable grandiose display of gold plate and gold goblets. Rushes were strewn on the floor, while embroideries and painted curtains decorated the walls.

In Alexandrova Sloboda the Tsar lived in great state in a court much smaller and more manageable than the court in Moscow, and more responsive to his whims. The leading members of this court were the boyar Alexey Basmanov and Prince Afanasy Viazemsky. Basmanov, whom Prince Kurbsky blamed for many of the horrors of the Oprichnina, came from an ancient family and was chiefly remarkable for his extraordinary courage in the service of the Tsar; and Basmanov's son Fyodor, an exceptionally handsome youth, was also in the Tsar's trust. Basmanov was intelligent and totally unscrupulous, and the son was worthy of the father. He was a dissolute young man, and sometimes shared Ivan's bed.

Prince Afanasy Viazemsky descended from one of the minor princely families and unlike the Basmanovs, who had known Ivan intimately for the past six years, he had only recently come to the Tsar's attention. He had been living in the western provinces and therefore had no connection with the established court nobility. He owed his present position to his charm and his gift for flattery. Peter Zaitsev was another unscrupulous adventurer. He was one of the three men commanded to murder Prince Ivan Belsky in 1542 and his lack of scruple commended him to the Tsar. The Basmanovs, Viazemsky, and Zaitsev constituted the Council of Four who superintended the day-to-day operations of the oprichniki. There was also a body of councillors called the *Oprichnina Duma*, presided over by Prince Mikhail Temriukovich, the brother of the Tsaritsa.

Recruiting for the Oprichnina was a cumbersome and time-consuming process. Some 6,000 provincial nobles appear to have been interviewed, and their genealogies and those of their wives were cautiously examined. They were asked questions about their relationships with other princes and boyars, and interrogated about their loyalty to the Tsar. If they were approved, and if four trusted nobles from their own districts vouched for them, they were admitted into the ranks of the oprichniki. Never before had there been such a close investigation of provincial nobles. Ivan demanded and received absolute loyalty from these chosen members of the nobility, and if they were poor, he rewarded them with handsome estates expropriated from other nobles.

It was a time of massive expropriations and endless journeys. Those whose lands were expropriated were given new estates, usually far away. They were ordered to make their way to these new estates in the clothes they stood in, and no one was permitted to help them. The orders were harsh: "If any citizen in the towns or any peasant in the villages give shelter even for an hour to the sick or to noblewomen about to give birth, then he shall be executed without mercy and his body not buried, but left for the birds, the dogs and wild animals." The new estates given by the Tsar were no more than areas marked on a map scores of miles from the nearest cities. Once wealthy landowners and their families appear to have made the long journey on foot, living on the charity of peasants.

Young provincial noblemen, possessing no land, suddenly found themselves owning estates teeming with villages, because the Council of Four was satisfied that they would perform any deed demanded of them in the Tsar's name. Once accepted into the confraternity of the oprichniki, these nobles uttered a solemn oath to defend the Tsar at all costs. The oath, which has survived, read as follows:

> I swear to be loyal to my Lord the Tsar and to his kingdom, to the young Tsareviches and to the Tsaritsa, and I swear not to be silent about any evils I know of, those that I have heard or will hear about, which are meditated by this or that person against the Tsar and

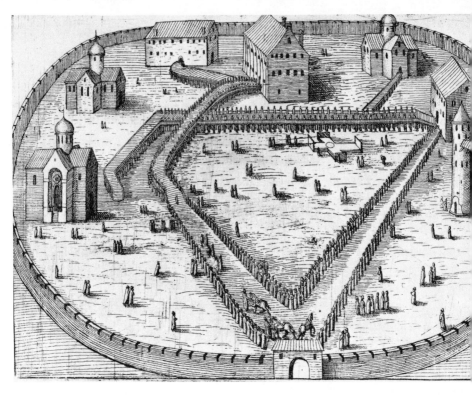

Alexandrova Sloboda, the walled fortress-palace. There were many more buildings than this rough sketch suggests. (From Jacob Ulfeld, *Legatio Moscovitica*, 1608, courtesy, the New York Public Library)

Grand Prince, his kingdom, the young Tsareviches and the Tsaritsa. I also swear on oath that I shall not eat or drink or have any dealings with, or have anything in common with, anyone from the Zemshchina. On this I kiss the Cross.

This was perhaps the milder form of the oath introduced at the beginning of the Oprichnina. In his *History* Prince Kurbsky speaks of a more fearful oath, which called upon the oprichnik to break away completely from his parents and relatives, his friends and brethren, so that he could serve the Tsar with total devotion.

Once admitted into the oprichniki, the nobleman found himself in a secret conspiratorial organization of vast scope and unlimited power. His life was organized to the last detail, but his rewards were commensurate with his duties. He was above the law, with power of life and death over everyone he encountered. His lawlessness was a right and privilege which he earned by entering the magic circle of

Alexandrova Sloboda, the dining room..The Tsar with the Tsarevich on his right sits at the center table. Five Danish diplomats can be seen sitting against the wall at top right. (From Jacob Ulfeld, *Legatio Moscovitica*, 1608, courtesy, the New York Public Library)

the Tsar; and his reward was wealth and power and as much blood as he cared to spill.

The oprichniki at Alexandrova Sloboda resembled the Knights Templar in their double roles as monks and warriors. All, including Ivan, wore the simple black robes of monks. They rose early, long before dawn, to attend the morning service where Ivan presided, and woe betide those who failed to appear! Unless they were excused by sickness, they were punished with eight days of penance or a brutal beating. The service lasted for three hours, from four to seven o'clock in the morning, and there was an hour's rest. The service was resumed at the stroke of eight and continued until ten o'clock, when they all breakfasted. Ivan, assuming the role of the watchful abbot, remained standing, while the rest sat. When they addressed him, they called him "brother," and he addressed them in the same way. They ate and drank well, and when they had finished, Ivan sat down to eat alone. So it went on day after day the long religious service followed by a breakfast where Ivan stood and watched and waited.

What he was waiting for was the opportunity to wreak vengeance on his imagined enemies. Hundreds of people had been rounded up by the oprichniki and led off to the prison chambers of Alexandrova Sloboda. Having eaten, Ivan made his way to the torture chamber where he would himself interrogate the victims and order those whose answers were unsatisfactory to be tortured. He took great pleasure in watching them in their agony. "He was always gay and cheerful and spoke excitedly when he attended these interrogations and tortures," report Taube and Kruse, two foreign mercenaries who joined the oprichniki. Albert Shlichting was another observer who carefully watched the behavior of the Tsar in the dungeons:

> The tyrant habitually watches with his own eyes those who are being tortured and put to death. Thus it happens frequently that blood spurts onto his face. He is not in the least disturbed by the blood but on the contrary he is exhilarated by it and shouts exultantly: "Goida! Goida!" ("Hurrah") and then all those around him shout: "Goida! Goida!" But whenever the tyrant observes someone standing there in silence, he immediately suspects that he is sympathetic to the prisoner, and asks why he is sad when he should be joyful, and then orders him to be cut to pieces. And every day people are killed at his orders.

Taube and Kruse relate that scarcely a day passed without the killing of twenty to forty people at Alexandrova Sloboda.

In the art of killing, the Tsar had become a master who exulted in his powers. If sufficiently roused, he would kill with his own hands but he preferred to let others do the killing for him. Sometimes he would read out the names of the people he wanted killed while he was in church, during the service, and there would be a written order with the name and manner of execution: strangling, drowning, burning, hacked to pieces. There were no special executioners. All the oprichniki were liable to be called upon to perform these offices at a moment's notice. They carried long black staffs with

...arp iron points with which they could knock a man off his feet ...nd then transfix him to the ground, while beneath their garments ...ng knives "the length of a forearm or even longer" were ...ncealed, and with these they could hack a man to pieces. "No ...ne protested against these executions," wrote Taube and Kruse. ...on the contrary they considered themselves fortunate to be able ...o do this good and holy work."

Ivan luxuriated in torture, pools of blood, stiffening corpses. This ...as the world where he was most at ease and enjoyed his greatest ...iumphs. More than one of the oprichniki attested to his full-...roated joy when the blood of his victims spurted on his face. It ...as as though he was happy only when he was inflicting the ...ltimate degradation on defenseless and innocent peoples. He was ...ad and evil, and there was no remedy for his madness. The evil ...ould endure through all the remaining years of his reign.

Sometimes we are given small clues to the nature of his madness. ...lbert Shlichting wrote that he always found it difficult to ride into ...lexandrova Sloboda because of the stench of the corpses. We ...now that the corpses often remained unburied for many days, and ...is happened because Ivan ordered it, because he believed that ...aitors deserved more than death, and because the decomposing ...odies were a warning to others. It was part of the punishment that ...ey should receive the ultimate degradation of being refused ...hristian burial.

Understandably he did not sleep well, and we are told that he ...ad to be coaxed to sleep by storytellers. They were three blind ...en who recited fables and ancient histories until at last he fell into ...fitful sleep.

Outwardly, when he went on pilgrimage or traveled through the ...ountry, Ivan presented himself as a man of imperturbable dignity. ...ery few people outside the ranks of the oprichniki knew what was ...appening at Alexandrova Sloboda. Thus when Ivan set out from ...loscow on September 21, 1565, for the annual pilgrimage to the ...roitsa-Sergeyevsky Monastery, he was greeted with the usual ...eference and respect. There were the usual gifts to the monks and ...eartfelt prayers for his safety. He went on to Rostov, Yaroslavl, ...nd Vologda, which he proposed to transform into a powerful base ...f operations for the Oprichnina, and then, following the pattern of ...arlier pilgrimages, he rode as far north as St. Kirill's Monastery near Beloozero. He returned to Moscow on December 27 to lear that Devlet Guirey, the Khan of the Crimea, had threatened th Russian fortress at Bolkhov on the southern frontier but had bee repulsed. Prince Ivan Belsky and Prince Ivan Mstislavsky, i command of the main army on the Oka River, had sent reinforce ments to the fortress only to learn that they were not needed. Ther was therefore nothing to fear from the Tatars.

By the spring of 1566 Russia was learning to adapt itself to th strange invention of the Oprichnina, which divided the country int arbitrary segments at the whim of the Tsar. The system was no working well, but the resources of the country were such that eve worse depredations could be tolerated. Ivan himself was please with his experiment and was quite prepared to moderate some o the penalties he had imposed on the nobility. When the Metropoli tan Afanasy and the Boyar Council petitioned him to permit Princ Mikhail Vorotynsky to return from his exile in Beloozero, h graciously assented and Prince Vorotynsky's vast estates were give back to him. Similarly he repealed the order to the nobles who ha been exiled to Kazan. They had only just settled in Kazan and wer now once more uprooted; and the complicated redistribution o their estates would occupy the government for many years to come Some got back their estates immediately, but most of them had t wait until bureaucracy had finished its work. The Estates Office i the Kremlin was working overtime.

Suddenly, while the Tsar was away from Alexandrova Slobod inspecting the southwest frontier, the Metropolitan Afanasy sub mitted his resignation "on account of an infirmity," and it wa sometimes thought that the infirmity he suffered from was too grea a knowledge of Ivan's crimes. Afanasy retired to the Chudo Monastery inside the Kremlin, and when Ivan returned from hi tour of inspection he appointed Herman Polev, Archbishop o Kazan, a distant descendant of the princes of Smolensk, to be th new Metropolitan. Prince Kurbsky described him as "a man o great physical stature, of pure and holy life, well versed in th Scriptures," adding that he was kind to the poor and steadfast i time of trouble.

Such a man would inevitably find himself at odds with the Tsar and this happened much sooner than anyone had expected Herman engaged the Tsar in a long conversation on the subject o he oprichniki immediately after his appointment; he spoke about God's punishment for men's sins, the Last Judgment, and the necessity for a Tsar to act justly in the eyes of all. The Tsar was impressed and recounted this conversation to the oprichniki, who were alarmed and frightened. If the Tsar followed Herman's advice, then the oprichniki would be disbanded and reduced to insignificance. Now they basked in the Tsar's favor and had full power to murder and rob as they pleased. Alexey Basmanov worked on the Tsar's sense of authority and convinced him that the new Metropolitan should be deprived of his office. The ceremonies of induction had not yet been performed; it was therefore a comparatively easy matter to unseat him. "You have not yet assumed office," the Tsar told him, "and yet already you are trying to make me your captive!" After being Metropolitan for two days, Herman Polev returned to Kazan to resume the conversion of the Tatars to the true faith.

It remained to appoint a new Metropolitan, and to the surprise of many Ivan chose a man who was even more saintly than Herman Polev. His choice fell on Philipp Kolychev, Abbot of Solovetsky Monastery, in the far north. The monastery lay on the small island of Solovki in the White Sea. Ivan did not immediately announce his choice; the abbot was first summoned to Moscow so that Ivan could have the benefit of his "spiritual counselling."

When he reached Moscow early in July 1566 the abbot was dumbfounded to learn that he was about to be appointed the Metropolitan of all Russia. He refused, saying, "The Tsar should not entrust a great cargo to so small a ship." He then asked to be allowed to return to his monastery in the far north, but Ivan insisted that no one else could fill the position. Finally Philipp Kolychev agreed, making one condition: that the Oprichnina be abolished. "I will obey your wish," he said, "but you must first satisfy my conscience. There must be no Oprichnina. I cannot give you my blessing, seeing that the country is in so much anguish." With great difficulty the Tsar succeeded in controlling his anger. "Do you not know," he said, "that my people desire only to devour me? There are people close to me who are preparing to destroy me!"

Such words indicated that Ivan was in the grip of an obsession for which there was no cure, and Philipp Kolychev sensibly returned to the subject of the Oprichnina, thinking that its abandonment might at least help the Tsar to live more peacefully. The Tsar lost patience and ordered him to be silent. The meeting ended in a deadlock: both the Tsar and the priest had laid down their conditions, which were irreconcilable. This became known to the boyars and bishops, who were desperate to have Philipp Kolychev as their Metropolitan on any conditions, even the condition that he maintain silence about the Oprichnina, for they hoped that his presence would act as a shield against oppression. If he rejected the pleas of the boyars and the bishops, he lay open to the charge that he was proud and obstinate. If he accepted the position on the Tsar's terms, he could expect to live dangerously. Finally on July 20 he signed a document in which he promised not to interfere "in the Oprichnina and the Tsar's domestic affairs" and five days later he was consecrated Metropolitan of all Russia in the Uspensky Cathedral.

After the consecration the Metropolitan delivered a sermon in which he said that rulers should act justly, reward those who merited rewards, and be fatherly toward their subjects. He spoke of "the abominable flatterers" who crowd around the throne and seek to blind the mind of the ruler, to pamper him, to pander to his passions, to praise those who are unworthy of praise and disparage those who are praiseworthy. He went on to speak of the transitoriness of earthly glory and of the victories of "unarmed love" which are accumulated through good deeds and are more glorious than victories on the battlefield. He said, "Silence may bring the soul to sin and cause the death of the entire people." The words were barbed, but the Tsar listened quietly and showed only courtesy to the new Metropolitan.

The battle was engaged, but in silence. The Metropolitan Philipp, armed with spiritual weapons, would continue to wage a strange underground war against the Tsar, armed with weapons of terror and oppression. There could be only one end to this war: the martyrdom of the Metropolitan. It was a fate which he appears to have accepted cheerfully, believing that by quietly opposing the Tsar he was serving the Russian people.

Meanwhile Ivan continued to refine and embellish his ideas on the Oprichnina. He was determined to push these ideas to their furthest limits and thus to alienate himself completely from the people. He was no longer in his own eyes the ruler of Russia but only of a segment of Russia that resembled pieces of a jigsaw puzzle, selected by him without any coherent boundaries to be his own private domain. He had abandoned the Kremlin palaces but decided to build a new Oprichnina Palace nearby, just outside the Kremlin wall, in the Oprichnina region of Moscow beyond the Neglinnaya River. In May 1556 the architectural plans were ready and he gave orders for the new palace to be built in the quickest possible time. Whole streets of houses were expropriated and then torn down, and by the end of the year the palace was almost completed. The walls were eighteen feet high and formed a square whose sides measured eight hundred feet. There were three gates each surmounted by carved emblems representing a double-headed eagle between two lions. The eagle was painted black and the lions' eyes were set with mirrors. Exactly what he intended to convey by this new emblem was unclear, but Heinrich Staden, a German mercenary who described the Oprichnina Palace at some length, says the lions had wide-open mouths. Perhaps the lions represented the spirit of the oprichniki roaring out their defiance of the world around them.

Within that vast square there were the usual appurtenances: a debtors' prison, kitchens, cellars, bathhouses, ice houses, stables, and administrative quarters. Staden adds the curious information that Ivan had a small cottage built in one corner of the square and it was his practice to take breakfast and lunch in this cottage. The wall near the cottage was a little lower than elsewhere, so that there was more sunlight and so that he could catch the morning breeze. Because the square was damp, it was strewn with white sand.

Although the palace and all the other buildings were made of wood, only the best workmen were employed and only the best materials were used, with the result that it was prodigiously costly. Staden says that it cost so much that some of the Zemshchina people wished it would burn down, and when he heard of this Ivan told his oprichniki that he would give them a fire that they would not quickly put out.

While the Oprichnina Palace was being built, in August or early September, some three hundred people led by Prince Vasily Pronsky, Ivan Karamyshev, and Krestianin Bundov took their lives in their hands and presented a petition to the Tsar, urging that the

Oprichnina be abolished. Prince Pronsky belonged to a famous and well-established princely family, Karamyshev to the nobility, Bundov to the lesser nobility. They therefore represented the entire spectrum of the nobility. Albert Shlichting has preserved the sense and perhaps the words of the petition:

> Most illustrious Tsar and Lord, why have you given orders to kill our innocent brethren? We have all served you loyally and spilled our blood for you! This is the way you reward us for our services. You throw the oprichniki at our throats, they pluck our brethren and blood relatives from our midst, they commit outrages against us, they beat, stab, and strangle us, and in the end they will kill us all.

No doubt there was a good deal more of this, none of it especially palatable to Ivan, who flew into a rage and ordered the entire deputation arrested. Five days later, having mastered his anger sufficiently to enable him to determine how many of them should be punished and what the punishments should be, he gave them over to the oprichniki. Pronsky, Karamyshev, and Bundov were decapitated, others had their tongues cut out, while some lost their arms and legs, and still others were set free; and some days later, remembering that he had let so many free, he ordered them rearrested and cut to pieces. Prince Kurbsky wrote that about two hundred nobles and officers in the army met their deaths for having petitioned the Tsar to put an end to the Oprichnina.

So large a massacre could not be concealed, and Ivan seems to have been concerned about the effect of these massacres on people abroad; and when in February 1567 he sent ambassadors to Lithuania, he cautioned them to explain that Prince Pronsky and Ivan Karamyshev had been executed justly because they were found plotting against the Tsar. They were to say, "The Tsar is indeed merciful and guilty men must always face execution."

As always, the Tsar was so certain that people were plotting against him that he scarcely troubled to think seriously about the plotters. Outside the Oprichnina, whose members had sworn a special oath of loyalty to him, everyone could be assumed to be guilty. When he told the Metropolitan Philipp, "Do you not know that my people desire only to devour me?" he was saying what, in his overheated mind, he firmly believed.

All through this period he was relentlessly suspicious, apprehensive, and murderous. Danger lay everywhere; there was safety only in flight, in finding some hiding place beyond the reach of his enemies. He spoke of leaving Russia or of becoming a simple monk or of abdicating and becoming a private citizen. Rumors of these unformed plans reached the Zemshchina and generated talk about the succession, and when the Tsar heard that people were talking about his successor, he became more apprehensive than ever. The oprichniki, who feared for their own safety if the Tsar abandoned the throne, did everything possible to keep the Tsar's suspicions at fever pitch. They invented rumors, imagined plots, produced false witnesses, and murdered at their leisure. The Tsar's enemies were much closer to him than he knew.

On January 12, 1567, he made his ceremonial entry into the new Oprichnina Palace, which had been built at such vast expense. Three weeks later, grown weary of the palace, he left Moscow and set out on a long pilgrimage which brought him at last to St. Kirill's Monastery in the far north. To the abbot he confided his desire to abandon the throne and to become a monk, and he gave the abbot 200 rubles for the preparation of his cell. Since it was unthinkable that he would find peace of mind in a plain, undecorated cell, he arranged later in the year to send gold plate, icons, and crosses to the monastery "for the furnishing of his cell." During the journey he spent some time at Vologda, where stone walls and towers were being built and the whole city was being transformed into a powerful fortress. A new cathedral in honor of St. Sophia was also being built. Of the three Oprichnina fortresses—the new palace in Moscow, Alexandrova Sloboda, and Vologda—the last was by far the strongest, and it was here that he expected to fight his last ditch battle against his enemies.

When he returned to Moscow at the end of June 1567 he was confronted with a real plot instigated by King Sigismund Augustus. He learned that four of the greatest dignitaries in Russia—Prince Ivan Belsky, Prince Ivan Mstislavsky, Prince Mikhail Vorotynsky, and the boyar Ivan Cheliadnin—had received messages from the King inviting them to come over to the other side. The families of Belsky and Mstislavsky belonged originally to a long line of Lithuanian princes and were distantly related to Sigismund Augustus; it was therefore not altogether surprising that an attempt should have been made to wean them away from Russia. These letters, brought to Moscow by Ivan Kozlov, a former Muscovite who served as a secret envoy of the King, were at once shown to Ivan, who proceeded to compose suitable replies in his own characteristic style. Sigismund, reading the letters, would have no difficulty recognizing their real author. Simultaneously the four Russian dignitaries had received letters from Gregory Hotkevich, the commander of the Lithuanian army, and Ivan wrote answers to these letters, ordering that they should be signed by the Russians who received them. Altogether Ivan wrote eight separate letters.

Disgusted, indignant, enraged, Ivan wrote in tones of unrelieved fury, as though calling upon God to witness the treachery of a foreign King. Pretending to be Prince Belsky, he wrote:

> We have carefully read your letter and we understand it well. You have written in the manner of a procurer, swindler and scoundrel. Surely it is beneath the dignity of a great ruler to start a quarrel between sovereigns in this way! What you cannot acquire in honest battle you try to achieve by surreptitious means, darting snakelike upon your prey!
>
> You should know that the will, the mercy and the hand of God uphold the autocracy of our Tsar, and bless us who are his worthy councillors. We cannot be destroyed by a little gust of wind or even by a great storm because we stand upon the strong foundations of the Church, which was established by Christ, and the very gates of Hell will not overcome it. That is why our autocratic Tsar and we who are his principal councillors do not fear destruction. As His Majesty the Tsar, who is our lord, grants favors to his loyal councillors and shows them the appropriate honor, so do we, who form his Council, demonstrate our loyalty and deepest submission to the unconstrained power of the Autocrat.

At every point Ivan betrays his authorship, and there can even be detected a note of wry amusement mingled with overweening pride as he paces the floor of the royal apartment and dictates those letters which, pretending to come from his subordinates, celebrate his own majesty, his power, his glory, and his obsessions.

One of his chief obsessions was free will, or rather the total lack of free will in a world which must obediently follow God's designs. Thus when King Sigismund Augustus mentioned in his letter to Prince Belsky that God gave men freedom and dignity, Ivan replied angrily that God gave Adam freedom but all later generations were deprived of their freedom as a result of Adam's sin; and if Sigismund Augustus did not understand this, he was palpably ignorant. Ivan wrote:

> You say that God created man and gave him freedom and dignity, but what you have written is far from the truth. Truly Adam, the first man, was granted power and free will, but God commanded him not to eat the fruit of the tree. Since he broke this commandment, he was severely punished. In this way his power was taken from him and he fell from grace: from light into darkness, from naked splendor to garments made of skins, from leisure to hard labor for his daily bread, from immortality to mortality, from life to death. And later God sent the Flood on the unclean people, and after the Flood he commanded that no soul should eat blood, and then after they raised the Tower of Babel he scattered the people, and then commanded Abraham to be circumcised as a sign of faith, and then to Isaac and later to Jacob he uttered his commandments, and then He gave to Moses the tablets of the law for the justification and purification of men, and in *Deuteronomy* He proclaimed damnation unto death to transgressors, and this same truth was established by Jesus Christ, who also ordered the punishment of transgressors.
>
> So now, Brother, you see there never was any freedom and what you have written is far from the truth. And what good is it, Brother, if your nobles have freedom to make you a swindler and urge you to append your signature to these follies?

Ivan was clearly enjoying himself as he wrote these interminable vituperative letters concerning the sinfulness of men, especially the Lithuanians, and the ultimate virtue of the autocrat "who acts for the good of his subjects, while those who lack the Tsar's authority stumble like drunken men and do no good to anyone." The Tsar stood above all men, as God stood above the Tsar. It was a lesson he hoped Sigismund Augustus would learn by heart.

Again and again Sigismund Augustus had argued that Ivan had brought so much evil to Russia that good and sensible men had only one recourse: to escape, to come over to his side. So, pretending to be Vorotynsky, Ivan thundered that there was no evil, there was no Oprichnina, no one was being harmed so long as he obeyed the law, and only traitors were being executed. Only the malicious and the envious could harbor such thoughts. As for Sigismund Augustus, he was no better and no wiser than "the godless kings" of the past like Nebuchadnezzar, Sennacherib, and Chosroes, men of devilish pride and appalling ambitions. Ivan pretending to be Vorotynsky, writes to Gregory Hotkevich concerning Sigismund Augustus's belief that Ivan had brought about a reign of terror in Russia:

> Being possessed by the devil, you wrote that your king heard tales about the senseless cruelty of our Tsar and about his unjust persecutions and merciless rages against his Christian subjects. What kind of diabolical nonsense is this? Is it permitted, does God allow other men to dictate the laws of a foreign country? And as for you who are ignorant of the law and not only criminals but apostates as well, how can it be permitted to you? How dare you speak, you whelp of the devil, in such an improper manner about His Majesty the Tsar? Our Tsar is a true Orthodox ruler and wisely directs his country; he favors the good and punishes the bad, and of course traitors are executed in all countries.

As we watch Ivan writing these letters, we observe a strange transformation: he is grimacing with rage, but painted on his face there is another and larger grimace. The rage is real but the greater rage is artificial, as he whips himself up into a prodigious and calculated fury. The insults, the innuendoes, the diatribes are all timeworn; he has used them so often before that they no longer startle. The rhetoric was becoming mechanical, and he was more dangerous than he had ever been.

In September 1567, not long after writing these letters, Ivan set out to attack Lithuania, staying first at the Troitsa-Sergeyevsky Monastery to pray at the tomb of St. Sergius, and then joining the Zemshchina army at Novgorod. He went with a large retinue which included the Tsarevich Ivan, Prince Afanasy Viazemsky, Peter Zaitsev, and the young Fyodor Basmanov. The names of two other oprichniki appear on the official lists of his retinue: they were Maliuta Skuratov and Vasily Griaznoy. At this time they occupied very minor positions, though they were destined to supplant his favorites and to become the most dreaded men in Russia. Maliuta Skuratov came from the petty nobility and owned hereditary estates seventy miles from the Lithuanian frontier. Vasily Griaznoy—his surname means "muddy"—also came from the petty nobility and owned hereditary estates in the province of Rostov

A large army stood poised at Novgorod for an attack on
Lithuania. There was an atmosphere of ferocious excitement at the
prospect of war with a well-armed and well-disciplined foe, and
then quite suddenly the excitement was dissipated in frustration.
The Tsar abruptly cancelled the invasion. He had, in fact, excellent
reasons for doing so—the weather was bad, sufficient artillery had
failed to arrive in time, a plague was raging in Livonia, and there
was an absence of provisions in the border towns. Worse still,
Sigismund Augustus was known to be preparing an invasion of
Russia and it was thought advisable that the Russian army should
go over to the defensive. Ivan returned to Alexandrova Sloboda in
an unusually somber mood. For some time nothing had been going
well, frustrations were piling on frustrations, he was at odds with
the world.

At such times Ivan had recourse to his most powerful weapon—
murder. He was not content to murder those who had served him
well, but he must bring about the destruction of their entire
families, kill all their servants, burn and pillage their houses and
estates. A new and even more terrifying campaign of mass murder
was now unleashed on Russia.

The Blood Flows

IF WE COULD LOOK into Ivan's mind when he returned t
Alexandrova Sloboda, we would find it choked with suspicions an
alive with cruelties. There had once been some brightness in hi
mind, but now it gleamed fitfully, like the small flames that danc
over the dying embers, flickering and menacing. He could still g
through the motions of ruling, but there was something strangel
mechanical in all his actions. Murder, too, had become mechanica
He was not so much acting as reacting to ever-present frustration
and an overwhelming sense of his own unworthiness.

At the age of thirty-seven he had become an alien in his ow:
land. The sense of alienation, his difference and remoteness fror
ordinary people, had of course always been there and he coul·
never entirely escape from the knowledge of his own majesty. Bu
now there could be detected a new and more profound alienatio·
which expressed itself in a desire to escape from Russia altogethe·
in his creation of a separate kingdom, and his repeated hints that h·
would give the crown to a foreigner. He was playing with th·
thought of abandoning the world he had known since his child
hood, and found comfort in the idea of living in a monk's cell o:
the shores of the White Sea. All the ceremonies of power wer·
becoming meaningless as he searched without success for an escap·
route worthy of an emperor. But there are no escape routes worth·
of an emperor except on the battlefield. He was a physical coward
and therefore a glorious death on the battlefield never appealed t·

him. He must continue to live, and there were few satisfactions in living. But he could give himself up to cruelties that excite the nerves and discover strange consolations in the contemplation of people dying in agony. This was the drug he employed to ease the pain of living, and it was provided in abundance by the oprichniki. Terror became his entertainment, and during the following years he destroyed people more ruthlessly and in greater numbers than ever before.

He now stood so far above the laws that it was as though the law had no existence, and so far above the flesh that it was as though flesh and its sorrows had no existence. Torture, which had always fascinated him, now obsessed him. He was continually inventing new and more excruciating forms of torture, while he filled the emptiness of his life with imaginary enemies, imaginary plots, imaginary crimes.

In later years he would say that the oprichniki had misled him and that he was as much their victim as the innocent people they tortured to death. He claimed that he had never really ordered those innumerable executions and he would pretend to a grief he had never felt when he wrote to the monasteries asking the monks to pray for the souls of the dead. Finally he would turn against the oprichniki and destroy them as calmly and mechanically as he had destroyed the poor devils who were tortured to death in the cellars of the Oprichnina Palace. He had no mercy for anyone, and this total absence of mercy was only another sign of his alienation from the world.

In time a myth grew up that Ivan was pursuing a carefully formulated social and political policy to bring about the annihilation of the boyar class. It was a myth that gave some comfort to Stalin, who was engaged in liquidating the *kulaks*, the more prosperous peasants who rejected the idea of working in the collective farms. The Russian historian Robert Wipper wrote a book idealizing Ivan for his wide-ranging understanding of the social forces at work and for his determination to destroy the oppressive boyars and to inaugurate a new and more egalitarian social system. But in fact Ivan had no understanding of the social forces at work; he destroyed blindly, impassively, scarcely caring who was destroyed, like a maniac.

Ostensibly the reason for the new wave of terror was the

discovery of another plot implicating high officials of the court. The oprichniki told Ivan that Prince Belsky and Prince Mstislavsky were implicated. Ivan was not convinced of the guilt of these two princes of royal blood, saying, "I and these two comprise the three pillars of Moscow and on us rests the whole state." But beyond the circle of royal princes he permitted himself to believe there was treachery everywhere.

The mild-mannered Kazarin Dubrovsky, the assistant secretary of the treasury, was executed. He was sitting quietly in his house with his two sons when the oprichniki broke in, killed them, and threw the bodies into the well. They also killed his servants and retainers, and went on to kill Dubrovsky's brothers and their entire families.

Ivan Cheliadnin, the former governor of Moscow, renowned for his kindness and gentleness, had long been in disfavor with Ivan who sent him to govern Polotsk to get him out of the way. He was one of those who received letters from King Sigismund Augustus and Gregory Hotkevich. Heinrich Staden said of him: "He willingly helped the poor to find justice quickly." He was now about sixty and had a great career behind him. Suddenly Ivan summoned him to Moscow, dispossessed him of all his valuables, his clothes, his properties, even his household utensils, and then ordered him to fight the Tatars. Cheliadnin, now a pauper, begged a horse from a monk and set out for the southern front, where he remained until on September 11, 1568, he received another summons to Moscow.

He must have known he was doomed, for he said farewell to his wife and close friends before he went to the Kremlin palace, but he could not imagine the fate reserved for him. The Tsar ordered him to be dressed in royal robes and to mount the throne with the scepter in his hands. Thereupon the Tsar doffed his hat and knelt before Cheliadnin in homage, saying, "This is what you have been wanting all along—to be Grand Prince of Moscow in my place. Now rejoice and enjoy the power you were thirsting for!" There was a pause, and then the Tsar rose to his feet, and said, "Just as it is in my power to establish you on the throne, so it is in my power to remove you from it!" Then he seized a dagger and struck Cheliadnin several times in the chest. Then, seeing that he was not yet dead, Ivan ordered the guards to finish him off.

Russian cavalry. (From Herberstein's *Rerum Moscoviticarum Comentarii*)

At the Tsar's orders the body of Cheliadnin was unceremoniously dragged across the Kremlin and dumped in the middle of the
Red Square for all to see. There followed for six weeks a reign of
terror directed against all the nobles who might conceivably have
some connection with Cheliadnin. For some reason the Tsar was
merciful toward Cheliadnin's wife, who was sent off to a nunnery,
but all Cheliadnin's servants were killed by drowning. Some three
hundred people living on his estate at Kolomna were also drowned.
The oprichniki were permitted to go on a long rampage. The estates
of the nobles around Moscow who were known to be friendly to
Cheliadnin were devastated in sudden raids, and at the Tsar's
orders the wives were abducted, thrown into waiting carts, and
carried off in triumph to Moscow. Prince Afanasy Viazemsky,
Maliuta Skuratov, and Vasily Griaznoy were placed in charge of
these expeditions, which usually took place at night and with the
assistance of small armies of musketeers. The houses of officials,
merchants, and scribes were also devastated and their wives, too,
were thrown into the carts.

The Tsar took the more beautiful wives to himself and distributed the rest among his entourage. Some were passed on to the
musketeers. Albert Shlichting relates that of some five hundred
women gathered in these expeditions, the Tsar kept fifty for himself
and five hundred horsemen were commanded to guard them. Those
who pleased him he kept; the rest were thrown into the river. From
time to time the survivors of the women who had been rounded up
for the pleasure of the Tsar and the oprichniki were returned to
their homes, always at night and in great secrecy. Some women
killed themselves, while others died of shame.

In Ivan's eyes the wives of traitors deserved to be raped, and in
taking these women he was simply inflicting a necessary punishment.

Ivan himself rode with the oprichniki on some of these expeditions, gave orders, and saw that executions took place in the
manner he desired. Thus when he came to one of Cheliadnin's
estates he sought out the soldiers, ordered them to be stripped
naked, locked them up in a house, and blew up the house with
gunpowder.[1] Shlichting says the Tsar was greatly amused with this

---

[1] Ivan Cheliadnin owned vast estates—in the province of Beloozero alone he owned 120

new form of execution and the sight of the bodies flying through the air. For the women on the estate he invented still another form of execution. They were stripped and herded into the woods like cattle, and then the oprichniki went hunting after them, torturing and killing all of them. Another form of entertainment was to bring chickens to the execution ground, and when the chickens were let loose, the naked women and girls were ordered to catch them. While they were running after the squawking chickens, they were shot down with arrows.

On one occasion a nobleman, Nikita Kazarinov, was arrested and brought to Alexandrova Sloboda wearing a monk's robes. Ivan gazed at him speculatively and said: "He is an angel, and therefore it is proper that he should fly to Heaven." Then he ordered the man to be tied to a barrel of gunpowder and blown up. Ivan, as a connoisseur of mass murder, had learned that it is easier to kill when the victims are deprived of their human dignity.

All through the summer and autumn the reign of terror continued. The oprichniki were now in the ascendant, murdering, looting, raping as they pleased. Secret death lists were compiled, and every day small groups of privileged assassins, numbering from ten to twenty, sallied forth from the Oprichnina Palace to carry out their orders. They rode on swift horses, wore coats of mail under their long black cloaks, were armed with heavy axes and swords, and carried the familiar emblems—the broom stuck in a quiver and a dog's head tied to the saddle. They were the privileged agents of the terror. "None of the victims," wrote Taube and Kruse, "knew what crime he had committed, or when he would die, or whether he had been condemned to death. Thus each man went unsuspectingly to work, to the courts and the offices, and suddenly the oprichniki would descend upon him, strangle him or cut him to pieces in the street, at the gates, or in the marketplaces, although he was quite innocent. The bodies were left to lie on the ground and no one was permitted to bury them. The marketplaces and the streets were so filled with corpses that the people, and the foreigners too, could not go about their work, not only because they were afraid but also because of the unbearable stench."

---

villages. On every estate there were men trained for military duty who were called up in the event of war.

Mass murder had become a habit recklessly pursued by a Tsar who cared only for inflicting punishment on his own people. As usual, he busied himself thinking up refinements to murder, and he discovered a surprisingly large number of them. A woman was hanged on her own gatepost. He ordered that her husband should pass through the gate without showing any sign of emotion, otherwise he too would be hanged. A woman was hanged from the roof beam above her dining table, and her family was ordered to take their meals at the table. This kind of thing went on all over Russia.

Only one person was in a position to protest and to be listened to. This was the Metropolitan Philipp, who begged the Tsar to put an end to these meaningless massacres. The Tsar answered, "Those who are close to me have risen up against me and seek to do evil to me. Then what business of yours is it to give me advice?" Philipp answered that it was a sin to encourage evil men and that the Tsardom was in danger as a result of their actions. He attempted to convene a synod of bishops who would deliver a public warning to the Tsar, but only Herman, Archbishop of Kazan, supported him. The others were too terrified to act, and one of them, Pimen, Archbishop of Novgorod, reported secretly to the Tsar that Philipp was behaving treacherously. The bishops remained silent; the Tsar was forewarned; the fate of Philipp was sealed.

Philipp's opportunity to confront the Tsar publicly came on Sunday, March 22, 1568, in the Uspensky Cathedral. The Tsar and his guard of oprichniki entered the cathedral dressed in black, with black cloaks and high-peaked black caps. The Tsar made his way to the Metropolitan's throne and stood there, awaiting a blessing. There was no blessing. The Metropolitan was gazing at an icon of the Savior, refusing to pay any attention to Ivan, although conscious of his presence. Finally some boyars came up and said, "Holy father, the Tsar is here! Give him your blessing!" And then the Metropolitan turned slowly toward Ivan and in the presence of all the clergy and the boyars he said:

"I do not recognize the Orthodox Tsar in this strange dress, and I do not recognize him in the actions of his government. To what limits have you gone, O Tsar, to place yourself beyond the reach of a blessing? Fear the judgment of God, O Tsar! We are now offering up the bloodless sacrifice to the Lord, while the blood of innocent

hristians is being spilt beyond the altar! Since the day when the
un first shone in the heavens, no one has ever seen or heard a
god-fearing Tsar persecuting his own countrymen so ferociously!"

The words of the Metropolitan, preserved in the chronicles
written by priests, were remembered also by Taube and Kruse, who
recorded the same words with only slight variants. The Metropolitan's voice was harsh and somber as he went on:

"Even in heathen kingdoms law and justice prevail, and there is
compassion for the people—but not here! Here the lives and
possessions of the people are unprotected, everywhere there is
pillage, everywhere there is murder, and all this is perpetrated in the
name of the Tsar! You sit high on your throne, but there is a God
who judges us all. How will you stand before His judgment seat,
stained with the blood of the innocent and deafened by their
screams under torture! Even the stones under your feet cry out for
vengeance! I speak, O Tsar, because I am a shepherd of souls and I
fear only the one and only God!"

Trembling with fury, Ivan struck the ground with his iron-tipped
staff.

"Do you dare to challenge my will?" he shouted. "It would be
better for you if you were more in agreement with us!"

"Then where would be my faith?" the Metropolitan answered.
"The sufferings of Our Saviour and His commandments were vain,
I remained silent. I am not grieving for those innocents who have
suffered—they are God's martyrs! I am grieving for your soul!"

Ivan was too angry to speak, and therefore made menacing
gestures. Once again he struck the ground with his staff. Then when
he had sufficiently composed himself to say what was on his mind,
he said in a terrible voice: "Up to now I have spared you traitors to
no purpose! From now on I shall behave as you depict me!"

The Metropolitan showed no sign of fear.

"I am a stranger and a pilgrim on the earth, like all the priests,"
he answered, "and I am ready to suffer for the truth. And if I
remained silent, where would be my faith?"

Hearing this, the Tsar stormed out of the cathedral, followed by
the oprichniki in their black gowns.

On the following day Ivan ordered the arrest of all the principal
members of the Metropolitan's court. They were tortured and
interrogated, but no incriminating evidence was found. It was

decided to invoke the assistance of Pimen, the Archbishop
Novgorod, who dearly wanted to be installed as Metropolitan of
Russia. One day Pimen confronted the Metropolitan in tl
cathedral and said: "You are making accusations against the Ts
and all the time you are committing evil." The Metropolita
replied: "You are trying to seize my throne—you, who will soc
lose your own!" It was becoming increasingly clear to Ivan that
attempts to depose Philipp would fail unless extraordinary mea
ures were taken. It was necessary to act cautiously because tl
Metropolitan was venerated and revered by the people of Moscov

On July 28, 1568, a strange incident occurred at the Novodevicl
Monastery, where the Metropolitan was presiding over the celebr
tions in honor of the feast day of the monastery. Ivan and h
bodyguard of oprichniki attended the celebrations and took part
the customary procession around the monastery walls led by pries
bearing crosses, icons, and banners. During the procession tl
Metropolitan turned and observed that one of the oprichniki w
wearing the round skull cap worn by the Tatars. Since it was alwa
the custom for the laity to remain bareheaded while taking part
processions and since the skull cap was associated with Islam, tl
Metropolitan concluded that the oprichnik was deliberately moc
ing the Christian faith, and in his anger he turned to the Tsar ar
said, "When we are glorifying our God and His words are beii
read in affirmation of our Christian faith, it is proper that m
should remain uncovered. Whence comes this Tatar custom? L
not all of us who are present profess the same faith?"

"Who has dared to do this?" Ivan asked.

"Someone in your suite," the Metropolitan answered.

Already the man had slipped the Tatar cap off his head, ar
when Ivan turned round he saw that all the oprichniki we
bareheaded. It occurred to him that the Metropolitan had simp
invented the incident in order to admonish him and he began
abuse Philipp, calling him a liar, a traitor, and an evildoer, cursii
him and threatening to expose him. Yet, for the moment, he cou
do nothing. To rid himself of the Metropolitan it was necessary
have the Church on his side, and the Church was still devoted to
saintly Metropolitan.

But the Tsar was determined to depose Philipp, however long
took, and there were some churchmen who were prepared to ass

im. He decided to send a delegation of church officials to the
olovetsky Monastery, where Philipp had lived for thirty years, to
iscover whether there had been any scandalous conduct on the
art of the Metropolitan. The delegation consisted of Pafnuty,
ishop of Suzdal, and Feodosy, the Abbot of the Andronikov
Ionastery, some clerics, and an armed guard under the command
f Prince Vasily Temkin-Rostovsky, who had only recently re-
irned from captivity in Lithuania. Prince Temkin-Rostovsky had
een given a high rank in the Oprichnina army, and his presence
as intended to emphasize the importance of the mission.

Neither Pafnuty nor Feodosy were able to obtain any evidence of
rongdoing by the Metropolitan from the monks at the Solovetsky
Ionastery. They protested that he had always behaved in the most
intly manner and not a single impious or unpatriotic thought had
er crossed his mind. Unhappily, however, Abbot Paissy of the
lovetsky Monastery was an ambitious man who was quite
epared to sign a fabricated catalogue of misdeeds performed by
e Metropolitan. The list was compiled by Prince Temkin-Ros-
vsky with the assistance of Abbot Feodosy. Bishop Pafnuty
fused to have anything to do with it.

By the beginning of November 1568 everything was ready for the
ial of the Metropolitan. The Tsar had read the list of misdeeds
id was satisfied with it. Philipp was summoned to meet his
cusers in the presence of the Boyar Council. He appeared in his
aborate vestments, wearing the white cowl of a Metropolitan and
rrying his staff of office, an austere and commanding figure.
bbot Paissy read out the catalogue of misdeeds and crimes.
iilipp listened in silence, refusing to defend himself. Herman,
rchbishop of Kazan, spoke strongly in his defense, but to no avail.
iilipp gazed at the abbot and said: "The evil you have sown will
it bring you the fruits you desire," and then he addressed himself
the Tsar, saying:

"Tsar and Grand Prince, you must not think that I fear you or
at I fear death. No, I am an old man who has led a blameless life
the monastery, free of rebellious passions and worldly intrigues,
id in that innocence I desire to surrender my soul to God, who is
ur God as well as mine. It is better that I should leave behind the
emory of a man who died innocently affirming the truth of his
ith than that I should remain the Metropolitan silently submitting

to a reign of terrible lawlessness! Do with me as you will! Here i
my shepherd's staff, here is my white cowl, here is the mantle wit
which you once desired to exalt me!"

Then he turned to the assembled churchmen and said: "You
bishops and abbots and all who serve at the altar, look faithfull
after the flock of Christ, prepare to give an account of yourselve:
remember to fear the Tsar in Heaven more than the Tsar on earth!

With these words the Metropolitan turned to leave, havin
removed his cowl and mantle and having laid down his staff, as
sign that he had resigned from his high office. Ivan was infuriate
and called him back, shouting that he had behaved with imper
missible haste, the judgment and the punishment had not yet bee
pronounced, and he must put on his robes again. He als
commanded the Metropolitan to conduct the services at th
Uspensky Cathedral on the feast day of the Archangel Michae
which would take place on November 8. Only after he ha
conducted these services would he be permitted to lay down h
office. Clearly the Tsar wanted more time to think up an appropr
ate punishment for a man he regarded as a declared enemy.

For Ivan there was only one appropriate punishment: tortu
unto death. The Metropolitan knew he was doomed, but neither h
nor Ivan yet knew what tortures would be inflicted on him. Durin
the four days between the trial and the feast of the Archang
Michael, the decision was taken. It was a very simple decision. Th
oprichniki would be let loose on him.

The Metropolitan was conducting mass when the armed oprich
niki burst into the cathedral, led by Alexey Basmanov and Maliut
Skuratov. The Metropolitan's crimes were read out and he wa
judged unworthy of his high office. Then the oprichniki hurle
themselves on him, tore the crown from his head, jostled him, an
stripped him of his vestments. Then they dressed him up in
monk's tattered robe and ran him out of the cathedral, waving the
brooms at him. They threw him on a sleigh and drove him acro
the Kremlin and into the Red Square and then to the near
Bogoyavlensky Monastery. All the time people came running up t
the Metropolitan, demanding a blessing. At the gate of th
monastery the sleigh stopped long enough for him to make
farewell speech: "Children, I have done all I could, and but for th
love I bear you I would not have remained a day on th

Metropolitan's throne. Have faith in God's mercy. Guard your souls in patience." Then they hurried him away and put him in a cell in the monastery.

But this was not quite the punishment which, according to Ivan, he deserved. Inevitably he would be executed, but something must first be done to degrade and humiliate him. He must be insulted and the last vestiges of human dignity must be removed from him by placing him on trial before his peers in his patched and tattered gown, the former Metropolitan reduced to the status of a beggar in rags. On the following day Ivan showed how little he understood the mentality of Philipp, who was brought back to the Kremlin and once more confronted his accusers. Pimen, Archbishop of Novgorod, advanced new charges. Abbot Paissy added new slanders. Philipp was condemned to perpetual imprisonment. It appeared that his chief crime was that he had practiced sorcery.

Of all those who attacked him, Abbot Paissy was the one who was most distasteful to Philipp. Once, looking at Paissy, who had been his pupil at the monastery, he said: "God's grace on your lips, my son! False lips are speaking against me! Have you not heard the words of God that 'whosoever is angry with his brother shall be in danger of hell fire.' [2] And there is another text in Holy Scripture: 'Whatsoever a man soweth, that shall he also reap.' " Then he added: "These are not my words—they are the words of the Lord!"

While there was breath in him, Philipp was determined to protest. The Tsar was present, and Philipp had the opportunity to say for the last time those things that had been in his mind for many months.

"Do not torture your people!" he said. "Remember always the hour of your death. Depart, O Tsar, from godless acts, and remember the fate of former rulers, for those who did good were blessed after their deaths and those who ruled evily were remembered without pity. Therefore you should endeavor to follow in the paths of those blessed ones, for high rank does not secure a person from death, which inexorably sinks its teeth into all things! Therefore, before the coming of death, you should offer the fruits of goodness and thus gather for yourself treasures in Heaven. Remember that all the treasure you amass on earth remains on earth, and all of us will have to answer for our lives!"

[2] The first text comes from *Matthew*, V, 22, the second from *Galatians*, VI, 7.

Philipp spoke in this way because it was the only way the Tsar could be made to understand the enormity of his crimes. The God-fearing Tsar might conceivably be brought to contemplate the wrath of God. Instead, the Tsar was incensed because the boyars and churchmen all listened silently and reverently, and because Herman, Archbishop of Kazan, once more defended Philipp, saying he was innocent in spite of the false witnesses brought against him. It was Archbishop Herman's last official act, for on the following day the oprichniki, at the Tsar's orders, entered his house and cut off his head. The official version was that he had died suddenly of the plague. Prince Kurbsky, in his history of the reign of Ivan IV, wrote that he was either poisoned or strangled. The exact manner of his death was learned when the Soviet government permitted his tomb to be opened.

In the eyes of the Tsar Archbishop Herman was a traitor, while Philipp was guilty of an even more outrageous crime—he had dared to call God's wrath upon the Tsar. It was therefore necessary that he should be given a punishment worthy of his crime. According to Prince Kurbsky, he was loaded with heavy chains around his arms, legs, and loins, and carried off to prison where he was placed in a dark and narrow cell. Orders were given that he should receive no food, and it was hoped he would starve to death. Some days later officials from the Kremlin entered his cell. A miracle had taken place, the chains had fallen away and Philipp was standing there with his hands above his head, singing psalms. The officials fell to their knees, sobbing. When they reported what they had seen to the Tsar, he cried out, "Spells, spells has he cast! My enemy! My traitor!"

More miracles were recorded. It was said and firmly believed by Prince Kurbsky and many churchmen that the Tsar ordered a wild, half-starved bear to be led into the bishop's cell, and on the following morning the Tsar himself came to peer into the cell, expecting to see Philipp's bones lying there. Instead he found him standing in prayer, while the bear lay quietly in a corner of the cell. As he went away, the Tsar was heard muttering, "Spells! The Bishop casts spells!"

The Tsar was sufficiently impressed by these incidents to pay attention to a petition signed by the Church Council, which begged him to spare Philipp's life. For some reason the Tsar decided to take him out of the prison and place him in a cell in the Monastery of Nikola Stary, across the Red Square from the Kremlin and close to the Bogoyavlensky Monastery. Crowds assembled outside the monastery from morning to night, all eagerly discussing the fate of the beloved Metropolitan and the miracles performed by God in order to save him. The Tsar, afraid that there would be riots, ordered him transferred to the Otroch Monastery near Tver.

Many strange stories were told about Philipp while he was in the Monastery of Nikola Stary. A close friend and relative of his called Ivan Kolychov came under suspicion and the Tsar ordered his execution. Execution by gunpowder was now much favored by the Tsar, who gave precise instructions on how Ivan Kolychov was to die. He was hoisted up and roped to the roof beam of his house. Kegs of gunpowder were rolled into the cellar and the house was blown up. Miraculously Ivan Kolychov survived, for after the explosion he was found sitting on the ground, dazed but alive, with one arm roped to a great beam. The Tsar was present and saw what had happened. Such miracles were not permitted, and so one of the oprichniki rode up to the man, cut off his head and presented it to the Tsar, who ordered that it should be placed in a leather bag and shown to Philipp. Accordingly a messenger was sent to the monastery with the bag, with instructions to present the head to Philipp with the words, "Here is the head of your favorite cousin! Your spells were of no avail to him!"

Philipp received the head in his hands, kissed and blessed it, and returned it to the messenger.

He was the last of the heroic Metropolitans. Those who followed him were self-serving, without courage, doing what was demanded of them. Philipp was followed by Kirill, who died in his bed and was followed by Anthony. They flitted like shadows through the last somber years of Ivan's reign.

The chroniclers describe how the reign of terror spread across Russia, and no one, rich or poor, noble or peasant, was immune to it. The purpose of the terror was to make everyone afraid of the Tsar, and it accomplished its purpose. Inevitably people hoped for a change, and from time to time the Tsar himself seemed to hope that the burden would be removed from him. But while he was on the throne, he destroyed anyone suspected of having any designs on it. Toward the end of 1568 his suspicions fell on his cousin Prince Vladimir of Staritsa, who was totally without ambition, but there was not the least doubt that he was popular among the Muscovites, who would have rejoiced if, by some miracle, he was elevated to the throne. The oprichniki fanned Ivan's suspicions, and he was soon engaged in discussions with his favorites about the best way of getting rid of his cousin.

The plot was involved and intricate. Hopefully, Prince Vladimir would enter the trap at a moment when he was least aware that he was doing so. The first step was taken early in 1569 when the Tsar learned that the Tatars were preparing a campaign against Astrakhan and Kazan. He ordered Prince Vladimir to proceed to Nizhni-Novgorod to take command of the army, with the boyar Peter Morozov as his second in command. Spies were sent out to follow Prince Vladimir's progress to Nizhni-Novgorod, and they reported back that the Prince had been welcomed in Kolomna with more than the usual marks of affection, a fact which may or may not have had some connection with a recent punitive raid on Kolomna by an oprichnik army. At the gates of the city Prince Vladimir was welcomed by priests with banners and crosses, and he was offered the traditional bread and salt. While he continued his journey to Nizhni-Novgorod, all those who had played prominent roles in welcoming him were rounded up, tortured, and murdered In Ivan's eyes they were his supporters and therefore traitors. All this, of course, became known to Prince Vladimir, who now realized that he was in extreme danger.

Ivan continued to unfold the plot cautiously. Fish were plentiful in Nizhni-Novgorod, and Ivan began to send his cooks to the city to examine the fish and bring back the best for his table. Nothing could be more innocent than a cook selecting fish for the royal table, but when one of these cooks reported that he had met Prince Vladimir and received poison and a gift of fifty rubles to pour the poison on the Tsar's food, the plot thickened. The cook was arrested and interrogated, and the poison was pronounced to be deadly. Although Ivan had himself concocted the plot with the help of the oprichniki, he came easily to the belief that Prince Vladimir was his mortal enemy and was intent on destroying him.

The next step was to find a pretext to invite the Prince to Alexandrova Sloboda. No satisfactory pretext being found, it was decided to ask him to come to Alexandrova Sloboda to discuss the invasion plans of the Tatars. It was now late in September; Prince Vladimir had taken no part in the sporadic fighting during the summer; and the season for Tatar invasions was long since over. Nevertheless he set out from Nizhni-Novgorod with his wife, his four children, his court, and his bodyguards, "knowing nothing whatsoever about his misfortune and his approaching death." Just outside Alexandrova Sloboda, near a village, a camp was prepared for him, and there he spent the night of October 8, 1569.

The next morning a small army of oprichniki, led by the Tsar, rode up to the camp and surrounded it. There was a good deal of noise, trumpets blared, kettle drums were being beaten. The Tsar, according to his custom, slipped away into one of the village houses, leaving to Maliuta Skuratov and Vasily Griaznoy the task of confronting Prince Vladimir with the evidence of his crimes. Skuratov and Griaznoy announced that the Tsar no longer regarded him as a brother because he, Prince Vladimir, had made an attempt on the Tsar's life and on his throne. The cook who said he had received poison and fifty rubles from Prince Vladimir was produced. The Prince denied everything. He knew now that he was caught in a trap and was doomed. His wife and children were weeping. He was told that the Tsar would soon receive him and pronounce judgment.

Then they were taken to the house in the village where Ivan had installed himself. Prince Vladimir protested his innocence and offered to renounce the world and spend the rest of his life in a monastery. Ivan remained unmoved. He said that since the Prince had attempted to poison him, it was proper that he should pay the penalty. He must die, and his family with him. A goblet was presented to him, but he pushed it away, saying, "I refuse to kill myself." His wife reminded him that by drinking the poison he was not committing suicide. "Dear husband," she said, "by drinking the poison you are suffering execution at the hands of him who offers you the poison. The Tsar himself is your murderer. God is just, and on the Day of Judgment the Tsar will be called to account for your innocent blood." Then Prince Vladimir bade farewell to his wife, blessed his children, prayed that God would receive his soul, and drank the poison. He died in agony fifteen minutes later.

Princess Evdokia, the second wife of Prince Vladimir, took the poison, and so did one of her daughters; another daughter survived.

Two children by the Prince's first wife were spared. Having accomplished his purpose, the Tsar was in a mood to be magnanimous, and he summoned the Princess's ladies-in-waiting, pointed to the bodies lying around the room, and said that if they would beg for mercy, he would spare them all, although he regarded them as guilty. To his surprise they refused to beg for mercy. One of them said, "We do not desire your mercy. We would rather be with God in Heaven, cursing you until the Day of Judgment, than remain under your tyrannical rule. Do with us as you will!" He had expected them to throw themselves at his feet. Instead they stood there proudly and defiantly.

The Tsar had ways of dealing with such people. Enraged, he ordered that all these women should be stripped naked, led out of the house and set upon by dogs, and the oprichniki were finally allowed to put them out of their misery by shooting them. The bodies were left where they fell, for the birds and wild animals to peck at. Many of the officials of Prince Vladimir's court were also summarily dealt with. The Tsar had not forgotten the Prince's mother, Princess Efrosinia, then living as a nun in the distant Convent of the Resurrection at Beloozero. Eleven days later, on October 20, 1569, she was drowned at the Tsar's orders.

Ivan's ferocious rage during those terrible days may have been brought about by an event that took place on September 6. On that day his wife, the Circassian princess who became the Tsaritsa Maria Temriukovna, died. Ivan himself spread the rumor that she had died as a result of the machinations of his secret enemies. Apparently he had come to dislike her, and for a long time they had been estranged. He ordered court mourning to be observed. No one walked in cloth of gold; instead dark mourning clothes of plain damask and velvet were worn, without any gold in them. Funeral services for the Tsaritsa were held throughout Russia, alms were given to the poor, donations were made by Ivan to monasteries and churches. Maria Temriukovna was buried in the Voznesensky Monastery within the Kremlin beside all the dead Grand Princesses and Tsaritsas of Russia, and Ivan was lonelier than ever.

All around him Ivan created a wilderness, a no-man's-land, where no enemies could dwell. Princes, boyars, nobles, and common people were being executed for no better reason than that he felt safer when they were dead. In his diseased and illogical mind he saw his enemies crowding upon him and he knew exactly how to deal with them. He would destroy them all, to the very last of them. And not only people: cities, too, must be destroyed. In ever-widening circles he would reduce Russia to destruction. During that winter he planned the most breathtaking and the most infamous of his many massacres.

Massacre

Lord Novgorod the Great—such was the proud name the citizens of Novgorod gave to their rich and beautiful city with its gilded domes and white-walled churches, its huge warehouses, and fleets of merchant ships. Novgorod, meaning "new city," was one of the most ancient cities in Russia, having come into existence long before there was a settlement in Moscow. For six hundred years it was an independent principality ruling over a vast area of northern Russia, acquiring over the centuries so much wealth, so much prestige, and so many settled habits and traditions that it had come to be regarded as the chief city of Russia, sending its ambassadors to half the kingdoms of Europe and trading with all of them. To the cultivated Novgorodians tyranny was anathema, and they conducted their affairs through an elected council. Only when they were at war did they permit a prince to rule over them, and even then the councillors met regularly and decided upon all issues concerning the business of the city.

The city took the shape of two half-moons lying on the banks of the swift-flowing Volkhov River a few miles north of Lake Ilmen. On one side was the red-walled Kremlin dominated by the six domes of the Cathedral of St. Sophia and the Archbishop's palace; on the other side was the Market Side teeming with huddled streets, where most of the working population lived. Moats, high walls, and watch towers protected the city, and a wide wooden bridge connected the two half-moons.

At the end of the fifteenth century Ivan III sent a large army against Novgorod and conquered it. He confiscated many of its treasures, divided the lands belonging to the See of St. Sophia among his nobles, and expelled most of the nobles and merchants of the city. All together nearly three million acres of arable land were granted to the Muscovite nobility on condition that they serve the Grand Prince of Moscow. Nevertheless Novgorod succeeded in retaining its original character; the monks, the workmen, the common people had not been uprooted, and in many subtle ways they succeeded in conquering their conquerors. Novgorod preserved its separateness and individuality.

In the eyes of Ivan IV, who knew Novgorod well, for he had visited the city several times, the separateness and individuality of the Novgorodians smacked of treason. They were a people who spoke their minds, and they complained bitterly about the exactions of the Muscovite army in its wars against Livonia. Special levies and special taxes were raised to support the army; the army was usually billeted in Novgorod before it set out against Livonia; trade with foreign countries came to a standstill while the wars were being fought. It appeared that the Novgorodians were more concerned with trade than with enlarging the boundaries of the Muscovite empire. Ivan decided to punish them.

When Ivan punished his officers of state, he rarely gave precise reasons. It was enough that his suspicions had been aroused, that they had acted in a manner incomprehensible to him, that he had taken a sudden and unreasoning dislike for them. He believed he had a good nose for smelling out treachery and he thought he could recognize a traitor even before he became treacherous. So with Novgorod; he felt under no necessity to proclaim the reasons that led him to believe that Russia would benefit by a general massacre of the inhabitants. The reasons could be invented later, if anyone dared to ask for them.

Nevertheless certain macabre rituals had to be performed before he could order the oprichniki to march against Novgorod, and a *casus belli* had to be found. This was provided, according to the Novgorod Chronicle, by a certain Peter Volynets, who had been brought before the courts of Novgorod for a crime and severely punished. He had a score to settle with Novgorod. After his release he journeyed to Alexandrova Sloboda and succeeded in convincing the Tsar that Archbishop Pimen headed a conspiracy to bring all the Novgorod territories under the sway of King Sigismund Augustus, who was both King of Poland and Grand Prince of Lithuania. According to Peter Volynets there existed proof of the conspiracy in the form of a letter signed by Archbishop Pimen on behalf of the people of Novgorod. Where was the letter? It was concealed in the Cathedral of St. Sophia in Novgorod. Peter Volynets suggested he should be permitted to return to Novgorod in the company of one of the trusted officers of the Tsar's court and in his presence retrieve the letter which lay behind an icon of the Virgin directly facing the Archbishop's throne. In this way he would offer demonstrable proof of the letter's existence. Ivan professed to be deeply impressed by the story of the hidden letter, and Peter Volynets was sent to Novgorod with orders to bring back the letter as soon as possible. This was done. Ivan was overjoyed, for the letter provided him with the visible proof that his long-smoldering suspicions and desires were justified.

Not all the oprichniki appear to have been in favor of the expedition against Novgorod. Three of them, Prince Afanasy Viazemsky and the two Basmanovs, Alexey and Fyodor, seem to have been reluctant to attack the city. What was to be gained by a general massacre? Prince Viazemsky was especially close to Ivan, and they had no secrets from one another. The prince always acted as the taster when the court physician, Dr. Arnolfo, prescribed medicines for Ivan. But among the prince's proteges was a certain Gregory Lovchikov, who attracted Ivan's attention and was soon high in his favor. Lovchikov was ambitious, prepared to sacrifice anyone to his ambitions. Although he owed his position at court to Prince Viazemsky and was therefore in duty bound to serve him loyally, he became an informer against him. One day in late November or early December 1569 he informed Ivan that Prince Viazemsky had already divulged to the Novgorodians the secret plans for the attack on their city. There was no truth in the story, but Ivan had his own reasons for believing it. Prince Viazemsky's lack of enthusiasm was now sufficiently explained.

For an extraordinary crime an extraordinary punishment was appropriate. Ivan's solution was simple. He gave orders to his bodyguard to ambush and murder the prince's servants, a few each day. Every day the prince would come to confer with Ivan, and when he returned home he would find some of his servants lying dead in the courtyard. Terrified, the prince said nothing about the dead servants to Ivan. Day followed day, and at last there were no more servants left. Next it was the turn of the prince's brothers. They, too, were murdered, and still the prince attended the daily conferences with Ivan. Suddenly he panicked and fled to the house of Dr. Arnolfo. Ivan knew where he was, allowed five days to pass, and then ordered the prince into his presence. "You can see for yourself that all your enemies are conspiring to destroy you," Ivan said. "If you are wise, you will flee to Moscow and await my coming!"

By this time Prince Viazemsky was almost mad with fear. He knew he was in mortal danger. His only hope of salvation lay in blind obedience to Ivan's orders. He galloped from Alexandrova Sloboda as fast as his horse would carry him, and because he knew Ivan's mind and was afraid of being ambushed, he attacked and killed everyone he encountered on the Moscow road.

The Basmanovs, father and son, were also suspected of having dealings with Novgorod. They were not punished at this time, but were placed under arrest to await the hour of their execution. Only a short time before Fyodor Basmanov had commanded the Oprichnina army sent to guard the southern frontier against the Tatars, but his services in the field were of no avail to him. Power within the Oprichnina fell more and more into the hands of Maliuta Skuratov and Vasily Griaznoy.

At a secret meeting held in the throne room at Alexandrova Sloboda Ivan announced that he had formed the irrevocable decision to punish Novgorod, and not only Novgorod, for Pskov and all the towns of the former Grand Principality of Tver also deserved punishment. He had proof that they were all in secret communication with King Sigismund Augustus and preparing to swear allegiance to him. He had decided to march against these towns in the greatest secrecy in order to preserve them for the empire of Muscovy.

In the third week of December the Tsar set out from Alexandrova Sloboda for the march against Novgorod, westward across the snow. It was the worst time of the year, and therefore the most propitious for the Tsar, who hoped to fall on his enemies unawares. He was accompanied by the members of his court, by the Tsarevich

Ivan, who was not yet fifteen years old, and by an army of about 15,000 men, of whom about 1,500 were armed with muskets. There was also a small detachment of Tatar mercenaries.

In the normal course of events the army would pass through Moscow. Ivan ordered a wide detour, chiefly because he was afraid that if the Muscovites learned his intentions they would warn the Novgorodians. The army moved along the forest pathways silently, stealthily, killing everyone encountered along the way, for it was necessary that the existence of the army should be kept secret. In this way they came to Klin, a small unfortified town on the frontier of the former principality of Tver. Here Ivan himself gave the signal for a general massacre of the inhabitants, sparing neither women nor children. The streets and houses were filled with the dead and dying. A few weeks earlier he had given orders that about a hundred families from Pereyaslavl should take up residence in Moscow, and by ill fortune the exiles happened to be passing through Klin when the Oprichnina army arrived. They were killed, and someone took the trouble to count the corpses. All together 470 exiles from Pereyaslavl were killed. No record was made of the number of people of Klin who died on the same day.

Before leaving Klin Ivan ordered that all the treasure from the local churches and monasteries should be carried away; and the baggage carts were loaded with icons, vestments, golden candelabra, and altar screens as the army marched northward.

Secrecy was the watchword: no one was permitted to know Ivan's intentions. Six hundred oprichniki rode ahead to clear the way; six hundred rode behind, and on both flanks there were six hundred. Their orders were to kill everyone they encountered. If a luckless peasant stumbled into the Tsar's camp, he was seized, stripped naked, and rolled in the snow until he died. If one of the oprichniki left the camp, even if it was only to obtain provisions, he was killed. The officer in charge of preparing the camp each night was told during the morning where the camp would be; then, with three hundred armed men, he rode ahead to prepare the site. Woe betide the captain who did not prepare the new camp to the Tsar's perfect satisfaction.

It was a simple matter to kill the people of Klin, but it was considerably more difficult to kill the people of Tver, who lived in a large and handsome city well-protected with towers and wooden walls. In the fourteenth century the Grand Principality of Tver rivalled Moscow for supremacy over the Russian states and could put an army of 30,000 men in the field. Now, although it no longer possessed an army, it was still an important city, and the Tsar therefore approached it with extreme caution and secrecy. No one in Tver had yet heard about the killings. It was necessary to lull the people into a false sense of security. Ivan established his court in the nearby Otroch Monastery and commanded the oprichniki to stand guard outside the city walls and on no account to make their way inside. Meanwhile he lived royally in the well-appointed monastery, attended divine services, and conducted himself as though he were merely on a tour of inspection.

The most distinguished resident in the monastery was the former Metropolitan Philipp. He lived in a small secluded cell, and was not permitted any communication with the monks. An old man, alone with his God, Philipp had no fear of death and least of all did he have any fear of Ivan. When Maliuta Skuratov entered the cell and asked Philipp to bless the undertakings of the Tsar and to grant a special blessing on the expedition to Novgorod designed to punish Archbishop Pimen for his treachery, Philipp refused and went on to denounce the crimes of the Oprichnina army, saying, "Only those who are good and perform good deeds may be blessed." From the expression on Maliuta Skuratov's face, Philipp knew that his words were a death sentence, and he said quietly: "I have long awaited death. Let the Tsar's will be fulfilled." Saying this, he turned away and began reading the service for the dying. Maliuta Skuratov, who knew that Philipp possessed an inflexible will and would never change his opinion of the Tsar, did what was demanded of him. He strangled Philipp or smothered him with a pillow, and then summoned a meeting of the community of the monks, where he announced that the former Metropolitan had regrettably died "as a result of the unbearable heat in his cell." He gave orders that the body should be buried immediately, and this was done. Without any ceremony the terrified monks dug a grave behind the altar and buried him.

Ivan remained in the Otroch Monastery for five days. On the first day, December 22, he laid his plans. On the second day Philipp was murdered, thereafter to be remembered as a martyr and a saint. On the third day Ivan gave orders that all the treasure of the monastery should be collected and piled into baggage carts; everything valuable, even the possessions of the monks, must be removed to Alexandrova Sloboda, together with all the treasures from neighboring monasteries. The people of Tver imagined that Ivan was in a rage with the monks, and would leave ordinary people alone. For the next two days Ivan remained quiet and on the sixth day he gave the order for the massacre.

A massacre is not merely a general slaughter; it follows complex laws, and goes through complex stages. Ivan's intention was to punish Tver for its crimes of treachery and *lèse-majesté*, and it was therefore not sufficient merely to kill the inhabitants. First, he must make them conscious of their sins. Secondly, he must abase them. Thirdly, he must kill them. Since Tver was a rich city, the first step involved the capture of their treasure and the destruction of everything that could not be carried away. The oprichniki were ordered to seize the treasure and destroy the rest. They broke down the doors of houses, smashed the furniture and the household utensils, and carried off the stores of lard, wax, grain, and furs to the courtyard and made bonfires out of them. In this way the rich were reduced to penury and the poor to starvation. Ivan emphasized that any officer who failed to carry out these orders would be treated like a common criminal, which meant that he would suffer the fate of the people of Tver.

Since Ivan was bent upon acquiring the utmost amount of treasure, the rich suffered most. Those who refused to say where they had hidden their money and valuables were tortured until they had confessed, and then hanged. Women and children were not spared; the old were not respected. Some Livonians and some exiles from Polotsk were living in Tver. Ivan ordered them to be rounded up and brought to the banks of the Volga, where they were summarily executed in his presence and their bodies pushed under the ice of the river. About 9,000 people died during this two-day reign of terror. Something very like this massacre had taken place in Tver in 1327, when Khan Uzbek sent 50,000 Tatars against the city, but the cruelties of a Khan were only to be expected. The cruelties of the Tsar were totally unexpected, and therefore all the more terrifying.

Ivan resumed his journey to Novgorod, killing and pillaging along the way. At the town of Torzhok there were two prisons, one

filled with prisoners-of-war from Livonia, the other with captured
Tatar nobles. Ivan gave orders that all the Livonians should be
executed. This was done, and he then turned his attention to the
Tatars, who had somehow learned about the execution of the
Livonians and knew what to expect when the Tsar, Maliuta
Skuratov, and a well-armed detachment of oprichniki entered the
prison courtyard. There had been five hundred Livonian prisoners;
they were bound and shackled, and many old men, women, and
children were included among them; and he watched the executions with the certain knowledge that no harm would come to him.
There were only nineteen Tatar prisoners, and he expected they
would be dispatched in a few seconds. He did not know they were
armed with long knives concealed in their sleeves, and they were
neither bound nor shackled. When they realized they were about to
be executed by the armed oprichniki, the Tatars hurled themselves
upon them and succeeded in killing two of them and severely
wounding Maliuta Skuratov. According to a contemporary record,
he was knifed in the stomach. One of the boldest of the Tatars
hurled himself on Ivan, but was cut down just in time. Ivan hurried
away after ordering that musketeers should be sent to the prison to
shoot down the surviving Tatars.

These murders were merely minor divertissements to provide him
with entertainment during the journey. More serious matters lay
ahead. On January 2, 1570, while the army was two day's march
from Novgorod, he ordered the advance troops to race ahead,
surround the city, set up guard posts and barriers along all the
roads leading to it, and ensure that no one left it. This time there
was no pretense that he was on a tour of inspection or that he was
leading an army against the Livonians. The city was effectively
sealed off, to await its punishment.

Because Ivan believed, or pretended to believe, that Archbishop
Pimen and his priests and monks were responsible for the terrible
act of treachery which had brought him to embark on this punitive
expedition, he reserved a special fate for the churchmen. Once they
had sealed off Novgorod, the oprichniki were under orders to seal
off the surrounding monasteries. The abbots and monks were led
away, and the Tsar's seal was placed on the monastery gates. About
500 abbots and monks were brought to Novgorod, where they were
beaten from morning till night. Meanwhile the priests and monks

living within Novgorod were rounded up and they were also beaten, and all the churches and monasteries were sealed off. The houses of nobles and prominent citizens were sealed off in the same way, and these citizens were put in chains and kept under guard together with their wives and children. For twenty Novgorod rubles, a very large sum, any monk or priest living within the city could go free. If he could not pay the money, he was beaten mercilessly or put in irons.

The Tsar deliberately slowed down his march, and it was not until January 6 that he arrived with his army within sight of the city. It was a Friday, and the Feast of the Epiphany, but no bells were ringing. Novgorod was frozen in the silence of fear.

The Tsar's camp was established on raised ground about a mile and a half from the city walls, on the right bank of the Volkhov River. The site was chosen carefully, for here were the ruins of the Gorodishche, the ancient castle and settlement built by Rurik, the founder of the Russian state and the ancestor of the Tsar. According to the legend, the Novgorodians had summoned to their city the Varangian chieftain Rurik, saying, "Our land is great and rich, but there is no order in it. Come and rule over us." Here, where his ancestor had brought order, Ivan was about to bring chaos.

His first command was that all the abbots and monks who had come from the outlying monasteries should be beaten to death with clubs. The mangled bodies could be returned to the monasteries for burial. Abbesses and nuns shared the same fate. His intention was to create a wasteland around Novgorod, for these monasteries were also trading centers, storehouses, and potential centers of resistance. Novgorod must be reduced to impotence before he struck out with all his available force.

The order to club the monks to death was given on Saturday, January 7. Since the following day was a Sunday, he decided to attend divine service in the Cathedral of St. Sophia within the walls of the Kremlin of Novgorod. The murder of about 500 monks and nuns rested lightly on his conscience, and he proposed to go to church as though nothing had happened.

On Sunday he set out with the Tsarevich and a large detachment of his army for the Cathedral. He rode along the right bank of the Volkhov River, entered the Merchants' District, and then began to

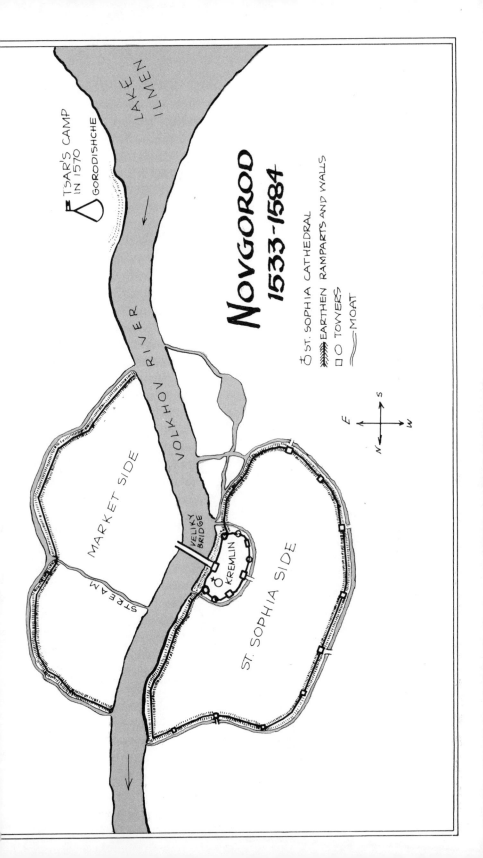

NOVGOROD
1533-1584

☩ ST. SOPHIA CATHEDRAL
🌲 EARTHEN RAMPARTS AND WALLS
□ ○ TOWERS
〰 MOAT

TSAR'S CAMP
IN 1570
GORODISHCHE

LAKE ILMEN

VOLKHOV RIVER

MARKET SIDE

STREAM

VELIKY BRIDGE

KREMLIN

ST. SOPHIA SIDE

ride across the great wooden bridge which led to the Kremlin wall. At this moment Pimen, Archbishop of Novgorod, accompanied by all the clergy of the Cathedral armed with golden crosses, icons, and brilliantly colored banners, came across the bridge to meet him. The Tsar and the Tsarevich led the armed procession coming from the east and the Archbishop led the procession coming from the west. The Archbishop held out the cross, thus attempting to offer the Tsar a blessing, but the Tsar drew back, for he had no intention of being blessed by the man he was about to destroy. The Third Chronicle of Novgorod records the words Ivan shouted from the bridge:

> Because you worship evil, you have no holy cross in your hands. Instead, you are carrying a weapon, and this weapon, together with your evil thoughts, your monks and the citizens of Novgorod, is an instrument designed by you for the surrender of Novgorod the Great, which is our patrimony, to the enemy, the foreigner, the King of Poland, Sigismund Augustus!
>
> So you are no longer the shepherd, nor the teacher, nor the holder of the Archbishopric of St. Sophia. No, you are a wolf, a predator, a destroyer, a traitor, an enemy of our crown!

Having spoken these words in a terrible rage, Ivan ordered the Archbishop to turn back and celebrate mass in the Cathedral. During the mass Ivan was seen to be praying fervently. Afterward, followed by the Tsarevich and the oprichniki, he rode to the Archbishop's palace for the midday meal and for a while he seemed to be on his best behavior. It was believed that his rage had subsided. Suddenly he stopped eating and began screaming at his soldiers, telling them they must take the Archbishop's treasury and strip the palace of all its valuables. As for the Archbishop, his nobles, servants, and attendants, all of them must be placed under arrest. The Cathedral of St. Sophia must be plundered and left a barren shell. Icons, sacred vessels, embroidered robes, even the great doors must be piled onto the baggage carts. The famous bronze bell weighing 18,000 pounds, which summoned the people of Novgorod to church, that too must be removed to Alexandrova Sloboda. The Kremlin of Novgorod was to be pillaged of all its treasures.

Archbishop Pimen was wearing gold-embroidered robes and a

closely fitting white cowl surmounted by a gold crucifix. Enraged by the spectacle of the Archbishop in full episcopal attire, Ivan ordered the oprichniki to remove the cowl and the robes. He was made to stand in his underwear.

"You have no right to be an Archbishop!" Ivan shouted. "You would be better if you were dressed up like a clown, and I'll find a wife for you!"

No man could become an Archbishop unless he had led a chaste and virtuous life, and these last words were therefore especially offensive. The abbots of twenty-seven monasteries had accompanied Ivan to the midday feast. Nearly all the monks from these monasteries had already been slaughtered. To these abbots Ivan addressed himself: "Come, be my guests! I invite you all to contribute to the expenses of the wedding!" It appeared that the expenses of the wedding were extraordinarily high, and each abbot was assessed according to the wealth of his monastery.

Ivan had not yet finished with the Archbishop. He ordered the servants to produce a white mare, and it became clear that the Archbishop was to be married to the mare.

"Here is your wife!" the Tsar said. "Saddle her, mount her at once, and ride off to Moscow! When you have reached Moscow, add your name to the register of clowns!"

Archbishop Pimen climbed on the mare, and Ivan then gave instructions that his feet should be tied to it. The Archbishop was then told to ride off in the direction of Moscow, but a moment later Ivan had a better idea: he had thought of some new indignity for the long-suffering Archbishop. A musical instrument attracted his attention. It was a kind of lyre with strings and bellows. Ivan thrust the instrument into the Archbishop's hands, saying: "Since you now have nothing else to do and since you have taken a wife, here's something for you to play with!"

There was a good deal of mirthful laughter. The Archbishop was in his underwear; the oprichniki were crowding around him; Ivan was enjoying the degradation of a churchman who was far from being saintly but had genuinely attempted to rule his flock justly. As he rode away on the white mare in the direction of Moscow with a strong bodyguard, the Archbishop plucked the strings and blew the bellows.

A few days later Ivan wrote to the Metropolitan Kirill in

Moscow that "Archbishop Pimen may not perform any services in the church, but his style and dignity are not to be removed from him until he has been judged and sentenced by the Church Council."

The sacking of the Cathedral of St. Sophia and of the Archbishop's palace, and the degradation of the Archbishop, put Ivan in a good temper. He sent an order to the people of Novgorod telling them to go about their affairs as usual and he urged them to sell their goods to the oprichniki at a just price.

When he returned to the Gorodishche later in the afternoon, his mood was somber and threatening. The time had come to confront the people with their sins. Men, women, and children were brought to him to be interrogated. He wanted evidence of treachery. How, and why, had it come about that the Novgorodians had sent secret messages to King Sigismund Augustus, asking him to rule over them? Since they had not done so, no evidence was forthcoming. The evidence therefore had to be manufactured. Under torture some of the prisoners confessed to imaginary crimes, incriminating one another, and invented totally untrue stories, and were sentenced to death. Roped together and tied to the backs of sleighs, some with ropes round their necks and others with ropes round their legs, they were dragged across the snow to the wooden bridge across the Volkhov River to await their punishment.

Ivan cherished the refinements of punishment. He ordered a high platform to be built on the wooden bridge. Some were to be thrown off the platform, others from the bridge. The ice had been broken below the bridge, and there was a dark pool of water below. The arms and legs of the victims were bound, and it was thus impossible for them to swim away, and even if they could swim, it would not have helped them. Underneath the bridge the oprichniki, armed with boat-hooks, pikes and axes, were waiting for them in boats. The victims thrown from the bridge sank in the water and then rose to the surface; the oprichniki then hacked and chopped them with axes, or thrust at them with the pikes and boat-hooks, until the bodies sank again.

The chroniclers have recorded one curious detail. They say the men were thrown off the bridge, while the women and children were thrown from the high platform. The Tsar was accustomed to eing men being killed, but the sight of women and children being urled to their deaths was an unaccustomed diversion.

For nearly four weeks the killings continued. What the chroniers called "the unabatable fury of the Tsar" brought about the eaths of about 30,000 people. On some days a thousand people ere thrown into the river and then stabbed and axed to death. ccasionally the figure rose to fifteen hundred; sometimes it fell to ve or six hundred. Ivan had discovered an efficient way of isposing of the corpses, for they were carried downstream under e ice and left no trace. Mass murder was being practiced at little xpense, hygienically, with a minimum of death-dealing instruents, and without any complications.

While the waters under the bridge were the principal execution rounds, Ivan had recourse to novel methods of killing in order to lieve the monotony. High picket fences were erected round a eld, and some Novgorod merchants were then led into the field. van, wearing armor, mounted his horse, lowered his lance and harged them. He derived so much satisfaction from spitting a erchant on the end of his lance that he invited the Tsarevich to in him. After killing a few merchants, he left the field to the prichniki, ordering them to chop up the remaining merchants and row the pieces into the Volkhov River. In this way he killed erhaps twenty merchants with his own hands. Maliuta Skuratov laimed to have killed 1,490 Novgorodians with his own hands, xcluding the fifteen he shot with a musket. The wound he had eceived at Torzhok from a Tatar knife had evidently healed apidly.

Two desires worked on Ivan: the desire to massacre, and the esire to acquire treasure and loot. One of the richest merchants in Novgorod was a certain Fyodor Syrkov, known for his munificent ndowment of monasteries. He had hidden his wealth and refused o divulge where he had hidden it. The Tsar had no difficulty in aking him reveal the hiding place. First, Syrkov was thrown into he ice-cold river at the end of a long rope. Before he could drown, e was pulled out and taken before the Tsar.

"Did you see anything in the water?" the Tsar asked him.

Syrkov was a brave man and answered: "Yes, I saw the evil pirits living in the deep waters of the Volkhov River, and they were bout to rise to the surface to steal your soul from your body!"

Ivan had no liking for bold men and ordered the oprichniki to stand him up to his knees in a caldron of water. A fire was lit beneath the caldron, and long before the water had reached boiling point the unhappy Syrkov revealed the hiding place of his treasure amounting to 12,000 silver rubles, which was equivalent in purchasing power to more than a million dollars of today's money. The revelation did no good to Syrkov, for Ivan ordered him to be chopped to pieces and thrown into the river.

Before the end of the first week of February 1570 Ivan decided that the massacres at Novgorod had gone far enough. About a third of the population had been killed, and most of the wealth of the city was in his hands. He needed a change of air, and more exercise, and therefore set out on a tour of inspection which would take him to all the great monasteries in the neighborhood. The monks had been killed, but the treasuries had been left intact and the buildings themselves were under seal. He spent a day in each monastery superintending the removal of costly fabrics, sacred vessels, icons, bells, and whatever else he could lay his hands on. His rage for destruction extended to the granaries, which were burned, and all the horses and cows belonging to the monasteries were slaughtered. Then he returned to Novgorod gorged with his loot.

The final punishment took the form of a general sack of the city. The shops and warehouses were looted and burned down. The stalls in the marketplaces were smashed, the private houses were invaded, the young women were raped and sometimes carried off by the oprichniki, and all the valuables were removed. Heinrich Staden, who was present throughout the campaign against Novgorod, wrote as follows about Ivan's last days in Novgorod. "After the pillage of the monasteries the sack of the city began. Nothing was allowed to remain in the city and everything that the soldiers could not carry away was either thrown into the river or burned. If any of the Zemskiye people retrieved anything from the water, he was hanged. All high buildings were torn down, and all the beautiful doorways, stairs, and windows were destroyed." By this time the oprichniki had grown weary of massacre, and perhaps no more than a thousand died during these last days.

Suddenly, in the early morning of February 13, 1570, Ivan decided to make his peace with Novgorod. The time was propitious, for it was the Monday of the second week of Lent. At sunrise he ordered messengers to announce that by the Tsar's orders every street in Novgorod must send its leading citizen to the Gorodishche. There could be no question of disobeying the Tsar's orders, and the messengers returned to the Gorodishche with about sixty elders, who believed themselves as good as dead. Clearly there would be another massacre, and another, and another, until no one in Novgorod was left alive. To their surprise they found the Tsar in an accommodating mood. According to the chronicler, the Tsar gazed upon them with merciful and kindly eyes, and said:

> Men of Novgorod the Great, all those of you now remaining in this city, I pray you to beseech the all merciful, ever generous and most loving God, and His pure Mother and all the saints, on behalf of our Tsardom, and my children Ivan and Fyodor, and my Christ-loving army, so that Our Lord may grant us victory over our enemies whether visible or invisible. God shall judge Archbishop Pimen, who is a traitor to me and also to you, and all his evil collaborators, and they will be held accountable for this bloodshed. But you must not grieve any more. Go, and be thankful!

Why was he saying this? Perhaps it was because he had punished them enough. Perhaps it was because he wanted a breathing space or because the stench of the dead was more than he could bear, or because the ultimate humiliation of the injured lay in making them bless the name of the one who does the injury. He was asking that his victims pray for him, his sons, and his Christ-loving army, which was still murdering wantonly, still scouring the countryside and creating havoc in the villages.

Even now he continued to punish the people of Novgorod. A large amount of their wealth consisted of goods and supplies stored in the warehouses at Narva. Accordingly, he sent five hundred oprichniki to Narva with instructions to set fire to the warehouses and kill anyone who attempted to save anything from the flames. Their bodies were to be thrown into the river and all their property was to be burned. This appears to have been the last order given by the Tsar before he set out for Pskov.

When the Tsar said, "Go, and be thankful," he was speaking with massive irony. Even before he arrived in Novgorod there was a shortage of foodstuffs and during the time he stayed in the city all the available grain including seed grain and all the domestic animals were destroyed at his orders. As a result Novgorod suffered from a terrible famine which was followed by pestilence. The chroniclers report that in September of that year ten thousand people were buried in a mass grave in Novgorod and in May 1571 another mass grave was dug. So many people had been killed or had died as a result of starvation and the plague that Ivan ordered people to be transferred to Novgorod from all over Russia.

Carts loaded with all the treasure plundered at Novgorod set out for Alexandrova Sloboda. Gold and silver, pearls and precious stones, holy icons, furs and silks, and even the great bell from the Cathedral of St. Sophia and the great bronze doors carved in 1336 were sent under guard to Alexandrova Sloboda, the treasure being sealed up in the vaults under the two new churches built to celebrate his victory over the people of Novgorod. It occurred to Ivan that the bronze doors of the Cathedral of St. Sophia would serve as an admirable decoration to his own cathedral at Alexandrova Sloboda, but they proved to be too large and had to be cut down to size. The less valuable booty was loaded on sledges, driven to a monastery outside Novgorod, and distributed among the oprichniki.

No one was ever able to count the number of the dead at Novgorod. John Horsey wrote that 700,000 were killed, but this is clearly an error, for the population of Novgorod including the children cannot have numbered much more than 100,000. By comparing all the available estimates it is possible to reach a figure of about 30,000 people killed while the oprichniki were occupying the city, and at least 20,000 died in the ensuing famine and pestilence.

The Tsar's attitude throughout these murders was one of calm condescension, implying that he had conferred a favor on the people of Novgorod by rescuing them from treason. That there was not the slightest evidence of treason was a matter of indifference to him. There was a plan, and everything must be carried out according to the plan. The city must be emptied of its traitors, and all available means were to be used against them. He liked his orders to be carried out calmly, methodically, without passion. The river, in his eyes, became a conveyor belt quietly removing the people from the scene. It did not happen like that. The river,

hoked with the dead, became the prime source of the plague that
hreatened to engulf all Russia in the following months.

Albert Shlichting tells the story of the beggars of Novgorod who
vere expelled from the city to wander about in the snowy wastes.
'hey were unharmed, perhaps because Ivan felt there was some
anctity in extreme poverty. Some of the citizens, seeing that the
beggars were allowed to go free, disguised themselves in rags and
scaped. But there was no food to be found in the snow and most of
hem perished. The more daring ones returned secretly to the city at
tight to feed off the corpses, which they kept salted in barrels. In
ime Ivan himself learned about this practice. It interested him. He
sked his officers to inquire into it and to bring some of the
annibals into his presence. According to Shlichting he was
nterested in the purely technical question of why they kept the
bodies salted in barrels. They did not answer his question; they said
only that they were dying of starvation and ate the bodies to keep
live. He ordered them to be thrown into the river.

Before leaving the city Ivan took possession of the Torgovaya
torona or Market Side, which contained most of the warehouses
nd shops. Here he built a palace where he resided whenever he
visited Novgorod. Accordingly, a month after he departed for
Pskov, when the ice was beginning to melt, the builders set to work
o dig the foundations of his new palace, which was splendidly
urnished.

He was well content with himself. The oprichniki had served him
vell; all his orders had been obeyed; he had punished the enemy
and acquired a vast treasure; and it remained only to make the
vestward journey to Pskov, the white-walled city, as rich as
Novgorod and almost as powerful, where the processes of murder
and plunder would be repeated with whatever refinements he felt
necessary.

Five days later, on February 18, he came in sight of the virgin
city. Exhausted by the long journey, he decided not to enter it that
day and spent the night in the Monastery of St. Nicholas just
outside the walls. The monastery was built like a fortress and
offered him all the protection he needed. It was a Saturday, and on
Sunday he intended to remind the people of Pskov that he was their
Tsar and that they owed everything, even their lives, to him.

A Blood Bath in
the Red Square

Once Pskov was the capital of an independent republic where th
people elected their rulers and stoutly maintained their independ
ence with the help of a prince chosen by the Popular Assembly. Th
prince, who was charged with the defense of the city, was usually
descendant of Rurik or one of the princes of the Lithuanian roya
family, and he was not permitted to interfere in the affairs of th
city. The government with its Boyar Council and Popular Assembl
and with its elected mayor and commander of the citizen militi
was overthrown when Pskov was annexed to Muscovy in 151c
Thereafter it was ruled by a governor sent from Moscow, whos
word was law.

What was chiefly remarkable about Pskov was its beauty an
strangeness, for unlike any other city in Russia it was built of ston
from the local limestone quarries; and this stone, of a soft yellow o
pinkish white, gave it an extraordinary glow. Moscow had ston
walls, but only around the Kremlin and Kitay Gorod. Pskov ha
stone walls everywhere. The sunlight lingered and flashed on them
and the shadows melted on them. All the other Russian cities wer
built of wood and had a somber look about them; they were heav
and dark, while Pskov was all lightness and grace. The people wer
aware of the beauty of the city and took great care of it.

They were a mercantile people trading in flax, stone, corn, tallow
smoked fish, skins, tar, pitch, honey, and timber for shipbuilding
The flax, used chiefly for the making of sails, was noted for it

quality and in great demand. So, too, were the ceramic tiles with an apple-green glaze, which were exported all over Russia. When Ivan decided to rebuild Kazan, he sent for stone masons from Pskov. Thus the city had many sources of revenue and there was little poverty. They were a practical people, deeply religious, eminently law-abiding, possessing a system of laws so elaborate that other cities marveled. They were a people who cherished their freedoms and guarded them even when they were being ruled by princely governors sent from Moscow.

Since it was a mercantile community the merchant guilds, housed in the great halls of Dovmont Castle, acquired enormous powers. The castle was named after Prince Timotheus Dovmont, a Lithuanian warrior who fortified the city against the army of Novgorod and secured its independence. A German traveler who visited Pskov in the sixteenth century wrote approvingly of the people's pride in their city, their friendliness and open-mindedness. They were the most civilized Russians he had ever encountered.

Partly, of course, this was because Pskov was the most westernized of all Russian cities and because ancient Russian civilization had developed here unhindered by the Tatars. By way of Lake Chud the people of Pskov had direct access to the Gulf of Finland and thus to the Baltic. They were accustomed to seeing foreign merchants and were not suspicious of them. Nor did they suffer from any feeling of inferiority in the presence of foreigners. They possessed their own traditions, their own way of life, their own schools of architecture and painting. They remembered, too, that Pskov was the home of the first Christian Princess of Russia, St. Olga, who was baptized by the Byzantine Emperor in Constantinople.

Suddenly the people of Pskov were confronted with something completely outside their experience. For many days they had known about the events taking place in Novgorod. Survivors who fled to Pskov had recounted in great detail the mass executions on the river, the murders in the streets, the incessant looting, the reign of terror which Ivan organized so coldly, so dispassionately, that he seemed to be not a man but an incarnate devil. They knew, too, that when Ivan had finished with Novgorod, he would turn immediately on Pskov. They debated among themselves and came to no conclusions except that they must throw themselves on the mercy of the Tsar. They did not arm themselves and they made no special arrangements for the coming of the Tsar and his army of oprichniki. They waited in fear and trembling, knowing that only a miracle could save them.

The Tsar was elated by the prospect of new massacres and vast booty; so were the oprichniki who formed their own private armies and raped, murdered, and looted as they pleased. The Tsar had promised that large shares of booty would be divided among them, but so far he had not kept his promise. They therefore took the law in their own hands and organized their own expeditions. No one knows how many of them embarked on these murderous adventures, but it would appear that all those who felt they were in the Tsar's good graces murdered and robbed at their pleasure. Heinrich Staden, who had every reason to believe that he was well-favored by the Tsar, has recounted his own exploits after leaving Novgorod. He wrote:

> I began to assemble an army of retainers from the poor, naked wretches around me, and I gave them clothes, which was much to their liking. I then undertook my own expeditions and found they were loyal to me. So when we came to a monastery or a church, they would go in and capture someone and ask him politely where the money was hidden and where we could find good horses. And if the man who was captured did not want to respond agreeably, they held him and tortured him until he spoke. In this way they got money and valuables for me.

It was laughably simple, and Staden enjoyed these easy triumphs and collected a considerable amount of booty, which was carted away to his own estate. But sometimes people grew weary of being robbed and murdered, and fought back. There were places between Novgorod and Pskov where an officer of the Oprichnina was advised to tread delicately. Here Staden recounts what happened when he blundered into a small town which refused to submit to the exactions of freebooters:

> We came to a town where there was a church, and my retainers entered it and took away the icons and other frivolous things, while I remained mounted outside. Suddenly I saw six horsemen who were being chased by three hundred Zemskie people, and I did not know who the six horsemen were, whether they were from the Zemshchina

or the Oprichnina, and so I summoned my retainers to mount their horses. By this time I realized what was happening—the six horsemen were oprichniki and they were being pursued by all those people. They cried out for help and so I attacked. And when the Zemskiye saw so many of my people emerging from the church they fled to the Prince's estate. I shot one of them, broke through the crowd, rode quickly through the gates. From the upper floor of the house stones were hurled at me. With one of my retainers called Teshata, I ran up the stairs, an ax in my hands. I was met by a Princess whose sole desire was to throw herself at my feet, but when she observed the anger written on my face she turned back to enter her own room. I struck her in the back with an ax and she fell through the doorway. Then I sprang over her and greeted the ladies who attended her.

Later, when I hurried from the women's room into the courtyard, the six oprichniki fell at my feet, saying, "We will inform our master about this and he will tell the Grand Prince how nobly you have borne yourself against the Zemskiye people. We observed your courage and cautiousness with our own eyes." I said to my retainers, "Take what you can, and get out quickly."

We rode through the entire night and came at last to an unfortified settlement. I did no harm to anyone there. I was resting. After two days of lying low I learned that five hundred musketeers of the Oprichnina had been killed by the Zemskiye people in that place.

Staden had no moral sense whatsoever and he told the story as ʤough he was the hero of an absorbing adventure. What he ᵣemembered most vividly was the Princess falling through the ᵈoorway with an ax in her back, but he also remembered other ᵗʰings—that he had to ride throughout the night to escape the ᵤemskiye people and that he had to lie very low when he came to ᵗʰe unfortified settlement. Nevertheless he was able to accumulate ᶠorty-nine horses and twenty-two of them were used to pull the ˢleighs heaped with the valuables he had stolen from churches and ᵖrivate houses.

When Ivan reached the Monastery of St. Nicholas on the ᵒutskirts of Pskov, he had the firm intention of drowning the city in ᵇlood. The people of Pskov were, in his eyes, just as guilty of ᵗreachery as the people of Novgorod and deserved a similar fate. It ᶜost him nothing to destroy a city. Indeed, the destruction of a city ʷas always highly profitable, for the booty became his private ᵖroperty.

The people of Pskov were too terrified to sleep that night. The comforted and bade farewell to one another, for they expected die. Children were told that the wrathful Tsar had arrived at the gates and that strange things would soon be happening; meanwhi they must be brave. Husbands solemnly bade farewell to the wives and to their children, and then the whole family proceeded church. That night the churches were crowded. It was a Saturday the second week of Lent, and on the Sunday it was expected the the Tsar and the oprichniki would enter the city.

All that night the church bells tolled and the people praye before the icons with tears streaming down their cheeks. The soun of the church bells reached the Monastery of St. Nicholas, and was said that the Tsar's heart was softened by the distant bells the clear winter night. This, however, was unlikely, for he was not man whose heart was often softened. Meanwhile Prince Yur Tokmakov, the governor of Pskov, addressed the people and tol them to set up outside their houses tables full of meats. When th Tsar entered the city, he must find them all kneeling, holding out him the traditional welcoming gifts of bread, salt, and good foo Men, women, and children would be kneeling side by side.

For some reason the Tsar decided to enter Pskov through th Varlaamsky Gate, which stood on the north of the city. This mean a long ride under the northern walls of the city and in order reach the Krom or Kremlin he would have to pass through th poorer part of the city. Perhaps he took this circuitous route to giv himself a longer time to relish the prospect of destroying the cit Messengers had been sent ahead to announce the route he woul take, and there were priests to welcome him at the Church of S Varlaam near the Varlaamsky Gate. Among these priests wa Abbot Kornely of the Pechersky Monastery and a monk calle Vassian Muromtsev. Both the monk and the abbot had incurred th displeasure of the Tsar and were likely to be punished. They ha been friends of Prince Andrey Kurbsky. They had been correspondence with him, and they still possessed some influenc He ordered their arrest.

As he drove through the city on a sleigh, he observed that th people were all kneeling outside their houses with bread and salt their hands. They were chanting words of prayer and submissiv ness. "Our Lord and Tsar, we are all your loyal subjects," the

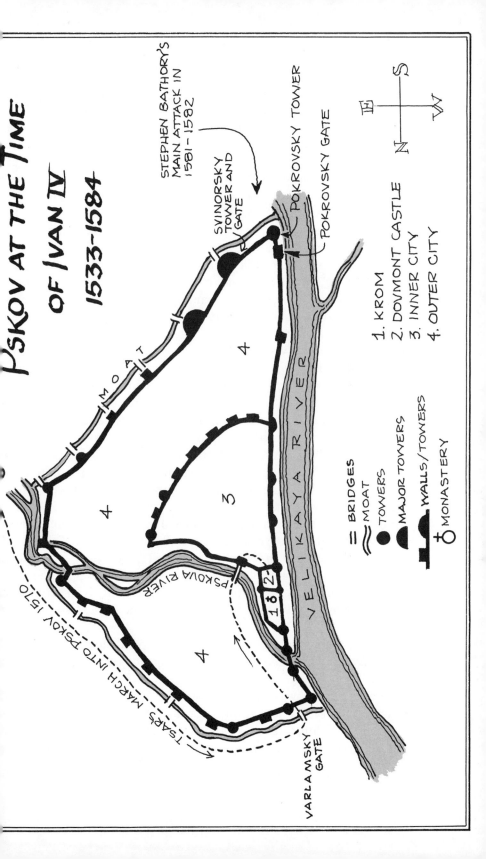

Pskov at the Time of Ivan IV
1533-1584

STEPHEN BATHORY'S MAIN ATTACK IN 1581-1582

SVINORSKY TOWER AND GATE

POKROVSKY TOWER

POKROVSKY GATE

N E S W

MOAT

4

4

3

4

1 & 2

PSKOVA RIVER

VELIKAYA RIVER

TSAR'S MARCH INTO PSKOV 1570

VARLAMSKY GATE

= BRIDGES
≈ MOAT
● TOWERS
⬤ MAJOR TOWERS
▬ WALLS/TOWERS
⚲ MONASTERY

1. KROM
2. DOVMONT CASTLE
3. INNER CITY
4. OUTER CITY

chanted. "With love and fervor we offer you this bread and salt. Do as you wish with our lives and possessions, for both our lives and our possessions belong wholly to you, O Great Autocrat." It was said that the Tsar was pleased by this unexpected expression of humility, but it is more likely that he regarded it as perfectly normal behavior and was surprised only because the humility was so well organized. Prince Yury Tokmakov had done his work well.

In the Cathedral of the Holy Trinity, within the walls of the Krom, the Tsar and his entourage attended the morning service. For a while Ivan prayed at the tomb of St. Vsevolod, the first prince of Pskov, who died in 1138. Near the prince's tomb hung the great sword he had used in many battles, inscribed with the words, *Honorem meum nemino dabo,* meaning "I shall surrender my honor to no one." It was observed that Ivan gazed at the sword for a long time.

Once the service was over the real work of the oprichniki began. Some thirty or forty members of the petty nobility who had earned Ivan's displeasure were arrested and executed. Abbot Kornely and the monk Vassian Muromtsev were also executed. The order went out to the oprichniki to despoil all the churches and monasteries, and Ivan especially asked them to remove the finest bells.

The blood bath was about to begin when it occurred to Ivan to visit the *yurodivy* Nikolay Salos, known as Mikula, a holy man famous throughout the region. Ivan approached the house where Mikula was living and suddenly there came a voice like thunder through the window, saying, "Ivashka! Ivashka! How much longer will you continue to shed innocent Christian blood? Take care! Leave at once, or a great misfortune will befall you!" Instead of leaving at once, Ivan entered the house and confronted the holy man, who thrust in his hands a slab of raw meat. Ivan refused to accept the meat, saying, "I am a Christian. I do not eat meat during Lent."

"You do much worse!" the holy man replied sternly. "You feed upon human flesh and blood, forgetting not only Lent but God Himself!"

While Mikula was speaking, the sky suddenly grew overcast, thunder rumbled and lightning flashed. Mikula raised his hands toward the lightning and exclaimed, "A thunderbolt will strike you dead if you or any of your oprichniki touch a hair of the head of the smallest child in Pskov! Know that we are being protected by an angel of God for a better fate than murder! Leave Pskov at once, or face the wrath of God!"

The story goes on to relate how Ivan begged Mikula for forgiveness and for his prayers, and was answered with more curses. About this time Ivan's favorite horse fell dead. This story was told by the chroniclers and also by the three foreign mercenaries, Staden, Taube, and Kruse, who joined the oprichniki and therefore had no reason to portray the Tsar in an unfavorable light. Sir Jerome Horsey also told the story, adding that he had himself seen the holy man: "I saw this impostor or magician, a foul creature, [who] went naked both in winter and summer. He endured both extreme frost and heat, did many strange things through the magical illusions of the devil, much followed, feared, and reverenced, both of prince and people."

Something very strange had happened: a naked holy man had said "No" to Ivan, and the Tsar, deeply aware of his guilt and the powers of holy men to bring down curses from Heaven, obeyed and left the city with all his oprichniki a few hours later, taking with him such spoils as had already been removed from the churches but otherwise leaving the city untouched. One man had stood between Ivan and innumerable murders.

Pskov was saved by the miracle of holiness. Ivan's determination to fill the deep and swift-flowing Velikaya River with corpses was abandoned hurriedly in the face of threats uttered by a holy man. But if Pskov was saved, it was not entirely saved. Orders went out to the people to serve the Tsar by dragging heavy guns up to the Livonian frontier, to construct bridges, and to mine saltpeter and sulphur for the making of gunpowder. In effect, a heavy war tax was levied on them. Some who were ordered to drag guns simply vanished in the forests and others died miserably of cold and famine. Even this was better than dying at the hands of Ivan's executioners, and the vast majority of the people of Pskov remained alive to sing the praises of Nikolay Salos, who had stood between them and Ivan's vengeance.

The expedition against Novgorod and Pskov was now over, and the army rode south to Staritsa where, as Staden says, "the Tsar had decided to muster his forces to see how they had borne up and how many remained with him." Ivan was well pleased with what he saw and in good humor. Staden, who had excelled himself as a private freebooter, found himself, as he expected, in the Tsar's good graces. Henceforth the German who struck an ax in the back of a Russian princess was permitted to call himself Heinrich von Staden. Having distributed other awards to his faithful followers, Ivan hurried on to Alexandrova Sloboda to survey the treasures plundered from Novgorod and to build the two churches which celebrated his two victories.

In an age of religious fervor Ivan was one of the most deeply religious men. He was exuberant in his prayers and utterly devoted to Christ, the Virgin, and his favorite saints. He spent long hours in contemplation of the holy icons, attended all the services of the Orthodox Church, and was continually engaging in theological arguments with the priests attached to his court. When he removed the church bells, icons, and carved doorways from Pskov and Novgorod, and took them into his private keeping in Alexandrova Sloboda, he appears to have genuinely believed that he had increased his store of divinity. They belonged to him by right of conquest; the question of his right of possession was never raised. Was he not God's annointed, the sole possessor of the Russian land?

Although Ivan was firm in the Orthodox faith, he was perfectly prepared to listen to the arguments of theologians belonging to other persuasions. He believed they were heretics and were damned, but this belief did not prevent him from inquiring very seriously into their arguments. He listened to them courteously even when they aroused only horror in his breast. He did not punish them, though he sometimes called them "dogs." He knew a great deal about Islam and the Catholic Church, but he appears to have known very little about Protestantism until the arrival in Moscow in May 1570 of a Polish-Lithuanian embassy led by Jan Krotowski, a Hussite who hoped that the doctrines of Jan Huss, "the pale thin man in mean attire," would be received with approval in Russia. Huss had been burned at the stake by the Catholic Church. Krotowski was a man of substance who admired Ivan and wanted him to become King of Poland and Grand Prince of Lithuania on the death of King Sigismund Augustus, who was known to be ailing. Huss had a large following among the Polish and Lithuanian nobility and gentry, and Krotowski believed that

Ivan's candidacy would be more palatable to them if he permitted the dissemination of the new faith and gave it his blessing. The ambassador even hoped that Ivan would be converted.

The embassy, of course, dealt with many matters unconnected with Hussite beliefs, but in the eyes of Krotowski it was abundantly necessary that Ivan should be well-informed about them. He therefore brought with him a famous Hussite preacher called Jan Rakita. Ivan agreed to listen to one of Rakita's sermons, promised the preacher immunity from any punishment that might arise from the expression of heretical doctrines, and promised that if Rakita provided him with a written copy of his sermon, he would answer it in detail. This was done. Rakita's sermon is lost, but a copy of Ivan's answer, written on eighty-four parchment sheets, placed in a jewel-studded box and solemnly handed to Rakita before his departure, has survived. With some difficulty Rakita's ideas can be guessed by studying Ivan's vehement denunciations. For example, we know that Rakita upheld the Ten Commandments because Ivan replied: "You believe in the Ten Commandments as set down in the second book of Moses. Know that the Apostles changed all these commandments except two: Thou shalt love thy God with all thy soul and thy neighbor as thyself. These two you do not observe." [1] Rakita declared that all men are delivered unto death because of Adam's sin and therefore the Word of God took flesh and dwelt among us. Ivan replied that this was an error. "Until the birth of Christ the just also were delivered unto death and descended into hell," he wrote. "But when Christ was brought forth into the light, then the power of death was broken." Again, when Rakita charged that in the Orthodox Church the Apostles are considered to be divinities, Ivan, quoting from *Corinthians*, answered brusquely: "Know this concerning the Apostles: we are far from considering them as divinities. One of them said: 'I have planted, Apollos watered; but God gave the increase.' " Ivan knew the Pauline texts by heart and used them to advantage. He could always bend the difficult texts for his own purposes and on occasion he could write paragraphs which have the effect of precise sermons. Here he attacks Rakita for misunderstanding faith and works:

[1] I *Corinthians*, III, 6.

You wrote that we are forgiven and our sins are blotted out freely not because of any human works, and our errors are expunged by grace. But if works do not come first, why should Christ say in the Gospel: "If any man does not leave his father, and mother, and wife, and children, and brethren, and sisters, and his possessions, and deny himself, he is not my disciple, and he that taketh not up his cross, and followeth after me, is not worthy of me." [2]

By the cross he means to be crucified to all the things of this world, that is, to hold of little account all earthly desires, to abstain from acquiring wealth, possessions, food, drink, to desire nothing and to be content with whatever befalls us, joyfully and prayerfully. The cross means to love your enemies, those by whom you are oppressed, to pray to God for those who torment us, to treat your possessions as if you did not possess them, and to have no care for them.

The cross means to be unremitting in prayer, fasting, observing the divine commandment as it befits the lives of pilgrims, or as Paul says, to seek after possessions to come and to desire to live in that eternal paradise.

This is what it means to carry one's cross, to be crucified to the world, to follow Christ.

Ivan's attitude toward Rakita is one of contempt and derision. How amazing, how stupid, that someone should exist who does not understand the simple truths of the Orthodox faith! From time to time he rounds on Rakita with an ill-tempered rebuke: "Since you are a dog and an enemy of Christ's cross, I don't want to have anything to do with you!" Nevertheless he continues to argue with him, to confound his arguments, and to press home with his own triumphant conclusions. Since he was accustomed to having priests around him and was well versed in theological hair-splitting he had no difficulty in reducing Rakita's arguments to absurdities. He was a man who prided himself on his cleverness. He appears not to have realized that if he had simply kept quiet, accepting Rakita's arguments for what they were worth, he might have earned the respect of the Polish and Lithuanian nobility and gentry, and acquired the crown of Poland and the Grand Principality of Lithuania. The sermons of Rakita and Ivan were political events of the first magnitude, but it is unlikely that Ivan realized how many political advantages he threw away in his trouncing of Rakita's beliefs.

[2] *Matthew*, 10:37–8, *Luke*, XIV, 26.

We know Ivan's writings best through his letters to Prince Kurbsky, full of fire and sudden explosive violence. They are passionate letters written in an extremity of passion, and yet half-concealed behind the frenzy there can be observed a cool and calculating mind. It is as though down below the smooth-running destructive engines were at work belching out so much smoke and steam and flames that it is almost impossible to see the shape of the machinery. We expect him to be fierce in every utterance and he does not disappoint us. So it comes as a surprise to discover that he could on occasion tell stories from the apocryphal gospels and the writings of the Church Fathers with a kind of carefree grace. He believed devoutly in miracle-working images and especially in the Icon of the Virgin of Vladimir which he believed had been painted by St. Luke; and so, very calmly, as though he was telling a friend how it had happened, he tells Rakita this story about holy statues and icons:

Consider the woman having an issue of blood. Christ healed her, and she made a life-size bronze statue of Him. This statue, up until the time of Julian, King of the Greeks, accursed apostate and devil-worshipper, cured many people of their illnesses. It is the same with the temple in Lydia founded by the Apostles. On top of a column at the north gate, there was an image of the Mother of God and her eternal Son. This image was not the work of human hands, but divinely made. It was revealed in order to show who were Christians and who were pagans. It was proper that there be a church where this miracle occurred. When the Apostles invited the Mother of God to the dedication of the church, she replied, "You go, my children, for I shall be there with you." When the Apostles arrived at the church and saw the image, they wept and were filled with joy and they offered thanks to God the Creator of all.

After a while the Mother of God herself came to the place. When she saw that the image was most faithful, she said, "My help and my grace will remain there." The filthy Julian later tried to destroy this place. When the masons were trying to break down the walls and tear down the painting, the image was strengthened by God and remained more firmly embedded in the wall, and so the violators abandoned the task of destroying it. Although they struck it with hammers, it remained unblemished and in no way were they able to destroy it: they had merely dusted it. After these affronts certain upright men came and cleansed it, and in this way it remained unharmed with all its colors preserved.

There is also the story of the famous Jenaeus, who was restored to
health by Peter and John, and erected a beautiful temple. In this also
there was an image of the Virgin Mary, which was made by him in
accordance with her own desire and which worked great miracles.
Blessed Luke painted it and brought it to the Mother of God. When
she saw it, she said, "May my power and favor be with this image."
As long as this image is preserved in Moscow in our realm, so long
shall the Christian faith remain whole.

There is no reason to think that Ivan regarded any of these
statements as fantasies. Stories about icons "not made by hands"
were believed implicitly in his time, and since some of the most
famous wonder-working images were in his possession and had
abundantly demonstrated their power over the Tatars, and other
enemies, he had no reason to doubt their efficacy. Icons were
sources of immense spiritual and earthly power, like the bones of
the saints. The prayers of the faithful also generated power, and he
found in himself, as the successor of St. Vladimir, Grand Prince of
Kiev, who had brought the Christian faith to Russia, still another
source of power. Rakita was left in no doubt that Ivan regarded
himself as a spiritual and earthly ruler. Thus power resided in him
and around him, and belonged to him by right of succession, and
was everywhere at his command: he was speaking as a theologian
but also as a man who knew himself to be if not at the right hand of
God so close to divinity that it made very little difference. In his
lifetime, in spite of all his crimes, Ivan regarded himself as the
shepherd of the Orthodox faith.

When he spoke to Rakita in the Great Palace of the Kremlin
sitting on his high throne and confronting the Hussite preacher who
stood on a dais covered with carpets, he was speaking from the
heights of infallible wisdom. As spiritual ruler, he consigned Rakita
to damnation, saying, "I regard you as a heretic, because your
teaching is depraved and clearly contrary to the teaching of Christ
and the Church. Not only are you a heretic, but a servant of
Antichrist raised up by the devil!" But Ivan had not the slightest
interest in persecuting the heretic. He was familiar with many
Protestants, found them more congenial than Catholics, permitted
them to practice their religion freely, and once fined the Metropolitan of Moscow a stupendous sum for insulting a German Protes-
tant. Ivan kept his promise of letting Rakita go free. He appears to

have regarded the debate as a pleasant interlude in the hard task of governing Russia.

The Polish and Lithuanian ambassadors left Moscow on July 3, 1570, and almost immediately the hard work of governing took the form of secret trials followed by public executions.

Ivan's well-mannered behavior toward the ambassadors was the expression of deliberate policy; he enjoyed entertaining foreigners, learning about their countries, debating with them and seeking from them those assurances of friendship which were the necessary fruits of his foreign policy. But the main, all-consuming passion of the Tsar had little enough to do with foreign policy. What chiefly concerned him was the rooting out of traitors among the ranks of the boyars, the princes, and the nobility.

Since those who were condemned to death for treachery were brought to trial in secret, we do not always know why they were condemned. Many, perhaps most of them, were the innocent victims of agents provocateurs or of private malice. Thus we have no information whatsoever about the reasons that brought about the execution of Prince Peter Serebriany on July 20. He had been one of the heroes of the battle for Kazan and was highly respected in the Boyar Council. It was known that for some weeks he had been in disfavor. Quite possibly in an unguarded moment he had protested against the crimes committed in Novgorod and Pskov. Ivan's method of execution was unusual. He ordered Maliuta Skuratov to go to the prince's residence, hack off his head, and bring it back to the Oprichnina Palace in Moscow, where he was then staying. Maliuta Skuratov did as he was told. The prince's head was cut off in his own courtyard. Maliuta Skuratov ran to the palace and laid the head at Ivan's feet, saying, "Tsar, the work you commanded me to do has been done!" The Tsar exclaimed, "*Goida!*" and all the oprichniki around him shouted in chorus.

A day or two later Ivan ordered the execution of a hundred and sixty-five Polish and Lithuanian prisoners. They were being held in three towers, apparently within the confines of the Oprichnina Palace. According to the chroniclers there were fifty-five prisoners in each tower and Ivan himself superintended the executions and killed the first two prisoners by thrusting a long spear through the bars. He was attempting to kill a third, bungled it and gave the job to his son, the Tsarevich Ivan, who had no difficulty killing a defenseless prisoner. These killings were acts of imbecile brutality and ferocity, all the more inexplicable because only a few days before Ivan had signed a three-year truce with the Polish and Lithuanian ambassadors.

Ivan's attitude toward prisoners was one of contempt. They deserved to die because they were prisoners. During his campaign against Novgorod and Pskov, he ordered the execution of prisoners wherever he found them. It is related that among the hundred and sixty-five prisoners were many notables whose lives could have been usefully exchanged with the lives of Russian prisoners, but Ivan was rarely interested in such transactions. It is related, too, that after all the prisoners were dead, he returned to the palace and gave himself up to musical entertainments. At sunset he remembered the dead and ordered that they should be piled onto carts and taken to the cemetery reserved for foreigners.

Early on the morning of July 25, 1570, a troop of oprichniki arrived on the Red Square and began to hammer twenty heavy stakes into the ground. Then logs were roped to the stakes in such a way that they formed a continuous horizontal line, each log touching the next. Then they lit fires and over each fire they set a caldron of water, which was soon boiling. The people who had been walking about the Red Square grew alarmed, for it was obvious that these strange preparations could have only one purpose—more executions. The news from Novgorod and Pskov had terrified the people of Moscow, who reasoned that Ivan was perfectly capable of doing to them what he had already done in the north; and suddenly there were no more people left on the square.

The news that the people had vanished was brought to Ivan, who decided to investigate. He arrived on the square in full armor, with a helmet, sword, bow and quiver full of arrows, and a bodyguard of similarly armed oprichniki. About the same time fifteen hundred mounted musketeers rode onto the square and took up their places round the scene of execution. Seeing that the square was deserted, Ivan with an escort rode up and down the side streets exhorting the people to be of good heart and to come to the square, where no harm would befall them. Previously he had arranged that there should be food prepared for the citizens in some of the houses overlooking the Red Square.

These attempts to lure the people into the square failed at first;

they were all hiding from Ivan in fear and trembling. Finally it was decided to send several old men, who did not care very much what happened to them because they were close to death, to find out Ivan's intentions. Ivan received them kindly, and they reported on their return that there was nothing to fear from him.

Meanwhile, three hundred of his victims, many weakened by torture and hunger, and some with broken legs and arms, were led out onto the square and tied with ropes to the logs, to await their fate. The common people who began to emerge from the side streets saw them and went hurrying back to their houses to report that a mass execution was about to take place. It was observed that not many people had appeared on the square, that they moved hesitantly, and that they turned away as soon as they saw the prisoners. Ivan was enraged, for he wanted them all to attend, and as he rode up and down the square, he shouted that they were all beholden to him, they had a duty to attend the executions and to come as close as possible to the prisoners, and although he had intended to destroy the people of Moscow, as he had destroyed the people of Novgorod, nevertheless he felt no anger toward them and they had nothing to fear.

So between threats and blandishments, and appeals for more and more people to present themselves, Ivan and his attendants managed to bring a large crowd onto the Red Square and those who came late watched from the roofs. The proceedings began with Ivan appealing to the people.

"Is it right for me to punish traitors?" he shouted, and there came the answering shout, "Long live the good Tsar! It is right for you to punish traitors according to their crimes!"

Ivan then moved to a place reserved for him near a boiling caldron and did something totally unexpected. He ordered the release of a hundred and eighty-four prisoners, who had been judged the least guilty. Addressing himself to the boyars, he said, "I give them to you, accept them, and take them away," according to the formula which meant that the boyars were now made responsible for them. These prisoners were allowed to make their way through the ranks of mounted musketeers guarding the place of execution.

Vasily Shchelkalov, the Tsar's secretary, then began to read out the names of those who had been condemned to death. When this was completed, Ivan Viskovaty was brought forward. He was a man of humble origin who for more than twenty years had been the Secretary for Foreign affairs when he was not actively pursuing diplomatic affairs abroad. He was Russia's chief diplomat, the architect of Russian foreign policy, known for his resourcefulness and courage. In 1561 he was promoted to Keeper of the Privy Seal, and in the following year he was sent on an embassy to Denmark. Whatever his title, he remained Ivan's chief adviser on foreign affairs.

When Ivan returned from his campaigns against Novgorod and Pskov, Viskovaty took his life in his hands by presenting a petition demanding an end to all the bloodshed. He urged Ivan to think about his responsibility toward God and the people. There were rumors that Ivan proposed to murder all the boyars: this, too, must not be allowed to take place. He urged the Tsar to consider two points especially: Who will be left to help him defend the country? Who will he live with after executing so many brave people?

Ivan was stunned by the petition and what particularly seems to have disturbed him was that Viskovaty knew of his intention to murder the boyars.

"I have only just begun to rid myself of you people!" Ivan shouted. "I shall make it my business to destroy all of you root and branch, so that not even a memory of you remains! I truly hope to do this, but if the worst comes to the worst and God punishes me and I am forced to surrender to a foreign enemy, then I would rather surrender something of great importance than become the laughingstock of you, who are my servants!"

The Tsar's unreasoning hatred of the boyars, his fear of intrigues against him, his suspicions about the growing influence of the seventeen-year-old Tsarevich, all these had led him on his return to Moscow to contemplate desperate actions. He had shown that he was perfectly capable of ordering bloodbaths on a hitherto unprecedented scale, and the extermination of the boyars was only part of a plan which involved his own possible abdication. But first he was determined to administer such ferocious punishment on the Russian people that they would remember him for ever afterward. He was a man who found it almost impossible to conceal his intentions and he had publicly proclaimed his plans for a violent theatrical coup which would shake Russia to her foundations. He was planning another and more extensive bloodbath which might or might not be followed by his abdication and the installation of a foreign prince on the throne of Russia.

It was at a reception given to Prince Magnus of Denmark that Ivan made his intentions known. The Boyar Council and the foreign ambassadors were present; so was the Tsarevich Ivan and the entire court. Suddenly Ivan turned to Prince Magnus and said, "Your Illustrious Highness, after I am dead, you shall be my heir and the ruler of my country—and I shall tear up my unworthy subjects by the roots and humble them and trample them underfoot!" The reception, which was given in the Great Kremlin Palace in June 1570, was luxurious and sumptuous to the highest degree. Ivan was fond of the handsome thirty-year-old prince, to whom he had just given the crown of Livonia and the hand of Princess Evdokia, the daughter of Prince Vladimir of Staritsa. The crown of Livonia was not in his keeping, but that was a small matter. Princess Evdokia died and Prince Magnus was later given Maria, another of the daughters of Prince Vladimir of Staritsa, and this too was a small matter. But Ivan was well aware of the solemnity of the occasion: a crown was being offered, a prince was being betrothed. He chose this occasion to announce that Prince Magnus would inherit the throne and that he would wreak a terrible vengeance on the Russian people. There was a threefold curse on them: they would be uprooted, humbled, and trampled underfoot.

The mind of the psychopath in power moves in predictable ways. Once he has tasted the joys of destruction he cannot stop, for there is nothing to prevent him. He publicly proclaims his intentions, and the proclamation of the coming terror is almost as satisfying as the terror itself. He kills those who are closest to him and those who are indifferent to him, and those who resist him must die many times over.

Ivan Viskovaty, the man who resisted the Tsar, was about to die many times over.

Vasily Shchelkalov read out the crimes committed by the prisoner from a long scroll. He said:

> This man Ivan, an officer of the Tsar and Grand Prince, has been unfaithful and has acted without loyalty. He has been in communication with the King of Poland and has promised to hand over to him

the fortresses of Novgorod and Pskov. That was his first act of treason.

At this point Shchelkalov struck Viskovaty with a whip, thus indicating that he was enraged by the prisoner's crimes. He went on:

> Your second act of treason and duplicity took place when you wrote to the Sultan of Turkey urging him to send armies against Kazan and Astrakhan. Your third act of treason took place when you wrote to the Khan of the Crimea, commanding him to devastate the land of the Tsar and the Grand Prince with fire and sword. And so it happened that the Khan raided the land of Muscovy and caused great harm to the people and the country. You are the cause of this great calamity and thus you have committed treason against your sovereign.

Bleeding from several cuts from the whip, Viskovaty turned to Ivan and replied with words as courageous as any spoken in Russia: "Great Tsar, God is my witness that I am innocent. I deny that I have committed any of the crimes attributed to me. As befitted a loyal subject, I have always served you loyally. I entrust my affairs to God, before whom I am a sinner, and I leave the judgment to Him. In time to come He will be the judge of your acts and mine. Since you thirst for my blood, then take it and spill it, innocent though it is. Drink and eat my blood until you are sated with it!"

Viskovaty had not quite finished with Ivan. He admonished Ivan for secretly murdering so many boyars in the mistaken belief that they were attempting to usurp his power, and then he went on to reproach him for massacring so many innocent people. How many women and girls had been violated at his orders and then killed! And when some oprichniki went up to him and bade him confess his guilt and to beg the Tsar for mercy, Viskovaty answered: "Damnation upon your tyrant! What are you all but destroyers of the people and drinkers of human blood? You have your task—it is to utter falsehoods and to slander the innocent! But God will judge you, and in the next world you will be punished for your sins!"

Damnation upon your tyrant! Budte prokliaty s vashem tirannom! Never before had such words been uttered in the presence of Ivan, who immediately shouted, "Begin!" The oprichniki stripped off

Viskovaty's clothes, and hung him by the armpits to one of the horizontal logs. Maliuta Skuratov ran up to the Tsar and said, "Who will be the executioner?"

"Those who are most loyal to me!" the Tsar answered.

To prove his loyalty Maliuta Skuratov cut off Viskovaty's nose, another cut off an ear, and soon all the oprichniki were cutting off pieces of his flesh, as though he were butcher's meat. In his book *On the Russe Commonwealth* Giles Fletcher says that Ivan ordered him to be cut up as though he were a goose, cutting the lower parts of his legs and arms and finally cutting off his head, and all the time Ivan was taunting him, saying, "That's goose flesh—is it good meat?"

Viskovaty died, and then it was the turn of the treasurer, Nikita Funikov, who had loyally served the Tsar for a quarter of a century or more. Shchelkalov read out the list of his crimes and he answered that he was completely innocent but acknowledged the Tsar's right to execute him even though he was innocent.

"You will die!" the Tsar said, "but you will not die at my hands or at my instigation, and not by any fault of mine! You will die because you listened to your companion [Viskovaty] and were wholly dependent on him! Even if you committed no crimes, you must perish because you served him!"

The Tsar then gave the signal to the oprichniki to do their work. Funikov was stripped naked, and buckets of ice-cold water and boiling hot water were poured on him until his skin came off like an eel's.

The third to be executed was the cook who at the Tsar's orders had given poison to Prince Vladimir of Staritsa. There followed a hundred and thirteen executions, with the Tsar and the Tsarevich joining the executioners, stabbing the victims with spears or hacking at them with swords. There was, of course, no danger, for the victims were trussed to great balks of timber, and the Tsar and the Tsarevich could therefore move along the line with impunity. The killing went on for four hours, and then the ropes were cut and the dead were thrown into a heap. In the evening Ivan ordered them to be carted off and buried in a mass grave.

When they were all killed, the Tsar still had much to do. He first called at the house of Nikita Funikov, and ordered his bodyguard to seize the widow and torture her until she revealed the hiding place of her valuables. She died under torture and the valuable were given to the Tsar. Her daughter stood by, weeping and trembling. She was about fifteen, and very beautiful, but the Tsar was exasperated by her weeping and ordered his guards to kill her. As the oprichniki were about to seize her, the Tsarevich Ivan held her by the skirt and cried out, "Dear father, let me have her! I will keep her locked up!" Ivan ordered the oprichniki to let the girl remain in his son's keeping.

Even after the orgy of killing on the Red Square Ivan's thirst for blood was not satisfied. Three days later the wives and daughters of the dead men were clubbed to death and their bodies thrown into the river.

Among those who perished were most of the administrative heads of the government. Some of the leaders of the oprichnik were also under arrest. The Basmanovs, father and son, had been under arrest in Moscow during the expedition to Novgorod—they had shown insufficient enthusiasm for the project—and they too were killed. How and where they were killed remains unknown. Since they were high officers of the Oprichnina and the manner of their deaths would normally be reported in the chronicles, it must be assumed that they were killed secretly. In the following month the Tsar sent some money to the Troitsa-Sergeyevsky Monastery for the repose of their souls.

Some weeks later Afanasy Viazemsky, who had also incurred the Tsar's displeasure before the campaign against Novgorod, was placed under arrest and given daily beatings. As each day passed a new fine was imposed on him. One day the Tsar would demand a fine of three hundred rubles, on another day it would be five hundred or a thousand, according to the Tsar's pleasure. Viazemsky's body was bruised and swollen, but the fines continued. When he had no more money, he pretended that various rich merchants owed him money, and the oprichniki were sent to collect the debts. The beatings continued into the following year. The Tsar's vengeance reached out to Viazemsky's wife, who was the Mistress of the Seamstresses, an official post which gave her the supervision of forty young seamstresses who embroidered and sewed the robes of gold cloth worn at court. Finally the Tsar wearied of Viazemsky and sent him to prison at Gorodets where he was kept in chains.

What had long been predicted was now at last coming to pass.

The oprichniki, those anarchic and self-serving executioners who had been let loose upon the country, were about to be destroyed. In the past it seems never to have occurred to Ivan that they resembled a vast swarm of maggots eating away at his throne. When he finally turned against them it was because they proved to be totally inefficient. They were skilfull at butchering Russians but they showed no skill at butchering Tatars. They were a gang of murderers, and like all such gangs they were composed of cowards who ran away at the first sign of danger. Suddenly the Tatars invaded Muscovy, put Moscow to the flames, and carried off an immense treasure. The Zemshchina princes and the common people fought the Tatars, and the oprichniki ran for their lives.

Moscow in Flames

AT FIRST THERE WAS only a small cloud on the horizon. There was a growing sense of fear, as though everyone knew that disasters were fast approaching, but no one knew from which direction they would come. Moscow was suffering from famine, the July massacres on the Red Square were still vividly remembered, and Ivan was still issuing commands from the guarded seclusion of his palace at Alexandrova Sloboda. Nothing more was being heard about Prince Magnus's elevation to the throne, and it appeared that the Tsarevich was in the Tsar's good favor and therefore Prince Magnus was unlikely to be his successor. The threat to uproot and then trample the Russian people underfoot was not being carried out, but the people were too exhausted to care. The terrible Emperor was on the throne: lightning might strike out of a cloudless sky.

Early in September 1570 there came rumors that a large Tatar army was on the march. Since the Russians had ambassadors and agents in the various Tatar courts and usually knew in advance what they were up to, these rumors were treated seriously and Prince Ivan Belsky led an army to the Oka River. About ten days later, on September 16, Ivan himself set out from Alexandrova Sloboda at the head of an army of oprichniki, marching toward the fortress of Serpukhov, which lay on a tributary of the Oka River. Serpukhov was built of white stone and belonged to that chain of fortresses, mostly built of wood, which stretched along the Oka

.iver and its tributaries. Kashira, Kaluga, Tarusa, Alexin, and erpukhov were all minor fortresses compared to Kolomna, where ₁e main army was concentrated. Russian territory extended far to ₁e south, and beyond the Russian frontiers lay the *dikoye pole,* the ʻild plain, the no-man's-land where the tribesmen wandered. When ₁e Tatars drove up from the south they encountered no real ₚposition until they reached the Oka River. Now, as in previous ₑars, their aim was not conquest but the capture of loot and young ₗussians to sell in the slave markets of Kaffa and Constantinople. ᶠ by chance they captured members of the Russian nobility, they ʻere ransomed; and there existed a fixed scale of ransom payments ₑcording to their rank.

But once the Tsar arrived at Serpukhov, it became clear that this ʻas not the large Tatar army which had been expected, but a ᵧouting force of about 6,000 men. This small army arrived at the ʻontier town of Novosil, which belonged to Prince Mikhail ʻorotynsky, and after pillaging the town the Tatars withdrew. The ₗilitary commanders on the Oka River concluded that there was ₜtle danger of any further attacks that year, but for safety's sake it ʋas decided that the Zemshchina Army should retain its positions long the Oka River for two more weeks and that special efforts ₕould be made to reinforce the southern defenses. Prince Vorotyn ₖy was placed in charge of all the defense works, fortresses, guard ₒsts, and scouting operations. He was chosen because he was an ₓperienced general and also because he was the owner of vast ₛtates on the southwest frontier and could therefore be expected to ₚut his heart into defending the entire frontier. The decree, ₚpointing him to this new position, was not signed until early the ₒllowing year, but it is clear that he was given full powers by Ivan ₗuring his brief visit to Serpukhov. The decree mentions defense ₗnes, guard posts, ramparts made of earth and balks of timber, and ₒokout posts deep in no-man's-land. If the Tatars were going to ₙvade Russia, the defense was in good hands.

Ivan spent only a few days in Serpukhov. On September 22 he ₑturned to Alexandrova Sloboda.

What the Russians did not know until later was that the force of ,₀₀₀ men who reached as far north as Novosil had been sent to ₑst the Russian defenses in advance of a massive attack that was ₑeing prepared by Devlet Guirey, the Khan of the Crimea, whose

last invasion had taken place in 1565. He was an old man sufferin
from the infirmities of old age. Two years earlier the Russian envo
to the Khan's court reported that "the insides were falling out c
him and sometimes he cannot sit on a horse and during the farewe
audience he leaned back," by which the envoy meant that h
leaned back on the cushions and appeared to be exhausted. But th
Khan was not so ill that he was incapable of organizing a vas
army, leading it and inflicting terrible defeats on the Russians. I
seemed to him and to all the enemies of Russia a good time t
attack. Sultan Selim II, who attempted to capture Astrakhan i
1569 but failed miserably, was encouraging him. The Poles an
Lithuanians were complaining that for the past three years th
Tatars had inflicted no damage on Russia and therefore could no
expect the customary gifts. Old as he was, the Khan decided t
attack, with all the forces he could muster.

His army consisted of about 120,000 men, mostly from th
Crimea but including recruits from the Great Nogay Horde, wh
roamed the steppes east of the Volga, and from the Lesser Noga
Horde, who were established on the shores of the Sea of Azo
between the Don and the Kuban. There were other smalle
detachments of Tatars and a contingent of Turkish soldiers. O
April 5, 1571, the Khan led his two sons and his army across th
narrow isthmus of Perekop, which joins the Crimea to th
mainland, and marched north. His intention was to sack Mosco
and put it to the flames.

On the journey across the steppes the Tatars encountered som
Russian nobles who had fled from Russia to avoid execution. Fron
them the Tatars learned that the Tsar was at Alexandrova Sloboda
that Moscow was suffering from famine, and that the bulk of th
Russian forces were in Livonia. They advised the Khan to press o
to Moscow. A certain Kudiyar Tishenkov, a member of th
Russian provincial nobility, said he had heard that the Tsar wa
expected to arrive shortly at Serpukhov but his army was so smal
that it would provide no effective opposition. He offered to act a
the guide of the Tatars, and when he saw that one of the Tata
captains distrusted him, he replied, "If you fail to reach Moscow
then you can impale me! There is nothing standing in your way!"
Then two recently baptized Tatars were brought into the Khan'
presence and they too said that there was nothing to prevent hir

from arriving before the gates of Moscow. Accordingly it was decided to march on Moscow with Kudiyar Tishenkov acting as the guide.

Although the Russian envoy at the Khan's court was able to send a message to Moscow with the warning that the Khan's army had left Perekop and was advancing to the north, the news did not reach Ivan until too late. Suddenly the Tatars appeared at Tula, burned the town, and sped on toward Serpukhov. The Zemshchina forces on the Oka River consisted of about 50,000 men and were therefore heavily outnumbered by the enemy. The main army was stationed at Kolomna under Prince Ivan Belsky, the right wing was commanded by Prince Ivan Mstislavsky at Kashira, and the vanguard was at Serpukhov, where Prince Mikhail Vorotynsky had his headquarters. On May 16 Ivan set out with his oprichniki from Alexandrova Sloboda for Serpukhov, riding ahead with about 6,000 troops while the rest of his army, hastily organized, followed at a more leisurely pace. He knew that Tula had been attacked but did not know how large the Tatar armies were. He decided to pitch his camp some miles away from Serpukhov, and he was still in camp when he received one of the greatest shocks of his life, for he learned that a large Tatar army had crossed the Oka River and was only twenty miles away to the west.

Ivan was one of those men who find no difficulty in massacring defenseless civilians but he could not command armies, or fight, or show courage in adversity. He was inclined to lose his nerve whenever he was confronted with danger. So now, realizing that the Tatars were almost within earshot, he fled, stopping for only one night at Alexandrova Sloboda to collect his treasure chests full of jewels and gold and silver plate. The treasure represented wealth and power, an insurance against all emergencies; with it he could pay the expenses of his court, purchase military equipment from abroad, and perhaps—for his ultimate intentions are unknown—secure safe passage to England and live passably well on English soil.

He had no difficulty in justifying his flight. He complained later to the Polish ambassador that he had been led into a trap. "No one warned me about the Tatar army," he said. "My own subjects led me straight to them. There were 40,000 Tatars, while I had only six thousand of my own troops."

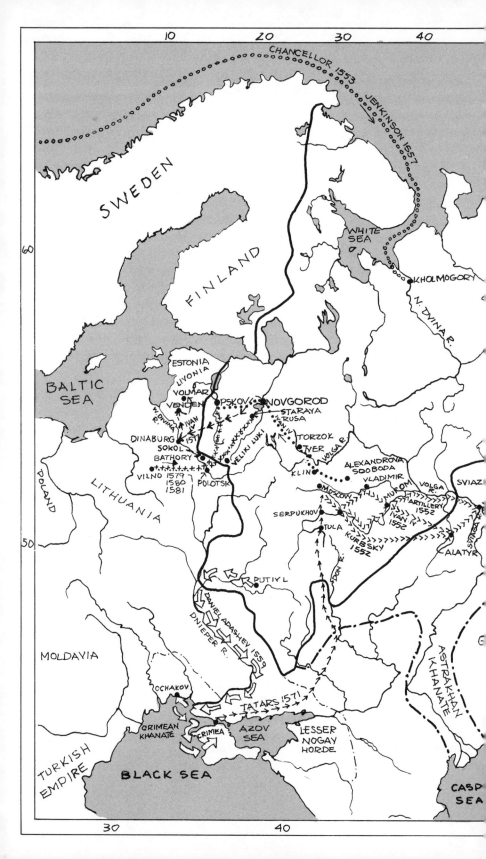

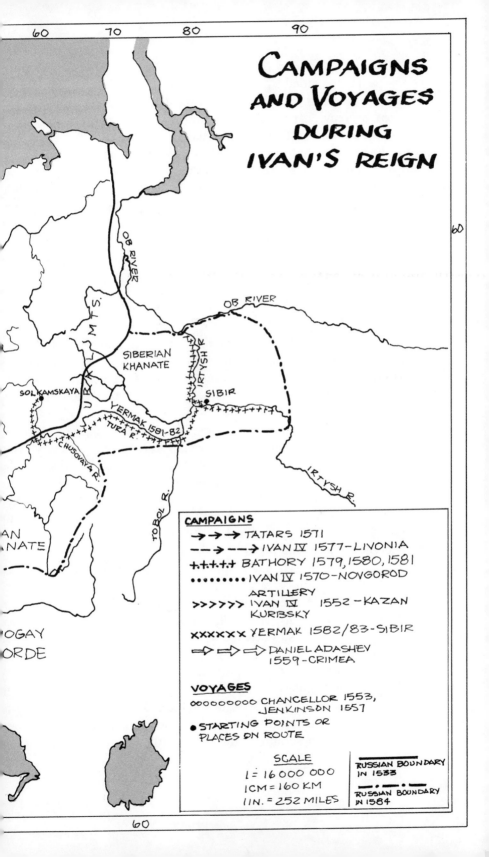

The Tatars, aided by Kudiyar Tishenkov, crossed the Oka River, quickly defeated a force of oprichniki, and continued to advance in great secrecy, carrying everything before them. Ivan was now completely cut off from the Russian armies on the Oka River. All he knew was that some dreadful calamity must have occurred. From Alexandrova Sloboda, with his two young sons, his treasure, his guards, and his household servants, he fled first to Rostov, then to Yaroslavl, and then to the Oprichnina stronghold at Vologda, surrounded by stone walls and permanently guarded by five hundred musketeers. There, planning to seek even greater safety, although he was already far in the north, he ordered the construction of river boats to carry him and his entourage to the White Sea by way of the Dvina River, and once he had reached the coast it would be a comparatively easy matter for him to arrange for one of the English ships to take him to England. Meanwhile he ordered the defenses of Vologda to be strengthened, apparently fearing that the Tatars would seek him out in this northern country or perhaps as Giles Fletcher suggested in his book because he feared that the Russian nobility and the officers of the army would hand him over to the Tatars.

Long before Ivan reached Vologda, the Tatars reached Moscow. Serpukhov, where they crossed the Oka River, was only a day's ride or about sixty miles from Moscow. As soon as they heard about the crossing, the Russian army turned right about and raced for the city, which it reached only a few hours before the Tatars. Prince Ivan Mstislavsky threw his troops into the western suburbs inside the loop formed by the Moskva River. Prince Ivan Belsky's army occupied the northern bank of the river from the Kremlin to the Yauza. Further east, across the Yauza, was the army of Prince Mikhail Vorotynsky, whose task was to guard the eastern approaches, while the Oprichnina quarter of Moscow was commanded by an army of oprichniki under the command of Prince Vasily Temkin-Rostovsky. He was one of those who took an active part in the July massacres and was seen to jump off his horse and cut off the heads of a man, his wife, and two sons, then he solemnly dragged the headless bodies and laid them before Ivan. Although the Princes were in a desperate situation, their armies far outnumbered by the Tatars; they had made a sensible distribution of their forces on the assumption that the battle for Moscow would be fought somewhere on the outskirts of the city. The fords nearest Moscow were well-guarded. The Kremlin itself, with the heavy cannon mounted on the walls, was virtually impregnable. Here and there, and especially in the Oprichnina quarter, wooden walls had been erected on the earthen ramparts, while the walls of the Kremlin and the Kitay Gorod with their towers and defense posts served as a powerful bulwark against the enemy.

The Tatars, driving up from the south, had not the least intention of fighting a pitched battle. Their intention was to destroy the city, acquire as much plunder as possible, and then return to their homeland. But in order to destroy the city it was necessary to come very close to it. Belsky's army took up positions south of the river on the edge of the region known as the Great Field and offered battle. There was some savage fighting. Belsky was severely wounded, and the Russians were forced back. Meanwhile the Tatars pressed closer to the city not only in the south but also in the west, where a whole army crossed the ford near the Novodevichy Monastery to attack the Oprichnina quarter, which they stormed and set on fire. There had been little rain for some weeks, a strong west wind was blowing, and the flames spread to the Kremlin. Soon nearly all the palaces and churches within the Kremlin walls were burning. The small wooden churches exploded; the iron girders supporting the walls of the Granovitaya Palata melted away; the bell towers caught fire and the bells melted; and afterwards the Russians remembered that all the church bells of Moscow were ringing and one by one the sound of the bells died away.

On the morning of May 24, 1571, the heart of Moscow perished, and only a few charred buildings survived the fire by a miracle. The flames from the Oprichnina quarter spread eastward and threatened to engulf the whole city. For a few hours it seemed that the Kitay Gorod would be spared, but a gun foundry caught fire and the flaming roof sailed into the air and fell over the walls of the Kitay Gorod, which was soon in flames. Whole streets burst into flame. People who took refuge in the cellars were suffocated to death. Others, who ran to the river for safety, carrying their valuables with them, were killed by the Tatars or drowned. A few survived by standing in the river up to their necks. So great was the fury of the fire that about sixty thousand people, half the population of Moscow, perished.

Prince Ivan Belsky was among those who took refuge in a cellar. He died of suffocation. Heinrich Staden was luckier; he found a cellar already occupied, forced half of the people out at sword-point, brought in his own servants, and then locked the iron door until the fire had abated. He survived unharmed.

"The entire city was burned down in three hours," says the Piskarevsky Chronicle. The chronicler relates that the first flames were seen three hours after sunrise and the fire had burned itself out by the early afternoon.

Devlet Guirey, the Khan of the Crimea, watched Moscow in flames from a safe vantage point on the Sparrow Hills. When it seemed that the fire might reach his encampment he sensibly took the precaution of moving away. He had seen what he had come to see. He had achieved two things which gave him immense satisfaction—he had humbled the Tsar and shown that the Russian army was no match for his Tatars. The armies of Mstislavsky, Belsky, and Temkin-Rostovsky had shown themselves to be incompetent; only Vorotynsky's army, which had not yet engaged the Tatars, threatened him. But it was a small threat, he could take it in his stride, and at the most Vorotnysky would be able to mount skirmishes against the Tatar rear guard. The Khan moved on to the Tsar's palaces at Kolomenskoye, which were pillaged and burned to the ground. Two days later, on May 26, 1571, the Khan ordered a general withdrawal. He plundered and took prisoners along the way, set fire to the wooden fortress of Kashira on the Oka River, devastated Kolomna and the entire province of Ryazan, and returned safely to the Crimea. Vorotynsky pursued him for a little way but soon gave up the fight. The Tatars had taken over 100,000 prisoners, who would bring good prices on the slave market.

Ivan's flight to Vologda showed that he was deathly afraid of falling into Tatar hands. He had also come to some serious conclusions about the oprichniki, who had demonstrated their total incompetence and therefore deserved severe punishment. He said later that he only heard about the destruction of Moscow ten days after it happened, but since horsemen were known to have made the journey from Moscow to Vologda in four days of hard riding, he may not have been telling the truth. Moscow had perished, but not all was lost. He was still the Tsar and Grand Prince of Russia, and he could detect no feeling against himself among the long-

uffering population. He decided to return to Alexandrova Sloboda
nd there, toward the end of the first week in June, he learned for
1e first time the full extent of the disaster. He immediately
ummoned the Metropolitan, the bishops, and members of the
ancient nobility" to a council. There is some significance in the
1ct that he called upon the long-established noble families for
dvice, since previously he had declared war on them and had
ounded the Oprichnina in the hope of destroying them.

The most urgent task was the rebuilding of Moscow, but first the
ead bodies had to be cleared away, all the more since it was high
ummer and nothing had been done to remove them. Most of the
urvivors fled in fear of the pestilence. The rivers were choked with
odies, and there were more to come, for Ivan gave orders to throw
ll the dead bodies found in the ruins into the river. The cure
roved worse than the disease. With more and more bodies thrown
ito it, the Moskva River was no longer a river; it changed its
ourse; and the likelihood of pestilence only increased. The wells
ere dry, there was no fresh water, and the situation was desperate.

The Muscovites who had fled were ordered back; people from
ar-off towns and villages were ordered to go to Moscow to dig
raves and help to rebuild the city. Masons, carpenters, and
raftsmen of all kinds were pressed into service and promised
eedom from all taxes and customs duties while the work was
oing on. It took four years to repair the damage. When the four
ears had passed, there was a new white wall of stone around the
Kremlin and the Kitay Gorod, and where there had been thou-
ands of gutted houses there was a new city.

Ivan refused to take any of the blame for the disaster. The fault,
5 he saw it, lay largely with the oprichniki who had not covered
1emselves with glory during the fighting and were unworthy of
im. Although they had sworn absolute loyalty to him, they had
ompletely failed him. In the past he refused to listen to any
riticisms of them; if they attacked, imprisoned, raped, or murdered
nyone, they had only to claim that the person was disloyal to the
sar to be relieved of all responsibility. Simply by being oprichniki
1ey were permitted the utmost license to commit as many crimes
5 they pleased. Now at last it was becoming evident that they had
ommitted altogether too many crimes; and from being the Tsar's
1ief defenders they became his chief liability.

Another bloodbath began: this time the oprichniki were th
victims. Ivan appears to have begun this bloodbath cautiously an
circumspectly, for there were now few public executions. Pete
Zaitsev, one of the original oprichniki, was "hanged from the cou
gates opposite his bedroom." Prince Vasily Temkin-Rostovsk
who had shown himself to be so pathetically incompetent when th
Tatars attacked the Oprichnina Palace in Moscow, was summaril
executed. Another commander of the palace forces was Princ
Mikhail Cherkassky, the brother of the Tsar's second wife, Mari
Temriukovna, who had died two years earlier, but his clos
relationship to the Tsar did not save him from execution. Som
high oprichnik officers were simply clubbed to death, and over
hundred died of the poisons administered by Ivan's doctor, Eliseu
Bomelius.

Bomelius, too, met the fate he deserved. He came originally fro
the town of Bomel in the Netherlands. At various times he was
Lutheran preacher in Westphalia, a doctor of medicine with
degree from Cambridge University, a practicing astrologer i
London, and a convicted felon in the King's Bench prison. He wa
by all accounts a quack, a mischief-maker, a man learned in man
arts and unscrupulous in all of them. He came to Russia in the trai
of the Russian ambassador to England and immediately set abou
working on Ivan's weaknesses. He claimed to foretell the future, t
be able to cure all diseases and to possess magical powers. The Tsa
was impressed and rewarded him handsomely. He was able to sen
his wealth to the town of Wesel in Westphalia, where he intende
to retire. He was a superb poisoner. Taube and Kruse report tha
when Ivan returned to Alexandrova Sloboda he began to ri
himself of many highly placed oprichniki. "The Tsar," the
reported, "gave written instructions to the doctor on the length o
time the poison should take effect. Sometimes he wanted it to tak
effect in half an hour, at other times he wanted it to take effect i
one, two, three, or four hours." The doctor performed these tasks t
Ivan's complete satisfaction. Four years later he decided to leav
Russia secretly, lined his pockets with gold, and reached Psko
where he was recognized and placed under arrest. Brought back t
Moscow, he was accused of intriguing with the Kings of Polan
and Sweden, tortured on the rack until his limbs were out of join
whipped with iron wires, and finally bound to a spit and roaste

When he was taken down, there was still some life in him. Jerome
Horsey, visiting the Kremlin at the time, suddenly saw the roasted
wreck of a man being driven away in a sleigh. "I pressed among
many others to see him; cast up his eyes naming Christ; cast into a
dungeon and died there." Thus, graphically, Horsey described the
end of a man whom the Pskov chronicler described many years
later as a ferocious magician who "completely turned the Tsar
away from the faith, made him hate the Russian people, and caused
him to love foreigners."

That Bomelius exercised considerable powers over Ivan's mind is
not in doubt, but it may be questioned whether he succeeded in
completely turning the Tsar away from the faith. Eliseus Bomelius
had many uses as a doctor and prognosticator. As doctor and
poisoner he seems to have been as good as any in his time; as
prognosticator he failed as often as he succeeded. According to
Jerome Horsey he prophesied that Queen Elizabeth would eventually marry Ivan and thus encouraged him to persist in his suit.
Horsey, who knew him well, said "he lived in great favor and
pomp, a skillful mathematician, a wicked man, and practicer of
such mischief."

There were other practicers of mischief: among them was Devlet
Guirey, Khan of the Crimea, who sent his ambassador to Ivan on
June 15, 1571. Ivan was in no mood to receive the ambassador and
his entourage, but had no alternative. At all costs he was
determined to delay as long as possible another encounter with the
armies of the Khan, who now demanded the cities of Astrakhan
and Kazan as the price of peace. To forestall the surrender of these
two large jewels in his crown, Ivan was prepared to pay a high
price. A new army was being sent to the Oka River, careful plans
were being made by the military, and to avoid a war on two fronts
Ivan was preparing to sign a treaty of friendship with the Swedes,
who occupied part of Livonia. The ambassador, who was a prince
of the Crimean Khanate, arrived with an escort of nobles and
guards armed with bows and arrows and "curious rich scimitars."
They rode up to Ivan's palace at Bratashino on the road between
the Troitsa-Sergeyevsky Monastery and Moscow. At first Ivan
treated them roughly, feeding them on stinking horseflesh and
later, depriving them of proper sleeping quarters. He was obviously attempting to provoke them, but "they endured, puffed and

scorned" this base usage, for they were very sure of themselves and knew that Ivan would eventually grant them an audience. They had nothing to lose; the Tsar had much to gain.

The Tatars wore long black sheepskin kaftans and carried themselves with grave dignity. The ambassador was a man of consummate ugliness with a harsh, penetrating voice. He was taken into the throne room alone, guarded by four Russian soldiers, and the Tatar nobles who had accompanied him were allowed to look on through an iron grille. Ivan sat on a throne, wearing cloth of gold, with three of his crowns beside him. Probably they were the crowns of Muscovy, Astrakhan, and Kazan, which was especially beautiful with its curving petal-shaped leaves of gold. The ambassador wore a gown of cloth of gold and a rich cap given to him by the Tsar. He had much to say in his penetrating voice, and Ivan would have preferred not to listen to it.

The ambassador declared that he was the envoy of the Khan of the Crimea, "who rules over all the kings and kingdoms the sun shines upon." It was the Khan's pleasure to inquire about Ivan's feelings now that he had felt "the scourge of the Khan's displeasure by sword, fire and famine." It was a taunting speech, deliberately conceived to infuriate Ivan. The princely ambassador produced rusty gold-handled knife, which had belonged to the Khan, and he suggested that there was a sovereign remedy for all the ills that had befallen Russia. He gave Ivan the knife, hinting that he might like to cut his own throat with it.

"My Lord wanted to send you a horse," the ambassador went on when Ivan declined the knife. "But all our horses have become exhausted after riding so far across Russia."

Ivan succeeded in keeping his self-control. He commanded the ambassador to read the letter from the Khan of the Crimea. The ambassador began reading:

"I came to Russia, devastated the land and put it to the flames to avenge Kazan and Astrakhan. I desire neither money nor treasure, for they are of no use to me. As for the Tsar, I searched for him everywhere. I searched for him in Serpukhov and in Moscow, desiring his head and his crown. But you did not come to meet us, you fled from Serpukhov, you fled from Moscow, and still you dare to call yourself Tsar of Muscovy. You have no shame and are completely without courage. If you desire our friendship, then give is back Kazan and Astrakhan, and swear an oath on behalf of yourself, your children and your grandchildren that you will do as I command. And if you do not do these things, beware! I have seen the roads and highways of your kingdom and I know the way!"

The Tsar remained silent, in a mortal rage. The guards hustled the ambassador out of the throne room, attempting to remove the gold gown and rich cap which he wore so insolently, but he was able to take care of himself until his retinue came to the rescue. We are told that Ivan went into a state of shock. "He fell into an agony, sent for his ghostly father, tore his own hair and beard." The captain of the bodyguard offered to cut the ambassador and his entire retinue to pieces, but Ivan made no answer and the captain wisely concluded that it would be altogether too dangerous to kill the Tatars on his own responsibility.

Thereafter the Tatars were treated more tenderly. They were given good food and the best accommodation available, while the Tsar labored over the message to be sent back to the Khan of the Crimea. Finally the Tsar summoned the ambassador and gave him a message which Jerome Horsey has recorded in vigorous Elizabethan English:

> Tell the miscreant and unbeliever, thy master, it is not he; it is for my sins and the sins of my people against my God and Christ; he it is that has given him, a limb of Satan, the power and opportunity to be the instrument of my rebuke, by whose pleasure and grace I doubt not of revenge and to make him my vassal or long be.

Ivan was saying, as he had said so often, that God would grant him the ultimate victory before long, but meanwhile he was being made to suffer for his sins and the sins of the Russian people. Soon the Crimean Khan would become his vassal; the tables would be turned; the vanquished would become the victors. The ambassador in his thundering voice replied that he absolutely refused to give such a message to the Khan. There were no further incidents. He left the throne room and returned to the south.

Ivan's message, as recorded by Horsey, conveys exactly the tone of furious piety favored by him. It was inconceivable to him that the Khan was really responsible for so many disasters to Russia. Suffering arose from sin and from the wrath of God; the Khan was merely "the instrument of my rebuke." By prayer and pilgrimage he hoped to direct God's wrath upon the enemy.

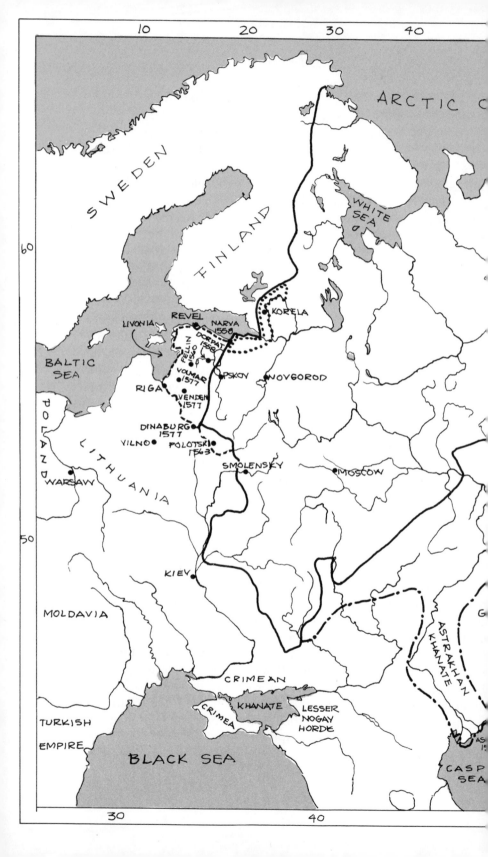

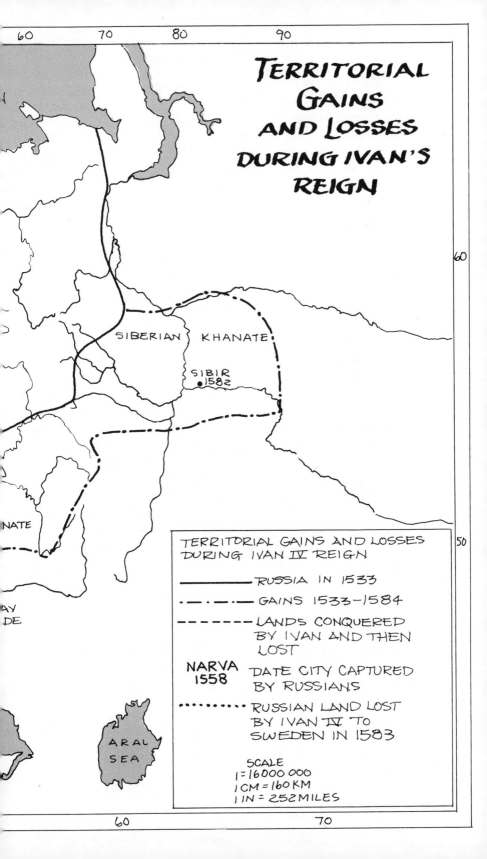

Meanwhile Ivan employed all his diplomatic skills against th Khan. Afanasy Nagoy, one of his best ambassadors, was sent t the Crimean court with instructions to speak softly and to prolon the negotiations as long as possible. The Khan would be offere Astrakhan, but only provisionally; if he sent his son to be Khan c Astrakhan, there must also be a Russian governor and the Russian in Astrakhan must be given full liberty to practice their trades an their religion as before. Ivan manufactured conditions and exulte in making them unacceptable. Afanasy Nagoy was instructed t ask whether the Khan of the Crimea would permit Ivan to place th crown of Astrakhan on his son's head, thus making him a vassal By concentrating on Astrakhan Ivan hoped that the subject o Kazan would not be raised.

By October 1571 the Crimean Khan had grown impatient. H wrote: "You offer Astrakhan, but Astrakhan is only part of wha we want. We want Kazan as well. Otherwise you will have th upper part of the river and we shall have only the lower part. This i intolerable."

Since it was clear that the Khan would not yield, Ivan continue to temporize. Letters from the Khan remained unanswered; th ambassadors were kept in seclusion and told that Ivan was engage in pressing business. In fact he was very busy. On December 24 1571, he reached Novgorod with an army which he intended t throw against the Swedes. Happily there was no fighting and he wa able to secure a truce with Sweden. He was back in Alexandrov Sloboda toward the end of January 1572. When a Tatar ambassa dor arrived on February 5, Ivan said he had just vanquished th Swedish army in battle. As for the question of Kazan, this was not matter which could be discussed lightly. High plenipotentiarie would have to meet, a peace treaty would have to be concluded, a offensive alliance against Poland and Lithuania would have to b signed. "The sword remains sharp only for a little while," Ivan reminded the ambassador. "Too much use blunts it, and it i possible that the blade might break." The Khan demande immense gifts, and the Tsar replied: "Our land is barren and w have nothing to give." All the time reinforcements were bein hurried toward the Oka River.

On October 28, 1571, the Tsar married for the third time. Th bride, selected from among two thousand beautiful girls from al parts of the country, was Marfa Sobakina from an ancient noble family of Tver. A week later the Tsarevich was also married. His bride was Evdokia Saburova of a well-known boyar family in Moscow.

When Ivan married Marfa Sobakina, she was ailing. He knew she was ill but believed that with God's help he could cure her sickness. Instead her illness grew worse and she died on November 13, 1571, sixteen days after her marriage, to the consternation of Ivan who believed that this was another sign of God's wrath. He would say that Anastasia died because evil persons cast a spell on her and poisoned her; that his second wife was also poisoned; that the third died as a result of evil spells. He thought of becoming a monk and putting the world behind him, but decided against it, saying that "Christians are being enslaved, Christendom is being destroyed, and my children are not yet grown up." In March 1572 he convoked a Church Council to advise on whether it was permissible to marry for a fourth time, having chosen Anna Koltovskaya, who belonged to the minor court nobility, as a prospective bride. The bishops deliberated and agreed to permit the marriage on condition that he did penance for a year. The Tsar always enjoyed doing penance and faithfully obeyed the bishops, who ruled that during the course of a year he would not be permitted inside the church to receive the Holy Sacraments but must remain outside.

The marriage to Anna Koltovskaya brought him no children. Four years later he abruptly divorced her and ordered her to spend the rest of her days in a nunnery in Tikhvin in the far north.

The Tatar invasions usually took place in the spring or early summer. The negotiations with the Crimean Khan had broken down and it was now evident that the Khan would attempt another massive invasion, and this time the consequences might be even more disastrous. In fact, the Khan was determined to reduce Russia to the status of a Tatar province. He intended to capture Ivan alive and bring him in triumph to the Crimea. Already the Tatar princes were being assigned principalities and the Sultan of Turkey had been promised "a huge gift of treasure" from Ivan's treasury for his help in providing heavy guns. This time the Khan intended to 'advance like a bloodthirsty lion, his ferocious jaws wide open to devour the Christians."

The Zemshchina forces on the Oka River had been working frantically for many months to improve the defense works. For a length of about 250 miles earthworks were being erected along the river banks, cannon were mounted wherever the Tatars might be expected to cross, the fortresses south of the river were strengthened, and trees were being cut down to delay the advance of the Tatar cavalry. The Russians had made careful plans to signal the approach of the Tatars long before they reached the Oka River and they were making plans to set fire to the steppes. Thanks to an improved system of reconnaissance the Russian commanders on the river bank believed they would be able to foretell exactly where the Khan would attempt to cross the river and crush him.

Although a Tatar invasion was expected for the early summer, Ivan refused to take command of the army in the south, but instead took the precaution of retreating to Novgorod with all the treasure he could lay his hands on. It was estimated that 10,000 *puds*, corresponding to 180 tons, of treasure were sent to Novgorod where he arrived on June 1, 1572, to be greeted by Archbishop Leonid with the customary fanfare. The Tsar lived quietly in his palace. He attended services in the Cathedral of St. Sophia which he had despoiled two years earlier and prayed for deliverance from the Tatars. On July 2 a great storm arose and the crosses on many churches, including the church attached to Ivan's palace, were blown down. This was a bad omen.

Ivan was devoured with anxiety. He knew the Tatars were determined to capture him alive and take his treasure, and he congratulated himself that he was now out of their reach and his treasure was safe, but his future as Tsar depended upon a Russian victory. It was doubtful whether he could continue on the throne if there was another disaster like the last. The generals on the Oka River sent him regular reports, but he half-distrusted them and preferred to have his own independent sources of information. Thus we find him writing to Evstafy Pushkin, the governor of Staritsa, on July 17:

> Tell me when the Khan is going to reach the river, and where he will cross, and in what direction he will be coming. You must let me know this without fail. You are not permitted to keep us waiting without news. Information should be sent to us by a courier with two

horses. You should also see that one or two people at Tver should be ready to bring us news of the coming of the Khan. At all costs keep us informed.

From Novgorod he sent his closest aide Prince Osip Shcherbatov to the Oka River, encouraging the army to hold fast and promising abundant rewards to the generals if they succeeded in destroying the Tatars. In this way, offering bribes and sunk in misery, he waited for the coming of the Tatars.

How deeply miserable he was we know from the will he wrote while in Novgorod. He was forty-two years old, but wrote like a man in extreme old age. Much of the will is concerned with advising his sons Ivan and Fyodor about their future behavior. They should love one another and the younger should loyally serve the older, the future Tsar. Remembering Christ's injunction, "This I command, that you love one another," he urged them to love all those who returned their love and to punish implacably all traitors. They must not punish in fury, as he had done. On the contrary they should sift the evidence cautiously and without rancor. They must learn statecraft, study the people, advise themselves about foreign affairs, and be well-informed about matters of Church and state, for others will snatch the power from them unless they are knowledgeable. They must especially study military affairs. "You should learn all those things that need to be learned, whether they pertain to the monasteries, the army, justice and the government of Moscow, and the daily life of the people. Then they will not tell you what to do, but instead you will tell them what must be done, and thus you will acquire mastery over your realm and your people." He seemed to be thinking of the days when his actions were guided by the Chosen Council and especially by Sylvester and Adashev, before he had taken full power in his own hands.

He also warned his sons against making the wrong friends. "You should love and favor those people who serve you loyally," he wrote. "Protect them from everyone so that no harm shall befall them, and they will serve you with greater loyalty." Nor should they strike in anger. Punishments, he explained, should be administered only after all the facts had been ascertained, not in a moment of rage. It was very late in the day for such discoveries.

The testament of Ivan is remarkable for the mood of somber

self-questioning. He was evidently fearful about the future and the fate reserved for his physical body and for his immortal soul. He was deeply aware that he had committed crimes so vile that they cried out for punishment. Self-pity, self-abasement, fear of the wrath of God all had their place in his confession. He wrote:

> My body has grown feeble, my spirit is sick, and the ills of my body and spirit have increased, but no doctor can cure me. I looked for someone to grieve with me, but found no one. I received evil for good and my love was answered with hatred. For my many sins God's wrath descended upon me, and the boyars in their wilfulness deprived me of my inheritance, and now I roam from place to place as God wills.

He went on to accuse himself of lascivious speech, unjustifiable rages, drunkenness, debauchery, thievery, murder, even fratricide for had he not committed the "sin of Cain" when he killed Vladimir of Staritsa? He had committed so many crimes that "although I am a living person, yet in the eyes of God my evil deeds have made me more putrid and more hideous than a corpse, and because of this am hated by everyone."

There remained the grant of the succession which went to his elder son Ivan, while the younger son Fyodor was to receive a huge principality which included whole provinces and the cities of Yaroslavl, Volokolamsk, Suzdal, and Kostroma.

Ivan wrote his testament in abject fear—fear of the Tatars, fear of betrayal by those around him, fear of the army which might hand him over to the enemy, and always the fear of God. He was writing in a city where he had murdered countless numbers of Russians. Hourly he expected news of defeat. Instead there came news of a resounding victory. On August 6 two noblemen sent by Prince Vorotynsky rode into Novgorod with the news that the Crimean army had been defeated at a small village halfway between Serpukhov and Moscow. As trophies they brought two Tatar swords and two bows and quivers captured from the enemy. The Tsar ordered that all the church bells should ring and that a solemn service should be held in the Cathedral of St. Sophia. The stern and saintly Archbishop Leonid presided over the service.

The Tsar rewarded the two noblemen and sent one of his closest advisers, Afanasy Nagoy, to the Russian Army with gifts and gold medals.

He learned that towards evening on July 26 a huge Tatar army had appeared on the south bank of the Oka River. Throughout the next day, a Sunday, they were held off by heavy cannon fire, but in the darkness of Sunday night the main Tatar army succeeded in crossing the river at Kashira. The Crimean Khan then led his troops toward Moscow, the Russians in hot pursuit. The Khan's progress was slowed up by his heavy cannon; the Russian vanguard caught up with the Tatar rear guard near the village of Molodi; and soon the main Russian army joined it and hastily threw up earthworks and palisades. Divey Mirza, the commander in chief of the Tatar army, hesitated between advancing on Moscow, now only fifteen miles from his advance forces, or turning back.

Finally Divey Mirza decided to give battle in Molodi. There were skirmishes, three thousand Russian musketeers in an advance position were wiped out by Nogay cavalrymen, but Divey Mirza was captured when his white horse stumbled and threw him. According to the Anonymous Chronicle he was not immediately recognized, but when the captured Tatar prince Shirinbak was being interrogated and asked about the plans of his commander in chief, he replied, "All our plans are with you, because you have captured Divey Mirza, who knows everything." The Russians then set about finding Divey Mirza among their captives. At last he was found and taken to Vorotynsky's tent, and when Prince Shirinbak threw himself down at Divey Mirza's feet, the Russians knew that the battle was half over.

Skirmishes continued through the week, but on Saturday, August 2, the Crimean Khan threw his army against the Russian palisades in an effort to rescue Divey Mirza. The Tatars, who fought best on horseback, were ordered to dismount before they reached the palisades. When they attempted to climb the wooden walls, their hands were chopped off. Meanwhile Prince Vorotynsky had succeeded in taking most of the main army out of his hastily erected fortress and moving it through a hidden valley to the rear of the Tatar forces. Then he pounced and simultaneously the heavy cannon inside the fortress opened fire on the Tatars, who broke and fled. Many, caught between two fires, were slaughtered. The Crimean Khan fled with his guards, in the words of the popular song, "not by the roads and not by the highways." The Novgorod Chronicle relates that a hundred thousand Tatars were left dead on the battlefield. Heinrich Staden, who claims to have been in the thick of the fighting, wrote that "every corpse that had a cross round its neck was buried at the monastery that lies near Serpukhov, while all the rest were left to be eaten by the birds." Soon people all over Russia were singing a song about the triumph of the Russian army over the Tatars:

> No mighty cloud covered the heavens,
> No mighty thunder roared from the sky.
> Where is he going, the dog, the Crimean Tsar?
> He is going to the mighty Tsardom of Muscovy.
> "Today we shall conquer stone-built Moscow:
> On the way back we shall take Ryazan."
> And when they reached the Oka River
> They pitched their white tents.
> "Now ask yourselves the keenest questions:
> Who shall sit in stone-built Moscow?
> Who shall sit in the city of Vladimir?
> Who shall sit in the city of Suzdal?
> Who shall keep old Ryazan?
> Who shall sit in the city of Zvenigorod?
> Who shall sit in the city of Novgorod?"
> Then Divey Mirza, son of Ulan, stepped forward:
> "Listen, our Lord Khan of the Crimea,
> You, our Lord, shall sit in stone-built Moscow,
> And your son shall sit in Vladimir,
> Your nephew shall sit in Suzdal,
> Your cousin shall sit in Zvenigorod,
> Your Master of the Horse shall sit in old Ryazan,
> But to me, O Lord, grant Novgorod:
> There in Novgorod lies my good fortune!"
> The voice of the Lord cried out from heaven:
> "Listen, you dog, Crimean Khan!
> Know you not the Tsardom of Muscovy?
> There are in Moscow seventy Apostles
> Beside the three Holy Fathers,
> And there is still in Moscow an Orthodox Tsar."
> And you fled, you dog, you Crimean Khan,
> Not by the roads and not by the highways,
> And without your banners, the black flags!

Rarely in the past had the Russians enjoyed so complete a victory over their enemies. So heavily punished were the Crimean Tatars that they mounted no further full-scale attacks for the rest of Ivan's reign. At the battle of Molodi the Russian army recovered its full strength and prestige. The news of the victory traveled all over Europe; the chronicles acclaimed it; and Ivan realized at last that the army was more important than the Oprichnina, which was now doomed.

Foul Stinking Dog

FOR THREE YEARS after the battle of Molodi the Tsar lived in comparative tranquillity. There were, of course, occasional executions and sudden outbursts of terrifying rage, but on the whole he found himself attempting to live like a civilized human being. The rages exhausted him, and the years of unrestrained ferocity sapped his energies. He was a sick man, suffering from a variety of maladies, and conscious that his physical and spiritual powers were on the wane. The slow processes of corruption had long been at work on him, and now at last he was paying the penalty for his outrageous crimes. "Sores of the flesh and the spirit multiply, and there is no doctor who can heal me."

Nevertheless, as he well knew, there was a doctor constantly in attendance. God dwelt in him, and around him, and His medications had proved efficacious. By the victory at Molodi God had ensured that he, Ivan, would reign for many more years as Tsar and Grand Prince of Russia. He saw God's awesome hand over the battlefield, and therefore owed no debt to Prince Mikhail Vorotynsky, the hero of the battle, and his courageous soldiers. He was grateful and relieved now that the victory had been won, and yet not so grateful that he did not believe he had no share in the victory. On the contrary, he had a full share in it. He, the Tsar, by his constant prayers to God, had helped to work this miracle.

He and the Russian people knew what would have happened if they had been defeated—they would have become the slaves of the

Tatars, who once were the masters of most of Russia, exacting tribute, ordering the princes to attend their courts and beg for favors. This had lasted for two hundred years. In the time of Ivan's grandfather the Tatars were finally expelled from Russia. Ivan, in his own time, had seen them so dangerously close to winning back their lost empire that he had fled twice to Novgorod, knowing that if they won his only recourse was to go to England and throw himself on the mercy of Queen Elizabeth.

There hangs in the National Museum at Copenhagen, in a small room devoted to sixteenth-century furniture, a small painting of Ivan on wood, which shows him troubled, perhaps anguished, the forehead deeply lined, the face very red, the hair receding, the nose very long and pendulous, thick sensual lips, a heavy red beard streaked with silver. He wears the sumptuous raiment of the court and a wide collar studded with emeralds, rubies and pearls.

What is surprising is the artist's success in making a credible portrait within the limits of a tradition of ecclesiastical painting. Saints must be shown stiffly, hieratically. But while Ivan is shown hieratically, he is not stiff; it is a human face burdened by the weight of fleshly cares. It is not an especially distinguished face. He might be a defrocked priest or carpet seller with an interest in religion. The deeply sunken eyes are speculative, the lips deride chastity. In that brooding face there is not a trace of imperial grandeur. Yet it is not easily forgotten, and it is not difficult to believe that this is an authentic portrait of the man who single-handedly plunged Russia into a long-lasting reign of terror. That he looked like a priest does not surprise us, and that he also looked like a carpet seller should surprise us even less. Morose, vindictive, avaricious, mean-spirited, totally self-centered, with no saving graces except his intelligence, he confronts us in the portrait and seems to be asking for our sympathy.

Not that sympathy was often given to him by a people who were mercilessly oppressed by him. Their feeling for him was one of awe amounting almost to terror before a divinely appointed ruler; he was history incarnate; he walked on the heights remote from the ordinary affairs of men; and if he punished them it was because in some mysterious way they were worthy of punishment. It seems never to have occurred to the Russians to do away with him, for we hear of no authentic attempts on his life. Ivan himself believed he was being threatened daily, and he executed thousands of men because he thought they were disloyal and therefore menaced his very existence. It was not true and he must have known it was not true; nevertheless he saw traitors everywhere.

After the battle of Molodi his violence subsided and his fear of treachery diminished. The victory was so complete, it was so obviously preordained and he was so clearly implicated that he lost his customary fear and gave himself up to a feeling of general well-being. The Swedes were troublesome; the truce had expired, and they were spreading rumors that he was about to sue for peace. While still in Novgorod, with the news of victory ringing in his ears, he wrote on August 11 a curious letter to King John III of Sweden, who had delayed sending his ambassador to Ivan perhaps because the outcome of the Tatar invasion was still uncertain:

> I had believed that you and your people, having felt the weight of my wrath, would act reasonably. I awaited your ambassadors, they did not arrive, and all the time you were spreading rumors that I was suing for peace. This shows you have no pity for the Swedish people and you put your trust in your great wealth.
>
> Look what happened to the Khan of the Crimea at the hands of my military leaders!
>
> We are now leaving for Moscow, but we shall return to Novgorod in December. Then you will see the Russian Tsar and his army sue for peace from the Swedes!

This letter was written in the midst of the victory celebrations. All over Russia there was rejoicing; solemn services of thanksgiving were held in all the churches and cathedrals; and in Novgorod there was a special service in honor of the victory at the Cathedral of St. Sophia followed by entertainments and feasts over which Ivan presided. On August 19, the day before he left for Moscow, the Tsar was feasted in the palace of Archbishop Leonid, who would soon learn that it was dangerous to be close to the man who believed that all victories and defeats come from God.

By the end of the month Ivan was in Moscow, his faltering power reestablished by victory. He was at the center of things, no longer in exile. His first task was to shower the army with rewards. To the leading commanders, and especially to Prince Mikhail Vorotynsky, went gold plates and other valuables from his treasury; lesser

Icon of Ivan IV probably painted shortly after his death and now in the National Museum in Copenhagen. The inscription at top left and right reads: "Tsar and Grand Prince Ivan Vasilievich of all Russia." (Courtesy, National Museum, Copenhagen)

rewards were given to the junior officers according to their rank and their accomplishments on the battlefield. Vorotynsky had become a popular hero, ballads were sung about him, and this too was dangerous. The newly discovered document known as the Anonymous Chronicle reports that "the Tsar began to hate him because he received so much praise from the people, and accused him of treason." In fact the accusation came many months later. It was not in the Tsar's nature to feel grateful toward those who saved him. Outwardly he remained on terms of close friendship with Vorotynsky; inwardly he seethed with indignation and planned to destroy his benefactor.

He had studied the arts of revenge with minute care. The place, the punishment, the disposal of the body, were not chosen arbitrarily. For every real or imagined crime against him there could be found suitable remedies.

Thus, when he received an envoy from the Khan of the Crimea on September 4, 1572, shortly after his return to Moscow, he deliberately arranged that the reception should take place in the house of a peasant in a small village called Luchinskoye outside of Moscow. In this way no honors need be paid to the envoy. The envoy presented the inevitable insulting letter from the Khan, who announced that he had never contemplated making war on Russia. On the contrary, he had entered Russia in order to conclude a lasting peace with the Tsar, and as for those unfortunate skirmishes, they only showed the superiority of the Tatar forces. He had returned to the Crimea only because the Nogay tribesmen claimed that their horses were worn out. He asked that Kazan and Astrakhan should be given to him; and if not both, then at least the Tsar should think seriously of offering him Astrakhan. The Khan added that he would accept no gifts of money or treasure from the Tsar because he could always raid the Lithuanians and Circassians "to avoid hunger." The calculated impudence was designed to enrage Ivan, who replied calmly that he had not the least intention of surrendering Kazan and Astrakhan. "We have one sword against us in the Crimea," he answered mildly. "If we give up Kazan, we shall have two swords against us, and if we give up Astrakhan we shall have three." The envoy was sent away empty-handed from the peasant's house in an obscure village. This, too, was part of the punishment.

More envoys arrived, this time from Poland and Lithuania. King Sigismund Augustus died on July 18, 1572, and the vexing question of the succession was once more being discussed. The envoys were toying with the possibility that the crown of Poland might be given to Ivan's second son Fyodor. The idea alarmed the Tsar, who wondered why Fyodor should be preferred to himself. He advanced his own claim to the throne at some length, pointing to his obvious virtues, his sense of implacable justice, his experience, and his love for the Polish and Lithuanian people. He was anxiously looking forward to the time when they would send plenipotentiaries with full powers to negotiate. He said:

> If the Polish and Lithuanian nobles, who are now without a King, decided to choose me for their King, then they would discover what a good ruler I am and how well I would protect them. The power of the Muslims would not increase but decrease, and not only the Muslims —no Christian kingdom would succeed in opposing us if God willed that our countries become united.

Ivan was well aware that he had a reputation for exacting stern punishments, and defended himself with the argument always used by dictators. "You say I am harsh and vengeful," he said. "It is true, but ask yourselves against whom I am harsh. I am harsh only with those who are harsh with me!" Then he touched the gold chain of kingly office that hung from his shoulders. "For those who are good to me—why, I would pluck off this chain and give it myself to a good servant!" At that moment Maliuta Skuratov, one of the most murderous of the oprichniki and still in high favor, decided to intervene. Skuratov was standing next to Ivan. He said, "Orthodox Tsar and Lord! Your treasury is not so poor! If you have need to reward someone for services performed, there are other things that can be found to give him!"

Skuratov was speaking in the authentic accents of the political toady. Ivan should be warned against making too many sacrifices for his people. This thought inspired Ivan to speak to the Poles and Lithuanians about his great wealth, pointing out that his treasury and the lands he had inherited from his father and grandfather had increased twofold during his reign. He added, "Of course, this is neither here nor there, but I thought I would mention it in passing."

Again and again he came back to the accusations of cruelty

which were being levelled at him from so many quarters. It was obviously a matter that deeply concerned him, and he had a whole quiverful of arguments to defend himself. He told them how he had almost fallen into the hands of the Tatars through the negligence and treachery of his army commanders. "Surely this was not a small act of treason!" he insisted. "Some were executed for it, and it was a just punishment! Don't you have executions in your own country?" He promised that if they made him King of Poland and Lithuania, they would find in him a merciful Lord.

He reminded his listeners that he had never shown anything but mercy to Prince Kurbsky, who fled Russia to become a prince of Lithuania. Prince Kurbsky had committed innumerable crimes and had even brought about the death of Anastasia—and here the Tsar pointed to his son, saying, "This boy's mother"—and yet it had never occurred to Ivan to punish this man. "I swear by God and by my word as Tsar that it never occurred to me to have him executed! All I wanted, because he had done wrong, was to bring him to obedience and to deprive him of his rank and privileges, and after this it was my intention to forgive him and return everything to him, but before I could do this he panicked and fled to Lithuania. You nobles should watch him for your own good lest he flee to another country and cause you great harm!"

Ivan was presenting himself as the mildest and most generous of emperors and also as a doting father who could not possibly let his son Fyodor become King of Poland because "I have only two sons, and they are like the eyes in my head, and if I give away one of them it is like plucking out the heart of a man."

In matters of religion, too, Ivan presented himself as a moderate. "There are Poles and Lithuanians who follow the Lutheran creed and destroy icons," he announced. "They do not want me for their ruler, but I shall say nothing about them since the Scriptures were given to us so that we shall not give way to violence and anger but so that we will show gentleness and meekness."

He portrays himself as the man of peace, the gentle executioner, the servant of God. By asking that Fyodor should become King of Poland, they were implying that they wanted a mild and compassionate ruler, for Fyodor was known to be reserved and gentle. As he went on speaking, Ivan grew more and more enamored at the prospect of adding two more crowns to the many he already possessed, and he said, "Remember all I have told you and tell it to your nobles! Let them send plenipotentiaries as soon as possible, so that this good matter shall not be allowed to grow stale!" Maliuta Skuratov, not to be outdone, echoed his master's words and added a half-concealed threat. "Your nobles should send plenipotentiaries quickly," he said, "so that this good cause shall remain good and so that nothing evil happens meanwhile."

The ambassadors departed, but they had seen enough of Ivan at close quarters to be dubious about his qualifications. The order to send plenipotentiaries quickly was not obeyed. Six months passed before the Lithuanians sent a plenipotentiary to Ivan's court, and about the same time the Poles apologized for not sending a representative, giving as their excuse the fact that a plague was ravaging the country. Mikhail Garaburda, an astute and experienced diplomat, maintained that the Lithuanian nobility were unable to make up their minds; they would accept either Ivan or Fyodor; the Tsar must decide. But the Tsar was in no mood to make decisions. He was too busy attending to the liquidation of the Oprichnina to assume any further responsibilities. Lithuania tempted him, but Livonia tempted him even more, and both harbored nests of traitors.

Ivan appears to have developed a great fondness for Novgorod, where he remained all winter and late into the spring. Here in the Cathedral of St. Sophia, on April 12, 1573, he attended the wedding of Prince Magnus to the thirteen-year-old Princess Maria, the daughter of Prince Vladimir of Staritsa. The Danish prince, now titular King of Livonia, had been betrothed to her elder half-sister, who died. Since Ivan was determined to marry Magnus into his own family and Maria was the only available princess, the wedding was merely a matter of convenience. Nor was Magnus especially happy about the arrangement. He was a king without power, living on an estate on the island of Oesel in the Baltic, with few soldiers and small revenue. He had been promised five trunkfuls of gold, but Ivan failed to send them. Instead, as a wedding present, he received several trunks full of clothes for himself and his bride and the deeds to the town of Karkus and the surrounding villages in Russian-occupied Livonia. Ivan hoped he would conquer the rest of Livonia and Magnus wondered why he received so little help.

Ivan enjoyed the wedding. The chroniclers relate that he danced with the guests and beat time to the music with his staff on the heads of the young monks, who were dancing merrily. As usual he was obsessed by the possibilities of treachery and spoke pointedly on the subject in the speech he delivered at the wedding. Two Livonian mercenaries, Taube and Kruse, had recently attempted an uprising at Dorpat with the intention of giving it to King Sigismund Augustus and Ivan professed to have been deeply shocked by the occurrence, even though the attempt had failed and Dorpat remained in Russian hands. So now, speaking very solemnly, he warned the young King that he could expect no new gifts until he had proved himself. He said:

> King Magnus, it is now time for you to return with your bride to your kingdom. There were other towns in Livonia I wanted to give you, and also a large dowry of money, but there came to my mind the thought of the treachery of Taube and Kruse, whom I had showered with favors.
>
> I know you are the son of a King and therefore I have more trust in you, but after all you are only human! If it should occur to you to betray me, then you will use my money to hire soldiers who will join forces with my enemies, and once again we shall be compelled to take Livonia with our blood!
>
> You will earn my continual favor only when you have proved your loyalty!

Magnus was disappointed, but there was nothing he could do. He returned sadly to his estate, living modestly and quietly, serving only three-course dinners and buying toys for his bride, his life of leisure interrupted by occasional border raids and skirmishes. More and more it seemed unlikely that Ivan would make him Tsar of Russia.

Meanwhile Ivan was still winding up the affairs of the Oprichnina which had proved to be so murderous, so useless, and so inefficient. It resembled a giant corporation which could not be wound up without dislocating innumerable businesses. The book work was formidable, for thousands of estates were now being returned to the original owners. Many documents had been lost in the fire of Moscow; it was necessary to examine distant archives, to inquire into inheritances, and to punish the guilty. In some cases the original families owning the sequestered estates had been wiped out. Sometimes the oprichniki had completely ruined the estates, which had to be replaced by other estates. A state of almost total bureaucratic confusion resulted. Confusion lay at the heart of the Oprichnina, and when it was liquidated, there was more confusion. The Oprichnina was dissolved because it had outlived any conceivable usefulness to Ivan, who now at last realized something that was obvious to his meanest subject: it was a cruel absurdity imposed upon the country by imperial power.

There was no date of death and there were no obsequies. The Oprichnina died slowly, piecemeal, in silence. By order of the Tsar no one was allowed to mention that it had ever existed. Heinrich Staden, one of the very few oprichniki to write his memoirs, wrote that if anyone so much as hinted at the existence of the Oprichnina, he was stripped to the waist and whipped through the marketplace. "All their estates were returned to the Zemskiye people because they had resisted the Khan of the Crimea and the Grand Prince could no longer do without them." It was as simple as that. All the murders, all the bloodbaths, all the miserable subterfuges, came to an end without anyone being officially told that it had come to an end. Where previously there had been a conspiracy of terror there was now a conspiracy of silence.

Of the people who had formed the inner council of the Oprichnina only Maliuta Skuratov and Vasily Griaznoy survived for a little while longer. Skuratov, Ivan's favorite, was killed while besieging the Livonian fortress of Paida on January 1, 1573. Griaznoy was captured by the Tatars on the steppes of the Upper Don River a few months later. Ivan offered a ransom of 2,000 rubles, but the Tatars thought he was worth more and refused to release him. They offered to exchange him for Divey Mirza, the general commanding the Tatar armies who was still in Russian hands, but Ivan felt it was not a fair exchange. Griaznoy had told his captors that he was a man of great importance in Ivan's court. It was his biggest mistake. Ivan wrote to him in his Crimean prison:

> Why did you say you were a man of great importance? Of course it is true that when we were confronted with the treason of the Boyars, we were compelled to surround ourself with people like you of lowly birth. But do not forget who your father and grandfather were! How then can you consider yourself the equal of Divey Mirza? Freedom will only give you a soft bed. If he goes free, he will raise his sword against the Christians.

You should have known your way, Vasiushka, when you rode after the Tatars. You should not have fallen asleep when you were reconnoitering. You rode out as though you were going hunting, and so you fell into a Tatar trap. Or did it cross your mind that in the Crimea everything would be as easy as cracking jokes at my table?

Griaznoy died in prison, a fate which he richly deserved. Prince Mikhail Vorotynsky died more barbarously, the victim of the intrigues of a thieving servant and of Ivan's implacable vengeance against the greatest military commander of his time.

Vorotynsky was arrested on the southern front, brought in chains to Moscow, and confronted in Ivan's presence with a servant he had dismissed. The servant had much to say, and Ivan professed to believe every word of it.

"Your servant," Ivan said, "has testified against you that you desired to place me under a spell and employed witches to work magic over me."

Vorotynsky was known to be especially devout, and witchcraft was not a subject which had ever interested him. He was a soldier, the hero of many battles, intelligent, and forthright. He was now about sixty years old, and he knew he was doomed.

"I never learned to practice magic, O Tsar," he said, "nor did I ever inherit any knowledge of it from my ancestors, and I know nothing of witchcraft. I learned to worship one God, who is glorified in the Trinity, and truly to serve you, my Tsar and Sovereign. The man who accuses me is a servant who escaped from my household after robbing me. You should not accept his evidence or put any trust in him, for he is doing evil by betraying me and bearing false witness against me."

Vorotynsky was condemned to death by burning. Ivan, according to his custom, attended the execution and amused himself by raking the burning coals with his iron staff. At the last moment when the great general's body was scorched with the flames and he was scarcely breathing, Ivan ordered a reprieve. Vorotynsky was to be sent to a prison at Beloozero in the far north, but he died when he was three miles outside Moscow.

In Vorotynsky's memory Prince Kurbsky, who had known him well, wrote a famous panegyric, praising him for his steadfastness, his superb intelligence, his heroism, and his innocence. "In the hands of the drinker of blood," he wrote, "you received a great suffering, and you shall receive from the hands of Christ our God the crown of martyrdom."

About the same time two other noblemen, Prince Nikita Odoevsky and the boyar Mikhail Morozov, were also executed together with their wives. Odoevsky was in command of the right wing of the army on the southern front, a young man, the father of three sons, with a distinguished career in front of him. Morozov had commanded the artillery at the siege of Kazan in 1552 and combined an army career with high office in the government, becoming successively governor of Smolensk and of Dorpat. He, too, had fought at the battle of Molodi. The two noblemen were accused of witchcraft, tortured, and sentenced to death. Prince Kurbsky relates that Odoevsky was killed in a very curious manner. "Many forms of torture were inflicted on him: they stuffed a shirt through his chest, tugged it to-and-fro, and he died immediately." Of the manner of Morozov's death nothing is known. Many years later, in 1583, Ivan sent a hundred rubles, an unusually large donation, to the Troitsa-Sergeyevsky Monastery for the prayers for the repose of Morozov's soul.

A few weeks later a long smoldering dispute concerning the treatment of well-known noblemen under sentence of banishment at the Kirillov Monastery in Beloozero began to occupy Ivan's attention. The dispute concerned questions of privilege. Were the nobles to be treated better than the monks? Was it permissible for them to live in aristocratic luxury while the monks lived simply? Ivan Sheremetev, a boyar, who had fought at Kazan and been second-in-command of the Tsar's bodyguard, a man with a distinguished record in the Boyar Council and in military affairs, was sentenced to prison in Beloozero after being tortured to make him reveal the place where he had hidden his treasures. At the Kirillov Monastery he adopted the name of Iona. Another boyar, Ivan Khabarov, was also living there under the name of Ioasaf. There was a third boyar, Vasily Sobakin, the father of Ivan's third wife Marfa Sobakina, and he was living under the name of Varlaam. It appears that Sobakin was infuriated by Sheremetev's high standard of living. There was an open quarrel, and one of the elders of the monastery reported the matter to Ivan in September 1572. Ivan wrote back that all the former boyars now living in the monastery must live frugally.

This was not the end of the matter, for in the summer of 1573 the Abbot of the Kirillov Monastery wrote to Ivan, saying that Sheremetev had been in ill-health and that was why he was permitted to eat well. Ivan replied with a long letter written in rage and self-disgust, by turns ironical, sarcastic, threatening, playful, venomous. The fury is undisguised and the self-abasement is prolonged beyond reason with the result that it becomes finally unconvincing, and no doubt was intended to be unconvincing. Mingled with the rage is the sound of full-bellied, raucous laughter.

> To the most pure Monastery of the Dormition of the most pure Mother of God and of the blessed, God-fearing and saintly Father Kirill and to their brethren in Christ, the Tsar and Grand Prince Ivan Vasilievich of all Russia sends greetings.
>
> Woe unto me the sinner! Woe unto me the accursed! Woe unto me the unclean! Who am I to venture to ascend these heights? For God's sake I pray you, fathers and teachers, to reconsider your decision.
>
> I am not worthy to call myself your brother, so let me be like one of your common laborers. I kneel before you and beg you to reconsider your decision for God's sake! For it is written, Angels are the light of monks, monks are the light of the laity. It is proper for you, our teachers, to enlighten us who have erred into the darkness of pride and into the mortal delights of pride, gluttony and intemperance. But I—foul stinking dog that I am—who can I teach? What can I instruct? How can I enlighten?
>
> If you desire enlightenment, then you have a teacher among you, the great light Kirill. Pray beside his tomb and he will give you guidance. You have his saintly disciples and his monastic rules. In them you will find an instructor and teacher. Learn from them. Forgive us who are poor in spirit and enlighten us, and for God's sake forgive us our boldness.

The Tsar was begging forgiveness for his boldness in writing to the Abbot. He explained that his effrontery was perhaps justified by the fact that once in a state of black depression brought about by alarms and treacheries in Moscow, he had thought very seriously of retiring from life and becoming a monk at the Kirillov Monastery. He had gone so far as to kneel before the Abbot while visiting the monastery to implore a blessing for his novitiate. "And thus it seems to me that I am half a monk and have dared to speak to you."

All this was merely the overture: the conjuring trick transforming "the foul stinking dog" into the novice who kneels imploringly in front of the Abbot. He had been asked for his judgment on the affair and felt an overmastering need to reply. According to the rules laid down by St. Kirill, everyone at the monastery must be treated equally and therefore there could be no distinction between the boyars and monks. Ivan wrote:

> When one takes monastic vows, one forsakes the world and everything in the world. But how can one call Sheremetev a monk? The tenth servant of his who lives in his apartment eats better than the monks who eat in the dining hall. The Russian saints have laid down the rules of monastic life leading to salvation, while the boyars who came to you introduced their own worldly ways. It is not they who have been tonsured by you, but you who have been tonsured by them.
>
> Yes, the rules of Sheremetev are good! Keep them! The rules of St. Kirill are not good, so set them aside! Today this boyar will introduce one of his worldly ways, and tomorrow another will introduce another, and little by little monastic rules will vanish and there will be only worldly rules. Remember that in all monasteries the founder introduced strict rules in the beginning, and then the worldly ones came along and overthrew them. . . .
>
> Because of Sheremetev you give us no peace! I have told you that Sheremetev and Khabarov must eat with the rest of the monks in the dining hall. If Sheremetev is really sick and not shamming, then he should eat alone in his cell. What about all these parties? Why is there feasting, and why are sweetmeats brought to his cell? In the old days, at the Kirillov Monastery, there was not even a spare needle and thread. What can be said about his store-house outside the monastery walls? All this is lawlessness and totally unnecessary. For food he should have bread, a piece of fish, and *kvas*. Beyond that, if you so decide, give him anything you wish, as long as he eats alone and there are no feasts or celebrations. If someone comes to him to converse on spiritual matters, let him not come at meal time, for there should be no eating or drinking during spiritual conversations.
>
> Or perhaps you are sorry for Sheremetev because his brothers even to this day continue to send messages to the Crimea urging the Muslims to wage war against Christians.

So, for page after page, Ivan inveighs with heavy sarcasm against the luxuries enjoyed by the boyars, the obsequiousness of the monks, the absurdity of it all. Like St. Chrysostom, from whom in this discourse he borrows unashamedly, he claims that all luxuries are designed to turn men away from God, forgetting that he lived himself in a state of luxury which beggared description. Poor Sheremetev! Poor Khabarov! How tragic their lives, and how ill-used they are! As for the poor Abbot, what can be expected of him since he permits the rule of Sheremetev to override the rule of St. Kirill? Ivan concludes his letter with a flourish:

> May the peace of God and the mercy of the most pure Mother of God and the prayers of the wonder-working Kirill be with you and with us, Amen! And we, O Fathers, bow to the ground before you

Ivan wrote this long letter with gusto and the appropriate savagery. It was a small matter, but he prolonged it beyond all probability and almost beyond endurance. He resembled those people who tell jokes and repeat them endlessly because they are in love with their own voices and because they tell jokes more to amuse themselves than to amuse the audience. Sometimes, as he describes the behavior of the boyars in the Kirillov Monastery, he seems to be overcome by a great weariness and disgust. When he spoke of himself as "a foul stinking dog," he was not being entirely ironical.

Many of the spurs of his action no longer existed. The victory of Molodi had settled the fate of the Tatars for many years to come. The dissolution of the Oprichnina was forced upon him by events, and the desperate stratagems, by which he maintained himself in power over a separate, private kingdom while simultaneously ruling over the whole of Russia, were no longer needed. For many years he had been living from one crisis to another; if there was no crisis he would create one. Now at last he seemed to weary of living on the vertiginous heights, and he grew quieter and less adventurous.

What disturbed him most, while the Russians were binding up their wounds after the seven-year nightmare of the Oprichnina, was the prevalence of witches. All over Russia, it seemed to him, powerful spells and magic charms were being uttered against him; the sorcerers were at work; enchantments were being practiced and ghosts were abroad. He was convinced that the sudden death of the

Tsaritsa Marfa had been brought about by magic spells and these spells had been uttered not only against the Tsaritsa but against himself and his children. He had survived by the mercy of God, but for how long? Two cousins of Marfa were executed on suspicion of practicing witchcraft. The fear of witches remained with him to the end of his life.

In January 1575 a large number of Russian prisoners returned from the Crimea, and Ivan interrogated them. He wanted to know whether there had been treachery in the ranks of the Russian army, and no doubt he discovered enough traitors to make the interrogations worth his while. Later in the spring he rid himself of his fourth wife Anna Koltovskaya, sending her into a nunnery, and for good measure he executed her relatives.

In the summer Ivan ordered the arrest of Leonid, Archbishop of Novgorod and Pskov. Significantly the archbishop's many crimes included "the keeping of witches." He was also accused of sodomy, counterfeiting money, and secret communication with the King of Poland. Prince Kurbsky describes him as "a gentle and distinguished man" and from the Novgorod Chronicle we learn that he once fined his deacons because they arrived late for a service. Of his fate we know nothing for certain except that he died miserably. According to the Pskov Chronicle the Tsar in a rage tore off his vestments, had him sewn in a bearskin, and set the dogs on him. Jerome Horsey, who was in Russia during this time, says the archbishop was lodged in a cell "with irons on his head and legs." Sentenced to everlasting imprisonment, he is said to have spent his days painting icons, combs, and saddles while living on a diet of bread and water.

The tempo of executions was much slower now. Instead of killing Ivan sometimes resorted to the practice of confiscating everything a man possessed, even his clothes. It was a kind of symbolic execution, and he practiced it on the boyar Nikita Zakharin, the brother of the adored Anastasia. Jerome Horsey, who lived next door to Nikita Zakharin on Varvarka Street in Kitay Gorod, left a vivid account of the sudden eruption of vandals in a quiet street:

> His majesty came to the city of Moscow; cast his displeasure upon some noblemen and governors thereof; set a parasite of his and sent with him two hundred gunners to rob Nikita Romanovich our next

neighbor, brother to the good empress Anastasia, his first wife, took from him all his armor, horse, plate, and goods, to the value of forty thousand pounds; seized his lands and left him and his so poor and needy as he sent to the English house the next day for as much coarse cotton as made him a gown to cover himself and children withal.

A similar but more bloody punishment was visited about the same time on Andrey Shchelkalov, the Grand Secretary, who was beaten until he disgorged five thousand rubles, and was left half-dead. He was not killed, but his faithful servant Ivan Lottych was murdered, apparently as a warning. Jerome Horsey relates that Shchelkalov was also forced to repudiate his young and beautiful wife and to gash her naked back with a scimitar as a sign of renunciation.

There were more sporadic executions in the late summer of 1575. The chroniclers report that Ivan ordered the heads to be thrown into the courtyards of Prince Ivan Mstislavsky, Andrey Shchelka-lov, the Metropolitan, and other high officials as a grizzly warning. It seemed that he could not live without killing but was growing weary of it.

He was also growing weary of life. "The foul stinking dog" would bark and bite, but the vigor was going out of him. He had no philosophy of life, no plans except to survive and to secure the survival of his dynasty, no military policy except to extend his frontier in Livonia with the assistance of King Magnus, who was proving to be totally incompetent. He was exhausted, his sails hung slack, and he drifted with the tide.

A Tatar Khan on the Throne

IN THE AUTUMN OF 1575 there occurred an event so strange, so unexpected, so out of keeping with Ivan's known behavior that the historians have failed to offer any convincing explanation. Quite suddenly, without warning, Ivan stepped down from the throne, gave a Tatar Khan all the rights and privileges of a Grand Prince, and set up his residence outside the Kremlin. He announced that henceforth the former Tsar Ivan would be known as Prince Ivan Moskovsky.

The man he placed on the throne was Sayin Bulat, Khan of Kasimov, the tiny Tatar enclave on the Oka River. As a young man in 1561 the Khan accompanied Princess Kocheney, the daughter of the Circassian Prince Temriuk, to Moscow when she was about to become the second wife of the Tsar. Since his own mother and the Circassian princess were sisters and it was the custom to invite all the relatives to the wedding, he attended as an official guest. He was then about sixteen years old, and it appears that Ivan was attracted by his good looks and noble bearing.

Sayin Bulat was one of the many Tatar princes to enter Ivan's court, but his close relationship to the new Tsaritsa gave him special prominence, and since he was totally loyal and obedient Ivan appointed him Khan of Kasimov, when the reigning Khan Shigaley died in 1566. This was a signal honor, demonstrating that Sayin Bulat was his favorite among all the Tatar Khans at court. The Russian envoy to the Sultan of Turkey was instructed to emphasize the power and freedom enjoyed by the Khans who possessed their own principalities within the Russian border, and none was more powerful and more free than the Tsarevich[1] Sayin Bulat. The envoy declared that "our master has placed Tsarevich Sayin Bulat on the throne of Kasimov and has ordered the building of mosques and madrasahs according to Muslim law, and in no way has our master placed any bounds on his freedom." No doubt this was an exaggeration. The Khans of Kasimov were always the vassals of the Tsar. Yet it is possible that Ivan out of his affection for the young Khan had given him more freedom than he gave to any of the other Tatar princes.

Inevitably the young Khan was called upon to perform military service for the Tsar. As a very young man he served as second-in-command of an army under his uncle Khan Tokhtomysh during the campaigns on the Livonian and Swedish fronts, and he commanded the vanguard during the Polotsk campaign of 1563. He was evidently a brave and resourceful general, being given bigger and bigger commands. In 1574 he commanded the Russian armies attacking Pernau in Livonia. By this time he had acquired a new name and a new religion. Sayin became Simeon at his baptism in July 1573. To this name was added Bekbulatovich, because he was the son of Bekbulat, grandson of Akhmad, the last Khan of the Golden Horde.

There was nothing at all unusual in the baptism and change of name of a Tatar Khan. Tatar royalty, flocking to Moscow, adopted the Christian faith whenever it suited their purpose. The Tatar Khans ranked above all the princes and boyars at court.

By the summer of 1575 the Tsarevich Simeon Bekbulatovich was a man of considerable importance, well-known in the circles of the nobility, a general with many victories to his credit. He was unmarried, in his early thirties and with a promising career in front of him. Ivan regarded him as a person of proven loyalty and trusted him implicitly. He was not implicated in the horrors of the oprichniki and he was liked by the princes and boyars. When the crisis came, Ivan turned to the still young Tsarevich, granted him the powers of a Grand Prince, and stepped down into a well-publi-

---

[1] The Russians generally addressed a Khan as Tsar. The sons and grandsons of Khans were addressed by the title of Tsarevich.

cized obscurity. Simeon appears to have accepted his new role quietly and undramatically, as befitted a man superbly conscious that the blood of Jenghiz Khan flowed in his veins.

Exactly what caused the crisis and how it came about remain unknown. What is certain is that Ivan felt an overwhelming desire to be relieved of the burdens of kingship. Perhaps it was no more than a desire to be relieved of day-to-day decisions and to avoid the meetings of the Boyar Council, which remained in office and attended to affairs of state even when Ivan was behaving most autocratically and fancied he was the sole ruler, the single arbiter of Russia's destiny. Or perhaps he had grown weary of bloodshed: the disembowelings, the slow stranglings, the impalings, the beheadings, the throwing of his victims into the bear-pits. For a long time he had been chief judge and executioner, and he may have wanted a rest from his labors. Many theories have been advanced, but none is satisfactory. Probably there was not one reason but a whole cluster of reasons. An obscure illness, a chance meeting with a *yurodivy,* a half-formed plan to leave the country and take refuge in the court of Queen Elizabeth, or simply the knowledge that he was living through one of those rare periods when the country was in no danger from its external enemies—the Tatars were unnaturally quiet, a long smoldering revolt in Kazan had been quashed, and the Livonian wars were at a standstill—and there was a breathing space when it scarcely mattered whether there was a Tsar on the throne. Any one or any group of these might have brought about the profound malaise which led him to enter into private life.

The popular imagination took a somewhat simpler view of these events. Some believed he abandoned the throne after receiving a warning from a soothsayer: "If you remain Tsar during this year, you will surely die!" Others believed he suspected a plot by which his son Ivan might attempt to seize the throne. The recently discovered Anonymous Chronicle notes that at this time "the Tsar and Grand Prince Ivan Vasilievich of all Russia began to suspect that his son Tsarevich Ivan had designs on the throne, and therefore the Tsar decided to thwart him." Still others were of the opinion that he was scotching a plot by which the boyars hoped to gain power. But all these were surmises. The reality was that a Tatar Khan was on the throne of all the Russias, issuing orders and wearing the proper vestments. Simeon Bekbulatovich became the Grand Prince of Russia.

The investiture of Simeon Bekbulatovich as Grand Prince took place in the Uspensky Cathedral in the presence of Ivan and all the nobles of the court. It appears that he was not crowned, but the jewel-studded *barmy*, the shoulder-mantle always worn by the Grand Princes at their coronations, was solemnly placed on him by the Metropolitan Anthony and the appropriate anthems were sung. Thereafter in theory he possessed in full measure all the autocratic powers of a Grand Prince, while Ivan became Prince Ivan Moskovsky, a leading boyar. Ivan left his palace in the Kremlin and took up residence on Petrovka Street in a residential suburb north of the Kremlin. He was often seen riding in his private carriage between his house and the Kremlin, and when he attended meetings at the Kremlin he deliberately chose to sit as far away as possible from the new Grand Prince to emphasize his inferior station.

But all this was a polite fiction and the reality was very different. Ivan surrendered his power in such a way that he retained the possibility of regaining it whenever he pleased. He resembled a man who divorces his wife and continues to keep her as a mistress. The Grand Prince Simeon was not permitted to use the title of Tsar, and Ivan continued to regard himself as Tsar of Russia, and when writing to his lieutenants in Kazan, he called himself Tsar of Kazan. Just as previously he had split the country into two separate parts, the Zemshchina and the Oprichnina, so now he devised a formula by which the rule should be divided between two separate people, and he remained the senior partner while outwardly professing to be the junior partner. Prince Ivan Moskovsky was as powerful as ever. He was still Tsar; he still possessed great estates; he still ordered executions; he still received ambassadors; he still presided over his own court; but now there were advantages previously denied to him: he was more inaccessible than before and he could now work mysteriously in the background without anyone knowing what he would do next. He had achieved a state of perfect irresponsibility.

Nevertheless the polite fiction was pursued. If Prince Ivan Moskovsky wanted anything from the Grand Prince, it was necessary for him to write a petition couched in the usual terms of

bject supplication, with the petitioner naming himself in the most
umble way. Characteristically, when Prince Ivan Moskovsky
petitioned the Grand Prince Simeon Bekbulatovich, he omitted his
own title and represented himself as Ivanets Vasiliev, Ivanets being
humble form of Ivan and Vasiliev being such a name as a
ommoner might bear if his father was called Vasily.

Although Ivan quite seriously maintained that he had entered
private life, he still needed to have his own courtiers and favorites
round him. It was therefore necessary to come to some arrangement with the Grand Prince concerning the courtiers who remained
n the Kremlin and those who served in the court on Petrovka
treet. A new apportionment had to be made, and accordingly Ivan
ddressed himself to the Grand Prince:

TO THE LORD,
THE GRAND PRINCE SIMEON BEKBULATOVICH

Ivanets Vasiliev together with his sons Ivanets and Fedorets
humbly petition for permission to apportion the members of the
court, the boyars, the court nobility, the provincial nobility, and the
attendants. We petition further that some may be kept and others
dismissed and submit that all this may be arranged with the help of
the Lord's officers. Also, we request permission to make our choice
from all the members of the court. Also, we crave permission to rid
ourselves of those who are not wanted by us. And when we have
sorted the people out, then, O Lord, we shall submit their names to
you and thereafter we shall take none without Your Lordship's
express permission. And we request, O Lord, your favor in not
sequestering the private estates of the people who come to us, as was
done previously in the case of the appanage princes. We urge you to
let them remove from their estates granted to them by the government their money, their harvested corn, and their movable be-
longings. We ask that they should be allowed to leave the estates
without being robbed.

We request that you will show mercy to those who desire to join us
and that they will be permitted to leave without incurring your
displeasure and that they will not be taken away from us. And as for
those who desire to leave us in order to join you, we request, O Lord,
that you will show favor to us and be merciful to us by not taking
them into your court and not accepting their petitions.

Do us also, O Lord, the kindness of granting us a decree in your

name showing what provisions should be made for the cour
attendants, whether by letters patent of our clerks, or by charte
signed by us, or would you demand a full bond? Let us know, (
Lord, the terms of your decree.

Thus do we petition you! Show us your mercy and favor, O Lord

Ivan's petition, full of blandishments and commands, is a strange
document to be written to a reigning Grand Prince. What Ivan was
saying clearly enough was that he proposed to take a select group
of boyars and nobles into his service, leaving Simeon Bekbulato
vich with the rest.

Ivan also chose a wife for the Grand Prince. She was Anastasia
the daughter of Prince Ivan Mstislavsky, who was descended from
both Ivan III and Khan Ibrahim of Kazan. Since Prince Mstis
lavsky ranked first among the Russian princes, the choice was no
made lightly. The wedding took place in the Uspensky Cathedra
with the splendor that accompanied all royal weddings. Ivan
himself gave the bride away and his son, the Tsarevich Ivan, acted
as chief usher. Simeon Bekbulatovich could regard this arranged
marriage as still another sign of the high favor in which Ivan held
him, a reaffirmation of Ivan's intentions regarding him. The
marriage took place a few days after his investiture as Grand
Prince.

On November 29, 1575, in his house on Petrovka Street, Ivan
gave an audience to Daniel Sylvester, the Englishman sent by
Queen Elizabeth to appease his wrath, for Ivan had been extremely
displeased with the results of his embassies to England. Elizabeth
paid no attention at all to his suggestion that both sovereign
should agree to grant refuge to one another in the event of interna
disorders; or rather, she offered him asylum but did not request
asylum for herself. Ivan was infuriated by her lack of reciprocity
her assumption that she was in no need of his help. He had
therefore made life very difficult for the English merchants in
Russia. But the audience with Sylvester was friendly as he
discussed, among many other things, the reasons that led him to
abandon the throne. Sylvester was an intelligent man; he knew
Russian well; and he gives the impression of a man who reported
quite accurately what Ivan told him. Ivan explained that the real
reason why he conducted these negotiations with Queen Elizabeth

was that he "highly foresaw the variable and dangerous estate of princes," and had therefore come to suspect his "own magnificence," by which he meant that he had begun to doubt whether he would long remain on the throne. He went on to say:

> We have resigned the estate of our government which hitherto hath been so royally maintained into the hands of a stranger who is nothing allied unto us, our land or crown. The occasion whereof is the perverse and evil dealing of our subjects who murmur and repine at us, forgetting loyal obedience they practice against our person. The which to prevent we have given them over unto another prince to govern them but have reserved in our custody all the treasure of the land with sufficient train and place for their and our relief.

In a characteristically Russian way Ivan insisted that Queen Elizabeth had been prevented from understanding the real purport of his letter because traitors had "interpreted our meaning to their pleasure and misinformed our sister." The truth was that his sister knew exactly what he meant. Ivan hinted at conspiracies and spoke darkly of Queen Elizabeth's agent in Lübeck who had obviously poisoned her mind against him: evidently there were so many misunderstandings that the cause was hopeless. But Ivan remained affable throughout the audience and Daniel Sylvester would later be given another opportunity to present Queen Elizabeth's case to him.

The audience was doubly important, for it showed Ivan wrestling with two problems which were quite separate yet linked together by his desperate need for safety in an uncertain and dangerous world. Queen Elizabeth had offered him asylum but on terms that were quite unacceptable, for she had not accepted his own offer of asylum to her. For the moment his safety was assured by the fact that he had resigned in favor of a stranger who was "nothing allied unto us, our land or crown." This was stretching the truth: Simeon Bekbulatovich was distantly related to him by marriage and was in no sense a stranger. Moreover he could be relied upon to be abjectly obedient to Ivan's purposes. On one subject Ivan spoke truthfully: he had reserved in his custody all the treasure of the land. The reins of power were still in his hands and he alone possessed the keys to the treasury.

About the same time that Ivan was speaking to Daniel Sylvester

there arrived, on the frontier between Russia and Lithuania, the
ambassadors of Maximilian II, the Holy Roman Emperor. Maximilian and Ivan were on friendly terms and both professed to be
shocked by the St. Bartholomew's Day massacre of 1572. "Dear
brother, you grieve over the blood that was shed," Ivan wrote to
Maximilian. "It is seemly for a Christian sovereign to grieve over
the inhuman treatment of so many people by the King of France
and over the blood he spilt without cause." Ivan was not being
disingenuous: he regarded religious quarrels among Christians as
relatively unimportant. When he committed his own massacres, he
maintained that they were necessary in order to extirpate treason.

The imperial ambassadors, Hans Kobenzl and Daniel Printz, had
not come to Russia to discuss massacres. They wanted to discuss a
vast range of important subjects from the election of a King of
Poland to a joint attack on the Turkish Empire. This was not an
ordinary embassy, for the ambassadors were empowered to conduct the most far-reaching negotiations. Maximilian did not know
there was a new Grand Prince on the throne, and for a while Ivan
appears to have been in a quandary. Should he, or should he not
receive the ambassadors? Since he was now Prince Ivan Moskovsky, did he have any right to receive them? As usual, in such
circumstances, he procrastinated and kept them kicking their heels
on the border, where they remained for about six weeks. Such
behavior was insulting to the Emperor, and in December Ivan
writing from what he called "the Tsar's Palace in Moscow," urged
them to be patient. He wrote:

> You should not be alarmed because we have not yet received you
> Certain important and difficult matters having arisen in our territory
> it has become encumbent upon us to investigate them. As quickly as
> possible We shall arrive in our city of Mozhaisk and We shall give
> instructions to have you escorted to this place where you will be
> received in audience.

"The important and difficult matters" that occupied Ivan's
attention were perhaps connected with the furnishing of his house
in Mozhaisk in a manner suitable for receiving ambassadors. It was
also necessary to arrange for the most sumptuous foods, the most
magnificent vessels, and the most splendid clothes for his courtiers.
At all costs he must appear in his utmost magnificence and the

ambassadors must be left in no doubt that he was the real ruler of Russia.

All this took time, and it was not until the middle of January that the audience took place. The ambassadors were staggered by the opulence and cultivated good taste of the court, all the more so because they had been warned when traveling through Poland that they were about to enter a country where intolerable crudity was the rule. In his report to Vienna Kobenzl wrote that he had visited the courts of the Kings of Spain, France, Hungary, Bohemia, and of the Grand Dukes of Tuscany, but never had he set eyes on so much treasure as he saw at Mozhaisk. Ivan, wearing his gold crown and golden robes, received the ambassadors graciously. The ambassadors were led from one vast hall to the next, and each hall gleamed with treasure.

Only four brief descriptions of Ivan's personal appearance have survived. One of the most convincing was supplied by Daniel Printz in his report to the Emperor:

> He is very tall and physically very powerful, though somewhat tending to fat. He has large eyes which are perpetually darting about, observing everything thoroughly. He has a red beard with a somewhat black coloring and wears it rather long and thick. But like most Russians he wears the hair of his head cut short with a razor.

Although Ivan was on his best behavior throughout the embassy, Printz soon learned about his formidable temper. "They say that when he is in the grip of anger he foams at the mouth like a stallion and appears close to madness. When he is in this state, he rages against everyone he encounters." Printz also observed that the whole court, but especially Ivan, were continually crossing themselves and gazing at the icons. Whenever Ivan lifted up his goblet or began to eat one of the dishes set before him, he made a large, expansive sign of the cross while gazing at an icon of the Virgin or of St. Nicholas, who was especially venerated in Mozhaisk.

The ambassadors carefully observed Ivan's eating habits. He sat at his high table with the Tsarevich beside him and the great nobles sitting at the same table some distance away. He liked to see the meats and poultry before they were carved, and so processions of young noblemen entered the dining hall bearing platters and passed below his table for his approval. At one of these dinners the main course consisted of swans. Ivan approved, and then the swans were taken away so that the carvers could go to work. Meanwhile Ivan offered bread to his guests, first turning to the Tsarevich, then to the nobles, and finally to the ambassadors, who were told, "The Tsar and the Grand Prince present this loaf to you." Thereupon they rose and thanked Ivan for the gift of bread and they also thanked the nobles who brought it to them. Soon the swans, carved up placed in smaller dishes and garnished with onions, were served First Ivan received his portion, and then the nobles, and then the ambassadors, who rose and thanked the Tsar. All through the long dinner which went on late into the night, the ambassadors were bobbing up and down to thank Ivan, who sat with his elbows firmly planted on the table, smiling indulgently at the procession of food bearers, for he had a hearty appetite.

Then as now a Russian banquet involved innumerable toasts The Tsar drank to his son, to his nobles, to the ambassadors, and the toasts were repeated. The ambassadors wisely permitted themselves the luxury of not drinking everything that was offered them. They observed that Ivan was provided with a taster who stood behind him. Wine or mead would be poured into Ivan's goblet and then into the taster's goblet. Only after the taster had drunk the wine would Ivan drink.

The Poles had warned the ambassadors that they were about to enter a rude and barbarous country. In one respect this was true. Everyone ate with his fingers, tearing off the portion of meat he wanted and throwing the rest back in the dish. The ambassadors, accustomed to knives, successfully borrowed a knife from a Russian noble and then shared it between them. But if the manner of serving was atrocious, and if there was too much garlic for their tastes, nevertheless they found nothing but praise for the cooks. Toward the end of the meal the Tsar presented a pickled plum to each of the nobles he wanted to honor. The granting of favors was not reserved to the Tsar; the nobles in their turn would give choice morsels to their favorites.

In the intervals of feasting the ambassadors negotiated with the Tsar. These negotiations were curiously unreal; they bargained for properties they did not possess and made plans to attack enemies they had no intention of attacking. Sigismund Augustus, King of Poland and Grand Prince of Lithuania, the last of the Jagellon

Sigismund II Augustus, King of Poland and Grand Prince of Lithuania.

dynasty, died on July 18, 1572, without issue and the question of his successor was discussed at great length. The French had their candidate: Henry of Valois, the son of Catherine de Medici. The Emperor Maximilian thought his son, the Archduke Ernst, was a more suitable candidate. Ivan did not present his son as the candidate but thought seriously of acquiring Lithuania for himself. In fact Henry of Valois had been crowned King of Poland in the Cathedral at Cracow but proved to be preposterously incompetent and soon returned to Paris. There remained the claims of Ivan and Maximilian. According to Ivan, Lithuania must be permanently united to Muscovy; also Livonia and Kiev belonged to him; and if these matters were agreed to, he would permit the Archduke Ernst to become King of Poland. He had no passionate convictions regarding Poland, which was far away and inhabited by Roman Catholics. Kobenzl, or perhaps Maximilian speaking through him, conveyed the substance of many wild dreams by which Maximilian and Ivan would acquire new empires. The East lay at their mercy, Constantinople was within reach, the Sultan could be hurled out of Europe and Asia Minor into the deserts of Arabia. Ivan was not encouraged by the prospect of fighting the Ottoman Empire; he was more concerned with Livonia and Lithuania, for above everything else he wanted a window on the Baltic. The imperial ambassadors offered him the empire of the ancient Greeks and the Ottoman Sultans, while Ivan would have been perfectly happy to have Riga and Reval.

The negotiations concerning the Kingdom of Poland were being conducted without the advice and consent of the Poles, who were conducting their own negotiations. Their choice fell on Stephen Bathory, Prince of Transylvania, a vassal of the Sultan and a man of remarkable courage and resourcefulness. They made one stipulation: they would welcome him as King if he married the Princess Anna, the sister of Sigismund Augustus, thus maintaining a link with the beloved Jagellon dynasty. Stephen Bathory accepted the condition. He was crowned on May 1, 1576, and immediately afterward celebrated his marriage with the Princess.

Although rumors that Stephen Bathory was being considered for the throne of Poland had reached Mozhaisk, neither Ivan nor the ambassadors attached much importance to them. It was not to be believed that the Poles would elect their own King without the consent of the Tsar and the Emperor. So the long negotiations continued—they lasted from January 14 to January 27, 1576—and all the time they concerned matters that had very little relation to reality. There were polite discourses, many toasts, interminable meals. The main purpose of Ivan appears to have been to ensure that the Emperor would not meddle with his affairs in Livonia.

The ambassadors departed after signing a treaty of friendship.

A few weeks later Ivan sent his own ambassador to the Emperor Maximilian in Vienna. He chose Prince Zakhary Sugorsky, formerly the governor of Astrakhan and an ambassador to the court of the Crimean Khan. He was graciously received by the Emperor, who doffed his hat to the ambassador. Prince Sugorsky expected the Emperor would then extend his hand to be kissed. He waited; no hand was extended; and the ambassador showed signs of being deeply troubled until it was explained that the German Emperor was not accustomed to extending his hand. Finally the Emperor, following the Russian custom, extended his hand and the ambassador kissed it.

There survives a contemporary woodcut showing the Russian ambassador and his retinue at the court of Maximilian. The Russians are dressed in their finery, and Prince Sugorsky is shown defying tradition by not wearing a beard.

On January 29, 1576, Ivan gave an audience to Daniel Sylvester,

Prince Zakhary Sugorsky (second from left) and his retinue on his way to offer his sealed credentials to the Emperor Maximilian. The Russian ambassador's credentials are being carried by the young man at right. (From a contemporary German engraving)

the English envoy, in his house on Petrovka Street in Moscow. Sylvester was about to leave for England and wanted to receive Ivan's final message to Queen Elizabeth. Fresh from what he regarded as a brilliant victory at Mozhaisk, Ivan was in a belligerent mood, accusing Queen Elizabeth of "a kind of haughtiness" which he found insufferable because she demanded "the abasing of our self towards her." Since he was not accustomed to abasing himself toward anyone, he raged against her until Sylvester interrupted with a request that the Tsar should "certify" his "great dislike," meaning that he should list the reasons why he had come to have such a low opinion of her. It transpired that the chief reason was that she did not have total confidence in him, even though he had behaved with extraordinary liberality towards the English merchants in Russia and shown them countless favors. The question of asylum was still uppermost in his mind. The Tsar had had no difficulty in extracting from the ambassadors the promise that if he needed asylum in the territories of Maximilian, it would be granted to him, and similarly, if Maximilian ever had occasion to seek refuge in Russia, Ivan guaranteed him asylum. The doctrine of reciprocity was established. The crime of Queen Elizabeth was that she had refused to entertain the thought that she would ever be in need of asylum at Ivan's court. She had demonstrated her "haughtiness," thus placing him in the position of a suppliant, and this was intolerable to him.

Then, so that there should be no doubt about who was the real ruler of Russia, Ivan went on to explain that Simeon Bekbulatovich, although he had been "enthroned in the imperial dignity," had not been crowned. He reigned at the Tsar's pleasure and was therefore merely the temporary occupant of the throne. Ivan retained the imperial regalia, the scepter and the seven crowns, and as long as they were in his possession the real power belonged to him. "At our pleasure we can take the dignity unto us again," Ivan said, "and will yet do therein as God shall instruct us, for that the same is not confirmed unto him by order of coronation nor he by assent elected, but for our pleasure." Such were the Tsar's words as Daniel Sylvester wrote them down immediately after the audience. They provide the only certain testimony concerning the Tsar's reasons and intentions when he elevated Simeon Bekbulatovich to the throne. It was done "for our pleasure," and could be undone "at our pleasure." The Tsar had taken all the precautions necessary to ensure that while Simeon Bekbulatovich was given certain limited powers, he was little more than a figurehead. Daniel Sylvester was to convey to Queen Elizabeth the information that he was still the supreme ruler of Russia and with this warning he dismissed the English envoy, who kissed his hand and the hand of the Tsarevich, who was present throughout the speech from the throne.

Only a few decrees signed by Simeon Bekbulatovich as Grand Prince of all Russia have survived. One of these decrees concerns a certain Ivan Liubovnikov, who petitioned against the Board of Internal Revenue that he was being made to pay all the taxes on a property in Murom when in fact he owned only half the property. Simeon decreed that "it shall be as Ivan petitioned us." The decree was sealed with the Grand Prince's seal on March 27, 1576.

Meanwhile Ivan continued to appear at court, ostentatiously assuming a humble role and permitting Simeon Bekbulatovich to precede him both in the council chamber and in the cathedral. When the summer came, the Tsar ordered the Grand Prince to sign a decree commanding Ivan to serve with the troops on the Oka River. The decree was read out by the Secretary for Military Affairs in the presence of the Boyar Council. It read simply: "Prince Ivan Vasilievich Moskovsky! The Grand Prince Simeon Bekbulatovich of all Russia commands you to serve at the river bank against the coming of the Khan of the Crimea."

On the following day, pleading poverty, Ivan submitted a petition for a grant-in-aid in order to outfit an army. The petitioner no longer called himself Ivanets Vasiliev, as he had done when he petitioned about the apportionment of the two courts. He wrote:

TO THE LORD, THE GRAND PRINCE
SIMEON BEKBULATOVICH OF ALL RUSSIA

We, Prince Ivan Vasilievich Moskovsky and my son Prince Ivan Ivanovich, hereby submit this petition. Having received your command to serve on the river bank, we request that you should favor us with the means to serve you, as God shall instruct you.

This petition was solemnly handed to Simeon Bekbulatovich, who handed it to the Secretary for Military Affairs, who then read it aloud to the Boyar Council. The Secretary, who had already discussed the matter with Ivan and Simeon, then announced that the petition had been granted, saying, "Prince Ivan Vasilyevich and Prince Ivan Ivanovich! The Grand Prince Simeon has decided to grant you 40,000 rubles for your services." Ivan and the Tsarevich then bowed to Simeon, and a few days later they set out for the southern front.

Ivan and his son spent the summer at the fortress town of Kaluga on the banks of the Oka River, accompanied by the great nobles of his court. The main army was commanded by Prince Ivan Mstislavsky, the father of the Grand Princess. A very powerful force, largely financed by the grant of 40,000 rubles—an immense sum in those days—stood guard on the river bank, but the expected battles did not take place, for the Tatars failed to attack. Ivan spent a pleasant summer holiday with the army and returned to Moscow late in August. The long, lazy days in camp had given him time for reflection and when he finally returned to Moscow he had decided to put an end to the rule of Simeon Bekbulatovich.

He issued a series of decrees, appointing himself once more Grand Prince of all Russia, and he granted Simeon Bekbulatovich the rank and style of Grand Prince of Tver in reward for his services, thus reviving a grand principality that had become extinct at the end of the fifteenth century. Thereafter Simeon Bekbulatovich vanished from the scene and little more was ever heard of him.

Ivan was once more Tsar and Grand Prince of all Russia at the age of forty-six. The strange year-long charade was over, and he now resumed the task given to him by God, that task which he found so burdensome, so terrible, so satisfying, and so delightful.

Good News from England

ONE OF THE PIECES of unfinished business that loomed large in Ivan's mind was the conquest of Livonia, which he regarded as a perpetual thorn in his side. One of his first tasks therefore after he had resumed the throne was to prepare for an invasion of Livonia on a massive scale, to put an end once and for all to the pretensions of those who claimed to be its rulers. Northern Livonia was now being claimed by the King of Sweden, and southern Livonia by the King of Poland. Preparations for the invasion of Livonia occupied most of the spring and early summer of 1577. In May, accompanied by his sons Ivan and Fyodor, he set out from Moscow for Novgorod, and in the middle of June he left Novgorod and advanced on Pskov, where King Magnus was waiting for him. There the final plan of conquest was worked out. Magnus was to attack the heavily fortified city of Venden while Ivan was to march south against Lithuanian Livonia. Surprise was all the easier to achieve because Russia and Lithuania had signed a truce which would not expire until later in the year.

Ivan's army carried everything before it. The terror of his name, the suddenness of the attack, and the unpreparedness of the Livonians led to easy victories. When the army appeared before Marienhausen, the town surrendered without a fight on the promise that the garrison would be allowed to leave unharmed. It was the same at the heavily fortified town of Dinaburg (Dvinsk). Sometimes the garrisons left before the army arrived. But when the garrison at

Chestvin failed to surrender, the punishment was swift and terrible, for heavy guns were brought up, the fortress was demolished, all the soldiers were executed, and the women and children were sold into slavery to the Tatars.

King Magnus was also winning victories. He captured Venden and went on to capture so many other towns that he came to regard himself as the rightful king of Livonia, owing allegiance to no one. He wrote to Ivan, commanding him to desist from any further conquests in Livonia. Outraged, Ivan advanced on the nearest German town claimed by Magnus, executed the entire garrison, and wrote off an angry letter:

> To Magnus the king, our vassal. I sent you from Pskov to take only Venden, but following the advice of evil persons or your own stupidity, you want everything. Know that we are close to you. I have many soldiers and can act efficiently. Either obey or go back beyond the sea. I can send you to Kazan. I can take Livonia without your help.

Ivan was a master of the threatening letter, and Magnus felt properly chastised. He hoped his impolitic letter would be forgotten, but Ivan never forgot. At the head of the Russian army, Ivan advanced on Venden, sending messengers ahead to demand that Magnus come out and meet the Tsar and make his submission. Unwisely Magnus sent two ambassadors with his apologies. Infuriated, Ivan had the two ambassadors whipped with birch rods and sent them back with instructions to Magnus to present himself immediately to the Tsar. Magnus hesitated; he was afraid for his life; and it was only when the citizens convinced him that the fate of the whole city depended upon his compliance that he summoned up enough courage to ride out with an escort of high officials to meet the Tsar. He had reason to be afraid. Ivan had learned that he was already negotiating with King Stephen Bathory and was preparing to swear allegiance to the King of Poland. In Ivan's presence Magnus fell on his knees and begged forgiveness. Ivan raised him up and gave him a tongue-lashing:

> Fool! So you dared to think of your Livonian kingdom! You—a poor vagabond, who was received into my family, married to my beloved niece, given clothes by me, given money and cities by me—only to betray me, your lord, your benefactor, your father!

Wall painting in Svyazhsk Cathedral. Ivan is in center.

Answer me! How many times have I heard about your wicked schemes, and yet I did not believe them and was silent! Now everything has been revealed to me! It was your intention to betray me, take Livonia from me, and become the vassal of the King of Poland! But God is merciful, for he protected me and gave you into my hands!

Now return to me what is mine, and sink once more into insignificance. If you had not been a king's son, I would have taught you a lesson for opposing me and taking my cities away from me!

Having admonished Magnus, Ivan ordered that he should be imprisoned with his escort in an empty mansion, where they spent the following days and nights. Later, Magnus was let out so that he could arrange for the formal entry of the Russian troops into Venden. Lodgings in Venden were prepared for Ivan and orders were given that there should be no molestation of the citizens by the Russian troops. At all costs there must be a peaceful entry. But neither Ivan nor Magnus had paid any attention to the German garrison still in command of the fortress. The fortress guns opened fire, some Russian soldiers were killed, and Ivan predictably ordered all his heavy guns to be brought up to reduce the fortress to rubble. No mercy would be shown to the Germans. The bombardment continued for three days. When the Germans realized that the fortress could no longer hold out and that the survivors would inevitably be tortured to death, they decided to blow themselves up. The three hundred defenders therefore filled the cellars with gunpowder, received the last sacraments from their pastors, embraced their families, and watched in silence while Heinrich Boysmann, formerly a member of the court of King Magnus, threw a lighted torch to the gunpowder. On that day, September 20, 1577, the entire garrison of Venden perished.

Within a few weeks all the other towns and castles claimed by King Magnus surrendered to Ivan, and all the cities of Livonia, with the exception of the important ports of Riga and Reval, fell into his hands. One surrender especially delighted him—Volmar, where Prince Andrey Kurbsky had taken refuge after his flight from Dorpat. Ivan therefore took this occasion to write a long letter to Kurbsky full of his griefs, his agonies and triumphs, accusing his former friend of murders and treacheries without number, enumerating his own sins which were legion, and confusing all issues with sudden outbursts of paranoiac rage. Prince Kurbsky was out of his reach, and Ivan seems to have felt that the very vehemence of his rage would be sufficient to strike Kurbsky dead. Implicit in the letter is the desire to torture his former friend to death. At the same time, to compensate for so many remembered wounds, Ivan continually vaunted his triumphs.

The violence of Ivan's rage knew no bounds. Speaking of the boyars who had oppressed him and, as he firmly believed, wished to bring about his downfall, he spits out one violent accusation after another. He accused Kurbsky of causing the death of Anastasia and of wanting to give the crown to Prince Vladimir of Staritsa. There was no truth in these accusations, but Ivan half-believed they were true. He saw himself as a man continually bedeviled by conspiracies which he had scotched just in time. He wrote:

> I could not endure these vexations any longer, and so I defended myself, and then you began to act against me and betray me still

more. And so I set myself against you with greater severity. I wanted you to submit to my will, and because of this—how you defiled and outraged the sanctity of the Lord! Having become angered with a man, you have struck against God! . . .

Behold, O Prince, the ways of the Lord. God giveth power to whomsoever He wills. You and the priest Sylvester and Alexey Adashev speak boastfully like the devil in *Job*, saying: "I have been going to-and-fro in the earth, and walking up and down in it, and I have brought all things under the sky under my feet." But God said to him: "Hast thou considered my servant Job?" Just so did you think of having all Russia under your feet! But all your conspiracies have come to nothing by the will of God! . . .

You said: "There are no people left in Russia—no one stands firm." Well, you are not here now, and who do you think is conquering the German fortresses? The fortresses are falling before the power of the life-giving Cross, which defeated Amalek and Maxentius! The German cities do not even make preparations for battle; they merely bow their heads at the sight of the life-giving Cross. And when it so happened, due to our sins, that the life-giving Cross did not appear, then we gave battle. . . .

And so we have been brought by God to Volmar, where you had hoped to rest from all your toils. Yea, by God's will, we caught up with you in your resting-place, and forced you to ride further afield. . . .

Written in our patrimony, the land of Livonia, in the year 1577, the forty-third year of our reign, and of our tsardoms: the thirty-first year of our Russian tsardom, the twenty-fifth of our Kazan tsardom, the twenty-fourth of our Astrakhan tsardom.

Having put his seal to the letter, Ivan placed it in the hands of the Lithuanian Prince Alexander Polubensky, the man who had revealed to him the treachery of King Magnus, with instructions that it should be dispatched immediately to Prince Kurbsky. As for King Magnus, Ivan was surprisingly lenient. He was pardoned, made to renew his oath of allegiance, and given several cities in central Livonia. Then Ivan returned to Alexandrova Sloboda, leaving behind some verses which he ordered to be translated into German and hung prominently in all the Livonian churches. The verses read:

> I am Ivan, lords of the many lands
> Enumerated in my title. I worship

The faith of my ancestors,
Which is the true Christian faith
According to the teachings of St. Paul,
And this is the same faith
Which is followed by the good people of Moscow.
I am their hereditary Tsar.
I neither begged for this title
Nor did I purchase it.
My Tsar is Jesus Christ.

With this German doggerel Ivan put the seal on his Livonian conquests. Twenty-seven towns and cities had surrendered to him or had been battered into submission. To his regret Riga remained in the hands of Stephen Bathory and Revel remained in the hands of John III, the King of Sweden.

A red-hot iron rake had been dragged across Livonia; thousands of soldiers and peasants had been slaughtered; the life and economy of the country were completely disorganized; and all to no avail. The Swedes and the Lithuanians were now more determined than ever to avenge Ivan's insults. Dinaburg fell to the Lithuanians by a ruse. They sent barrels of wine to the Russian garrison, waited till they were drunk, then scaled the walls and massacred them. A German force attached to the army of King Stephen Bathory advanced on Venden, acquired the keys to the main gateway, opened the gate, and crept stealthily into the city. Other towns and cities fell to the Swedes. Ivan had enjoyed a hollow victory. Once more the patchwork quilt was being torn to shreds.

Predictably, too, King Magnus went over to the enemy. He concluded a secret treaty with King Stephen Bathory and went into hiding in Courland.

The loss of Venden stung Ivan to a massive retaliation. Prince Ivan Golitsyn with an army of 18,000 men besieged the city in the fall of 1578. The siege was broken off when a combined force of Germans, Lithuanians, and Swedes attacked the Russians. Prince Golitsyn fled into the night, taking his cavalry with him, but leaving his artillery and foot soldiers behind. There was a spectacular slaughter, the Russian gunners hanged themselves from their cannon to avoid a worse fate if they were captured, and a third of the Russian army perished.

This victory at Venden provided Prince Kurbsky with a suitable occasion for admonishing the Tsar for so much deplorable boasting. "As for your vaunting and boasting that you conquered the Livonians by the power of the life-giving Cross, I do not know nor do I understand how this accords with the truth—the thief's flag would be more appropriate," Kurbsky wrote, and went on to describe the Russian generals captured at Venden who were put in chains and led off to Poland where they were "mocked and jeered at by all, to your criminal and everlasting shame and to the shame of Holy Russia and to the disgrace of the people, the sons of the Russian land."

Kurbsky's letter was hard-hitting, with a bitter humor. Of those life-giving Crosses which gave so much comfort to Ivan he wrote, "Those Crosses of yours have been broken in many places." Remembering Ivan's accusation that he was one of those who brought about the death of Anastasia, he wrote, "In my family we are not accustomed to destroying our relatives, unlike the rulers of Muscovy."

But the kernel of the letter is a single sentence written in hot blood. "You have transformed the tsardom of Russia into a fortress in Hell by closing the frontiers and suppressing freedom." It was an accusation which could be made against many of Ivan's successors.

Ivan's campaign against Livonia, embarked upon so lightheartedly, produced many bitter fruits. Polotsk, once an important city in Kievan Russia, fell to the Lithuanians in the spring of 1579. It was a year of bad omens. They said a tombstone fell on Moscow with some indecipherable lettering, and the Tsar ordered it to be smashed. They said, too, that thunder was heard out of a cloudless sky. Moscow trembled when it heard of the loss of Polotsk and the neighboring town of Sokol. For once Ivan decided that it was best to make a clean breast of it, and the state secretary, Andrey Shchelkalov, was ordered to address the people on the Red Square and admit defeat. Dressed in somber black, Shchelkalov read out the words dictated by Ivan:

Good people! Know that the King has taken Polotsk and put Sokol to the flames! I bring you melancholy news. Prudence demands that we remain firm, nothing is permanent in the world, fortune betrays even the greatest of rulers.

Although Polotsk is in Stephen's hands, all of Livonia remains in ours. We have lost some Russians, but the Lithuanians have lost more. In this minor misfortune let us console ourselves with the memory of the many victories and conquests of the Orthodox Tsar.

The women of Moscow shouted that they wanted their husbands returned to them. Failing that, they demanded that the state secretary should give them new husbands. They could not be quieted until Shchelkalov ordered men with birch rods to drive them away.

While all these battles were taking place, Ivan himself seemed strangely unaffected. He continued to live in great state, held audiences with his councillors and with ambassadors, and conducted himself as though he had no cares. Jacob Ulfeld, an ambassador from Denmark, visited him in August 1578, when he was living at Alexandrova Sloboda, and later wrote a detailed account of the audience.

The Danes arrived in great state, the ambassador being provided with a retinue of 106 persons. Accommodation was provided for them outside Alexandrova Sloboda, and they were a little surprised to discover that the road from their residence to the palace was heavily guarded by two thousand musketeers. This was a sure sign that the negotiations which concerned Danish claims in Livonia would be difficult.

Jacob Ulfeld was a remarkably observant man and his account of his embassy includes some drawings which provide us with the only surviving contemporary pictures of Alexandrova Sloboda. Unfortunately these drawings leave much to be desired. Although they are evidently based on quick sketches made at the time, they cannot be taken as accurate depictions of the scene. The drawings, which are reproduced in this book, show cavernous halls and some oddly isolated buildings. We see watch towers, raised causeways, three churches, three stone houses. It is quite obvious that there must have been many more buildings and that they were more richly ornamented than they are depicted. The interiors are more satisfying. Here is Alexandrova Sloboda as Jacob Ulfeld remembered it some years later—the Tsar at his high table, the solemn processions, the youths in white silk guarding the throne, and the great officers of state in their long golden robes. But the overwhelm-

g impression is one of awkwardness and discomfort, as though it
as all taking place in a vast cow barn.

As they were about to enter the audience chamber, the Danes
ere warned that they must on no account fail to recite all the
sar's titles with the proper respect. They found the Tsar and the
sarevich Ivan sitting on their thrones. Ivan wore a gown of yellow
:lvet sewn with jewels with a gold jewel-studded collar. His gold
·own was surmounted with a velvet cap sparkling with precious
ones, and he wore jeweled rings on all his fingers. The Tsarevich
ore a red velvet gown, and this too was studded with jewels. As
Ilfeld approached the throne, Ivan stretched out a glittering hand
ι welcome. Ulfeld was not quite sure what was expected of him,
nd the herald said, "Jacob! Ivan Vasilievich is so gracious toward
ou that he offers you his hand. So go up to him and give him your
and!"

Ulfeld did as he was directed and then gave his hand to the
sarevich. Other members of the embassy did the same. Then the
sar inquired about the health of the King of Denmark, and after
:ceiving a satisfactory answer he permitted Ulfeld to make his
pening speech. The ambassador carefully recited the long cata-
ιgue of Ivan's titles, and he observed that a change came over the
sar's face. His eyebrows rose, he puffed himself up, and he looked
leased. But when the ambassador began to talk about the serious
ιatters which had brought him to Russia, Ivan stopped him, saying
ιat these would have to be discussed with his advisers. "Thus,"
·rote Ulfeld, "we were unable to tell him what the King of
)enmark had ordered us to say to him."

Ivan told them to sit down, and then a herald came up and said,
The Tsar invites you to feast with him today. So stand up and
ιank His Majesty." This they did, feeling more and more like
ιarionettes on strings. Then they were ordered into another room
ι begin negotiations with the four councillors of state, Bogdan
Ielsky, Ivan Cheremisinov, Andrey Shchelkalov, and Andrey
herefedinov. Bogdan Belsky was the Tsar's new favorite; he was
ιot related to the Belsky princes and had acquired his high position
ιrough his cousin Maliuta Skuratov. The negotiations were
ιonducted "while the tables were being laid." When they saw Ivan
gain he wore a simple gown of dark silk and a small red cloth cap
ewn with precious stones, and the Tsarevich wore white. During

the feast the Tsar followed his familiar custom of presenting dish
to the members of his court, and Ulfeld noted that the first di
went to Prince Ivan Mstislavsky and the second to Niki
Zakharin, the brother of Anastasia. After that it was the turn of tl
Danish ambassador and some of the members of his suite, and the
the Tsar resumed his offering of dishes to the nobles. Ulfe
counted the number of times the Tsar presented these dishes ar
came to a grand total of sixty-five. Malmsey was poured from
gold beaker into a glass; the Tsar sipped the wine, and then sent tl
glass to Ulfeld, who concluded that he had received a special mar
of the Tsar's favor. "I know you have had a long journey by lan
and sea," the Tsar said through an interpreter, "and you hav
suffered great hardships. I shall see that you have everything yo
need."

On the tables the dishes and glasses were so crowded that
would have been impossible to add any more. Once more Iva
presented Ulfeld with wine—this time it was mead in a silve
beaker. But these marks of favor had no effect on the negotiation
which continued to be difficult. And Ulfeld observed that the Tsar
table manners left much to be desired.

On August 25 Ulfeld and his suite were summoned to the palac
greeted by Ivan, who wore a gown of green velvet, and then sent o
to continue their negotiations. The Russians were not pliable; the
refused to cede any points and were incapable of compromise; an
the Danes found it hard going. The negotiations broke off and wer
resumed two days later. Around midnight on August 27, 1578, Iva
indicated that he wanted several changes in the agreement and th
Danes reluctantly agreed, and on the following day, in the morning
Ivan requested that the document should be read. The readin
lasted an hour, and at the end Ivan gave his assent to it. As usua
he was crowned and bejeweled, and Ulfeld, who was standing clos
to him, could not help observing that the orb "was the size of a
boy's head and covered on all sides with precious stones." Ther
was a gilded casket beside Ivan, and he would sometimes place th
orb in it, and there was another casket for his crown.

While the treaty was being read, Ivan paid not the slightes
attention. He talked with some of his nobles and once h
summoned Bogdan Belsky to his side and showed off his beautifu
rings and the gold scabbard and gold belt which he wore under hi

outer garment. But this display of total disinterest came to an end when the reading was over. With great solemnity Ivan placed the two copies of the treaty in a casket and then a crucifix was placed on the top copy. He kissed the casket and swore to abide by the treaty and then called the Danish ambassador to his side and made him place his hands on a New Testament open at the Gospel of St. John and kiss the book and swear in the name of the King of Denmark that he would abide by the treaty. When this was done, he gave each of the Danes three glasses of mead, bade them greet the King of Denmark on his behalf, and let them go. Some time later forty-three servants brought farewell gifts to the Danes. These consisted of furs, and were intended for the ambassador, his suite, and the King of Denmark.

On the following day, at two o'clock in the afternoon, the Danes learned that they were expected to leave at once. They packed hurriedly, for such peremptory demands could not be denied. They therefore set out on the return journey to Denmark at nine o'clock in the evening and traveled throughout the night without sleeping.

While Ivan presented himself as a man of august majesty, scarcely interested in such mundane things as treaties and embassies, he was becoming increasingly aware that the Livonian war had become a costly mistake. It was draining Russia of its youth, its wealth, its guns. The landed gentry, who supplied the bulk of the army, were being ruined; the peasants were running away from the estates to avoid being taxed and conscripted as laborers; the entire social system was being disrupted. By the winter of 1579 the Tsar had come to the conclusion that the Church, which owned vast properties, must be made to disgorge some of its wealth. He therefore summoned the leading bishops, abbots, and archimandrites to a council in the Kremlin to decide how the wealth of the Church should be put to the service of the State.

In his opening speech Ivan spoke of the nation's desperate need, his unavailing efforts to replenish the exhausted treasury, the incessant dangers that confronted the country. It was one of the best speeches he ever made. Sir Jerome Horsey, who clearly had a copy of the speech in front of him, translated it into Elizabethan prose:

> He told them that which he was to say was best known to
> themselves; he had spent the most part of his time, wits, vigor and

youth in warfaring for their wealth and safety, preservation, and defense of his kingdoms and people; what dangers and troubles he had passed was not unknown to them, above many others. They apart to whom he makes his moan, have only reaped the benefi thereof. By which his treasures have been exhausted and their increased; their safeties, peace, and tranquillity preserved, and his lessened and daily endangered by foreign enemies and practices, both at home and abroad, which he was very sensible they were too well acquainted with. How could he or they any longer subsist without their essential assistance.

Their willingness must be the touchstone and trial of their fidelity, as well as their contemplations, which proved of no force. Their pretended prayers prevailed not; whether for their iniquities, his sins and people's, or both, he leaves to the divine knowledge.

The utility of their holy thoughts and actions must now be the supply out of their infinite abundance; yea, the urgent necessity and miserable estate both of him and people doth now require their devotion; the souls of their own patrons and donors, saints and holy workers of wonders, for redemption of their souls and sins, commands it. Prepare therefore your thoughts with holy resolutions, without sophistical or exorcisms of refusal.

Ivan's demands were robed in ecclesiastical flattery; the words flowed like prayers; a knife was concealed in them. As they debated among themselves how to placate him, his spies among them reported the progress of their thoughts. It was clear that they aimed to surrender as little as possible of their wealth. Ivan lost patience and summoned forty of the most distinguished prelates and urged them to remember the example of King Henry VIII and the fate that befell Ananias and Sapphira. He commanded them under pain of terrible penalties to produce "a faithful and true inventory what treasure and yearly revenues every of your houses have in their possessions," reminding them pointedly that they had accumulated a third of the wealth of all Russia "by your witchery and enchantments and sorcery." And what had they done to deserve so much wealth? In a towering rage he enumerated their crimes:

> You buy and sell the souls of our people. You live a most idle life in all pleasure and delicacy, commit most horrible sins, extortion, bribery, and excess usury. You abound in all the bloody and crying sins, oppression, gluttony, idleness, and sodomy, and worse, if worse, with beasts.

If the Church had been sensible, it would have offered Ivan a good half of its possessions. The Church was not sensible, Ivan lost patience, and inevitably had recourse to the weapons he knew best. The fattest monks, seven in number, were arrested and the entire Church Council was invited to watch them being clawed to death one by one in a bear-pit. Each monk was provided with a five-foot-long spear, but none of them had any experience in fighting bears. A monk from the Troitsa-Sergeyevsky Monastery showed that he had some inkling of the proper method to be employed when confronting a bear, for he so planted the spear in the ground that the bear's chest was split open, but unfortunately the bear still had enough life in him to devour the monk.

Ivan let it be known that this was only the beginning. He proposed to burn seven more monks at the stake unless a full inventory was forthcoming. An inventory was quickly drawn up, and on January 15, 1580, the Church Council agreed to pay three hundred thousand marks into the Tsar's treasury, to surrender all mortgaged lands in their possession together with all the patrimonial lands of the princes which had been purchased or bequeathed to the Church, and to acquire no further lands. Ivan's treasury was now brimming over.

Ivan had won his battle against the Church but he had not solved the problems of the ruined nobles. By tradition and custom their peasants were free to leave the estates every year after harvest time. They were free agents; they might serve whatever master they chose. On November 26, St. George's Day, there was always a great coming and going among the peasants, who had no difficulty finding new landowners to work for. A good peasant, even if he was in debt to his former landowner, would take service under a new landowner, who would cheerfully pay his debts. To save the nobles, Ivan now decreed that during the period of emergency no peasant would be allowed to leave his master's service. In this way, as a result of the Livonian wars, Russia took the first dangerous step which led to the serfdom of the peasants.

As usual, when confronted with disasters, Ivan imagined himself surrounded by traitors and conspirators. Famine and pestilence were abroad; his armies had been mauled by King Stephen Bathory; the country faced economic ruin. All this could be explained only by treason. The people feared a new bloodbath.

Instead, on Ascension Day, the anniversary of the day in 157
when the Crimean Tatars sacked and burned Moscow, Iva
delivered himself of a three-hour speech in which he first an
nounced the forthcoming marriage of his second son Fyodor t
Irina Godunova, and then launched into a ferocious denunciatio
of his disloyal and treacherous subjects. He threatened to abando
them, leaving them as a reproach to all the nations of the earth
Russia was doomed. "God and his prodigious creatures in th
heavens fight against us!" he roared, and went on to point out tha
the famine was God's punishment on "a naked, a disloyal, an
distressed people." Sir Jerome Horsey, who acquired a copy of th
speech, concluded that it was too long to quote. "Little wa
answered, less done, at this assembly," he noted. This was all to th
good, for Ivan exhausted himself with the speech and had n
energy left for murdering his poor subjects. Everyone prostrate
himself before the Tsar, wished him long life and happiness, an
called upon God to bless the marriage of Fyodor and Irina. The
he dismissed them "with good words and more favorable counte
nance, which was held for a mutual reconciliation and forgivenes
of all."

In the summer of 1580, shortly after Fyodor's marriage to Irina
Ivan married Maria Nagaya, from a family of boyars who ha
served the former Grand Princes of Tver before becoming member
of the court nobility in Moscow. Jerome Horsey believed that th
marriage was forced upon him because it had become known tha
he was seriously thinking of abandoning Russia and taking refug
in England, and it was necessary that he should perform some ac
to show his intention to remain in Russia. "To put out all jealousy
thereof in their minds," wrote Horsey, "he married again the fifth
wife, the daughter of Fyodor Nagoy, a very beautiful young maide
of a noble house and great family, of whom he had a third so
called Dmitry Ivanovich." [1]

Horsey himself was becoming more and more indispensable to

[1] Russian historians usually credit Ivan with seven marriages. (1) Anastasia Romanovna
d. 1560, (2) Maria Temriukovna, d. 1569, (3) Marfa Sobakina, who married Ivan in Octobe
1571 and died sixteen days later, (4) Anna Koltovskaya, who was sent to a nunnery in 1575
(5) Anna Vasilchikova, d. 1577, (6) Vasilissa Melentieva, who was sent to a nunnery in
1577, (7) Maria Nagaya, who married Ivan in 1580 and survived him. The marriage with
Marfa Sobakina was never consummated and there appears to have been no formal marriage
ceremony with the beautiful widow Vasilissa Melentieva.

the Tsar. He knew many court secrets, embarked on many intrigues, acted as a double agent, spying for both Elizabeth and Ivan, and was at ease in everyone's company. He had a quick tongue, a lively imagination, and had learned to speak Russian, Polish, and Dutch with considerable fluency. Ivan, desperately needing ammunition, sent him to England for gunpowder, saltpeter, lead, and brimstone. Shortly before Horsey left Moscow for London he had an audience with Ivan, who asked him whether he had seen the ships that were being built at Vologda. Many people believed the ships were intended to carry the Tsar and his treasure to England. Horsey said he had seen the ships, and there was the following conversation:

Tsar: What traitor hath showed them to you?

Horsey: The fame of them was such, and people flocked to see them upon a festival day, I ventured with thousands more to behold the curious beauty, largeness, and strange fashion of them.

Tsar: Why, what mean you by those words, strange fashion?

Horsey: For that the portraiture of lions, dragons, eagles, elephants, and unicorns were so lively made and so richly set forth with gold, silver, and curious colors of painting.

Tsar: It is true; you seem to have taken good view of them; how many of them?

Horsey: It please your majesty I saw but twenty.

Tsar: You shall see forty, ere long be, no worse. I commend you. No doubt you can relate as much in foreign place, but much more to be admired if you knew what inestimable treasure they are inwardly to be beautified with. It is reported that the queen, my sister, hath the best navy of ships in the world.

Horsey: It is true, and please your majesty.

Tsar: Why have you dissembled with me then?

Horsey: For strength and greatness to break and cut through the great ocean, turbulent seas.

Tsar: How framed so?

Horsey: For art, sharp-keeled, not flat-bottomed, so thick and strong-sided that a cannon shot can scarce pierce through.

Tsar: What else?

Horsey: Every ship carries cannon and forty brass pieces of great ordnance, bullets, muskets, powder, chainshot, pikes, and armor of defense, wild fireworks, stanchions for fights, a thousand mariners and men at arms, soldiers, captains, and officers of all sorts to guide and govern; discipline and daily divine prayers, beer, bread, beef, fish, bacon, pease, butter, cheese, vinegar, oatmeal, aqua-vitae, wood, water, and all other provisions. . . . [Horsey then gives a lengthy list of the sails, flags and musical instruments on board the English ships.]

Tsar: How many such hath the queen as you describe?

Horsey: Forty, and please your majesty.

Tsar: It is a good royal navy, as you term it. It can transport forty thousand soldiers to a friend.

Ivan's last statement was especially significant, because it showed clearly that he expected Queen Elizabeth to come to his help when needed. In his overheated imagination her navy existed in order that forty thousand Englishmen should come to his rescue. He was wrong on all points, and not least in his estimate that each English ship could carry a thousand troops. Nevertheless his faith in Queen Elizabeth remained unbounded; England was his anchor, the protecting hand that would save him in his worst extremity; the forty ships at Vologda and the forty ships of the English fleet would soon be at his disposal. Such were his hopes as he sent Horsey on a secret mission to Queen Elizabeth.

Since it was winter and the sea route from the White Sea around Scandinavia would be frozen, it was decided that Jerome Horsey should make the dangerous journey through Livonia and take ship from Hamburg. Ivan delighted in secret stratagems and discussed with Savva Frolov, his secretary of state, the best way to conceal the letter. They hid it in the false side of a wooden bottle filled with aquavitae, and since the bottle was not worth three pennies and would be hidden under the horse's mane, they thought no one would pay any attention to it. Horsey's expenses for the journey were sewn into his boots and his old clothes—they amounted to four hundred gold ducats. At his farewell audience, Ivan insisted that Horsey should not read the document addressed to Queen Elizabeth until he had reached safety for fear that it might become known to his enemies, and said, "Always be thou trusty and faithful, and thy reward shall be my goodness and grace from me hereafter."

Hearing these words, Horsey fell prostrate with his head on the Tsar's foot, his heart heavy with the thought of all the dangers ahead.

That night with twenty servants and a high-ranking official in attendance he drove by sleigh to Tver, where he stopped long enough to acquire provisions and fresh horses. Then he sped on to Novgorod, Pskov, and Neuhausen. He claimed that he traveled six hundred miles in three days. Arriving near the frontier of Livonia, he dismissed his companions and drove off alone into enemy territory. He was arrested several times but always succeeded in talking his way out of danger. At Arensburg he was arrested and lodged in a wretched house infested with snakes and hens. He was brought before the governor, and was in danger of being shot as a Russian spy, but it happened that the governor's granddaughter, Madelyn van Uxell, was a prisoner in Moscow. Horsey had befriended her, and her letters home had been full of his praises. From being a prisoner he became an honored guest, feasted, magnificently entertained, and provided with passports. He rode on to Pilten, where he was entertained by King Magnus, who was drinking heavily, having lost most of his possessions in riotous living. The King had a poor opinion of Horsey's drinking capacity; Horsey had a poor opinion of the royal spendthrift. For the rest of the journey to Hamburg Horsey was treated with all the honors due to an ambassador. By day he hid the wooden bottle under his cloak, and by night it was his pillow.

At last, reaching England, Horsey broke open the bottle and found that the documents smelled strongly of aquavitae. There was nothing he could do about it. When he handed them to the Queen, she remarked upon their smell, and was pleased by his explanation. He was sworn esquire of her body, and she gave him her picture and he kissed her hand.

What Ivan asked for in his letter was provided by the Queen in ample measure. Thirteen English ships laden with copper, lead, gunpowder, saltpeter, brimstone, and much else to the value of £ 9,000, set out for Russia by the northern route. At the North Cape some Danish ships attempted an ambush but were fought off. All the ships arrived safely at the White Sea bay of St. Nicholas in the early summer of 1580, only five or six months from the day when Horsey set out with the wooden bottle from Moscow.

At Alexandrova Sloboda Ivan welcomed his secret messenger promised payment as soon as he reached Moscow, and carried ou his promise. A letter from Queen Elizabeth was placed in the Tsar's hands secretly, by which Horsey meant that he was alone with the Tsar when the letter was handed over. He was commended for his speed, his loyalty, his diplomacy, and basked in the Tsar's favor Thirteen shiploads of military supplies found their way into the Tsar's warehouses in Moscow.

They came just in time. Soon the Tsar's armies would be reeling from the blows of King Stephen Bathory and Russia was in greater danger than ever.

Murder of the Tsarevich

KING STEPHEN BATHORY was a man with a methodical mind, calm, vigorous, and without illusions. They said he had studied at the University of Padua, but there was little of the scholar about him. They said, too, that he suffered from epilepsy and there was a strange unhealing wound on his leg, but these were perhaps legends invented to suggest that he was more vulnerable than he appeared to be. He was a short, thickset man, with high cheekbones, a long pointed nose, and a very low forehead. He did not look like a king; he looked like a Hungarian peasant. He had risen out of almost total obscurity to become the voyevoda of Transylvania, owing allegiance to the Sultan of the Ottoman Empire, and he had been elected King of Poland and Grand Prince of Lithuania because the Poles and Lithuanians saw in him a superb administrator. That a Hungarian commoner should become the ruler of vast territories in eastern Europe was surprising enough; what was even more surprising was that he made no effort to learn the languages of his subjects and yet was beloved by them. He was more than their king; he was their conscience.

From the beginning he had taken Ivan's measure and knew how to deal with him. Ivan's cruelties, his Byzantine pretensions, his vanity, his dependence upon his whims rather than any carefully thought-out plans were all proof of an inner weakness. Force, and force alone, would make him change his course. In 1579, the King had captured Polotsk and was now preparing to attack Russia itself. In the summer of 1580 he was forty-seven, three years younger than Ivan, and at the height of his powers.

During that summer Ivan was in a state of panic. He knew that a massive attack on Russia was being prepared, but he did not know where the blow would fall. He was striving for a truce on almost any terms. He invited the King to send ambassadors to Moscow, but the King refused, saying that Russian ambassadors must come to Vilno. He laid down conditions: the ambassadors must arrive in Vilno during the five weeks beginning June 14, 1580. Ivan replied that it would take five weeks for his ambassadors to reach the Lithuanian frontier and many more days for them to reach Vilno. The King answered that this was a matter of indifference to him. After five weeks he would be in the field in command of his army, and if they wanted to, and if they could find him, the ambassadors could reach him in his headquarters.

Knowing that war was imminent, Ivan ordered inspectors to comb the land for the nobles who had gone into hiding. Once found, they were to be beaten and then sent under guard and with guarantees of good behavior to Pskov or Novgorod, to serve in the army. To the envoys who were continually being sent to Poland and Lithuania he sent precise instructions: "If you want anything, you must ask your hosts for it courteously without swearing and without making threats. If you are granted permission to buy provisions, buy them; if permission is refused, you must endure. If the King does not enquire about the Tsar's health and does not rise when you greet him in the Tsar's name, do not complain." Such mildness was not characteristic of Ivan. The King had sent him an ultimatum: there could be peace only if Russia surrendered all of Livonia and the cities of Pskov, Novgorod, and Veliki Luki.

In despair Ivan sent an urgent message to all the monasteries, urging the monks to pray to God, the Mother of God, and all the saints to preserve Russia from the invaders. Not knowing where the blow would fall, he scattered his troops in a dozen different places: at Pskov, Novgorod, Smolensk, on the Western Dvina River, in the few remaining strongholds in Livonia, especially in northern Livonia, where he feared an attack by the Swedes, and he was careful to maintain a large army on the Oka River far in the south in case the Tatars took it into their heads to attack at the same time as the Poles and Lithuanians. The King sent a column of 9,000 men

gainst Smolensk. It was only a feint. The real attack was directed
n Veliki Luki, which was reached by long circuitous roads through
orests and marsh lands. Some 50,000 Polish, Lithuanian, German,
nd Hungarian troops stood outside the walls of a city defended by
,000 Russians.

Russian ambassadors attended upon King Stephen Bathory in
is camp outside Veliki Luki. The King sat on his throne and
aughtily greeted the ambassadors, who begged him to call off the
iege, promised to surrender twenty-four towns in Livonia if he
vould agree to a truce, and said they were agreeable to the
urrender of Polotsk. This was strange, for Polotsk had been
aptured by the King the year before. The King repeated his
lemand for Pskov, Novgorod, and Smolensk, and the ambassadors
eft for Moscow for further instructions.

With its wooden outer wall and wooden watchtowers Veliki Luki
vas especially vulnerable to the flaming cannon balls used in the
King's army. The Russians had time to cover the walls with earth,
ut the King sent his men right up to the walls to remove the earth
nd then blew them up with charges of gunpowder. With the walls
n fire, the King issued an ultimatum. If they laid down their arms
nd marched peacefully out of the city, their lives would be spared,
therwise they would all be massacred. The defenders accepted the
ltimatum and were beginning to march out when the Hungarian
roops, fearing to be deprived of their legitimate booty, broke into
he burning city and slaughtered everyone in sight. On that day,
eptember 7, 1580, Veliki Luki fell to the enemy. A month later the
King, who was unwell, called off the campaign and returned to
Vilno. The loss of Veliki Luki was, for the moment, a sufficient
unishment for the Russians.

Battles and skirmishes continued through the winter. Staraya
Rusa, an ancient city forty miles south of Novgorod, fell to the
Lithuanians. The Swedes blockaded the fortress of Padis in
northern Livonia for thirteen weeks, starving the Russians into
urrender, and then slaughtered them. Russian ambassadors who
vent in search of the King were ill-treated, subjected to continual
ndignities, given neither food nor fodder for their horses, and some
f their horses died of starvation while many of their servants were
obbed and beaten. Ivan treated his enemies in this way; now the
ables were turned. The Russian ambassadors and envoys, once so

arrogant, found themselves at the mercy of Polish and Lithuania officials who were even more arrogant. When they complained the were receiving no fodder for their horses, they were told: "Fodder Fodder! You are always asking for fodder! You know we are at wa and the money allotted for fodder is needed for other things!"

Ivan was forced to eat humble pie. When in the spring of 1581 h sent two new ambassadors, Ivan Pushkin and Fyodor Pissemsky, t the King's court, they received instructions to behave with perfec humility. If abused or beaten, they were to accept punishmer quietly; if insulted or provoked, they were to remain silent. If th Polish King objected to the word "Tsar" in the treaty, he was to b told that the Russian sovereign, to obtain peace among Christian would not insist on being addressed by this title. As for Livoni Ivan was prepared to surrender the entire country except for fou cities including Dorpat and Narva.

King Stephen Bathory had long ago made up his mind that h would accept nothing less than all of Livonia, Smolensk, Novgoro(and Pskov. Realizing that Ivan was in serious difficulties he adde for full measure an indemnity of 400,000 gold Hungarian ducats t pay for his military expenses. These escalating demands rouse Ivan to a remarkable exhibition of self-pity. In a long letter to th King, dispatched on June 30, 1581, Ivan complained bitterly of th ill-treatment he was receiving at the hands of the King, who ha violated the truce, permitted Russian traitors to enter his servic(used treasure from the captured cities to pay for mercenaries, an burned down whole cities with firebombs—a dastardly weapo which no civilized ruler would use. Ivan explained patiently that h possessed one single overriding aim—to prevent the shedding c Christian blood. It was an odd claim from a man who had she(more Christian blood than any of his contemporaries. He declare(that he had sent only small armies into Livonia; then why was th King sending vast armies against him? He was the hereditary rule of a great nation fighting against a mere elected official who thirste(for blood, and he went on to remind the King that life-givin(Crosses were protecting Russia and her Tsar. He wrote:

> Then what kind of peace do you want? You stole our treasur(enriched yourself, impoverished us, hired soldiers with our money captured Livonian territory, crammed it with your soldiers, and the

with an even larger army than before, you marched your soldiers against us to take whatever was left. What is clear is that you want perpetual war, not peace.

What was equally clear was that Ivan's letter provided a remarkable self-portrait of a man in a frenzy of self-pity, terrified by the approach of the King's armies, capable of deluding himself about the real situation to an extent that was breathtaking, and incapable of intelligent argument. Sometimes in the letter he said things that were better left unsaid, for they invited crushing rejoinders. Ivan accused the King of allowing his soldiers to abuse the dead. The King replied:

> You accuse me of abusing the dead. I did not abuse them. You, however, torture the living. Which is worse?
>
> You condemn me for allegedly breaking the truce! You, the falsifier of treaties, changing them in secret and secretly adding new paragraphs to them in order to satisfy your insane lust for power! . . .
>
> We have not set eyes on your face, nor on the flags embroidered with the Cross which you boast about. You do not frighten your enemies with your Crosses—you frighten only the poor Russians.
>
> Why did you not come and meet us at the head of your army? Why did you not protect your subjects? Even the humble hen covers her chicks with her wings to protect them from the falcon and the eagle. But you, the double-headed eagle—for such is your insignia—you go into hiding!
>
> You say you sorrow over the loss of Christian blood. Well then, choose a time and place and meet me on horseback and we shall fight one another! God will crown the better one with victory!

The King's hard-hitting letter was not calculated to sweeten Ivan's temper. Too many accusations hit their mark: Ivan was a notorious abuser of the dead, an equally notorious falsifier of treaties, and a physical coward who would not dare to engage in single combat. The King sent Ivan a present consisting of two books written in Latin and recently published in Germany concerning the state of Muscovy and its ruler with special reference to passages showing that Ivan was not descended from Augustus Caesar but from princelings who paid tribute to the Khan of the Crimea. "Read what they say about you in Europe," the King wrote.

The King's letter was dispatched by messenger and read aloud to the Tsar, who listened in silence. When the entire letter had been read out, he said quietly, "Send greetings to your sovereign from us." Normally a royal messenger would be offered food from the Tsar's table. Ivan thought it imprudent to feed someone who had brought so much bad news.

Implicit in the letter was the worst news that Ivan had heard for some time. War was imminent, huge forces would soon be advancing against Russia under command of a man who was fearless, ruthless, and completely sure of himself. Nothing would deter him, and unless a miracle happened he would carry every thing before him.

One hope—a very slender hope—remained with Ivan. He had convinced himself that Pope Gregory XIII and the German Emperor Rudolph, the successor of Maximilian, were his natural allies and that both of them were alarmed by King Stephen Bathory's close friendship with the Sultan of the Ottoman Empire. He wrote to both, urging an alliance against the King who "was shedding Christian blood in alliance with Moslem rulers." Rudolph was not impressed with the argument; Gregory XIII saw the opportunity to begin a dialogue with Russia which might end with the conversion of the Russians to the Catholic faith. Istoma Shevrigin, Ivan's ambassador at large, reached Rome on February 26, 1581, and was received like a long-lost child. The Jesuits were especially intrigued by the possibilities of mass conversion; the Pope was solicitous; a Jesuit, Antonio Possevino, who had worked in Poland, was given the task of mediating between King Stephen Bathory and the Tsar, who came to believe that the Pope was actively engaged in supporting his cause.

The Pope, of course, was engaged in supporting his own causes and Possevino was an intelligent papal agent. He reached Lithuania early in July 1581 and was almost immediately closeted with the King, who had just received Ivan's strange letter accusing him of shedding Christian blood and abusing the dead. It was not the best time to discuss arbitration. Possevino had three audiences with the King, and then set out for Russia, meeting Ivan at Staritsa on August 20. Characteristically Possevino showed very little interest in discussing the war. What he wanted to discuss was the possibility of converting the Russians to Catholicism, a matter which Ivan regarded with distaste. He insisted that they should discuss peace negotiations. It was already too late. On August 25 the Russians in the watchtowers of the northern city of Pskov saw a huge cloud of dust moving across the sky. It was being blown towards them by a strong south wind—King Stephen Bathory was advancing on the city.

The cloud of dust was terrible enough; a few hours later the whole horizon was filled with the King's troops.

Ivan had not guessed where the blow would fall, though he knew it was coming. The main Russian army, under the command of Simeon Bekbulatovich, was established at Staritsa. Some fifteen miles to the west stood the vanguard army under Prince Mikhailo Katyrev-Rostovsky. These two armies thus covered the approaches to Moscow, which was defended by a garrison force under Prince Ivan Mstislavsky. Another large army defended the Oka River against a simultaneous attack by the Tatars. The remaining Russian strongholds in Livonia were protected by garrison troops, and there was a powerful force at Novgorod under the command of Prince Ivan Golitsyn, the governor of the province. Prince Ivan Shuisky was placed in charge of the defense of Pskov, having sworn to defend the city to the death in an impressive ceremony in front of the Icon of the Virgin of Vladimir in the Uspensky Cathedral. The oath was repeated when he reached Pskov and assembled the entire populace, calling on them to swear before icons and crosses that they would die before surrendering the city.

King Stephen Bathory was a man who enjoyed solving difficult problems. Warned by a Russian traitor that Pskov was impregnable because of its stone walls and powerful defenses, and that he would be well advised to lay siege to Smolensk instead, he simply dismissed the advice as unworthy of a great general. No doubt the capture of Pskov presented difficulties, but if they were solved he could expect every other city to fall to his army at the first blow. The Krom, the castle of Dovmont, the fortress towers, the inner and outer walls—all were of stone. The King was certain that he could batter down the stone walls with his heavy guns, and then the infantry would pour through the debris of the walls and capture the whole city. It was a challenge which he found irresistible.

Prince Ivan Shuisky was a stern, capable, and devoted general whose chief characteristic was one he shared with his Russian soldiers—endurance. The fortifications were strengthened and the suburbs beyond the outer walls were fired to prevent the King's forces from entering them and using them as a base for attacking the city. With its wide moats, twenty-eight towers, forty-foot-high walls, and its underground galleries reaching far beyond the outer walls, Pskov was, if not impregnable, at least better protected than any other city in Russia. In addition, it lay under the protection of the holy relics of St. Vsevolod which, at Prince Shuisky's orders, were carried in procession round the walls followed by the entire population.

On the day when the King's army was first seen, Prince Shuisky ordered a general attack. The gates swung open, the Russian soldiers poured out, engaged the enemy, took many prisoners and were themselves taken prisoner, and by nightfall they returned to the city, realizing that the sortie had resulted only in a few inconclusive skirmishes. Nothing had been gained and little had been lost.

Uncharacteristically the King was acting cautiously. He had an army of 100,000 Poles, Lithuanians, Germans, and Hungarians, and the defenders of Pskov probably amounted to no more than 40,000. His army was so well-trained and so well-equipped that the ambassador from the Sublime Porte, who visited him in his camp, observed: "If the Sultan and Bathory were to act together, they would conquer the world." To breach the gates and walls the King ordered trenches dug; along these trenches gabions could be advanced to the city walls. The defenders took the precaution of building a second wall within the outer wall. For nearly two weeks, until sunrise on the morning of September 7, 1581, the King continued to make his preparations. Then, as the sun came over the horizon, twenty heavy cannon bombarded the city. On the following day, after further bombardment, the order was given for the attack. At several places the walls had crumbled under the bombardment and the King genuinely believed that by nightfall he would be the master of the city. Two of the great towers had been captured by the Germans and Hungarians, and the King's flag flew over them. Poles and Lithuanians were fighting the Russians along the walls and pressing them back. "We shall dine tonight in the citadel of Pskov!" the generals said. It was learned that Prince Shuisky had been wounded and that the Russians were retreating.

The King was congratulating himself that Pskov was about to fall into his hands after only two days of fighting.

Covered with blood and shouting at the top of his lungs, Prince Shuisky became the incarnate spirit of endurance and resistance, the embodiment of Russian courage. The holy icons and relics were brought to him; the enemy began to give way. One of the towers captured by the Germans and Hungarians suddenly crumbled into a heap of rubble; the Russians had blown it up with a heavy charge of gunpowder placed in one of the underground galleries. The fighting continued, but now it was outside the city walls.

Women and children hurried to bring water to quench the thirst of the soldiers; some came with ropes to drag away the cannon captured at the gates, and others armed themselves with pikes and joined the battle. By sunset the enemy was retreating to prepared positions and the Russians were streaming back to the city with captured standards, captured trumpets, and many prisoners. They had lost over 800 men and twice as many were wounded, but the King had lost more than five times as many. That night, in the candle-lit Cathedral of the Trinity, Prince Shuisky addressed his soldiers, saying:

> Thus the first day has gone by, a day of labor, valor, tears and joy. Let us complete what we have begun! Our powerful enemies have fallen, while we, the weak, stand in our armor before the altar of God. The proud giant has been deprived of his bread, while we in our Christian humility have been fed with heavenly mercy!

On the following day, in a message shot by arrow into Pskov, King Stephen Bathory urged Prince Shuisky and his generals to surrender. He promised them extensive freedoms and privileges, the freedom to trade where they wished, the freedom to retain their ancient customs, their property, and their faith. Prince Shuisky shot back an answer, "We do not betray Christ nor the Tsar nor the Fatherland." The King threatened to destroy the entire population of Pskov unless they surrendered, and Prince Shuisky replied, "We fear no threats. Come and fight. The victory is in God's hands."

With all the advantages of a powerful and well-trained army, heavy guns, vast stores of ammunition, and superb generalship, the King failed to take Pskov. Throughout September and October he made repeated assaults on the city, dug nine separate tunnels under the walls, hurled countless firebombs into the city, and massed his cannon in the hope of breaching the walls and destroying the towers. On November 2, 1581, after five days of continuous bombardment, he threw his entire army across the frozen Velikaya River in a last despairing effort to capture the city, and watched them straggling back over the ice. A month later he was still there, hoping to starve the city into surrender.

Although Pskov held out, Ivan deserved little credit. Once more he had been saved by his soldiers. At his headquarters in Staritsa he was protected by two huge armies. No effort was made to relieve Pskov or to supply food and ammunition to the beleaguered city. Ivan was sunk in the stupor of inertia.

The King's raiding parties penetrated deep into Russia. One particularly daring raid, led by Christophor Radziwill, reached Rzhev, only fifteen miles from Staritsa, where Ivan had his headquarters. This raid by a small cavalry detachment reached Rzhev in early November 1581. Ivan panicked and hurried off to the safety of Alexandrova Sloboda.

He had scarcely reached Alexandrova Sloboda when a deputation of nobles came and presented him with a humble petition. They were brave men, for Ivan had his own way of dealing with petitioners. They knelt before him while one of them read out the words of the petition:

> For three years our enemies have been invading the Fatherland, which it is our bounden duty to defend. We are ready to shed our blood, lay down our lives, and sacrifice our property for the sake of the Fatherland. Therefore, O Lord and Master, send your eldest son to the war!

Ivan entirely misunderstood the petitioners, flew into a rage, tore off his crown and the jeweled *barmy* around his shoulders and threw them to the ground, called them all traitors, and told them they had better choose another Tsar. Since the Tsarevich was present, he evidently thought they liked the Tsarevich more than they liked the Tsar. They answered that they were not traitors, they did not want the Tsar to abandon the throne, they only wanted the Tsarevich to lead them to victory. Apparently they left Ivan's presence without being punished, for we hear nothing more about the petitioners.

Some hours later, still simmering with rage, Ivan ordered the Tsarevich into his presence and loudly berated him, saying: "You poor fool! How dare you seek to commit treason and sedition? How dare you defy me?" The Tsarevich stood his ground and denied that he had ever surrendered to a single treacherous thought; all he wanted was an army; his only aim was to defeat Stephen Bathory. His opinions about the calamitous three-year campaign against Stephen Bathory were well-known and it was unlikely that he was in any great danger. Then, as so often when he was troubled, the Tsar began to talk about the great collection of gold plate and jewels in his treasury. The Tsarevich, short-tempered like his father, answered that he cared nothing for all these jewels and regarded courage and valor as being worth infinitely more than the entire contents of the treasury. In this rebuke lay an explicit condemnation of Ivan's cowardice and the futility of all his actions during the three-year war. Ivan was so enraged that he raised his heavy iron-pointed staff as though to strike his son. Boris Godunov, who was present, rushed forward and seized Ivan by the arm. This, too, was unpardonable, and Boris Godunov found himself reeling backward while Ivan jabbed at him with the sharp point of the staff, drawing blood. Then, so enraged that he scarcely knew what he was doing, the Tsar brought down the heavy end of the staff on his son's skull, striking him in the temple and felling him to the ground. The blood was pouring out of the Tsarevich's head, and Ivan thought he was dead.

There was a moment of stunned surprise and shock, and suddenly Ivan threw himself down beside his son, embraced and kissed him, and attempted to staunch the flow of blood, weeping uncontrollably, and calling out for a doctor to come immediately.

"I have killed my son!" he groaned, and it was observed that his face had turned deathly white.

He had committed many crimes, but it was beyond belief that he would crown all these crimes with the murder of his own son. Nevertheless it was so.

Ivan cried out for forgiveness and his prayer was answered. The Tsarevich could still talk, although the wound was fatal. He said, "I have always been loyal," and as a sign of forgiveness he kissed his father's hand. Then he was carried away and laid on a bed, while the Tsar remained in a trance of shock and grief, refusing to remove his clothes spattered with his son's blood, now sitting by the bedside, now leaning helplessly against the wall. For three days Ivan went without sleep or food.

The doctors came, but they could do nothing. The Tsarevich lingered on for three days. He died three hours before sunrise in the early morning of Sunday, November 19, 1581. He was twenty-seven years old.

Although married three times, the Tsarevich left no children. His widow, the Tsarevna Elena, spent the remaining years of her life as a nun in the Novodevichy Monastery. She took the name of Leonida and was given the township of Lukh and a large estate to support her widowhood.

Three days after the Tsarevich's death, the cortege set out from Alexandrova Sloboda for Moscow. The Tsar and all his entourage wore black; the Tsar walked beside his son's coffin all the way. At the funeral service in the Cathedral of Michael the Archangel the Tsar threw himself against the coffin, uttering terrible cries. Before the coffin was sealed, a king's ransom of jewels was poured into it, and every night twelve good citizens of Moscow kept watch on the tomb.

For many months Ivan remained grief-stricken. He slept fitfully, and tossed so violently that he sometimes fell off the bed to spend the rest of the night on the floor, shouting and moaning, growing silent only when he became exhausted. At such times attendants would spread a mattress on the floor and give him a pillow; and then, lying quietly, he would await fearfully the coming of the dawn.

During those months he was afraid to show himself to the people. One day he announced to his boyars that God had so cruelly punished him that there remained nothing for him but to leave the world and spend the remaining days of his life in a monastery. Since his son Fyodor was incapable of governing, they must choose a successor and immediately grant him the throne and the regalia. But the boyars were cautious. They knew his temper, his habit of suddenly announcing his abdication only in order to smoke out his enemies, and they also knew that any successor they might choose would be confronted with extraordinary difficulties and dangers, and when they met Ivan again they announced that they wanted no

Ivan presenting the Icon of the Virgin to the Danilov Monastery in Moscow, circa 1564. The Tsarevich Ivan is standing behind him. This is the only contemporary portrait of the Tsarevich that has survived.

other Tsar but Ivan and his son Fyodor. Ivan pretended to accept their petition reluctantly and remained on the throne.

He was only a shadow of himself. The man who had once roared like thunder became strangely quiet. He no longer wore jeweled robes and no longer flourished the jeweled scepter; even his many crowns, which delighted him so much that he would sometimes wear two or three different crowns during the course of a single meal, were put away as a grown man puts away childish things. He wore black robes like a monk. Suddenly in the midst of the most ordinary conversation he would burst into a fit of weeping for no reason at all or because someone had said something that reminded him of the dead Tsarevich. For the rest of his life he was somber, morose, and given to sudden bouts of hysteria.

He had learned long ago that the donations to the monasteries and the prayers of the monks had the power to assuage grief and diminish the sense of guilt. So he scattered money widely and many monasteries and churches received gifts in commemoration of the dead Tsarevich. To the Troitsa-Sergeyevsky Monastery he sent the vast sum of 5,000 rubles for prayers to be said in perpetuity for the repose of his son's soul, and a further 10,000 rubles were distributed among the Patriarchs of Constantinople, Antioch, Alexandria, and Jerusalem, and the abbots of the monasteries of Mount Athos and Sinai for the same purpose. On January 6, 1583, when visiting the Troitsa-Sergeyevsky Monastery for the Feast of the Epiphany, he threatened that unless prayers were spoken for the Tsarevich and special services were held for him "so long as the monastery remains standing and until the end of time" he would confront them all at the Last Judgment and curse them. At all costs the murdered Tsarevich must be saved. It was remembered that when he demanded that the monks should never forget to pray for his son, he knelt and bowed before them six times in succession, and all the time he was weeping.

About this time, or a little later, he began to compile those strange lists known as *sinodiki* in which he enumerated the people he had killed and urged that prayers should be said for their souls. The lists were long and comprehensive; armies of scribes were employed to write down the names of the victims and the circumstances of their executions; the Tsar's private archives and those of his ministries were combed in order to discover the names of the dead; and in addition he consulted the death lists compiled for the use of the Oprichnina. Killing had been his passion, and now his passion was to be subjected to mathematical analysis, as though he wanted to learn the grand total of his sins. In the early months of 1583 these *sinodiki* began to arrive at monasteries all over Russia, together with handsome donations to be used for the support of the monks.

Very often it happened that the entire estates of people he had killed fell into his hands. Now, perhaps because he knew that death was approaching and he would soon be called to the Judgment Seat, he began to divest himself of those immense properties and stores of treasure which had accumulated over so many years. In addition to the names of the people he had executed, the dates, and the manner in which they died, it became necessary for the scribes to value and record the value of all the properties, culling them out of ancient estate records. Hundreds of secretaries were employed. The inventories were not always to be found in Moscow; appraisers were sent out to examine inventories all over Russia; complex and difficult problems had to be solved; an entire new industry was being created. Ivan was determined not to appear before God burdened by the vast wealth that had come to him by murder, and so to the mathematics of killing there was added the mathematics of estate accounting.

The dead were entering his life: at all costs their ghosts must be appeased. He proposed to divide their wealth among the two hundred monasteries of Russia, each monastery getting its proper share, and this too demanded many weeks of concentrated mental application. Since the matter ultimately affected the fate of his immortal soul, he took care that the work was done accurately and expeditiously. In fact the task was so arduous that it was not completed until after his death.

No single complete *sinodik* has survived, but ten fragmentary lists have been found in the monasteries, where the monks copied out the names of the victims and sometimes omitted to include the circumstances of the execution, although these, when known, were usually provided in the original *sinodik*. Fortunately for historians the monks sometimes included a few relevant details. Strangely the Tsar sometimes included the names of people who were not killed but merely disgraced and sent into exile. Sometimes, too, the Tsar simply abandoned a hopeless task, gave a rough count of the people killed, adding, "Thou Thyself, O Lord, know their names."

The *sinodik* of the Monastery of St. Kirill enumerates 3,470 victims, but this is far from being the complete total. Among all the partial lists, supplementary lists, and special lists no estimate of the total is given. Ivan must have known how many people he killed, but the secret died with him.

A *sinodik* preserved in a monastery would begin in this way:

In 1583 the Tsar and Grand Prince Ivan Vasilievich of all Russia sent to the monastery this list of names to be prayed for, giving orders that they should be remembered during the litanies, liturgies and funeral services in God's church daily.

Remember, O Lord, the souls of Thy departed servants, the princes and princesses and boyars and all Orthodox Christians, both male and female, who have been killed together with those whose names are not recorded.

Those who are not listed by name in the *sinodik* but in groups of ten, twenty or fifty, they are also to be prayed for. Thou Thyself, O Lord, know their names.

Often only the Christian names are given. Thus we read: *"Nikita, Ivan Viskovaty, Vasily, his wife and two sons, Ivan, his wife and three daughters. . . ."* By comparing different lists it is possible to identify many of these people, and so we learn that Nikita refers to Nikita Funikov, the treasurer, that Vasily is Vasily Stepanov, a secretary, and that Ivan is Ivan Bulgakov, also a secretary and that all of them were killed in Moscow in July 1570. Titles are sometimes recorded: "The pious appanage princess and nun Efrosinia, mother of Vladimir, was drowned in the Sheksna River, together with twelve people, including nuns." There follows a list of the names of the people killed with her, the last being a fisherman named Korypan. Elsewhere the catalogue of death remains impenitently anonymous:

At Ivanovo Bolshoye seventeen people were killed, fourteen of whom met their deaths struck down by hand. At Ivanovo Menshoye thirteen people were killed, three of them struck down by hand. In Chermnev three people were killed, and two in Soslavl. At Bezhetsky Verkh sixty-five people were killed, twelve of them struck down by hand. Thou Thyself, O Lord, know their names.

Sometimes, too, we learn the names of the killers, and sometimes the killers themselves later appear among the dead. Sometimes there is a hint of drama: "Kazarin Dubrovsky with his two sons, and ten men who came to his help." We would like to know more about the ten brave men who came to his help. A strange silence shrouds these lists, as stark and impersonal as a landscape covered with snow. Time has long ago obliterated the features of these people who died in so much terror and agony, but even today these lists can still haunt us, as they haunt the Russians who have never completely succeeded in erasing them from their memory.

The compilation of so many lists of people and so many ruined estates occupied many of the last months of Ivan's life. He had

Tsar Fyodor, who succeeded Ivan on the throne.

Seventeenth-century portrait of Ivan.

become the chief registrar, the chief accountant. Dimly he appears to have realized the full measure of his criminality, the enormity of his evil deeds. In the past he had often beaten his breast and confessed to infamous murders and debaucheries, but there had always been an element of theatricality in these confessions. Now the theatrical gestures were abandoned—now there were only the lists, the names, the number of sons and daughters killed, the value of the estate, strange account books which recorded no profit, only a continual loss. These account books were almost abstractions of death, as Ivan himself was almost an abstraction of pure evil. In his dark robes he resembled a shadow melting into shadows. The lights were going out and soon he would be swallowed up in the darkness.

Portrait of a Lady

THERE REMAINED for Ivan less than two and a half years of a life that had grown burdensome. He continued to sleep badly, at the mercy of his nightmares, and the days were no more endurable than the nights. He tried not to think of his dead son and carefully avoided all the places associated with his son's death. He had killed the Tsarevich at Alexandrova Sloboda and therefore orders were given that the place should be shut down. Once it was the capital of his empire, the seat of power, with its dungeons, torture chambers, and vast treasuries, and now it was given back to the surrounding forests.

He was weary of life, weary of murders, weary of wars. King Stephen Bathory was still sending raiding parties into Russia and hoping to starve Pskov into surrender, and Ivan was hoping the war would go away. He sued for peace, rejecting all suggestions that he should send an army to the relief of embattled Pskov. On December 13, 1581, less than a month after the death of the Tsarevich, the negotiations began at Yam Zapolsky, a small town deep inside Russian territory, some fifty-five miles southeast of Pskov, in the midst of a region devastated by the long war. A mediator, the papal emissary Antonio Possevino, presided over the negotiations. At whatever the cost in territory Ivan wanted the negotiations to succeed, if only to give himself the satisfaction of establishing a peace which was certain to be insecure; for whenever territory is surrendered to the enemy, he can be expected to demand more. Ivan's secret dispatches to the Russian envoys during the peace parlays have not survived, but we can sometimes guess the contents. We know, for example, that he ordered all the Russian delegates to be splendidly dressed and to ride beautifully caparisoned horses. They were ordered to make a show of wealth and the assurance that comes from wealth. Into that desolate region where even the heavy snowfall could not conceal the miseries of war, merchants were sent from Moscow to set up their shops, displaying their costly wares in tents. No one must know that Russia was impoverished and exhausted by the three-year war.

The Lithuanians knew the real situation better than Ivan. They were not especially impressed by the gaudy display of the Russians. They made harsh demands. All of Livonia must be surrendered by Russia. Henceforward Polotsk, Veliki Luki, and all the other important towns would be included within the empire of King Stephen Bathory, and in addition they demanded a war indemnity of 400,000 Hungarian gold crowns. Ivan hoped to retain Dorpat and some other towns, which would give him access to the sea. Impressive efforts were made to convince Antonio Possevino of the rightness of the Russian cause. Meat was brought down from Novgorod especially for his use, and it was explained to him that unless the Russians possessed a seaport on the Baltic, they would be unable to form alliances with the Pope and the Emperor against the Moslems. The papal intermediary played his cards well; he pretended to be neutral and showed signs of favoring both sides while demonstrating an inevitable partiality for Catholic Poland and secretly hoping to convert the Protestants of Lithuania to Catholicism. The negotiations continued for three weeks, with nothing accomplished. Suddenly the besieged fortress of Pskov erupted. Prince Ivan Shuisky had already sent out forty-five sorties in the hope of breaking the siege. On January 4, 1582, he gave orders for a forty-sixth sortie. His cavalry and infantry fought so ferociously that the Poles and Lithuanians concluded that the Russian army would never surrender the city. Prepared to sue for peace, they announced that on the orders of King Stephen Bathory they were breaking off negotiations. Both sides were bluffing. On January 15, 1582, they agreed to a ten-year truce on condition that Russia cede the whole of Livonia to the Poles and Lithuanians. King Stephen Bathory waived the indemnity of 400,000 Hungarian gold crowns and returned Veliki Luki to the Russians but kept Polotsk. Ivan lost Dorpat, but was saved from greater humiliation by the heroic defense of Pskov, which saved Russian honor. Ivan by his cowardice and pusillanimity had no share in these triumphs. The loss of Livonia was a disaster of the first magnitude and most of the blame must be laid at Ivan's door.

Soon after the signing of the Treaty of Yam Zapolsky, the papal intermediary, who had worked so successfully on behalf of the Poles and Lithuanians, arrived in Moscow. His purpose was to discuss religious matters with Ivan, who was sunk in gloom. "I found the Tsar in deep despair," Possevino wrote. "The court, formerly so splendid, now resembled an abode of monks, their black gowns showing evidence of the Tsar's somber spirits." Ivan felt that nothing would be gained by religious discussions; they would lead to arguments; and arguments would lead to hatred. Possevino appears to have embarked on the discussions with misgivings and only because Pope Gregory XIII insisted that one last attempt should be made to unite the Orthodox and Catholic faiths under himself as the Supreme Pontiff. Ivan was rarely long-suffering, but he showed toward Possevino an unusual charity. We find him speaking in the tones of a very old and experienced man who harbors no desire to quarrel with anyone and desires only to be left in peace. He said:

> Antony, we are already fifty-one years of age. We were brought up in our Christian faith and we have reached maturity, thanks to God's grace! At this age we have no desire to change our faith, nor do we desire a greater kingdom to rule over. The Roman faith would not be in agreement with many articles of belief in our Orthodox Christian faith. We do not want to talk about it because we do not want any quarrels. Besides, we cannot take upon ourselves even to discuss such a serious matter without the blessing of our father, the Metropolitan, and the Church Council.

Possevino had the Jesuit temper, charming, ruthless, absolutely certain of the rightness of his cause; and he pressed hard. Ivan had his own ways to escape from his adversary's arguments. Someone had told him that the Pope was often carried on a portable throne and Crosses were sown onto his shoes for the people to kiss. "In our church," said Ivan, "it is not the custom to wear the Cross below he belt." Possevino was puzzled and made a long speech on the necessity to revere Popes and Emperors, and bowed very low to Ivan to show how much he revered the supreme ruler of Russia. Reverence, even extreme reverence, was perfectly proper, he suggested until Ivan cut him short. "This man who calls himself the co-ruler with Christ orders people to carry him on a throne as if he were on a cloud, as if he were an angel, and does not live according to the teachings of Christ—well, that Pope is not a shepherd but a wolf!"

So it had come out at last, all the pent-up emotion of the Orthodox confronted with the Roman Catholic mind. Possevino was deeply shocked.

"If the Pope is a wolf," he said sternly, "then I have nothing more to say."

Ivan did his best to make amends.

"You see," he explained, "when we talk about religion we only provoke each other. I do not call Pope Gregory XIII a wolf but I call a wolf a Pope who does not follow the teachings of Christ!"

Characteristically, in attempting to make amends, Ivan only made matters worse. He realized this, laid his arm on Possevino's shoulder and permitted him to withdraw. Later that day he sent meats from his own table to the papal emissary.

Three days later, on February 24, 1582, Possevino was again summoned to an audience with the Tsar, who bade him sit down opposite the throne and said in a loud voice, so that all the people in the audience chamber could hear him: "Antony, please forget what I said about the Popes that so annoyed you! We do not agree on matters of faith, but I want to live in peace with all Christian rulers, and I shall send my officers to accompany you to Rome, and for the services you have rendered I offer you my gratitude."

In this way the Tsar made his amends, and Possevino was permitted to continue his discussions on religion with a group of boyars. Since he had very little knowledge of the Russian character he continued to be something of a nuisance, making absurd requests. He asked for the expulsion of all Lutheran pastors and was told that all men were free to practice their faiths in Russia on condition that they made no attempt to convert the Orthodox Christians. He asked for permission to erect a Catholic church and was told that the Catholics were permitted to worship freely and bring their priests into Russia, but the building of churches was not permitted. Possevino then raised the question of a combined Catholic and Orthodox crusade against the Muslims, and Ivan let it be known that he would gladly join such a crusade if all the other crowned heads of Europe would do the same, an unlikely event, and therefore one that did not greatly concern him. Possevino was not so much outmaneuvered as placed in a position where he seemed to be continually out of step, and Ivan drew some wry satisfaction from watching the papal emissary as he became increasingly confused.

On the first Sunday of Lent Ivan once more summoned Possevino to an audience. In the silkiest tones he invited the representative of the Pope to attend an Orthodox service. He said:

> Antony, I know you want to see the customs of our Church, and so I have arranged to have you escorted to the Uspensky Cathedral at a time when I myself will be present, and you will then see the beauty and majesty of a true service to God. There, in the Cathedral, we adore the heavenly, not the earthly, and we honor our Metropolitan without holding him aloft in our hands. The Apostle Peter was not carried aloft by the faithful; instead he walked without shoes—and your Pope calls himself God's Viceroy!

Possevino was outraged, but kept his temper. He explained that there could be no communication between himself and the Orthodox Church until there was communication between the Pope and the Metropolitan; and he refused to attend the service. But the Uspensky Cathedral was next door to the palace, and at a signal all the nobles swept out of the audience chamber and made their way to the Cathedral, and Possevino found himself being carried forward by the crowd, until he was safely deposited on the doorstep of the Cathedral. Ivan shouted after him: "Antony, be careful that no Lutherans follow you into the cathedral!" He was pleased with this little gambit, but Possevino was able to slip away. Ivan was surprised, for he thought he had done everything possible to ensure that the papal emissary would attend the service. He rubbed his forehead with his hand and said, "He has a strong will!"

The trick had failed, but Ivan continued to deal with him courteously, even sending him a gift of seven black sables, for himself and the Pope. Possevino left Moscow on March 15, 1582, accompanied by Russian envoys to the papal court dressed in black. If they were asked why they wore such somber costumes, they were instructed to reply that they were in mourning for the Tsarevich Ivan. They were also instructed to deny that the Tsar had ever called the Pope a wolf.

Thus ended Possevino's hopeless attempt to bring the Roman Catholic and Orthodox churches together, with Ivan as an amused spectator and his boyars as confederates in his amusement. The times were bitter and these amusements were rare enough to become memorable.

The wars were not over yet. The Nogay Tatars were becoming increasingly troublesome, the Cheremiss were rising, threats of another invasion from the Crimea were being taken very seriously. King John III of Sweden had captured Narva and was sending raiding parties into Russian territory. Happily he was on bad terms with King Stephen Bathory and there was very little possibility of concerted action by the Swedes, the Poles, and the Lithuanians. Having concluded peace with King Stephen Bathory, Ivan attacked the Swedes with the express purpose of capturing Narva, and then abruptly called off the war and invited the enemy to negotiate a peace treaty. He was clearly unsure of himself and terrified by the possibility of a Tatar invasion. In May 1583 he concluded a two-month truce with Sweden, which was later extended for three years. Sweden kept Narva and a large part of the former Russian coast of the Gulf of Finland.

Given adequate leadership, it is likely that the Russian army would have carried everything before it. But Ivan was not a war leader. Senile, guilt-ridden, suffering from various undiagnosed diseases, he was a pitiful remnant of the man who had once conquered Kazan. Among his many fantasies was one concerning England. He believed that England might become an invaluable ally; she would provide him with weapons and ammunition, and she would do this all the more readily if he were allied by marriage to a close relative of the Virgin Queen. English guns, English gunpowder, an English wife—armed with these, there were no enemies he could not conquer.

One of Ivan's many doctors was Dr. Robert Jacoby, who at some period of his life appears to have encountered the family of Francis, the second earl of Huntingdon, whose large family included a

daughter Mary, known as Lady Mary Hastings. It occurred to Dr
Jacoby that Lady Mary Hastings would make a suitable bride for
Ivan, who was still married to his seventh wife. The doctor had
arrived from England in 1581 with a letter of recommendation from
Queen Elizabeth testifying to his great skill, and Ivan trusted him
implicitly, listened to his stories about the court, and became
infatuated with a woman he had never seen. According to Dr
Jacoby, she was a niece of the Queen. This was not true, but neither
the Tsar nor the doctor was concerned with the truth. Lady Mary
Hastings did belong to one of the most powerful families in
England and there had been a time when her father thought of
himself as a future King.

On August 11, 1582, Fyodor Pissemsky, ambassador and envoy
extraordinary, was sent by Ivan to negotiate a close alliance
between Russia and England and simultaneously to negotiate his
marriage to Lady Mary Hastings. His instructions, which were
voluminous, were also precise. Pissemsky was instructed to commu-
nicate the Tsar's intentions in a private audience with the Queen;
he must acquire a painting of the lady, meet her, describe her at
length, and learn her exact relationship to the Queen, the number
of her brothers and sisters, and her father's rank. If Queen
Elizabeth objected that the Tsar was already married, she was to be
told that the present Tsaritsa had no royal blood, and furthermore
he did not like her and would soon rid himself of her in favor of the
Queen's niece. Pissemsky, arriving in London a month later, had
some difficulty approaching the Queen because it was a plague year
and she had vanished into the seclusion of Windsor Castle. Finally,
on November 4, 1582, a reception was given for him at the Castle
and he was accorded all the honors due to him. The Queen rose
graciously when the Tsar's name was mentioned, and she stepped
forward to receive from Pissemsky's hands the gifts and letters from
the Tsar. Smiling, she said she regretted her ignorance of the
Russian language; she asked after the Tsar's health, and she said
she had been saddened by the death of the Tsarevich. When
Pissemsky said that the Tsar loved her above all the other
sovereigns of Europe, she answered, "I love him no less and
sincerely hope one day to see him with my own eyes."

The conversations between a sovereign and an ambassador are
usually predictable. The Queen asked Pissemsky how he liked

ІОАННЪ ВАСИЛЬЕВИЧЬ
Царь и Самодержецъ всероссійскій.
Joann Wassiljewicz
Tzaar et Autocrator totius Russiae

Seventeenth-century portrait of Ivan.

England, and he answered that he found every virtue and ever imaginable grace in the country where he had the honor of bein the Russian ambassador. Then the Queen asked him wheth Russia was now quiet, and he replied predictably that it was ver quiet, adding that all seditions had been stamped out, the rebe had repented, and the Tsar had dealt with them mercifully. The were the introductory pleasantries; the real business of the embass would come later.

On December 18, 1582, Pissemsky had his first formal meetin with Queen Elizabeth's ministers. The ambassador announced tha he had been entrusted by the Tsar with the task of negotiating defensive and offensive alliance; England was to make commo cause with Russia in peace and war; and in the event of war th Queen was expected to furnish troops for the Tsar, or failing tha to render financial assistance and to send military supplies. Ther were long discussions on the precise terms of the treaty and on th English claim to the exclusive right of trading on the White Sea. N final agreement was reached, and exactly a month later, on Januar 18, 1583, the ambassador had his first private audience with th Queen on the subject of Ivan's marriage to Lady Mary Hastings. transpired that according to the Queen the lady was not beautif enough to be worthy of Ivan and in addition she had recentl suffered from smallpox which left her with a blemished skin. Late when she had recovered, arrangements would be made to let th ambassador see her and a picture would be painted. Four month passed, and on May 18, 1583, the ambassador first set eyes on th lady.

The occasion was carefully stage-managed and resembled a slav market with the ambassador representing the prospective pur chaser. Lady Mary Hastings was exhibited in a tent set up in th gardens of York House, the palatial residence on the Thame Embankment that had formerly belonged to the Archbishop o York. She was attended by young noblemen and maids of hono and Pissemsky appears to have approached her in trepidation. "Sh put on a stately countenance," wrote Sir Jerome Horsey, and h describes how the ambassador behaved in her presence. "Cas down his countenance; fell prostrate to her feet, rose, ran bac from her, his face still towards her, and the rest admiring at h manner. Said by an interpreter it did suffice him to behold the ange he hoped should be his master's spouse; commended her angelical countenance, state, and admirable beauty." In his description of the lady, written for the Tsar, Pissemsky omitted to mention that she was beautiful. He wrote that she was "tall, well-shaped, slender, white of face, her hair dark blond, and she has a straight nose, and her fingers are long and slender." It was an admirable portrait of a dignified and rather plain-looking English woman of the aristocracy. Queen Elizabeth in her forthright way commented on the confrontation a few days later when talking to the ambassador.

"I do not think your Sovereign will like my niece," the Queen said, "nor do I think that you liked her."

"It seemed to me that your niece is very beautiful," the ambassador replied diplomatically. "Now it all rests in the hands of God."

He had waited for many months for a glimpse of the future Tsaritsa; it had been granted to him; and he was satisfied. The Queen, too, appears to have thought she would lose nothing by marrying off an obscure kinswoman to the Tsar. Lady Mary Hastings was not averse to becoming an empress. Later, when she learned more about Ivan's character, she changed her mind and begged Queen Elizabeth to put an end to the proceedings. For the rest of her life her friends amused themselves by calling her "the Empress of Muscovy."

Just before the Russian ambassador left England, he was the guest of honor at a banquet given by Queen Elizabeth at her palace at Greenwich; and when he took his leave she placed in his hands two letters addressed to Ivan. In one letter she thanked him for his proposals for an alliance, and in the other expressed her pleasure at his intention to visit England not because of any danger arising in his country but simply because he genuinely desired to meet her. She promised to prove to him that England would be a second Russia for him. These diplomatic niceties were designed to prepare her own ambassador's diplomatic efforts toward acquiring substantial trading privileges. The ambassador was also commanded to inform the Tsar as diplomatically as possible that the Queen had no interest in concluding an offensive alliance with Russia and that Lady Mary Hastings suffered from poor health and would not be able to make the long and arduous journey to Moscow. Also her relatives did not want to be parted from her.

Sir Jerome Bowes.

The English ambassador was well chosen. Sir Jerome Bowes was a proud, peppery, rough-humored man, who permitted no nonsense from anyone and was quite capable of standing up to the Tsar. He possessed an exaggerated sense of his own importance, but in dealing with Ivan it was always useful to feel important. From the moment Bowes arrived in Moscow he was a power to be reckoned with.

The two ambassadors set out for Russia together, arriving at Rose Island in St. Nicholas Bay on July 23, 1583. Here in the far north Pissemsky separated from Bowes and hurried overland to Moscow, bearing the letters of Queen Elizabeth and the painting of

Lady Mary Hastings, while Bowes went by ship, sailing up the Northern Dvina River as far as Vologda, where horses and provisions were furnished to him by the Tsar; and again at Yaroslavl he was given two fine horses at the Tsar's orders. It was evident that he was going to be treated with quite extraordinary respect.

When he reached Moscow he was given an escort of three hundred well-appointed gentlemen of the court on horseback, led by Prince Ivan Sitsky, a man who had served Ivan in many high positions and most notably as an ambassador to the court of King Stephen Bathory. They accompanied him to his lodging where he received food from the Tsar's table and was told that the Tsar was anxious to see him, but since no doubt he was tired from the long journey he would be permitted two days' rest before his first audience. Bowes therefore rested and prepared himself for the ordeal of meeting a man who was even prouder and more rough-tempered than himself.

On October 24, 1583, at nine o'clock in the morning, Bowes in the company of Prince Sitsky and the same three hundred gentlemen of the court on horseback rode off to the Kremlin Palace. Accompanying him were thirty of his own servants, who carried the costly gifts intended by Queen Elizabeth for the Tsar. Bowes was peppery from the beginning, for he saw that Prince Sitsky rode on a better horse than the one provided for him and he insisted upon being as well horsed as the prince. But Bowes behaved well in the palace and in the Tsar's presence he was permitted to sit close to the throne on a bench draped with a carpet. Ivan sat with his three crowns in front of him, and there were the inevitable four guards wearing silver clothes. There were the usual questions about Queen Elizabeth's health and they were answered in the usual way. Soon Bowes was dismissed, and Ivan, who was favorably impressed by the ambassador's demeanor, ordered that two hundred dishes be sent to his lodging. The embassy had begun well; it remained only to work out the details of the treaty with the help of a commission which consisted of Nikita Zakharin, Bogdan Belsky, and Andrey Shchelkalov.

But of course it was not simply a question of working out a simple treaty. Ivan wanted things his own way: the Queen must do his bidding. He proposed that a special clause be inserted in the treaty, reading: "Queen Elizabeth must either persuade Bathory to conclude a genuine peace with Russia, forcing him to return Livonia and the Province of Polotsk to Russia, or else she must attack Lithuania with us." Bowes had no intention of accepting such a one-sided clause and vehemently reminded the commissioners that he had no authority to grant the request. "I cannot return with it," he said bluntly. "The Queen would think me a fool if I did!"

Then there was the question of the special privileges granted to the English, permitting them the sole right to trade with the ports on the White Sea. The commissioners sensibly asked him whether he expected the Russians to abandon trade with all the other sovereign states, and Bowes replied that they were forgetting that the English were the first to discover the route to the White Sea and therefore were entitled to this special privilege. When Ivan finally agreed that the English should have the greater share of trade with the White Sea, but proposed that France and the Netherlands should also be accorded trading facilities, Bowes continued to demand exclusive privileges.

Then Ivan raised a curious matter which needed explanation. He wanted to receive embassies from the Pope and from the sovereign rulers of Catholic countries. Could they not pass through England and travel to the White Sea on English ships? Bowes was sure that Queen Elizabeth would not permit it. Ivan's boyars replied sensibly, "Faith does not interfere with friendship. Look, your Queen and our Tsar are of different faiths, but he desires to keep her as his friend above all other sovereigns." Ivan agreed that the Queen might have good reason to keep a papal ambassador out of her country, but he could not understand what was harmful about an ambassador from a Catholic country stepping foot on English soil for a few days before embarking for northern Russia.

The negotiations were going along badly, and Bowes attempted to cut through the knots by seeking private audiences with Ivan. In this he was helped by Dr. Robert Jacoby. But these audiences were sometimes noisy. Once, annoyed by Queen Elizabeth's refusal to agree to a treaty on his terms, Ivan flew into a temper and shouted that he did not reckon the Queen of England to be his fellow, and there were others who were her betters. Bowes was appalled and answered heatedly, and the following exchange took place:

Bowes: The Queen my mistress is as great a prince as any in Christendom, equal to him who thinks himself the greatest, well able to defend herself against his malice whosoever, and counts no means to offend any that either she had or should have cause to be enemy unto!

Tsar: Yea, how sayest thou to the French King and the King of Spain?

Bowes: Mary! I hold the Queen my mistress as great as any of them both!

Tsar: Then what sayest thou to the Emperor of Germany?

Bowes: Such is the greatness of the Queen my mistress as the King her father had not long since the Emperor in his pay, in his wars against France!

Ivan did not relish the idea that an English King could buy the services of a German Emperor and became even more enraged. He ordered Bowes to leave the Kremlin Palace at once, adding, "If you were not the ambassador, I would throw you out of the doors!" Sometime later, when he had calmed down, the Tsar said, "Pray God that I should have such a loyal subject!"

These uneasy conversations continued. One day Bowes was summoned to a meeting with the Tsar and his closest advisers. Present were Nikita Zakharin, Dmitry Godunov, Bogdan Belsky, Andrey Shchelkalov, Prince Fyodor Trubetskoy, two secretaries and three other nobles of the Boyar Council. These men were the rulers of the Russian state, and three of them—Nikita Zakharin, Bogdan Belsky, and Andrey Shchelkalov—stood near the apex of power. These three therefore were ordered to come close to the throne to discuss with Bowes a matter of the utmost importance: the Tsar's marriage to Lady Mary Hastings.

It appeared that Ivan was well satisfied with the lady's portrait and was determined to marry her. But would Queen Elizabeth consent to the bride joining the Orthodox faith? There were also other questions to be decided, and the Tsar seemed to be on the verge of declaring the date of the wedding. Bowes, who knew exactly what Lady Mary Hastings thought about the wedding, demurred. He said she was ill and it was unlikely that she would become an Orthodox Christian. The Tsar was bitterly disappointed, saying, "I see you have come here not to do business but to refuse! So I will no longer speak to you about the matter!" Bowes realized he was in danger of jeopardizing the main purpose of his embassy, which was to obtain exclusive trading privileges for English merchants in northern Russia, and he attempted to appease the Tsar by suggesting that Lady Mary Hastings was a very distant relative of the Queen and furthermore there were many others who were much prettier.

"Who are they?" the Tsar asked.

Bowes replied that he was not at liberty to reveal their names. He needed the permission of the Queen, and could do no more than assure the Tsar that they existed. This was bad news, and the Tsar relapsed into ill humor, saying, "Then what instructions do you have? We cannot conclude the treaty as the Queen of England desires!"

Bowes saw that he must appease Ivan once again, and he arranged through Dr. Jacoby for another private audience. This was granted, and Ivan immediately asked him whether he had received further instructions.

"I have no other instructions," Bowes replied. "But the Queen ordered me to listen to whatever you will wish to say and to repeat your words to her."

Bowes appears to have spoken haughtily, for Ivan immediately impressed upon the English ambassador the fact that he was the Tsar and all communications with him should take place through his boyars. If the Queen of England came to Moscow, then she could speak to him as an equal. Ivan continued: "You talk a good deal, but say nothing to the purpose. You tell us you have no instructions, but yesterday Dr. Robert told us you wanted to speak with us privately. So say what you want to say!"

Once again Bowes avoided the main issue. He told Ivan that when he was ambassador to France, he did not deal with lesser mortals but spoke directly to the King. Ivan wanted to get down to hard facts.

"Tell us what the Queen instructed you to say to us about the marriage. As for France, this tells us nothing. In our country we do not talk to ambassadors in this way."

Nevertheless he was talking with the ambassador face to face; he was asking questions and pleading for an answer; and there was no answer. Bowes was saying: "Queen Elizabeth desires your friendship more than she desires that of any other sovereign, and my

esire is to serve you." It was a brilliant improvisation designed to
rolong the agony. Ivan said sternly: "Tell me who are the maidens
ho are the Queen's nieces, and I'll send my ambassador to look at
hem and make their portraits."

Bowes offered to provide accurate portraits, but since he could
ot provide a single maiden Ivan remained frustrated and embit-
ered. When he saw Bowes a few days later he shouted: "You are
n ignoramus! From the moment you arrived here you have
ccomplished nothing!" This was not quite true, for Bowes had
ontrived a successful delaying action and still believed he would
e successful in getting the treaty he wanted. When Ivan became
specially angry, Bowes complained that he was being ill-used: they
ad given him only pork, which he detested, and demanded lamb
nd chicken. He placed the blame on Andrey Shchelkalov, and the
sar immediately gave orders that Shchelkalov should have no
urther dealings with Bowes, and the merchants who contracted to
end food to Bowes were thrown into prison, while Bogdan Belsky
vas ordered to apologize on behalf of Ivan for the verbal abuse
owes had suffered at court. Ivan was especially anxious that
owes would pardon him for saying he was an ignoramus.

There were altogether about six meetings with Bowes, the last of
hem taking place on February 20, 1584. They were always spirited,
ronical, curiously graceful, like a dance. At one of these last
neetings Ivan announced that he was so determined to marry one
f Queen Elizabeth's kinswomen that he had come to the conclu-
ion that he must himself go to England and claim his bride, and he
dded that he would take his treasure with him. He seems to have
elt that Queen Elizabeth would be so dazzled by the splendor of
is treasury that she would give him everything he wanted.

In those last weeks of his life he was infatuated with an unseen
nd unknown English woman. England beckoned to him, and for
im that mysterious island shone like a vision of paradise. Since he
vas not a man who permitted anyone to oppose his will, he would
ave made the long and difficult journey from Moscow to London
or no other purpose than to choose a wife distantly related to the
Queen of England. Less than a month after his last meeting with
Bowes the Tsar died quite suddenly, and history was deprived of
he spectacle of the Tsar walking hand in hand with Queen
Elizabeth through the gardens of Windsor Castle.

Andrey Shchelkalov was a man of vast experience and prove loyalty who often suffered savage beatings at Ivan's hands. He hel the office of Chancellor and was therefore one of the most powerf men in Russia, but this did not save him when Ivan flew into one c his rages. He was genuinely puzzled by many of Ivan's policies; h had no love for Englishmen, disliked Bowes, and sometime wondered why Ivan wanted an English bride. On the day of Ivan death he hurried to Bowes' house. He had information of grea importance and it was necessary that it should be phrased in th proper way. He said: "Your English Tsar is dead!"

Triumph and Defeat

ɔURING HIS LIFE IVAN COMMITTED every imaginable crime and he
vas rewarded with astonishing triumphs. The gods favored him,
ɣranting him most of his desires. Scarcely an enemy went unpun-
shed; his victories on the battlefield would be remembered
hroughout recorded Russian history; and to the empire he had
nherited from his father he added vast new territories. These
riumphs sometimes took place without his knowledge; he was not
esponsible for them, and they often occurred in spite of him rather
han because of him; and he took full credit. Thus it happened that
he Russian army soundly defeated the army of the Crimean Tatars
t a time when Ivan was taking refuge in the north. He returned to
Moscow to enjoy the victory celebrations and thereafter regarded
nimself as a great conqueror. In the last years of his life the pattern
vas repeated. He scarcely lifted a finger and the vast new empire of
Siberia fell into his hands.

This new empire was given to him by the powerful and wealthy
merchant family of the Stroganovs, whose landholdings reached
rom the Northern Dvina River to the Ural Mountains. Originally
hey were merchants of Novgorod; they became Russia's first
arge-scale industrialists. They possessed saltworks, lumberyards,
smithies, and forges, and traded in wood, iron, salt, fish, grain, furs.
As they moved eastward, they were granted charters authorizing
hem to colonize unoccupied land and to conquer territories
ɔccupied by the Tatars, Voguls, and Ostiaks who lived there. The

Stroganovs had their own private armies, their own fortresses, thei own capital at Solikamsk. Sporadic fighting between the smal Stroganov armies and the armies of Kuchum, Khan of Siberia beginning in 1573, had become continual, and by 1581 th Stroganovs had concluded that they would be best served b destroying the khanate. Khan Kuchum was descended from Princ Shiban, one of the younger sons of Jenghiz Khan. His capital wa the town of Sibir on the Irtysh River, which flows into the evei longer Ob River. Both rivers had their source in the mountains o Outer Mongolia.

Ivan welcomed the decision to conquer Siberia, but offered ver little help. The Stroganovs were permitted to conquer at their owi risk. To lead the expedition they chose Yermak Timofeevich, wh had formerly earned his living by brigandage on the lower reache of the Volga River. He had a rather flat face, a heavy black beard broad shoulders, and he carried himself with an air of authority His army consisted of 540 Cossacks and about 300 volunteers, al armed with muskets, and in addition they were provided with thre field cannon. The Stroganovs also provided them with food anc banners with holy images painted on them. The total cost of th expedition was 20,000 rubles.

Yermak set out for Siberia on September 1, 1581, from a bas camp on the Chussovaya River, sailing up the river toward the Ura Mountains, passing beneath fierce cliffs and dense forests. After si days his men dragged the boats ashore and began to carry then over a pass. Here, in the pass, they built a fortified camp where the remained throughout the winter, and in May they broke camp lowered their boats on the Tagil River, and sailed eastward into th domain of Khan Kuchum, raiding Tatar settlements along the way Once, when they captured an important Tatar officer, they sent hin ahead to Sibir where he reported to the Khan that the Cossacks hac weapons that "spewed out flame and smoke with a sound lik thunder." The muskets and the three cannon terrified the Siberians but they continued to fight.

Yermak fought a whole series of engagements on the way tc Sibir. Progress was slow; many of his men were killed, and man more were wounded. He fought his first pitched battle against th Tatars on October 23, 1582, when winter was already coming down. There had been so many losses in the previous engagement that many of his men wanted to return to Russia. "If we retreat, we shall be filled with shame for not having carried out our promise to the Stroganovs," Yermak answered, and he ordered the attack on the Tatar camp, protected with felled trees, which guarded the approaches to Sibir. The Tatars were armed with bows and arrows, and were no match for the Cossacks with their cannon and muskets. But the battle was hard fought, the Tatars darted out from behind the felled trees to engage the Cossacks in hand-to-hand fighting, and the issue was still in doubt when Mametkul, Khan Kuchum's nephew commanding the Tatar forces, was wounded and had to be carried away to the farther bank of the Irtysh, and then the Tatars lost heart. Shortly afterward Khan Kuchum, who had been watching the battle from a hill some distance away, rode off to Sibir, not to put the town in a state of defense but to gather up his treasure before escaping eastward.

The Russians had lost about two hundred men in the previous engagements, and they lost over a hundred more in the battle for Sibir. Three days later they entered the abandoned town. A few days later the Ostiaks and the Tatars began to return, having been promised that no punishment would fall on them. Yermak threatened his Cossacks with death if they so much as touched the local inhabitants. Yermak was well aware of the importance of his conquest, for the way was now open for the conquest of the rest of Siberia to the Pacific Ocean.

For his own reasons Yermak delayed his report to Ivan, and it was not until the end of the year, on December 22, 1582, that Ivan Koltso, his second in command, set out from Sibir for Moscow, together with fifty of the Cossacks. They took with them a larger number of furs and skins as presents for the Tsar—there were sixty bundles of sables, forty pelts to a bundle, twenty black fox skins, and fifty beaver skins. They also carried long letters from Yermak addressed to Ivan and to the Stroganovs with a full account of their exploits. To the Tsar Yermak wrote that he had undertaken the expedition to expiate his sins of brigandage, and now that he had succeeded in conquering the Khanate of Siberia, which will remain in Russian possession "for ever and ever, so long as God lets the world stand," he hoped and prayed for a free pardon for himself and his Cossacks. If no free pardon was granted, he promised to offer his life heroically on the scaffold.

The long letter, which had taken two months to write, finally reached Ivan at the end of January or the beginning of February 1583. The church bells rang, and there were services of thanksgiving to celebrate the new conquest. In the streets of Moscow the people could be heard congratulating one another with the words, "God has given a new kingdom to Russia." Everyone shared in the excitement, remembering that there had been little good news in Russia for many years. Ivan Koltso became the hero of the hour, feted by everyone, and welcomed in the throne room of the Kremlin Palace, where he bowed before Ivan and kissed his hand. The misdeeds of the Cossacks were forgotten; they were showered with gifts. Ivan ordered that Yermak should be presented with a special coat of mail with a golden double-headed eagle emblazoned on the accompanying cuirass.

Siberia passed into possession of the Tsar. The Bishop of Vologda was commanded to send ten priests, together with their families, to Siberia. Ivan Koltso was authorized to seek new settlers for the conquered land. Prince Simeon Bolkhovsky was ordered to proceed at once with five hundred musketeers to Sibir to establish the Tsar's authority. Yermak himself was granted the title Prince Sibirsky.

The Stroganovs too found themselves in high favor. Ivan summoned them to court, heaped praises on them, presented them with new lands and estates on the Volga, and permitted them to trade without paying any taxes or duties in all their towns and villages. This was a princely gift, representing vast new wealth, a proper reward for having added a new empire to Ivan's vast territories.

About the same time that Ivan Koltso was being feted in Moscow, in February 1583, the Cossacks succeeded in capturing Mametkul, the nephew of Khan Kuchum. Yermak received him kindly, but kept him under strong guard, for he was a brave and daring commander and had caused much havoc during the previous three months. When Ivan heard of the capture of Mametkul, he ordered that the Tatar prince should be brought to his court, received him well, and according to the long-established custom granted him the rights enjoyed by all the Tatar princes who swore an oath of loyalty to him and entered his service.

Meanwhile Khan Kuchum roamed the steppes of central Asia,

determined at all costs to regain his lost kingdom, continually plotting. Once conquered, the Tatars often rebelled. They had many advantages: they outnumbered the Russians, they traveled lightly, and they did not suffer from scurvy, which killed off half of Yermak's Cossacks. An uprising, led by a certain Karacha, spread across Siberia, and Sibir, now a heavily defended fortress town, was surrounded by Karacha's forces. On the night of June 12, 1585, the Cossacks crept out of the town, attacked Karacha's forces while they were sleeping, killed many of them and sent the rest fleeing along the Irtysh River. The Tatars were quite capable of using the same trick. On August 5, less than two months later, Yermak himself was resting in his camp only two days' march from Sibir when he was surprised by a force commanded by Khan Kuchum. During the night it rained heavily, a strong wind rose, and Yermak gave his men permission to sleep, for it was inconceivable that the Khan would attack on such a night. He did not know that the Khan's spies had been following him closely and knew exactly where he was. In the middle of the night Khan Kuchum's Tatars fell on the camp, which was set in an ancient Tatar burial ground, and slaughtered all the Cossacks except for two men who succeeded in escaping. One of the men succeeded in regaining Sibir, the other was Yermak, who dived into the swift-flowing Irtysh River in full armor, hoping to reach the place where the Cossack boats were moored. But weighed down by the armor emblazoned in gold with the double-headed eagle, he drowned. On that same night forty-eight of his Cossacks were killed in the burial ground.

Thus died Yermak, the thickset, broad-shouldered, black-bearded conqueror of Siberia, having ruled over his conquest for less than three years. Dead, he entered into legend. Songs were sung and stories were told about him, and some of them had little enough relation to historical truth but were all the more truthful for being imaginative. After the conquest of Siberia, he never returned to Russia, but the popular imagination demanded that he should be seen confronting the terrible Tsar, and so they sang:

> Then Yermak and all the Cossacks departed from Sibir
> And made their way to the stone city of Moscow,
> To the terrible Tsar Ivan Vasilievich,
> And the Lord Tsar spoke to him, saying:

"Well, Yermak Timofeevich, where have you been?
How many people have you been robbing?
How many innocent souls have you killed?
How did you capture the Tatar Khan?
How did you bring the Tatar army into my power?"

Then Yermak fell to his knees,
Bowing low before the terrible Tsar,
And thrust a letter into the Tsar's hands
And with the letter went the accompanying words:
"Before you, O Lord, I profess my guilt.
We have been brigands on the blue waters!"
And the Lord Tsar was not in the least angered,
And showed great mercy to the sinner,
And ordered him to be loaded with gifts.

Then Yermak was sent back to the land of Sibir
With orders to collect tribute from the thieving Tatars
So that the Tsar's treasury should be filled up,
And he returned with his Cossacks to Siberia
To fulfill the orders of the Tsar
To extract from the thieving Tatars
The necessary tribute and to bring them
Even more under the Tsar's authority,
And they did so with the utmost eagerness.

Inevitably Yermak became a folk hero and suffered the strange
transformations that occur to heroes. In legend he became the man
who almost single-handedly opened up Siberia to the Russians, and
it was forgotten that at the time of his death there was scarcely a
single Russian left alive in Siberia. Yermak had opened the way;
his successors fought the descendants of Khan Kuchum for nearly
a hundred years before they had all of Siberia in their grasp.

Ivan, too, became a legend in his own lifetime. In the songs he
was always "the terrible Tsar Ivan Vasilievich," the man who
exulted in terrible deeds, uttering violent curses like Beelzebub in
the old English morality plays, given over to violence and rapine,
and then exulting in his grief. Here the Tsar addresses his people:

"Ho, there, my boyars and princes,
Put on your clothes of mourning,
Come to the morning service,
Come to the funeral service of the Tsarevich.
I will boil you all in a caldron!"

And throughout all white-walled Moscow,
And throughout the Tsardom of Muscovy,
He gave orders that the people should fast
And go to God's church and pray
And put on their clothes of mourning.

Soon, much sooner than anyone expected, they would be putting on the clothes of mourning for the Tsar himself.

Although he was only fifty-three, Ivan had the appearance of an old man in the winter of 1583. He was swollen with dropsy and riddled with diseases of many kinds and many origins. His excesses had at last caught up with him; and his fears, for he was a man who always feared greatly, now gathered around him in huge and ungainly flocks. In the past he had always succeeded in containing his despairs by destroying people; now he knew that he was himself about to be destroyed, and he found no satisfaction anywhere.

One day, early in 1584, he was standing on the Red Porch of the Kremlin Palace when he saw a comet shaped like a fiery Cross hanging in the sky between the Cathedral of the Annunciation and the great tower known as Ivan's Belfry. He gazed at it for a long time, and then he said, "This sign foretells my death."

He had always possessed faith in witchcraft, necromancy and magic, and now, but too late, he hoped to use the dark powers for his own advantage. Lapland was famous for its witches and soothsayers, and at his orders some sixty Lapp magicians were brought to Moscow and placed in the care of Bogdan Belsky, the Tsar's favorite. They cast spells, consulted oracles, studied the stars. Belsky visited them daily and reported their findings to Ivan. Unhappily their findings continued to be unsatisfactory; they pronounced that their own spells were powerless against the signs of the stars. They were even able to foretell the date of his death—March 18. Belsky kept this information for himself, regarding himself as a contender for the throne, and promised the witches that he would have them burned if their prophecy proved to be wrong. On March 10 Ivan gave orders that a Lithuanian embassy should be stopped on its way to Moscow, and about the same time he wrote to all the monks of St. Kirill's Monastery at Beloozero pleading for their prayers in his extremity. He wrote:

> To the great and most pure Monastery, to the saintly and blessed
> monks, to the priests, deacons, elders and choristers, and to those

who are bedridden in their cells and to all the brethren, the Grand Prince Ivan Vasilievich sends his greetings.

He bows to your feet and prays kneeling before your blessedness, begging you to favor him, whether you are assembled together or in your cells alone, with prayers to God and the most pure Mother of God on behalf of my most sinful self that I may be released, great sinner that I am, of all my sins by virtue of your blessed prayers and that I may be granted recovery from my present mortal sickness and made well.

In whatsoever we have transgressed against you, we ask from you the favor of forgiveness, and in whatsoever you have transgressed against us, God will forgive you all.

There was a good deal more of it, and Ivan did not forget to remind the monks of the many benefactions he had granted to the monastery. He had provided oil for their lamps, food for their tables, and alms for their poor. They owed him something, and it was time they repaid the debt.

On the same day that he ordered the Lithuanian embassy to be stopped, he wrote his last will and testament, appointing his sweet-tempered and simpleminded son, the Tsarevich Fyodor, to be his successor. To help Fyodor govern the country, he appointed a Council of Regents of four men. They were Prince Ivan Mstislavsky, Prince Ivan Shuisky, Nikita Zakharin, and Boris Godunov. Ivan's younger son Dmitry was to be given the principality of Uglich.

In his will Ivan paid tribute to the boyars and voyevodas, whom he described as "my friends and collaborators," in his victories over the Tatars, the Livonians, and the Turks. He bade the Regents avoid war with Christian powers, pointing to the unfortunate consequences of his wars with Lithuania and Sweden, which brought about the exhaustion of the country. He ordered taxes reduced and the release of all Lithuanian and Livonian prisoners of war. And he bade Fyodor to reign in the fear of God, with love and mercy.

He knew he was dying, but he could not acquiesce to his own death. The comet still hung in the sky, and in addition a strange bird hovered over Moscow at night, cawing loudly, proclaiming his death. It was said that the bird was of enormous size and that it would continue its loud cawing until the moment he died. And so it happened.

IOVAN
BASILLI
GRĀ DVCA
DI MOSCOVIA
stampato nouamente·

Ivan in old age, a seventeenth-century portrait.

He hoped he would die quietly, without pain, but with just sufficient warning to enable him to offer up his prayers for salvation at the last moment. Many years before he had written a hymn to the Archangel Michael, "the leader of the heavenly hosts and guardian of all mankind," in which he asked that every day and most especially when he lay dead and his body was giving off a fearful stench, this hymn would be chanted. The terrible emperor addressed the terrible angel:

> Before thy fearful and terrible coming,
> Pray for thy sinful servant.
> Let me know when my time comes,
> That I may repent of my evil deeds
> And throw off my burden of sin.
> I shall travel a long journey with thee.
> O fearful and terrible angel,
> Do not terrify me, for I am helpless.
>
> O holy angel of Christ, O terrible leader of the hosts,
> Have mercy upon me, thy sinful servant.
> When, O angel, the time comes to summon me
> And to separate my soul from my wretched body,
> Then come gently, let me look upon thee joyfully,
> And dost thou look upon me reassuringly.
> O fearful and terrible angel,
> Do not let thy coming terrify me.

There were many more anguished verses, and it was clear that he had thought deeply about death and his inevitable encounter with the terrible angel. Indeed, death was the one subject he knew best.

Yet life still stirred in him; he still lusted after women. When the beautiful Tsarevna Irina, the wife of Fyodor, entered his bedroom to inquire after his health, he half-rose from the bed and attempted to throw his arms round her. She screamed and ran from the room. He still lusted after his wealth, and every day he was carried in his chair into the treasury to gaze upon the accumulated wealth of the Tsars. On one of these occasions, only a few days before his death, he beckoned to Jerome Horsey to accompany him. Horsey observed that Ivan had begun "grievously to swell of the cods, with which he had most horribly offended above fifty years altogether, boasting of a thousand virgins he had deflowered and thousands of children of his begetting destroyed."

In the treasury Ivan discoursed on his treasures. They included loadstones, which possessed the "great and hidden virtue" of enabling mariners to navigate their ships and to keep the tomb of the Prophet Mohammed hanging in midair in the mosque at Derbent. He then ordered some needles to be touched with the loadstone and marvelled to see them hanging together in a chain. Then he ordered coral and turquoise to be placed on his hand and arm, and observed that they suddenly grew pale, a sure sign that his death was imminent. "I am poisoned with disease," he said, and went on to contemplate a unicorn's horn which he called "my royal staff," and which like so many of his treasures was studded with diamonds, rubies, sapphires, and other jewels. This unicorn's horn had cost a fortune of seventy thousand marks sterling paid to the great banking family of the Fuggers at Augsburg. For many centuries it was believed that the unicorn's horn was wonderfully equipped to indicate the presence of poisons, but it could no longer cure the poisons in his blood. His mind darting, he turned to a wooden board, and ordered his court physician, Johan Eylof, a Dutchman, to scrape a circle on it with the horn and place a spider within the circle. The spider died; another died a little later; a third ran outside the circle and survived. Ivan was in despair. Of the unicorn's horn he said, "It is too late. It will not preserve me." [1]

Jerome Horsey was watching everything that happened with the intensity of a man who knows that strange things are spoken by dying emperors. Ivan was casting a long, last, helpless look at his treasures, and the Englishman remembered his words:

> "Behold these precious stones. This diamond is the Orient's richest and most precious of all other. I never affected it; it restrains fury and luxury and abstinacy and chastity; the least parcel of it in powder will poison a horse given to drink, much more a man." Points at the ruby. "O! this is most comfortable to the heart, brain, vigor, and memory of man, clarifies congealed and corrupt blood." Then at the emerald. "The nature of the rainbow, this precious stone is an enemy to uncleanness. Try it; though man and wife cohabit in lust together, having this stone about them, it will burst at the spending of nature.

---

[1] The belief in the miraculous power of the unicorn's horn against poison was widespread in Europe. Supposedly the horn sweated and changed color in the presence of poison. Queen Elizabeth possessed such a horn valued at £100,000. As late as 1789 a unicorn's horn was used to detect poison at the French court.

The sapphire I greatly delight in; it preserves and increaseth courage, joys the heart, pleasing to all the vital senses, precious and very sovereign for the eyes, clears the sight, takes away bloodshot, and strengthens the muscles and strings thereof." Then takes the onyx in hand. "All these are God's wonderful gifts, secrets in nature, and yet reveals them to man's use and contemplation, as friends to grace and virtue and enemies to vice. I faint; carry me away to another a time."

On March 17, 1584, Ivan felt better, took a bath, and sent out orders that the Lithuanian embassy which had been detained at Mozhaisk because of his illness should proceed at once to Moscow. It would take them two or three days to make the sixty-mile journey and by that time he thought he would be in better shape to receive them. On the following afternoon he read his will again, and sent Bogdan Belsky to see the Lapp magicians. Horsey tells us that the Lapps were quite certain he would die that day, and when Belsky reminded them that he was "as heart whole as ever he was," they replied, "Sir, be not so wrathful. You know the day is come and ends with the setting of the sun."

Meanwhile Ivan ordered his apothecary and physicians to prepare for his "solace," by which he meant that they should give him the various potions for his diseases, and afterward he took another bath. They heard him singing in his bath; he was evidently in high spirits. Returning from his bath, wearing a loose gown, shirt and linen hose, he sat down on his bed and called to Rodion Birkin, a nobleman from Ryazan, to bring out a chessboard. Bogdan Belsky, Boris Godunov, and other high officers of the court were standing around him. Jerome Horsey, who appears to have been present, relates that Ivan set the pieces on the board but could not make the king stand up properly. Suddenly he fainted and fell backward across the bed.

During these last years he had often suffered from fainting spells, but it was clear that this was no ordinary fainting spell. There was a lot of shouting and running about. Someone sent for brandy, someone else called the doctors and the apothecary, rose water and marigold were brought to him, but it was all in vain. Within a few minutes, in Sir Jerome Horsey's words, "he was strangled and stark dead."

Yet there were some who still believed there might be some life in him. Twice before he had suffered from strokes, and had recovered.

Therefore the court officials remained silent, afraid that if they gave way to grief or rejoicing the Tsar would hear them. Only Feodosy Viatka, the Tsar's confessor, seemed to know exactly what should be done. He dressed the dead man in a monk's robe and put a monk's cowl on his head, and gave him a new name, and performed the ceremony appropriate for a living man who enters the community of monks. Ivan had hoped that like his father he would become a monk before dying. Instead he became a monk after his death, acquiring the new name of Iona.

The four Regents were all in Moscow and the transfer of power took place quietly and efficiently, with the overwhelming use of military power. All the Kremlin gates were closed, all the gunners on the walls were ordered to be ready to fire at a moment's notice to put down any rebellion by a usurper who might attempt to seize the throne. The treasury was sealed off; the guards were mounted; the matches for firing off the great cannon were lit. On the terrace of the Kremlin Palace Boris Godunov gave out orders. When Sir Jerome Horsey hurried up to him, and offered himself, his servants, powder and pistols to the new lord protector of Russia, his services were accepted. "Be faithful and fear not!" Godunov said with a cheerful countenance. He and the other Regents had long ago mapped out the strategies of the transfer of power.

The Tsarevich Fyodor entered the bedroom where Ivan lay in his monk's habit. He wept uncontrollably, and was followed by the Metropolitan with a train of priests, who also wept. The Metropolitan chanted:

> Where is the city of Jerusalem?
> Where is the wood of the life-giving Cross?
> Where is our Lord Tsar, the Grand Prince Ivan
>   Vasilievich of all Russia?
> Why hast thou left thy Russian Tsardom and thy
>   noble children and left us all orphans?

Having uttered the conventional and yet deeply moving complaint, the Metropolitan set about consoling the Tsarevich and the nobles in the bedroom, urging them to place their trust in God and not to forget that a new Tsar would soon be on the throne. The Metropolitan hurried away to his palace to write letters to the archbishops and bishops all over Russia, summoning them to

The graves of Ivan the Terrible and his two sons Ivan (left) and Fyodor (right) in the Cathedral of Michael the Archangel in Moscow.

Moscow to attend the funeral and the coronation of the Tsar's successor.

For two days the body lay in an open coffin and the people crowded to see the man who could no longer punish them. They saw him wearing a monk's habit and there was an embroidered apron on his chest depicting the Crucifixion. They wept unrestrainedly not because they had any affection for him but because they were aware that an age died with him and because they were aware that the future might be even more terrible than the past. For fifty years they had known no other Tsar, and they wept too because they were bereft of a familiar figure, a known presence. They wept more for themselves than for the dead Tsar.

After the funeral service the coffin was laid beside the tomb of Tsarevich Ivan. Then it was bricked over, and in time a bronze sepulcher was fashioned, bearing his name and titles. Songs were sung about him and he entered into legend, suffering that strange process by which the legend escapes from history altogether. His virtues and vices were reassembled, and the people recreated a figure which bore little resemblance to the real Ivan. They saw him against the moonlight, gleaming with a fierce moonlit brightness, heroic and terrible, haunting their dreams. In the streets of Moscow they sang:

> O bright moon, O father moon,
> Why didst thou not shine as in former times,
> As in the ancient times long ago?
> It happened to us in Holy Russia,
> In stone-built Moscow, in the golden Kremlin,
> In the Uspensky Cathedral,
> In the Cathedral of Michael the Archangel.
> They struck the great bell
> And the echoes spread over all the moist Mother Earth.
> All the princes and boyars came together,
> All the warriors rode up together
> To offer prayers in the Uspensky Cathedral.
> There stood the newly fashioned cypress wood coffin,
> And in the coffin lay the Orthodox Tsar—
> The Orthodox Tsar, Ivan Vasilievich, the Terrible!
> The life-giving Cross stood at his head,
> And beside the Cross lay the Tsar's crown,
> At his feet the sharp and terrible sword.
> Everyone prays to the life-giving Cross,
> Everyone bows to the golden crown,
> Everyone looks trembling at the terrible sword.
> Around the coffin the wax candles are burning,
> And the priests and patriarchs all stand before the
>   coffin,
> Chanting and singing the service for the dead.
> Thus they bade farewell to our Orthodox Tsar—
> The Terrible Tsar—Ivan Vasilievich.

It was his fate to be remembered as the bearer of the sharp and terrible sword, the strange avenger who punished men for crimes they had never committed, the symbol of ruthless majesty let loose upon a people who yielded to him because he claimed to be their divinely appointed ruler. He had played with them like a small boy tearing off the wings of flies, and they bore him no resentment. He had spilled more Russian blood than any other Tsar, and they were proud they had so much blood to spare. Sometimes, in the troubled years following his death, they sang another song which showed that they wanted him back again:

> You have shone, O father moon!
> You shine, O moon, throughout the dark night—
> Light up, O moon, the stone city of Moscow!
> In the stone city of Moscow, in Holy Russia,
> Beside the Uspensky Cathedral,
> A young soldier is standing guard.
> He is standing guard and praying to God,
> He is praying to God and tearfully he cries:
> "O turbulent winds, hurl yourselves down from the
>   mountains!
> O winds, scatter the yellow sands!
> O moist Mother Earth, split open!
> Lift up, O tomb stone!
> Burst open, O thin white shroud!
> Rise up, rise up, O Orthodox Tsar,
> Our Orthodox Tsar, Ivan Vasilievich!"

The prayers of the young soldier remained unanswered, and there was no second coming of Ivan the Terrible. On April 23, 1953, a few weeks after the death of Stalin, his tomb was opened and the skeleton, with shreds of the monk's gown still clinging to it, was examined by Soviet authorities. They found little more than they had expected to find: the remains of a tall, barrel-chested, heavy-set man with a low forehead and long arms. From the examination of the bones it was clear that he had suffered from a peculiarly painful form of arthritis. They found traces of arsenic and quicksilver, but these were not sufficient to suggest he had been poisoned, for they were used in the medicaments of the time. A plaster cast was made of the skull and a sculptor attempted on the basis of the skull to reconstruct the features of the Tsar. Then, still wearing the shreds of his monk's robe and the embroidered apron depicting the Crucifixion, the remains of Ivan the Terrible were removed from the laboratory table and replaced in the coffin in the presence of movie cameras which recorded the scene for posterity. Then they covered him with sand and sealed the coffin.

Such was the second coming of Tsar and Grand Prince Ivan Vasilievich, known as Ivan the Terrible, who was descended from the ancient line of Rurik and from Byzantine emperors and from many obscure forefathers, a tormented man who visited his torments on his people. His greatest gift to the Russian people was his own death. By his mere presence, during the second half of his reign, he corrupted all the life around him, poisoning and defiling everything he touched. He left his country in disarray, exhausted by his savagery. He did all this with wide-open eyes, knowing at every moment what he was doing, his fierce intelligence undimmed by the knowledge that he was causing irremediable harm. In his own lifetime he was called "the Terrible," and he was more terrible than anyone can imagine. Not until our own time did anyone arise who could be compared with him.

The Great Seal of Ivan IV, 1583. The small circles represent his principalities and kingdoms. Kazan is represented by the winged chimaera, upper right.

Vasily II Tyomny,
Grand Prince of Moscow.
Born 1415,
died 1462.
Married Princess Maria of Borovsk, granddaughter of Fyodor Kosh
Maria died in 1485.

Ivan III	Anna
Grand Prince of Moscow and all Russia.	died 1501.
Born January 22, 1440,	Married Vasily,
died October 27, 1505.	Grand Prince of R
Married Sophia Palaeologina, died 1503.	From their daught
	descend the Princes

Vasily III	Yury
Grand Prince of all Russia.	Prince of Dmitrov.
Born March 25, 1479,	Born March 23, 1
died December 3, 1533.	died August 3, 153
First wife Salomonia Saburova,	in prison.
married 1505, divorced 1525 and	
forced to become a nun.	
Second wife Elena Glinskaya	
daughter of Prince Vasily	
Glinsky of Lithuania.	
Elena died April 3, 1538.	

Ivan IV	Yury
Tsar and Grand Prince of all Russia.	Prince of Uglich.
Born August 25, 1530,	Born October 30,
died March 18, 1584.	died June 24, 1563

of Staritsa.
ugust 5, 1490,
d February 2, 1533,
ecember 10, 1537,
n.

ir
of Staritsa.
ıly 9, 1535,
d October 9, 1569.
ife Evdokia,
er of Alexander Nagoy.
d September, 1550.
wife Evdokia, daughter
ce Roman Odoevsky.
d 1555. Odoevskaya was
d with her husband.

Evdokia
Born 1492,
Married Prince Kudaikul
(Pyotr Ibrahimovich)
of Kazan in 1506,
died 1513.

Two more sons and
two daughters.
Died before 1533.

Anastasia*
Married June 6, 1538,
Vasily Shuisky, the Regent.

Anastasia*
Married 1526,
Fyodor Mstislavsky

Ivan Mstislavsky
Born 1527 or 1528,
died 1586.

: wife,

of Dmitrov
552,
73 or 1574.

Evdokia
Born around 1553,
died November 20,
1570.

By second wife,
Maria
Born after 1555,
Married April 12, 1573
to Prince Magnus of
Denmark.

A Daughter,
executed in
1569 with her
parents.

Both daughters of Evdokia had the same name.

Ancestors of Ivan IV's Mother, Princess Elena Glinsk

IAKSHA   = NN   NN = N
Serbian voyevoda.
Died around 1453.

STEPHAN IAKSHICH   =   **MILITSA**
Voyevoda of Serbia.   Died afte
Died January 1489.   1506.

ANNA IAKSHICH
Married Vasily
Glinsky about
1500. Died after
1547. (In 1547 she was
accused of setting fire
to Moscow.) She was
Ivan IV's grandmother.

MIKHAIL GLINSKY   **YURY GLINSKY**
Died 1559.   Killed 1547.

Prince Boris = widow of   ESMAN = NN
Ivanovich | Prince Ivan   RAIEVSKY
GLINSKY | Koribut of
Died about | Lithuania.
1457.

PRINCE LEV GLINSKY = RAIEVSKAYA
He died in 1485.

Prince VASILY GLINSKY
His brother was the powerful
Mikhail Glinsky.
He died about 1515.

NA GLINSKAYA
ied in 1526 Grand Prince
y. Elena was the mother
an IV. She was Regent from
to 1538.

GENEALOGICAL TABLE III

showing descent of Ivan's grandmother, Sophia Palaeologina.

MANUEL II PALAEOLOGUS = HELEN DRAG
Emperor of Byzantium | daughter of
1391–1425 | Constantin
| Dragosh of
| Macedonia

THOMAS PALAEOLOGUS
Despot of Morea
1409–1465
married Catherine
Zaccaria in January 1430.
Thomas was the
younger brother of
the two Emperors
John VIII and
Constantine XI, the
last Emperor of
Byzantium.

From these three genealogical tables it can be seen that Ivan IV had Rus
Greek, Serbian, Genoese, Lithuanian, and, through Elena Glinskaya, pei
Tatar blood.

CENTURIONE ZACCARIA = CREUSA
Baron of Arcadia and   TOCCO
Prince of Achaia   daughter
Died 1432   of Leon-
The Zaccarias   ardo II
were originally   Tocco,
Genoese.   Lord of
                              Zante.

CATERINA ZACCARIA
Heiress of
Achaia
Died 1462.

IA (ZOE) PALAEOLOGINA
d Ivan III and was the
r of Vasily III

Glossary

Appanage Prince.	A Prince possessing his own state within the Grand Principality of Moscow, with his own army and court of boyars, nobles, and officials. The state was virtually independent, but foreign affairs were in the hands of the Grand Prince.
Boyar.	Boyars were members of the Grand Prince's council chosen from among the most important nobles' families. These families were known as the boyar families. Originally the boyar families were untitled. Then in the sixteenth century, after Moscow had absorbed all the other Russian states, the dispossessed prince of these states came to serve the Grand Prince of Moscow. The most important of these princes became members of the Boyar Council and their families merged with the old untitled boyar families of Moscow.
Kvas.	A Russian drink made from black bread and malt.
Lobnoye Mesto.	Literally, Upper Place. From *lob*, meaning forehead. The Lobnoye Mesto was on the crest of the ridge that cut across the Red Square.
Oprichnina.	Formerly a portion of an estate set apart for

the widow's use. From *oprich*, meaning separate. The *oprichniki*, or separated ones, were nobles and boyars selected by Ivan to serve him when he created his separate kingdom early in 1565. The Oprichnina was the vast area claimed by Ivan as his private and personal possession.

Serdechniki. People who remove hearts from corpses. From *serdtse*, meaning heart. The word appears to be unknown before 1547, when the Chronicles relate that hearts were being removed in Moscow and other towns.

Sinodiki. Books used in Orthodox churches inscribed with the names of the dead. These names were read out during the services with prayers to bring peace to their souls.

Skomorokhi. Entertainers, players, clowns, jugglers, musicians and singers who were invited to weddings and other celebrations. Appears to be derived from Scaramuccio ("skirmish"), a stock figure in Italian farces. Scaramuccio was beaten by Harlequin for his boasting and cowardice.

Terem. The private apartments of the Tsar and Tsaritsa, usually on the upper floors of their palaces. Also the women's part of a house.

Voyevoda. Military commander. Connected with *voina*, meaning war. Later used for a governor of a province.

Yurodivy. God's fools. Literally, foolish, crazy. It was believed that they wore their foolishness as a disguise and that their strange and unpredictable actions possessed deep spiritual meaning.

Zemshchina. From *zemlya*, meaning land. The territory that was not included in the Oprichnina. The *Zemskiye* were the people who lived in the Zemshchina.

Chronology

THE RUSSIAN CHRONOLOGY *has been used throughout. During the sixteenth century this was nine days behind the western calendar. Thus Ivan's birthday is given here as August 25, 1530, but according to the western calendar this would be September 3, 1530. Some complications occur because the Russian year was regarded as beginning in September. In documents of the period the Russians follow the Byzantine practice of dating all events from the creation of the world, which was supposed to have taken place in 5508 B.C. In contemporary documents the year of Ivan's birth is therefore given as 7038.*

1479	March 25	Birth of Vasily III
1505	September	Marriage of Vasily III to Salomonia Saburova
1526	January 21	Vasily III marries Elena Glinskaya
1530	August 25	Birth of Ivan
1532	October 30	Birth of Ivan's younger brother Yury
1533	December 3	Death of Vasily III
1533	December 11	Arrest of Ivan's uncle Yury
1534	August 3	Flight of Simeon Belsky to Lithuania
1534	August 5	Arrest of Mikhail Glinsky, the uncle of Grand Princess Elena
1534– 1537	July– January	War with Lithuania

1535	July 9	Birth of Ivan's cousin, Vladimir of Staritsa
1536	August	Death in prison of Ivan's uncle Yury
1536	September 15	Death in prison of Mikhail Glinsky
1537	June 2	Arrest of Ivan's uncle Andrey of Staritsa
1537	December	Death in prison of Andrey of Staritsa
1538	April 3	Death of Grand Princess Elena
1538	April 9	Arrest of Ivan Ovchina-Obolensky and of his sister Agrafena
1538	April–November	Vasily Shuisky in power
1538	October	First arrest of Ivan Belsky
1538–1540	November–July 25	Ivan Shuisky in power
1539	February	Metropolitan Daniel deposed by the Shuiskys
1539	February 6	Ioasaf Skrypitsyn becomes Metropolitan
1540–1542	July 25–January 3	Ivan Belsky in power
1541	July–August	Invasion of the Crimean Tatars
1542	January 3	Second arrest of Ivan Belsky by the Shuiskys
1542	January 3	Metropolitan Ioasaf deposed by Ivan Shuisky
1542	January 3–May	Ivan Shuisky again in power until his death
1542	March 16	Makary, Archbishop of Novgorod and Pskov, made Metropolitan
1542–1543	May–December 29	Andrey Shuisky in power
1542	May	Ivan Belsky dies in prison in Beloozero
1543	December 28	Andrey Shuisky arrested by Ivan's orders and killed
1543–	December–	Fyodor Vorontsov in favor

1545–1546	October–July	Struggle for power: Kubensky and the Vorontsovs against the Glinskys
1546	July 21	Execution of the boyars Ivan Kubensky, Fyodor and Vasily Vorontsov
1546–1547	July 21–June	The Glinskys in power
1547	January 16	Coronation of Ivan
1547	February 3	Marriage of Ivan and Anastasia Zakharina
1547	June 21	Great Fire of Moscow
1547–1560		Alexey Adashev, Sylvester, and the Chosen Council in power
1547	December	The Tsar's First Campaign against Kazan
1549	February 27	Convocation of clergy, boyars, and nobles in the Kremlin Palace
1549	March 3	Ivan's speech to the people on the Red Square
1549	February	Establishment of the Office of Petitions
1549	February 28	Powers of the provincial governors reduced
1549	August 10	Birth of Ivan's first child Anna
1549	November 24	The Tsar's Second Campaign against Kazan
1550	June	New Code of Laws compiled
1551	February 23	The Stoglav Council
1551	May	The building of Sviazhsk
1551	August 16	Shigaley made Khan of Kazan
1551	September	Ivan's throne placed in the Cathedral of the Assumption
1552	March 6	Shigaley leaves Kazan
1552	June 16	The Tsar's Third Campaign against Kazan
1552	June	Crimean Tatars invade Russia
1552	October	Capture of Kazan
1552	October	Birth of Ivan's son Dmitry
1553	March	Ivan's illness

1553	June	Death of Dmitry
1553	June	Coming of the English
1554	March 28	Birth of Ivan's second son Ivan
1554	July 2	Conquest of Astrakhan
1558	January	Beginning of the Livonian War
1558	May 11	Capture of Narva by the Russians
1559	Spring	Daniel Adashev's raid against the Crimean Peninsula
1560	August 7	Death of Anastasia
1560	Winter	The fall of Alexey Adashev and Sylvester
1561	August 31	Ivan's marriage to Princess Kocheney (Maria Temriukovna)
1562	March	War with Lithuania resumes
1563	February 15	Ivan captures Polotsk
1563	Spring	First executions: relatives of Alexey Adashev
1563	November 24	Death of Ivan's brother Yury
1563	December 31	Death of the Metropolitan Makary
1564	January 30	Murder of Mikhail Repnin
1564	March 5	Ivan's confessor Andrey Protopopov becomes Metropolitan Afanasy
1564	March	*Apostol* printed by Ivan Fyodorov
1564	April 30	Flight of Andrey Kurbsky
1564	May	Kurbsky's first letter to Ivan
1564	July 5	Ivan's reply to Kurbsky
1564	July	Dmitry Ovchina-Obolensky strangled at Ivan's orders
1564	Summer	Protests are made by Metropolitan Afanasy and the boyars
1564	November	Rafaello Barberini visits Ivan
1564	December 3	Ivan leaves Moscow
1565	January	Establishment of the Oprichnina
1565	February	Second period of mass executions: Prince Alexander Gorbaty-Shuisky and other important nobles
1566	May 19	Metropolitan Afanasy retires
1566	May	Herman, Archbishop of Kazan, ap-

		pointed Metropolitan and removed two days later
1566	June 28–July 2	Council concerning peace with Lithuania
1566	July 25	Philipp Kolychov, Abbot of Solovetsky Monastery, becomes Metropolitan
1566	Summer	A deputation of nobles asks Ivan to abolish the Oprichnina
1566	Fall	Third period of mass executions: nobles who asked that the Oprichnina be abolished
1567	Spring–Summer	Letters from King Sigismund II Augustus of Poland and Lithuania to Ivan Belsky, Ivan Mstislavsky, Mikhail Vorotynsky, and Ivan Cheliadnin
1568	Most of the year	Fourth and worst period of mass executions
1568	March 22	First public confrontation between Ivan and Metropolitan Philipp
1568	July 28	Second public confrontation between Ivan and the Metropolitan, at Novodevichy Monastery
1568	September 11	Murder of the boyar Ivan Cheliadnin
1568	November 4	Trial of the Metropolitan Philipp
1568	November 6	Murder of Archbishop Herman
1568	November 8	Metropolitan Philipp arrested in church and deposed
1568	November 11	Kirill, Abbot of Troitsa Sergeyevsky Monastery, made Metropolitan
1569	September 6	Death of Maria Temriukovna
1569	October	Fifth period of mass executions: execution of Vladimir of Staritsa, his wife and daughter, and their noblewomen (October 9); execution of Vladimir's mother Efrosinia (October 11); executions of vari-

		ous other persons connected with the Staritskys
1569	November–December	Fall of the chief oprichniki Alexey and Fyodor Basmanov and of Afanasy Viazemsky
1569–1570	December–March	Sixth period of mass executions: punitive expedition against Novgorod, Pskov, Tver, and other towns
1569	December 23	Metropolitan Philipp murdered by Maliuta Skuratov
1570	May	Jan Rakita's dispute with Ivan on religion
1570	June	Prince Magnus of Denmark made King of Livonia by Ivan and betrothed to the daughter of Vladimir of Staritsa
1570	June	Peace with Lithuania
1570	July	Seventh period of mass executions: execution of Ivan Viskovaty and many other prominent officials
1571	May	Tatar invasion and the flight of Ivan to Vologda
1571	May 24	Tatars burn Moscow
1571	June	Eighth period of mass executions: execution of chief oprichniki
1571	October 28	Ivan marries Marfa Sobakina, his third wife. She dies shortly thereafter
1572	April	Ivan marries Anna Koltovskaya, his fourth wife
1572	June 1	Ivan goes to Novgorod to escape an expected Tatar invasion
1572	July 26–August 2	Invasion of Russia by the Crimean Tatars and their defeat at Molodi
1572	July 18	Death of Sigismund II Augustus, King of Poland and of Lithuania
1572	Fall	Abolition of the Oprichnina
1573	Summer	Mikhail Vorotynsky's arrest and death

1574–1575	Late or Early	Dr. Eliseus Bomelius executed
1575	May	Ivan's fourth wife, Anna Koltovsk-aya, sent to a nunnery
1575		Ivan marries Anna Vasilchikova, his fifth wife
1575	Summer	Arrest of Archbishop Leonid of Novgorod and Pskov
1575	Fall	Ninth and last period of mass execu-tions: execution of about 40 no-bles and priests in Moscow
1575	Fall	Simeon Bekbulatovich made Grand Prince of all Russia by Ivan
1576	February	Ivan receives the ambassadors of the Emperor Maximilian II at Mo-zhaisk
1576	May 1	Stephen Bathory crowned King of Poland
1576	Fall	Simeon Bekbulatovich removed by Ivan
1577		Death of Anna Vasilchikova, and in the same year Ivan marries Vasil-isa Melentieva, his sixth wife
1577		Ivan invades Livonia and takes all of it except for Riga and Reval
1577	September 12	Ivan's second letter to Andrey Kurb-sky from the Livonian city of Volmar
1578	August	Danish ambassador Jacob Ulfeld at Alexandrova Sloboda
1578	October 21	Defeat of the Russian army at the Livonian city of Venden
1578	October–November	Andrey Kurbsky's third letter to Ivan
1579	August 30	Stephen Bathory's First Campaign against Ivan and the capture of Polotsk
1579	September 3	Andrey Kurbsky's fourth letter to Ivan, from Polotsk

1579	September 29	Andrey Kurbsky's fifth letter to Ivan
1579–1580	Winter	Ivan summons Church Council and demands contributions for the war
1580	Winter–Summer	Jerome Horsey's mission to England to obtain war supplies
1580	Summer	Ivan marries Maria Nagaya, his seventh and last wife
1580	September 7	Stephen Bathory's Second Campaign against Ivan and the capture of Veliki Luki
1581–1582	August–January	Stephen Bathory's Third Campaign and the siege of Pskov
1581	Fall	Narva captured by the Swedes
1581	September 1	Yermak Timofeevich sets out against the Khan of Siberia
1581	November 19	The Tsar kills his son Ivan
1582	January 15	Peace between Ivan and Stephen Bathory
1582	February–March	Religious discussions between Ivan and Possevino
1582–1583	August–June	Pissemsky's mission to England to arrange the marriage between Ivan and Mary Hastings
1582	October 19	Birth of Ivan's fourth son Dmitry
1582	October 26	Yermak takes the Khan's capital of Sibir
1583	February	Ivan Koltso brings news of the conquest of Siberia to Moscow
1583	July	Jerome Bowes' embassy to Moscow
1584	March 18	Death of Ivan

Bibliography

The following abbreviations have been used:

AE   Arkheografichesky ezhegodnik
AIK   Annales de l'Institut Kondakov
ANORYaS   Akademiya Nauk, Otdeleniye russkogo yazyka i slovestnosti, SPB
Chteniya   Chteniya, Obshchestvo Istorii i Drevnostey, Moscow, Universitet
GBL   Gosudarstvennaya biblioteka im. Lenina
IA   Istorichesky Arkhiv
IZ   Istoricheskiye Zapiski, Moscow
L   Leningrad
LGPI   Leningradsky gosudarstvenny pedagogichesky institut
LZAK   Letopis Zaniatiy Arkheologicheskoy Kommissii
M   Moscow
M-L   Moscow-Leningrad
OSP   Oxford Slavonic Papers
OCP   Orientalia Christiana Periodica, Rome
PDPI   Pamiatniki Drevney Pismennosti i Iskusstva, St. Petersburg
PSRL   Polnoye Sobraniye Russkikh Letopisey
RAOS   Russkoye Arkheologicheskoye Obshchestvo v Yugoslavii, Sbornik
RIZ   Russky Istorichesky Zhurnal
SEER   Slavonic and East European Review
SK   Seminarium Kondakovianum
SR   Slavic Review
SPB   St. Petersburg
TODRL   Trudy otdela drevnerusskoy literatury
UZ   Uchonye Zapiski
VY   Vestnik Yevropy
VI   Voprosy istorii
ZMNP   Zhurnal ministerstva narodnogo prosveshcheniya
ZNRIB   Zapiski russkogo nauchnogo instituta v Belgrade

Aleksandro-nevskaya letopis. PSRL, XXIX. M, 1965.

Alekseeva, O. B. et al., eds. *Istoricheskiye pesni XVII veka.* M–L, 1966.

Alpatov, M. V. *Art Treasures of Russia.* New York: Harry N. Abrams, n.d.

Alshits, D. N. "Ivan Grozny i pripiski k litsevym svodam ego vremeni." IZ, (1947), 251–289.

———. "Istochniki i kharakter redaktsionnoy raboty Ivana Groznogo nad istoriey svoego tsarstvovaniya," *Trudy otdela rukopisey Gos. pub. bibl. im. M. E. Saltykova-Schedrina,* Vol. I (IV) L, 1957, 119–146.

———. "Proizkhozhdeniye i osobennosti istochnikov povestvuyushchikh o boyarskom miatezhe 1553 goda." IZ, 25 (1948), 266–292.

———. "Tsar Ivan Grozny ili diak Ivan Viskovaty?" TODRL, XVI, M, (1960) 617–625.

Andreyev, N. "Filofey and his Epistle to Ivan Vasilievich," SEER, 90 (1959), 1–31.

———. "Inok Zinovy Otensky ob ikonopochitanii i ikonopisi," SK, 8 (1936), 259–278.

———. "Interpolations in the Sixteenth Century Muscovite Chronicle." SEER, 84 (1956), 95–115.

———. "Ioann Grozny i ikonopis XVI veka." AIK, 10 (1938), 180–200.

———. "Kurbsky's Letter to Vassian Muromtsev." SEER, 81 (1955), 414–436.

———. "Literatura i ikonopis. K istorii idey v Moskovskoy Rusi." In *To Honor Roman Jakobson.* The Hague, Mouton, 1967.

———. "Mitropolit Makary kak deyatel religioznogo iskusstva." SK, 7 (1935), 227–244.

———. "Mnimaya tema—o spekuliatsiakh E. Kinana." *Novy Zhurnal,* No. 109 (1972), 258–272.

———. "Ob avtore pripisok v litsevykh svodakh Groznogo." TODRL, 18 (1962), 117–148.

———. "O dele diaka Viskovatogo." SK, 5 (1932), 191–241.

———. *Studies in Muscovy. Western Influences and Byzantine Inheritance.* London, 1970.

Antipin, G. G. *Zariadiye.* M, 1973.

Artsikovsky, A. B. *Drevnerusskiye miniatiury kak istorichesky istochnik.* M, 1944.

Astakhova, A. M., et al., eds. *Istoricheskiye pesni XIII–XVI vekov.* M–L, 1960.

Badigin, K. S. *Korsary Ivana Groznogo.* Roman—khronika vremen XVI veka. M, 1973.

Bakhrushin, S. V. *Ivan Grozny.* M, 1945.

———. "The Problem of Feudalism in Lithuania, 1506–1548." SR, 21 (1962), 639–659.

Barberini, Raffaello. "Relatione di Moscovia." In A. Olearius, *Viaggi di Moscovia.* Viterbo, 1658, 192–222.

Barenbaum, I. E., and Davydova, T. E. *Istoriya knigi.* M, 1971.

Barsov, I. V. *Drevne-russkiye pamiatniki sviashchennogo venchaniya tsarey na tsarstvo. Slavistic Reprintings,* The Hague, Mouton, 1969. i–xxxv, 1–90.

Barsukov, A. *Rod Sheremetevykh.* SPB, 1881–1904. 8 vols.

Belokurov, S. A. *O posolskom prikaze.* M, 1906.

Belov, E. A. "Ob istoricheskom znachenii russkogo boyarstva do kontsa XVII veka." ZMNP, 243 (1886), 68–127; 244, 29–75.

Berry, L. E. and Crummey, R. O., eds. *Rude & Barbarous Kingdom. Russia in the Accounts of Sixteenth Century English Voyagers.* Madison, Wisc.: University of Wisconsin Press, 1968.

Bibikov, G. N. "K voprosu o sotsialnom sostave oprichnikov Ivana Groznogo." In *Trudy GIM,* 14. M, 1941, 5–28.

Blum, J. *Lord and Peasant in Russia from the Ninth to the Nineteenth Century.* Princeton, Princeton University Press, 1961.

Bobrinskoy, Count A. *Dvorianskiye rody vnesennye v obshchy gerbovnik vserossiiskoy imperii.* SPB, 1890.

Bocharov, G. N., and Vygolov, V. P. *Aleksandrovskaya Sloboda.* M, 1970.

Bode-Kolychov, M. L. *Boyarsky Rod Kolychovykh.* M, 1886.

Bogdanovsky, N. "Inzhenerno-istorichesky ocherk osady Kazani v 1552 g," *Inzhenerny zhurnal*, 8 (1898), Pt. I, 1021–1055; 9 (1898), Pt. I, 1149–1178.

Bogoyavlensky, S. K. "Dopros Tsaria Ivana Groznogo russkikh plennikov vyshedshikh iz Kryma." *Chteniya*, 2 (1912), Smes 26–33.

———. "O pushkarskom prikaze," *Sbornik statey v chest Liubavskogo*. SPB, 1917.

———, and Novitsky, G. A. eds. *Gosudarstvennaya oruzhevnaya palata*. M, 1954.

Bond, Sir Edward A. *Russia at the Close of the Sixteenth Century*. London, Hakluyt Society, 1856.

Budovnits, I. U. *Monastyri na Rusi i borba s nimi krestian v XIV–XVI vekakh*. M, 1966.

Buganov, V. I. "Dokumenty o srazhenii pri molodiakh v 1572 godu." IA, 4 (1950), 166–183.

———, ed. *Razriadnaya kniga 1475–1598 gg*. M, 1966.

———, "Povest o pobede nad Krymskimi tatarami v 1572 g." AE (1961), 259–275.

———, and Koretsky, V. I. "Neizvestny moskovsky letopisets XVII veka iz muzeynogo sobraniya GBL," *Zapiski otdela rukopisey*, 32. M, 1971, 127–167.

Bukadorov, I. F. *Istoriya kazachestva*. Vol. I. Prague, 1930.

Burdey, G. D. "Molodinskaya bitva 1572 goda." In *Iz istorii mezhslavianskikh sviazey*, 26. Uchenye Zapiski Instituta Slaviano-vedeniya, 1973, 48–79.

Bushchik, A. P. *Illiustrirovannaya istoriya SSSR XV–XVII vekov*. M, 1971.

Chadwick, N. K. *Russian Heroic Poetry*. Cambridge, England: Cambridge University Press, 1932.

Chaev, N. S. "K voprosu o syske i prikreplenii krestian v Moskovskom gosudarstve v kontse XVI veka." IZ 6 (1940), 149–166.

———, "Teoriya 'Moskva—Tretii Rim' v politicheskoy praktike Moskovskogo pravitelstva XVI veka." IZ, 17 (1945).

Cherepnin, L. V. *Obrazovaniye russkogo tsentralizovannogo gosudarstva v XIV–XV vekakh*. M, 1960.

———. "Zemskiye sobory i utverzhdeniye absoliutizma v Rossii." In *Absoliutizm v Rossii*. M, 1964, 92–133.

Chernov, A. V. *Vooruzhenye sily Russkogo gosudarstva, v XV–XVII vv.*, M, 1954.

Cowie, Leonard W. *The Reformation of the Sixteenth Century*. New York, G. P. Putnam's Sons, 1970.

Culpepper. J. M. "The Kremlin Executions of 1575 and the Enthronement of Simeon Bekbulatovich." SR, 24 (1965), 503–506.

Daen, M. E., "Novootkryty pamiatnik." In O. I. Podobedova et al., *Drevnerusskoye iskusstvo*. M, 1970, 206–225.

Dal, V. *Tolkovy slovar zhivogo velikorusskogo yazyka*. 2d ed. SPB, 1880–1882; reprint, 1955. 4 vols.

Demkova, N. S. and Droblenkova, N. F. "K izucheniyu slavianskikh azbuchnykh stikhov." In TODRL, Vol. XXIII, L, 1968, 27–61.

Denisova, M. M. *Russkoye oruzhiye XI–XIX vv*. M, 1953.

Dewey, H. W. "The Decline of the Muscovite Namestnik." OSP, 12 (1965), 21–39.

———. "The White Lake Charter." *Speculum*, 32 (1957), 74–83.

Diakonov, M. A., *Ocherki obshchestvennogo i gosudarstvennogo stroya drevney Rusi*. 3d ed. SPB, 1910.

———, *Vlast Moskovskikh gosudarey*. SPB, 1889.

Dictionary of National Biography. London, Oxford University Press, 1967.

Dmitrieva, R. P. *Skazaniye o kniaziakh Vladimirskikh*. M-L, 1955.

Dovnar-Zapolsky, N. V. "Torgovlya i promyshlennost Moskvy v XVI–XVII vv." In *Moskva v proshlom i nastoyashchem*. Vol. VI M, n.d., 5–67.

Dukhovnye i dogovornye gramoty velikikh i udelnikh kniazey XIV–XVI vekov. Edited by S. V. Bakhrushin and L. V. Cherepnin. M-L, 1950.

Eaton, Henry L. "Cadasters and Censuses in Muscovy." SR, 26 (1967), 54–69.

Eckardt, H. von. *Ivan the Terrible*. New York: Alfred A. Knopf, 1949.

Entsiklopedichesky slovar. SPB, Brockhaus-Efron, 1890–1904.

Ermolinskaya letopis (up to 1533), PSRL, XXIII, SPB, 1910.

Evgenieva, A. P. and Putilov, B. N. *Drevniye rossiiskiye stikhotvoreniya sobrannye Kirsheyu Danilovym*. M-L, 1958.

Fedotov, G. P. *The Russian Religious Mind*. Cambridge, Harvard University Press, 1966.

——. *Sviatye drevney Rusi*. Paris: YMCA Press, 1931.

——. *Sviatoy Filipp, mitropolit moskovsky*. Paris: YMCA Press, 1928.

Fekhner, M. V. *Torgovlya russkogo gosudarstva so stranami vostoka v XVI veke*. M, 1956.

Fennell, J. L. Jr., ed. *The Correspondence Between Prince A. M. Kurbsky and Tsar Ivan IV of Russia, 1564–1579.* Cambridge: Cambridge University Press, 1955.

——, ed. *Prince Kurbsky's History of Ivan IV*. Cambridge, Cambridge University Press, 1965.

Findeizen, N. *Ocherki po istorii muzyki v Rossii*, I. M-L, 1928.

Fisher, Alan W. "Muscovy and the Black Sea Slave Trade." *Canadian-American Slavic Studies*. University of Pittsburgh, Volume 6, No. 4, winter 1972, 575–594.

Fisher, R. H. *The Russian Fur Trade 1550–1700*. Berkeley, University of California Press, 1943.

Fletcher, G. "Of the Russe Common Wealth." In E. A. Bond, ed., *Russia at the Close of the Sixteenth Century*. London: Hakluyt Society, 1856.

Florinsky, M. T., *Russia: A History and Interpretation*. New York: Macmillan, 1955.

Gerasimov, M. M. *The Face Finder*. Translated by A. Broderick. London, Hutchinson, 1971.

Golubinsky, E. E. *Istoriya russkoy tserkvi*. M, 1900–1917. 2 vols. (2 parts to each vol.)

Gorbachevsky, N. *Arkheograficheskiy kalendar na dve tysiachi let*. Vilna, 1869.

Gorsky, S. *Zhizn i istoricheskoye znacheniye kniazia Andreya Mikhailovicha Kurbskogo*. Kazan, 1858.

Grabar, I. E., ed. *Istoriya russkogo iskusstva*, Vol. III. M, 1955.

Graham, Stephen. *Ivan the Terrible*. Hamden, Archon Books, 1968.

Grekov, B. D. *Krestiane na Russi*, Vol. II, 2nd ed. M, 1954.

Grey, Ian, *Boris Godunov*, New York, Charles Scribner's Sons, 1973.

——, *Ivan the Terrible*. London: Hodder and Stoughton, 1964.

Grigoriev, G. L., "Zaveshchaniye Ivana Groznogo." VI, 4 (1972).

G.S.Sh. *Kniaz Afanasy Danilovich, syn kniazia Daniila Aleksandrovicha Moskovskogo*. SPB, M. M. Stasiulevich, 1908.

Gudzy, N. K. *Istoriya drevney russkoy literatury*. 7th ed. M, 1962.

——. *Khristomatiya po drevney russkoy literature XI–XVI vekov*. M, 1962.

Gumilevsky, Dmitry (Archbishop Filaret), *Obzor russkoy dukhovnoy literatury*. Vol. I, 3rd edition, SPB, 1884.

Hakluyt, Richard. *The Principal Navigations Voyages Traffiques and Discoveries of the English Nation*. 2 vols. London: J. M. Dent; New York: E. P. Dutton, 1926.

Halecki, O. "Possevino's Last Statement on Polish-Russian Relations," OCP (1953), 261–302.

Hamel, J. V. *Russia and England*. London, 1854.

Hammerich, L., R. Jakobson et al., eds. *Tonnies Fenne's Low German Manual of Spoken Russian*. Pskov, 1607; Copenhagen, 1961.

Heidenstein, R. *Zapiski o Moskovskoy voine (1578–1582)*. SPB, 1889.

Hellie, Richard, *Enserfment and Military Change in Muscovy*, The University of Chicago Press, 1972.

Herberstein, Sigmund von. *Commentaries on Muscovite Affairs*. Edited and translated by O. P. Backus. Lawrence, University of Kansas Press, 1956.

———. *Description of Moscow and Muscovy, 1557*. Edited by Bertold Picard and translated by J. B. C. Grundy. London. Dent & Sons, 1969.

———. *Rerum Moscoviticarum Commentarii*. Translated by E. H. Major. London: Hakluyt Society, 1851.

Hopf, Charles, *Chroniques Gréco-Romaines*, Berlin, Librairie de Weidman, 1873.

Horsey, Sir Jerome. "Travels." In E. A. Bond, ed. *Russia at the Close of the Sixteenth Century*. London: Hakluyt Society, 1856. Reprint, New York: Burt Franklin, n.d.

———. *Zapiski o Moskovii XVI veka Sera Dzheroma Gorseya*. Translated N. A. Belozerskaya. Foreword by N. I. Kostomarov. SPB, 1909.

Howes, R. C. *The Testament of the Grand Princes of Moscow*. Ithaca, Cornell University Press, 1967.

Hulbert, E. "The Zemsky Sobor of 1575; A Mistake in Translation." SR, 25 (1966), 320–322.

Iasinsky, A. N. *Sochineniya kniazia kurbskogo kak istorichesky material*. Kiev, 1889.

Istoriya Moskvy. Period feodalizma, XII–XVI vv. Vol. I. M, 1952.

Kapitokhin, A. A., and Yakovlev, I. V. *Pokrovsky sobor*. M, 1970.

Kappeler, Andreas. *Ivan Groznyj im Spiegel der ausländischen Druckschriften seiner Zeit. Ein Beitrag zur Geschichte des westlichen Russlandbildes.* Herbert Lang, Bern, Peter Lang, Frankfurt/M, 1972.

Karamzin, N. M. *Istoriya gosudarstva rossiiskogo*. 4th ed. SPB, A. Smirdin, 1833–1835. Vols. 7–10.

Karger, M. K. *Novgorod Veliky*. M-L, 1961.

Karlinsky, S. "*Domostroy as Literature.*" SR 24 (1965), 497–502.

Kashtanov, S. M. *Sotsialno-politicheskaya istoriya Rossii kontsa XV–pervoy poloviny XVI veka*. M, 1967.

———. "Finansovaya problema v period provedeniya Ivanom Groznym politiki udela." IZ (1968), 82, 243–272.

Kazakova, N. A. *Ocherki po istorii russkoy obshchestvennoy mysli. Pervaya tret XVI v.* L, 1970.

———. *Vassian Patrikeev*. M-L, 1960.

Kazanskaya istoriya. Compiled by G. N. Moiseeva. Edited by V. P. Adrianova-Peretts.

Kazansky letopisets. PSRL, XIX. SPB, 1903, M, 1954.

Keenan, Edward L. *The Kurbskii-Groznyi Apocrypha*. Cambridge, Harvard University Press, 1971.

Khoroshevich, A. L. "Byt i kultura russkogo naroda po slovariu Tonni Fenne 1607 g." In *Novoye o proshlom nashey strany*. M, 1967, 200–217.

Khrushchev, I. *Issledovaniye o sochineniyakh Iosifa Sanina*. SPB, 1968.

Kirchner, W. *Commercial Relations Between Russia and Europe, 1400–1800*. Bloomington, Indiana University Press, 1966.

Kireevsky, P. ed. "Russkiye narodnye pesni," *Chteniya*, 1848, No. 9, Book 22, Part IV, 145–226.

Klevanov, Alexander, trans. "Kritiko-literaturnoye obozreniye puteshestvennikov po Rossii do 1700 goda i ikh sochineniy Fredrika Adelunga. *Chteniya*, M. 1848, No. 9, Book 22, Part III, 1–48.

Klibanov, A. I. *Reformatsionnye dvizheniya v Rossii v XIV–pervoy polovine XVI vekov*. M, 1960.

Kliuchevsky, V. O. *A History of Russia*. Translated by C. J. Hogarth. Vol. II. New York: E. P. Dutton, 1912.

———. *Boyarskaya duma drevney Rusi*. 3d ed. M, 1902.

———. *Drevnerusskiya zhitiya kak istorichesky istochnik*. M, 1871.

———. "Kharakteristika Tsaria Ivana Groznogo." *Rodnaya rech*. 1917, No. 81.

———. *Sochineniya*. Vol. II. M, 1957.

Kobrin, V. B. "Sostav oprichnogo dvora Ivana Groznogo." AE (1959), M, 1960, 16–91.

Kondakov, N. P. *The Russian Icon.* Translated by E. H. Minns. Oxford: Clarendon Press, 1927.

Kopanev, A. I. "Naseleniye russkogo gosudarstvo v XVI veke." IZ, 64 (1957), 233–254.

——, "Nezemledelcheskaya volost v XVI–XVII vv." In *Krestianstvo i klassovaya borba v feodalnoy Rossii.* L, 1957.

Koretsky, V. I. *Zakreposhcheniye krestian i klassovaya borba v Rossii.* M, 1970.

Koroliuk, V. D. *Livonskáya voina.* M, 1954.

Korotkov, I. A. *Ivan Grozny: Voennaya deyatelnost.* M, 1952.

Koslow, Jules, *Ivan the Terrible.* New York, Hill and Wang, 1961.

Kostomarov, N. "Lichnost Tsaria Ivana Vasilievicha Groznogo." VY, Vol. 5 (Oct. 1871), 500–571.

——, *Russkaya istoriya v zhizneopisaniyakh ee glavneyshikh deyateley.* 2d ed. SPB, 1881. 2 vols.

Kozanchikov, D. E., ed. *Stoglav.* SPB, 1863.

Krestinin, Vasily. *Istoricheskiye nachatki o Dvinskom narode, drevnikh, srednikh, novykh i noveishikh vremen.* SPB, 1784.

——, *Istorichesky opyt o selskom starinnom domostroitelstve Dvinskogo naroda v severe.* SPB, 1785.

Kuntsevich, G. Z. *Istoriya o kazanskom tsarstve ili kazansky letopisets.* LZAK, Vol. XVI, SPB, 1905.

——, ed. *Sochineniya Kniazia Kurbskogo.* SPB, 1914.

Kurat, A. N. "The Turkish Expedition to Astrakhan in 1569 and the Problem of the Don-Volga Canal." SEER, 94 (1961), 7–23.

Kurbsky, Prince Andrey M. "Predisloviye mnogogreshnogo Andreya Yaroslavskogo na knigu siyu dostoynuyu naritsatisia Novy Margarit." In *Skazaniya kniazia Kurbskogo.* Edited by Ustrialov, N. SPB, 1886, 269–277.

Kusheva, E. N. "K istorii khlopovstva v kontse XVI—nachala XVII vekov." IZ, 15 (1945), 70–96.

——. *Narody severnogo kavkaza i ikh sviazi s Rossiey v XVI–XVII vekakh.* M, 1963.

Kuznetsov, I. I. *Sviatye Blazhennye Vasily i Ioann Khrista radi moskovskiye chudotvortsy.* M, n.d.

Lappo, I. I. *Velikoye kniazhestvo Litovskoye za vremia ot zakliucheniya Liublinskoy unii do smerti Stefana Batoriya (1569–1586).* Vol. I, SPB, 1901.

——. *Zapadnaya Rossiya i ee soedineniye s Polshiey.* Prague, 1924.

Latysheva, G. L. and Rabinovich, M. G. *Moskva i moskovsky kray,* M. 1973.

Latysheva, G. P. and Rabinovich, M. G. *Moskva v dalekom proshlom.* M, 1966.

Lazarev, V. N., ed. *Drevnerusskoye iskusstvo XV—nachala XVI vekov.* M, 1963.

——. *Old Russian Murals and Mosaics from the XI to the XVI Century.* London: Phaedon Press; Greenwich, Conn.: New York Graphic Society, 1966.

Lebedevskaya letopis, PSRL, XXIX. M, 1965.

Leonid, Arkhimandrite, "Evangeliye 1564–1565 gg. Bibliograficheskoye izsledovaniye." PDPI, XXXVII, 1882.

——. "Poslaniye k neizvestnomu protiv liuterov, tvoreniye Parfeniya Yurodivogo, pisatelia XVI veka." PDPI, LX, 1886.

Leontiev, A. K. *Obrazovaniye prikaznoy sistemy upravleniya v Russkom gosudarstve.* M, 1961.

Letopis po voskresenskomy spisku (from 1354 to 1541). PSRL, VIII, SPB, 1859.

Letopisets nachala tsarstva tsaria i velikogo kniazia Ivana Vasilievicha. PSRL, XXIX, M, 1965.

Likhachev, D. S. *Chelovek v literature drevney Rusi.* M, 1958.

——. "Kanon i molitva angelu groznomu voevode Parfeniya Yurodivogo (Ivana Groznogo)." In *Rukopisnoye nasledstvo drevney Rusi.* L, 1972, 10–27.

————. *Kultura Rusi: epokha obrazovaniya russkogo natsionalnogo gosudarstva. konets XIV—nachalo XVI vv.* L, 1946.

————. *Kultura russkogo naroda* X–XVII v. M, 1961.

————, "Kurbsky i Grozny—byli li oni pisateliami?" In *Russkaya literatura*, 4. L (1972), 202–209.

————. *Natsionalnoye samosoznaniye drevney Rusi: ocherki iz oblasti russkoy literatury XI–XVII* v. M, 1945.

————, ed. *Puteshestviya russkikh poslov XVI–XVII vekov.* M-L, 1954.

————, *Tekstologiya* (na materialakh russkoy literatury X–XVII vv.). M-L, 1962.

———— and Dmitrieva, L. A. *Izbornik.* M, 1969.

Likhachev, N. P. *Biblioteka i arkhiv moskovskikh gosudarey v XVI stoletiye.* SPB, 1894.

————, *Razriadniye diaki XVI veka.* SPB, 1888.

Lileev, N. V. *Simeon Bekbulatovich.* Tver, 1891.

Liubovsky, M. K. *Ocherk istorii Litovsko-Russkogo gosudarstva do Liublinskoy unii vkliuchitelno.* 2nd ed., M, 1915.

Lurie, Ya. S. *Ideologicheskaya borba v russkoy publitsistike XV–XVI veka.* M-L, 1960.

————. *Povest o Drakule.* M-L, 1964.

Lvovskaya letopis, PSRL, XX; SPB, 1910 (Part 1 from 858 to 1533), 1914 (Part 2 from 1534 to 1560).

Lyzlov, A. I. *Skifskaya istoriya*, I, III, M, 1787.

Makary (Bulgakov), Metropolitan. *Istoriya Russkoy tserkvi.* SPB, 1877–1891. 12 vols.

Maksimovich, E. F. "Tserkovno-zemsky sobor 1549 goda." ZRNIB, 9 (1933), 1–15.

Malinin, V. *Starets Eleazarova monastyria Filofey i ego poslaniya.* M, 1901.

Malyshev, V. I., ed. *Povest o prikhozhed[y]e Stefana Batoriya na grad Pskov.* M-L, 1952.

Markevich, A. I. *Istoriya mestnichestva v Moskovskom gosudarstve v XV–XVII vekakh.* Odessa, 1888.

Massa, Isaak. *Kratkoye izvestiye o Moskovii v nachale XVII v.* M, 1937.

Mazurinsky letopisets, PSRL, XXXI. M, 1968.

Melnikov, N. M. *Yermak Timofeevich.* Asmere, Seine, 1961.

Miliukov, P. N. *Ocherki po istorii russkoy kultury*, 7th ed. M, 1918.

Miller, V. F. *Istoricheskiye pesni russkogo naroda XVI–XVII vekov.* ANORYaS, SPB, 1915.

Mirsky, D. S. *A History of Russian Literature: From the Earliest Times to the Death of Dostoyevsky.* New York: Alfred A. Knopf, 1927.

Mneva, N. E. *Iskusstvo Moskovskoy Rusi.* M, 1965.

Moiseeva, G. N., ed. *Kazanskaya istoriya.* M-L, 1954.

————, *Valaamskaya beseda—pamiatnik russkoy publitsistiki serediny XVI veka.* M-L, 1958.

Moleva, N. M. *Pskov.* M, 1969.

Morfill, W. R. *Russia.* London, T. Fisher Unwin, 1890.

Moskva v ee proshlom i nastoyashchem. Izdaniye posviashchennoye pamiati istorika Moskvy I. Ye. Zabelina. 6 volumes. M, Obrazovaniye, n.d.

Muraviev, A. N., *A History of the Russian Church*, London, 1842.

Myachin and Chernov, *Moscow.* M, 1967.

Nasonov, A. N. *Istoriya russkogo letopisaniya XI—nachala XVIII veka. Ocherki i issledovaniya.* M, 1969.

————. "Novye istochniki po istorii kazanskogo vziatiya." AE (1960), M, 1962.

———— ed. et al. *Ocherki istorii SSSR. Period feodalizma—konets XV—nachalo XVII v.* M, 1955.

————. *Pskovskiye letopisi.* M, 1941–1955, 2 vols.

Nechayev, V. V. "Ulichnaya zhizn Moskvy v XVI–XVII vv." In *Moskva v ee proshlom i nastoyashchem.* Vol. III. M, n.d., 56–80.

Nikolaevsky, P. B. "Russkaya propoved v XV–XVI vv." ZMNP, 2 (1868).

Nikonovskaya letopis. PSRL, XIII, SPB, 1904. (Nikon Chronicle)

Nosov, N. E. *Ocherki po istorii mestnogo upravleniya russkogo gosudarstva pervoy poloviny XVI veka.* M-L, 1957.

——. "Sobor primireniya 1549 goda i voprosy mestnogo upravleniya." In *Vnutvenniaya politika tsarizma* (seredina XVI—nachalo XX vv). L, 1967, 5–69.

——. *Stanovleniye soslovno-predstavitelnykh uchrezhdeny v Rossii. Izyskaniya o zemskoy reforme Ivana Groznogo.* L, 1969.

Novgorodskaya tretiya letopis. PSRL, III, SPB, 1841, 207–305.

Novgorodskaya vtoraya (arkhivskaya) letopis. PSRL, III, SPB, 1841, 121–201, PSRL, XXX, M, 1965.

Novgorodskiye letopisi. SPB, 1879.

Novodvorsky, V. *Borba za Livoniyu mezhdy Moskvoyu i Rechiyu pospolitoy* (1570–1582). SPB, 1904.

Novoselsky, A. A. *Borba Moskovskogo gosudarstva s tatarami v pervoy polovine XVII veka.* M-L, 1948.

"Novoye o proshlom nashey strany." In *Pamiati akademika M. M. Tikhomirova.* M, 1967.

Novy letopisets. PSRL, XIV, M, 1965.

Obnorsky, S. P., and Barkhudarov, S. G. *Khrestomatiya po istorii russkogo yazyka,* I. M, 1952.

Obolensky, Prince M. "Porozheniye moskvitian i osada goroda Vendena." *Chteniya,* M. 1847, No 3, book 16, part III, 43–58.

Olearius, A. *Opisaniye puteshestviya v Moskoviyu.* Preface, translation, and notes by A. M. Loviagin. SPB, 1906.

Otryvok russkoy letopisi (from 1445 to 1552). PSRL, VI, SPB, 1853.

Pamiatniki kulturnikh i diplomaticheskikh snosheny Rossii s Italiey. edited by E. F. Shmurlo. Bk I, Fasc. 1. L, 1925.

Pavlenko, N. I. "K istorii zemskikh soborov XVI veka." VI, 5 (1968), 82–105.

Peresvetov, I. *Sochineniya I. Peresvetova.* Edited by D. S. Likhachev and I. I. Zimin. M-L, 1956.

Peresvetov, R. T. *Po sledam nakhodok i utrat.* M, 1963.

Pernstein, John. "Doneseniye o Moskovii." *Chteniya,* I, 1–20, M, 1876.

Petrei, Peter. "Podlinnoye i podrobnoye opisaniye russkikh gosudarey." *Chteniye,* 1866 I, Pt. 4, 112–167.

Pierling, P. *Bathory et Possevino.* Paris, 1887.

Pipes, R., ed. *Of the Russ Commonwealth. Giles Fletcher.* Cambridge, Mass., Harvard University Press, 1966.

"Piskarevsky letopisets." Edited and annotated by O. A. Yakovleva. *Materialy po istorii SSSR,* 2. M, 1955, 23–175.

Pisma russkikh gosudarey. M, 1848.

Platonov, S. F. *Ivan Grozny.* SPB, 1923.

Podobedova, O. I. "K voprosu o sostave i proizkhozhdenii litsevogo letopisnogo svoda vtoroy poloviny XVI veka." In *Problemy istochnikovedeniya.* Edited by A. N. Nasonov. Vol. IX. M, 1961, 280–332.

——. *Miniatiury russkikh istoricheskikh rukopisey.* M, 1965.

——. *Moskovskaya shkola zhivopisi pri Ivane IV.* M, 1972.

Pokrovsky, N. N. *Aktovye istochniki po istorii chernososhnogo zemlevladeniya v Rossii XIV-nachala XVI v.* Novosibirsk, 1973.

Polosin, I. I. *Sotsialno–politicheskaya istoriya Rossii XVI–nachala XVII v.* M, 1963.

Pomerantseva, E. V., and Mints, S. I. *Russkoye narodnoye poeticheskoye tvorchestvo.* M, 1959.

Portal, Roger, *The Slavs.* A Cultural and Historical Survey of the Slavonic Peoples. Trans. from French by Patrick Evans. New York, Harper & Row, 1969.

Poslaniya Ivana Groznogo. Commentary by Ya. S. Lurie, D. S. Likhachev, et al. M-L, 1951.
Possevino, Antonio. *Commentarii di Moscovia.* Mantova, 1596.
Presniakov, A. E. *Tsarstvennaya kniga, ee sostav i proizkhozhdeniye.* SPB, 1893.
————. "Moskovskaya istoricheskaya entsiklopediya XVI v." In *Izvestiya otdela russkogo yazyka i slovesnosti.* 1899, Bk. 4, 824–876.
Prinz, Daniel. "Nachalo i vozvysheniye Moskovii." *Chteniya* (1876), 3, 1–46; 4, 47–73.
Prodolzheniye Aleksandro-nevskoy letopisi. PSRL, XXIX, M, 1965, 315–355.
Pronshtein, A. P. "K istorii vozniknoveniya kazachikh poseleniy i obrazovaniya sosloviya kazakov na Donu." In *Novoye o proshlom nashey strany.* M, 1967, 158–173.
Pskovskaya pervaya letopis. PSRL IV, SPB, 1848, 173–360.
Pushkarev, S. G, *Sviato-Troitskaya Sergieva Lavra.* Prague, 1928.
Razriadnaya kniga 1475–1598 gg. Edited by V. I. Buganov. M, 1966.
Riazanovsky, N. V. *A History of Russia.* New York, Oxford University Press, 1963.
Riazanovsky, V. A. *Obzor russkoy kultury. Istorichesky ocherk.* New York 1947–1948.
Rice, D. T. *Russian Icons.* London–New York: King Penguin Books, 1947.
Roginsky, M. G., trans. "Poslaniye Taube i Kruse." RIZ, 8 (1922), Petrograd, 8–59.
Rozanov, S. P. "Iz istorii russkikh pchel." PDPI, CLIV, SPB, 1904.
Rubinstein, N. L. *Istoriya Tatarii.* M, 1937.
Russky biografichesky slovar. SPB, 1896–1918. 25 vols. incomplete.
Rzhiga, I. S. *Peresvetov-publitsist XVI veka.* M, 1908.
Rzhiga, V. F. "Opyty po istorii russkoy publitsistike XVI veka. Maksim Grek kak publitsist." TODRL, Vol. I, 2, 1934.
Sadikov, P. A. *Ocherki po istorii oprichniny.* M–L, 1950.
————. "Pokhod tatar i turok na Astrakhan v 1569 g." IZ, 22 (1947), 132–166.
Sakharov, A. M. *Obrazovaniye i razvitiye Rossiiskogo gosudarstva v XIV–XVII vv.* M, 1969.
————. ed. *Sbornik dokumentov po istorii SSSR.* Chast III, XVI vekh. M, 1972.
Samokvasov, D. I. *Arkhivny material. Novootkrytye dokumenty pomestno-votchinnykh uchrezhdeny Moskovskogo gosudarstva XV-XVII vv.* Vols. I-II, M, 1905–1909.
Samsonov, N. G. *Drevnerussky yazyk.* M, 1973.
Savva, V. I. *Moskovskiye tsari i vizantiiskiye vasilevsy.* Kharkov, 1901.
————. *O posolskom prikaze v XVI veke.* Kharkov, 1917.
Sazonova, Yu. *Istoriya russkoy literatury,* II. New York. Chekhov Publishing House, 1955.
Scherbatow, Prince Alexis. *The Answer of Tsar Ivan IV to Rakita: a Neglected Source on the Russian Attitude towards Protestantism in the Second Part of the Sixteenth Century.* 1964, unpublished.
Scherbatov, Prince M. M. *Istoriya Rossiyskaya ot drevneyshikh vremen,* Volume V, SPB, 1786, 1903.
Selifontov, N. N. *Opyt bibliograficheskogo ukazatelia . . . dlia istorii predkov Tsaria Mikhaila Fyodorovicha Romanova.* SPB, 1900.
————. *Sbornik materialov po istorii predkov Tsaria Mikhaila Fyodorovicha.* SPB, 1898.
Seredonin, S. M. *Sochineniya Dzhilsa Fletchera kak istoricheskiy istochnik.* SPB, 1891.
Shcheglova, S. A. "Pchela, po rukopisiam kievskikh bibliotek." PDPI, CLXXV, SPB, 1910.
Shcherbachev, Yu. "Kopengagenskiye akty." *Chteniya* (1916), II, No. 182.
Shlichting, Albert. *Novoye izvestiye o Rossii vremeni Ivana Groznogo. "Skazaniye" Alberta Schlichtinga.* Tr. A. I. Malein, 2d ed. L, 1934.
Shmidt, S. O. "Chelobitny prikaz v seredine XVI stoletiya." *Izvestiya Akademii Nauk SSSR. Seriya istorii i filosofii.* Vol. VII, 5, M, 1950.
————. "K istorii soborov XVI v." IZ, 76 (1964), 121–151.
————. "K istorii zemskoy reformy (sobor 1555/1556)." In *Goroda feodalnoy Rossii.* M, 1966, 125–134.

———. Kogda i pochemu redaktirovalis litsevye letopisi vremeni Ivana Groznogo."
Sovetskiye arkhivy, 1, 2 (1966).

———. "Miniatiury Tsarstvennoy knigi kak istochnik po istorii Moskovskogo vosstaniya 1547." In *Problemy Istochnikovedeniya*. Vol. V. M, 1956.

———. "O Moskovskom vosstanii 1547 goda." In *Krestianstvo i klassovaya borba v feodalnoy Rossii.* M, 1967, 114–130.

———. ed. *Opis tsarskogo arkhiva XVI veka; arkhiva Posolskogo prikaza 1614 goda.* M, 1960.

———. "O vremeni sostavleniya' Vypisi, o vtorom brake Vasiliya III." In *Novoye o proshlom nashey strany.* M, 1967, 110–122.

———. "Pravitelstvennaya deyatelnost A. F. Adasheva." UZ, 167, M, 1954.

———. "Prodolzheniye khronografa redaktsii 1512 goda." IA, Vol. VII, M, 1951, 254–299.

———. "Sobory serediny XVI veka." *Istoriya, ASSR,* IV (1960).

———. *Stanovleniye rossisskogo samoderzhavstva. M, 1973.*

———. "Zametki o yazyke poslaniy Ivana Groznogo." TODRL, XIV, M-L, 1958.

Shmurlo, E. F. *Rossiya i Italiya.* Vol. II. 2d ed. SPB, 1913.

Skrynnikov, R. G. "Dukhovnoye zaveshchaniye Tsaria Ivana Groznogo." TODRL, XXI, M–L 1965, 309–318.

———. "Kurbsky i ego pisma v Pskovo-Pecherskii monastir." TODRL, XVIII, M-L, 1962, 99–116.

———. *Nachalo oprichniny.* L, 1966.

———. "Oprichnaya zemelnaya reforma." IZ, Volume 70, 1961.

———. "Oprichnina i posledniye udelnye kniazheniya na Rusi." IZ, 76 (1964), 152–174.

———. "Oprichny razgrom Novgoroda." In *Krestianstvo i klassovaya borba v feodalnoy Rossii.* L, 1967, 157–171.

———. *Perepiska Groznogo i Kurbskogo, paradoksy Edvarda Kinana.* L, 1973.

———. "Samoderzhaviye i Oprichnina." In *Vnutrenniaya politika tsarizma (seredina XVI–nachalo XX vv).* L, 69–99.

———. "Vedeniye oprichniny i organizatsiya oprichnogo voiska v 1565 g. i Sinodik opalnykh tsaria Ivana Groznogo kak isticheskii istochnik," UZ, LGPI, 278 (1965), 3–86.

Smirnov, I. I. *Ocherki politicheskoy istorii russkogo gosudarstva 30—50kh godov XVI veka.* M-L, 1958.

———. *Rossiya i Turtsiya v XVI-*XVII vekakh. M, 1946. 2 vols.

———. "Sudebnik 1550 goda." IZ, 24, 1947, 266–352.

Smirnov, P. P. *Posadskiye liudi i ikh klassovaya borba do serediny XVII veka.* Vol. I. M-L, 1947.

Sobraniye gosudarstvennykh gramot i dogovorov, I. M, 1813; II. M, 1819; III. M, 1828.

Sokolov, Y. A. *Russian Folklore.* Translated by C. R. Smith. Hatboro, Folklore Associates, 1966.

Soloviev, S. M. *Istoriya Rossii s drevneyshikh vremen.* Edited by L. V. Cherepnin. M, 1959–1966. 29 vols.

Spegalsky, Yu. P. *Pskov.* L-M, 1963.

Speransky, M. "Iz istorii otrechennykh knig: Part I, Gadaniya i psaltiri," PDPI, CXXIX, SPB, 1898.

———. "Part II, Trepetniki." PDPI, CXXXI, SPB, 1899.

———. "Part III, Lopatochnik." PDPI, CXXXVII, SPB, 1900.

———. "Part IV, Aristotelevy vrata ili tainaya tainykh." PDPI, CLXXI, SPB, 1908.

Sreznevsky, I. I. *Material dlia slovaria drevnerusskogo yazyka.* I–III. SPB, 1893–1903.

Staden, Heinrich von. *Aufzeichnungen über den Moskauer Staat.* Edited by Fritz Epstein. Hamburg, 1962.

——. *The Land and Government of Muscovy.* Translated by T. Esper. Stanford, Calif., Stanford University Press, 1967.

Stefanovich, D. *O stoglave. Ego proizkhozhdeniye, redaktsiya i sostav.* SPB, 1909.

Stepennaya kniga tsarskogo rodosloviya. PSRL, XXI, SPB, Part I, 1908, Part II, 1913.

"Stikhiry, polozhennyia na kriukovye noty. Tvoreniye Tsaria Ioanna Despota Rossiiskogo," Leonid, Archimandrite. PDPI, LXIII, 1886.

Strokov, A. A. *Istoriya voennogo iskusstva.* M, 1955.

Sukhotin, L. M. "Ivan Grozny do nachala oprichniny." RAOS, 3 (1940), 67–100.

——. *K peresmotru voprosa ob oprichnine.* Belgrade, 1931.

——. "Moi raboty po istorii oprichniny." *Novy Zhurnal,* 20 (1948), 294–300.

——. "Spisok oprichnikov." *Novik,* 3, 27 (1940), 19–25.

——. "Yeshche k voprosu ob oprichnine." RAOS, 265–289. Yubileiny Sbornik.

Sylvester, Archpriest. *Domostroy.* Edited by A. Orlov. Russian Reprint Series. The Hague, Europe Printing, 1967.

Sytin, P. V. *Iz istorii Moskovskikh ulits.* M, 1958.

Tatishchev, V. N. *Istoriya rossiiskaya,* vol. 6. M-L, 1966.

Taube, Baron M. A. "Iogann Taube, sovetnik tsaria Ivana Groznogo." *Novy Zhurnal,* 71 (1963), 170–189.

Tcherepnin, A. *Anthology of Russian Music.* Bonn: M. P. Belaieff, 1966.

Tedaldi, Giovanni. *Izvestiye o Rossii.* Edited by E. Shmurlo. SPB, 1891 (pamphlet, 35 pages).

Tikhomirov, E. *Pervy tsar moskovsky Ioann IV Vasilievich Grozny.* 2 volumes, SPB, 1888.

Tikhomirov, M. N. *Drevnerusskiye goroda.* M, 1956.

——. *Istoricheskiye sviazi Rossii so slavianskimi stranami.* M, 1969.

——. *Kratkiye zametki o letopisnykh pamiatnikakh v rukopisnykh sobraniyakh Moskvy.* M, 1962.

——. "Maloizvestnye letopisnye pamiatniki: povest o poimanii kniazia Andreya Ivanovicha Staretskogo." IZ, 10, 1941, 85–90.

——. *Novoe o proshlom nashey strany.* Pamiati akademika M. N. Tikhomirova. M, 1967. Edited by V. A. Aleksandrov, S. O. Shmit et al.

——. "Piskarevsky letopisets kak istorichesky istochnik." *Istoriya SSSR,* III (1957), 112–122.

——. *Rossiiskoye gosudarstvo XV–XVII vekov.* M, 1973.

——. *Rossiya v XVI stoletiye.* M, 1962.

——. *Russkaya kultura X–XVIII vekov.* M, 1968.

——. *Soslovno-predstavitelnye uchrezhdeniya (zemskiye sobory) v Rossii XVI veka.* M, 1958, No. 5.

——. *Srednevekovaya Moskva v XIV–XV vekakh.* M, 1957.

——, ed., et al. *U istokov russkogo knigopechataniya,* M, 1959.

—— ed "Zapiski o regenstve Eleny Glinskoy i boyarskom pravlenii, 1533–1547 gg." IZ, 46 (1954), 278–288.

Tikhomirov, N. Ya, and Ivanov, V. N. *Moskovsky kreml.* M, 1967.

Timofeev, Ivan. *Vremennik.* Edited by V. P. Adrianova-Peretts, commentary by O. A. Derzhavina. M-L, 1951.

Tipografskaya letopis (up to 1534), PSRL, XXIV, Petrograd, 1921.

Tolstoy, Alexey K. *Kniaz Serebriany. Povest vremen Ioanna Groznogo.* M. 1966.

——. *A Prince of Outlaws.* New York: Alfred Knopf, 1927.

Tolstoy, Dmitry "Rech Tsaria Ivana Vasilievicha Groznogo k Polskim i Litovskim Panam-Radam." *Chteniya,* M. 1848, No. 9, Book 22, Part 4, 296–302.

Tolstoy, Yury, V. *Pervye sorok let snosheniy mezhdu Rossieyu i Anglieyu 1553–1593.* SPB, 1875.

Trofimov, I. V., *Pamiatniki arkhitektury. Troitse-Sergievskaya Lavra.* M, 1957.

Trofimov, Vladimir. *Pokhod pod Kazan, ee osada i vziatiye v 1552 g.* Kazan, 1890.

Tsvetayev, D. *Maria Vladimirovna i Magnus Datsky.* ZMNP, 196 (1878), 57–85.

Turgenev, Alexander, ed. *Historica Russiae Monumenta,* 3 vols., SPB, vol. I, 1841; vol. II, 1842; Supplementum, 1848.

Ulanov, V. Ya., "Polozheniye nizshikh klassov v Moskovskom Gosudarstve v XVI–XVII veke." In *Moskva v ee proshlom i nastoyashchem.* Vol. IV. M, n.d., 85–106.

———. "Zapadnoye vliyaniye v Moskovskom gosudarstve v XVI–XVII vv." In *Moskva v ee proshlom i nastoyashchem.* Vol. VI. M, n. d., 68–96.

Ulfeld, Jacob. "Opisaniye puteshestviya v Rossiyu." *Chteniya,* X, 1883, 1–55.

———. *Legatio Moscovitica,* 1608.

Ulukhanov, I. S. *O yazyke drevney Rusi.* M, 1972.

Uspensky, N. D. *Drevnerusskoye pevcheskoye isskustvo,* M, 1971.

Ustrialov, N., ed. *Skazaniya kniazia Kurbskogo.* SPB, 1886.

Vallotton, Henry, *Ivan le Terrible.* Paris, Arthème Fayard, 1959.

Vasiliev, S. *Aleksandrovskaya Sloboda,* M. 1971.

Vasilievsky, V. G. *"Polskaya i nemetskaya pechat."* ZMNP, 1889, 127–167; 350–390.

Veliaminov-Zernov, V. V. *Issledovaniya o Kasimovskikh tsariakh i tsarevichakh.* SPB, 1863–1887. 4 vols.

Velikiya Minei Chetii. Sobrannyia vserossiiskim mitropolitom Makariyem. M, 1868–1914.

Vernadsky, G. *A History of Russia.* (5th rev. ed., New Haven, Conn., Yale University Press, 1961). Vol. 4, 1959, Vol. 5, Pt. 1, 1969.

———. "Ivan Grozny i Simeon Bekbulatovich." In *To Honor Roman Jakobson.* The Hague, Mouton, 1967, 151–169.

———. "Serfdom in Russia." In *Relazioni del X Congresso Internationale di Scienze Storiche.* Vol. 3, Firenze, 1955.

Veselovsky, N. I. *Tatarskoye vliyaniye na posolskiy tseremonial v Moskovskiy period russkoy istorii.* SPB, 1911.

Veselovsky, S. B. *Issledovaniya po istorii oprichniny.* M, 1963.

———. *Feodalnoye zemlevladeniye v severo-vostochnoy Rusi.* M-L, 1947.

Vilinsky, S. G. *Poslaniya startsa Artemiya XVI veka.* Odessa, 1906.

Vodovozov, N. V. *Istoriya drevney russkoy literatury.* M, 1958.

Vologodsko-permskaya letopis. PSRL, XXVI, M, 1959.

Vvedensky, A. A. *Dom Stroganovykh v XVI–XVII vekakh.* M, 1962.

Vyssotsky, A. N. *Astronomical Records in the Russian Chronicles from 1000 to 1600 A.D.* Lund, Sweden, Meddelande frän Lunds Astronomika Observatorium, Ser. II, 26, 1949.

Waliszewski, K. *Ivan the Terrible.* Hamden, Archon Books, 1966.

Weinberg, Peter. *Russkiye narodnye pesni ob Ivane Vasilieviche Groznom.* SPB. 2d ed., 1908.

Wipper, R. *Ivan Grozny.* M, 1947.

Yakovleva, O. A., ed. "Piskarevsky letopisets." In *Materialy po istorii SSSR,* 2. M, 1955, 23–175.

Yankovsky, P, "Pechalovaniye dukhovenstva za opalnykh," *Chteniya,* 1876, Bk 1, 168–205.

Yuriens, I. A. *Vopros o livonskoy dani,* Warsaw, 1913.

Zabelin, I. E. *Domashny byt russkogo naroda v XVI i XVII stoletiakh.* M, 1872, 2 vols.

———. *Domashny byt russkikh tsarits v XVI–XVII stoletiakh,* M, 1869.

———. *Istoriya goroda Moskvy.* M, 1905.

Zaozerskaya, E. I. *U istokov krupnogo proizvodstva v russkoy promyshlennosti XVI–XVII vekov.* M, 1970.

Zarinsky, Platon, Archpriest, *Ocherki drevney Kazani.* Kazan, 1877.

Zenkovsky, S. A., ed. and trans. *Medieval Russian Epics, Chronicles and Tales.* New York: E. P. Dutton, 1963.

Zernov, Nicolas, *Moscow the Third Rome.* London, 1944.

————. *The Russians and their Church.* London, 1945.

Zharkov, I. A., ed. "Maloizvestnaya razriadnaya zapis serediny XVI veka." AE, M, 1961, 255–258.

Zimin, A. A. "Antichnye motivy v Russkoy publitsistike kontsa XV veka." In *Feodalnaya Rossiya vo vsemirnoistoricheskom protsesse.* M, 1972, 128–138.

————. *Kholopy na Rusi.* M. 1973.

————. "Khoziaitvenny krizis 60–70 kh godov XVI veka, i russkoye krestianstvo." *Istoriya Zemledeliya SSSR,* Vol. V, M, n.d., 11–20.

————. "Kogda Kurbsky napisal 'Istoriyu o velikom kniaze Moskovskom?'" TODRL, XVIII, 1962.

————. "O politicheskikh predposylkakh vozniknoveniya russkogo absoliutizma." In *Absoliutizm v Rossii.* M, 1964, 18–49.

————. *Oprichnina Ivana Groznogo.* M, 1964.

————. *Peresvetov i ego sochineniya.* M, 1956.

————. *Peresvetov i ego sovremenniki.* M, 1958.

————. *Reformy Ivana Groznogo.* M, 1960.

————. *Rossiya na poroge novogo vremeni.* M, 1972.

————. "Sostav bioarskoy dumy v XV–XVI vekakh." AE for 1957, M, 1958, 41–87.

————. *Tysiachnaya kniga 1550 goda i Dvorovaya tetrad 50 kh. godov XVI veka.* M, 1950.

————. "Zemsky Sobor 1566 goda" IZ, 71 (1962), 196–235.

———— and Lurie, Ya. S., eds. *Poslaniya Iosifa Volotskogo.* M-L, 1959.

Notes

REFERENCES ARE GIVEN IN A SHORTENED FORM. Thus Veselovsky's work *Issledovaniye po istorii oprichniny* is listed in the notes as Veselovsky, *Issledovaniye*. The works of Karamzin, Soloviev, Tatishchev, and Vernadsky, to which frequent reference is made, are listed under the authors' names. The full titles of the books are given in the bibliography.

The following abbreviations have also been used: PSRL = *Polnoye Sobraniye Russkikh Letopisey*; NL = *Nikonovskaya Letopis*; PPL = *Pskovskaya Pervaya Letopis*; RBS = *Russky Biographichesky Slovar*.

Page

1   For Vasily's mother, see Soloviev, III, 55–64; Vernadsky, IV, 18–26.

1   "Whom do I resemble?": PPL, PSRL, IV, 295; Soloviev, III, 285.

1   For Vasily's character, see PPL, PSRL, IV, 298–299.

2   For Vasily's reign, see Zimin, *Rossiya*; Soloviev, III, 218–352; Karamzin, VII, 1–225; NL, PSRL, XIII, 1–77, 409–418; Herberstein, *Commentaries*.

2   For Salomonia and her divorce, see Zimin, *Rossiya*, 267–299; Soloviev, III, 285–287; Karamzin, VII, 128–131; Fennell, *History*, 4–5; Vernadsky, IV, 135, 158–159.

2   "If you should . . .": Karamzin, VII, 129, footnote 268; Shmidt, *O vremeni*, 110–122; Zimin, *Rossiya*, 293–294.

2   For Mikhail Glinsky, see Soloviev, III, 239–246; RBS, G, 324–330; Karamzin, VII, 61–62.

2   For Elena Glinskaya and her family, see Vernadsky, IV, 138–139; RBS, G, 317–318.

4   For the marriage ceremony, see Karamzin, VII, 211–214: Latysheva, G. P. and Rabinovich, M. G., *Moskva i moskovsky kray*, 226–230.

4   "Lord, come to the place: ibid., 212.

5   "The will of the Tsar: Kliuchevsky, *Sochineniya*, II, 137.

5   For the new idealogy, see Vernadsky, IV, 165–170.

5   For the Boyar Council, see Kliuchevsky, *Boyarskaya Duma*; Zimin, *Rossiya*, 409–411.

5   For clerks, see Fennell, *History*, 96–97.

6   For the Grand Prince leaving the boyars and secretaries in charge of the government, see Buganov, *Razriadnaya kniga*, 44, 53, 69.

7   For life in sixteenth century Moscow, see Latysheva and Rabinovich, *Moskva v dalekom proshlom*, 90–247; Staden, *The Land and Government*; Sytin, *Iz istorii*; Nechayev, "Ulichnaya zhizn," 56–80; Ulanov, "Polozheniye," 85–106; Dovnar-Zapolsky, "Torgovlia," 5–67; Ulanov, "Zapodnoye vliyaniye," 68–96; Hakluyt, *Principal Navigations*, I, 418–438.

8   "All the burden: Hakluyt, *Principal Navigations* (Everyman), 417.

9   "Their speech is: Berry and Crummey, *Rude & Barbarous Kingdom*, 199.

9   For youths practicing fisticuffs, see Herberstein, *Description*, 42; Nechayev, "Ulichnaya zhizn," 78.

9   For birth of Ivan, see NL, PSRL, XIII, 49.

9   For the storm, see *Vtoraya novgorodskaya letopis*, PSRL, VI, 287–288; Karamzin, VII, 150.

10   For Ivan's baptism, see NL, PSRL, XIII, 49–53; Karamzin, VII, 150.

10   "O Sergius, by your prayers: NL, PSRL, XIII, 49–53; Karamzin, VII, 150.

11   "had been sent by God: NL, PSRL, XIII, 49–53.

11   "because a loving mother: ibid.

11   For Ivan's first public appearance, see ibid., 59.

11   For the visit to Kolomenskoye, see ibid., 65.

12   For the birth of Yury, see ibid., 66.

12   "From Grand Prince Vasily Ivanovich: *Pisma russkikh gosudarey*, 3–5.

12   "From Grand Prince Vasily Ivanovich: ibid.

13   For illness and death of Vasily, see NL, PSRL, XIII, 75, 410 ff.

15   "like hail or rain": ibid., 410.

15   For the "possessors" and "nonpossessors," see Vernadsky, IV, 130–133, 150–151; Riazanovsky, *A History*, 135–137; Soloviev, III, 197, 327–334.

18   "As you well know: NL, PSRL, XIII, 76, 413; Karamzin, VII, 159; Soloviev, III, 289–290.

19   "Brethren, Nikolay has: NL, PSRL, XIII, 414.

19   "Pray, father for: Soloviev, III, 290; Karamzin, VII, 161.

19   "My son is young: NL, PSRL, XIII, 415.

19   "Guard my son: ibid.; Karamzin, VII, 161–162.

20   "Brother, do you: NL, PSRL, XIII, 417–418.

20   On Shigona's vision, see ibid., 76, 418.

21   For burial of Vasily, see NL, PSRL, XIII, 76–77, 418–419; Tatishchev, VI, 138–139; Karamzin, VII, 163–164; Soloviev, III, 293–294.

24   "May God bless you: PPL, PSRL, IV, 299; Nasonov, *Pskovskiye letopisi*, 106; Soloviev, III, 395–396; Karamzin, VIII, 3.

24   For population of Russia, see Kopanev, "Naseleniye," 233–254.

29   For Mikhail Glinsky, see Soloviev, III, 239–246; RBS, G, 324–330.

32   For arrest of Prince Yury, see NL, PSRL, XIII, 78–79, 420; *Letopisets nachala tsarstva*, PSRL, XXIX, 10–11; Karamzin, VIII, 3–6; Tikhomirov, "Zapiski," 283.

33   For arrest of Mikhail Glinsky, see NL, PSRL, XIII, 83; RBS, G, 330;

Karamzin, VII, 8; Soloviev, III, 400; Zimin, *Reformy*, 230–231; Tikhomirov, "Zapiski," 283.

34   For Andrey Shuisky's governorship of Pskov, see PPL, PSRL, IV, 304.

34   For the Shuiskys, see RBS, Sh, 504–515; for the Belskys, see RBS, B, 663–674.

35   For Andrey of Staritsa, see NL, PSRL, XIII, 91–97, 428–431; *Vologodsko-permskaya letopis*, PSRL, XXVI, 317–318; Tikhomirov, "Maloizvestniye letopisnye pamiatniki," 84–87; Soloviev, III, 401–404; Karamzin, VIII, 8–12; Zimin, *Reformy*, 243–248; Tikhomirov, "Zapiski," 284.

37   "My Lord, you have: Soloviev, III, 402.

39   "Thus by God's will: Fennell, *Correspondence*, 72–73; NL, PSRL, XIII, 124; RBS, Sh, 509.

40   The source for the footnote is Soloviev, III, 71, 302, 308.

41   For the first arrest of Ivan Belsky, see NL, PSRL, XIII, 126, 431–432; Karamzin, VIII, 44–45 and footnote 70; Soloviev, III, 423; Zimin, *Reformy*, 251–252.

42   For the banishment of Metropolitan Daniel, see Tikhomirov, "Zapiski," 83; Zimin, *Reformy*, 253; Karamzin, VIII, 45–46; Fennell, *Correspondence*, 74–75; NL, PSRL, XIII, 127.

42   For the release of Ivan Belsky, see NL, PSRL, XIII, 132; Zimin, *Reformy*, 257; Karamzin, VIII, 51–52; RBS, B, 668.

44   For relations with Lithuania, 1533–1538, see NL, PSRL, XIII, 81–89, 94–96, 99, 107–108, 110–116, 420–424, 427; Soloviev, III, 268, 406–411; Zimin, *Reformy*, 243–244; Karamzin, VIII, 18–21, 25, 29–31.

47   For Khanate of Kasimov, see Vernadsky, *History*, III, 330–332.

47   For flight of Simeon Belsky, see NL, PSRL, XIII, 83; Soloviev, III, 406; Zimin, *Reformy*, 232, 240–243; Karamzin, VIII, 6–7; RBS, B, 674.

48   For Crimean invasion of 1541, see NL, PSRL, XIII, 99–114, 137–139, 433–438; *Letopisets nachala tsarstva*, PSRL, XXIX, 40–41; Buganov, *Razriadnaya Kniga*, 101; Tatishchev, VI, 148–153; Karamzin, VIII, 56–64; Soloviev, III, 443–447; Zimin, *Reformy*, 259–260.

48   "I shall come: NL, PSRL, XIII, 110, 433.

49   "Oh, most holy: NL, PSRL, XIII, 434.

49   "a bright candle: ibid.

49   "Our Grand Prince: ibid., 434–435.

49   For the meeting of the Boyar Council to prepare for the invasion, see NL, PSRL, XIII, 434–435; Soloviev, III, 444–445; Karamzin, VIII, 57.

50   "But if it should: NL, PSRL, XIII, 106, 435–436.

50   "We are well armed: ibid.

51   "I was told: ibid., 109.

52   "because the Khan: ibid., 112–113.

53   For the second overthrow of Ivan Belsky and the return to power of Ivan Shuisky, see NL, PSRL, XIII, 140–141, 439–440; Tikhomirov, "Zapiski," 285; *Letopisets nachala tsarstva*, PSRL, XXIX, 42; Karamzin, VIII, 64–67; Soloviev, III, 425; Tatishchev, VI, 154; Fennell, *History*, 10–11; Fennell, *Correspondence*, 78–79; Zimin, *Reformy*, 260–261.

54   Ivan receives Lithuanian ambassadors, see NL, PSRL, XIII, 141; Karamzin, VIII, 68 and footnotes 109 and 114; Soloviev, III, 453.

55   "The Shuiskys treated us: Fennell, *Correspondence*, 74–75.

56   For death of Ivan Belsky, see NL, PSRL, XIII, 141, 440; Tikhomirov, "Zapiski," 85.

56   For Andrey Shuisky, see RBS, Sh, 506–507.

56   For arrest of Fyodor Vorontsov, see NL, PSRL, XIII, 443; Fennell, *Correspondence*, 78–79; Karamzin, VIII, 71; Soloviev, III, 427.

58   For arrest and death of Andrey Shuisky, see NL, PSRL, XIII, 145, 444–445; Zimin, *Reformy*, 267, footnote 3. Another chronicle stated that Andrey Shuisky was killed "by the keepers of the hounds near the Kuriatny Gate on the orders of the boyars, and lay naked at the gate for two hours." See Shmidt, "Prodolzheniye," 289. This shows that certain boyars were involved in the arrest and death of Andrey Shuisky.

58   "The Grand Prince: NL, PSRL, XIII, 444.

58   "The boyars committed: ibid.

58   "From this time: ibid., 145, 444.

58   "and became obedient: ibid., 444.

59   It was observed: Fennell, *History*, 10–11.

59   There were always flatterers: ibid.

60   "some rude words: NL, PSRL, XIII, 147, 446.

60   Later, Ivan appears: Buganov, *Razriadnaya kniga*, 157, 198–199, 208, 223, 226.

60   Fyodor Vorontsov's crime: NL, PSRL, XIII, 147, 449; Karamzin, VIII, 78; Soloviev, III, 430; Zimin, *Reformy*, 268. One suspects the hand of Ivan's maternal relatives, the Glinskys, in this because of later events and because they had easy access to the young Grand Prince.

61   For the enthronement of Shigaley as Khan of Kazan, see NL, PSRL, XIII, 148, 447; Soloviev, III, 448. It should be noted that at the time of Grand Prince Vasily III, Kazan was nominally a vassal state but then it became independent again; see Soloviev, III, 264, 416, 418, 442.

61   For Ivan's games at Kolomna, see Tikhomirov, "Piskarevsky letopisets," 115; Yakovleva, "Piskarevsky letopisets," 73–74.

61   For Ivan at Kolomna, see NL, PSRL, XIII, 149, 448; Tikhomirov, "Zapiski," 286.

61   For description of the city of Kolomna, see Tikhomirov, *Rossiya*, 146.

62   For the Novgorodian musketeers, see NL, PSRL, XIII, 448–449; Zimin, *Reformy*, 268, footnote 8.

      For the execution of the Vorontsovs, see NL, PSRL, XIII, 149, 448–449;
63   *Aleksandro-nevskaya letopis*, PSRL, XXIX, 147; Tikhomirov, "Zapiski," 286; Tatishchev, VI, 160; Soloviev, III, 430–431; Zimin, *Reformy*, 268–269 and footnote 8 on p. 268.

64   "the root of all evil: Fennell, *History*, 14–15.

64   The *Tsarstvennaya Kniga* is a part of the *Nikonovskaya letopis* covering Ivan IV's reign from 1533 to 1553.

64   "The Glinsky's were close: NL, PSRL, XIII, 456.

64   For Ivan's journey to Novgorod and Pskov, see PPL, PSRL, IV, 306–307.

65   For Spiridon Savva and his works, see Vodovozov, *Istoriya*, 207–212.

65   For the legend of Vladimir Monomakh's coronation, see ibid., 210; NL, PSRL, IX, 144.

66   For Filofey and the "Third Rome" theory, see Vodovozov, *Istoriya*, 212-213; Andreev, "Filofey," 6–9, 21, 28–31; Golubinsky, *Istoriya*, II, 765–766.

66   For the coronation of Dmitry, see NL, PSRL, XII, 246–247; Barsov, *Drevne-russkiye pamiatniki*, 33–37.

66   For the enthronement of Russian Grand Princes in the past, see Barsov, *Drevne-russkiye pamiatniki*, XIII–XIV.

67   Both Ivan's father and grandfather occasionally used the title of Tsar and were addressed as Tsar. But Ivan was the first to be crowned officially as Tsar. See Vernadsky, V, 1, 20; Zimin, *Rossiya*, 140, 157.

67   For Ivan's coronation, see Barsov, *Drevne-russkiye pamiatniki*, 1–90; NL, PSRL, XIII, 150–151, 450–452; Karamzin, VIII, 82–87; Tatishchev, VI, 161–162; Vernadsky, V, 1, 30; Zimin, *Reformy*, 274–277.

67   "Father, Most Holy Metropolitan: Barsov, *Drevne-russkiye pamiatniki*, 73.

68   "Here I am, O Lord: ibid., 84.

68   showered him with gold and silver coins: ibid., 89; NL, PSRL, XIII, 453.

68   Another tradition places the origin of the Zakharin family in Novgorod, where they were boyars. Roman Zakharin was not a fully fledged boyar but had the rank of a boyar-okolnichi.

69   For Andrey Kobyla, see NL, PSRL, XII, 17.

69   For Ivan's marriage to Anastasia, see ibid., XIII, 151–152, 450, 453; Karamzin, VIII, 89.

70   For pilgrimage, see NL, PSRL, XIII, 453; Karamzin, VIII, 88–89.

70   For hatred of the Glinskys, see Fennell, *History*, 191; NL, PSRL, XIII, 456.

70   For the deputation from Pskov, see PPL, PSRL, IV, 307.

71   For the great bell, see NL, PSRL, XIII, 453–454; Tikhomirov, *Kratkiye zametki*, 13.

72   For *serdechniki*, see Tikhomirov, "Zapiski," 288.

72   For the great fire of June 1547, see NL, PSRL, XIII, 152–154, 454–455; *Mazurinsky letopisets*, PSRL, XXXI, 130–131; *Aleksandro-nevskaya letopis*, PSRL, XXIX, 151–153; Tikhomirov, "Zapiski," 287–288; PPL, PSRL, IV, 307; Tatishchev, VI, 163–165; Karamzin, VIII, 91–95; Soloviev, III, 433–435; Vernadsky, V, I, 31–33; Fennell, *History*, 14–17; Fennell, *Correspondence*, 82–83; Zimin, *Reformy*, 295–299; Shmidt, "O Moskovskom vostanii."

74   "The fire came to an end: NL, PSRL, XIII, 154, 455.

75   "Princess Anna Glinskaya: NL, PSRL, XIII, 456.

76   "Who would be so mad: Fennell, *Correspondence*, 82–83. See also *Poslaniya*, 35.

78   "In this way perhaps: Fennell, *History*, 16–17.

80   For Alexey Adashev, see Shmidt, *Pravitelstvennaya deyatelnost*.

80   "governed the Russian land: Tikhomirov, "Piskarevsky letopisets," 114. Yakovleva, "Piskarevsky letopisets," 55–56.

80   Historians are unable to agree whether these marginal notes were written by Ivan himself or by Ivan Viskovaty, his secretary of foreign affairs. For examples of these notes, see NL, PSRL, XIII, 443–445, 448–449, 455–456. For discussion on this subject see Zimin, *Oprichnina*, 67–71; Andreev, "Interpolations" and "Ob avtore"; Alshits, "Ivan Grozny" and "Tsar Ivan Grozny."

80   "Sylvester was all powerful: NL, PSRL, XIII, 524.

81   For the early and later membership of the Chosen Council and its relationship to the Boyar Council, see Zimin, *Reformy*, 316–325; Smirnov, *Ocherki*, 139–163, 194–263; Vernadsky, V, I, 36–37.

81   For bad harvests, see Shmidt, "Prodolzheniye," 294; Zimin, *Reformy*, 313. Bad harvests began in 1547 and became worse in 1548 and 1549.

81   For Ivan's campaign against Kazan in winter of 1547–1548, see NL, PSRL, XIII, 155–156, 457–458.

81   For defeat of Tatars before Kazan, see ibid., 156–157, 458–459; Tatishchev, VI, 166–167; Karamzin, VIII, 109–110; Soloviev, III, 449.

81   For attack by Khan of Crimea on Astrakhan, see Karamzin, VIII, 112.

81   "You were young: ibid., 112–113.

82   For arrest of Crimean ambassador, see ibid., 113.

82   For Safa and Utemish Guirey and for Kazan affairs in 1549, see ibid., 113; NL, PSRL, XIII, 157, 459; Soloviev, III, 455, 449; Tatishchev, VI, 167.

82   For Adashev and petitions, see Zimin, *Reformy*, 326–328; Yakovleva, "Piskarevsky letopisets," 56. The Office of Petitions was established in February 1549 in the Kremlin near the Cathedral of the Annunciation, most probably in the treasury building.

82   For Prince Yury's marriage, see NL, PSRL, XIII, 154, 457.

82   For flight and arrest of Glinsky and Turantay-Pronsky, see ibid., 154–155; Shmidt, "Prodolzheniye," 293.

83   For reformers, see Zimin, *Peresvetov*.

83   For Artemy of Pskov, see ibid., 155–156, 167–168; Vernadsky, IV, 283; also V, 1, 26, 71, 73, 75, 77; Golubinsky, *Istoriya*, II, I, 832–837.

83   "he was invited: Zimin, *Peresvetov*, 156.

83   For Ermolay Erazm, see ibid., 126–141; Vernadsky, V, 1, 26–28; Grekov, *Krestiane*, II, 210–219.

84   "The monks," he wrote: Zimin, *Peresvetov*, 132.

84   "In this way: ibid., 141.

84   For reforms of the Chosen Council, see Zimin, *Reformy*, 316 ff.; Nosov, *Stanovleniye*; Vernadsky, V, 1, 48, 84–85; Soloviev, IV, 36–37; Nosov, "Sobor," 12, 49–50.

85   For convocation of February 1549, see Shmidt, "Prodolzheniye," 295–296; Zimin, *Reformy*, 325; Nosov, "Sobor," 8–9; Vernadsky, V, 1, 39; Shmidt, *Stanovleniye*, 133–196.

85   "I have no rancor: Shmidt, "Prodolzheniye," 296.

85   For the convocation of the people on Red Square, see Nosov, "Sobor," 39–40; Karamzin, VIII, 98–99 and footnote on 159; Soloviev, III, 437–438.

85   "I was very young: Soloviev, III, 437–438; Karamzin, VIII, 98–99 and footnote on 159.

87   For Peresvetov and his works, see Zimin, *Peresvetov*, 270 ff.; Vernadsky, V, 1, 26, 28, 40; Vodovozov, *Istoriya*, 223–226; Grekov, *Krestiane*, II, 219–221; Sazonova, *Istoriya*, II, 347–355; Soloviev, III, 713; Rzhiga, *Peresvetov*.

88   For the reasons behind the Church reforms, see Soloviev, IV, 76–78, 83; Zimin, *Reformy*, 380, 384.

88   For the *Stoglav*, see Zimin, *Reformy*, 378–391; Vernadsky, V, I, 44–50; Soloviev, IV, 76–98; Kozanchikov, *Stoglav*; Stefanovich, *O stoglave*.

88   "No one can describe: Soloviev, III, 435; Karamzin, VIII, 105; Vernadsky, V, I, 45.

89   For musicians, clowns, and fortune-tellers, see Soloviev, IV, 83–84; Zimin, *Reformy*, 381.

90   For icon painters, see Soloviev, IV, 79–80; Vodovozov, *Istoriya*, 220.

90   For decrees limiting acquisition of property by the monasteries and abolition of tax privileges, see Zimin, *Reformy*, 389–390; Vernadsky, V, 1, 47; Soloviev, IV, 88–89.

90   For education, see Vodovozov, *Istoriya*, 218–219; Soloviev, IV, 80; Vernadsky, V, 1, 48; Demkova and Droblenkova, "K izucheniyu," 27–61.

90   For copying of manuscripts, see Vodovozov, *Istoriya*, 119–120; Soloviev, IV, 79–80; Vernadsky, V, 1, 48.

91   For Ivan's second campaign against Kazan, see NL, PSRL, XIII, 158–160, 460–462; *Aleksandro-nevskaya letopis*, PSRL, XXIX, 156–157; Soloviev, III, 455–456; *Letopisets nachala tsarstva*, 57–58; Karamzin, VIII, 113–118; Tatishchev, VI, 168–169.

91   "You should not be: NL, PSRL, XIII, 159, 461.

92   "On this hill: Karamzin, VIII, 115–116.

92   Ivan spent a month: NL, PSRL, XIII, 160–161, 462.

92   the Nogay Tatars raided: ibid., 161, 462.

92   "the prince of princes: Karamzin, VIII, 117.

92   For Ulan Korshchak, see ibid., 120.

92   Utemish Guirey was born in 1546 and died in 1566.

92   For the third campaign against Kazan, for the building of Sviazhsk, and for the enthronement of Shigaley, see NL, PSRL, XIII, 162–169, 462–470; *Aleksandro-nevskaya letopis*, XXIX, 159–164; *Letopisets nachala tsarsva*, XXIX, 59–67; Tatishchev, VI, 171–177; Karamzin, VIII, 117–124; Soloviev, III, 456–457; Vernadsky, V, 1, 53–54.

93   For attack on suburbs of Kazan, see NL, PSRL, XIII, 163–164, 465.

93   For building of Sviazhsk, see ibid., 164, 466.

93   For the Cheremiss and other tribes, see Vernadsky, III, 209; V, 1, 53.

93   For Cheremiss sent against Tatars, see Karamzin, VIII, 119–120; Soloviev, III, 456–457.

94   Flight and capture of Ulan Korshchak, see NL, PSRL, XIII, 166, 468; Karamzin, VIII, 120–121. Soloviev, III, 457.

94   Tatar embassies arrived: NL, PSRL, XIII, 166–167, 468.

94   "If you do this: Karamzin, VIII, 122.

94   For Suyun Beka, see ibid., 122–123; NL, PSRL, XIII, 168, 468, 469.

94   For enthronement of Shigaley, see ibid., 169, 470.

95   For release of Russian slaves, see ibid., 169–170, 470; Vernadsky, V, 1, 54; Karamzin, VIII, 124.

95   For massacre of Tatar nobles by Shigaley, see NL, PSRL, XIII, 172, 472; Karamzin, VIII, 125; *Kazansky letopisets*, PSRL, XIX, 355–357.

96   Shigaley leaves throne of Kazan, see NL, PSRL, XIII, 174, 474; *Kazansky letopisets*, PSRL, XIX, 355–357; Karamzin, VIII, 127–128.

96   "You wanted to kill me: NL, PSRL, XIII, 174, 474.

96   For Mikulinsky's failure to enter Kazan, see NL, PSRL, XIII, 175–177, 474–476; Karamzin, VIII, 128–130; Soloviev, III, 460–462.

97   About the arrival of Yediger Makhmet, see NL, PSRL, XIII, 179, 478; *Kazansky letopisets*, PSRL, XIX, 376–377.

97   For the incident with the women at Sviazhsk and Makary's sermon, see NL, PSRL, XIII, 180–183, 479–482; Karamzin, VIII, 137–138; Tatishchev, VI, 186–189.

98   "Blessings from the: NL, PSRL, XIII, 180, 479.

98   "Let them go: ibid., 181, 480.

100 "O merciful Creator: Nasonov, "Novye istochniki," 10.

101 Ivan prays in the Uspensky Cathedral, see ibid., 12–13.

102 "so that our enemies: ibid., 13.

102 "Wife, it is my wish: ibid., 13–14; NL, PSRL, XIII, 184–185, 483.

103 For the Tsar's march to Kolomna and the attack of the Crimean Tatars, see NL, PSRL, XIII, 186–190, 484–488; *Aleksandro-nevskaya letopis*, PSRL, XXIX, 178–181; *Letopisets nachala tsarstva*, 80–84; Tatishchev, VI, 192–195; Nasonov, *Novye istochniki*, 14–16; Karamzin, VIII, 140–144; Soloviev, III, 463–464.

103   For the council of war at Kolomna, see *Aleksandro-nevskaya letopis*, PSRL, XXIX, 181; NL, PSRL, XIII, 191, 488; Trofimov, *Pokhod*, 41–42.

107   Complaints of the Novgorodians, see NL, PSRL, XIII, 191, 488, Karamzin, VIII, 144; Soloviev, III, 464.

107   For march from Kolomna to Kazan, see NL, PSRL, XIII, 191–192, 489, 494–499; *Aleksandro-nevskaya letopis*, XXIX, 181–182, 187–190, *Letopisets nachala tsarstva*, XXIX, 85–86, 91–95; Soloviev, III, 465–466; Karamzin, VIII, 146–151; Trofimov, *Pokhod*, 45–49; Fennell, *History*, 30–35.

    Makary's letter, see NL, PSRL, XIII, 192–197; 489–494.

108   Ivan's reply, see ibid., 197–198, 494.

108   Kurbsky's description, see Fennell, *History*, 30–31.

109   "From the Sura River: ibid., 32–33.

109   For appearance of Sviazhsk, see Karamzin, VIII, 147–148.

109   "like coming home: Fennell, *History*, 32–33.

111   For letters to Yediger Makhmet and Tatars, see NL, PSRL, XIII, 201, 498; Karamzin, VIII, 149.

112   For description of Kazan, see Fennell, *History*, 34–35; Trofimov, *Pokhod*, 52–59; Tikhomirov, *Rossiya*, 498–499.

113   For siege of Kazan, see NL, PSRL, XIII, 202–220, 498–514; *Aleksandro-nevskaya letopis*, PSRL, XXIX, 190–206; *Letopisets nachala tsarstva*, PSRL, XXIX, 94–111; *Lvovskaya letopis*, PSRL, XX, 516–33; *Kazansky letopisets*, PSRL, XIX, 412–462; Nasonov, "Novye istochniki," 17–26; Korotkov, *Ivan Grozny*, 31–38; Trofimov, *Pokhod*, 50–114; Fennell, *History*, 34–71; Ilovaisky, III, 193–203; Tatishchev, VI, 204–218; Soloviev, III, 466–472; Karamzin, VIII, 150–180; Bogdanovsky, "Inzhenerno-istoricheskiy ocherk," 1021–1055; Strokov, *Istoriya*, 370–376; Vernadsky, V, 1, 55–57.

113   For Tatar forces, see Strokov, *Istoriya*, 372; Korotkov, *Ivan Grozny*, 28–39.

113   For the army and its commanders, see Buganov, *Razriadnaya kniga*, 134, 137–138.

113   It appears that Mikhail Vorotynsky was the more talented. The *Kazansky letopisets*, PSRL, XIX, 466, says that Mikhail Vorotynsky was a great general.

116   "Therefore strive together: NL, PSRL, XIII, 203, 499.

117   For Tatar attack, see ibid., 204, 500; Fennell, *History*, 36–37.

118   For the storm, see NL, PSRL, XIII, 205.

118   For Yapancha's breakout, see ibid., 207.

120   For Tatars practicing magic spells, see Fennell, *History*, 52–53.

121   "They could not even eat: ibid., 44–45.

121   A Danish historian has suggested that Razmysl was really a Danish engineer called Rasmussen. Karamzin, VIII, 161, suggested that Razmysl was not a name at all, but meant "engineer" from the verb *razmyshliat*, to think out.

122   For igniting of gunpowder and defeat of Yapancha, see NL, PSRL, XIII, 208–210, 504–506.

122   For Gorbaty-Shuisky's expedition, see ibid., 210–211, 506–507; Fennell, *History*, 48–51.

123   "Glory to Thee: Nasonov, *Novye istochniki*, 18–19.

124   "I have been appointed: ibid., 8.

125   For the liberation of the Russians, see ibid., 19.

125   "I am doing this: ibid., 21.

125   For the siege engine, see NL, PSRL, XIII, 507; Fennell, *History*, 54–55.

126   "A candle burns up quickly: Evgenieva and Putilov, *Drevniye Rossiiskiye stikhotvoreniya*, 196.

"Those who suffer: *Kazansky letopisets*, PSRL, XIX, 443–444.

"There shall be one fold: Nasonov, *Novye istochniki*, 22; NL, PSRL, XIII, 216, 511.

"Lord, the time has come: NL, PSRL, XIII, 217, 512.

"his councillors took: Fennell, *History*, 60–61.

"I had so many grievous: ibid., 66–67.

For surrender of Yediger Makhmet, see Fennell, *History*, 64–65; Karamzin, VIII, 176.

"by the grace of God: NL, PSRL, XIII, 513–514.

"Tell them that according: Buganov and Koretsky, "Neizvestny moskovsky letopisets," 141–142. For Yediger Makhmet prostrating himself, see *Kazansky letopisets*, PSRL, XIX, 464–465.

The few surviving Tatar chronicles briefly describe the defeat. Here is the account of one Tatar chronicler: "After the massacre the Russian Khan took Kazan and established his power in its territories. This happened in the year 961 from the Hegira, the year of the Mouse, on the second day of the Constellation of the Scorpion, on a Sunday in the year 1552 according to the Christians" (Rubinstein, *Istoriya Tatarii*, 95).

A somewhat lengthier account is given by another chronicler: "At last misfortune turned its face upon the Muslims. They lost their homes and became captives. They had fought courageously but to no avail. At the head of the Russian Army was Ivan Vasilievich, called the Terrible. Before this, he built a strong fortress on the Sviaga River, which served as his base. Here he kept his guns and provisions, and his soldiers were always ready to attack. The heart of Islam was destroyed, and countless numbers of believers were killed. The emirs and all their treasures and their wives fell into Russian hands and suffered dishonor. To save themselves from the Russians some fled and sought refuge in the Crimea and the Kuban, and became inpoverished, while others, tempted by worldly riches, received high rank and gifts of peasants from the Russians and gave up their faith. And many unfortunate Muslims from hunger gave up their faith and were enslaved. Many of these people now live in the lands of Kazan. Thus the unbelievers were victorious (Rubinstein, *Istoriya Tatarii*, 123).

For Ivan's entrance into the city, see NL, PSRL, XIII, 220, 515.

One sixteenth-century source says that about 190,000 Tatars, men, women, and children, were killed. The same source gives the number of Russians killed as 15,355. See *Kazanskaya istoriya*, 159.

"They are not Christians: *Kazansky letopisets*, PSRL, XIX, 467–468; Karamzin, VIII, 179.

"With my own eyes: Nasonov, "Novye istochniki," 23.

For processions around Kazan, see Nasonov, "Novye istochniki," 24.

For Gorbaty-Shuisky as governor, see NL, PSRL, XIII, 221.

For Kurbsky's views on the Tsar's policy, see Fennell, *History*, 72–75.

For Tatar uprisings, see ibid., 90–95; *Lvovskaya letopis*, PSRL, XX, 540–541, 546–547, 552–554.

For Tsar's return journey, see NL, PSRL, XIII, 222–223, 516–518; *Kazansky letopisets*, XIX, 471–473; Fennell, *History*, 74–75.

"After God in His: Fennell, *Correspondence*, 92–93.

"Long live our God-fearing: NL, PSRL, XIII, 223, 518.

"Before I set forth: ibid., 223–225, 518–520.

"The grace of God: ibid., 225–227, 520–521.

140   For Ivan's visit to churches, see *Kazansky letopisets*, PSRL, XIX, 477.

141   For the banquet: NL, PSRL, XIII, 227–228, 522.

142   "God protected me from you: Fennell, *History*, 72–73.

142   For the baptism of Prince Dmitry, see NL, PSRL, XIII, 522–523. For th baptism of Utemish Guirey and Yediger Makhmet, see ibid., 229.

143   For Ivan's illness and the troubles concerning the succession, see NL, PSRI XIII, 238, 523–532; *Aleksandro-nevskaya letopis*, PSRL, XXIX, 211–214; Fennel *Correspondence*, 94–95, 192–193, 210–213; Zimin, *Reformy*, 406–414; Andreev "Interpolations" and "Ob avtore"; Alshits, "Proizkhozhdeniye" and "Tsar Iva Grozny"; Karamzin, VIII, 197–207; Soloviev, III, 524–528; Vernadsky, V, 58–63.

145   "At the time of: NL, PSRL, XIII, 238.

145   "God knows, and so dost thou: ibid., 524.

146   "If you will not: NL, PSRL, XIII, 524–525.

146   "Yesterday you swore: ibid., 525.

146   "And you Zakharins: ibid.

147   "Tell me why: Fennell, *Correspondence*, 192–193.

147   if he recovered he would go: Fennell, *History*, 74–75. For journey to St. Kirill' see ibid., 74–91; NL, PSRL, XIII, 231–232.

148   Fighting had broken out near Kazan: *Aleksandro-nevskaya letopis*, PSRI XXIX, 215.

148   For Ivan's companions, see Fennell, *History*, 80–81; Buganov and Koretsk "Neizvestny moskovsky letopisets," 150.

149   "You have made a vow: Fennell, *History*, 76–79.

150   "I must go: ibid., 78–79.

150   "If you do: ibid., 80–81.

151   "How may I rule: ibid., 82–83.

152   For drowning of Dmitry, see ibid., 90–91; Buganov and Koretsky, "Neizvestn moskovsky letopisets," 150; NL, PSRL, XIII, 232.

152   For burial of Dmitry, see NL, PSRL, XIII, 232.

152   For marriage of Yediger Makhmet, see ibid., 235.

152   For Fyodor Adashev becoming a boyar, see Zimin, "Sostav," 66.

153   For the birth of Tsarevich Ivan, see NL, PSRL, XIII, 239.

153   For the conquest of Astrakhan, see NL, PSRL, XIII, 235, 242–244, 274–27' Soloviev, III, 482–487; Karamzin, VIII, 216–220. After the capture of Astrakha in 1554 the Russians installed the vassal Khan Derbish. After the Khan attempted rebellion in 1556, a Russian governor was appointed.

154   For will of May 1554, see Karamzin, VIII, 210–211 and footnote on 318.

155   For Cabot's instructions, see Hakluyt, *Principal Navigations*, 232.

156   "Yea and though they lie: ibid., 259.

158   "There was a majesty: ibid., 280.

160   "We shall doe all that is: ibid., 317.

163   That done, the people: Berry and Crummey, *Rude & Barbarous Kingdom*, 5

165   For Vishnevetsky's raid, see NL, PSRL, XIII, 288, 296. Vishnevetsky cam from Lithuania and entered the Tsar's service in 1557.

165   For the Tatar invasion, see ibid., 314; Soloviev, III, 494–495.

165   For Daniel Adashev's raid into the Crimea, see NL, PSRL, XIII, 315, 318–32 *Lebedevskaya letopis*, PSRL, XXIX, 277, 279–280; Soloviev, III, 495; Karamzi 291–293.

166   "As a result of: NL, PSRL, XIII, 319.

166   For Vishnevetsky's second raid, see ibid., 318, 320.

166   For Cossack raids and famine in Crimea, see ibid., 322–323; Soloviev, III, 495; Karamzin, VIII, 249, 294.

166   For prohibition of travel in Russia of skilled artisans, see Soloviev, III, 498–499; Karamzin, VIII, 252–253.

167   For Dorpat tribute, see Yuriens, *Vopros o livonskoy dani*, 9–10, 13–14, 16, 57. In former times Dorpat, known as Yuriev, was a Russian city. In 1224, when the Germans captured it, the German bishop of the city agreed to pay tribute to Russia. The Russians maintained that this agreement was still in effect.

167   For the Livonian war, see Soloviev, III, 499–502; Karamzin, VIII, 252–256, 262–263; Yuriens, *Vopros o livonskoy dani*, 47, 49, 51; NL, PSRL, XIII, 280, 286–287; *Lebedevskaya letopis*, PSRL, XXIX, 254, 259, 260–261; Fennell, *History*, 106–121.

167   For the capture of Narva, see Soloviev, III, 502–503; Karamzin, VIII, 266–270; Fennell, *History*, 109–115; *Lebedevskaya letopis*, PSRL, XXIX, 264.

168   "My house and my ears: Karamzin, VIII, 280.

169   For capture of Ringen, see ibid., 282; Fennell, *History*, 118–119.

169   "Since the days of: Soloviev, III, 509.

170   "God knows, and: Karamzin, VIII, 299–300, and footnote on 498; Soloviev, III, 519.

170   "You call Livonia yours: ibid.

170   "He led me into: Fennell, *History*, 136–137.

170   For the Livonian campaign of 1560, see Fennell, *History*, 142–147; Karamzin, IX, 20–24; Soloviev, III, 566–568.

171   "the last defender: Fennell, *History*, 142–143.

171   "You are attempting: ibid., 148–149.

172   "Serves you right: Karamzin, IX, 25; Soloviev, III, 568.

172   For the peasant uprising, see Soloviev, III, 569.

172   "You can certainly: Staden, *The Land and Government*, 112–113.

172   For Anastasia's journey to Kolomenskoye, see NL, PSRL, XIII, 328; *Lebedevskaya letopis*, PSRL, XXIX, 287.

173   For death of Anastasia, see ibid. The chroniclers say nothing about the place of her death, but it seems likely to have been at Kolomenskoye.

174   "This empress became wise: Berry and Crummey, *Rude & Barbarous Kingdom*, 264–265, 299.

174   Concerning Ivan's order to end the mourning period, see NL, PSRL, XIII, 329; Fennell, *Correspondence*, 190–193; Karamzin, IX, 13–14.

175   For Vasily Blazhenny (St. Basil), see Fedotov, *Sviatye drevney Rusi*, 199–202.

175   For construction of the cathedral, see *Lebedevskaya letopis*, PSRL, XXIX, 235; NL, PSRL, XIII, 251–252, 320, 334.

176   "they, by God's: Kapitokhin, *Pokrovsky sobor*, 2.

176   For Postnik and Barma, see Myachin and Chernov, *Moscow*, 92.

177   For consecration of cathedral, see NL, PSRL, XIII, 320.

178   For Church of St. John the Baptist at Dyakovo, see Grabar, *Istoriya*, III, 435–439.

183   For frescoes in Zolotaya Palata, see Podobedova, *Moskovskaya shkola*, 10–22, 59–69; Zabelin, *Domashny byt*, 129–133.

185   For Ivan Viskovaty's objections, see Andreev, "O dele," 47–98; Vernadsky, V, 1, 75–76.

186   For icon of St. John the Baptist, see Daen, "Novootkryty pamiatnik," 207–225.

180   For Tsar's throne, see Mneva, *Iskustvo*, 131–132; Podobedova, *Moskovskaya shkola*, 22.

180   For crown of Monomakh, see Vernadsky, III, 386, and for crown of Kazan see Bogoyavlensky and Novitsky, *Gosudarstvennaya oruzheynaya palata*, 157–159, 514; *Kazansky letopisets*, XIX, 467, footnote. The crown was made in 1553. Historians hold various views about it. Some think it was made for Yediger Makhmet after he was baptized and received the honorary title of Khan of Kazan, while others believe that Ivan made it for himself.

186   For Ivan as a good singer and choir master, see Uspensky, *Drevnerusskoye pevcheskoye iskustvo*, 186. For the teaching of singing and the introduction of part-song, see ibid., 153, 169, 223–227.

188   For Ivan's hymn to the Virgin, see Leonid, *Pamiatniki*, No. 428, Vol. 63; Uspensky, *Drevnerusskoye pevcheskoye iskustvo*, 187–191, 357–362.

190   For St. Peter of Moscow, see Muraviev, *A History*, 51–57, and for the Hymn to St. Peter, see Leonid, *Pamiatniki*, loc. cit., and Tcherepnin, *Anthology*, 13, xxx.

193   For *Domostroy*, see Sylvester, *Domostroy*; Sazonova, *Istoriya*, II, 338–347; Vodovozov, *Istoriya*, 230–233; Soloviev, IV, 173–181.

194   "whip your child: Sylvester, *Domostroy*, 13–15.

195   "When rising in: Sylvester, *Domostroy*, 11–12.

196   For book printing in Ivan's time see Tikhomirov, *U istokov*, 10–40, 234–247; Barenbaum and Davydova, *Istoriya*, 55–65; Soloviev, IV, 187–188; Grabar, *Istoriya*, III, 610–625.

199   The *skomorokhi*—the word comes from the Scaramouche of the *Commedia del' Arte*—consisted of entertainers, buffoons, clowns, and musicians, who regularly attended feasts, weddings, and wakes. They traveled about and sometimes gave public performances. The Church objected to them primarily for their lewdness, and their activities were criticized by the Church Council of 1551. Under the Chosen Council they were banned from court, to the satisfaction of Prince Andrey Kurbsky, but after the fall of Adashev and Sylvester Ivan brought them back. See Nasonov, *Ocherki*, 402–403; Fennell, *History*, 22–23; Nechayev, "Ulichnaya zhizn," 78–79.

199   "The Tsar came: Fennell, *History*, 288.

200   For Ivan at Mozhaisk, see NL, PSRL, XIII, 320–322; Fennell, *History*, 136–137; Fennell, *Correspondence*, 96–99.

200   For Sylvester's retirement, see Fennell, *Correspondence*, 98–99; Fennell, *History*, 160–161.

201   For banishment of Adashev, see ibid., 158–159; Veselovsky, *Issledovaniya*, 98.

201   For trial of Sylvester and Adashev in their absence, see Fennell, *History*, 152–159. For burial of Adashev, see Tikhomirov, "Piskarevsky letopisets," 114.

202   "there was a great peace: Tikhomirov, "Piskarevsky letopisets," 114.

202   "kept scores of sick: Fennell, *History*, 178–179.

202   For Ivan's second marriage, see NL, PSRL, XIII, 329–333; *Lebedevskaya letopis*, PSRL, XXIX, 288–289, 291–292; Soloviev, III, 702; Karamzin, IX, 43; Vernadsky, V, 1, 103; Bond, *Russia*, 158. There exists very little information about Ivan's second wife. According to Staden, she advised Ivan to establish the Oprichnina. See Staden, *The Land and Government*, 17–18.

203   For the displeasure at court over Ivan's second marriage, see Zimin, *Oprichnina*, 90.

203   "God grant that: Pomerantsev and Mints, *Russkoye narodnoye, poeticheskoye tvorchestvo*, 378.

203   "One could see: Soloviev, III, 702.

203   On the confirmation of the Tsar's title by the Patriarch, see NL, PSRL, XIII, 334–339; Fennell, *History*, 274–279; *Lebedevskaya letopis*, PSRL, XXIX, 292–296.

204   For the arrest of Ivan Belsky, see ibid., 297; NL, PSRL, XIII, 340; Zimin, *Oprichnina*, 91–92; Veselovsky, *Issledovaniya*, 112.

204   For the King of Poland's letter to the Khan of the Crimea, see Soloviev, III, 574; NL, PSRL, XIII, 340; Karamzin, IX, 32–33.

204   For Ivan at Mozhaisk, see NL, PSRL, XIII, 341.

204   For arrest of Mikhail Vorotynsky, see ibid., 344; Zimin, *Oprichnina*, 90 and footnote 1.

204   For arrest of Kurliatev, see NL, PSRL, XIII, 344; Fennell, *History*, 182–183.

205   "And Kurliatev—why: Fennell, *Correspondence*, 190–191.

205   For Ivan's campaign of 1562–1563 and the capture of Polotsk, see NL, PSRL, XIII, 345–365; *Lebedevskaya letopis*, PSRL, XXIX, 301–319.

205   For death of Shakhovskoy, see Fennell, *History*, 190–191.

206   "a small single angry word: Fennell, *Correspondence*, 22–23.

206   For Kurbsky's banishment, see Andreyev, "Kurbsky's Letter," 426; Skrynnikov, "Kurbsky," 104; Zimin, *Oprichnina*, 102–103.

206   For the alleged treason and for the execution of Adashev's relatives, see Skrynnikov, "Kurbsky," 104; Zimin, *Oprichnina*, 103; Fennell, *History*, 179; Veselovsky, *Issledovaniya*, 110.

206   For the prosecution of the Sheremetevs, see Zimin, *Oprichnina*, 109–110. This took place in the spring of 1563 after the capture of Polotsk. Ivan Sheremetev was pardoned in the spring of 1564.

206   "His torture chamber: Fennell, *History*, 208–209.

207   "Adashev, Sylvester and Sheremetev: Zimin, *Oprichnina*, 110. These instructions were given to the Russian ambassador to the Crimean Khan in April 1563.

207   For the death of Vasily, see NL, PSRL, XIII, 366.

207   For the death of Yury, see ibid., 372.

207   For the death of Makary, see ibid., 374; Golubinsky, *Istoriya*, II, 744–875; Muraviev, *A History*, 101–112.

208   For the *Minei Chetii*, see Gumilevsky, *Obzor*, I, 147–155; *Velikiye Minei Chetii*.

208   For Makary's testament, see NL, PSRL, XIII, 374–377.

208   For Vladimir of Staritsa and his secretary, see NL, PSRL, XIII, 368; Zimin, *Oprichnina*, 104–106.

208   "After the capture: Shlichting, *Novoye izvestiye*, 16.

209   For release of the Poles, see NL, PSRL, XIII, 363.

209   For Molchan Mitkov, see Fennell, *History*, 290–291.

210   For Mikhail Repnin and Yury Kashin, see ibid., 180–181.

210   "Why," he asked: Fennell, *Correspondence*, 2–3.

210   For Kurbsky's and Ivan's letters, see Fennell, *Correspondence*; *Poslaniya*; Kuntsevich, *Sochineniya*.

       In 1971 Professor Edward Keenan, wrote a book called *The Kurbskii-Groznyi Apocrypha*, in which he attempted to show that the correspondence between Ivan IV and Andrey Kurbsky was not written by them but by certain persons in the 17th century. Professor Nikolay Andreyev of Cambridge, Professor Dmitry S. Likhachev of Moscow and Professor Ruslan G. Skrynnikov of Leningrad have published criticisms of Keenan's hypotheses. They pointed out numerous errors and inconsistencies. Professor Keenan's hypothesis rests on the fact that there are no sixteenth-century copies of the correspondence. All internal and external evidence goes to prove the authenticity of the Kurbsky-Ivan correspondence and Kurbsky's *History of Ivan IV*.

211 For Kurbsky's flight, see NL, PSRL, XIII, 383; *Prodolzhenie*, PSRL, XXIX, 334; Zimin, *Oprichnina*, 112–113; Skrynnikov, "Kurbsky," 110; Andreyev, "Kurbsky's Letters," 418, 428; Karamzin, IX, 56; Soloviev, III, 543.

211 For Kurbsky's wife, see Karamzin, VIII, 56.

211 For Yuliana becoming a nun, see NL, PSRL, XIII, 382; *Prodolzhenie*, PSRL, XXIX, 334.

212 "the Tsar, exalted above all: Fennell, *History*, 2–3.

212 For Vasily Shibanov, see Skrynnikov, "Kurbsky," 115; Karamzin, IX, 56–57, 59–60.

212 For Kurbsky's family relationship to Anastasia, see Fennell, *Correspondence*, 210–211.

212 For Kurbsky and Maxim the Greek, see Kurbsky, *Predisloviye*, 273–274.

212 For Kurbsky's literary activity and life in Lithuania, see Ustrialov, *Skazaniya*; Kuntsevich, *Sochineniya*; Gorsky, *Zhizn*; RBS, K, 585–600.

213 "It is always proper: Fennell, *Correspondence*.

213 "If thou considerest: ibid., 20–21.

213 "a leprous conscience: ibid., 2–3.

213 "As for blood: ibid., 66–67.

213 "I boast not: ibid., 152–153.

214 For Ivan's quotation from Dionysius, see ibid., 144–147.

214 "If it is sweet: ibid., 146–147.

215 "Why do you not: ibid., 246.

215 Kurbsky's *History of the Grand Prince of Moscow* appears to have been completed in 1573. Later Kurbsky added to it, see Zimin, "Kogda Kurbsky napisal 'Istoriyu o velikom kniaze Moskovskom'?"

215 For the deaths in Kurbsky's family, see Ustrialov, *Skazaniya*, 271–272.

216 For Ovchina-Obolensky and for the protests of the Metropolitan and the boyars, see Shlichting, *Novoye izvestiye*, 16–17.

217 "The Tsar," he wrote: Barberini, "Relatione," 207–208.

218 For the establishment of the Oprichnina, see NL, PSRL, XIII, 391–396; *Prodolzheniye*, PSRL, XXIX, 341–345; Yakovleva, "Piskarevsky letopisets," 75–76; Roginsky, "Poslaniye," 31–36; Shlichting, *Novoye izvestiye*, 18; Staden, *The Land and Government*, 17–19; Veselovsky, *Issledovaniya*, 134–143; Zimin, *Oprichnina*, 127–135; Sadikov, *Ocherki*, 19–25; Soloviev, III, 550–553; Karamzin, IX, 70–79; Shmidt, *Stanovleniye*, 211–246; Skrynnikov, "Oprichnaya zemelnaya reforma," 223–226; Skrynnikov, "Vvedeniye," 7–11; Kliuchevsky, *Sochineniya*, II, 172–176; Vernadsky, V, I, 107–109; Waliszewski, *Ivan the Terrible*, 237–247.

For the names of the oprichniki and the composition of the Oprichnina court, see Kobrin, "Sostav oprichnogo dvora," 16–91; Bibikov, "K voprosu," 5–28; Sukhotin, "Spisok," 19–25; Sukhotin, "K peresmotru."

218 For Ivan's regulated daily life, see Fennell, *Correspondence*, 90–93.

219 "My soul is satiated: Shlichting, *Novoye izvestiye*, 18.

220 For Ivan removing his robes and crown, see Roginsky, "Poslaniye," 31.

220 For Ivan plundering the Moscow icons, see ibid., 31–32.

220 For Ivan's leave-taking, see ibid., 32; NL, PSRL, XIII, 391; Staden, *The Land and Government*, 18; Zimin, *Oprichnina*, 127–128; *Prodolzheniye*, PSRL, XXIX, 341; Veselovsky, *Issledovaniye*, 134; Soloviev, III, 550–551.

221 For Ivan at Troitsa-Sergeyevsky Monastery, see NL, PSRL, XIII, 392.

221   For dress of oprichniki, see Roginsky, "Poslaniye," 38; Staden, *The Land and Government*, 18; Tikhomirov, "Piskarevsky letopisets," 115; Karamzin, IX, 83–84; Sadikov, *Ocherki*, 22.

221   For the boyars being sent back naked, see Roginsky, "Poslaniye," 32.

222   For Ivan's letters to Moscow, see Zimin, *Oprichnina*, 129–130; NL, PSRL, XIII, 392; *Prodolzheniye*, PSRL, XXIX, 342.

222   "wherefore the Tsar: NL, PSRL, XIII, 392.

222   "If God and the weather: Roginsky, "Poslaniye," 32.

223   For Ivan's letter to the people, see NL, PSRL, XIII, 392.

223   "Woe unto us who have sinned: ibid., 393.

224   "With grave reluctance: Roginsky, "Poslaniye," 32.

225   For the delegation and their reception, see NL, PSRL, XIII, 392; Roginsky, "Poslaniye," 32.

226   "Thus," commented a Livonian: Roginsky, "Poslaniye," 34.

226   For the Oprichnina part of Moscow and the Kremlin, see NL, PSRL, XIII, 395.

227   For Ivan's speech to the boyars, see Roginsky, "Poslaniye," 34–35; NL, PSRL, XIII, 395.

228   For arrests and executions, see NL, PSRL, XIII, 395–396.

228   For money for prayers, see Veselovsky, *Issledovaniye*, 147.

228   For death of Gorensky, see Shlichting, *Novoye izvestiye*, 36. According to another account he was hanged, see Roginsky, "Poslaniye," 35.

229   For death of Simeon Rostovsky, see Shlichting, *Novoye izvestiye*, 20–21.

231   For description of Alexandrova Sloboda, see Bocharov and Vygolov, *Aleksandrovskaya Sloboda*; Karamzin, IX, 84; Vasiliev, *Aleksandrovskaya Sloboda*. For life there see Roginsky, "Poslaniye," 39–40; Shlichting, *Novoye izvestiye*, 25–27.

232   For young Basmanov being Ivan's bedmate, see Shlichting, *Novoye izvestiye*, 17; Staden, *The Land and Government*, 125.

233   For the recruiting of the oprichniki, see Roginsky, "Poslaniye," 35–36.

233   "If any citizen: ibid., 35.

233   "I swear to be loyal: ibid., 35. See also Staden, *The Land and Government*, 18, 30, 104–105. For Kurbsky's version of the oath, see Fennell, *History*, 249–251.

234   For power and abuses of the oprichniki, see Staden, *The Land and Government*, 19, 32–34, 80, 109; Roginsky, "Poslaniye," 37–38.

236   "The tyrant habitually: Shlichting, *Novoye izvestiye*, 25.

236   Taube and Cruse relate: Roginsky, "Poslaniye," 40.

237   For Shlichting at Alexandrova Sloboda, see Shlichting, *Novoye izvestiye*, 26.

237   Concerning the policy of refusing Christian burial, see Veselovsky, *Issledovaniya*, 325–336, especially 334–336.

237   For the story-tellers, see Roginsky, "Poslaniye," 40.

237   For the Tsar's pilgrimage, see NL, PSRL, XIII, 399–400.

238   For Tatar raid, see ibid.

238   For the provinces and townships taken into the Oprichnina, see ibid., 394–395; Roginsky, "Poslaniye," 35–36; Zimin, *Oprichnina*, 306–341; Skrynnikov, "Oprichnaya zemelnaya reforma," 223–350; Veselovsky, *Issledovaniye*, 156–177.

238   For Vorotynsky being pardoned, see Zimin, *Oprichnina*, 161.

238   For the pardon given to the nobles exiled to Kazan, see Skrynnikov, "Oprichnaya zemelnaya reforma," 249.

238   For the resignation of Afanasy, see NL, PSRL, XIII, 401; *Prodolzheniye*, PSRL, XXIX, 350; Zimin, *Oprichnina*, 240–241.

238 "a man of great: Fennell, *History*, 244–245. For Polev, see Zimin, *Oprichnina*, 240–241.

239 For the appointment of Philipp Kolychev, see Karamzin, IX, 91–94; Zimin, *Oprichnina*, 244–247; Muraviev, *A History*, 114–115; NL, PSRL, XIII, 403.

239 "I will obey your wish"; Karamzin, IX, 91–92.

240 For Metropolitan Philipp's sermon, see Karamzin, IX, 94; Muraviev, *A History*, 115.

241 For the Oprichnina Palace, see NL, PSRL, XIII, 401–406; Staden, *The Land and Government*, 48–52; Skrynnikov, "Samoderzhaviye," 83, and footnote 40.

242 For the petition to abolish the Oprichnina, see Shlichting, *Novoye izvestiye*, 38–39; Zimin, *Oprichnina*, 202–203; Sadikov, *Ocherki*, 29; Yakovleva, "Piskarevsky letopisets," 76; Petrei, "Podlinnoye i podrobnoye Opisaniye," 137.

242 For the execution of the petitioners, see Fennell, *History*, 192–193; Shlichting, *Novoye izvestiye*, 39.

242 "The Tsar is indeed merciful: Zimin, *Oprichnina*, 203; Veselovsky, *Issledovaniye*, 432.

242 "Do you not know: Karamzin, IX, 92; Zimin, *Oprichnina*, 249.

243 For Ivan's fears and plans of flight, see Skrynnikov, "Samoderzhaviye," 84–85; Tolstoy, *Pervye sorok let*, 40.

243 For the oprichniki keeping Ivan's suspicions at fever pitch, see Skrynnikov, "Samoderzhaviye," 84.

243 For Oprichnina Palace, see NL, PSRL, XIII, 401–406.

243 For retiring to monastery, see Skrynnikov, "Samoderzhaviye," 84.

243 For fortifications of Vologda, see NL, PSRL, XIII, 406.

243 For messages to the four boyars from Sigismund Augustus, see Zimin, *Oprichnina*, 267–268.

244 "We have carefully read: Poslaniya, 418–419.

245 "You say that God: ibid., 419–420.

246 "Being possessed by: ibid., 438.

246 For Ivan setting out against Livonia, see Zimin, *Oprichnina*, 265–267.

250 "I and those two: Shlichting, *Novoye izvestiye*, 23; Skrynnikov, "Samoderzhaviye," 85; Skrynnikov, "Vvedeniye," 37–42.

250 For the death of Dubrovsky, see Shlichting, *Novoye izvestiye*, 24; Zimin, *Oprichnina*, 272–273.

250 For the Cheliadnin affair, see Shlichting, *Novoye izvestiye*, 21–22; Staden, *The Land and Government*, 19–20; Zimin, *Oprichnina*, 273–284; Skrynnikov, "Vvedeniye," 37–41; Roginsky, "Poslaniye," 41–42.

250 "This is what you: Shlichting, *Novoye izvestiye*, 22.

252 For the reign of terror against those connected with Cheliadnin, see Roginsky, "Poslaniye," 41–42; Fennell, *History*, 314–217.

252 For the punitive expeditions against Cheliadnin's estates, see Shlichting, *Novoye izvestiye*, 22–23, 37; Staden, *The Land and Government*, 21; Skrynnikov, "Vvedeniye," 38–39, 68–71.

253 "None of the victims: Roginsky, "Poslaniye," 41.

For punitive raids on villages in the far north, see Kopanev, "Nezemledelcheskaya volost," 176–194.

For punitive raids against fortresses in the south, see Fennell, *History*, 224–229.

254 For the conflict between the Tsar and Metropolitan Philipp, see Yankovsky, "Pechalovaniye dukhovenstva," 186–198; Zimin, *Oprichnina*, 248–257; RBS, F, 116–121; Muraviev, *A History*, 114–117; Karamzin, IX, 99–106; Roginsky, "Poslaniye," 43–44; Fennell, *History*, 233–241.

254   "Those who are close: Yankovsky, "Pechalovaniye dukhovenstva," 190.

254   For Philipp's proposal to convene a synod, see Zimin, *Oprichnina*, 249–251.

254   "Holy father, the Tsar: Karamzin, IX, 100.

255   "Even in the heathen kingdoms: Karamzin, IX, 101–102.

255   "Do you dare challenge: ibid., 102; Yankovsky, "Pechalovaniye dukhovenstva," 192.

255   "Up to now: Roginsky, "Poslaniye," 43.

255   "I am a stranger: Yankovsky, "Pechalovaniye dukhovenstva," 192.

255   For the arrest of the Metropolitan's court, see Roginsky, "Poslaniye," 43.

256   "You are making: Yankovsky, "Pechalovaniye dukhovenstva," 192.

256   "When we are glorifying: ibid., 193.

257   For the delegation to the Solovetsky Monastery, see ibid., 194–195.

257   "The evil you have; ibid., 194–195.

258   For the attack against Philipp in the Cathedral, see ibid., 195.

258   "Children I have done: Yankovsky, "Pechalovaniye dukhovenstva," 195.

260   For Archbishop Herman Polev and his death, see Zimin, *Oprichnina*, 250, 255–256.

260   "Spells, spells has he cast!" Fennell, *History*, 238–239.

261   For the Tsar's fear of riots, see Yankovsky, "Pechalovaniye dukhovenstva," 197.

261   "Here is the head: Fennell, *History*, 217.

262   For the affair of Vladimir of Staritsa, and his death, see Roginsky, "Poslaniye," 45–47; Staden, *The Land and Government*, 21, 28; Karamzin, IX, 136–140; Zimin, *Oprichnina*, 289–292; Skrynnikov, "Vvedeniye," 45–46; Fennell, *History*, 192–193.

263   "knowing nothing whatsoever: Roginsky, "Poslaniye," 46.

264   For the death of Efrosinia, see Karamzin, IX, 140; Zimin, *Oprichnina*, 292.

267   For Peter Volynets and the forged letter of treason, see Zimin, *Oprichnina*, 294; *Novgorodskiye letopisi*, 485; Karamzin, IX, 142.

269   For the downfall of the Basmanovs and Viazemsky, see Vernadsky, V, 1, 123; Zimin, *Oprichnina*, 442.

269   For the fall of Viazemsky, see Shlichting, *Novoye izvestiye*, 32–33.

269   "You can see for yourself: ibid., 33.

269   Only a short while before: Staden, *The Land and Government*, 125.

269   Concerning the passing of power to Maliuta Skuratov and Vasily Griaznoy, see Skrynnikov, "Samoderzhaviye," 89.

269   For the secret meeting, see Roginsky, "Poslaniye," 47; Zimin, *Oprichnina*, 294 and footnote 1.

270   For the punitive expedition against Novgorod, see Zimin, *Oprichnina*, 294–303; Skrynnikov, "Oprichny razgrom Novgoroda," 157–171: *Novgorodskaya tretiya letopis*, 254–262: Roginsky, "Poslaniye," 47–50; Staden, *The Land and Government*, 25–27; Fennell, *History*, 245–247; Karamzin, IX, 141–149; Shlichting, *Novoye izvestiye*, 27–32; Soloviev, III, 558–560; Bond, *Russia*, 161–163; Berry, *Rude & Barbarous Kingdom*, 268–269.

270   For size of Oprichnina forces, see Roginsky, "Poslaniye," 48.

271   "Only those who are good: Karamzin, IX, 143.

273   For the Tatar prisoner's attack on the Tsar, see Roginsky, "Poslaniye," 49.

274   For *Gorodishche*, see Tikhomirov, *Drevenerusskiye goroda*, 22–23.

276   "Because you worship: *Novgorodskaya tretiya letopis*, 256–258.

276   For the pillage of the cathedral, see ibid., 257–259.

277   "You have no right: Shlichting, *Novoye izvestiye*, 29–30.

277   "Here is your wife!" ibid, 30.

277   Concerning the musical instrument, see ibid., Karamzin, IX, 148.

278   "Archbishop Pimen may not: Skrynnikov, "Oprichny razgrom Novgoroda," 165.

278   For women and children being thrown off the bridge, see *Novgorodskaya tretiya letopis*, 260.

278   For Ivan's part in the killings, see Shlichting, *Novoye izvestiye*, 29.

279   Concerning Maliuta Skuratov and his victims, see Skrynnikov, "Vvedeniye," 49–50.

279   "Did you see anything: Shlichting, *Novoye izvestiye*, 30.

280   For the plunder of the monasteries outside Novgorod, see *Novgorodskaya tretiya letopis*, 259, 261.

280   For the sack of the city, see *Novgorodskaya tretiya letopis*, 261.

280   "After the pillage: Staden, *The Land and Government*, 27.

281   "Men of Novgorod the Great: *Novgorodskaya tretiya letopis*, 261–262, 259–260.

282   For people dying of pestilence and famine, see *Novgorodskiye letopisi*, 101, 106.

282   For the booty, see Staden, *The Land and Government* 28, 119; Roginsky, "Poslaniye," 49–51; Shlichting, *Novoye izvestiye*, 31.

282   For Horsey's fantastic number, see Bond, *Russia*, 162.

283   For bodies stored in barrels, see Shlichting, *Novoye izvestiye*, 31–32.

283   For the Market Side being incorporated in the Oprichnina, see *Novgorodskiye letopisi*, 100, 110; Zimin, *Oprichnina*, 339.

284   For the annexation of Pskov, see Karamzin, VII, 25–41; Zimin, *Rossiya*, 112–123; Soloviev, III, 233–238.

284   For life in Pskov, see Tikhomirov, *Rossiya*, 317–321; Spegalsky, *Pskov*; Moleva, *Pskov*; Hammerich and Jakobson, *Tonnies Fenne's Low German Manual*; Khoroshevich, "Byt i Kultura," 200–217.

286   They waited in fear: Karamzin, IX, 149–151.

286   For the plundering by the oprichniki, see Staden, *The Land and Government*, 119–121, see also 33–34.

286   "I began to assemble: ibid., 119–120.

286   "We came to a town: ibid., 120–121.

287   For Ivan's punitive expedition against Pskov, see Karamzin, IX, 149–151; Skrynnikov, "Oprichny razgrom Novgoroda," 167–168; Zimin, *Oprichnina*, 302–303; Soloviev, III, 561, 734 and footnote 91; Shlichting, *Novoye izvestiye*, 32.

288   For Vassian Muromtsev being among those who met Ivan, see Zimin, *Oprichnina*, 302–303.

288   "Our Lord and Tsar: Karamzin, IX, 150.

290   For the Tsar gazing at the sword of Prince Vsevolod, see ibid., IX, 151.

290   For the execution of forty local nobles, see Skrynnikov, "Oprichny razgrom Novgoroda," 67.

290   "Ivashka! Ivashka!" See Roginsky, "Poslaniye," 50; Staden, *The Land and Government*, 27–28.

290   "I am a Christian: Karamzin, IX, 151.

290   "A thunderbolt will: Bond, *Russia*, 161.

291   For horse falling dead, see Soloviev, III, footnote 91 to page 734.

291   For the heavy war tax, see PPL, PSRL, IV, 318.

291   For muster at Staritsa, see Staden, *The Land and Government*, 121.

292   For Staden being in the Tsar's good graces, see ibid., 121. At the muster at

Staritsa the Tsar said to Staden, "You shall be called Andrey Vladimirovich." As a result Staden believed he was now a noble as only important men were addressed with their patronymic and began calling himself Heinrich von Staden. In 1572 he commanded 300 oprichnik petty nobles, thus confirming his new position, see ibid., 130.

292   For Krotowski's embassy and his hopes, see Vernadsky, V, 1, 127.

293   "You believe in the Ten Commandments: Scherbatow, *The Answer*, 14, from whose unpublished manuscript the remaining quotations from Ivan's answer to Rakita are taken.

297   For the departure of the Polish and Lithuanian embassy, see Vernadsky, V, 1, 128; Zimin, *Oprichnina*, 436.

297   For the death of Peter Serebriany, see Shlichting, *Novoye izvestiye*, 44–45.

297   For the executions in Moscow, see Shlichting, *Novoye izvestiye*, 44–49; Staden, *The Land and Government*, 28; Roginsky, "Poslaniye," 51; Petrei, "Opisaniye," 141–144; Zimin, *Oprichnina*, 436–444; Skrynnikov, "Vvedeniye," 53–58; Karamzin, IX, 152–158.

298   For preparations on the Red Square for the executions, see Shlichting, *Novoye izvestiye*, 45–46; Petrei, "Opisaniye," 141.

299   "Is it right for me: Shlichting, *Novoye izvestiye*, 46.

300   For Viskovaty's petition to the Tsar, see Shlichting, *Novoye izvestiye*, 62; Skrynnikov, "Samoderzhaviye," 88.

300   "I have only just: Shlichting, *Novoye izvestiye*, 62.

300   For Ivan's suspicions concerning the Tsarevich Ivan, see Skrynnikov, "Samoderzhaviye," 88–89; Shmurlo, *Rossiya i Italiya*, II, 230. At the end of 1570 it was reported in Poland that "a serious disagreement and rift had occurred between the Tsar and his eldest son, and that there were many important persons well disposed to the father and many others were well disposed to the son."

301   "Your Illustrious Highness: Skrynnikov, "Samoderzhaviye," 88, footnote 58; Shcherbachev, "Kopengagenskiye akty." *Chteniya*, II, III, 34.

301   Evdokia was sometimes mistakenly called Eufimia. She died that same year on November 20, 1570; see Zimin, *Oprichnina*, 433, footnote 5.

301   Magnus married Maria on April 12, 1572 in Novgorod, see Zimin, *Oprichnina*, 433, footnote 5: Tsvetayev, *Maria Vladimirovna*, 57–85.

301   "This man Ivan: Shlichting, *Novoye izvestiye*, 46–47.

302   "Your second act: ibid., 47.

302   How many women and girls: Petrei, "Opisaniye," 143.

302   "Damnation upon your tyrant!; Shlichting, *Novoye izvestiye*, 47.

303   "That's goose flesh: Berry, *Rude & Barbarous Kingdom*, 165.

303   "You will die!; Shlichting, *Novoye izvestiye*, 48.

303   For execution of the cook, see ibid., 48.

303   Concerning the Tsarevich Ivan spearing the victims, see Roginsky, "Poslaniye," 51.

304   "Dear Father, let me have her!; Shlichting, *Novoye izvestiye*, 57, footnote 49.

304   For the execution of the prisoners' wives, see Skrynnikov, "Vvedeniye," 56.

304   For the death of the Basmanovs, see Zimin, *Oprichnina*, 442–443; Staden, *The Land and Government*, 35; Fennell, *History*, 288–289.

304   For the punishment and imprisonment of Viazemsky, see Shlichting, *Novoye izvestiye*, 33; Zimin, *Oprichnina*, 443. Later Viazemsky was released from prison and in the reign of Ivan's son he was serving in Kazan. But he never regained any influence. See Buganov, *Razriadnaya Kniga*, 494.

307   For the Tsar's departure for the Oka River, see Zimin, *Oprichnina*, 451.

307   For Serpukhov and other fortresses on the Oka, see Tikhomirov, *Rossiya*, 137–155. For defense of the southern frontier, see Zimin, *Oprichnina*, 251.

307   For the fixed scale of ransom, see Veselovsky, *Issledovaniya*, 214.

307   For the force of 6,000 Tatars, see Zimin, *Oprichnina*, 450–451.

307   For Novosil and other possessions of Mikhail Vorotynsky in the south, see Skrynnikov, "Oprichnina," 163.

308   For the Tatar invasion of 1571 and the fire of Moscow, see Karamzin, IX, 176–183; Soloviev, III, 606–608; Zimin, *Oprichnina*, 450–452; Buganov, *Razriadnaya Kniga, 239*–240; Staden, *The Land and Government*, 46–48, 51, 83–84, 129; Bond, *Russia*, 163–168; Berry, *Rude & Barbarous Kingdom*, 270–274; Roginsky, "Poslaniye," 52–54; NL, PSRL, XIII, 300–301; Tikhomirov, "Maloizvestnye letopisnye pamiatniki," 225; Yakovleva, "Piskarevsky letopisets," 79–80; Tikhomirov, "Piskarevsky letopisets," 116–117; Novoselsky, *Borba Moskovskogo gosudarstva*, 26–27, 32, 430. For Ivan's own account, Tolstoy, "Rech," 298; Soloviev, III, 620; Turgenev, *Historica*, Vol. I, 230.

308   "the insides were falling; Novoselsky, *Borba*, 26–27.

308   For the Turkish expedition against Astrakhan, see Karamzin, IX, 123–128.

308   For the size of the Khan's army, Zimin, *Oprichnina*, Karamzin, IX, 176.

308   "If you fail to reach Moscow: Zimin, *Oprichnina*, 452.

309   For the size of the Russian forces on the Oka River, see Novoselsky, *Borba Moskovskogo gosudarstva*, 430.

309   For Ivan's flight, see Zimin, *Oprichnina*, 453; NL, PSRL, XIII, 301; Bond, *Russia*, 165. Turgenev, *Historica*, Vol. I, 221.

309   "No one warned me: Tolstoy, "Rech," 298; Soloviev, III, 620.

312   For Giles Fletcher, see Berry, *Rude & Barbarous Kingdom*, 191–192.

312   For the disposition of the Russian forces around Moscow, see Zimin, *Oprichnina*, 454.

312   For Temkin-Rostovsky, see Kobrin, "Sostav," 76–77.

313   Stone walls only existed around the Kremlin and Kitay Gorod, around the rest of the city there were earthern ramparts with moat and wooden bridges. See Sytin, *Ulitsy*, 68, 118, 288. There may have been gates.

313   For the battle south of the river and the wounding of Belsky, see Tikhomirov, "Maloizvestnye letopisnye pamiatniki," 225.

314   "the entire city: Yankovleva, "Piskarevsky letopisets," 79.

314   For Staden forcing people out of the cellar, see Staden, *The Land and Government*, 129.

314   For the Khan on Sparrow Hills, see Karamzin, IX, 180.

314   For the number of prisoners taken by the Tatars, see Zimin, *Oprichnina*, 457. According to reports from Poland received from the Crimean ambassador, the Tatars took 60,000 prisoners and killed 60,000 Russians, loc. cit.

315   For council at Alexandrova Sloboda, see Karamzin, IX, 180; Bond, *Russia*, 166.

315   For the rebuilding of the city, see Bond, *Russia*, 167–168.

315   For the Tsar losing faith in the oprichniki, see Staden, *The Land and Government*, 34–35.

316   For the execution of the oprichniki, see Zimin, *Oprichnina* 460–462; Staden, *The Land and Government*, 35; Roginsky, "Poslaniye," 54.

316   "Hanged from the court gates: Staden, *The Land and Government*, 35.

316   For Bomelius, see *Dictionary of National Biography*, 796–797; Berry, *Rude &*

Barbarous Kingdom, 274, 279, 292–293; PPL, PSRL, IV, 318; Roginsky, "Poslaniye," 54.

316   "The Tsar," they reported: Roginsky, "Poslaniye," 54.

317   "I pressed among many: Berry, *Rude & Barbarous Kingdom*, 293.

317   "completely turned the Tsar: PPL, PSRL, IV, 318.

317   "he lived in great favor: Berry, *Rude & Barbarous Kingdom*, 279, 293.

317   For the defensive preparations on the Oka in the event of another Tatar invasion, see Burdey, "Molodinskaya bitva," 53–54, 60, 62.

317   For truce with Sweden, see ibid., 64.

317   For the Tsar's meeting with the ambassador of the Crimean Khan, on June 15, see Karamzin, IX, 180–182; Soloviev, III, 607–608; Bond, *Russia*, 166–167.

318   "I came to Russia: Karamzin, IX, 181–182: Soloviev, III, 607–608.

319   "He fell into an agony: Bond, *Russia*, 167.

322   For Ivan's policy of prolonging the negotiations, Karamzin, IX, 182; Soloviev, III, 608.

322   "You offer Astrakhan: Soloviev, III, 608.

322   For Ivan's journey to Novgorod and the truce with Sweden, see Zimin, *Oprichnina*, 467.

322   "The sword remains sharp: Soloviev, III, 609.

322   For Ivan's third marriage and for the marriage of Tsarevich Ivan, see Karamzin, IX, 183–184; Zimin, *Oprichnina*, 466.

323   "Christians are being enslaved: *Mazurinsky letopisets*, PSRL, XXXI, 138.

323   For Ivan's fourth marriage to Anna Koltovskaya, see ibid., Zimin, *Oprichnina*, 470, for Anna becoming a nun, see Skrynnikov, "Vvedeniye," 63.

323   "advance like a bloodthirsty: Fennell, *History*, 194–195, Staden, *The Land and Government*, 58, 76; Zimin, *Oprichnina*, 472.

324   For defensive preparations, see Burdey, "Molodinskaya bitva," 53–54, 63.

324   For Ivan's move to Novgorod, see *Novgorodskiye letopisi*, 108, 110, 113–116; Karamzin, IX, 196; Zimin, *Oprichnina*, 470.

324   "Tell me when the Khan: Veselovsky, *Issledovaniya*, 313.

325   For Ivan's message to the army, see Burdey, "Molodinskaya bitva," 63; Buganov, "Dokumenty," 179.

325   For Ivan's will, see *Dukhovnye i dogovornye gramoty*, 426–445; Zimin, *Oprichnina*, 471–472, Veselovsky, *Issledovaniya*, 302–322; Skrynnikov, "Dukhovnoye zaveshchaniye," 309–318. Skrynnikov believes that the will was written in the winter of 1564–1565, but most historians are of the opinion that it was written in Novgorod in the summer of 1572. Vernadsky, V, 1, 135–137; Grigoriev, "Zaveshchaniye," 210–214.

326   "My body has grown feeble: *Dukhovnye i dogovornye gramoty*, 426.

326   "although I am: ibid., 426.

327   For the invasion and the battle of Molodi, see Buganov, "Dokumenty," 168–183 and "Povest," 259–275; Burdey, "Molodinskaya bitva," 48–79; Staden, *The Land and Government*, 53–55, 129–130: Karamzin, IX, 198–201; Buganov and Koretsky, "Neizvestny Moskovsky letopisets," 142–143.

327   "All our plans: Buganov and Koretsky, "Neizvestny Moskovsky letopisets," 143.

328   "every corpse that: Staden, *The Land and Government*, 55.

328   "No mighty cloud: Zenkovsky, *Medieval Russian Epics*, 424–425.

332   "I had believed: Karamzin, IX, 200–201; Soloviev, III, 640–641.

332   For services and celebrations in Novgorod, see *Novgorodskiye letopisi*, 120.

332   For the Tsar handing out rewards, see Buganov and Koretsky, "Neizvestny Moskovsky letopisets," 143; Buganov, "Documenty," 181.

334   "The Tsar began to hate: Buganov and Koretsky, "Neizvestny Moskovsky letopisets," 143.

334   For Ivan receiving the Tatar envoy, see Karamzin, IX, 206–207.

334   "We have one sword: ibid.

335   "If the Polish and Lithuanian: Tolstoy, "Rech," 297; Karamzin, IX, 209–210; Soloviev, III, 620.

335   For Ivan's speech to the Polish and Lithuanian delegates, see Tolstoy, "Rech," 297–302; Karamzin, IX, 211–213; Soloviev, III, 619–623; Turgenev, *Historica*, Vol. I, 229–232.

337   For the wedding of Magnus and Maria in Novgorod, see Karamzin, IX, 216–217; Likhachev, "Kanon i molitva," 20.

338   "King Magnus, it is now: Karamzin, IX, 217.

339   For the end of the Oprichnina, see Staden, *The Land and Government*, 34–35, 52, 130; Bond, *Russia*, 166; Berry, *Rude & Barbarous Kingdom*, 273; Zimin, *Oprichnina*, 473; 476–477; Veselovsky, *Issledovaniya*, 190–199; Sadikov, *Ocherki*, 134–138; Karamzin, IX, 202–204: Vernadsky, V, I, 135–139.

339   "All their estates: Staden, *The Land and Government*, 52.

339   For the death of Skuratov, see Zimin, *Oprichnina*, 477; Kobrin, "Sostav oprichnogo dvora," 23–24.

339   For Vasily Griaznoy's death, see Veselovsky, *Issledovaniya*, 214–215; Karamzin, IX, 207–208; according to Karamzin the Tsar in the end ransomed Griaznoy.

339   "Why did you say: Veselovsky, *Issledovaniya*, 215; Karamzin, IX, 207; Obnorsky, *Khrestomatiya*, 252–253.

340   For arrest and death of Vorotynsky, see Vernadsky, V, I, 140–141; Fennell, *History*, 196–199; Karamzin, IX, 262–263; Veselovsky, *Issledovaniya*, 369–370.

340   "Your servant, Ivan said: Fennell, *History*, 196–199.

341   For the death of Odoevsky, see Fennell, *History*, 199.

341   For the death of Morozov, see ibid., 230–231.

341   For the Tsar's donation, see Veselovsky, *Issledovaniya*, 416–417, 367.

341   For the Tsar's letter, see *Poslaniya*, 161; Sazonova, *Istoriya*, 368–372; Gudzey, *Khrestomatiya*, 300–304; Obnorsky, *Khrestomatiya*, 260–265.

341   The Tsar's statement that the Sheremetev brothers urged the Tatars to attack Russia was pure fantasy. See Zimin, *Oprichnina*, 464.

341   For the Sobakins, see Skrynnikov, "Vvedeniye," 62; Veselovsky, *Issledovaniya*, 445–446.

345   For the interrogation of returning prisoners, see Zimin, *Oprichnina*, 464; Bogoyavlensky, "Dopros," 29–30.

345   For Anna Koltovskaya, see Skrynnikov, "Vvedeniye," 63.

345   For Leonid, Archbishop of Novgorod, see Bond, *Russia*, 187–188; Berry, *Rude & Barbarous Kingdom*, 292–293; Nasonov, *Pskovskiye letopisi*, II, 262; *Novgorodskiye letopisi*, 148, 345; Buganov and Koretsky, "Neizvestny Moskovsky letopisets," 163, footnote 20. According to Jerome Horsey the arrest of Leonid was connected with the arrest of Eliseus Bomelius.

345   "His majesty came to the city: Bond, *Russia*, 194; Berry, *Rude & Barbarous Kingdom*, 298–299; Buganov, "Neizvestny Moskovsky letopisets," 145.

346   For Andrey Shchelkalov's punishment, see Berry, *Rude & Barbarous Kingdom*, 299.

346   For the heads thrown in courtyards, see Yankovleva, "Piskarevsky letopisets," 81.

346   For the sporadic executions, see ibid.; Buganov and Koretsky, "Neizvestny Moskovsky letopisets," 145.

347   For Sayin Bulat's arrival in Russia, see NL, PSRL, XIII, 333.

347   For Tatar princes in Russian service, see Vernadsky, V, I, 92–94, 142.

348   For Simeon Bekbulatovich, see RBS, S, 465–471; Vernadsky, V, I, 142–146; Lileev, *Simeon Bekbulatovich*; Vernadsky, "Ivan Grozny," 151–169; Buganov and Koretsky, "Neizvestny Moskovsky letopisets," 132–134, 145–146.

348   For Novosiltsev's report to the Sultan, see RBS, S, 466.

349   "If you remain Tsar: Yakovleva, "Piskarevsky letopisets," 82.

349   "The Tsar and Grand Prince: Buganov and Koretsky, "Neizvestny Moskovsky letopisets," 145.

350   For the enthronement ceremony, see Prinz, "Nachalo," 29; Tikhomirov, "Piskarevsky letopisets," 17; Sadikov, *Ocherki*, 42.

350   For Ivan's title of Prince Moskovsky, see Buganov and Koretsky, "Neizvestny Moskovsky letopisets," 132–134, 146.

350   For Ivan's house on Petrovka Street, see Soloviev, III, 564–565; Sytin, *Iz istorii Moskovskikh ulits*, 420.

350   For Ivan's messages to Kazan, see Kashtanov, "Finansovaya problema," 245.

351   "Ivanets Vasiliev together with: RIB, XXII, II, 76–77.

352   For Simeon's marriage, see Buganov and Koretsky, "Neizvestny Moskovsky letopisets," 145; Sadikov, *Ocherki*, 41–42.

352   For the treaty, see Tolstoy, *Pervye sorok let*, 39, 179, Bond, *Russia*, xxvi–xxxix.

353   "We have resigned the estate: Tolstoy, *Pervye sorok let*, 179–182.

354   For the relations between Maximilian II and Ivan, see Karamzin, IX, 231–232.

354   "Dear brother, you grieve: Karamzin, IX, 232.

354   For the embassy of Maximilian II, see Prinz, "Nachalo," 27–29, 50–56; Pernshtein, "Doneseniye," 1–20.

354   "You should not be alarmed: Prinz, "Nachalo," 50–51.

355   "He is very tall: ibid., 27.

355   "They say that: ibid.

357   For Henry of Valois in Poland, see Soloviev, III, 629.

358   For the negotiations, see ibid., 636–637.

359   For the second meeting with Sylvester, see Tolstoy, *Pervye sorok let*, 183–185.

360   "At our pleasure: Tolstoy, *Pervye sorok let*, 184–185.

361   For the decrees issued by Simeon Beckbulatovich, see Kashtanov, "Finansovaya problema," 244–247.

361   For Ivan Liubovnikov, see Likhachev, *Razriadniye diaki*, 472.

361   "Prince Ivan Vasilievich Moskovsky, Buganov and Koretsky, "Neizvestny Moskovsky letopisets, 146.

361   "To the Lord: "Neizvestny Moskovsky letopisets," 146; Likhachev, *Razriadniye diaki*, 65.

362   For Simeon Bekbulatovich becoming Grand Prince of Tver, see Buganov and Koretsky, "Neizvestny Moskovsky letopisets," 146; RBS, S, 470–471.

363   For sources of Ivan's campaign of 1577, see Soloviev, III, 645–646; Karamzin, IX, 246–260; Buganov, *Razriadnaya Kniga*, 281.

363   For truce, see Karamzin, IX, 251.

364   For women and children sold into slavery, see ibid.

364   "To Magnus the king: ibid., 253; Soloviev, III, 645.

364   "Fool! So you dared: Karamzin, IX, 255; Soloviev, III, 645.

366   For Ivan's letter to Kurbsky from Volmar, see Fennell, *Correspondence*, 186–197.

366   "I could not: ibid., 192–197.

367   "I am Ivan: Karamzin, IX, 260.

368   For sources for the events after Ivan's campaign of 1577, see Karamzin, IX, 276–282; Soloviev, III, 646–649; Ulfeld, "Opisaniye," 48, 50; Vernadsky, V, I, 150–151.

369   "As for your vaunting: Fennell, *Correspondence*, 212–215.

369   For Stephen Bathory's campaign of 1579 and the fall of Polotsk, see Karamzin, IX, 287–300; Soloviev, III, 652–655; Vasilievsky, "Polskaya i nemetskaya pechat," 131–139; Heidenstein, *Zapiski*, 38–87.

369   For the tombstone from the sky, see Polosin, *Sotsialno-politicheskaya istoriya*, 205.

369   "Good people! Know that: ibid., 205–206; Karamzin, IX, 300, footnote 519.

373   For the disastrous situation in Russia, Shmidt, "K istorii," 146; Zimin, "Khoziaistvenny krizis," 11–20.

373   "He told them that: Bond, *Russia*, 174–180; Berry and Crummey, *Rude & Barbarous Kingdom*, 280–285.

374   "You buy and sell: ibid., 282; Bond, *Russia*, 176.

375   For the arrest of the seven monks, see ibid., 178; Berry, *Rude & Barbarous Kingdom*, 283–284.

375   For the Church Council, see ibid., 285; Bond, *Russia*, 179; Karamzin, IX, 302; Vernadsky, V, I, 156–157.

375   For the peasants, see Vernadsky, V, I, 157; Staden, *The Land and Government*, 33, 67. Staden added that "a number of peasants in the country have a lot of money, but they do not brag about it . . ," ibid., 67.

376   For Ivan's speech on Ascension Day, see Bond, *Russia*, 188–189; Berry, *Rude & Barbarous Kingdom*, 293–294.

376   For the Tsar's marriage to Maria Nagaya, see Karamzin, IX, 312; Bond, *Russia*, 181; Berry, *Rude & Barbarous Kingdom*, 286.

377   Concerning the Tsar needing war supplies, see Berry, *Rude & Barbarous Kingdom*, 290; Bond, *Russia*, 184–185.

377   For the Tsar's conversation with Horsey, see Bond, *Russia*, 185–186; Berry, *Rude & Barbarous Kingdom*, 290–291.

378   For Horsey's travels, see Bond, *Russia*, 189–194; Berry, *Rude & Barbarous Kingdom*, 294–298. Many historians believe that Horsey returned only in the summer of 1581. In fact he could have made the journey there and back in six months. He was traveling very fast. For example he reached the island of Oesel from Moscow in ten days.

382   For Ivan's efforts to make peace with Bathory, see Karamzin, IX, 303–305; Soloviev, III, 655–656.

382   "If you want anything: Karamzin, IX, 305; Soloviev, III, 656.

382   For Bathory's ultimatum, see Karamzin, IX, 305.

382   For Tsar's message to the monasteries, see Soloviev, III, 657.

383   For Bathory's campaign of 1580, see Heidenstein, *Zapiski*, 97–160; Soloviev, III, 657–659; Karamzin, IX, 306–310.

383   For the siege and capture of Veliki Luki, see Karamzin, IX, 307–309; Soloviev, III, 657–658.

383   For the capture of Padis by the Swedes, see Soloviev, III, 659; Karamzin, IX, 310–311.

384   "Fodder! Fodder!"; Soloviev, III, 660.

384   For Ivan's instructions to Pushkin and Pissemsky, see Karamzin, IX, 315; Soloviev, III, 661.

384   "Then what kind of peace: Karamzin, IX, 315–316; Soloviev, III, 661–662.

385   "You accuse me of abusing: Soloviev, III, 663; Karamzin, IX, 317 and footnote 547.

385   "Read what they say: Karamzin, IX, 318 and footnote 548.

386   "Send greetings: Soloviev, III, 663; Karamzin, IX, 318.

386   For Ivan's letters to the Pope and the arrival of Possevino, see Karamzin, IX, 305–306; Soloviev, III, 665–668; Vernadsky, V, I, 162–163. For the papers of Possevino on his mission, see Turgenev, *Historica*, Supplement, 1–125.

387   For Bathory's campaign of 1581 and the siege of Pskov, see Karamzin, IX, 321–345; Soloviev, III, 663–664; Vernadsky, V, 1, 163–165; Malyshev, *Povest*; Heidenstein, *Zapiski*, 198–260; Buganov, *Razriadnaya Kniga*, 317–318.

387   Warned by a Russian traitor: Karamzin, IX, 327–328.

388   For the size and composition of Bathory's army, see Soloviev, III, 663; Karamzin, IX, 326.

388   "If the Sultan: Karamzin, IX, 326.

389   "Thus the first day: ibid., 330–331.

389   "We do not betray: ibid., 332.

390   For Radziwill's raid, see Karamzin, IX, 336–337; Vasilievsky, "Polskaya i nemetskaya pechats," 373–377.

390   "For three years our enemies: Polosin, *Sotsialno-politicheskaya istoriya*, 207.

391   For the events leading up to the death of Tsarevich Ivan, see Polosin, *Sotsialno-politicheskaya istoriya*, 207–208; Karamzin, IX, 349; Heidenstein, *Zapiski*, 242; Berry, *Rude & Barbarous Kingdom*, 300; Bond, *Russia*, 195; Soloviev, III, 703; Vernadsky, V, I, 165; Veselovsky, *Issledovaniya*, 337–339.

391   For the presence of Godunov, see Karamzin, IX, 349.

391   According to Possevino, the Tsar visited the wife of the Tsarevich, who was expecting a child, became angry with her and began to beat her. The Tsarevich came running in and tried to stop his father. The Tsar was enraged and struck his son. As a result of the blow the Tsarevich later died and the Tsarevna Elena had a miscarriage that night. See Antonio Possevino, *Commentarii*, 39.

391   "I have killed my son! Karamzin, IX, 349.

391   "I have always: Karamzin, IX, 349.

392   Tsarevna Elena was the third wife of Tsarevich Ivan and the daughter of the boyar Ivan Vasilievich Sheremetev the Younger. The first wife was Evdokia Saburova, who was made a nun and sent to the Pokrovsky Monastery; his second wife was Feodosia Solovova, who was sent to a nunnery in Beloozero. See Buganov and Koretsky, "Neizvestny Moskovsky letopisets," 149.

392   For the funeral, see Karamzin, IX, 349; Berry, *Rude & Barbarous Kingdom*, 300; Bond, *Russia*, 195.

392   For the Tsar's announcement about abdication, see Karamzin, IX, 351.

394   For Ivan's visit to the monastery, see Veselovsky, *Issledovaniya*, 339–340.

394   For the *sinodiki*, see Veselovsky, *Issledovaniya*, 340–354. For the names listed, see ibid., 354–478; Skrynnikov, "Vvedeniye," 3–86.

395   "In 1583 the Tsar: Skrynnikov, "Vvedeniye," 67; Veselovsky, *Issledovaniya*, 352–253.

397   "Nikita, Ivan Viskovaty: Skrynnikov, "Vvedeniye," 81.

397   "At Ivanovo Bolshoye: ibid., 69. These were the estates of the boyar Ivan Cheliadnin, devastated in 1568, see ibid., 38.

397   "Kazarin Dubrovsky with: ibid., 67.

400   For the negotiations at Yam Zapolsky, see Karamzin, IX, 339–345; Soloviev, III, 669–670, 723.

401 For Shuisky's last sortie, see Karamzin, IX, 343.

401 For date of truce, see Vernadsky, V, I, 165.

402 For the discussions between Possevino and Ivan, see Karamzin, IX, 353–363; Soloviev, III, 671–673; Possevino, *Commentarii*, 72 and ff.

402 "I found the Tsar: Karamzin, IX, 353–354.

402 "In our church," Soloviev, III, 672.

403 "This man who calls: Karamzin, IX, 359.

405 For the Russian envoys dressed in black, see Karamzin, IX, 364, footnote 621.

405 For the Cheremiss uprising, see Karamzin, IX, 410–411; Buganov and Koretsky, *Razriadnaya Kniga*, 331, 335, 340; Buganov, "Neizvestny moskovsky letopisets," 149–150.

405 For the war and peace with Sweden, 1582–1583, see Karamzin, IX, 407–409; Vernadsky, V, I, 165–166; Soloviev, III, 673–674.

405 For Dr. Jacoby, see Bond, *Russia*, xlviii–xlix; Karamzin, IX, 414–415.

406 For Pissemsky's embassy to England, see Bond, *Russia*, xlviii–liii; Karamzin, IX, 415–422; Soloviev, III, 676–679.

406 "I love him: Karamzin, IX, 416.

406 For Pissemsky's private audience with the Queen, see ibid., 419.

408 For Pissemsky's interview with Mary Hastings, see ibid., 420–421; Bond, *Russia*, 196; Berry, *Rude & Barbarous Kingdom*, 301.

408 "Cast down his countenance: Bond, *Russia*, 196.

409 "tall, well shaped, slender: Karamzin, IX, 421.

409 "I do not think: Soloviev, III, 678.

409 "the Empress of Muscovy: Bond, *Russia*, 196.

409 For the letters given to Pissemsky, see Karamzin, IX, 422.

410 For the instructions to Bowes, see Tolstoy, *Pervye sorok let*, xxxvii; Bond, *Russia*, lii; Soloviev III, 679; Karamzin, IX, 423.

410 For the embassy of Jerome Bowes, see Karamzin, IX, 422–427; Soloviev, III, 679–683; Bond, *Russia*, liv–lv; 196–198; Berry, *Rude & Barbarous Kingdom*, 301–303.

411 For the reception of Bowes, see Bond, *Russia*, 197–198.

412 "Queen Elizabeth must: Karamzin, IX, 423.

412 "Faith does not interfere: Soloviev, III, 680.

413 For exchange between Bowes and Ivan, see Karamzin, IX, 424; Bond, *Russia*, liv.

413 "Pray God that I: Karamzin, 424.

413 For the ambassador's meeting with the Tsar to discuss marriage, see Karamzin, IX, 425–426.

413 "I see you have: Soloviev, III, 680.

414 "Who are they?": ibid., 681.

414 "Then what instructions: ibid.

414 "You talk a good deal: ibid.

414 "Tell us what the Queen: ibid.

415 "You are an ignoramus!: ibid., 582.

415 For Bowes' complaints against Shchelkalov, see ibid.

415 Concerning the Tsar's hope of going to England, see Bond, *Russia*, liv–lv.

416 "Your English Tsar is dead!" Tolstoy, *Pervye sorok let*, xxxix; Vernadsky, V, I, 168.

418 For the conquest of Siberia, see Karamzin, IX, 365–406, X, 17–20; Soloviev, III, 686–702, 715–723, IV, 279–280; Vernadsky, V, I, 175–183; Vvedensky, *Dom Stroganovykh*, 15–111; *Mazurinsky letopisets*, PSRL, XXXI, 142–144.

418 For the Stroganovs' decision to invade Siberia, see Vernadsky, V, 1, 179.

418 For Yermak's earlier life and brigandage, see Vvedensky, *Dom Stroganovykh*, 88.

418 For the description of Yermak, see Karamzin, IX, 403.

418 For Yermak's forces, arms and provisions, see Vvedensky, *Dom Stroganovykh*, 97.

418 "spewed out flame: Soloviev, III, 700.

419 "If we retreat: ibid.

419 For the triumphal arrival of Ivan Koltso in Moscow, see Karamzin, IX, 391–392.

419 "for ever and ever: ibid., 391.

420 For the Prince of Siberia, see *Mazurinsky letopisets*, PSRL, XXXI, 143. The chronicler wrote, "the Tsar ordered a letter to be sent to Yermak not to the ataman but to the Prince of Siberia."

420 For the reception of the Stroganovs by the Tsar, see Karamzin, IX, 392, 394.

420 For capture of Mametkul, see Karamzin, IX, 387, 397.

420 For Khan Kuchum's flight into the steppes, see ibid., 388.

421 For the death of Yermak, see ibid., 402; Soloviev, IV, 280; Vernadsky, V, 1, 181. Ivan Koltso died in the spring of 1585.

421 "Then Yermak and all the Cossacks: Evgenieva and Putilov, *Drevniye rossiiskiye stikhotvoreniya*, 89–90. For more songs about Yermak, see ibid., 86–87; Chadwick, *Russian Heroic Poetry*, 201–202; Melnikov, *Yermak Timofeevich*.

422 "Ho, there, my boyars: Pomerantseva and Mints, *Russkoye narodnoye poeticheskoye tvorchestvo*, 379.

423 "This sign foretells my death." Karamzin, IX, 428; *Novy letopisets*, PSRL, XIV, 34.

423 Concerning the witches from Lapland, see Berry, *Rude & Barbarous Kingdom*, 304; Bond, *Russia*, 199.

423 "To the great and most pure: Peresvetov, *Po sledam Nakhodok i utrat*, 118–119; Soloviev, III, 704.

424 Concerning the Tsar's will, see Karamzin, IX, 428–429; Soloviev, III, 704.

424 For the great bird, see Yakovleva, "Piskarevsky letopisets," 85.

426 For Ivan's attack on Tsarevna Irina, see Karamzin, IX 430; Petrei, "Opisaniye," 158.

426 "Before thy fearful: Likhachev, "Kanon i molitva," 22–23.

426 "grievously to swell: Berry, *Rude & Barbarous Kingdom*, 304; Bond, *Russia*, 199.

427 Concerning Ivan's talk about his treasures, see Berry, *Rude & Barbarous Kingdom*, 304–306; Bond, *Russia*, 199–201.

427 "Behold these precious stones: Bond, *Russia*, 200–201; Berry, *Rude & Barbarous Kingdom*, 305–306.

428 For Ivan taking baths, see Berry, *Rude & Barbarous Kingdom*, 306; Bond, *Russia*, 201; Karamzin, IX, 431.

428 For Ivan's death at the chessboard, see Berry, *Rude & Barbarous Kingdom*, 306; Bond, *Russia*, 201; Karamzin, IX, 431. Russian chronicles usually had only a brief mention of Ivan's death, for example, "In the year 1584 on the fourth Saturday of Lent died the Tsar and Grand Prince Ivan Vasilievich of all Russia. He reigned for many years and was married seven times. Tsar Ivan died suddenly. Some say that those who were close to him gave him poison." See Buganov and Koretsky, "Neizvestny moskovsky letopisets," 150.

428   For fainting spells, see Petrei, "Opisaniye," 157–160.

429   For events immediately after Ivan's death, see Karamzin, IX, 431–432; Buganov and Koretsky, "Neizvestny Moskovsky letopisets," 150–151; Berry, *Rude & Barbarous Kingdom*, 306; Bond, *Russia*, 201.

429   "Where is the city: Buganov and Koretsky, "Neizvestny moskovsky letopisets," 150–151.

430   They wept: Karamzin, IX, 432.

431   "O bright moon; Weinberg, *Russkiye narodnye pesni*, 60; Morfill, *Russia*, 89.

432   "You have shone: Weinberg, *Russkiye narodnye pesni*, 205–206.

432   For the opening of Ivan's tomb, see Gerasimov, *The Face Finder*, 184–189.

Index